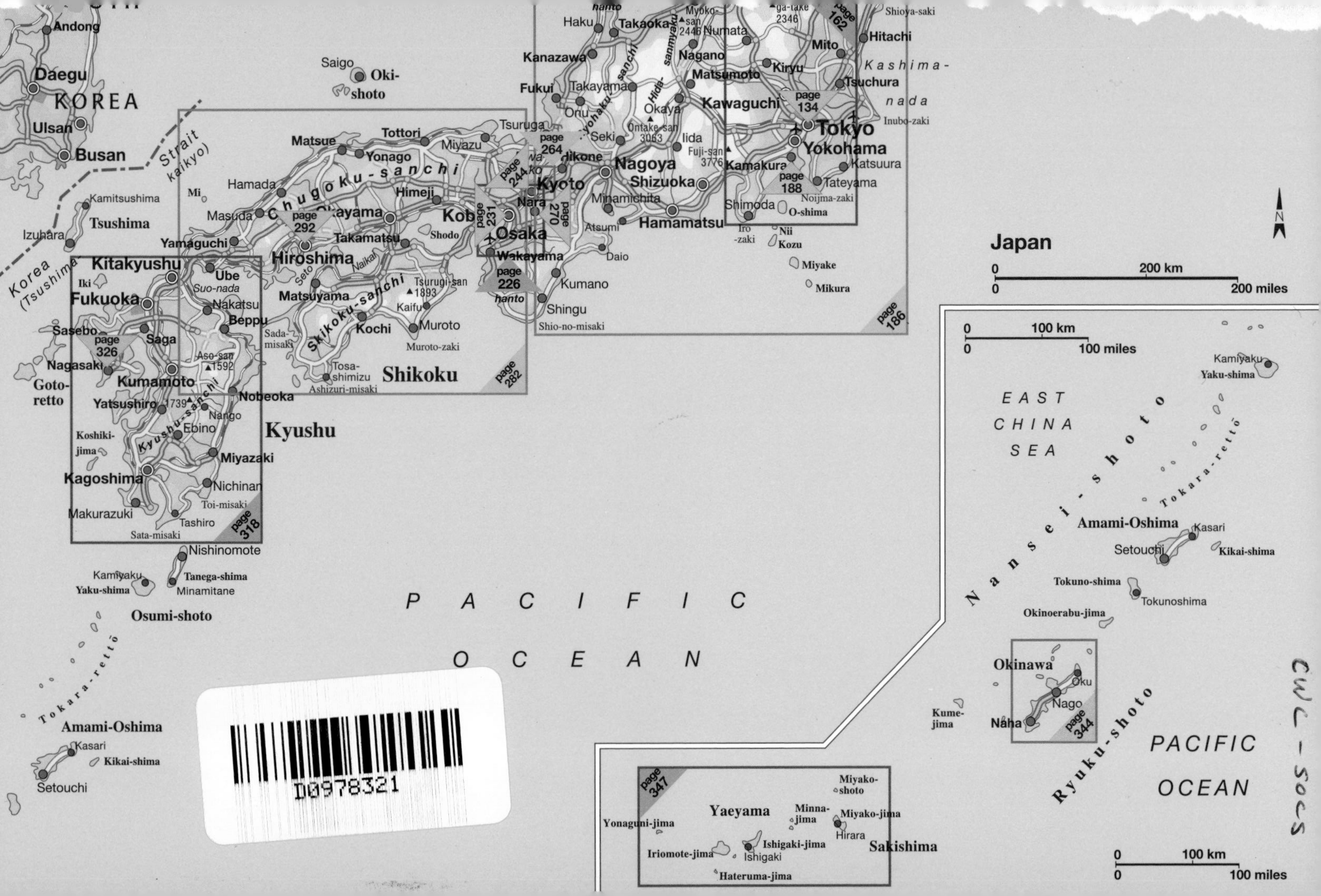
Japan
0 200 km
0 200 miles
KOREA
Andong
Daegu
Ulsan
Busan
Korea Strait (Tsushima kaikyo)
Tsushima
Kamitsushima
Izuhara
Saigo
Oki-shoto
Kitakyushu
Fukuoka
Iki
Sasebo
Saga
Nagasaki
Goto-retto
Kumamoto
Yatsushiro
Koshiki-jima
Kagoshima
Makurazuki
Sata-misaki
Kyushu
Kyushu-sanchi
Ube
Suo-nada
Nakatsu
Beppu
Aso-san 1592
1739
Nobeoka
Nango
Ebino
Miyazaki
Nichinan
Toi-misaki
Tashiro
Nishinomote
Tanega-shima
Minamitane
Kamiyaku
Yaku-shima
Osumi-shoto
Tokara-retto
Amami-Oshima
Kasari
Kikai-shima
Setouchi
Mi
Hamada
Masuda
Yamaguchi
Matsue
Yonago
Tottori
Chugoku-sanchi
Hiroshima
Okayama
Takamatsu
Himeji
Kobe
Miyazu
Tsuruga
Shodo
Seto Naikai
Matsuyama
Shikoku-sanchi
Kochi
Tsurugi-san 1893
Kaifu
Muroto
Muroto-zaki
Sada-misaki
Tosa-shimizu
Ashizuri-misaki
Shikoku
Osaka
Wakayama
Kii-hanto
Kyoto
Nara
Hikone
Kumano
Shingu
Shio-no-misaki
Haku
Takaoka
Kanazawa
Fukui
Takayama
Oniu
Hida-sanmyaku
Ryohaku-sanchi
Okaya
Ontake-san 3063
Seki
Nagoya
Iida
Fuji-san 3776
Shizuoka
Hamamatsu
Minamichita
Atsumi
Daio
Myoko-san 2446
Numata
Nagano
Matsumoto
Kiryu
Mito
Hitachi
Shioya-saki
Tsuchura
Kashima-nada
Inubo-zaki
Kawaguchi
Tokyo
Yokohama
Kamakura
Katsuura
Tateyama
Noijma-zaki
Shimoda
Iro-zaki
O-shima
Nii
Kozu
Miyake
Mikura
page 162
page 134
page 188
page 186
page 264
page 244
page 231
page 270
page 226
page 282
page 292
page 326
page 318
PACIFIC OCEAN
EAST CHINA SEA
0 100 km
0 100 miles
Nansei-shoto
Tokuno-shima
Tokunoshima
Okinoerabu-jima
Okinawa
Oku
Nago
Naha
page 344
Kume-jima
Ryuku-shoto
PACIFIC OCEAN
page 347
Yaeyama
Yonaguni-jima
Iriomote-jima
Ishigaki-jima
Ishigaki
Hateruma-jima
Minna-jima
Miyako-shoto
Miyako-jima
Hirara
Sakishima

INSIGHT GUIDES

JAPAN

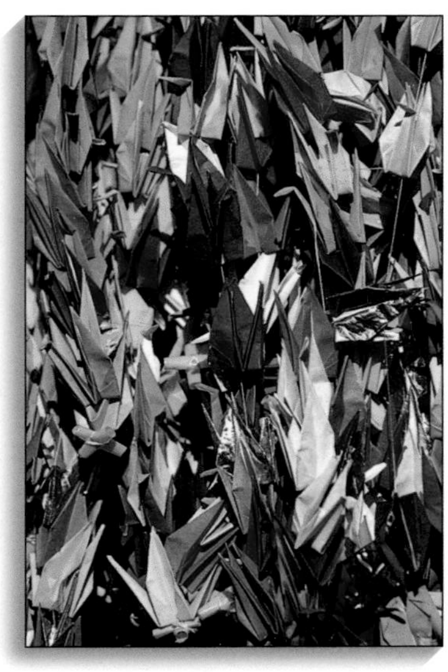

APA PUBLICATIONS
Part of the Langenscheidt Publishing Group

INSIGHT GUIDE
JAPAN

About This Book

The first Insight Guide pioneered the use of creative full-colour photography in travel guides in 1970. Since then, we have expanded our range to cater for our readers' need, not only for reliable and practical information about their chosen destination but also for a real understanding of the history, culture and workings of that destination. Now, when the internet can supply us with inexhaustible (but not always reliable) facts, our books marry text and pictures to provide those much more elusive qualities: knowledge and discernment. To achieve this, they rely heavily on the authority of locally based writers and photographers.

In this, the latest edition of *Insight Guide: Japan*, we journey to one of the most captivating, confounding and intriguing of nations. An archipelago of ancient enigmas and exquisite art, Japan offers a traveller densely packed cities, a delicate cuisine, diverse environments, and unfamiliar culture. This book unlocks the complexities.

Editorial
Project Editor
Alyse Dar
Updater
Stephen Mansfield
Series Manager
Rachel Fox

Distribution
North America
Langenscheidt Publishers, Inc.
36–36 33rd Street, 4th Floor
Long Island City, New York 11106
orders@langenscheidt.com
UK & Ireland
GeoCenter International Ltd
Meridian House, Churchill Way West
Basingstoke, Hampshire RG21 6YR
sales@geocenter.co.uk
Australia
Universal Publishers
1 Waterloo Road
Macquarie Park, NSW 2113
sales@universalpublishers.com.au
New Zealand
Hema Maps New Zealand Ltd (HNZ)
Unit 2, 10 Cryers Road
East Tamaki, Auckland 2013
sales.hema@clear.net.nz
Worldwide
Apa Publications GmbH & Co. Verlag KG (Singapore branch)
7030 Ang Mo Kio Avenue 5
08-65 Northstar @ AMK
Singapore 569880
apasin@singnet.com.sg

Printing
CTPS - China

First Edition 1992
Third Edition 1999
Updated 2006; Revised 2008
Reprinted 2010

CONTACTING THE EDITORS
We would appreciate it if readers would alert us to errors or outdated information by writing to:
Insight Guides, P.O. Box 7910, London SE1 1WE, England.
insight@apaguide.co.uk

www.insightguides.com

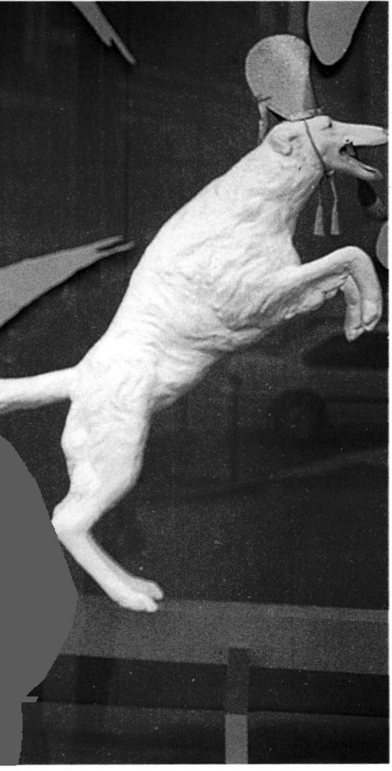

How to use this book

The book is carefully structured to convey an understanding of Japan and its culture and to guide readers through its sights and attractions:

◆ The Features section, with a yellow colour bar, covers the country's history and culture in lively authoritative essays written by specialists.

◆ The Places section, with a ...e bar, provides full details of ...he sights and areas worth ...g. The chief places of inter- ...e coordinated by number ...ecially drawn maps.

...ravel Tips listings section, with an orange bar and at the back of the book, offers a convenient point of reference for information on travel, accommodation, restaurants and other practical aspects of the country. Information is located quickly using the index printed on the back cover flap, which also serves as a handy bookmark.

The contributors

This new edition, supervised by Insight editor **Alyse Dar**, builds on earlier editions edited by **Scott Rutherford**, who lived in Japan for a number of years and wrote most of the Tokyo coverage, and **Malcom Davis**.

The book has been comprehensively updated by British-born resident of Japan, **Stephen Mansfield**. In addition to revising the text, Mansfield also expanded many of the Places chapters, contributed to the Japanese gardens picture story and wrote the information panels on manga, architecture and sake. **Paula Soper** edited the text.

Contributors from earlier editions whose work suvives in this one include **Ed Peters**, **Hugh Paxton**, **Mason Florence**, **Bill Williams**, **Matsutani Yuko**, **Kim Schuefftan**, **Steve Usdin**, **John Carroll**, **Alex Kerr**, **Davis Barrager**, **Mark Schreiber**, **David Benjamin**, **Anthony J. Bryant**, **Bruce Leigh**, **Rich Blumm**, **Peter Ujlaki**, **Peter Hadfield**, **Arturo Silva**, **Gail Feldman**, **Evelyn Corbett**, **Wayne Graczyk**, **Robert McLeod** and **Otani Eiho**.

The book was proofread by **Sylvia Suddes** and indexed by **Penny Phenix**.

Map Legend

- International Boundary
- National Park/Reserve
- Ferry Route
- Airport: International/Regional
- Bus Station
- Parking
- Tourist Information
- Post Office
- Church/Ruins
- Monastery
- Mosque
- Synagogue
- Castle/Ruins
- Archaeological Site
- Cave
- Statue/Monument
- Place of Interest

The main places of interest in the Places section are coordinated by number with a full-colour map (e.g. ❶), and a symbol at the top of every right-hand page tells you where to find the map.

Photo: collecting alms on a pilgrimage in front of a department store.

INSIGHT GUIDE
JAPAN

CONTENTS

Maps

Introduction

History

Features

Tokyo, from Tokyo Bay.

Insight on ...

Information panels

Travel Tips

♦ **Full Travel Tips index is on page 353**

Places

THE BEST OF JAPAN

From family outings and unique attractions to historic sights and hot springs, here, at a glance, are our recommendations, plus some money saving tips that even the Japanese won't always know

ONLY IN JAPAN

- **Department Terminals** A fascinating consumer concept – train platforms feeding passengers straight into department stores. Accessible station-store interfaces are found in Nihombashi, Ikebukuro, Shibuya and elsewhere.
- **Capsule Hotels** Seal your door and fall into a contented sleep in these cosy, weightless cells, or sweat with claustrophobia. You either love or hate Japan's capsule hotels. *Page 358*
- **Vending Machines** It's the number and range that's unique to Japan: over 20 million on the last count, dispensing everything from disposable underwear to noodles.

ABOVE: sitting tight in a capsule hotel.
BELOW: making friends at Universal Studios Japan.

BEST FOR FAMILIES

- **Kiddyland** In the Aoyama district of Tokyo, five floors stuffed with toys and characters like Hello Kitty and Pokemon, time spent here with the kids could well lead to a temporary cash flow problem. *Page 380*
- **National Children's Castle** Extensive facilities for young children in Tokyo's Aoyama area. Playhouses, a music room, a roof play port, and a huge jungle gym. Lots of rainy day activities. *Page 380*
- **DisneySea** An addition to Tokyo Disneyland but requiring a separate ticket and a full day is recommended, the themes here are all connected to water. *Page 183*
- **Universal Studios Japan** Hollywood special effects and fun rides, Osaka's theme park replicates its Los Angeles prototype. *Page 380*
- **Sony Building** Older kids will want to check out the latest gadgets, especially on the 6th floor devoted to the PlayStation. *Page 143*

BEST ARCHITECTURE

- **Fuji TV Building** A Kenzo Tange masterpiece, this TV studio in Tokyo's man-made island Odaiba, and its suspended dome made of reinforced tungsten, seem to resemble the inside of a television set. *Page 152*
- **Tokyo Big Sight** You'll probably do a double take when you see the inverted pyramids of a building in Tokyo's Odaiba, that seems to defy gravity and common sense, but is still standing. *Page 152*
- **Umeda Sky Building** A striking skyscraper in Osaka's Umeda district, this soaring building is pierced by a large hole at one point in its structure. *Page 231*
- **ACROS Centre** Fukuoka is quite a laboratory for new architecture. ACROS, a culture centre, stands out for its ziggurat form and stepped terraces covered in hanging plants, creating the impression of a sci-fi jungle ruin. *Page 321*
- **Global Tower** Beppu's own piece of futurism, a curving sliver of steel and light with an observation platform at the top. *Page 152*

BEST PARKS AND GARDENS

- **Koishikawa Botanical Garden** Although landscaped, the grounds of this fine Edo-period green haven have a natural and informal feel. The oldest garden in Tokyo. *Page 146*
- **Shinjuku Gyoen** Enjoy the many species of plants, trees and flowers in a Tokyo park divided into different garden styles. There is a large botanical greenhouse for chilly days. *Page 157*
- **Daitoku-ji** A complex of immeasurably beautiful Kyoto gardens. The most famous is Daisen-in. *Page 256*
- **Ritsurin-koen** Completed in 1745, Ritsurin Park on Shikoku Island, is one of the finest stroll gardens in Japan. *Page 306*

ABOVE: Shinjuku Park, in the midst of frenetic Shinjuku, is a delightful oasis to stroll in.
BELOW: Venus Fort, an indoor shopping street with an ever-changing artificial sky.

MOST ORIGINAL TOKYO STORES

- **Tsutsumu Factory** Countless original designed sheets of wrapping paper, including thick *washi*, traditional Japanese gift paper, in a small Shibuya store. *Page 377*
- **Tokyu Hands** A fun Shibuya hardware store stocking things you may never have heard of. Fancy dress costumes, trinkets and other novelty goods add to the wonder world. *Page 376*
- **Venus Fort** A Greco-Roman shopping complex with an artificial sky that changes from sunrise through lightning to dazzling sunlight. *Page 152*

LEFT: the Fuji TV Building.

Best Pottery Towns

- **Mashiko** A major ceramic making centre, with over 300 kilns, pottery shops, markets and a museum. A great introduction to the craft. *Page 183*
- **Hagi** The town provides a lovely old setting for *hagi-yaki*, one of Japan's most esteemed ceramic ware. The glazed, pastels and earth colours, either smooth or with the contouring of lemon rind, are exquisite. *Page 299*
- **Saga** Ceramic enthusiasts can enjoy a circuit of Saga prefecture, taking in the pottery towns of Arita, Imari and Karatsu, three very distinctive styles. *Page 324*

Best Hot Springs

- **Dogo Onsen** These hot springs in Shikoku are the oldest in Japan. They are mentioned in the *Manyoshu*, the ancient collection of Japanese poetry (*circa* 759). *Page 310*
- **Beppu** A very busy spa town with eight different hot spring areas each with different properties. The open-air "hell ponds" of boiling mud are a crowd-puller. *Page 332*
- **Noboribetsu** There are 11 kinds of hot spring water at this spa resort in Hokkaido, including salt (for soothing pain), iron (for relieving rheumatism) and sodium bicarbonate (to attain a smoother skin). *Page 310*
- **Naruko** This once sacred site in Tohoku is over 1,000 years old. It is well known for its fine medicinal waters. *Page 204*

Best Temples and Shrines

- **Asakusa Kannon Temple (Senso-ji)** Tokyo's most visited temple hosts dozens of annual events and festivals. Nakamise, the approach street is full of craft and dry-food goods. *Page 150*
- **Kanda Myojin Shrine** One of Tokyo's liveliest shrine compounds, especially on Saturdays when weddings, rituals and festivals are held. Bright and cheerful architecture. *Page 145*
- **Meiji Shrine** An amazing setting at the centre of a forest in the middle of Tokyo. Gravel paths lead to the shrine, an example of pure Shinto design. *Page 155*
- **Yamadera** Tohoku's most sacred temple complex, a veritable labyrinth of steps, pathways and stone stairways across a rocky hillside. Built in the 9th century to last. *Page 210*
- **Koya-san** A complex of temples, monasteries and necropolis deep inside a mountainside forest. Bags of atmosphere. *Page 276*
- **Itsukushima-jinga** Fabulously located on stilts and pillars rising 16m (52 ft) above the waters of Miyajima, the walkways and platforms of this splendid, magical shrine seem to float in space. *Page 295*

Above: Hagi earthenware pottery.
Right: sweeping leaves at Yamadera temple complex.

BEST CASTLES

- **Himeji-jo** Of Japan's twelve surviving orginal castles, Himeji-jo certainly impressed UNESCO, who added it to their World Heritage list in 1993. Known as 'Shirasagi-jo,' or the 'white egret castle.' its graceful lines are said to resemble the bird as it is about to take flight. *Page 285*
- **Nijo-jo** The massively fortified exterior of this castle in central Kyoto, belies the delicate art treasures within. *Page 249*
- **Hikone-jo** Surrounded by over 1,000 cherry trees, the views across lake Biwa from the upper storeys of this castle are magnificent. *Page 263*
- **Matsue-jo** Built in 1611, Matsue-jo is another original castle. Among the castle's martial aspects are low windows for dropping boiling oil. *Page 300*

BEST ZEN

- **Engaku-ji** Founded in 1282, Engaku-ji is one of Kamakura's best-loved temples, beautifully situated among ancient cedar trees and discreet gardens, Engaku-ji is a good example of classic Zen architecture. *Page 170*
- **Ryoan-ji** Built in 1499, this famous Kyoto garden was created as both a tool for meditation and as a work of art. Arrive early in the morning before the crowds descend to appreciate the true Zen experience. *Page 257*

ABOVE: spend a day at Himeji-jo.
LEFT: Ryoan-ji.

MONEY-SAVING TIPS

Cheap to sleep: Providing you eschew top-end hotels, restaurants and the use of taxis, Japan can be a surprisingly affordable country to travel around. Accommodation in budget inns and business hotels range from as little as ¥3,000–6,000.
Travel: Buying a Japan Rail Pass beforehand can save you a huge amount of money. The JR passes are also useful for some lines into and through cities like Tokyo. Overnight buses, allowing you to save on sleeping accommodation, are cheaper than trains.
Shopping spree: Some department stores offer a 5 percent discount to foreign visitors.
Set lunch: Food can be good value with so many restaurants in competition. Look out for lunch set specials, which can be as cheap as ¥650. Fast food joints have sets for as little as ¥350.
Look at that: Great free views of Tokyo are afforded from the observation room at the Tokyo Metropolitan Government Office in Shinjuku.
Cheers: Drinks at music clubs and discos are sometimes included in the ticket price, and if not, are often cheaper anyway than in pubs and bars.
No tips: Tipping is almost non-existent in Japan, something that helps to offset daily costs.
Fill up: Family restaurants such as Denny's, Cocos and Volks often have a free coffee refill service after the first cup.
Film: Cinemas are expensive, but many offer half-price discounts on the first Monday of every month. Look out for "Women's Day Tickets" on Wednesday (half price).

A UNIQUE PLACE

Some see the Japanese turning into Westerners. Others see a Zen-like serenity. The reality is more complicated

A traveller roaming amongst the islands of Japan is usually seeking the exotic, or the wondrous, or the unconventional. And indeed, Japan is often so, in both the cities and along the back roads. Sometimes what's encountered seems illogical or of dubious purpose, but that is a bias of culture and outlook. The traveller will inevitably compare Japan with the West when confronted with the obvious examples of suits and ties on Japan's *sarariman* – the "salary man" or white-collar worker – and the proliferation of fast-food franchises nearly everywhere. The near-cult status of Western pop icons can lull the outsider into believing that East has met West. (Even the Japanese language, as different as it is, uses English loan words, an estimated 10 percent of all words used in daily conversation.) The traveller thinks, *Japan has become like the West.*

Big mistake. In its history, Japan has adopted many things, taking what it wants or needs, adapting, and then discarding that which is of no use. Over the centuries, the Japanese have adopted Chinese writing and philosophy, Korean art and ceramics, and most recently, Western technology, clothes and fast-food. Indeed, since it yielded to Perry's Black Ships in 1853, Japan has adopted things foreign with gusto. Yet that which it adopts from the West or elsewhere somehow becomes distinctly Japanese. A foreign word is chopped in half, recombined with the second half of another bisected foreign or even Japanese word, and – *voilà*, a new word in the Japanese language.

Although Japan derives most of its culture from its Asian neighbours and most of its modernity from the West, the Japanese continue to cultivate a self-image of an almost divine uniqueness. The Japanese repeatedly refer to Japanese things – including themselves – as "special" or "unique" and thus beyond an outsider's understanding. The special Japanese snow once kept out French skis, as did the special Japanese digestive system keep out American beef.

Japan is special, of course. It has become the world's second-strongest economy while evenly – and in comparison with most of the world, uniquely – distributing a growing wealth without creating a significant lower class. Yet, having done so, it has made itself into a uniquely expensive place. While Japan radiates an international image of sophistication and efficiency, the home country is oddly behind the times. Just two-thirds of Japanese dwellings are connected to a modern sewage system, for example. Bureaucrats in the Kasumigaseki government district of Tokyo issue vague, verbal suggestions for corporate guidance that somehow become the equivalent of regulatory edicts. Japanese companies understand the system and

PRECEDING PAGES: bamboo grove in Kamakura; 360-degree views from the Mori Tower, Tokyo.
LEFT: helping a grandson for *shichi-go-san*, when children are blessed at shrines.

its nuances, but foreign companies trying to start a business in the country are like fish out of water.

There is the nagging legacy of World War II, not to mention the uniquely Japanese forgetfulness regarding it. Other than of the atomic bombings of Nagasaki and Hiroshima, the Japanese don't talk about that war much. Yet, increasingly, neighbouring countries do, and Japan's relations with Korea and China are often rich with the undercurrents of the past. Most recently, national self-confidence weakened after a collapsing, superheated economy suffered a decade-long recession. There was also the 1995 Kobe earthquake that killed over 5,000 people and destroyed a supposedly earthquake-proof infrastructure, and a poison gas attack on Tokyo's subways, right in the heart of the government district in Tokyo.

Nonetheless, the Japanese are rightly proud of their country – current self-doubts aside – and of the sophistication and depth of its heritage. Much of its progress and advances have been the result of an inward-looking dedication and spirit. As an island nation, Japan is often focused inwards, as when the evening television news leads off with a cherry-blossom story and the remainder of the world is shoved to the end.

The Japanese are perhaps more appreciative of the subtleties of the changing seasons than any other people. Rural people will know if the dragonflies that appear in late spring are three days early this year, or if the *tsuyu*, the rainy season, is dragging on two days longer than normal. There is a delicate charm and serenity in such observations. It is a quality indicative of people with a strong sense of place.

There are those, Japanese and foreigners alike, who retain an image of a Japan of Zen-like serenity. It is a wistful image, a nostalgic retreat. The novelist and nationalist Mishima Yukio, who revered the old Japan and chose to rebel and then kill himself for those old-guard principles, wrote that "Japan will disappear, it will become inorganic, empty, neutral-tinted; it will be wealthy and astute." Who knows? Cultures change, shift, disappear. On its surface, Japan appears to be changing. Underneath, one wonders if it is capable of doing so, or if it wants to change. Even Japanese don't know. But for the traveller, Japan as it is today is a supremely embracing and fabulous – and, yes, special – experience.

A note on style

Wherever possible, we use Japanese terms for geographical names, appearing as suffixes to the proper name. For example, Mt Fuji is referred to as Fuji-san. Mountains may also appear with *-zan*, *-yama,* and for some active volcanoes, *-dake*. Islands are either *-shima* or *-jima*, lakes are *-ko*, and rivers are *-gawa* or *-kawa*. Shinto shrines end in *-jinja*, *-jingu*, or *-gu*. Temples are Buddhist, with names ending in *-tera*, *-dera*, or *-ji*. When referring to individuals, we follow ithe Japanese style: family name first, given name second. ❑

RIGHT: purification before praying at a Kyoto temple.

A NATION OF ISLANDS

An archipelago formed by the meeting of tectonic plates, Japan's thousands of islands are often rugged and violent, accented by soothing hot springs

N*ihon-retto,* the islands of the Japanese archipelago, were formed from the tears of a goddess. Where each tear fell into the Pacific there arose an island to take its place. So goes the legend. But no less poetic – or dramatic – is the geological origin of this huge archipelago that stretches from the subtropical waters of Okinawa – not far from Taiwan – to the frozen wastes of northern Hokkaido. The islands were born of massive crustal forces deep underground and shaped by volcanoes spitting out mountains of lava. The results seen today are impressive, with snow-capped mountain ranges and 27,000 km (16,800 miles) of indented coastline.

The archipelago consists of four main islands – Kyushu, Shikoku, Honshu and Hokkaido – and about 3,900 smaller islands extending from southwest to northeast over a distance of some 3,800 km (2,400 miles) off the east coast of Asia. Honshu is by far the largest and most populous of all the islands. The main islands are noted for their rugged terrain, with 70 to 80 percent of the country being extremely mountainous. Most of the mountains were uplifted over millions of years as the oceanic crust of the Pacific collided with the continental plate of Asia. The oceanic crust submerged beneath the thicker continental crust, buckling the edge of it and forcing up the mountain chains that form the backbone of the Japanese archipelago and that of the Philippines to the south.

Volcanoes and earthquakes

Other singular peaks in Japan – including Fuji, the highest – are volcanic in origin. They were formed from molten lava that originated far below the earth's surface as the oceanic crust sank into the superheated depths of the upper mantle. The molten rock was forced up through fissures and faults, exploding onto the surface. Weather and glacial action did the rest.

PRECEDING PAGES: the active Sakura-jima volcano, Kyushu. **LEFT:** Cape Sata, southernmost point of Kyushu. **RIGHT:** Mt Fuji.

One of the attractions of a visit to Japan is the possibility of seeing the milder geological forces in action. About 60 of Japan's 186 volcanoes are still active in geological terms, and occasionally they make their presence felt. Mihara on Oshima, one of the isles of Izu near Tokyo and part of Metropolitan Tokyo, exploded as

GEOGRAPHY IN JAPANESE

Japan:	*Nihon*	**village**:	*-mura*
world:	*sekai*	**city ward**:	*-ku*
country:	*kuni*	**lake**:	*-ko*
island:	*-shima*	**pond**:	*-ike*
mountain:	*-yama*	**river**:	*-kawa*
volcano:	*-dake*	**bay/gulf**:	*-wan*
valley:	*-tani*	**forest**:	*-shinrin*
cape:	*-misaki*	**hot spring**:	*onsen*
peninsula:	*-hanto*	**north**:	*kita*
prefecture:	*-ken*	**south**:	*minami*
city:	*-shi*	**east**:	*higashi*
town:	*-machi*	**west**:	*nishi*

recently as 1986, forcing thousands of residents to evacuate the island. A few years later, Unzen-dake on Kyushu violently erupted and devastated hundreds of kilometres of agricultural land. Sakura-jima, also on Kyushu and just a few kilometres from the city of Kagoshima, regularly spews ash – and an occasional boulder the size of a Honda – onto the city.

Earthquakes

Earthquakes are far more frequent than volcanic eruptions, especially around the more seismologically active areas near Tokyo. They are also a more serious threat and the Japanese Government currently spends billions of yen annually on earthquake detection – not that it works particularly well. Complacency is a common problem anywhere and certainly was in Kobe, which had been declared to be outside any significant earthquake zone. Nevertheless, in 1995 a massive quake hit the city, killing over 5,000 people and toppling high-rises.

Most Japanese tend not to dwell on the morbid aspects of the islands' geological activity, preferring to enjoy its pleasures instead. *Onsen*, or hot springs, are a tangible result of the massive quantities of heat released underground. For centuries hot springs have occupied a special place in Japanese culture until the pleasures of the *onsen* have become a national pastime.

Despite the dominance of mountains in these islands, the Japanese are not a mountain people, preferring instead to squeeze onto the coastal plains or into the valleys of the interior. Consequently separated from each other by mountains, which once took days to traverse, the populated areas tended to develop independently with distinct dialects and other social peculiarities; some local dialects, such as in Tohoku or Kyushu, are completely unintelligible to other Japanese. At the same time, isolation and efficient use of land meant that agriculture and communications evolved early in the country's history.

The highest non-volcanic peaks are in the so-called Japan Alps of central Honshu. Many of the landforms in these mountain ranges were sculpted by glaciers in an ice age over 27,000 years ago. Cirques, or depressions, left where glaciers formed, are still a common sight on some higher slopes. Debris brought down by melting ice can also be seen in lower regions.

Fauna and flora

To the Japanese, people are a part of nature and therefore anything people have constructed is considered part of the environment. The Japanese can look upon a garden – moulded, cut, sculptured and trimmed to perfect proportions –

and still see it as a perfect expression of the natural order, not something artificial.

The result of this philosophy has generally been disastrous for the wildlife and ecosystems of Japan. The crested ibis, for example, once considered to be a representative bird of Japan and common throughout the archipelago 100 years ago, is reduced today to less than a dozen individuals. The Japanese crane *(tancho)* is also close to extinction, though the bird was once common in Hokkaido. Fish such as salmon and trout are no longer able to survive in Japan's polluted rivers and lakes. Brown bears have been hunted almost to extinction, and only recently have hunting laws been amended and the animal recognised as an endangered species.

NO PLACE FOR BEARS

A few hundred wild bear remain, only on Hokkaido. Most of Japan's bears are confined in amusement parks, with dozens of bears often crowded into small concrete pits.

Of the other land mammals, the Japanese monkey, or macaca, is by far the most common in Japan. Originally a creature of the tropical rainforests, the macaca has adapted to the more temperate climates of these islands and can now be found throughout Kyushu, Shikoku and Honshu, although its numbers have been sharply reduced since the 1950s. During the winter months, macacas in Nagano and Hokkaido take to bathing in local hot springs.

In the far south of Japan, the islands of Okinawa have a distinctive fauna and flora. Here, the natural forests are subtropical, but many of the indigenous species of fauna have become rare or even extinct. The most spectacular characteristic of these islands is the marine life. Most of the islands are surrounded by coral, home to a rich and colourful variety of warm-water fish. Yet once again the rapid growth of the tourist and leisure industry – especially that of scuba diving – has led to the destruction of much of this natural coral.

In Hokkaido, the greater availability of space and natural moorland vegetation has led to the growth of the cattle and dairy industries. Meat is gradually becoming a more important part of the Japanese diet, just as rice is declining in popularity. In a sense, this is symptomatic of the way Japanese culture is changing. Younger generations are gradually turning away from the fish-and-rice diet to eat more meat and bread as Japan becomes more affluent, urbanised, and Western in outlook.

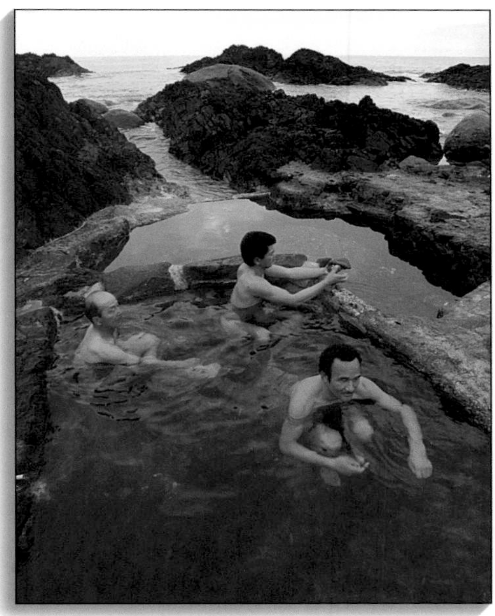

LEFT: Kyushu's Sakura-jima. **ABOVE:** protective barriers on Sakura-jima, and hot spring.

Climate

As any visitor will soon discover, an obsessive pastime with Japanese is discussing the weather. As a matter of routine, people nearly always greet each other by commenting on the weather, and the changing seasons still attract an unwarranted amount of attention by the television and print media in what is, after all, a largely urban society. If the blooming of the plum trees or cherry blossoms is a few days late this year, it will be a lead story on the news.

The two extremities of Japan, from the coral reefs of Okinawa to the ice floes of northern Hokkaido, are in very different climatic zones.

TYPHOONS

Generally three or four typhoons hit Japan during the season, smaller ones in August building up to larger ones in September. The southern or Pacific side of Japan bears the brunt of these ferocious winds, which are quite capable of knocking down houses and wrecking ships. Fortunately for Japan, however, most typhoons have expended their energy in the Philippines or Taiwan before reaching the archipelago. While more frequent than Atlantic hurricanes or Indian Ocean cyclones, the Asian typhoons are also considerably smaller in size and strength. The Japanese don't use names for typhoons, just numbers.

Because of the high mountain ranges running along the spine of Honshu, there are also major climatic differences between the Sea of Japan coast and the Pacific Ocean coast.

Japan's seasons are similar to those of Europe and North America. The coldest months are December to February, when the Sea of Japan sides of Hokkaido and Honshu experience heavy falls of snow as the cold air from Siberia picks up moisture over the Sea of Japan. The Pacific Ocean side, by contrast, is very dry during the winter months. This is accentuated in Tokyo by urban growth, which has tended to reduce evaporation, causing a further drop in winter precipitation. Winter water shortages are now becoming a serious problem in the capital.

Cherry blossom time

The southern areas of Kyushu and Okinawa have a relatively mild winter and are the first to experience the coming of spring. This manifests itself with the flowering of the cherry blossom – *sakura* – an event which the Japanese like to celebrate with a festival called *hanami*. Like the weather, the blossoming of *sakura* (and the autumn changing of leaves) is followed in the national media like the advance of an attacking army. The cherry trees flower in Kyushu towards the end of March; the phenomenon moves northward, finally reaching Hokkaido about the second week in May.

Alas, the burst of spring that follows is all too short. Soon after the cherry blossoms have fallen, about a week after they open, they are blown around by strong, southerly winds that bring with them occasional rain and precede the start of *tsuyu*, the rainy season. Temperatures rise quickly, and continuous but moderate rains begin to fall about two months after the end of the cherry-blossom season. (The Japanese are very definite about their seasons. A weather forecaster once announced on television: "The rain you are now experiencing is not the rainy-season rain – the rainy season will start as soon as this rain finishes".)

Once again, the central mountains of Japan define the boundaries of the rain fronts. On the Pacific Ocean coast of Honshu, the *tsuyu* rain is soft and drizzly. Further south and on the Japan Sea coast, it is hard and much more tropical in nature. In the southern areas especially, the rain is often accompanied by typhoons. Hokkaido, however, has a very indistinct rainy season. The rains ease around late June on the Pacific Ocean side and make way for the hot, humid summer. Temperatures reach a peak in August, when many city dwellers escape to the cool comfort of the mountains. Nonetheless, the city of Yamagata, which is buried under 1 metre (3 feet) of snow in the winter, once recorded Japan's highest summertime temperature: 41°C (105°F).

The warm body of water around Japan causes the heat of summer to linger into September, with occasional balmy days in October. But as the warm air mass moves south, the rains return on the backs of devastating typhoons.

Natural resources

There are coal mines in Hokkaido and Kyushu, but coal production peaked in 1941 and many coal-mining communities are now in serious decline. Nearly all of Japan's other raw materials, such as oil, minerals and metal ores, are imported. Timber is one resource Japan has in abundance, as most of the country's mountains are covered in natural or plantation forest. The natural cover varies from subarctic conifers in Hokkaido to deciduous and evergreen temperate broad-leafed trees throughout the other three main islands. Yet despite a soaring demand for timber – used in the construction industry and for paper and disposable chopsticks – domestic production has actually fallen. The Japanese prefer to buy cheap, imported timber from the tropical rainforests of Southeast Asia, a practice that is causing considerable concern among many environmentalists as the rainforests of Borneo and Burma, and until recently Thailand, are being reduced to barren slopes.

Fishing is another rural occupation that has declined in activity, mainly because of a decline in fish stocks as a result of over-exploitation. Japanese fleets now operate in international waters far away from home, and ports that once supported fishing fleets are turning towards other endeavours. One of the most lucrative of these is tourism. As the urban Japanese become more affluent and seek recreation outside the cities, ports and harbours are becoming leisure marinas, hotels and resorts are springing up all over the countryside, and mountains are being levelled in order to make way for golf courses. Yet, to Westerners, there is a paradox with the Japanese approach to ecology. It has been one of the proud boasts of Japanese that they live close to and in harmony with nature – a strong theme in Japanese poetry and reflected in the Japanese preoccupation with the weather.

LEFT: rice field near Kyoto. **ABOVE:** autumn harvest of vegetables in northeastern Hokkaido.

Urban zones

By far the largest of Japan's few flat spaces is the Kanto Plain, an area centred on Tokyo Bay and formed by a build-up of sediments resulting from Ice Age-induced changes in sea level. Other extensive areas of flat land occur in the Tohoku region, Hokkaido, and along the Nagoya–Osaka industrial belt.

Such is the concentration of resources in these plains that most of Japan's people, factories, farmland, housing and public facilities are all crowded onto approximately 20 percent of Japan's total land area. Thus, very little of what one might call countryside exists on the plains.

Cities, towns and villages tend to merge into an indistinct urban blur that stretches endlessly across the flat land, with fields and farms dotted in between. In general, the plains are monochromatic, congested, and less than aesthetic.

The main industrial regions are the Kanto and Kansai areas, which are centred on Tokyo and Osaka, respectively. The Kanto area alone produces nearly a third of Japan's entire gross domestic product. If it were an independent nation, it would produce more goods and services than the United Kingdom.

Once again, it is the Kanto region and Tokyo in particular that has benefited from Japan's prosperity since World War II. Metropolitan Tokyo now has a nominal population of more than 12 million, but in fact the city spreads beyond its political boundaries north, south and west to form a massive urban complex that stretches across the entire Kanto Plain. The actual population of this megalopolis is estimated at around 30 million people.

Metropolitan Tokyo and Yokohama are the first and second cities of Japan, respectively. Third in size is Osaka, with a population of 2.5 million, followed by Nagoya with a little over 2 million. These cities have experienced phenomenal growth since World War II as Japan's urban industrialisation and rural mechanisation drew people off the farms and into the cities.

Many rural communities are now suffering from an increasingly aged population, and some have become virtual ghost towns as young people have fled the rural lifestyle. The situation is serious. A shortage of women in the countryside results in male farmers going on organised urban field trips in search of mates wanting to escape the city.

An ageing population

This demographic problem is not one that will in the future be restricted to the countryside. Japan as a whole has one of the slowest population-growth rates in the world, at less than 1 percent annually, and many analysts believe that the problem of an ageing population will, more than anything else, eventually lead to Japan's demise as a world economic leader as the economy shifts to support a population with at least 25 percent of it in retirement.

The reasons for this low growth rate are not hard to find. The average Japanese enjoys the longest life expectancy in the world. But the overcrowded cities, where couples live in cramped apartments, often with parents, are not conducive to large families, nor are the phenomenal costs of education and urban life. The alternative – the countryside – lacks appeal and job opportunity. Farming on the typically tiny Japanese farms is inefficient and backward, made profitable only by heavy and politically motivated subsidies from the government. Unlike most other industrial nations, Japan has few natural resources and depends heavily upon manufacturing for wealth and employment. ❑

LEFT: urban congestion in central Tokyo lacks aesthetic appeal. **RIGHT:** snow in northern Hokkaido.

Decisive Dates

RISE OF CIVILISED JAPAN

10,000 BC Jomon culture produces Japan's earliest known examples of pottery.

3500–2000 BC Population begins migrating inland from coastal areas.

300 BC Yayoi Period begins with the migration of people from Korea, who introduce rice cultivation.

AD 300 Start of Kofun Period as political and social institutions rapidly develop. The imperial line, or the Yamato dynasty, begins.

500–600 Buddhism arrives in Japan from Korea.

TIME OF THE WARLORDS

710 A new capital is established in Nara.

794 The capital is relocated to Kyoto. While the court expands, rural areas are neglected.

1180s Estate holders respond to the imperial court's disinterest in the rural areas by developing military power. Conflict amongst warlords ends Heian Period.

1185 Minamoto Yoritomo is victor of the estate-lord struggles and is granted the title of shogun. He establishes his base in Kamakura. The weakened imperial court, however, stays in Kyoto.

1274 Mongols from China unsuccessfully attempt an invasion, landing on Kyushu.

1333 Muromachi Period begins as shogun Ashikaga Takauji returns capital to Kyoto, confronting the imperial court and further eclipsing its influence.

1467 Relations between shogun and provincial military governors break down, leading to the chaotic Age of Warring States. Power of feudal lords increases.

1573 Warlord Oda Nobunaga overruns Kyoto and conquers the provinces, thus beginning the process of unifying the islands.

1582 Nobunaga is assassinated and replaced by Toyotomi Hideyoshi.

1590 All of Japan is under Hideyoshi's control.

1597 Hideyoshi attempts an invasion of Korea, but dies a year later.

1600 Edo Period begins as Tokugawa Ieyasu takes control after the Battle of Sekigahara.

1603 Tokugawa moves capital to Edo (present-day Tokyo), beginning 250 years of isolation from the rest of the world. Edo becomes the world's largest city.

1639 The beginning of the national seclusion policy.

1707 Mount Fuji erupts, dropping ash on Edo.

1720 The ban on importing foreign books finally lifted.

1853 Perry arrives with US naval ships and forces Japan to accept trade and diplomatic contact. The shogunate weakens as a result.

RETURN OF IMPERIAL RULE

1868 Meiji Restoration returns the emperor to power. The last shogun, Yoshinobu, retires. The name of the capital is changed from Edo to Tokyo (Eastern Capital).

1872 Samurai class is abolished by imperial decree.

1877 The Satsuma Rebellion is crushed.

1889 New constitution promulgated.

1895 Japan wins the Sino-Japanese War.

1904–6 Japan wins Russo-Japanese War.

1910 Japan annexes Korea.

1918 Japan is hit hard by economic chaos. Rice riots.

1923 Great Kanto Earthquake hits Tokyo area, killing tens of thousands and nearly destroying the city.

1926 Taisho emperor dies. Hirohito ascends the throne to begin the Showa Period.

1931 The Japanese occupy Manchuria and install China's last emperor, Pu-yi, as leader of the new Manchuguo. Japan leaves the League of Nations.

1936 A bloody military uprising, one of many during the 1930s, almost succeeds as a *coup d'état*.

1937 Japan begins a brutal military advance on China.

1941 Japan attacks Pacific and Asian targets. Within a year, Japan occupies most of East Asia and the western Pacific.

1945 American bombing raids destroy many of Japan's major cities and industrial centres. In August, two atomic bombs are dropped on Hiroshima and Nagasaki. A week later, Japan surrenders.

1946 A new constitution places sovereignty with the people rather than the emperor.
1951 San Francisco Peace Treaty settles all war-related issues and Japan is returned to sovereignty, except for some Pacific islands, including Okinawa. Japan regains its pre-war industrial output.
1955 Socialist factions merge to form Japan Socialist Party; in response, the Liberals and Democrats join to create the Liberal Democratic Party (LDP).
1964 The Summer Olympics are held in Tokyo.
1972 US returns Okinawa to Japan.
1980s Japan's economy blossoms into the world's second most powerful.
1989 Hirohito dies, replaced by his son Akihito.

END OF THE DREAM

1990 The so-called "economic bubble" of overinflated land values and overextended banks begins to deflate.
1991 Completely dependent on imported oil, Japan receives international criticism for not contributing its share to the Gulf War against Iraq.
1992 Japan's worst postwar recession begins.
1993 After a series of publicised scandals, LDP members are replaced by independents. A coalition government lasts seven months, replaced by another coalition led by the Japan Socialist Party.

PRECEDING PAGES: a warm, country smile.
LEFT: Prince Shotoku Taishi with two princely escorts.
ABOVE: 1964 Summer Olympics in Tokyo.

1995 An earthquake hits the Kobe area, killing over 5,000 and leaving 300,000 homeless. A religious cult releases nerve gas in the Tokyo subway, killing 12.
1996 The Liberal Democratic Party return to power.
1998 The Winter Olympics are held in Nagano. The world prods Japan to resuscitate its economy, essential to bring Asia out of economic recession. The Chinese president berates Japan on a state visit for not sufficiently apologising for World War II.
1999 Several die in Japan's worst ever nuclear accident at a uranium reprocessing plant in Tokaimura.
2000 G8 summit hosted in Okinawa and Kyushu.
2001 Junichiro Koizumi becomes LDP leader and prime minister. He visits South Korea and apologises for their suffering under his country's colonial rule.
2002 Japan co-hosts the football World Cup.
2003 Japan records the highest unemployment figures in its post-war period. Government announces intention to install a defensive missile system.
2004 The country sends an unarmed peacekeeping mission to Iraq in support of the US-led coalition.
2005 A Japanese textbook which glosses over Japan's World War II record sparks anti-Japanese protests in China and relations with Beijing deteriorate.
2006 World economists trumpet the revival of the economy, but the Japanese take a wait-and-see attitude.
2007 Koizumi's successor, Shinzo Abe, steps down after serving only one year as prime minister.
2008 Prime Minister Fukuda resigns in September. ❑

JAPAN'S EARLY CENTURIES

Migrations of people from the mainland across now-submerged land bridges evolved into a feudal system of warlords and an aesthetic of profound elegance

Shinto mythology holds that two celestial gods, descending to earth on a "floating bridge to heaven", dipped a spear into the earth, causing drops of brine to solidify into the archipelago's first group of islands. As one of the male gods was washing his face in the fertile sea, the sun goddess, Amaterasu, sprung from his left eye, bathing the world in light. Japanese mythology claims its first emperor, Jimmu, a direct descendant of the sun goddess. Conferring on him the title Tenno, Lord of Heaven, all emperors up to the present day have been addressed in this way. As recently as the early 1940s, it was ordained that the emperor was traced back to Jimmu, descendant of the sun goddess, and the emperor was officially considered divine. Archaeologists could dig but not counter the myth.

Today, the claim of the emperor's descent from the sun goddess is made by only a few Japanese, notably right-wing nationalists.

What we can say with certainty is that the lands that are now the Japanese archipelago have been inhabited by human beings for at least 30,000 years, and maybe for as long as 100,000 to 200,000 years. The shallow seas separating Japan from the Asian mainland were incomplete when these people first came and settled on the terrain. After people arrived, however, sea levels rose and eventually covered the land bridges.

Whether or not these settlers are the ancestors of the present Japanese remains a controversy. Extensive archaeological excavations of prehistoric sites in Japan only began during the 1960s, and so a clear and comprehensive understanding of the earliest human habitation in the archipelago has yet to emerge.

It is generally agreed that Japan was settled by waves of people coming from South Asia and the northern regions of the Asian continent, and that this migration very likely occurred over a long period.

LEFT: a clay figure, or *haniwa*, from the Jomon Period. **RIGHT:** earthenware, Jomon Period.

Jomon Period (circa 10,000–300 BC)

The earliest millennia of Neolithic culture saw a warming in worldwide climate, reaching peak temperature levels between 8000 and 4000 BC. In Japan, this phenomenon led to rising sea levels, which cut any remaining land bridges to the Asian mainland. At the same

time, the local waters produced more abundant species of fish and shellfish. New types of forest took root, sprang up, and thrived. These natural developments in the environment set the stage for the Early Jomon Period. Japan's earliest pottery – belonging to the Jomon culture – has been dated at about 10,000 BC, possibly the oldest known in the world, say some experts.

The Early Jomon people were mostly coastal-living, food-gathering nomads. Dietary reliance on fish, shellfish and sea mammals gave rise to the community refuse heaps known as shell-mounds, the archaeologist's primary source of information about these people. The

Early Jomon people also hunted deer and wild pig. Artefacts include stone-blade tools and the earliest known cord-marked pottery (*jomon,* in fact, means cord-marked).

Grinding stones, capped storage jars and other Middle Jomon artefacts indicate a much more intense involvement with plant cultivation. Middle Jomon came to an end when tree crops in inland hilly areas failed to provide sufficient sustenance.

The Late Jomon Period, dating from around 2000 BC, is marked by a resurgence amongst villages of coastal fishing along the Pacific coasts of the main islands.

Yayoi Period (circa 300 BC–AD 300)

Named after an archaeological site near Tokyo University, the Yayoi Period was a time of significant cultural transition and was ushered in by peoples who migrated from rice-growing areas of the Asian mainland, starting around 300 BC, into northern Kyushu via Korea and, most likely, Okinawa. (Northern Japan, in fact, lingered behind the rest of the archipelago, with the Jomon culture persisting well into northern Japan's early historic periods.)

In a brief 600 years, Japan was transformed from a land of nomadic hunting-and-gathering communities into one of stationary farming villages: tightly knit, autonomous rice-farming settlements sprang up so rapidly in Kyushu and western Honshu that by AD 100 settlements were found in most parts of the country, except for the northern regions of Honshu and Hokkaido.

Kofun Period (circa 300–710)

The break with Yayoi culture is represented by the construction of huge tombs of earth and stone in coastal areas of Kyushu and along the shores of the Inland Sea. *Haniwa*, hollow clay human and animal figures *(see picture on page 32)*, and models of houses decorated the perimeters of these tombs. These were made, some experts have speculated, as substitutes for the living retainers and possessions of the departed noble or leader.

Political and social institutions developed rapidly. Each of the community clusters that defined itself as a "country" or "kingdom" had a hierarchical social structure, subjected to increasing influence by a burgeoning central power based in the Yamato Plain, in what is now the area of Osaka and Nara. The imperial line, or the Yamato dynasty, was most likely formed out of a number of powerful *uji* (family-clan communities) that had developed in the Late Yayoi Period.

Buddhism came to Japan in the 6th century from Korea. Although it is said that writing accompanied the religion, it may be that Chinese writing techniques preceded the religion by as much as 100 to 150 years. In any case, it was literacy that made the imported religion accessible to the nobility, also exposing them to the Chinese classics and to the writings of sages such as Confucius. Social and political change naturally followed an increase in literacy.

The power of the Soga clan was enhanced by exclusive control of the imperial treasury and granaries and by the clan's monopolistic role as sponsor for new learning brought in from the Asian mainland. Their consolidation of political power culminated with Soga daughters being chosen exclusively as the consorts of emperors, and with Soga clansmen filling important court positions. The reforms they introduced were aimed primarily at strengthening the central government and reducing the power of other clans at the imperial court. The reforms were far-reaching, including changes in social structure, economic and legal systems, provincial boundaries, bureaucracy and taxes.

Nara Period (710–794)

An empress in the early 8th century again constructed a new capital, this one in the northwest of the Yamato Plain and named Heijo-kyo, on the site of present-day Nara. The century that followed – the Nara Period – saw the full enforcement of the system of centralised imperial rule based on Chinese concepts (the *ritsuryo* system), as well as flourishing arts and culture.

With the enforcement of the *ritsuryo* system, the imperial government achieved tight control, placing administrative control in a powerful grand council. All land used for rice cultivation was claimed to be under imperial ownership, which later led to heavy taxation of farmers.

Heian Period (794–1185)

In the last decade of the 8th century, the capital was relocated yet again. As usual, the city was built on the Chinese model and was named Heian-kyo. It was the core around which the city of Kyoto developed. Its completion in 795 marked the beginning of the glorious 400-year Heian Period. Kyoto remained the imperial capital until 1868, when the imperial court moved to Edo, soon to be renamed Tokyo.

The strength of the central government continued for several decades, but later in the 9th century the *ritsuryo* system gradually began to crumble. The central government was interested in expanding the area of its influence further and further from the capital, but provincial government became harder to manage under the bureaucratic system.

This was modified so that aristocrats and powerful temple guardians could own large estates *(shoen)*. Farmers, working imperial lands but faced with oppressive taxation, fled to these estates in large numbers. Thus the estate holders began to gain political – and military – power in the provinces.

Provincial areas were neglected by the imperial court. Banditry became widespread and local administrators were more interested in personal gain than in enforcing law and order. The result was that the lords of great estates continued to develop their own military power, eventually engaging in struggles amongst themselves. The fighting ended the Heian Period dramatically and decisively.

LEFT: bronze vessel from the Yayoi Period.
RIGHT: Minamoto Yoritomo of Kamakura Period.

Kamakura Period (1185–1333)

The victor of the struggles, Minamoto Yoritomo, was granted the title of shogun. He set up his base at Kamakura, far from Kyoto and south of where Edo would arise. He established an administrative structure and military headquarters, creating ministries to take care of samurai under his control. He had, in effect, come to dominate the country by assuming control of justice, imperial succession, and defence of the country. He remained in Kamakura, refusing to go to the imperial capital.

Nevertheless, he convinced the emperor to sanction officials called *shugo* (military governors) and *jito* (stewards) in each province. The former were responsible for military control of the provinces and the latter for supervising the land, as well as collecting taxes. Both posts were answerable directly to the shogun himself, and thus government by the warrior class, located at a distance from the imperial capital, was created.

This governing system was based on obligation and dependency, not unlike that of medieval Europe, and so it can be called a true feudal system known as *bakufu*, or shogunate. The imperial court was, in effect, shoved into a corner and ignored. The court remained alive, however, though subsequent centuries saw its impoverishment. Still, it kept an important function in ritual and as a symbol until 1868, when the emperor again became the acting head of state.

Although the Kamakura Period was relatively brief, there were events and developments that profoundly affected the country. A revolutionary advance of agricultural techniques occurred that allowed greater production of food.

Consequently, there was a significant increase in population and economic growth, with more intense settlement of the land, improved commerce and trade, the expansion of local markets, and the beginnings of a currency system. Contact with the Chinese mainland resumed on a private basis.

Strong Buddhist leaders arose who preached doctrines that appealed to both the samurai and the common people, and Buddhism became a popular religion, whereas in the past it had been the monopoly of the aristocracy.

The complexities of civil rule became top-heavy; the system of military governors and stewards started to crumble. More strain was added by the defence of the country against the two Mongol invasions in 1274 and 1281, both of which were unsuccessful due in great measure to the fortuitous occurrence of typhoons that destroyed the invading Mongol fleet.

Muromachi Period (1333–1568)

A subsequent shogun, Ashikaga Takauji, returned the capital to Kyoto, bringing the shogunate nose to nose with the imperial court and effectively eclipsing any power, political or economic, that the court may have retained. At the same time, the Ashikaga shogun and vassals, in the age-old pattern of conquering warriors anywhere, caught aristocratitis and actively delved into such effete pursuits as connoisseurship and cultural patronage after the manner of the old aristocracy.

The name of the period, Muromachi, comes from the area of Kyoto in which a later Ashikaga shogun, Yoshimitsu, built his residence. His life represents perhaps the high point of the Ashikaga shogunate. Yoshimitsu took an active role in court politics as well as excelling in his military duties as shogun.

Overall, the Muromachi Period introduced the basic changes that would assure the economic growth and stability of the coming Edo Period. Agricultural techniques were improved, new crops were introduced, and irrigation and commecial farming expanded. Guilds of specialised craftsmen appeared, a money economy spread, and trade increased markedly. Most importantly, towns and cities arose and grew; such development was accompanied by the appearance of merchant and service classes.

A later Ashikaga shogun was assassinated in 1441, which started the decline of the shogunate; the relationship between the shogun and the military governors of the provinces broke down. A decade of war and unrest marked the total erosion of centralised authority and a general dissolution of society. It ushered in the Age of Warring States, a century of battle that lasted from 1467 until 1568.

The almost total decentralisation of government that occurred in the Age of Warring States saw the development of what might be called a true type of feudal lord, the *daimyo*. The need to defend territory by military might meant that the political unit became contiguous with its military potential. The *daimyo* became what he was by right of conquest and might, backed up by vast armies.

During this century of warfare, with its ethic of ambition and expansion by force of arms, it is not surprising that the idea of unifying – or subduing – the entire country occurred to a few of the warriors, leaders of vision and ability.

Momoyama Period (1568–1600)

This short Momoyama Period is somewhat of an historian's artefact, more the climaxing of the Muromachi Period. But it has been accorded a name, perhaps because the Ashikaga shogunate ended in 1573 (the Muromachi Period is when the Ashikaga shogun ruled), notably when Oda Nobunaga (1534–82), the first of three leaders to go about the business of unifying the country, overran Kyoto. The other leaders were Toyotomi Hideyoshi (1536–98) and Tokugawa Ieyasu (1542–1616).

Nobunaga conquered the home provinces in a rigorous manner. He eliminated rivals in the usual military fashion and is known particularly for razing the temples of militant Buddhist sects around Kyoto that opposed him. Temple burning aside, he had a flair for culture.

Although he brought only about one-third of the country under his control, Nobunaga laid the foundation for the unification that would later follow. He was assassinated by a treacherous general in 1582.

Hideyoshi, Nobunaga's chief general, did away with Nobunaga's murderer and set himself up as Nobunaga's successor. With military brilliance, statesmanship, and a certain amount of brass, he proceeded vigorously with the job of unifying Japan. By 1590, all territories of the country, directly or by proxy, were essentially under his control. But the government was still decentralised in a complex network of feudal relationships. Hideyoshi's hold on the country, based on oaths of fealty, was slippery at best. Still, he effected sweeping domestic reforms. The action that perhaps had the longest-lasting social impact on Japanese history was his "sword hunt", in which all non-samurai were forced to give up their weapons. (To this day, there are strict regulations on weapons of any sort in Japan, whether knives or guns.) A class system was also introduced. In some areas, rich landlords had to make a difficult choice: declare themselves to be samurai and susceptible to the demands of the warrior's life, or else remain as commoners and thus subservient to the samurai class.

Hideyoshi made two attempts to conquer Korea, in 1592 and 1597, with the aim of taking over China. His death in 1598 brought this megalomaniacal effort to an end.

The cultural achievements of these three decades were astonishing. The country was in political ferment, yet glorious textiles, ceramics and paintings were produced. ❑

LEFT: *sumi-e* (ink painting) from Muromachi Period.
ABOVE: a painted mural of the Battle of Osaka Castle.

THE EDO PERIOD

The rise of the great shogunates and their samurai warlords instilled in the Japanese culture ways of thinking and behaviour that persist even today

The political, economic, social, religious and intellectual facets of the Edo Period (1600–1868) are exceedingly complex. One often-cited general characteristic of this time is an increasingly prosperous merchant class occurring simultaneously with urban development. Edo (now modern-day Tokyo) became one of the world's great cities and is thought to have had a population in excess of 1 million at the beginning of the 18th century – greater than London or Paris at the time.

The Tokugawa shogun

For many years, the shogun Hideyoshi had bemoaned his lack of a male heir. When in the twilight of Hideyoshi's years an infant son, Hideyori, was born, Hideyoshi was ecstatic and became obsessed with founding a dynasty of warrior rulers. So he established a regency council of leading vassals and allies, foremost of whom was Tokugawa Ieyasu (1542–1616), who controlled the most territory in the realm after Hideyoshi. Members of the council swore loyalty to the infant; the boy was five at the time of Hideyoshi's death.

The death of Hideyoshi was naturally an opportunity for the ambitions of restless warlords to surface. Tokugawa Ieyasu had about half of the lords who were allied with Hideyoshi's son sign pledges to him within a year of Hideyoshi's death. In 1600, however, he was challenged by a military coalition of lords from western Japan. He won the encounter in the Battle of Sekigahara (near Kyoto) and became the islands' de facto ruler.

In 1603, Tokugawa Ieyasu was given the title of shogun by the still subservient but symbolically important emperor. He established his capital in Edo, handed his son the shogun title in 1605, and then retired to a life of intrigue and scheming that was aimed at consolidating the position of his family. (Ieyasu himself would die in 1616.)

The primary problem facing Ieyasu was how to make a viable system out of the rather strange mix of a strong, central military power and a totally decentralised administrative structure. Eventually he devised a complex system that combined feudal authority and bureaucratic administration with the Tokugawa shoguns as supreme authority from whom the various lords, or *daimyo*, received their domains and to whom they allied themselves by oath.

While the military emphasis of the domain was curtailed, each *daimyo* had considerable autonomy in the administration of his domain. The system sufficed to maintain peace and a growing prosperity for more than two centuries. Its flaws were in its inability to adapt well to social and political change, as would later be seen.

Ieyasu was Napoleonic in his passion for administration, and he thought of every device possible to assure that his descendants would retain power. Wanting to keep an eye on the *daimyo*, in 1635 he established the *sankin kotai* system, which required staggered attendance in Edo for the 300 independent feudal lords.

The shogunate set up a rigid class hierarchy – warriors, farmers, artisans, merchants – and adopted a school of neo-Confucianism as the theoretical basis for social and political policy.

Whether in Edo or the countryside, every individual knew exactly what his or her position in society was and how to behave accordingly. For most of the Tokugawa decades, Japan's doors were closed to the outside. Long years of isolated peace slowly replaced the warrior's importance with that of the merchant. The standards of living for all classes increased, but at times the shogunate quelled conspicuous consumption among merchants.

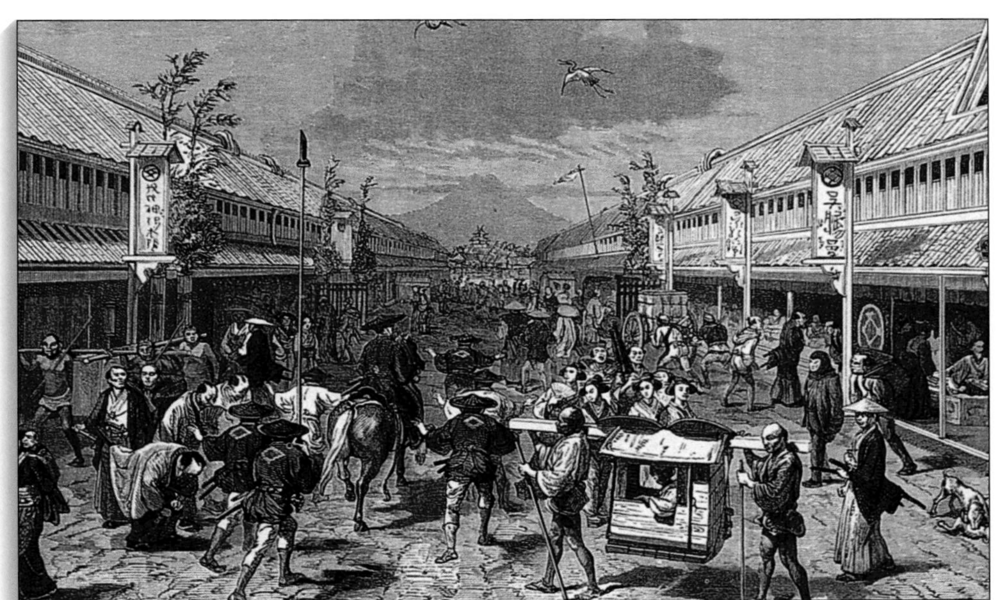

Growth of Edo

When Ieyasu first settled down in what would eventually become modern Tokyo, the area was little more than a collection of scattered farming and fishing villages. The little town of Edo-juku, at the mouth of the Hirakawa River, contained only about 100 thatched huts in the shadow of a dilapidated castle, built in 1457 by the minor warlord Ota Dokan. A sophisticated poet and scholar, in 1485 he was betrayed and butchered at the behest of his own lord.

Ieyasu brought with him to Edo a ready-made population of considerable size. Huge numbers of peasants, merchants and *ronin* (masterless samurai) poured into the new capital of the shogun to labour in the construction of the castle, mansions, warehouses and other infrastructure required to run the giant bureaucracy. The courses of rivers were changed, canals were dug, and Hibiya Inlet, which brought Tokyo Bay lapping at the base of the castle hill, was filled in.

When the major *daimyo* and their entourage were in town, the samurai portion of the city's population probably topped 500,000, maybe even outnumbering the commoners. The samurai allot-

LEFT: Tokugawa Ieyasu, the first Tokugawa shogun.
ABOVE: street life in Edo (Tokyo).

A SAMURAI'S WAY OF LIFE

The way of the samurai – *bushido* – was a serious path to follow, "a way of dying" to defend the honour of one's lord or one's own name. Often that meant *seppuku*, or ritual disembowelment. An unwritten code of behaviour and ethics, *bushido* came to the foreground during the Kamakura Period. In the Edo Period, *bushido* helped strengthen *bakufu*, or the shogunate government, by perfecting the feudal class system of samurai, farmer, artisan and merchant. The ruling samurai class was by far the most powerful. Only when the economy shifted from rice-based to monetary did the merchants take control of Edo, leaving the samurai increasingly in debt.

ted themselves over 60 percent of the city's land. Another 20 percent went to hundreds of shrines and temples, which formed a spiritually protective ring around the outer edges of the city.

By the early 1700s, an estimated 1 to 1.4 million people lived in Edo, making it by far the largest city in the world at the time. During the same period, Kyoto had a population of 400,000, and Osaka 300,000. In 1801, when Britain's navy dominated the seas, Europe's largest city, London, had fewer than a million inhabitants. Japan's population hovered around 30 million for most of the Edo era; less than two million belonged to the samurai families.

THE 47 MASTERLESS SAMURAI

In 1701, a warlord named Asano from near Hiroshima became angered at the taunting of a *hatamoto* named Kira, who had been assigned to teach him proper etiquette for receiving an imperial envoy. Asano drew his sword and wounded Kira. Asano was ordered to commit ritual disembowelment, or *seppuku*. He did so. His lands were confiscated and his samurai left as *ronin*, or masterless warriors. A year later, the *ronin* took revenge by attacking Kira's Edo mansion. Chopping off Kira's head, they took it to Asano's grave so that his spirit could finally rest. In turn, the 47 *ronin* were ordered by the shogun to commit *seppuku*, which they did as a group.

In general, the samurai gravitated to the hilly parts of the city, or Yamanote, while the townspeople congregated – or were forced to do so – in the downtown lowlands, or Shitamachi, especially along the Sumida River. More than half of Edo's residents were crammed into the 15 percent of the city comprising Shitamachi, with a population density of about 70,000 people per square kilometre. Almost from the start, both Yamanote and Shitamachi began to encroach through landfill onto Tokyo Bay. (Even today in the modern city of Tokyo, these two districts retain distinctive characteristics.)

The Edo castle

The grounds of Ieyasu's huge castle, including the defensive moat system, were extensive. The complex was not actually completed until 1640 but was razed by fire seven years later.

But the shogun's capital must have been a truly impressive city, backed by Fuji-san and laced with canals. It is often forgotten nowadays that most of Edo's supplies came by sea, especially from Osaka. In fact, one of the reasons Ieyasu had chosen the area for his capital was its easy access to the sea. But the swampy shore of Tokyo Bay itself was unsuitable for building docks and wharves; instead, canals and rivers threading inland from the bay served as ports.

This is not to suggest that the five great highways from the provinces, and especially from Kyoto, converging on the city were not also important. They were, especially the famous Tokaido, or East Sea Road, along which most of the feudal lords from Osaka and Kyoto travelled to Tokyo for their periodic and mandated stays in Edo. Tokaido also formed the central artery of the city itself between Shinagawa and Nihombashi.

The dichotomy between the refined – albeit somewhat constipated – culture of upper-class Yamanote and the robust, plebeian art and drama of lower-class Shitamachi (which Edward Seidensticker aptly dubbed respectively as the "high city" and "low city") has been a consistent feature of life in Edo. The Edokko (Children of Edo) took delight in delight, and this appreciation of pleasure is grandly reflected in the popular culture of the time – the colour and splash of *kabuki;* the *bunraku* puppet drama; *ukiyo-e* woodblock prints depicting the world of actors, sumo stars, courtesans and geisha; the pleasure quarters, licensed and unlicensed; and the vigorous publishing world of both scholarship and trashy stories. All of these reflected the Edo pleasure in the material world and in a kind of high consumerism. The fact that men outnumbered women – two to one as late as 1721 – probably contributed to making the male population more than a bit rowdy and cantankerous. It would certainly explain the emphasis on catering to the sensual pleasures of men and in the rise of woodblock prints of a rather graphic if not exaggerated sexual nature.

SHIFTING VICES

The shogunate unsuccessfully tried banning both *kabuki* and prostitution. Eventually, the shogunate simply moved them to less desirable locations.

Rise of the merchants

The establishment of the shogunate caused many economic changes. After the shogunate eliminated international trade, merchants and the increasingly powerful commercial conglomerates *(zaibatsu)* turned their attention to domestic distribution and marketing systems. The highways built by the Tokugawas, along with their standardisation of weights, measures and coinage, helped with the rise of the *zaibatsu*.

The *samurai* received their stipends in rice, but the economy was increasingly dependent upon money – not to the shogunate's liking, as the shogunate's economic foundation was based upon taxes paid in rice. The result: the samurai borrowed from the merchants and increasingly went into debt.

Yet it was still controlled with rigid social and governmental systems. Internal pressures demanded change. Moreover, the world itself was not about to allow Japan to keep its doors closed. The industrial revolution was gaining momentum in Europe. The Western powers were casting about for more countries into which to expand economic influence.

While others had tried rattling Japan's doors, it was the United States that yanked them open in 1853 with Commodore Matthew Perry and America's East India Squadron – the famous "Black Ships". He reappeared the following year with additional ships to back up the action and was successful. In 1858 a treaty of friendship and trade was signed with the United States, followed shortly by treaties with other Western powers.

The turmoil and tumult of the 15 years from 1853 to 1868 have been well documented in many books. The sense of Japan afloat in a sea of hostile powers who possessed more technology and had voracious ambitions may have acted to direct domestic energies away from internal wrangling. The shogun was in a tight squeeze with the arrival of Perry. His consensus with the *daimyo* regarding how to respond to the Black Ships – encouraging them to strengthen and improve defences in their own domains – eventually diluted his control over the *daimyo*. At the same time, an anti-Tokugawa movement amongst lower-level *daimyo* was stewing near Osaka and Kyoto.

Rebel *daimyo* captured the then-powerless emperor and declared the restoration of imperial rule. Shogunate forces sought to reverse the situation in Kyoto but were defeated. The shogun yielded to the imperial court in 1868 – the Meiji Restoration. The emperor ascended again to head of state; the reign of the Meiji emperor would last from 1868 until 1912. ❑

LEFT: print by Utamaro.

RIGHT: Perry's American fleet at Uragawa.

THE MODERN ERA

Once militarism was replaced by consumerism, Japan rapidly became one of the world's richest, safest and most advanced countries

The Meiji Restoration of 1868, in which the ascension of the Meiji emperor as the nation's leader returned Japan to imperial rule, was a revolution of considerable proportions. Yet it was accomplished with surprisingly little bloodshed. The last shogun, Yoshinobu, in statesman-like fashion retired and gave up the Edo castle rather than precipitate a full-scale civil war. Power was officially returned to the emperor in the autumn of 1867.

But shogunate residue remained in Edo and not all the samurai gave up easily. At the Tokugawa family temple of Kan'ei-ji, most of which is now Tokyo's Ueno Park, 2,000 die-hard Tokugawa loyalists – the Shogitai – chose to make a last stand in a bloody, one-day battle. During this Battle of Ueno, the Shogitai burned most of the Kan'ei-ji complex to the ground. Hundreds of the Shogitai were killed, their bodies left to rot by the victors.

Meiji Period (1868–1912)

In 1868, an imperial edict changed the name of Edo to Tokyo, or Eastern Capital, and Emperor Meiji moved his court from the imperial capital of Kyoto to Tokyo. But before leaving Kyoto, the emperor issued an extremely important document proclaiming that "knowledge shall be sought throughout the world so as to strengthen the foundations of imperial rule... Evil customs of the past shall be broken and everything based upon the just laws of Nature".

Because at the end of the Edo Period the office of emperor had no longer been associated with a political system, the emperor's "restoration" could be used as a convenient symbol and vehicle for choosing from a wide range of governmental structures. The quality of the nation's new leadership, and the political, economic and cultural choices they made, can be seen as nothing less than spectacular.

In a few decades, Japan effectively restructured itself as a political entity. In retrospect, this seems astonishingly radical. Yet it did not happen overnight, but rather by a series of incremental modifications to the political system. The first new governmental structure was a compromise between old and new. It cleverly borrowed names from archaic imperial institutions to give an aura of tradition to what was hardly traditional.

Meeting the Western powers as an equal was one of the guiding concerns of the Meiji years. This meant adopting anything Western, from railways to ballroom dancing. The pendulum first swung to extremes, from a total rejection of all native things (including an urge to abandon the Japanese language) to an emotional nationalism after the excesses of initial enthusiasm for foreign imports. Japan took to Western industrialisation with enthusiasm. But the employment of numerous foreign advisors (upwards of 3,000) ended as soon as the Japanese sensed that they could continue perfectly well on their own.

PRECEDING PAGES: celebrating the emperor's birthday outside the palace. **LEFT:** Mutsuhito, the Meiji emperor. **RIGHT:** exposition in Ueno Park, Meiji Period.

After a number of unsuccessful drafts over the years, a new constitution for the country was promulgated in 1889. This Meiji Constitution helped Japan become recognised as an advanced nation by the West. Another factor was Japan's success in the Sino-Japanese War of 1894–95, which proved the country's ability to wage modern warfare.

But the clincher in making Japan a true world power was winning the Russo-Japanese War of 1904–06, the first time that an Asian nation had defeated a European power. It didn't stop there, however. In 1910, Japan annexed Korea, ostensibly by treaty but actually under military threat. It would occupy Korea until the end of World War II in 1945.

Of Emperors and Calendars

Japan has a British-style constitutional monarchy and parliament. Since the 1868 Meiji Restoration, there have been four emperors, since World War II a figurehead:

- **Meiji** (Meiji Period) 1867 (1868)–1912
- **Taisho** (Taisho Period) 1912 (1915)–1926
- **Hirohito** (Showa Period) 1926 (1928)–1989
- **Akihito** (Heisei Period) 1989 (1990)–present

Coronation dates in parenthesis.

Japan uses two methods for indicating the year: the Western system (i.e., 2007) and a system based on how long the current emperor has reigned (i.e., Heisei 18). The latter appears frequently on official documents.

Emperor Meiji died in 1912. By then, Japan had consolidated its economy, defined a political system, changed its social structure, and become an advanced nation in many ways.

Taisho Period (1912–26)

The short reign of Emperor Taisho saw the 20th century catch Japan in its grasp and carry it off on a strange and sometimes unpleasant odyssey.

World War I proved an enormous economic boom, and Japan seized the chance to enter Asian markets vacated by the European powers. But the inevitable deflation hit hard and there were major rice riots in Tokyo in 1918.

The following year, most politics became extremely polarised as the labour movement and leftists gained momentum. A new right, which believed in the politics of assassination rather than the ballot box, emerged from the political shadows.

A series of political murders, including of prime ministers and former prime ministers, followed over the next 15 years, helping to create the climate of violence that eventually would let the military intervene in politics.

The big event of the 1920s was the Great Kanto Earthquake. It struck around noon on 1 September 1923, when a good percentage of the city's charcoal and gas stoves were lit. Fire, not the quake itself, caused the most damage. Ninety percent of Yokohama was destroyed.

During the Taisho Period, Japan began to bubble intellectually. The growing prosperity (and the accompanying problems), the shrinking size of the world, and the relative youth of Japan as a world power contributed to the "Taisho Democracy", which was actually little more than a time of good, healthy, intellectual ferment. Nevertheless, this bright spot was important as a precursor to Japan's plunge into the dark period of militarism and war and as a foundation for the country's emergence afterwards.

Showa Period (1926–89)

With the death of the Taisho emperor in 1926, Hirohito succeeded to the throne to begin the Showa Period. Japan's isolation from World War I had kept the nation free of Europe's war-weary cynicism, and, too, of the horrors of such war. But within a decade, Japan itself would be sliding into world war. Whatever the political, economic and social forces that produced the military government and the aggressive war effort, some observations can be made. The distribution of wealth was still uneven. The establishment factions included big business (the *zaibatsu*), the upper crust of government, and the military interests.

Political power within the country favoured establishment interests; suffrage was not universal. Non-establishment interests were weak because they had little recourse for expression, other than through imported political concepts – socialism and communism – that were distrusted and feared.

Japan, still sensitive to Western righteousness regarding Asia even half a century after opening up to the West, felt insecure. This and domestic economic and demographic pressures made military hegemony seem a viable alternative, at least to the military. Indeed, the military and its supporters were increasingly frustrated by what they saw as ineffectual and compromising civilian policies.

LEFT: *ukiyo-e* print of the emperor promulgating the Meiji Constitution. **ABOVE:** busy street in Tokyo's Shibuya district in the early 20th century.

Militarism's rise and fall

The pivotal point was the Manchurian Incident of 1931, in which Japanese military forces occupied Manchuria and set up the state of Manchuguo. Protest over this action by the League of Nations resulted in Japan leaving the League and following a policy of isolation. Within the military itself, extremist factionalism grew, and during the 1930s several plots of one kind or another sought to take over power. The most famous is the 26 February Incident of 1936, a bloody military uprising that might have been a coup d'état had it not been based on vague, romantic ideas that did not include a practical plan of how to use power. This bolstered the civilian resistance to military involvement in politics. But in the summer of 1937 war erupted in China and Japanese troops began a brutal campaign against the Chinese, notably in the occupation of Nanjing and the slaughter of between 150,000 and 300,000 civilians.

Seeking to discourage Western intervention in Japan's Asian expansion, the Japanese military launched pre-emptive attacks not only on Pearl Harbor in December of 1941 but against European colonial holdings throughout Asia. In less than a year, Japan possessed most of East Asia and the western Pacific. Japanese occupation was often savage and inhumane.

But by early 1945, Japan was on the defensive. Ignoring the Geneva Convention ban, the US continued its campaign of terror bombings on civilian areas of Japanese cities. The air raids were of an unprecedented ferocity. Many of the firebombs fell on the populations of Sumida-ku and other wards to the east of Tokyo during the 102 raids that were launched between January 1945 and Japan's surrender in August. Robert McNamara, whose name would later be linked with the Vietnam War, took part in the planning of the raids, recalling later that "in a single night we burnt to death 100,000 civilians... men, women, and children."

SURRENDER PREVAILED

Evidence suggests that the Japanese military ignored civilian officials' pleas to end the war. Three days after the atomic bomb on Hiroshima, the imperial army's chief of staff assured the civilian government that a foreign invasion of Japan would be turned back. Informed of the second atomic bomb on Nagasaki, he repeated his claim. Still, on 14 August Hirohito prepared a surrender announcement. That night, 1,000 members of the army attempted a coup by surrounding the Imperial Palace, executing the emperor's guard commander, and searching for the emperor's surrender edict. The coup was thwarted, and Japan surrendered.

Despite Germany's defeat in May of 1945, Japanese military leaders would not yield. Japan's intransigence, combined with mounting pressure from the US scientific lobby keen to test the effects of their labour, saw the dropping, in mid-August of the same year, of atomic bombs on the cities of Hiroshima and Nagasaki.

On 15 August 1945, Emperor Hirohito spoke on the radio – the first time commoners had heard his voice – and declared an unconditional surrender. Japan lost its empire, its right to independent foreign policy, the emperor's claim to divinity, and the army. More than 6 million soldiers and civilians returned home to Japan. War-crime trials convicted several thousand Japanese; 920 of them were executed.

A new 1946 constitution issued under the mandate of Gen. Douglas MacArthur's occupation government guaranteed Western-style liberties, established a British-style parliamentary system, dismantled the pre-war industrial *zaibatsu*, and renounced war as national policy. With the signing of the 1951 San Francisco Peace Treaty, American occupation of the country ended and Japan regained its sovereignty a year later. Okinawa, however, remained under US control until 1972.

The sun rises again

Three significant characteristics help define post-war Japan up to the present day: government-coordinated industrialisation and spectacular economic growth; the mocking of democracy by politicians; and modern Japan's collective inability to recall much of Asia's history involving Japan between 1910 and 1945.

The decades following the war were of well-coordinated corporate and bureaucratic efforts to revive both business and the country. Protected by the American military umbrella, Japan was able to funnel full economic resources into its economy. Meanwhile, the provincial millions who continued to flow into Tokyo – its population more than doubled after 1950 – often found homes along the railway tracks leading from the main terminals of Shibuya, Shinjuku and Ikebukuro.

With the urban population's explosive rise, farming's importance dropped to a fraction of the nation's gross national product, although the farmers' political power actually increased. Unusual for a developing or developed country,

Japan's new national wealth was evenly distributed amongst the people, leaving almost no one in an economic lower class. Unemployment remained low. Industrial labour disputes and strikes were minimal.

During post-war reconstruction, government regulation had served Japan's interests well. But as Japan joined the advanced industrial economies in the 1960s and especially the 1970s, the one-way nature of Japan's markets strained relations with others, especially with the US, its largest market, and Europe. Over-regulation and chummy business-government relationships saddled consumers with ridiculously high prices for nearly everything except umbrellas, cheap in this rainy land.

High rates of household savings created excess capital, used by business and the government for funding massive infrastructure projects. The economy accelerated with uncanny momentum, surpassing every other country except the United States. Japan became the new global paradigm for success and potency. The stock market was on a trajectory that, in the late 1980s, momentarily exceeded the New York Stock Exchange in volume and vigour. Real estate in Japan became the planet's most valuable, and banks dished out money, securing the loans with highly over-valued land. Japan's rising sun seemed, for the moment, to outshine most of the world.

LEFT: a Japanese POW happy to read the headlines, "War Over".

ABOVE: schoolgirls wave blessings to the warriors from Kagoshima base, 1945.

Heisei Period (1989–)

Emperor Hirohito died in 1989, the longest-reigning emperor (62 years) in Japan's recorded history. His son, Akihito, took the throne and adopted the period name of *Heisei,* which means "attainment of peace". He and his family have made sustained efforts to humanise the imper-

WHAT KIND OF ARMY?

Article 9 of the postwar constitution, set up by the US, prohibits Japan from possessing or having the potential of an external military force. In place of a military is the *Jieitai*, or Self-Defence Forces (SDF). The SDF is a highly sophisticated military entity and one of the world's strongest armies, a situation that increasingly concerns Japan's neighbours. However, ships and planes in the SDF have limited operating range, and officially the SDF's responsibility extends 1,600 km (1,000 miles) from Japan's shores. Given Japan's past aggression, its military role today is a continuing and delicate debate, often inflaming right-wing nationalists and conservatives.

ial family and to tangentially deal with Japan's brutal past. But as a politically neutered figurehead, the emperor is not permitted to address politics, history, or his father's place in history.

Atop the cauldron of hyper-inflated land values, Japan's "bubble economy" superheated in the late 1980s, only to begin collapsing in 1990. The stock market lost half its value in a short time, banks lost still-unspeakable amounts on loans secured by now-deflated land values, and a blossoming Japanese self-righteousness as economic superpower took a cold shower. The country went into a recession that has continued into the new millennium.

But in politics, life at the very top remained very good. For nearly four decades, one political party has dominated Japan – the dubiously named Liberal Democratic Party, or LDP.

Institutionalised and immune to legal redress, *seiji fuhai,* or political corruption, festered unimpeded at the highest corporate and governmental levels. By the 1980s, *The Economist* opined, the ruling LDP government seemed to be "choking on its own corruption".

The LDP fell from grace in 1993 in an unusual backlash by voters, to be replaced by a coalition government. The LDP resuscitated itself by returning to control in 1996. By mid-1999 the

party had formed a coalition with the Liberal Party and the new Komeito Party.

Shaky foundations

Two events within two months in the mid-1990s eroded Japanese self-confidence and world opinion yet further. Approximately 10 percent of the world's earthquakes occur in Japan, and Tokyo and the surrounding Kanto Plain sit on geologically unstable ground.

In January of 1995, an earthquake hit Kobe,

Tokyo's Next Earthquake

Government studies in the 1990s estimated that there would be around 10,000 deaths and over half a million buildings destroyed in Tokyo if the 1923 earthquake were repeated today. Casualty estimates did not take into account subways. Three million people move in and out of Tokyo daily, mostly by train and subway, and should tunnels collapse, deaths in subways could reach tens of thousands alone. The Kobe quake was considerably more powerful than the 1923 earthquake that destroyed Tokyo. Official estimates have since been amended. Should a Kobe-strength earthquake hit Tokyo, casualties could approach 100,000.

Above: life goes on after the Kobe earthquake of 1995. **Right:** Seto Ohashi, between Shikoku and Honshu, during construction.

an important coastal port near Osaka. Kobe had been declared a low-risk area for earthquakes. The Great Hanshin Earthquake, as it has been named, killed more than 5,000 people and left 300,000 homeless. Fires from igniting gas mains (said to be earthquake-proof) incinerated entire neighbourhoods of poorly constructed residences; elevated expressways and *shinkansen* rails toppled over like matchwood. Subway tunnels collapsed. Moreover, the local and national government response was nothing short of inept and irresponsible. In the days that followed, the Japanese people were shocked by their government's inability to respond.

Two months after the Kobe earthquake, another event decimated Japanese confidence. In the heart of Tokyo, 12 people died and thousands were injured when the Tokyo subway system was flooded with sarin, a lethal nerve gas. It was in the middle of rush hour, and the prime target was Kasumigaseki Station, *the* subway stop for offices of the national government and parliament. The effect on the Japanese psyche cannot be described. The Japanese have long prided themselves on having perhaps the safest nation in the world, and believed that Japanese could not engage in lethal terrorism against other Japanese. But the nerve-gas attack

JUST BUILD AND NO ONE WILL COME

One of the major engines of growth in postwar Japan has been the construction industry. Following the war, most of Japan's infrastructure had to be rebuilt. Thirty years later, this development became institutionalised to the point that it is a major political tool. Much of this money comes from Japan's postal savings and pension funds. Public opinion has lately embraced the belief that many of these projects are useless efforts solely for politicians' gain and glory.

Bullet-train lines have been built to backwater towns. Two huge and quite expensive bridges between Shikoku and Honshu carry less than half the traffic that planners claimed, and tolls are more than US$50 one-way. The world's longest (9.5-km/6-mile) underwater tunnel, the Aqualine Expressway under Tokyo Bay that opened in 1998, is rarely used, perhaps because of a US$40 toll and because it goes nowhere important. In the 1980s, Tokyo's former governor initiated an immense "sub-city" in Tokyo Bay at an estimated cost of US$100 billion. The city intended to sell or lease reclaimed land for huge profits. The economy's collapse instead put Tokyo deep in debt.

Recent prime ministers have come to power on the platform of structural reform. The battle over who really runs the country, though, continues.

had been seemingly spontaneous and random.

In the days that followed, the chief of the National Police Agency was shot in front of his Tokyo home. Mysterious fumes sickened people at Yokohama Station and in nearby department stores. Shinjuku Station was seconds away from the release of enough hydrocyanic gas to kill 10,000 people. (A passer-by found the gas package in a toilet during the rush hour.)

The sarin gas attack – and other deadly deeds uncovered by investigators – were traced to a religious cult, Aum Shinrikyo, led by a nearly blind self-proclaimed prophet. On the day that its guru leader was arrested at the cult's main compound near Fuji-san, a parcel addressed to the governor of Tokyo exploded, which resulted in the hand of the governor's aide being blown apart.

GOVERNMENT DETAILS

Japan's government is called a parliamentary democracy. The prime minister, of the majority party, comes from the Diet. The emperor is head of state.

Persistent doldrums

Despite some promising economic indicators, such as a rallying stock market and high demand from China, Japan's recovery remains a matter of speculation. There have been many false dawns before.

The grimmest and most obvious fallout from Japan's economic decline, now well into its second decade, has been cynicism towards politicians, social destabilisation, and an increase in the levels of crime, suicide and homelessness. Aware of this new vulnerability, American and European companies have returned to Japan to buy up property and increase their market share of banking and other financial services.

If cleaning up Japan's bad loans and eradicating the so-called "zombie companies" is the main priority, why is this painful but necessary process not already underway? The old guard and the reformists have locked horns, resulting in half measures and inaction. A lack of political will and a reluctance to upset vested interests leave an essentially vibrant nation trapped in the machinery of obsolete institutions.

Giving cause for hope are Japan's enormous reserves of under-exploited private savings, its new willingness to at least discuss reform and enter into healthy public debate on how to revive a sclerotic nation, and the existence of large numbers of ambitious highly talented people capable, in the right environment, of leading the new Japan.

There is also the possibility of a "third great opening" as the media has dubbed the prospect of a hi-tech-driven recovery (the other two openings being Commander Perry's demand that Japan open to foreign trade, and General MacArthur's occupation-period initiatives). Finally, and perhaps the most significant of all, is the country's track record: its ability to bounce back from adversity. ❑

A WOMAN'S DESTINY?

Crown Prince Naruhito remained single until his early thirties. When he married, talk soon turned to an heir. His wife, Owada Masako, had a blossoming career in the diplomatic service. Younger Japanese women saw in her a modern woman – educated abroad, stylish, independent. Japanese agree, however, that marriage and the Imperial Household Agency have quenched Masako's independent ways. After eight years of marriage, Masako gave birth to a baby girl in December 2001. At the time of writing, the debate as to whether the post-war law stating that only males can assume the throne should be revised, has taken a step towards the acceptance of a female heir.

LEFT: female construction worker in Tokyo.
RIGHT: serious business.

YAMAHA

キン肉マン

THE JAPANESE PEOPLE

A place of rather strict rules and some unique ways of engaging life, Japan is beginning to embrace diversity and a more individual sense of identity

There is an insistence with cultural stereotypes that often makes them too conveniently well entrenched to bother disputing. In the case of Japan they are myriad. The country, we are told, is a rice culture, despite the fact that before this crop was introduced from China, wheat cultivation and hunting were the order of the day. The Japanese, we are assured, are a monolithic ethnic family, though facially the Japanese, representing a melting pot that takes its ingredients from as far afield as Mongolia and Polynesia, are perhaps one of the most ethnically diverse and therefore most interesting of the Asian races.

Stereotypically, of whatever size or purpose, the group defines for the Japanese a person's individual purpose and function. And the group known as the Japanese – *nihon-jin*, or if especially nationalistic, *nippon-jin* – is the mother of all groups. Not exactly an irreverent comment, given that Amaterasu Omikami, or Sun Goddess, is the mythological foremother of the Japanese themselves. Television commentators and politicians repeatedly refer to *ware-ware Nippon-jin,* or "we Japanese" and the implicit definition of what "we Japanese" are or aren't, do or don't do, believe or don't believe. The compulsion to define identity even shows up in advertising.

Origins

The Japanese sense of uniqueness extends down to a basic identity of a race and culture distinct from others – if not superior. But the objective evidence strongly points to origins from the mainland.

From the 3rd century BC, waves of human migration from the Asian continent entered the Japanese archipelago, bringing along rice cultivation (including the use of tools), metallurgy and different social structures. These migrations are now considered to have brought the ancestors of today's Japanese people, the Yamato, who displaced and pushed the resident – and decidedly different – Jomon population into the northern regions or other less desirable areas of the archipelago.

Theories regarding the racial origins of the Japanese cite both the north and the south – Manchuria and Siberia, and the South China or Indochina regions – as likely possibilities. Students of the subject differ as to which origin to favour. The southern physical type is, of course, the Malay; the northern type is the Mongolian. Today, both north and south Asia are considered equally valid as likely origins of the Japanese. Still, the precise configuration of the migrations and the cultural traits associated with areas of origin is subject to argument. (Toss in, too, other legitimate theories about migrations from Polynesia or Micronesia.)

There was substantial human immigration later – in addition to cultural and artistic influences – from the Korean peninsula, a point vehemently denied by Japanese nationalists and

PRECEDING PAGES: shellfish harvesting near Sendai. **LEFT:** proud yam harvesters, Kyushu. **RIGHT:** smiles at Kyoto temple during *shichi-go-san.*

racial purists despite the overwhelming archaeological and anthropological evidence. Whereas archaeology in many countries is considered the most neutral of disciplines, without political overtones of any kind, in Japan it is rife with factions and rivalries. One group of "experts" in Japan has steadfastly refuted and rejected most modern, scientific dating methods, particularly when they are used to authenticate theories proposing a Japan–Korea connection.

Some observers have dared to suggest that Japan's brutal occupation of Korea from 1910 to 1945 was an attempt to erase any historical Korean link – the Japanese forced Koreans to take Japanese names, convert to the Shinto religion, speak only Japanese, and tens of thousands of Koreans were brought to Japan as slaves to labour in mines and factories. The possibility of Korean ancestry, uncovered after researching mandatory family registries kept by regional governments, has spoiled marriage plans on more than isolated occasions.

It may also be possible that the Korean and Japanese languages were mutually understandable, if not identical, some 2,000 years ago and that the people on the Korean peninsula and the Japanese archipelago may have shared a common culture.

THE AINU

Today with a population of less than 20,000, the Ainu people of Hokkaido were early inhabitants of Hokkaido and also northern Honshu. Their origins are unclear; it was once thought that they were of Caucasian heritage, but blood and skeletal research strongly suggests connections with Siberia's Uralic population.

Today there are few speakers of Ainu, which has much in common with other northern Asian languages and also with languages of Southeast Asia and some Pacific cultures. Traditional Ainu culture was one of hunting and gathering. Bears and salmon had an especially sacred place in Ainu traditions.

Unique or arrogant?

Perhaps the most substantial insulator of Japan from the outside is the modern language, spoken only in the islands. In fact, the grammar and syntax are considerably easier than those of most Germanic or Romance languages. The Japanese will retort, however, that it is undoubtedly one of the world's most difficult. The language itself isn't, but the context of usage can be confusing and difficult for those not brought up within the Japanese culture.

There is an undercurrent in Japanese thinking and in Japanese traditions that all things Japanese, including the race, are "special", if not unique, among the world's things. And most Japanese believe that outsiders will never be able to fully appreciate, much less understand, the distinctions and nuances of *being* Japanese and of Japanese ways. There is much in the Japanese language that buttresses this fundamental notion.

Stay in Japan long enough, listen to the conversation and media, and it seems that only Japan has earthquakes, typhoons, tasty rice, misery, hot weather, bad memories of war, trees that change colour in autumn, snowfall, and fast trains. When French ski manufacturers first tried to export skis to Japan several decades ago, the Japanese government declared the skis unsuitable for the special and unique Japanese snow. Later, in the late 1980s when American beef producers were trying to increase exports to the Japanese market, the agriculture ministry argued that only Japanese beef was suitable for the special and unique digestive systems of the Japanese people. In the 1990s, respected university researchers even claimed that the Japanese were genetically unique in their ability to appreciate to the fullest the sounds of nature like crickets and waterfalls.

These days, with many Japanese enjoying extended periods abroad, contact with foreigners living in their midst, and an economy that is nothing if not global, many of these assumptions are being questioned and the sense of a uniquely different identity undermined.

LEFT: morning jog in Fukuoka.
ABOVE: the businessman *(sarariman)* often spends long hours after work continuing the office bonding.

Living on egg shells

In a country where physical crowding and complex interpersonal relationships have shaped the language and social manners over the centuries, even the slightest chance of offending, disappointing, or inconveniencing another person is couched in a shower of soft words, bows, and grave smiles. (Or worse, giggles, a sure signal of acute embarrassment or being uncomfortable.) That foreigners have sometimes stereotyped Japanese behaviour as insincere is, to the Japanese, ignorant and hurtful.

To some foreigners, the Japanese language is excruciatingly indirect, requiring finesse in extracting the proper message. Raised in this social and cultural context, the Japanese easily read between the lines.

Sometimes the Japanese are able to use this to their advantage. Notable, both for the linguistic hedging and for the insight into Japanese thinking, is the difference between how Japan and how the rest of Asia (if not the rest of the world) remember World War II. Recent prime ministers have made efforts to acknowledge the past despite the vociferous views of right-wing politicians, nationalists and university scholars. Yet the linguistic nuances, when properly translated and understood, reveal not the expected apology as it first seems to be when translated from Japanese, but rather a promise of "reflection" or "remorse concerning unfortunate events", hardly an admission of wrong action or a sincere apology. Much of this, however, is the official position. Engage individuals in discussion on these topics and very different, more informed and measured opinions will often emerge.

Obligations

If apologies are linguistic puzzles, other expressions of social necessity too are interesting, if not curious. Strangely, the very word for "thank you" – *arigato* – literally means "You put me in a difficult position". *Oki no doku,* which is an expression of sympathy, means "poisonous feeling". And who would think of expressing regret or apology with *sumimasen,* which in strictly literal translation means "This situation or inconvenience will never end"?

Then there is that virtually untranslatable word, *giri.* To violate *giri* is simply unthinkable. *Giri* is often translated as a sense of duty and

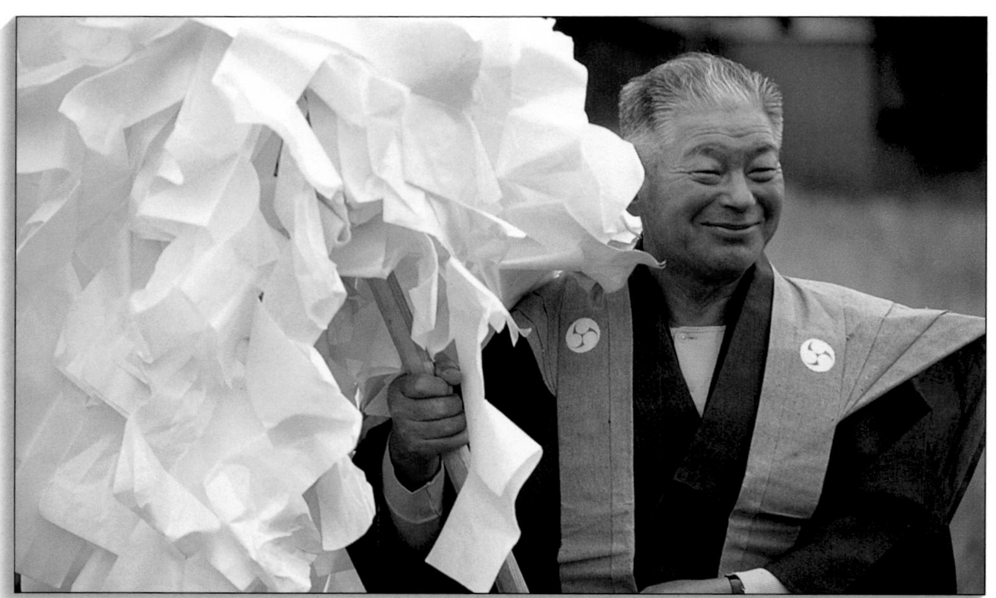

Language in Sex and Society

The Japanese *keigo*, or polite language, is a hold-over from the structured class system of feudal times when politeness was reinforced with a sword. In modern times, *keigo* has been preserved as a key element in the deeply rooted Japanese tradition of deference to one's superiors and of courtesy to guests.

Proper speech is a source of pride for most Japanese and the use of *keigo* can be an art in itself. Moreover, simply shifting the politeness level up a notch – or down – can have the effect of sarcasm or insult. (The younger urban generation, however, appears keen on dropping many of the complicated formal constructions.)

Perplexing to outsiders are the distinctions between the talk of males and females. Consider the first-person pronoun. Men have the option of several forms, the use of each dependent upon the situation and the people involved: *watakushi, watashi, boku,* or *ore*, from most polite to exceedingly casual. Women, of course, have fewer options. Modulation and tone of voice also tend to vary between the sexes. Men try to affect a deep rumble, which can approach theatrical proportions. Women often tend to inflect a high, nasalised pitch, said to be appealing and sexy to men. (Japanese women usually drop their voice to normal pitch when speaking a second language, however.)

honour, but such a definition ignores the subtle communal and personal responsibilities behind *giri*. In Japan, there are unspoken responsibilities inherent by acceptance and participation within a group, whether in a friendship or with coworkers in an office, or in the sharing of communal village life. When the responsibility beckons, and the member of any group can easily recognise it without articulating it, the individual must meet and honour that responsibility while putting aside his or her work or personal desires.

SUICIDE RATES

Japan's suicide rate is 18.1 deaths per 100,000 people annually, higher than the United States (12) and England (7.5) but notably lower than Finland (27.3).

Giri is the theme of many tragedies in Japanese literature and drama. A plot might turn on a daughter's obligation to put aside *ninjo,* or human feeling, and marry someone of her parents' choosing. If unable to reconcile her own desires with the obligations of *giri* to her parents, suicide is an accepted recourse. Of course, such recourse is rare today, but it still occasionally happens.

Family values

No doubt there's a proverb somewhere saying that obligation, like charity, begins at home. It's true, for example, that in Japan the eldest child (once only the male but now the female as well) is expected to care for aged parents. Likewise, it is still true that the estate, if any, of a deceased parent automatically passes to the eldest child. In fact, these mutual obligations were once inviolable. Today, however, disputes over care for the aged and for inheritance of wealth are increasingly common and often decided in favour not of the parents or children, but of the national government because of prohibitively high inheritance taxes.

Often cited as the core of Japan's traditional social stability, extended families are nowadays as far flung from the original homestead as education, job opportunities and jet planes can take them. And although nostalgia for the hometown and simpler living have taken on a trendy air in recent years, especially as affluence spreads, the urban family is increasingly defining the contours of Japanese life. On the surface, the family appears both paternal (the man is nominally the household head) and maternal (as women still control the household budget and child rearing). More opportunities for women in business, however, along with increased affluence and broader appetites for the good life, are slowly challenging this status quo.

In the Japan of pre-World War II, a young man often got married about the time his parents reminded him that he had reached the *tekireiki*, or appropriate marriageable age. His parents would take an active role in the selection of his bride, making sure she bore

the markings of a good wife, wise mother and self-sacrificing daughter-in-law. They interviewed the woman's parents. Even birth records were checked (and often still are), ensuring that the woman's family tree had no bad apples or embarrassing branches. Love rarely entered the picture. Parents knew that the couple would eventually become fond of each other and maybe become good friends. The wife, having severed the ties to her own family through marriage, adhered to the customs and practices of her husband's family. After all, throughout her upbringing, she had been taught that a woman found her greatest fulfilment in marriage. The mother-in-law – and often sisters-in-law – frequently added

LEFT: Shinto priests are an important part of village life. **RIGHT:** fishing experts untangling a line in Fukuoka.

to the wife's burdens by complaining about her shortcomings. And when the mother-in-law grew feeble, the wife would take care of her.

Despite the hardships, the wife generally chose to stay married. To divorce meant she had to face the censure – blame for the marital break-up was all hers – of her own family and that of the community.

XED-OUT EX

Batsu-ichi ("one X") is a nickname for those who are divorced. When a person gets divorced, an X is put through the spouse's name in the government's family registry.

The traditional wife follows a pattern that her grandmother followed in the pre-war years. Getting up earlier than her husband and children, she prepares the breakfasts

and makes sure everyone gets off to work or school on time. During the day, she does the housework, goes shopping and manages the daily household accounts. Occasionally, she takes part in activities of the neighbourhood association or of her children's school. She may also enjoy leisure activities such as learning a foreign language. At night, she and the children will eat together, since her husband comes home much later in the evening. Upon his return, she will serve him (and his relatives, if present) his dinner and sit with him while he eats. The wife knows better than to discuss family matters at those times. She waits until the weekends or when he appears less drained.

While the above is not as common or automatic as before, it is still a marital paradigm in both cities and rural areas. In many marriages today, the husband still maintains a higher status and exercises greater authority in the family by virtue of being the sole provider. He shows little inclination in helping around the house or taking care of the children, except when it suits him. Yet some husbands, like their wives, have been exposed to Western lifestyles and trends and make an effort at being liberated men in the Western sense, cultural biases aside.

Accelerating this process of change is the dramatic increase in the number of divorce cases since the 1990s, a reflection of the growing desire of spouses, particularly wives, to fulfil personal aspirations over those of the family. Some wives file for divorce when husbands retire from their jobs, demanding half of the husband's severance pay.

Some couples divorce before they even get started on a proper married life. It's called a Narita Divorce. Modern Japanese women have usually spent more time travelling overseas than their new husbands, who may never have been outside of Japan because of the emphasis on career. Their first jaunt overseas, perhaps a honeymoon, is ripe with tension and ends in disaster because the woman is more self-reliant than the man. After returning home to Narita, Tokyo's international airport, they divorce.

Essential education

In the 6th century, Japan adopted major elements of Chinese culture, including Chinese ideographs, Buddhism and Confucianism, not to mention a heavily bureaucratic system of government that persists today. Education was based on the meritocratic selection of talented individuals, later to be bureaucrats, who would then be taught to read and write the *Analects* of Confucius and works related to Buddhism. This Chinese system of education and civil service was absorbed within Japanese society. With the rise of the Tokugawa clan to power in 1603, the pursuit of Western knowledge was strictly limited and controlled, and the study of Buddhist works declined in favour of Confucian ethics.

During the feudal period, education was available to common people in *terakoya*. (*Tera* means temple and *koya* refers to a small room.) These one-room temple schools offered the masses instruction in the written language and certain practical subjects, such as the use of the abacus and elementary arithmetic. Texts were similar to the Chinese classics used by the samurai. Many of the teachers were monks.

Defeat in 1945 brought to Japan a total reformation of the educational system. The new model was essentially American in structure: six years of elementary school, three years of junior high school, and three years of high school. The first nine years were compulsory.

Entrance to higher education is determined by dreaded examinations, which are administered by the individual universities; for each school applied to for admission, a complete set of entrance exams must be endured. There is no universal university admissions exam. The more prestigious a school is, the greater the number of applicants seeking admission and the more difficult the examination.

To help them reach the goal of passing the examinations, parents will budget a considerable amount of their monthly income to send children to *juku,* or private cram schools, which are a multibillion-yen business. For the most disciplined of students, every night and weekend is spent at *juku* having their brains crammed with exam-passing information. It is all learned by rote and not deduction.

There is no doubt that the Japanese are united in a consensus that education is essential for social cohesion, economic prosperity and prestige in the international arena. Unfortunately, both in the primary and university levels, form and rote usually take precedence over function and knowledge. Students are taught not analysis and discourse, but rather only the information needed to pass exams for entrance into the next level of their schooling. There are exams for primary school, middle school and high school. And there are the exams for the university, the whole point of life up to this point.

Perhaps more importantly, schools reform undisciplined brats into responsible persons. Before starting school, children are often allowed to be unruly at home, the parents knowing this behaviour will be moderated in school.

LEFT: traditional values and modern trends unite.
RIGHT: Elvis impersonaters attract attention with an uninhibited performance.

Education is respected in Japan, and so are educators. In fact, the honourific for teacher – *sensei,* as in *Nakamura-sensei* – is the same as for physicians. Unfortunately, the responsibility and professional pressure is considerable upon teachers, especially at the high-school level when students are preparing for their university exams. Holidays are rare for the teachers.

Even the Japanese themselves admit their educational system's shortcomings. The excessive emphasis on entrance examinations is a cause of much national concern and debate, as is the alienation of significant numbers of young people, violence in schools and bullying of pupils. The effectiveness and desirability of many of these orthodox teaching approaches are increasingly being questioned, and reforms are being considered. In the field of English, for example, several thousand native speakers, applying more innovative, interactive methods of learning, are employed at both state and privately run schools.

Japan's Ivy League

Japanese social institutions in general, and schools in particular, are arranged hierarchically in terms of their ability to bestow economic and social status. No institution ranks higher in this regard than Tokyo University, or Todai. Even

Oxbridge and Yale pale beside Todai, an institute that inspires both awe and fierce competition for entrance. The few who make it past its hallowed gates are virtually guaranteed a life of privilege. To prove the point, 80 percent of postwar prime ministers hail from Todai, 90 percent of civil servants in the prestigious Finance and Home Affairs ministries call it their alma mater, the same number in the all-important Trade and Industry Ministry.

Such orthodoxy belies Todai's radical past. In 1969, students organised a protest against the university system, barricading themselves in the lecture hall. The stand-off only ended when riot police fully armed with tear gas moved in and arrested 600 students.

Although measures have been introduced to curb the excessive influence of Todai, favouritism towards its graduates and countless lost childhoods spent in swotting to get in continues, the problem compounded by parents, especially mothers, who see their offspring's place in a top university as an elevation of their own status. The other two heavyweights are Keio University and Waseda University, both also in Tokyo.

Juku are happy to pander to parental ambition; one typical train advertisement shows a Todai graduate with three small children beside him. The caption: "Whether you've aimed at a place in Todai for a year or since elementary school, this school will get you there."

Sweet uniformity

The idea that you are what you wear, that "these are my clothes, ergo this is my role", is nowhere more evident than in Japan. Conformism, still a powerful force in Japanese society, lends itself naturally to uniformism. Individuality as far as it exists, and it does, is generally of the kind that remains compatible with social rules. Even the radical urge is to be shared with others of a similar disposition.

Uniforms by their very nature unify, suggest strength in numbers – the perfect sartorial solution for a society that remains, despite all the surface experimentation, relatively rigid and tribal. Even Japanese youth, wearing clothes and accessories that highlight infinitesimal differences from the general pattern, have a way of suggesting that they are cut from the same cloth, part of a common weave.

Even the national costume, the kimono, categorises those who wear it into clearly

ABOVE: high-school students on a Kyoto excursion.
RIGHT: Meiji-era schoolboys sit up straight for the camera.

defined groups conforming to certain unwritten rules and conventions of dress: young women are encouraged to wear bright, vibrant colours that offset their youth, older women to don more muted hues that bespeak their maturity.

Shibuya, Harajuku and Shinjuku remain the centres of Toyko's theatre of dress. Harajuku in particular is the fusion point where the assertion of Western individualism gets absorbed into Oriental formalism. Here you will chance upon costumes reflecting almost every Anglo-Saxon popular culture fashion since the 1950s: from black-shirted Elvis clones, Minnie Mouse imitators, the checked shirts and chewed-up jeans of rockabilly hicks, the billowing, rainbow-coloured rags of hippie psychedelia, to post-punk and hip-hop.

While a few renegade brown and sand-coloured suits are occasionally glimpsed in commuter carriages, there isn't a great deal of colour on an average day, where black, gray and serge suits dominate among the male, white collar class, forming an almost unbroken uniformity of taste. The only member of an institution daring enough to wear a purple suit in public is the gang or syndicate-affiliated thug, who is also, as a special concession to his outlaw status, allowed to sport ties printed with surfboards, cocktail sticks and naked women.

Oldest society in human history

In 2003, the number of Japanese older than 100 reached over 25,000. In 1965, there were only 150 Japanese centenarians; in 1993, there were 5,000. Japanese are living longer and having fewer children, and the skewed demographics are worrying government planners. The birth rate of 1.4 children per woman is resulting in Japan becoming one of the world's oldest societies. The median age is around 40, matched in the world only by Germany. Japan's 65-plus generation, now at 15 percent of the population, will reach 25 percent by 2020. In contrast, that of the US will reach only 17 percent by 2020.

Of concern is the cost of providing retirement pensions and old-age benefits. It is estimated that to maintain the Japanese pension system, over the next 20 years it will be necessary to double basic income taxes. And as the population ages, the savings rate will drop, depleting the government's largest source of operating capital. ❑

OKINAWAN LONGEVITY

Few people know how to age better than Okinawa's old folks. Sharp minds and physical vigour among the advanced in age may be a rarity in other parts of the world, but in these southern islands it's commonplace. Okinawa in fact has the highest proportion of centenarians in the world, with 39.5 for every 100,000 people. That compares with about 10 to the same number of Americans. Two American authors of a best-selling book on longevity called *The Okinawa Program* discovered that elderly Okinawans have astonishingly clean arteries and low levels of cholesterol, and that heart disease, and breast and prostrate cancer are rare. The writers concluded that this enviable condition was attributable to the consumption of large amounts of tofu, seaweed and locally grown vegetables, regular exercise and a low-stress lifestyle.

Ironically for an age of better health care and treatment, the young are not expected to live as long as their grandparents. The prefectural government has launched its own programme, called "Healthy Okinawa 2010" in an effort to wean kids off burgers and cup noodles. School meals now include such tried and tested local dishes as stir-fried papaya, *goya* (bitter melon) and egg, boiled pork, and rice with *wakame* (soft seaweed), in an attempt to return to their culinary roots. A case, perhaps, of the wisdom of the ages?

RELIGION

To the outsider, the adaptability of worship and philosophy may seem contradictory and diffused. To the Japanese, beliefs are pragmatic and without hypocrisy

Polls asking Japanese in which religion they believe consistently yield results that total well over 100 percent – most say they are followers of both Shinto and Buddhism. The average Japanese thinks nothing of marrying at a Shinto shrine, burying loved ones in a Buddhist cemetery, or boisterously celebrating Christmas. Although the devout Christian or Muslim – each with a monotheistic god demanding unswerving fidelity – might find this religious promiscuity hard to fathom, the typical Japanese sees no contradiction.

Traditionally, nearly every home was once equipped with a *kamidana,* a god-shelf with Shinto symbols, or else a *butsudan,* a Buddhist household altar containing memorials for the family's ancestors before which offerings of flowers, food, drink, or incense are made daily. Most homes had both, and many still do.

The Japanese definitely seem to have a sense of religious piety and spiritual yearning, although it is very different from that in the West. The main difference seems to be that the line between the sacred and the profane is much less clearly drawn in Japan. In many ways, community life and religion are one and the same. Similarly, the distinction between good and bad, or sinful and righteous, is less clear in Japanese society. It is said that the West considers most things as black or white; in Japan, as elsewhere in Asia, there is a lot of grey.

Shinto

A basic understanding of the Japanese religious sensibility must begin with Shinto, which influences virtually every aspect of Japanese culture and society. It is hard to give any simple definition of Shinto (lit. way of the gods, or *kami*), since it is not a systematised set of beliefs. There is no dogmatic set of rules nor even any holy script. The term *shinto* was not even invented until after the introduction of Buddhism, a date traditionally given as AD 552, and then only as a way of contrasting the native beliefs with that imported faith.

In general, it can be said that Shinto shares with many other animistic beliefs the truth that all natural objects and phenomena possess a spiritual side. It is this animism – mixed with ances-

PRECEDING PAGES: Shinto shrine, marked by a *torii,* in Hokkaido. **LEFT:** Shinto priest reciting prayers. **RIGHT:** ringing the bell announces one to the gods.

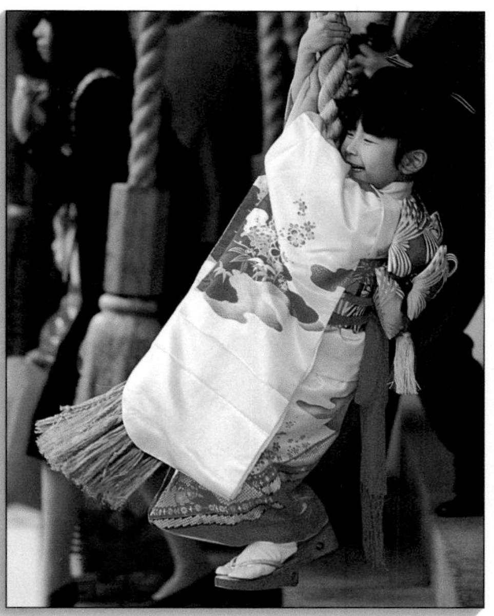

CONTROVERSIAL WORSHIP

Yasukuni-jinja, a large and controversial Shinto shrine just north of the Imperial Palace in central Tokyo, is an example (and a particularly notorious one) of the national shrines set up by the government authorities before World War II. It is here that the spirits of every soldier who has died in the name of the emperor since 1853 are enshrined (including war criminals executed by the Allies after World War II). Visits here – official or not – by the prime minister and members of government are usually made to appease right-wing nationalists and are vociferously denounced by neighbouring countries such as China and South Korea.

tor worship, a shared trait with Buddhism – that characterises Shinto. A tree, for example, was revered by the ancient Japanese as a source of food, warmth, shelter and even clothing. For that reason, when a great tree was felled to provide wood for the Buddhist temple complexes at Nara or Kyoto, it was not used for several years in order to give the spirit within time to depart safely. Mountains, forests and even the oceans were also revered.

It should be recognised that the term *kami*, although often translated as "god", is quite different from the Western concept of divinity. The classic definition, as originally understood in Japan, was made by the 18th-century scholar Moto-ori Norinaga: "Anything whatsoever which was outside the ordinary, which possessed superior power, or which was awe-inspiring, was called *kami*".

In ancient Shinto there was also a belief in a kind of soul – *tamashii* – that lived on after death. An unrefined form of ancestor worship also existed, remnants of which can be seen in the observances of the spring and autumn equinoxes and in the Obon festivities in early autumn, which in Japan have both Shinto and Buddhist overtones.

NO IMAGES

Prior to the arrival of Buddhism in the 6th century, Shinto lacked artistic or literary representation of beliefs and myths, and so it had no defined pantheon of deities.

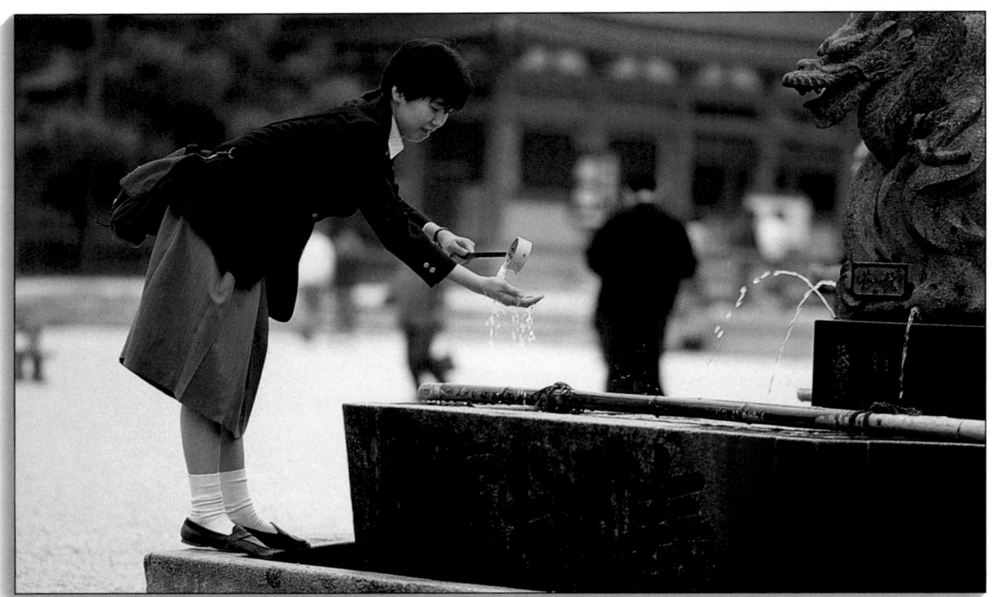

Early Shinto had concepts of heaven and hell as well, although they were hazily conceived at best. There was no concept of sin nor of divine retribution nor of absolution for offenses committed.

It was commonly thought that the dead would eventually be reborn into this world, just as spring returns after winter.

There are 13 mainstream Shinto sects and numerous subsects in Japan today, but since World War II, they have not been controlled by the government. In fact, it was only during the period from the Meiji Restoration of 1868 until the end of World War II that the state intervened in Shinto. During the Meiji Restoration, the government introduced *kokka* (national) Shinto as a political tool for controlling the people through the policy of *saisei it'chi* – the "unity of rites and politics".

Several shrines were established by the national government for various purposes as "national" shrines, including Yasukuni-jinja in Tokyo *(see box on page 69)* and the impressive Meiji-jingu, to the north of Shibuya in Tokyo, whose majestic architecture reminds the traveller that Emperor Meiji, enshrined within, was considered divine.

In fact, none of the national shrines – state inventions all – has much to do with traditional beliefs found within Shinto. Dismissing them as unimportant in the modern scheme of things, however, would be a sociological, if not religious and political, mistake.

Buddhism

The traditionally accepted date for Buddhism to have arrived in Japan is AD 552. While this may be true, it wasn't until centuries later that it ceased to be the exclusive province of aristocrats. This is somewhat ironic in view of the beliefs of the religion's founder, Sakyamuni – born a prince in eastern India (now part of Nepal) around 500 BC – who advocated a middle way between indulgence and asceticism.

The Buddha, as he came to be known (though this is a misnomer), blamed all the world's pain and discontent on desire and claimed that through right living, desire could be negated and the "self" totally done away with through entry into the blissful state of *nirvana,* or Buddhahood. Buddha's followers came to believe that one who really knows the truth lives the life of truth and thus becomes truth itself. By overcoming all the conflicts of the ego, one can attain a universal, cosmic harmony with all.

Mahayana, meaning Greater Vehicle, was the form of Buddhism that became established throughout most of East Asia. It holds that every being, sentient or non-sentient, shares a basic spiritual communion and that all are eventually destined for Buddhahood. Although all beings are separate in appearance, they are one and the same in reality. Every person's present situation is determined by past deeds, Buddhists believe. This is the principle of *karma.*

Since the main *Mahayana* sutras only appeared around 100 BC, it is not known the extent to which they reflect the original thoughts of the Buddha. However, by the time it reached Japan's shores through China, Buddhism had changed tremendously from Sakyamuni's simple message. The religion was to undergo even more radical change when it encountered the beliefs that were held in the Japanese archipelago.

As early as the 6th century, for example, *Ryobu* Shinto began to emerge as a syncretic compromise with Buddhism. In this hybrid belief system, *kamisama* were regarded as temporary manifestations of the Buddhist deities. In time, Buddhist thought became influenced by the indigenous beliefs, deviating so far from the original that some scholars doubt whether the Japanese version really deserves to be called Buddhism.

For example, although the goal of nirvana is to break the cycle of reincarnation, most Japanese Buddhists seem to believe that the souls of the dead are eventually reborn. As the famed folklorist Yanagida Kunio once pointed out, if asked where people go after they die, the typical Japanese will usually answer *Gokuraku*,

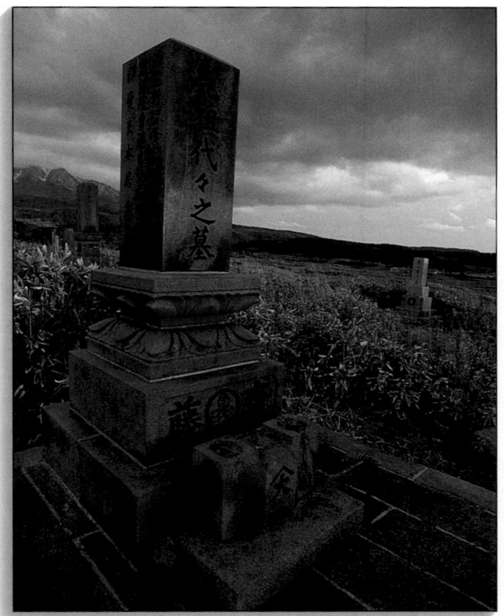

LEFT: purification at Heian-jingu, in Kyoto.
RIGHT: Buddhist tomb in northern Hokkaido.

NEW CULTS

The number of new religions and cults in Japan has proliferated since the 1970s. Many of these are quite legitimate, while others, though registered as religions, have raised concerns among the authorities.

The crackdown on cults began after AUM Shinrikyo's (AUM Supreme Truth) sarin gas attack on a Tokyo subway. Headed by a blind yoga instructor now in police custody, the group has reinvented itself with a new image, calling itself Aleph. Membership is said to be growing.

There are dozens more of these religious sects. The Japanese even have an expression for the phenomenon – the "Rush Hour of the Gods".

which translates as Paradise. Contrast this with the more orthodox Buddhist belief in death as a permanent state. In practice, however, Japanese usually return to their *furosato*, or ancestral home, for the two equinoxes as well as during the midsummer Obon, or Feast of the Dead, observances. The purpose of attending Obon is to be present when the family's ranking male ceremoniously offers food to the spirits of departed ancestors – spirits that return to earth for the occasion. From where do they return? Yanagida says most people will answer

VISUAL DEITIES

Under the influence of Buddhism and its vivid visual expression, Shinto's pantheon of deities gradually became tangible.

"the mountains", which hold a special place in Japanese religious lore. Certain peaks – Omine near Nara and, of course, Mt Fuji – are especially sacred.

Amida Buddhism

There are today an estimated 56 main divisions and 170 subdivisions in Japanese Buddhism. The single most popular sect is Jodo Shinshu, founded in the 13th century by Shinran, who preached an "easy road to salvation" by means of the *nembutsu* prayer to the Amida, a bodhisattva who made a vow eons ago to save all who placed faith in him or her and to guide them to the Blissful Land of Purity.

About half of Japanese Buddhists belong to either Jodo Shinshu or another form of Amidaism founded by Honen (1133–1212). Jodo Shinshu offers that it is not necessary to be "good" so to be reborn into the Western Paradise and that the laity can become Buddhas as easily as priests. Amidaism is the Buddhist form closest to core Japanese beliefs due to its concern for moral judgement and its exaltation of inclinations beyond the mere good and evil.

Zen emptiness

The impact of that particularly eclectic form of Buddhism called Zen on Japanese culture is considerable, reaching far beyond the temple and entering into interior design, gardening, ink painting, calligraphy, the tea ceremony, cuisine, and even military strategies.

Two Buddhist priests in the 12th and 13th centuries – Eisai, founder of the Rinzai Zen sect, and his disciple Dogen, who established the Soto Zen sect – brought the principle of "emptiness" into Japanese Buddhism.

Soto sect followers rely almost solely on *zazen*, or sitting meditation and seek to emulate Sakyamuni, who reached the state of enlightenment while meditating without conscious thought in such a position. In contrast, the Rinzai sect also utilises *koan* riddles, such as the famous "What is the sound of one hand clapping?" *Koan* must be tackled with something beyond logic and non-logic; the riddles' function is to stimulate (or perhaps divert) the mind into a similar state.

Zen was influenced by both Daoism and the Wang Yangming school of neo-Confucianism, which stressed the "prime conscience" and the importance of action. They would describe the "Great Ultimate" as being akin to the hub of a well: empty but the point from which all action flows. For various reasons, Zen sects proved better able than the others to satisfy the spiritual needs of the *samurai*.

Whether through *zazen* or the use of *koan* posed by the Zen master, the goal is for the disciple to be provoked, excited or irritated to the point where one makes a nonintellectual leap into the void and experiences reality. ❑

LEFT: Buddhist believer beneath sacred waterfall.

Shrines and Temples

Shrines are of the Shinto religion, and their names often end in the suffixes *-gu, -jinja* or *-jingu*. Temples, on the other hand, are Buddhist and usually end with *-ji, -tera* or *-dera*. Quite often, temples and shrines are found side by side, or a temple or shrine will have an complementary adjunct on the same sacred grounds.

Shinto shrines

The thousands of Shinto shrines in Japan vary in size from tiny roadside boxes to large compounds such as the Grand Shrines at Ise and the Tosho-gu at Nikko. But nearly all share certain features.

First, there is at least one *torii*, shaped somewhat like the Greek letter *pi*. This gateway may have evolved from a bird's perch – a certain kind of bird having been a religious symbol in many animistic cults – and it may be made of wood, stone, metal, or even concrete. Like the *shimenawa* (sacred straw festoon), zigzag cuts of white paper, mounts of salt, and cleanly-swept gravel, the *torii* serves to mark off areas considered sacred from those thought profane.

Often the largest building of the shrine is the inner sanctum called the *honden*. This is the main dwelling of the deity. It is usually elevated above the other buildings and reached by a staircase. It is likely to be off-limits to visitors, but other than a mirror or, on rare occasions, an image, there is little to see inside. These objects, by the way, are the *mitama-shiro* or *go-shintai*, serving as spirit substitutes for the deity *(kami)* being worshiped. In front of the *honden* is the often quite spacious *haiden* or worship hall, used for ritual ceremonies. Usually this structure is merely a roof supported by pillars and open on all sides.

There are no elaborate rituals or prescribed procedures in worshipping at a shrine. On entering the grounds there is a stone water basin, often with ladles balanced across it. One rinses mouth and hands in preparation for approaching the deity. It is customary to toss a small offering into the cashbox at the foot of the *haiden* before sounding the shaker to attract the attention of the god. Devout worshippers also clap their hands twice, making doubly sure the god is listening. Then, a deep bow is performed and held while the prayer is offered.

During *matsuri*, or festivals, the gods are taken out for rollicking rides through the streets in *mikoshi* (portable shrines) so as to bring the blessings of the *kamisama* to all the community. (This is one of the few times when Japanese collectively shed their social inhibitions and turn quite rowdy.)

Buddhist temples

Under the Tokugawa shogunate, Japanese Buddhism lost much of its vigour, leading cynics to charge that priests were good for nothing else but burying people. An exaggeration, no doubt, but crematoriums still provide a good part of the income for most temples. The main building *(hondo)*, library *(bunko)*, bell tower *(shoro)*, and other buildings of a temple complex can be exquisite architectural creations. But the one most easily admired is the pagoda, or *to*. The form in Japan is the result of evolution from the dome-shaped *stupa* (thought to represent an upside-down rice bowl), in which the bones of the Buddha and Buddhist saints were buried in India.

Images found in temples include Nyorai (Tathagata) Buddhas, such as Sakyamuni after Enlightenment and Maitreya (Miroku) or Future Buddhas, distinguished by a pose with one leg crossed over the other. Others include the *nio*, fierce-looking images flanking gates to many temples and derived from the Hindu gods Brahma and Indra. ❑

RIGHT: offering at the Great Buddha, Kamakura.

ART, CRAFTS AND LITERATURE

With an aesthetic that goes back scores of centuries, Japan's art and crafts of today retain the depth and layers of history, culture and outlook

The earliest preserved distinctly Japanese art works are those of the late Yayoi Period (300 BC–AD 300). These were small, tubular clay figurines called *haniwa*, some of which were set up like fences around imperial mausolea. Whatever their purpose may have been – substitutes for people buried alive in the tombs or magical instruments to ward off evil spirits or bandits – their immediate interest lies in their simplicity and charm. Although many of them are only cylinders, some of the *haniwa* (and there are hundreds) are figures of men and women *(see picture on page 32)*, horses, monkeys and birds. Most are very simple with only a few details of decoration – perhaps a sword or a necklace. They have large hollow spaces for the mouth and eyes, which prevented them from cracking when being fired and which adds not only to their charm, but to their mystery, too.

Aesthetic impulses

The *haniwa* figures are also important for another reason. We find in them – at the very beginning of the culture – many of the salient characteristics of almost all Japanese art. The *haniwa* are, so to speak, decorative. They are very much in this world, regardless of how much they may evoke the next. They are narratory – we want to create stories for them; as still in time as they are, we imagine a time before and after their mouths opened. And with their soft modelling and indolent lines they are recognisably human. These figures are not gods or angels: they smile, they shout, they gaze. In fact, there is little that is abstract about them. This is an "art of the real", which does not eliminate the fantastic or even the artificial.

The *haniwa* possess a beauty that seems almost uncannily to come from a natural aesthetic impulse. They occur during a lull in Japanese absorption of outside influences at a time when the culture was developing its own native hues.

LEFT: from the *Lotus Sutra:* a hermit reciting a sutra.
RIGHT: *Maple Viewers*, Muromachi Period.

Recognising the conventions

The viewer needs only a few moments to get used to looking at Japanese art. He or she will soon recognise the conventions – the raised roofs to reveal scenes (no perspective here), the hooks for noses and slits for eyes, the seemingly abstract patterns that resolve themselves into a

few variations on plants and birds and insects.

Just look a little closer and the clothes and faces will soon take on individual qualities. There is no reason either to fear that cliché "open space". There is and isn't any great metaphysical principle at work here – the idea is simple enough: like European Symbolist poetry of a millennium later, the Japanese knew that art evokes, it does not depict.

Nara and Kamakura sculpture

Before the Nara Period, there are some superb examples of sculpture such as the Miroku at Koryu-ji, in Kyoto. This is a delicately carved wooden statue of the Buddha of the Future.

In the Nara Period (646–794), with Japan's full-scale welcome of things Chinese, the native response to the real is fused with its spiritual aspirations without ever abandoning the former. Work is done in wood, clay, bronze, or by using the curious technique of hollow lacquer.

There are some fine early pieces to be seen in the Yakushi-ji, in Nara, but visits must especially be made to the Kofuku-ji and the Todai-ji to see the numerous sculptures of the Buddha, of guardian deities and of monks.

Genji's Loves

Tale of Genji, the masterpiece of Japanese literature, was written by the daughter of a courtier around 1010. It is about Genji, a Heian-Period courtier, and his pursuit of the art of love.

It was also during this time that the 16-metre-high (52-ft) bronze Daibutsu (Great Buddha) in Nara was created. It was originally gilded with bronze and incised with designs that can now only barely be discerned on some of the lotus petals upon which the figure sits.

The Nara Period ended with the move of capital to Kyoto. With that – the beginning of the Heian Period (794–1185) – Japanese sculpture declined as other arts ascended and did not revive until the Kamakura Period several centuries later.

While Nara Period sculpture was both human and ideal, that of the Kamakura Period (1185–1333) was primarily human, passionate, personal and emotional. For example, the Kamakura Period produced more portraits of monks and demons than of aloof gods. Many of these can be seen in Todai-ji and Kofuku-ji in Nara. The Kamakura Period also produced its Daibutsu, which, though somewhat smaller than that in Nara, is equally affecting. Now sitting uncovered in the Kamakura hills, its impressiveness has been enhanced by time.

Painting

In the Heian Period, life itself became an art, and works of art became its decorative attendant. Kyoto's Byodo-in may have been meant as a model of the next world, but it only showed that life in this one was already exquisite. Japanese painting had long existed, particularly in the form of long, rolled and hand-held scrolls, but it had not flowered into great sophistication. These paintings, known as *Yamato-e*, might depict the changing seasons, famous beauty spots or illustrate well-known stories.

The best *Yamato-e* were of the latter type and depicted popular legends, warrior tales, or works of great literature such as the *Ise Monogatari* and *Genji Monogatari*, or the *Tale of Genji*. The popular legends might include a satirical look at pompous officials turned into battling frogs and rabbits, or a man who can't stop farting. Post-Heian warrior tales drew on the many heroic or sentimental tales collected in the *Heike Monogatari* and other stories (as Western artisans drew on Homer and Virgil). The scrolls are easy to follow and with their delicacy of line reveal the Japanese gift of design.

In the Kamakura Period, war and religion came together. This was the great period of Zen art, when *suiboku* (water-ink, or painting with black *sumi* ink) comes to the fore. One of the world's masterpieces of *suiboku-ga* can be seen in the National Museum in Tokyo: Sesshu's *Winter Landscape*. Owing to the sense of composition and the moods he evokes, Sesshu seems at times to be a contemporary artist. In fact, he died in 1506 at age 86.

In addition to calligraphy, *suiboku-ga* includes portraiture and landscape. An example of the principle "the line is the man himself" in portraiture is the stark portrait of the priest Ikkyu, in the National Museum in Tokyo.

In *suiboku* landscape paintings, the emphasis is again on the real and on the visually pleasurable (Japanese landscape is rarely as profoundly mystical as that of China), and quite often also on the grotesque, the curious and the purely fantastic.

The Momoyama Period (late 16th century) is Japan's age of baroque. Filled with gold and silver, with very bright, flat colours (no shading or outlining), and embellished with lush scenes painted on screens and walls, it is one of the high points of Japan's decorative genius.

This is not to imply that monochrome was abandoned during the Momoyama Period. Far from it: there was a great deal of superb *sumi-e* (ink picture) screens and paintings done at this time. The overwhelming impression of Momoyama-Period art, however, is of brilliance and gold, as one can see in the Jodan-no-ma and other ceremonial halls in the Nijo Castle in Kyoto, with its painted walls and gilded ceilings, or at nearby Nishi Hongan-ji, to the south of Nijo Castle, in the rather expansive *taimensho* (audience hall) and *Konoma* (stork room).

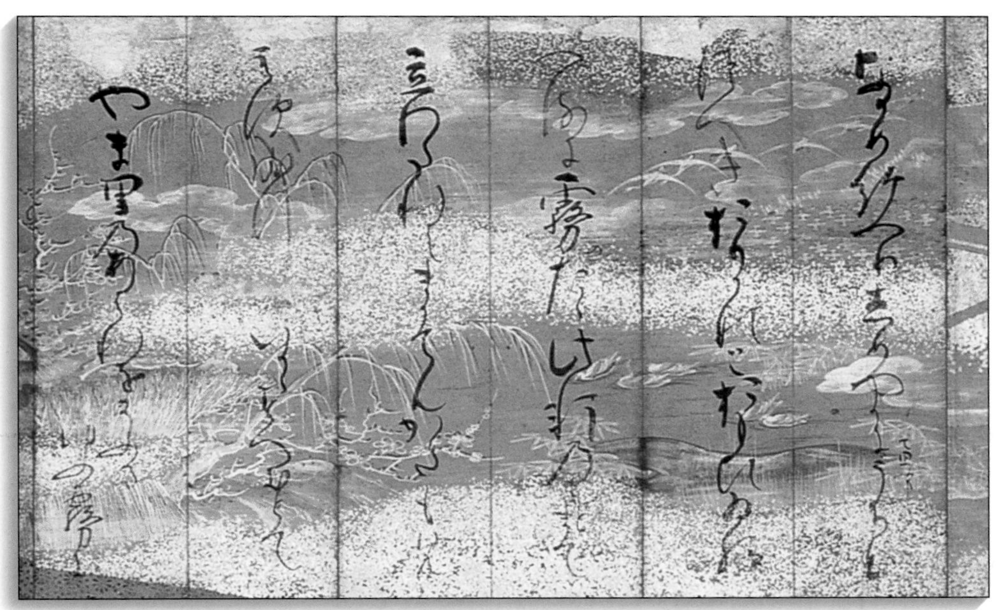

LEFT: Nara Period standing *bodhisattva*.
ABOVE: excerpts from *Tale of Genji*, 17th century.

Floating world

The Edo Period (1603–1868) is the great age of popular art, even though much great decorative art was being made for the aristocracy or the military classes, especially by Koetsu, Sotatsu and Korin. The latter's gorgeous *Irises* – all violet and gold – is an excellent example of the period art and can be seen at the Nezu Institute of Fine Arts in Tokyo.

In the rigid society of the Edo Period, the artisan was the third of the four social classes, one step above the merchant, who was at the bottom (in theory, but increasingly at the top in practice). This was the age of the unknown craftsman, whose tools, hands and skills were part of a tradition and who learned techniques as an apprentice. The merchant class, however, was developing its own pleasures in fiction, drama *(kabuki)* and art, and mass appeal soon became more important than ever before in most of the disciplines.

The art most associated with Edo Tokyo is *ukiyo-e* (lit. pictures of the floating world). Once again, the sublunary, fleshy human existence was a key element. Although woodblock printing had been used to reproduce sutras, for example, the technique first began to be used in a more popular vein in the early 18th century. At first, the prints were either monochromatic or hand-coloured with an orange-red. In time, two colours were used, then four, and so on.

Notable artists included Hiroshige Ando, Utamaro Kitagawa and Hokusai. Although the names of hundreds of *ukiyo-e* artists are known, it should be remembered that the production of these prints was a cooperative effort between many highly skilled people.

Early *ukiyo-e*, especially those by the first great master, Moronobu, are usually portraits of prostitutes from the Yoshiwara district of old Edo or else illustrations for books. With polychrome printing in *ukiyo-e*, a number of "genres" became established. There were, for example, portraits of prostitutes *(bijin ga)*, *kabuki* actors in famous roles, the ever-present scenes of renowned places, and of plant and animal life. Suffice to say that *ukiyo-e* is one of the world's great graphic art forms and in more ways than one. For example, the charmingly named *shunga* (lit. spring pictures) represent pornographic art of stupendous imagination and comprised a large part of every *ukiyo-e* artist's *oeuvre*. Ironically, *shunga* cannot be seen in Japan (too pornographic, even though it is considerably tamer than what is found in some magazines).

The Japanese have never considered *ukiyo-e* to be "art". It was a publishing form and not art until foreigners started collecting it. Only in the past few decades have Japanese collectors begun to realise the value of *ukiyo-e*. Yet the influence on Western artists has been considerable, especially amongst the Impressionists of the late 19th century. French engraver Félix Bracquemond fuelled the increasing interest in Japanese art – *Japonisme* – when he started distributing copies of Hokusai's sketches. Soon Manet, Zola, Whistler, Degas and Monet were both collecting *ukiyo-e* and adopting *ukiyo-e* motifs and themes in their own works.

Lacquerware

Japanese lacquer *(urushi)* is the sap of a certain tree (Rhus verniciflua) that has been refined and which may have pigment added. It has been used as a decorative coating on wood, leather and cloth for 1,500 years, but the earliest-known examples of lacquer in Japan – red and black lacquered earthenware pots – date back 4,000 years. Lacquerware *(nurimono)* is a community craft – no one person can do all of the 50 steps involved in the plain coating on a wooden bowl. Decoration may involve another 30. The most common Japanese examples of lacquerware are food bowls and serving trays – tableware known as *shikki*.

Ceramics

Japan is a treasure house of ceramic techniques, a craft that has long attracted many students from abroad. There are famous and numerous wares *(yaki)*, the names of which have a certain amount of currency in antiques and crafts circles throughout the world. In general, pottery in Japan is stoneware or porcelain, that is, high-fired wares.

Earthenware and low-fired pottery are found in small quantities, usually in the form of humble utensils, in *Raku-yaki* – a rustic style produced by hand and without the use of a potter's wheel – and in some of the enamelled wares of Kyoto and Satsuma, in southern Kyushu.

The porcelain industry still thrives, and much of it is hand-painted, though modern transfer processes are able to capture all the shades and nuances of hand-painted wares.

Textiles

This craft includes weaving and dyeing, as well as braiding *(kumihimo)* and quilting *(sashiko)*. Japan is a vast storehouse of textile techniques, one that Western craftspeople have yet to tap.

Of course, silks are the most famous and highly refined of Japanese textiles. The brocades used in *noh* drama costumes and in the apparel of the aristocracy and high clergy of

There are a number of unglazed wares, of which the most famous is *Bizen*, made from hard clay and with a bronze-like texture after firing. Traditional glazes are mainly iron (ash glazes), though feldspathic glazes are sometimes used.

Porcelains are decorated with underglaze cobalt and overglaze enamels. The decorated porcelains produced by numerous kilns in the Arita area of northern Kyushu, shipped from the port of Imari from the 17th to the 19th century, are still avidly sought by antiques collectors, as is the Kutani porcelain of the Kanazawa area.

LEFT: *shunga* erotic woodblock print.
ABOVE: Hagi ceramics.

MINGEI REVIVAL

Sensing a decline in Japanese folk crafts with the advent of the machine age, philosopher and art critic Yanagi Soetsu (1889–1961) set about reviving the production of simple, utilitarian but aesthetically beautiful objects, in a movement dubbed Mingei, or "ordinary people's art". Yanagi set up the Mingei-kan (Japanese Folk Craft Museum) in Tokyo in 1936. Besides being a venue for the display of bygone art, it also celebrated the works of living craftsmen, the textile designer Kiesuke Seizawa, the potters Kawai Kanjiro and Hamada Shoju, and the English ceramicist Bernard Leach among them. Thanks to Yanagi, and those who have followed, the movement today is alive and well.

bygone ages are among the highest achievements of textile art anywhere, as are the more humble but lyrical 16th-century *tsujigahana* "tie-dyed" silks.

Japanese folk textiles are a world unto themselves. Cotton, hemp and ramie are the most common fibres, but the bark fibres of the *shina* tree, *kuzu* (kudzu), paper mulberry, plantain (in Okinawa) and other fibres were used in remote mountain areas.

Indigo is the predominant colour, and the *ikat* technique (known as *kasuri*) is the most popular for work clothes, quilt covers, and the like. These white-on-blue textiles are durable.

Modern Literature

Japan has never been short of good writers. In over 1,000 years of literature, from *Genji Monogatari (The Tale of Genji)*, the world's first full-length novel, to the urban surrealism of Haruki Murakami's *The Wind-Up Bird Chronicle*, poets, playwrights and novelists have recorded the Japanese experience and the mutations of the human condition.

The publication of Natsumi Soseki's novel *Kokoro,* concerned with the conflict between the old and a newly emerging Japan, arguably marks the beginning of modern Japanese literature. The immediate post-war period, with its more liberal values, saw an extraordinary efflorescence of literary works. Not that everyone embraced unfettered change.

Jiro Osaragi's *The Journey* examines the upheavals of the American occupation of Japan, while Nagai Kafu, that great chronicler of Tokyo life, consistently rejected the contemporary in works of plangent nostalgia such as *Geisha in Rivalry* and *A Strange Tale from East of the River*. The doubtful role of Western culture in Japanese life surfaces in the popular nihilism of Osamu Dazai's *The Setting Sun* and *No Longer Human*, deeply troubled novels from a writer who, before he committed suicide, styled himself on the dissolute French poet Rimbaud.

An astonishing number of Nobel-quality writers are associated with the period from the 1950s to early 1970s. The great Junichiro Tanizaki, author of modern classics like *The Makioka Sisters* and *Diary of a Mad Old Man*, never won a Nobel, but two other writers associated with this period, Yasunari Kawabata and Kenzaburo Oe, did. Yukio Mishima was nominated for works like *The Golden Pavilion* and *Forbidden Colours*, whose controversial topics reflected the sensational life of the author himself, a brilliant, right-wing homosexual who would go on to stage an abortive coup d'état before finishing himself off in a well publicised, samurai-style suicide.

The Catholic writer Shusaku Endo is rightly admired for novels that are philosophical but strongly narrative. *Scandal* is a tale about muddled identities set in the Tokyo of the 1980s.

For a blistering look at modern Japan, its drug addicts, dropouts and dispossessed, Murakami Ryu's *Almost Transparent Blue* is hard to beat. Haruki Murakami is the best-known author outside of Japan for his wondrously offbeat stories, such as *Kafka on the Shore*.

Social issues are the stuff of a new wave of middle-aged writers, many of them women. Miyuki Miyabe's *All She Was Worth* and the recent *Shadow Family* are good examples of the Japanese social novel. The works of prize-winning novelist Kirino Natsuo, like all the titles mentioned here, have been translated into English. *Out*, a story of women working the night shift in a food packing company, is darkly feminist, right down to the murder and dismembering of an ingrate husband. ❑

LEFT: Nobel Prize winner, Yasunari Kawabata.

Demons of Manga

The term manga covers magazine and newspaper cartoons, comic strips and comic books. Like all cultural forms (and manga is recognised now as a modern art form), it has its historical antecedents. Comic drawings and caricatures have been found in the 7th-century temple complex of Horyu-ji in Ikaruga; in Toshodai-ji, an 8th-century Buddhist temple in Nara; and in the ancient scroll drawing called *Choju Jinbutsu Giga*, in which birds and other creatures satirise the aristocracy and clergy of the time.

The master woodblock artist Hokusai is credited with coining the expression manga to describe a form of adult story book popular in the Edo period (1600–1868).

The popularity of newspapers and magazines during the Taisho Period (1912–26) saw the dissemination of cartoons by popular illustrators such as Okamoto Ippei. A later artist, Osamu Tezuka, is credited as the "father of manga". Tezuka brought film techniques like panning, close-ups and jump cuts to manga, but is also credited with creating the unique look of Japanese manga, its characters singularly un-Japanese in appearance. From the early *Astro Boy*, Tezuka went on to explore more complex themes in *Black Jack*, about a brilliant, unlicensed surgeon, and *Adorufu ni Tsugu* (Tell Adolf), which examined anti-Semitism.

Successful manga like *Neon Genesis Evangelion* and *Chibi Mariko-chan* have been adapted into TV series. Some of these have been turned into internationally marketable films, or *anime* *(see page 95)*.

Manga are not just the preserve of testosterone seething adolescents. They appeal to all age groups and sexes. The late prime minister, Hashimoto Ryutaro, is said to have enjoyed quiet evenings at home with his wife reading manga. Though the appeal is broad, categories exist. *Shonen* (young boys) magazines often feature noble crusades or quests to win the heart of a seemingly unobtainable girl, while *shojo* (young girls) comics, though lighter in impact, take a closer, more refreshing look at human relationships, often bending or blurring gender lines. The *Shonen-ai* (boy's love) genre are popular with women who enjoy explicit images of gay couples. The much commented upon *hentai* (pervert) magazine, featuring violent sex and horror, in fact represent only a small part of the market.

Today's manga includes a range of subjects from flower arranging to how-to approaches to social relations, to abridged versions of classics like *The Tale of Genji*. Manga are often used to explain and simplify complex subjects like international finance. A special genre known as *benkyo-manga*, or "study comics", is aimed at students.

Needless to say, manga is a massive, multi-billion yen business. Sold in bookshops, convenience stores and vending machines, manga is everywhere, and successful illustrators have achieved the celebrity status of TV talents and pop *idoru* (idols).

Right: the ever-popular comic art of the Manga magazine.

They might be as thick as doorstops, but manga don't take long to read. Interestingly, an informal library of comic aficionados has sprung up on trains where, once read, the chunky tomes are left on the racks above seats, picked up by the next passenger and, once read, deposited back on the rack.

Because the manga style is so pervasive, it has influenced advertising, graphic and book design, and the appearance of the internet. Manga magazines, in fact, are decreasing in sales as the stories are effortlessly downloaded onto the more convenient handset of a mobile phone. As Donald Richie has said in his book *The Image Factory*, "eyes that were once glued to the page are now pasted to the palm of the hand". ❑

住友銀行

東洲齋寫樂畫

THE PERFORMING ARTS

Most of Japan's traditional performing arts look and sound otherworldly, if not sacred, to outsiders. Yet some were designed to entertain commoners

For many of the traditional Japanese performing arts, the distinction between dance and drama is tenuous. Most traditional Japanese drama forms today developed out of some form of dance, and all, accordingly, employ musical accompaniment. Several of the forms also involve vocal disciplines to some extent, but not enough to qualify as opera.

There are five major traditional performing-art forms in Japan: *bugaku*, *noh*, *kyogen*, *bunraku* and *kabuki*. Only *bugaku*, *noh* and *kyogen* could be called classical – all are tightly contained and formal entertainments performed originally for the aristocracy. Both *bunraku* and *kabuki* are traditional stage arts but derived from the vigorous common-folk culture of the Edo Period. Another form, *kagura,* needs to be mentioned as well. Although it falls within what could be called folk drama, there is no single form of *kagura*. Rather, these offertory dance-drama-story-religious performances, held on festival days before the deity, all differ greatly throughout the country, involving anything from religious mystery to heroic epics, to bawdy buffoonery and symbolic sexual enactments – or a combination of all these elements.

Bugaku

What the ancient indigenous dance and drama forms in Japan were is not known. There certainly must have been such expression before the cultural imports from the Asian mainland. During the 7th and 8th centuries, mainland culture from both Korea and China dominated the life of the archipelago's imperial court.

In AD 702, the court established a court music bureau to record, preserve and perform the continental music forms *(gagaku)* and dance *(bugaku)*. Influences included not only dance from China and Korea, but also from India and Southeast Asia. These dances are so highly stylised and abstract that there is little or no sense of story or dramatic event. The choreography is rigid and is usually symmetrical, since the dances are most often performed by two pairs of dancers.

The *bugaku* stage is a raised platform erected outdoors, independent of other structures and ascended by steps at the front and back. The performance area is carpeted with green silk, the stairs are lacquered black, the surrounding railings and posts are in cinnabar lacquer. Given that the *bugaku* repertoire has been preserved for almost 15 centuries, it is amazing to consider that about 60 different dances are known and performed today. These dances are categorised into "right" and "left", as was the custom in China. Left dances are slow, flowing and graceful, while right dances are relatively more humourous and spirited.

Masks are often part of a *bugaku* dance. Those used for the dances still performed (and many of those preserved in temples and other repositories associated with dances no longer performed) closely resemble some of the masks

PRECEDING PAGES: *kabuki* actor warms up, Tokyo. **LEFT:** the classic image of an 18th-century male *kabuki* performer. **RIGHT:** *noh* performer.

employed in religious performances in Bhutan.

Bugaku is classified into four categories: ceremonial, military, "running" and children's dances. The Imperial Household Agency (keeper and administrator of the imperial family) maintains a *bugaku* section for the preservation and performance, at certain times of the year, of this ancient form. Additionally, some shrines and temples have kept up *bugaku* performances as part of festivals and other yearly observances.

Noh and kyogen

What is called *noh* drama today dates from the early part of the 15th century. As an art form, its high degree of stylisation, monotonous-sounding vocal declamation (*utai*, a cross between chanting and dramatic narrative), and lack of overt action, makes it a distinctly acquired taste.

Such terms as classic dignity, grace and symbolism are used to describe the *noh* drama. It is said to have been developed from a dance-drama form called *sarugaku*. Little is known about *sarugaku*. There is evidence that would categorise it in the same way as *kagura* – a calling-down into physical manifestation and an offering to a deity or deities. Also, it seems there were wandering troupes who performed *sarugaku*. Considered part of the *noh* reper-

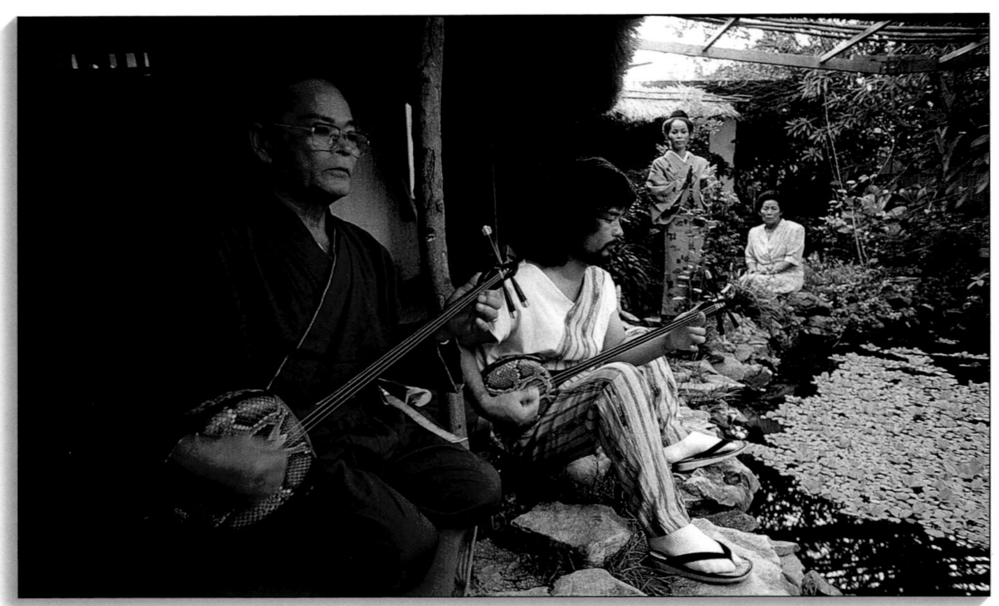

THOUSAND-YEAR-OLD MUSIC

There are solo or small-ensemble musical forms, particularly those featuring the harp-like *koto*, *shakuhachi* bamboo flute, *shamisen* and the numerous *taiko* (drum) and *minon* (folk singing) troupes. But the most authentic (if not typical) form of Japanese music performed apart from drama or dance is *gagaku* (lit. elegant music). It is a kind of orchestral music developed in the 9th century and little changed since.

Quite unlike the popular entertainments described elsewhere, *gagaku* was strictly court music, almost never performed in public before World War II, and only occasionally now.

It employs esoteric instruments resembling – sometimes identical to – those used in India and China long before high-tech instruments such as the *koto* or the *sitar* were developed. These include drums, nose-flutes and bowed, single-stringed droners. Together with a slow, "courtly" tempo, *gagaku* is ideal for (and to most Japanese ears, synonymous with) funeral music. In fact, probably the first and only time the Japanese public has heard it in recent times was during the televised funeral of Emperor Showa (Hirohito) in 1989. Devotees find tremendous excitement in *gagaku*'s extended, soulful sounds and unrelieved tensions.

toire, the sprightly dance *sanbaso* is performed by tradition as part of the rituals to invoke a felicitous beginning, such as for the upcoming new year or for a new company.

Whatever its origins, *noh* was perfected by Kan'ami Kiyotsugu (1333–84) and his son, Zeami Motokiyo, who were playwrights, actors and aesthetic theorists of the highest level. Together they created about one-third of the 240 *noh* plays known today.

Buddhism had a profound influence on the content and dramatic structure of *noh*. The veil of "illusion" that we perceive as everyday "reality" is, in a sense, pierced momentarily by *noh* to expose something more basic, something that subsumes the senses.

Masks, highly stylised sets and props (when such things do appear), a tightly controlled style of movement, a voice style that projects and declaims but does not entice, and musical accompaniment – *hayashi* – of a few types of drum and a piercing fife mean that this form of play relies mostly on imagery and symbolism for its dramatic impact. In contrast to this sparse and uncluttered form of drama, the textiles used for *noh* costumes are the diametric opposite. The world's most opulent and gorgeous gold and silver and polychrome brocades are what the *noh* actor wears on stage. And *noh* masks are an art form in themselves.

LEFT: *shamisen* players. **ABOVE:** Shinto dance performance and *bunraku* puppet and puppeteer.

As with Greek drama, the heavy and sober *noh* is performed in tandem with the light farces of *kyogen* (lit. crazy words), itself thought to reflect more directly the *sarugaku* antecedents it shares with *noh*. Although the dramatic methods have something in common with *noh*, *kyogen* does not use masks and is more direct and active. Traditionally, it is performed during intermissions of a *noh* performance, but today it is often performed by itself. These farces are both part of and independent of *noh* – lighthearted, concerned with nonsense, and simple.

Bunraku

Japan's glorious puppet drama is a combination of three elements, which, about 400 years ago, fused into a composite: *shamisen* music, puppetry techniques and a form of narrative or epic-chanting called *joruri*. The result is *bunraku*, the puppet drama that is considered to be an equal with live-stage theatre performance. Although *bunraku* developed and matured in the two centuries after its creation, the origin of the puppetry techniques used is still shrouded in mystery. There are folk-puppet dramas scattered throughout Japan, but the centre of *bunraku* puppet drama is in Osaka.

The *shamisen* (a banjo-like instrument) entered Japan from the kingdom of the Ryukyus (now known as Okinawa) sometime in the 16th century and was adapted and spread throughout the country very quickly. Although the instrument only has three strings, music produced by the *shamisen* has great versatility and, in particular, lends itself well to dramatic emphasis.

Bunraku puppets *(ningyo)* are manipulated directly by hand and are quite large – it takes three men to handle one of the major puppets in a play. The skills involved in manipulation of

bunraku puppets are considerable. The narrative style derives from classic epics of heroism chanted to the accompaniment of a *biwa*, a form of lute that made its way to Japan from central Asia at an early date. Although there may be more than one *shamisen* to give musical density to the accompaniment, there is only one chanter. He uses different tones of voice to distinguish male from female characters, young from old, good from bad. Accent and intonation convey nuances of feeling and indicate shifts of scene.

While *bunraku* and *kabuki* share many traits and have some plays in common, *bunraku* is the older of the two and it was *kabuki* that adopted elements of the puppet drama. The important point is that both *bunraku* and *kabuki* are popular theatre. *Bunraku* was for townspeople and intended as popular entertainment, much like Shakespeare's plays were in his day.

Kabuki

Plays for *kabuki* are still being written. Not many, granted, but the genre is alive, and like *bunraku* it is not "classical". *Kabuki* is the equivalent of cabaret spectacular, soap opera, morality play, religious pageant and tear-jerker. It is music and dance and story and colour and pathos and farce, everything any theatre-goer could want.

The highly stylised language of *kabuki*, the poses and posturing and eye-crossing for dramatic emphasis, the swashbuckling and acrobatics and flashy exits, instant costume changes and magic transformations – all are part of the fun.

Kabuki originated in the early years of the 17th century with a troupe of women who performed on the river bank at Kyoto what seems to have been a kind of dance (based on a dance performed at Buddhist festivals) and perhaps comic skits as well. Whether there was anything untoward in this performance probably will never be known, but the shogunal authorities seemed to think there was, and so in 1629 they banned women from appearing on stage. Male performers took their place, and to this day all *kabuki* performers are men; the discipline of the actor who takes female parts *(onnagata)* is particularly rigorous.

The female troupes were supplanted in short order by itinerant troupes of young men, who also got into trouble with the authorities. These groups were disbanded and the permanent theatre companies then developed in Kyoto, Osaka and Edo (now Tokyo) after the middle of the 17th century. *Kabuki* soon became the Edo Period's most popular entertainment.

The production of a *kabuki* play involves strict conventions: gestures and other movements, colours, props, costumes, wigs and make-up. Even the types of textiles used for costumes are determined. (But there are places in a play left for spontaneous ad-libs.) The audience directs much attention to the performer or performers. The story is secondary and it will be well-known anyway. *Kabuki* devotees want to see favourite stars in familiar roles. Indeed, *kabuki* has been actor-centred since its beginning.

The training of a *kabuki* actor starts at about the age of three, when children are left by their actor parents backstage. The children internalise the atmosphere and the music's rhythms. With this kind of training, *kabuki* naturally becomes part of one's core early on in life. This facilitates the years of rigorous apprenticeship and training that every *kabuki* actor must undergo.

The *kabuki* stage has a number of unique features. The most striking is the walkway that extends from the stage to the doors at the rear of the theatre at stage level. Actors enter and exit through this stage extension (*hanamichi*, meaning flower path), and it is sometimes used as a venue of action. Another feature is the curtain, decorated in vertical stripes of black, green and orange, opened from stage right to left. The *kabuki* theatre also featured a revolving stage long before the concept arose in Europe.

Kabuki Repertoire

There are some 240 plays in the *kabuki* repertoire of *jidai-mono*, or historical events and episodes, and *sewa-mono*, which deals with the lives of townspeople.

Dramatic pause

Both *noh* and *kabuki* show no clear-cut distinction between dance forms and stage movements. Still, *kabuki*'s grandiloquent gestures are a far cry from the austere containment of *noh*. The *kabuki* technique called *mie* illustrates the formalised beauty of performance. A *mie* occurs at certain climactic moments when the starring actor, projecting dramatic energy at top output, freezes into a statuesque pose with rigid stare and eyes crossed to emphasise a dramatic peak of intense emotional power. Glorious overkill, indeed. At such (and other) high points of a performance, shouts will ring out from the audience – the Japanese equivalent of "Do it, Eiho!" or "Kill 'em dead, Masayuki!" ❑

LEFT: *ukiyo-e* print of *kabuki* backstage.
ABOVE: *kabuki* performers.

Shock Dance

Performances may be announced at the last minute, venues moved from theatres to overgrown car parks, audiences exposed to sensory shocks. Welcome to *butoh*, Japan's most radical underground dance form. Stripped of the formalism of traditional Japanese dance, *butoh*'s intensity, the exposed nerve points and emotions it explores in almost total silence, the vision of semi-naked dancers smeared in white body paint, are definitely not for mainstream Japanese audiences. *Butoh*'s rejection of Western dance influences, its avowed aim to return to more elemental Japanese emotions, and its spurning of taboo subjects have ensured that it remains radical.

THE CINEMA OF JAPAN

Japanese cinema has always refused to embrace the values of Hollywood. In doing so, it has produced some of the world's most aesthetic and powerful films

The Japanese cinema has been pronounced dead so many times over the past few years – perhaps most often by Japanese critics and filmmakers – that its stubborn survival, if not full resurrection, comes as a relief. Just when it seemed that Japanese audiences had turned away from domestic product dealing with their country's amazing history, along came *Mononoke Hime (Princess Mononoke)* from Miyazaki Hayao, which smashed the previous all-time box-office record held by *E.T.* until *Titanic* came along. What was so heartening about the success of the Miyazaki film was that Japanese were indeed interested – in huge numbers – to see an epic historical fantasy about Japanese history, set in an ancient time filled with gods and demons, an era in which men and animals could still verbally communicate with each other. *Mononoke Hime* is a cartoon, or more accurately, anime *(see page 95)*, which has always been taken more seriously in Japan than in the West.

A difference in technique

Dramatically, the classic three-act structure of Hollywood holds little place in Japanese cinema. Character and mood, rather than plot, are what propel many of its best films. Stories often trail off by movie's end without a "proper" ending, storylines (especially in *jidai-geki*, or historical dramas) can be unbelievably convoluted and confusing, even to the most ardent devotees, and most Japanese films move at a considerably slower pace.

In a typical Japanese movie, dynamic action stands in contrast to long, sustained scenes of inactive dialogue, or just silence. The fundamental reason for this is that when engaging in conversation, the Japanese usually sit at *tatami*-mat level, stationary, without the pacing and arm-flailing common in Western conversation. The Japanese are also tremendously influenced by Zen Buddhist culture, whether consciously or not. Thus, directors not only take the time to smell the roses but to plant them, nurture them, and then watch them grow, quietly. Landscape and atmosphere also play key roles in Japanese cinema, perhaps tied into the other major religion of the country, the pantheistic Shinto. Floating mists, drops of water slowly falling into a stream, the soft, sad sound of cherry blossoms falling on an April day – all are familiar to Japanese audiences and alien to the rest of us.

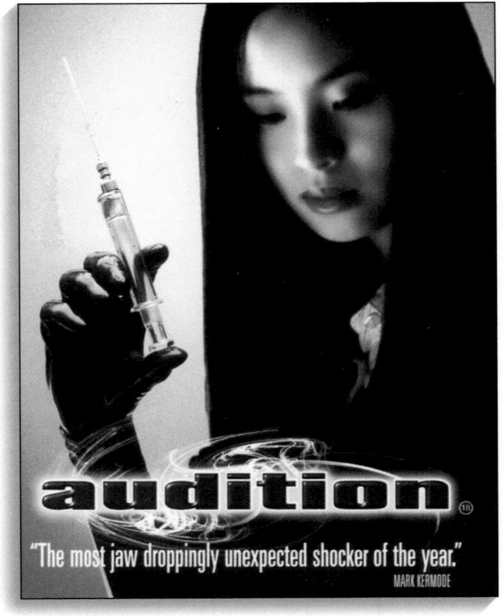

audition
"The most jaw droppingly unexpected shocker of the year."
MARK KERMODE

LEFT: *Godzilla vs The Smog Monster.* **RIGHT:** poster for the Japanese shock-horror film, *Audition* (1999).

Of course, it must also be said that such mass-market genres as *kaiju* (giant monster) and contemporary *yakuza* (gangster) movies are often just as breathlessly mounted as the latest dunder-headed Steven Seagal action flick.

There's also considerably more space in Japanese cinema for morally dubious protagonists since, in both the Shinto and Buddhist traditions, life is a balance between forces of good and evil, with both necessary to maintain life as we know it. Thus, a cold-blooded killer like the *ronin* (masterless *samurai*) Ogami Ito, who roams Japan with his tiny son Daigoro in a bamboo baby cart, dispatching others by decapitation and disembowelment in the popular *Sword of Vengeance* series of films, would absolutely baffle most Western audiences. Is he a good guy or a bad guy? Is he wearing a black hat or a white hat? The answer is both. And the dirty, amoral bodyguard portrayed by Mifune Toshiro in both *Yojimbo* and *Sanjuro* would also fit this bill quite beautifully. He was the prototype for Clint Eastwood's man with no name in Sergio Leone's operatic spaghetti Westerns *A Fistful of Dollars* (a remake of *Yojimbo*) and *The Good, the Bad and the Ugly.*

But what really makes Japanese film special isn't so much the bloodshed and ultra-violence, but rather the profound humanism and compassion ranging through its entire history. One would have to look deeply into other international cinemas to find efforts as profound as Kurosawa's *Ikiru* and *Ran*, Ozu's *Tokyo Story*, Kinoshita Keisuke's *Twenty-Four Eyes* or Mizoguchi's *The Life of Oharu*.

Age matters not

The great, golden age of Japanese film, which lasted from the postwar 1950s until the late 1960s when the burgeoning availability of television laid it to waste, is certainly gone. The three major studios still surviving – Toho, Shochiku and Toei – barely crank out enough domestic films in a year to fill a couple of the multiplexes that are suddenly springing up. But it's not over yet.

The death of Kurosawa Akira in 1998 was a particular blow. "Sensei", as he became known, almost single-handedly put Japanese film on the international map with *Rashômon*, which won top prize at the 1951 Venice Film Festival. His rising and falling fortunes over the next half century were emblematic of the Japanese industry itself. Endlessly frustrated by unreceptive Japanese studios and aborted projects,

OZU'S CAMERA EYE

Yasujiro Ozu (1903–63) was, arguably, Japan's greatest film director. In works like *Floating Weeds*, *But...* and *Record of a Tenement Gentleman*, Ozu's originality and technical skills are still admired by film buffs and students. Ozu's work is a good example of Japanese cinema's ability to define a style and approach through limitation. In Ozu's case this took the form of the lingering single, long shot. An aesthetic objectivity results from this restricted view. Ozu's best-known classic is *Tokyo Story* (Tokyo Monogatari), a wonderful work of directorial understatement routinely voted one of the best films of all time by bodies such as the British Film Institute.

Kurosawa attempted suicide after a box-office failure in 1970. Yet he would go on to make five more films, at least two of which – *Kagemusha* and particularly *Ran* – would be counted among his greatest works. However, Kurosawa repeatedly had to look outside Japan to Francis Ford Coppola, George Lucas, Steven Spielberg and Serge Silberman for support.

Imamura Shohei, one of Japan's acclaimed film makers, who died in 2006, brought a gritty realism to Japanese cinema, preferring to make films portraying people from the lower classes. He won the Palme d'Or at the Cannes Film Festival for *The Ballad of Narayama* (in 1982) and *The Eel* (in 1997).

Japanese film suffered a shocking and unexpected blow by the still inexplicable 1997 suicide-by-scandal of Itami Juzo. (A tabloid newspaper was about to reveal a supposed relationship between the filmmaker and a younger woman.) Itami was responsible for some marvellously smart and funny dissections of contemporary life, all of them starring his wife, Miyamoto Nobuko: *The Funeral*, *Tampopo*, and the societal exposés of the *Taxing Woman* films.

Another shock to the system was the 1996 death of actor Atsumi Kiyoshi, Japan's beloved Tora-san. Don't underestimate the impact of this character on the national consciousness (or Shochiku's box office take). Over the span of nearly 30 years and 47 films, this itinerant amulet seller was to Japan what Chaplin's Little Tramp was to the world during the Silent Era, only more so. Within the restrictive, often suffocating bounds of Japanese society, Tora-san's gypsy-like existence had strong appeal to the millions of train-riding 9-to-5 businessmen, and his endlessly disappointing romances held women in thrall.

Bright lights, new generation

Although filmmaking styles have been altered for scaled-down financial resources and changing audience tastes, there's much to recommend in Japan's younger generation of filmmakers. Suo Masayuki's delightful *Shall We Dance?* was the highest-grossing foreign-language film ever to play in US movie theatres at the time and would undoubtedly have won the Oscar for foreign films had it not been disqualified by one of the Academy's innumerable arcane rules.

The anarchic, dark, violent and often funny ruminations by "Beat" Takeshi Kitano – a tremendously successful and popular comedian, actor, game-show host, raconteur and moviemaker – have won international acclaim, particularly his most recent original effort, the alternately tender and cataclysmic *Hana-Bi* (*Fireworks*). And the first two films from Takenaka Naoto made a good impression: the wry and laconic *119* and *Tokyo Biyuri*, the moving but unsentimental film

about the difficult relationship between a photographer and his mentally unbalanced wife.

One step forward, two back

Curiously enough – although not so curiously, if one looks back to what occurred in the US during the Great Depression – Japan's economic downturn of the 1990s produced greater box-office revenues. As industry after industry reported dismal earnings, the business doing best was the movie business. Much of this can be attributed to foreign films such as *Titanic,* which in Japan accounted for more than 70 percent of the revenues of foreign films. Still, domestic product was also on the rise.

LEFT: the great Mifune Toshiro in *Yojimbo.*
RIGHT: poster for Beat Takeshi's 1997 *Hana-Bi* (Fireworks).

Elsewhere there was scrutiny and criticism from the Japanese and international media with another film, *Unmei no Toki (Pride)*, a big-budget, nationalistic biopic from director Ito Shunya that sympathetically portrayed Japan's wartime prime minister, Gen. Tojo Hideki. A storm of controversy erupted around the region upon the film's release. Asians were incensed that the man generally considered to be the prime instigator of Japanese Asian aggression – and the person responsible for what has become known as the Rape of Nanjing, in China – was depicted in the film to be battling for Asian interests against Western imperialism. *Pride* actually received a decent notice in *Daily Variety*, the primary American entertainment trade publication: "powerful, controversial, revisionist courtroom drama... [the film's] different spin on famous events of the Pacific war is at times quite disturbing but is nonetheless fascinating and makes for most effective drama". *Pride* was made for a huge (by Japanese standards) $11 million and starred the highly respected film and television actor Tsugawa Masahiko as Tojo.

Japanese films about World War II have always veered wildly between the powerfully pacifistic (Ichikawa Kon's harsh *Fires on the Plain* and the stunningly emotional *The Burmese Harp,* also directed by Ichikawa) and jingoistic flag waving. Often, war films try to have it both ways, especially in recent war movies in which popular teen idols, male and female, are cast in primary roles and then killed off tragically, much to the despair and tears of the young audiences.

Hollywood's Japan

The claim that the Japanese enjoy nothing more than seeing themselves through the eyes of the outside world is corroborated by a slew of well received Hollywood-made movies with Japanese locations and subjects. Hollywood had been fascinated with Japan as a setting for its dramas even before the 1958 John Wayne hit, *The Barbarian and the Geisha*, or the 007 thriller *You Only Live Twice*, but the last few years have witnessed a Japan boom that seems unstoppable.

Memorable films include Ridley Scott's *Black Rain,* filmed in Osaka, where a thriving criminal underworld provided theme and visual substance, and Paul Schrader's *Mishima*, which looked at the troubled but intriguing life of literary giant and right-wing imperialist Yukio Mishima.

Quentin Tarentino's 2003 *Kill Bill 1* and its sequel *Kill Bill 2*, were homages to the Japanese yakuza film; Tom Cruise's portrayal of a transplanted American Civil War veteran in *The Last Samurai* was a smash hit in Japan; Sophia Coppola's bizarre comedy *Lost in Translation*, filmed almost entirely in a Tokyo hotel, picked up an Oscar. The 2005 film version of Arthur Golden's novel *Memoirs of a Geisha* became a hit in Japan, where it was released under the title of its main character, *Sayuri*. Japan continues to inspire Hollywood. ❑

LEFT: Kurosawa in action.

GODZILLA

To the Japanese people, Godzilla isn't some huge, lumbering, atomic-born giant lizard. He's *their* huge, lumbering, atomic-born giant lizard. With the 22 movies since his debut in 1954's *Gojira* (a combination of the Japanese words for "gorilla" and "whale", anglicised to Godzilla for its US release two years later), this monster who towers above Tokyo smashing everything in his path is one of the most famous icons of postwar Japan. Naturally, despite (or perhaps because of) its special effects and far-fetched plot, the first of the many Godzilla movies became a huge hit, not only in Japan but throughout Southeast Asia, the US and Europe.

Anime

Sailor Moon. Dragonball Z. Doraemon. Pokémon. Evangelion. Gundam. Urusei Yatsura. Aeon Flux. My Neighbour Totoro. Akira. Princess Mononoke... The Diary of Anne Frank? Welcome to the fantastic, beautiful, grotesque, and always surprising world of anime, a cartoon universe peculiar to the Japanese imagination but now being accepted worldwide by legions of fanatical admirers. Born of manga *(see page 81)* – the thick comic books read by young and old in Japan – these feature-film and television cartoons are a stunning detour from the animated fare that most Westerners are raised upon.

In most of the world, cartoons are almost entirely the domain of the very young, and Japan certainly pays attention to that audience with several anime aimed squarely at children. The problem (for some Westerners and concerned Japanese parents as well) is that even the kid's anime is so visually frenetic that it makes good ol' Looney Tunes seem mellow by comparison.

As for the more adult fare... well, here's where the cultural differences between East and West are quite clear. Ultra-violence, raw sexuality and nudity, visionary and often apocalyptic views of the future, and extreme graphic style are the hallmarks of this genre, with most efforts falling into the science-fiction category. The better examples of these are truly stunning and original, such as Otomo Katsuhiro's 1989 classic *Akira* and, more recently, Oshii Mamoru's *The Ghost in the Shell*.

But there's an alternative to the endless parade of animated juggernauts and bare breasts – and his name is Miyazaki Hayao. A virtual font of creativity, Miyazaki heads the famed Studio Ghibli, which has been responsible for what many would consider to be the finest anime to emerge from Japan. Miyazaki got his start in TV anime, directing a popular multi-part version of *Heidi* before moving into features with *The Castle of Cagliostro*, based on a popular James Bondian character known as Lupin the Third. Since then, his films as director have included such fanciful, haunting and often humourous fantasy efforts as *Nausicaa of the Valley of the Wind, Laputa – The Castle in the Sky, Porco Rosso, My Neighbour Totoro, Kiki's Delivery Service,* and most recently, the gigantic box-office hit *Mononoke Hime*, or *Princess Mononoke (see picture above)*.

In addition to his penchant for pure entertainment, Miyazaki's concerns are also ecological and spiritual in a deeply Japanese way. Shinto strongly informs *Princess Mononoke* – a complex story that is essentially about the inevitable clash between humans and the deities of nature, in this case giant versions of boars and wolves endowed with the power of language – and the remarkable *Heise Tanuki Gassen Pompoko* (supervised by Miyazaki but directed by Ghibli's Takahata Isao), which is about raccoons fighting the destruction of their forest home in what would later become the Tokyo suburb of Tama. Miyazaki's last creation, *Sen to Chihiro no Kamikakushi* (Spirited Away) received an Oscar for best animated feature in 2003.

RIGHT: *Mononoke Hime*, or *Princess Mononoke*.

It's not too surprising that Miyazaki Hayao, often referred to as the Walt Disney of Japan, was finally discovered by Hollywood when the Walt Disney Company bought theatrical rights for *Princess Mononoke* and also made a deal to distribute on DVD several of Studio Ghibli's previous efforts.

There are other fine examples of ambitious anime that defy the supercharged sci-fi traditions, including of all things a very respectable 1995 two-hour version of *The Diary of Anne Frank*. While making the story palatable for a young audience, this film powerfully drove home the real-life drama against beautifully drawn backgrounds of 1940s Amsterdam and a score by Michael Nyman, who wrote the music for *The Piano*. ❑

ARCHITECTURE

With its post-and-beam construction, Japanese architecture allows flexibility with interior space and dissolves the rigid boundary between inside and outside

What kind of house would one build in Japan if one knew it might be blown away by winds or fall apart by movements of the earth? Besides typhoons and earthquakes, Japan also has severe rains, which often cause flooding and landslides. How would one make a palace or temple or hall, a farmhouse, or a gate to survive such destructive forces? These questions had to be faced by the designers of buildings in Japan's remote past and are still faced today.

The fact that Japan has the world's oldest wooden buildings (Horyu-ji, built about AD 670) and the world's largest wooden structure (at Todai-ji, some 50 metres/165 ft high and said to have been rebuilt at only two-thirds its original size) suggests that the architectural system adopted by the Japanese was at least partially successful in creating structures that last. On the other hand, at least in contemporary times, the devastation of the 1995 Kobe earthquake – thousands of homes, office buildings and expressways simply collapsed, while thousands more burned down in a matter of seconds – suggests otherwise. Indeed, rather than wind, earth and water, it is fire that is the greatest destroyer of buildings in Japan.

In any case, Japanese architecture has influenced architectural design throughout the world. Its concepts of fluidity, modularity, utilisation of limited space, and use of light and shadow have a great power and appeal, both aesthetically and as solutions to architectural problems in contemporary times.

Whatever factors determined how buildings were built in Japan – survival, tradition, aesthetics – some common characteristics can be found that define the tradition of Japanese architecture. Given the great range of climates and the complex topography of the archipelago, the persistence of such common architectural features is truly remarkable.

PRECEDING PAGES: open verandahs unite inside and outside. **LEFT:** traditional tools in use on a new shrine. **RIGHT:** imperial visit to Tokyo's Yasukuni Shrine.

The oldest Japanese dwellings are the pit houses of the neolithic Jomon culture, but the oldest structure to which the term "architecture" might be applied are the Grand Shrines of Ise *(see page 73)*. First completed in the 5th century, the shrines have been ritually rebuilt 60 times – every 20 years. Each rebuilding

takes years to accomplish, starting with the cutting of special cypress trees deep in the mountains, and it involves special carpentry techniques as well as time-honoured rituals.

Early influences

The introduction of Buddhism to Japan in AD 552 brought with it a whole raft of cultural and technical features, not least of which was the continental style of architecture. It is said that Korean builders came over to Japan and either built or supervised the building of the Horyu-ji (AD 607). The foundations of the vast temple that was the prototype of Horyu-ji can be seen in Kyongju, South Korea.

In the 7th century at the capital in Nara, Chinese architectural influence became quite obvious, not only in the structures themselves, but in the adoption of the north-south grid plan of the capital, based on the layout of the Chinese capital. At this time, both secular and sacred architecture was essentially the same, and palaces were often rededicated as temples. Both displayed red-lacquered columns and green roofs with pronounced upswinging curves in the eaves. Roofs were tiled.

Measured by Tatami

Room area is measured by the number of *tatami* mats (about 2 sq metres each). Combinations of mats are standard: 3, 4.5, 6, 8, 10 or 12 mats per room.

Evolving styles

The mutability of residence and temple held true in the subsequent Heian Period as well, as evidenced by the villa of the nobleman Fujiwara no Yorimichi (990–1074), which became the Phoenix Hall of Byodo-in, in Uji near Kyoto. The graceful *shinden-zukuri* style of this structure, utilised for the residences of Heian court nobles, is characterised by rectangular structures in symmetrical arrangement and linked by long corridors. The layout of Kyoto's Old Imperial Palace is similar, though it is a replica of this style.

When the imperial court at Kyoto lost the reins of power to the military government of the shogunate, located far to the west in Kamakura, the open and vulnerable *shinden* style was supplanted by a type of residential building more easily defended. This warrior style *(bukke-zukuri)* placed a number of rooms under one roof or a series of conjoined roofs and was surrounded by a defensive device such as a fence, wall or moat, with guard towers and gates. Tiled roofs gave way to either shingled or thatched roofs. This period also saw the importation of Chinese Song-dynasty architectural styles for temples, particularly the so-called Zen style, which is characterised by shingled roofs, pillars set on carved stone plinths, and the "hidden roof" system developed in Japan, among other features.

In the subsequent Muromachi Period, which saw the purest expression of feudal government and its breakup into the Age of Warring States (15th century), Zen Buddhist influence transformed the warrior style into the *shoin* style. This at first was little more than the addition of a small reading or waiting room *(shoin)*, with a deep sill that could be used as a desk, and decorative, built-in shelves to hold books or other objects. This room also displayed an alcove, the *toko-noma*, in which treasured objects could be effectively displayed. This *shoin* room eventually exerted its influence over the entire structure. Both the Golden Pavilion and the Silver Pavilion of Kyoto are examples of this style.

At the end of the Age of Warring States, firearms became common in warfare. In response to this, massive castles were built. Few original structures remain today. Himeji Castle, with white walls and soaring roof, is the finest example.

Political change brought the country into the Edo Period, and architecture saw a melding of the *shoin* style and teahouse concepts to produce the *sukiya* style, the grandest example of which is the Katsura Imperial Villa in Kyoto. This residential architecture displays an overall lightness of members, a simplified roof, and restrained, subtle ornamentation.

A box with a hat

The favoured material of building construction is wood. Walls, foundations of castles, the podia of some structures, and a few novel experiments saw stone in limited use, usually without mortar. Yet, undoubtedly because it was plentiful, wood remained the material of preference, particularly the wood of conifers. This is reflected in the reforestation laws of the shogunate and various feudal lords. The disappearance of certain types of large trees due to lumbering is reflected in certain historical changes in temple and shrine buildings.

This preference for wood is directly related to the fact that the basic structural system in Japanese architecture is post and beam. The structure is basically a box upon which a hat – the roof – rests. This system allows great freedom in the design of the roof, and the Japanese seemed to prefer large ones, sometimes exceeding one-half of the total height of a structure. Roofs also became elaborate, with generous eaves, and often very heavy.

Straight lines dominate Japanese architecture, seemingly a natural result of using wood and the post-and-beam system. There are few curves and no arches. Barrel vaulting is unheard of. Curves, when they appear as an integral part of a structure, are gentle and used as aesthetic relief from the predominantly flat, boxy construction. The curves on gables and eaves are a good example of this. On the other hand, carved and non-structural embellish-

LEFT: Shirakawa-go's unique style of architecture.
ABOVE: carpenters working on a new shrine relax over tea.

Surface Tensions

From the thin sliver of titanium that coats the soaring Global Tower in Beppu, through the Umeda Sky Building in Osaka, with its vaulting walls and great cavities of open, aerial space, to the honeycombed glass panels of the new Prada building in Tokyo, Japan is a dreamscape for the experimental architect.

What characterises many of these new creations more than anything else is their surfacing. The "bubble" years of the 1980s were characterised by a shift from industrial expansion to a post-industrial,

information-oriented society with software elements dominating over hardware ones. In the shift towards an information-based economy, buildings have become sounding boards, global-age transmitters. One can almost see on the surfaces of these buildings the alternating currents of the economy.

This flexible system of choreographed space, layers of artificial skin and surface, is achieved with hi-tech materials, which, at their most successful, create illusions of depth and space. This tendency is visible in the new surfaces and the floating contraptions surrounding the core of the building, in the use of lighter, non-durable, hi-tech industrial materials such as liquid crystal glass, polycarbon, Teflon, perforated metal and stainless-steel sheets.

The merits of insubstantiality, of surface units that can be replaced at will, are highly visible in the work of architect Fumihiko Maki, whose constructions are routinely sheathed in floating membranes of aluminium screen, perforated panels and light-reflecting surfaces. Tokyo's Cine Rise film complex, designed by Atsushi Kitagawara in 1986, is an early example of the attention to surface moulding. The stagey appearance of the building, with its cast aluminium drapery, "dissolving" roof and webbing of wire mesh, blends well with the cinematic pop quality of the area.

In acquiring the added function of advertising props, Japanese urban centres have been transformed into surfaces of running commercial text and scroll. In cities like Tokyo and Osaka, where pedestrians for the most part see one side of a building – the one overlooking the street – views are flattened into two-dimensional planes. Urban geographer Paul Waley has observed that "space in the Japanese city is conceived only in the context of the immediate visual field. This gives it an episodic quality...." If each panel is visualised as an episode, it is one in a narrative that is set on constant replay, or re-write.

Where a former age delighted more in the texture and tone of walls and other urban exteriors, in contemporary, space-depleted urban Japan, utility dominates the use of walls and other surfaces. The result is panels hung with a forest of signage. Commercial advertising inscribes the city in a deliberate, expressive manner. The textual quality of Japanese cities, from their daylight advertising to night-time electrographics, permits urban spaces to be scanned and read: the city as streaming text. Like the city itself, this commercial script can only be digested piecemeal, in lines of haiku length or even just a few syllables.

Signage in Japanese cities has developed to such an extent that, in some instances, entire buildings may be obscured by hanging objects and structures. Increasingly these are liquid constructions, façade-scale TV screens so carefully aligned and affixed that they appear as a seamless part of the building itself. These screens create, in what was hitherto an unassuming visual void, "a gate and a field within whose false depth a new, antithetical dimension of space and time opens up," as Vladimir Krstic has expressed it.

Are such liquid dreams the shape of things to come? For some, these seductive LCD screens may indeed be the writing on the wall. ❑

LEFT: one of Osaka's most striking skyscrapers, the Umeda Sky Building.

ment, especially on temples and other buildings that go in for opulent display, often shows a wild proliferation of scrolls, volutes and curvilinear motifs of many kinds, perhaps to offset the effect of this basic boxiness of the structure.

Post-and-beam boxes also may be combined and strung together in many ways to create fine aesthetic effects. The Katsura Imperial Villa in Kyoto represents the height of such architecture. Since posts or columns bear the weight of the roof, walls could be – and were – thin and non-supporting. This lightness of wall is another feature that makes traditional Japanese buildings top-heavy, and it was developed to the point that walls often ceased to be walls and became more like moveable partitions instead. (The main exceptions were buildings that were meant to have a protective or defensive function – storehouses and castles – which had thick walls of clay or wood.)

This is the origin of fluidity or modularity, perhaps the single most noteworthy aspect of Japanese buildings. Interior spaces were partitioned so that rooms could become more versatile, to be combined or contracted. The former was accomplished through the use of sliding and removeable door panels. A room could be divided by decorative standing screens, especially those with gold backgrounds to act as a reflective surface and bring light into gloomy castle or palace interiors. Corridor width was the necessary width for two people with serving trays to pass one another.

AMBIENCE COUNTS

A Japanese ceramic bowl and a kimono are very different when seen in a traditional Japanese room and in a room with plaster walls and glass windows.

ABOVE: traditional design of Kyoto's Nazen-ji, at the foot of Daimonji-yama.

Inside is outside

Also, in this approach, the distinction between wall and door often disappears. This applies to outside walls – the "boundary" between interior and exterior – as well. Outside walls are often nothing more than a series of sliding wooden panels that can be easily removed, thus eliminating the solid border between inside and outside, a feature very much welcomed in Japan's humid summer. The verandah thus becomes a transitional space connecting interior with exterior.

The ability to open up a house interior completely to external vistas contributed to the development of a heightened sensitivity to such vistas and to their manipulation.

Since the floors of traditional Japanese buildings are generally raised, house floor and ground surface are not contiguous (except in the case of the packed earth *doma*, the work and implement storage area of a farmhouse). In effect, this means that the indoor-outdoor fluidity is mainly visual and for circulation of air, not for movement of people in and out.

In rural areas, the veranda, when open, becomes a meeting place, to sit and talk with a neighbour.

WORLD HERITAGE HOMES

To see authentic, steep thatched-roofed, A-framed farmhouses *(gassho-zukuri)*, visit the villages of Shirakawa-go – made a UNESCO World Heritage Site in 1995.

Traditional materials

The materials used in traditional Japanese room interiors are few and limited, reflecting an ambivalence between interior and exterior, or perhaps a pleasure in harmonising rather than sharply demarking interior and exterior. Sliding door panels are either translucent *shoji* or the heavier, opaque *fusuma* paper screens, or of wood. Floors are of thick, resilient straw mats surfaced with woven reed (*tatami* mats), or of plain wood.

Supportive wooden posts remain exposed, and ceilings are generally of wood or of woven materials of various kinds. Wooden surfaces remain unpainted. In the few areas of the country where wooden architectural surfaces are lacquered, the lacquer enhances the material, letting it speak; covering it is "cheap".

Because of the generous eaves of Japanese buildings, interiors tend to be dark and often enough may be gloomy. The use of translucent paper *shoji* screens to diffuse soft light helps, but the soft, natural colours of the room materials generally absorb rather than reflect light. The colours, lighting and textures of traditional Japanese rooms influenced the qualities of all objects to be used in them, including clothing.

New principles

The artistic unity or harmony of a building extends to its properties as well. Master carpenters, who were both the architects and the builders of traditional buildings, developed aesthetic proportions that applied to all elements of a single structure, as well as to individual buildings in a complex. There are special and sophisticated carpenter's measures that apply this system of aesthetic proportion to construction.

The earth's oldest wooden buildings exist not too far from the Ise shrines, whose immortality is defined by their being ritually rebuilt exactly as the original every 20 years. Thus, the shrine is both ancient and new at the same time.

Teahouses show an awesome skill in building. Their lack of surface ornament, as seen in the rustic simplicity of unpainted wood, is itself a purely ornamental statement. Both the teahouses and the ornate shrines, temples and palaces shout out that they were built by skilled artists, the former emphasising taste but as a tool to contemplation and quiet, while the latter's primary message is loud, flaunting of skill, effort, money and power.

Historically, Japanese architecture shows a dialectic between imported, continental styles (mainly from China, but with some also from the Korean peninsula) and native Japanese styles. The borrowed styles from China and the Korean peninsula were constantly modified, adapted, and made into something clearly Japanese in taste. ❑

LEFT: a *ryokan* interior.
RIGHT: three-tiered pagoda in Kyoto.

THE ART OF LANDSCAPING

Compact, organised, and introspective: words stereotypically used to describe the Japanese might just as well be applied to their gardens

In Japan, gardening as a conscious art form can be traced to its introduction from China and Korea in the 6th and 7th centuries. The balance between nature and man-made beauty, with water and mountain as prototypical images, are the principles that form the basis for the traditional Japanese garden. Artfully blended with ponds, banks of irises and moss-covered rocks, carefully contrived Japanese gardens are objects of quiet contemplation. "In order to comprehend the beauty of a Japanese garden," the 19th-century writer Lafcadio Hearn wrote, "it is necessary to understand – or at least learn to understand – the beauty of stones." This is especially true of the *karesansui* (dry-landscape) garden. Zen Buddhism's quest for "inner truth", its rejection of superficiality and attachment embodied in the over-ornate styles of the day, gave birth to medieval temple gardens of a minimal beauty.

The stroll garden, however, was used to entertain and impress and creates an illusion of a long journey. As visitors strolled along carefully planned paths, around every twist and turn a new vista would appear. Famous scenes were recreated without the visitor having to undertake the arduous journey to the original sights. Among the views represented were miniaturised scenes from Kyoto, such as the hillsides of Arashiyama. The idea of confined space, combined with the Zen idea of discovering limitless dimensions in the infinitely small, saw the creation of the *kansho-niwa*, or "contemplation garden": gardens created as both tools for meditation and works of art. Carefully framed to resemble a scroll, they are intended to be appreciated like a painting that changes with the seasons.

◁ **LOTUS FLOWER**
The lotus flower, much seen in stroll and pond gardens, is a symbol of esoteric Buddhism and considered a divine and sacred plant. In the lotus pond of the Pure Land sect, the broad, pulpy leaves serve as seats for Amitabha Buddha.

△ **DAILY RIPPLE**
The Ryoan-ji rock garden in Kyoto is a fine example of *karesansui*. As part of the Zen daily ritual, white gravel is freshly raked in a circular pattern to represent the ripples of a flowing river. The emphasis is on the beauty of empty space.

△ **SMALL IS BEAUTIFUL**
Suizenji koen, in Kumamoto, is an example of *tsukiyama*, creating miniature reproductions of natural scenery. The spacious landscape garden represents the important, busy road (the Tokaido) from Edo (Tokyo) to Kyoto. The 53 post stations of the Tokaido are immortalised here, including a diminutive Mt Fuji.

▽ **BRIDGING THE GAP**
Traditionally arched wooden bridges, painted in vermilion, are a feature of Japanese gardens, and in earlier garden designs, often led to a central island. Function aside, crossing a bridge represents a journey between two worlds, the earthly one and the heavenly one.

△ **STROLL GARDEN**
The classic stroll garden at Rinno-ji temple is in the style of the Edo period. The carp pond is a distinctive feature. Water represents continuity and carp symbolise strength and perseverence.

△ **TIMELESS LIGHTS**
Introduced into tea gardens in the 16th century to add antiquity to the surroundings, as well as to guide nocturnal visitors, stone lanterns are a typical addition to a Japanese garden. The *hoju* (jewel) on top of the lantern is a symbol of enlightenment.

THE RIVERBANK PEOPLE

Although routinely ascribed to the prominent designers of the day, or to professional rock-setting priests, many Kyoto gardens were likely to have been built by *sensui kawaramono*, the much despised riverbank underclass. The "*mono*" of the designation stands for "thing", clearly stigmatising this pariah class as non-humans. A combination of Buddhist and Shinto taboos against the killing of animals and other sordid forms of work – slaughtering and skinning of animals, execution of criminals, burial of the dead – placed these people well beyond the sphere of a rigidly hierarchical class system with the nobility and clergy at the apex, descending to farmers, artisans and merchants. The trade of stripping and tanning hides required large quantities of water, forcing the *kawaramono* to build their abodes along the banks of the waterways. The *kawaramono* services became indispensable as they acquired greater skills in planting trees and in the placing of rocks. They were able to surpass their masters in the art of gardening. Ironically, it may be that some of Kyoto's "purest" gardens were created by the hands of men regarded as impure to the point of being inhuman.

SPORT

The most popular sports are sumo, baseball and soccer – one indigenous to the archipelago, the other two introduced from abroad. All are fanatically followed

Although baseball has long been the athletic obsession of Japan, occupying much more of the time and energy of the country's young athletes, sumo (pronounced s'mo) remains the "official" national sport. This is fitting, partly because of its history, which dates back as far as the third century, and also for its hoary, quasi-religious ritualism – but mostly because, in Japan, it's a more exciting sport.

While baseball and sumo are the two perennial spectator sports in Japan, professional soccer, introduced in the 1990s under the "J-League" banner, has proven its staying power in competing for the title of Japan's favourite sport.

Participant sports are few within Tokyo. It's just too expensive. Golf, the world knows, is fantastically popular in Japan, but only the rich can afford to play a proper round; the rest stand in cubicles at driving ranges and hit balls towards distant nets. Skiing is a fashionable sport and Japan has the mountains. But like most activities in which the Japanese engage, there are crowds and blaring loudspeakers everywhere, even on the slopes, making skiing here less than satisfying.

Baseball

A true national sport in terms of popularity and year-round interest, not to mention commercial importance, is the game of baseball. It was introduced in the early 1870s by university professors from the United States. Its popularity quickly spread and soon became the country's number one school sport. *Yakyu,* as baseball is technically called in Japanese (although *basuboru* is more common), rivals sumo as the national sport. The first professional baseball team was established in 1934. The two-league professional baseball system is a money-making industry, drawing more than 15 million spectators to stadiums.

Millions more watch on national television and train commuters devour the pages of Japan's daily national sports newspapers, from April to October, for details of the previous night's baseball league action. To put it mildly, Japan is a baseball-crazy country – even more so than the United States.

There are two major leagues in Japanese professional baseball, with teams owned by companies rather than being associated with cities, although a city's name sometimes figures in a team's official name. For top teams, the advertising and promotional value for the parent company (department stores, media giants and food processing companies) is considerable. The winners of each league pennant meet in Japan's version of the World Series, the best-of-seven Japan Series beginning the third week of October.

The Japanese rule allowing *gaijin* players in its professional leagues is one of the most interesting aspects of the system. Each Japanese team can list three foreign players on its 60-man roster, which includes the "major league" team and one farm team. There are critics who believe the teams should be allowed to employ as many foreigners as they wish and that the limitation rule should be abolished. Others have said *gaijin* players are not good for Japanese baseball and should be banned.

Most, however, feel the situation is fine as it is, since the colourful American players, with their quirks and occasional outbursts, make the Japanese game that much more interesting; the limit does, nonetheless, allow baseball in Japan to keep its identity as Japanese. Since the two-league system was begun in 1950, more than 300 foreign players have appeared in the Japanese leagues: some great , some mediocre, some who simply could not adjust to living in Japan or playing Japanese baseball.

The rules of Japanese baseball are generally the same as for the US. There are, however, several peculiarities such as the reversal of the ball-strike count in Japan making a full count 2-3, rather than 3-2. Teams have their own supporters' sections, with trumpets, drums and tambourines, headed by cheerleaders paid by the team. The resulting din shatters the eardrums.

Sumo

Some people say sumo is the national sport, some say it's the national spirit. Sumo wrestlers, or *rikishi,* would probably say it's a long, hard grind to fleeting glory.

Sumo is a fascinating phenomenon because it involves so many different things: physical strength, centuries-old ritual, a complicated code of behaviour, religious overtones, a daunting hierarchy system and feudalistic training regimes.

The *rikishi* wrestle on a raised square of mud and sand, the *dohyo*. A circle within the square, the *tawara*, is made of rice-straw bales. The wrestler's goal is to force his opponent to touch the surface of the *dohyo* with some part of his body (other than the feet), or to set foot out of the ring. This happens very fast. The average sumo bout lasts no longer than six seconds.

Appearances to the contrary, *rikishi* are not slabs of flab. They are immensely strong, rigorously trained athletes, with solid muscle often loosely covered in fat. The biggest *rikishi* in history (a Hawaiian named Salevaa Atisanoe, retired and now a Japanese citizen, and whose sumo name was Konishiki) reached 253 kg (557 lbs) before slimming down a bit for his wedding. Most grand champions, however, have ranged in weight from 110 to 150 kg (220–330 lbs).

There are no weight divisions. During a tournament, the smallest will fight the largest. Some bouts will have a *rikishi* wrestling another who weighs literally twice as much. Few holds are barred, but sumo tradition frowns on below-the-waist attacks. The waist itself is wrapped in sumo's only garment, a belt called the *mawashi*. The most dignified (and probably dullest) winning technique – called *yorikiri* – requires a two-handed grip on the *mawashi*, which allows the winner to lift and push his opponent out.

LEFT: foreign players are on nearly every team.
RIGHT: Bulgarian sumo champ, Kotooshu, riding high.

FOREIGN INVASIONS

It's no small irony that Japan's national sport, one replete with native Shinto-inspired rituals, should currently be dominated by foreigners. There has long been a sprinkling of Hawaiian and Fijian players, but recent years have seen the rise of Mongolian wrestlers into the very top ranks of sumo. The reigning champion, in fact, is a Mongolian. Some sports writers have made links between Mongolian wrestling and sumo. But what of Russian players, and even a European or two, a Bulgarian in one instance, making it to the semi-finals? Could it be that, like everything else Japanese, sumo is about to be embraced by the West not merely as a spectator sport, but a participant one?

Six two-week tournaments are held each year, three in Tokyo's Kokugikan, in the Ryogoku area in the eastern part of the city. The Tokyo tournaments are held in January, May and September.

Soccer

Like mountain climbing, soccer came to Japan via the enthusiasm of an Englishman, one Lieutenant Commander Douglas, a navy man who organised the first game here in 1873.

The turning point in Japanese soccer came much later though, with the establishment of the J-League in 1993, a costly undertaking that provided its national team with the players, just a few years later, to compete in Japan's triumphant co-hosting of the 2002 World Cup with Korea, in which Japan qualified for the first time in its soccer history for the quarter-finals. State-of-the-art stadiums, like those in Yokohama and Saitama, were built in readiness for the event and, if the game continues to draw the crowds as it currently seems to do, more such superb grounds are likely to be built in the coming years.

Oddly, Tokyo was excluded from the J-League when it was first founded, an omission that has since been rectified with the creation of the first-rate FC Tokyo and Tokyo Verdy 1969 clubs. These teams play at the Ajinomoto Stadium in Chofu City, just to the west of Tokyo, while the National Stadium is located right in the middle of the capital, in Shinjuku's Kasumigaoka district.

Starting off with ten teams, the J-League has grown to 28. A crop of cups, contests and tournaments, including the Yamazaki Nabisco Cup, the JOMO Cup and December's Emperor's Cup, have helped sustain the popularity of the game. Matches are played between March and October, with a summer break.

Standards are rising in the game, with several Japanese players now among the ranks of the major European squads. The ruling that Japanese teams can employ up to five foreign players has helped to both kindle interest in the game and to raise the quality of play.

Not to be sidelined, Japanese soccer fans have created their own counter-entertainment to the matches, with colourful pennants, painted faces, team-inspired costumes, and a barrage of drums and other musical instruments that provides a continuous soundtrack to the games and the well synchronised, good-natured frenzy of its supporters. Thankfully, hooliganism is still a foreign concept. ❑

ABOVE: Japanese soccer fans cheering their team.

The Martial Arts

A general term for various types of fighting arts that originated in the Orient, most martial arts practised today came from China, Japan and Korea. They all share common techniques, but there is no one superior style.

Two major martial arts evolved in Japan, the *bujutsu,* or ancient martial arts, and the *budo,* or new martial ways. Both are based on spiritual concepts embodied in Zen Buddhism. *Bujutsu* emphasises combat and willingness to face death as a matter of honour. It contains the philosophy and techniques of the samurai warriors and includes such arts as jujutsu and karate-jutsu. *Budo,* which started during the late 1800s, focuses on moral and aesthetic development. Karate-do, judo and aikido are all forms of *budo.*

Most of the martial arts end in the suffix *-do,* usually translated as "way" or "path". Thus, kendo is the way of the sword. *Do* is also the root of *budo* and of dojo – the place where one studies and practices a martial art.

The original form of **judo**, called jujutsu, was developed in the Edo Period (1603–1868). It was made up of different systems of fighting and defence, primarily without weapons, against either an armed or barehanded opponent on the battlefield. The basic principle of the judo technique is to utilise the strength of the opponent to one's own advantage. It is because of this that a person of weaker physique can win over a stronger opponent. The best known judo hall in Japan is the Kodokan in Tokyo, where one can observe judoists practising in early evenings.

Karate, meaning "empty hand" in Japanese, is a form of unarmed combat in which a person kicks or strikes with the hands, elbows, knees, or feet. In Japan, karate developed around the 1600s on the island of Okinawa. A Japanese clan had conquered the island and passed a strict law banning the ownership of weapons. As a result, the Okinawans – racially and culturally different from the Japanese – developed many of the unarmed techniques of modern karate.

Aikido is a system of pure self defence derived from the traditional weaponless fighting techniques of jujutsu and its use of immobilising holds and twisting throws, whereby an attacker's own momentum and strength are made to work against him. Since aikido is primarily a self-defence system and does not require great physical strength, it has attracted many women and elderly practitioners. By meeting, rather than blocking, a blow, one can redirect the flow of the opponent's *ki* (often translated as "mind" or "positive energy force"), dissipate it, and, through joint manipulation, turn it against the opponent until he or she is thrown or pinned down.

Kendo ("the way of the sword") is Japanese fencing based on the techniques of the samurai two-handed sword. Kendo is a relatively recent term that implies spiritual discipline as well as fencing technique. It is taught to most upper-level school children. (At the end of World War II, the US occupation authorities banned kendo on the basis of its use before the war to cultivate militarism. But in 1957, the practice of kendo was returned to Japanese schools.)

RIGHT: practising martial arts from an early age, a student of *kendo.*

Another martial art form that developed in Japan is **ninjutsu**, ("the art of stealing in", or espionage). People who practise ninjutsu are called *ninja.* Mountain mystics developed ninjutsu in the late 1200s. At that time, *ninja* were masters at all forms of armed and unarmed combat, assassination, and in the skilful use of disguises, bombs and poisons.

Although the rulers of Japan banned ninjutsu in the 1600s, the *ninja* practised it secretly and preserved its techniques. Today, ninjutsu is taught as a martial art with a non-violent philosophy. ❑

RIKISHI: LIFE ON THE BOTTOM AND ON TOP

Not only is the rikishi*'s training one of harsh days and a long apprenticeship, but competition at the top is without weight classes or handicaps.*

In sumo, life is best at the top. Only when a *rikishi*, or wrestler, makes it to the top ranks of *ozeki* or *yokozuna* (grand champion, the highest rank and rarely achieved) does life become easy. Those in the lower ranks become the *ozeki*'s or *yokozuna*'s servants and valets, doing nearly everything from running errands to scrubbing backs.

In most *beya* – the so-called stables in which wrestlers live a communal lifestyle with other *rikishi* – the day typically begins at 6am with practice, not breakfast. Harsh and tedious exercises work to develop the wrestlers' flexibility and strength, followed by repetitive practice matches amongst the *beya*'s wrestlers (the only time they wrestle one another, as wrestlers of the same *beya* don't compete during actual tournaments). Practice ends around noon, when the wrestlers bathe. Then the high-ranked wrestlers sit down to the day's first meal, served by the lower-ranked wrestlers. The food staple of the stable is *chankonabe*, a high-calorie, nutritious stew of chicken, fish, *miso*, or beef, to mention just a few of the possibilities. Side dishes of fried chicken, steak, and bowls of rice – and even salads – fill out the meal.

Financially, *rikishi* can be divided into two groups: those who earn a salary and those who don't. Lower-ranked wrestlers receive no salary, although they earn a small tournament bonus (and food and lodging are provided). When a wrestler reaches the *juryo* level, he becomes a *sekitori*, or ranked wrestler, and so worthy of a salary of at least US$7,000 a month. An *ozeki* receives at least $16,000 monthly, and a *yokozuna*, $20,000. The winner of one of six annual tournaments receives $100,000.

△ **THE GYOJI**
The referee of a sumo match is the *gyoji*, who shouts encouragement during matches.

▽ **MAWASHI**
The *mawashi*, or belt, is a single fabric 10 metres (30 ft) long and often used to toss out one's opponent.

AN ANCIENT SHINTO SPORT

Sumo has been around for at least 2,000 years. Japanese mythology relates an episode in which the destiny of the Japanese islands was once determined by the outcome of a sumo match between two gods. The victorious god started the Yamato imperial line.

While wrestling has always existed in nearly every culture, the origins of sumo as we know it were founded on Shinto rituals. Shrines were the venue for matches dedicated to the gods of good harvests. In the Nara and Heian periods, sumo was a spectator sport for the imperial court, while during the militaristic Kamakura Period, sumo was part of a warrior's training. Professional sumo arose during the 1700s and is quite similar to the sumo practised in today's matches.

Shinto rituals punctuate sumo. The stomping before a match *(shiko)* drives evil spirits from the ring (not to mention loosening the muscles) before a match. Salt is tossed into the ring for purification, as Shinto beliefs say that salt drives out evil spirits. Nearly 40 kg (90 lbs) of salt is thrown out in one tournament day.

◁ **HOPEFULS**
Sumo clubs nurture young hopefuls who might one day attain the adulation of a ranked wrestler.

▽ **IN THE RING**
The ring, made of a clay surface, is the *dohyo*, considered sacred ground and off-limits to women.

△ **TRAINING**
The wrestler undergoes years of rigorous training in the *beya*, or stable. All ranks train together.

▷ **TOP-RANKED GYOJI**
Gyoji follow a strict system of ranking. Higher-ranked *gyoji* wear elaborate kimono and *seta* (sandals) with *tabi* (Japanese-style socks).

淺草觀音
金龍山淺草寺御用
手焼せんべい箱入は
亀、無地、胡麻、のり
の四種類詰合せです
手焼せんべい
箱入
1.500エン
手焼せんべい
箱入
1.000エン
手焼せんべい厚亀 5枚
手焼せんべいのり 8枚 500円

胡麻 8枚 500円
手焼せんべい 無地 8枚 500円
手焼せんべい 亀 8枚

FOOD AND DRINK

The Japanese islands are home to what is probably the world's most eclectic, diverse, detailed, healthy and aesthetically appealing cuisine

Japan is a country of regional cuisines and, too, of seasonal cuisines. In fact, sampling local dishes is a fundamental purpose of travelling for many Japanese, whether it be a local *ekiben* box-lunch bought at the train station or an exquisite dinner at a remote *ryokan*. It would be foolish for this book to attempt a survey of the multitudinous regional and local cuisines. Even the Japanese don't try to know them all. But to sample them all, that would be a worthy life's goal.

In the cities, there are almost too many places from which to choose. Two types of places that particularly deserve attention for their pure Japanese atmosphere are the *izaka-ya*, or pub, often with a string of red lanterns above its door, and the *taishu-sakaba*, a much larger tavern-like establishment that may also sport red lanterns. These red lanterns *(akachochin)* signify a traditional Japanese place for eating and drinking. Specialities include fried fish, shellfish, broiled dishes, tofu (bean curd) dishes, *yakitori* (skewered and broiled meat), fried rice balls and simple sashimi.

Kaiseki ryori

At least one meal in Tokyo should be *kaiseki ryori*, a centuries-old form of Japanese cuisine served at restaurants or in *ryokan* in several elegant courses. Ingredients depend upon the season and region, and Japanese will travel great distances to sample a regional speciality. One might spend a lifetime sampling every regional variation. (Be warned that authentic *kaiseki ryori* is very expensive.)

Fastidiously prepared, *kaiseki ryori* is so aesthetically pleasing that it's virtually an art form in Japan.

Ideally, the food's visual appeal would be heightened by a proper setting for the meal, whether in the snow-blanketed mountains or on the sea shore. Some of the better restaurants serving *kaiseki ryori* have succeeded in creating exactly such an atmosphere regardless of outside environment, with brush works, flower arrangements, and views of waterfalls cascading over well-hewn rocks into placid pools. The effect elevates the senses and pleasure of *kaiseki ryori*.

The ingredients must be as fresh as the dawn. That's a prime requisite of good food in general, of course, together with a good recipe and a good cook. Rejoice in the fact that Japan has plenty of all three.

The taste of *kaiseki ryori* relies on the inherent taste of the food itself, not on spices or similar additions. Japanese cuisine focuses on flavour and its subtleties, and on the food's aesthetic presentation. Rather than create distinctive flavours for their dishes, Japanese chefs seek above all to retain the natural flavours. And rather than alter the appearance of their ingredients, they strive to enhance their visual appeal through artful arrangements.

PRECEDING PAGES: rice crackers for sale at Senso-ji.
LEFT: grilled octopus is a delicacy.
RIGHT: warm welcome at a neighbourhood *sushi-ya*.

Noodles

Japanese noodles are of three main types: *soba*, *udon* and *somen*. Made of buckwheat, *soba* noodles are thin and brownish, with a hearty consistency. *Udon* noodles, made of wheat, are usually off-white and thick, to very thick. *Somen* noodles, also made of wheat, are as thin as vermicelli. *Udon* is usually eaten in hot dishes, while *soba* and *somen* may be eaten hot or cold, depending upon season.

Another type of noodle called *hiyamugi* (iced noodles) is eaten only cold. *Hiyamugi* is made of the same ingredients as *udon* but much thinner.

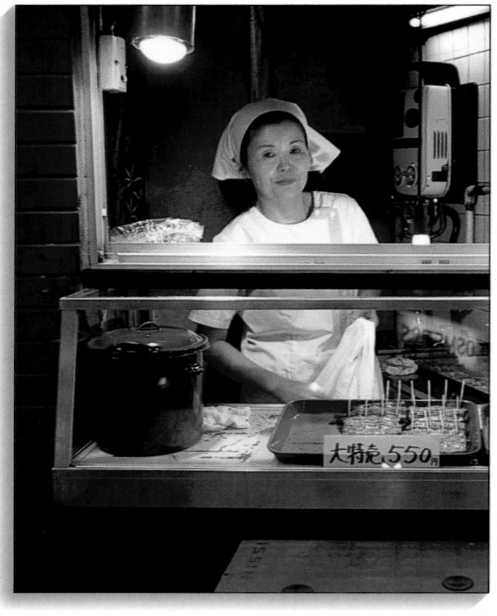

THE EELS OF SUMMER

Travellers will encounter many unusual dishes in Japan. Some fit in a category that Japanese commonly refer to as stamina *ryori*, or dishes intended to raise energy levels and "staying" power. Japan and especially Tokyo can be pretty enervating, so "stamina restaurants" (and drinks) are a common phenomenon. A popular summer dish is *unagi*, or broiled eel served on rice. It's said to help one withstand the hot and humid days of the Japanese summer – *doyo no iri*. Usually served with a sweetish *tare* sauce, *unagi* is rich in vitamins E and A, and it exceeds pork and beef in protein content yet contains fewer calories.

The most common type is *soba*, particularly delicious if not overburdened with non-buckwheat flour extender. *Soba* is usually served with wasabi (green horseradish), thinly sliced spring onions (scallions), a dip made of *mirin* (sweet sake), and *katsuobushi* (shaved flakes of dried bonito fish). *Soba* noodles in this form, when served chilled on a *zaru*, a type of bamboo tray, are called *zarusoba* and make a delicious summer meal. A rich source of vitamins B1 and C, *soba* is extremely nutritious, the more so the higher the buckwheat content in proportion to *sobako* (wheat flour).

Somen is another hot-weather favourite. Noted for its delicate flavour and adaptability to many garnishes it can be served *gomoku* ("five-flavour") style with strips of omelette, chicken and vegetables; *gomadare* style, with aubergine (eggplant), fish and *shiso* (beefsteak plant or Japanese basil); with fruit and hard-boiled swallow's eggs; or *hiyashi* style: cold, with nothing but soy sauce containing sesame oil. As a light, refreshing treat on a hot summer day, *somen* is hard to beat.

One of Japan's great cold-weather favourites is *udon* served in a hot, soy-based broth with an egg, spring onions and other vegetables. Unlike *soba* and *somen*, *udon* is not placed in a dip before being eaten. A real body-warmer, this noodle is prized for its excellent texture.

Not strictly a traditional dish, but one that is uniquely Japanese and that can be quite delicious, is *kare-udon*. As its name implies, it is *udon* served in the thick, somewhat spicy gravy that passes for curry in Japan. (Another popular curry dish is *kare-risu*, or curry rice. Look for it at large railway stations.)

Unlike pasta that's turned around on a fork, Japanese noodles are sucked into the mouth with chopsticks and slurped down. Noisily. In Japan that's how you do it, unabashedly and with total commitment. Experts say the noodles taste better that way. Although essentially Chinese, so-called *ramen* noodles are eaten so obsessively in Japan that to omit mentioning them would be remiss. *Ramen* is served very hot in soy-flavoured broth with savoury ingredients, most typically strips of bamboo and slices of spring onion and roast pork. Instant *ramen* is a mainstay of the home.

If short on time, try a *tachiguisoba-ya*, "stand-and-eat *soba*". Train stations always have them and a stand will sometimes be found on the platform. Prices are very reasonable, usually ranging from ¥200 or so for *kake-soba* (basic *soba* in broth) to somewhat higher for *tendama* (*soba* with raw egg and mixed ingredients fried together, tempura-style). Priced in between are tempura *soba*, *kitsune* (with fried *tofu*), *tanuki* (with tempura drippings), *tsukimi* (with raw egg), *wakame* (with kelp) and countless others.

At the *tachiguisoba-ya*'s low prices, you can't expect top-quality food, but on a cold, winter's day (or night) a bowl of hot *soba* is wonderfully warming. It's also an efficient use of commuting time.

Sushi and sashimi

Taste and visual pleasure converge in sushi and sashimi, both prepared with uncooked seafood. Japanese simply adore sushi and sashimi, and knowing the Western bias against raw fish or meat will often ask visitors – simply out of sheer curiosity – if they can eat one or the other.

A good sushi shop, or *sushi-ya*, can be both expensive and confounding if one doesn't know what to ask for. Try, instead, a *kaiten sushi-ya*, where small dishes of sushi pass by on a conveyor belt along the counter. It lacks a certain elegance, but in a *kaiten sushi-ya* the uninitiated can study the sushi offerings at leisure and sample it for less cost. Then later, armed with new-found expertise, visit a proper *sushi-ya*.

Good sushi requires that the ingredients should be of good quality and exceedingly fresh, that the rice be properly vinegared and steamed, and that the topping should be as fresh as possible. (Thawed-out frozen fish just doesn't cut it.) Those who prefer raw fish and seafood without rice should order sashimi, served in a tray or on a plate with attention to the appearance. Often small bowls of sauce will be offered for dipping the sashimi.

LEFT: vendor of *unagi* (eel), popular in summer.
ABOVE: counter fare can be fast and economical.

EAT AND DRINK AS THE LOCALS

At a traditional Japanese pub, the *izaka-ya*, try the likes of *saba* (mackerel) or *nijimasu* (rainbow trout). Eat them *shioyaki*-style (salt broiled), with a good, cold Japanese beer or a very dry sake.

Izaka-ya, essentially drinking places, serve a wide variety of Japanese snack foods but not complete meals, whereas *koryori-ya*, being essentially eateries, serve light Japanese meals. Both types of establishments serve beer and sake, often *shochu* (a vodka-like spirit), and sometimes whisky. Both *izaka-ya* and *koryori-ya* often feature regional foods, invariably served with rice. Eating at one is a very Japanese experience.

Nabemono

If hot-pot dishes are your favourite, Japan is the place to be in autumn and winter. Every part of Japan, without exception, has its own distinctive *nabe-ryori* (pot dishes).

Nabemono are typically winter dishes and include *ishikari-nabe* (Hokkaido Prefecture), containing salmon, onions, Chinese cabbage, tofu, *konnyaku* (a jelly made of root starch) and *shungiku* (spring chrysanthemum); *hoto* (Yamanashi), with handmade *udon*, *daikon* (white radish), *ninjin* (carrot), *gobo* (burdock), squash, onions, Chinese cabbage and chicken; and *chiri-nabe* (Yamaguchi), containing *fugu*

(blowfish) meat, Chinese cabbage, mushrooms, tofu, and starch noodles.

Popular for a quick meal and usually available in mini-marts is Tokyo-style *oden-nabe*, a potpourri containing potatoes, tofu, *konnyaku*, boiled eggs, octopus, carrots, *daikon*, kelp and many more ingredients. *Oden* are often presented as pick-and-choose right next to the cash register in convenience stores like 7-Eleven. It is a hearty dish and one of the better winter body-warmers.

Bento

Like most modern countries, Japan is increasingly a land of fast food. The traditional Japanese box lunch, *bento*, or more respectfully, *obento,* has become a form of fast food in itself, with both convenience stores and *bento-ya* offering wide selections to take out. A *bento* box, flat and shallow, is used with small dividers to separate rice, pickles and whatever else might be inside. *Bento* is eaten at work, school, picnics and parties.

Just about anything can be used in *bento*, including Western imports such as spaghetti, sausage and hamburger. Schoolchildren take *bento* to school for lunch.

A special type of *bento* that has become an art in itself, not to mention a pursuit for the connoisseur, is the *ekiben* (from *eki* for train station and *bento*). Japan is a nation of obsessed train travellers. Of all transport forms, the train is incontestably the most popular. Thus, some of Japan's most popular forms of food are those sold inside the stations.

Trains often make stops of just long enough duration to permit passengers to get off briefly and buy some of their favourite *meisanbutsu* (local specialities), especially the ubiquitous *ekiben*, to be eaten aboard the train. In 1885 the first *ekiben* appeared at Utsunumiyo station and rice balls with apricots inside *(umeboshi)* were sold to travellers.

Tsukemono

A Japanese meal always comes with *tsukemono*, or distinctive Japanese-style pickles. Pickles probably owe their origins to the practice of preserving foods in anticipation of famines. During the Edo Period, pickles came into their own and the *tsukemono-ya* (pickle shop) emerged as a new type of business. Ingredients used in Japanese pickles vary somewhat with the seasons. Common ingredients are Chinese cabbage, bamboo, turnips, *kyuri* (Japanese cucumber), hackberry, *daikon*, ginger root, *nasu* (Japanese aubergine), *udo* (a type of asparagus), *gobo* and many others.

Tsukemono add colour to a meal and offer a wide range of appealing textures, from crunch to squish, that might be missing from the main dishes. Pickles can serve to clear the palate for new tastes – such as in sushi, in which a bite of pickled ginger root rids the mouth of the aftertaste of an oily fish such as *aji* (mackerel) and prepares it for the delicate taste of *ebi* (prawn). ❑

LEFT: tasty treats at a grilled fish stand.

Spirits in Bottles

Although Sapporo Beer is probably Japan's largest liquid export these days, the quintessential Japanese drink remains sake.

A staple as much of Shinto ceremonies as of the rituals of the modern Japanese table, the quality of sake depends largely on the rice and water used in its fermentation. There are over 500 local sake breweries throughout Japan and those in Nigata prefecture are reckoned to be the best.

Sake is graded as *tokkyu* (special), *ikkyu* (first grade), and *nikyu* (second grade). Connoisseurs generally ignore these categories, established largely for tax purposes, in favour of the high- grade *junmaishu* (sake unmixed with added alcohol or sugar), and the very superior *ginjo-zukuri*, the purest sake on the market, a complex brew bulging with the kind of fragrance and fruity undertones associated with top French clarets. Serious drinkers tend to favour dry sake *(karakuchi)*, over the sweet variety *(amakuchi)*.

Besides the classic clear sake, there is a variety, *nigori-zake*, in which the rice solids have been left to sit in a thick sediment at the bottom of the bottle, resulting in a milky colour when shaken. A relative newcomer on the drinks scene, effervescent sake makes a lively end to a drinking session, or a light coda to a meal.

Unlike wine, sake does not age well and is best drunk within six months of bottling. Premium sake is at its best cold. Cheaper brands are often drunk hot during the winter.

A stronger tipple is *shochu*, a distilled spirit made from grain or potato. *Shochu* is often drunk with a soft drink or fruit juice, but recently straight, high-quality shochu has become *de rigueur* among young people. It can also be drunk *oyu-wari* (with a little hot water), which is a great way to warm up in cold weather.

ABOVE: casks of sake.

The drink hails from Kyushu, where the feisty people of Kagoshima have been drinking the potato variety since the 14th century. With the rise in popularity of the drink, Kyushu farmers have been under pressure recently from distillers who can't get their hands on enough potatoes. According to the papers, the resulting "potato wars" have witnessed some nasty scenes.

Okinawa has its own firewater, a spirit known as *awamori*. Much of this is still made from Thai rather than Japanese rice, a reminder that these islands once enjoyed a thriving trade with South East Asia. Devotees of *awamori* claim, the drink is hangover-free. At up to 60 percent proof, it's a theory you'll have to test with care. ❑

千社札広告札等の
みくじ 五十円

お札 お守
安産守

茨城県
すずらん
関茶店
アポロ写真館

PLACES

A comprehensive look at Japan's important destinations, with numbered cross-references to detailed maps

Spread like cultured pearls in the western Pacific, the islands of the Japanese archipelago lie off the coast of China, Russia and Korea. There are nearly 4,000 of these islands, strung out for over 2,800 km (1,700 miles) – from the remote mountains of the north, which look out across small stretches of water to Russian islands, to the southwest in Okinawa and nearly within sight of Taiwan. Covering 380,000 sq. km (147,000 sq. miles), Japan's land area is the size of Montana and a little larger than Italy, but twice as populous with more than 120 million residents – half the population of the United States.

The main islands of Hokkaido, Honshu, Shikoku and Kyushu are mountainous, cut through with narrow valleys. Fuji-san, the snow-capped 3,776-metre-high (12,388-ft) landmark, remains dormant and within sight of downtown Tokyo on a clear winter day. Overall, there are some 60 volcanoes in the archipelago considered to be active.

The Japanese transport system is known throughout the world, both for its efficiency and punctuality and for its rush-hour congestion within the train. The trains will take travellers nearly anywhere on the four main islands, even to the smallest villages, and with a punctuality which could be used to set chronometers.

The nation's capital, Tokyo, is on the main island of Honshu, which has the country's 10 largest cities, including the sprawling megalopolis of Tokyo-Kawasaki-Yokohama. The largest city outside of Honshu, Fukuoka, is far to the south on Kyushu.

It is expensive to travel within Japan. Trains aren't cheap and accommodation is costly. Indeed, it is cheaper for Japanese to take holidays in Hawaii or Sydney instead of within their own country. Yet they do travel within Japan, and they have made an art of travel that is often a bit too hierarchical and dogmatic for Westerners. Nevertheless, regardless of where one ends up, there are exquisite and delightful pleasures for the traveller, whether the *ekiben* box lunches at train stations or the precision with which a traditional *ryokan* pampers guests.

Naming conventions

Wherever possible, we use Japanese terms for geographical identifications. These appear as suffixes to the proper name. For example, Mount Fuji is referred to as Fuji-san. Mountains may also appear with other suffixes, including *-zan*, *-yama,* and for some active volcanoes, *-dake*. Islands are either *-shima* or *-jima*, lakes are *-ko*, and rivers are *-gawa.* Shrines are Shinto, and proper shrine names usually end in *-jinja*, *-jingu*, or *-gu.* Temples are Buddhist, with names usually ending in *-tera*, *-dera*, or *-ji*. ❑

PRECEDING PAGES: sunset along the Honshu coast near Hagi; Tokyo's Asakusa Kannon in late autumn; Tokyo's stock exchange.
LEFT: Daibutsu, the Great Buddha in Kamakura, south of Tokyo.

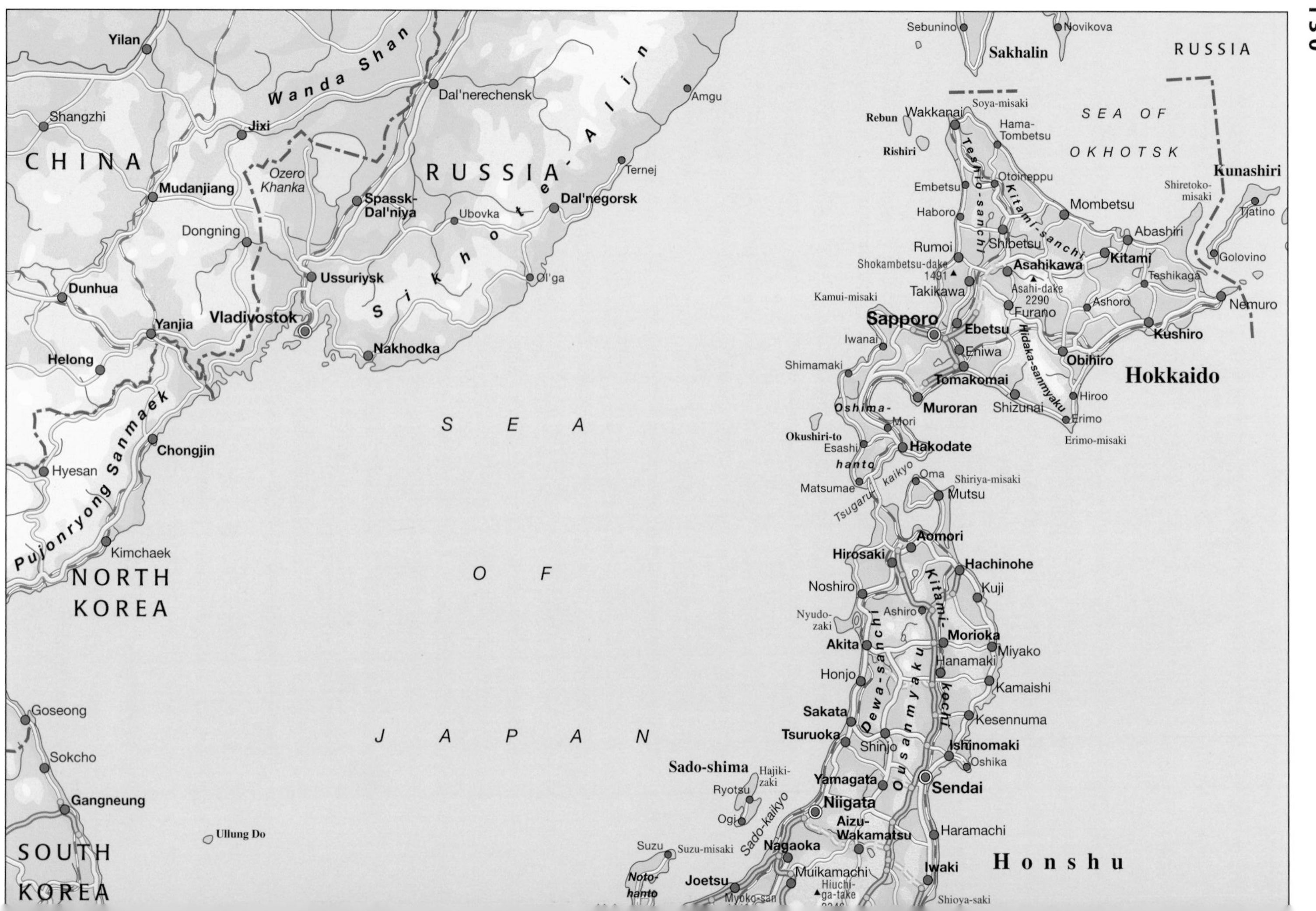
RUSSIA
SEA OF OKHOTSK
Sakhalin
Sebunino
Novikova
Kunashiri
Hokkaido
Rebun
Rishiri
Wakkanai
Soya-misaki
Sapporo
Asahikawa
Kitami
Abashiri
Mombetsu
Kushiro
Obihiro
Nemuro
Hakodate
Muroran
Tomakomai
Ebetsu
Otaru
Aomori
Hachinohe
Hirosaki
Noshiro
Akita
Morioka
Miyako
Kamaishi
Ishinomaki
Sendai
Yamagata
Niigata
Nagaoka
Joetsu
Iwaki
Sado-shima
Honshu
SEA OF JAPAN
RUSSIA
Sikhote Alin
Dal'nerechensk
Dal'negorsk
Spassk-Dal'niya
Ussuriysk
Vladivostok
Nakhodka
CHINA
Wanda Shan
Yilan
Shangzhi
Jixi
Mudanjiang
Dongning
Dunhua
Yanjia
Helong
NORTH KOREA
Chongjin
Hyesan
Kimchaek
Pujonryong Sanmaek
SOUTH KOREA
Goseong
Sokcho
Gangneung
Ullung Do

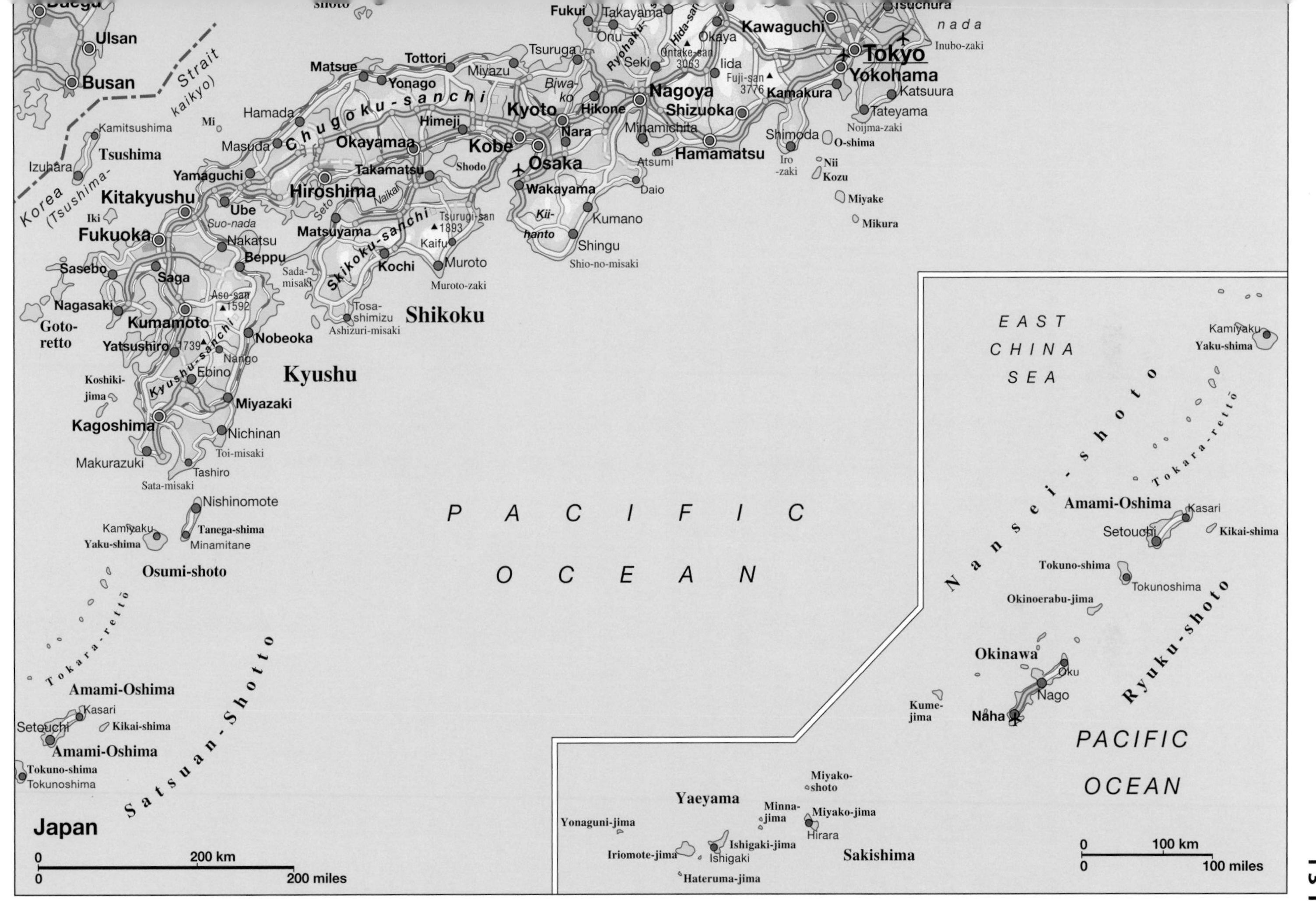
Japan
PACIFIC OCEAN
EAST CHINA SEA
Ulsan
Busan
Korea (Tsushima-kaikyo) Strait
Kamitsushima
Tsushima
Izuhara
Iki
Mi
Matsue
Tottori
Yonago
Miyazu
Tsuruga
Fukui
Takayama
Onu
Ryohaku-sanchi
Hida-sanmyaku
Okaya
Ontake-san 3063
Iida
Seki
Kawaguchi
Tokyo
Yokohama
Inubo-zaki
Fuji-san 3776
Kamakura
Katsuura
Tateyama
Noijma-zaki
Nagoya
Shizuoka
Biwa-ko
Kyoto
Hikone
Nara
Kobe
Osaka
Hamada
Masuda
Chugoku-sanchi
Himeji
Okayama
Minamichita
Shimoda
O-shima
Hamamatsu
Atsumi
Iro-zaki
Nii
Kozu
Miyake
Mikura
Shodo
Takamatsu
Yamaguchi
Kitakyushu
Ube
Hiroshima
Seto
Naikai
Suo-nada
Wakayama
Daio
Kii-hanto
Kumano
Shingu
Shio-no-misaki
Tsurugi-san 1893
Matsuyama
Shikoku-sanchi
Kaifu
Fukuoka
Nakatsu
Beppu
Kochi
Muroto
Muroto-zaki
Sasebo
Saga
Sada-misaki
Aso-san 1592
Tosa-shimizu
Ashizuri-misaki
Shikoku
Nagasaki
Kumamoto
Goto-retto
Yatsushiro
1739
Nobeoka
Nango
Kyushu-sanchi
Ebino
Kyushu
Koshiki-jima
Miyazaki
Kagoshima
Nichinan
Toi-misaki
Makurazuki
Tashiro
Sata-misaki
Nishinomote
Kamiyaku
Tanega-shima
Yaku-shima
Minamitane
Osumi-shoto
Tokara-rettō
Amami-Oshima
Kasari
Setouchi
Kikai-shima
Tokuno-shima
Tokunoshima
Satsuan-Shotto
Nansei-shoto
Okinoerabu-jima
Okinawa
Oku
Nago
Naha
Kume-jima
Ryuku-shoto
Miyako-shoto
Yaeyama
Minna-jima
Miyako-jima
Yonaguni-jima
Ishigaki-jima
Hirara
Iriomote-jima
Ishigaki
Sakishima
Hateruma-jima
0 200 km
0 200 miles
0 100 km
0 100 miles

鼓童
鼓童
鼓童
鼓童

CENTRAL HONSHU

The central part of Honshu contains not only a region known as Chubu, but also the Kanto region – and Tokyo

Descriptions of the Kanto region can be misleading. It is Japan's largest alluvial plain, but it is certainly not an area of wide-open spaces. None of the flat land extends far enough to offer a level, unbroken horizon. Most of Japan's longest rivers – the Tone, Naka, Ara, Tama and Sagami – all pass through the Kanto and empty into the Pacific, but few would call these concrete-lined conduits, managed and contained into near-obscurity, rivers at all.

Kanto is home to Tokyo, perhaps the world's most populated urban area. The Kanto plain wraps itself around Tokyo and its equally congested southern neighbours of Yokohama, Kamakura and Izu. To the southwest are Mt Fuji (or Fuji-san) and Hakone, and to the north is Nikko. There are six large prefectures in Kanto, not including Tokyo itself, which is a self-administrating entity. The area has a total population of well over 30 million people, most of them within the greater metropolitan area of Tokyo.

The average population density of the Kanto region is approximately 15,600 persons per square kilometre, three times that of Los Angeles but not so bad in comparison with Hong Kong, Mumbai, Jakarta or Mexico City. Yet many people think that Tokyo has grown too big, and recently talk has returned to the relocation of the national government's operations elsewhere, perhaps in Sendai, to the north in the Tohoku region.

Virtually nothing of interest about the region is recorded until Minamoto Yoritomo, the first Kamakura shogun, endowed Tokyo's Asakusa-jinja with 90 acres (36 hectares) of arable land around 1180. Later, in 1456, a village called Edo (Estuary Gate) was recorded when the first Edo castle was built by a small-time daimyo on the site of today's Imperial Palace. In 1600, a shipwrecked Englishman became the first foreign guest at Edo, tutoring Ieyasu Tokugawa. Three years later, Ieyasu started the 250-year Tokugawa dynasty.

Like all great cities, although perhaps even more so, Edo suffered its share of natural disasters, amongst them earthquakes and the last eruption of Fuji-san, in 1707, which covered Edo with 10 cm (4 inches) of volcanic ash.

In the area known as Chubu, beyond the Kanto, Japan is both highly industrial, as in Nagoya to the southwest, and rural, such as is found in the delightful Noto Peninsula and elsewhere along the Sea of Japan coast. There is also the historical city of Kanazawa, the mountainous resort city of Nagano, and the remoteness and drumming thunder of the island of Sado. ❑

Left: a Kodo drummer from Sado Island performs on a large *taiko*.

Tokyo Bayside
Tokyo
Shinjuku-ku
Kabukicho
Nishi-Shinjuku
Shinjuku
Shinjuku Gyoen (Imperial Gardens)
Shinanomachi
Chiyoda-ku
Yoyogi
Meiji-Jingu Gaien (Outer Gardens)
Shibuya-ku
Koen
Akasuka
Minami-Aoyama
Minato-ku
Aoyama Cemetery
Roppongi
Shibuya
Nishi-Azabu
Odaiba
Higashi Yashio
Higashi Shingawa
Aomi
Daiba
Tokyo Big Sight-Tokyo Kokusai Tenjijo
Fuji TV Building
Metropolitan Government Office
Shinjuku-eki (Station)
Harajuku-eki (Station)
Shibuya-eki (Station)
Meiji-jingu
NHK Broadcast Centre
Omotesando Hills
Mori Tower
Roppongi Hills
0 500 m
0 500 yds
0 1000 m
0 1000 yds

UENO KOEN
Tokyo Kokuritsu Hakubutsukan (Nat.Mus.)
Tosho-gu
National Science Museum
Zoo
Metropolitan Festival Hall
Shinobazu-no-ike
Kokuritsu Seiyo Bijutsukan (Mus. of Western Art)
Tokyo Daigaku (University)
Akamon (Red Gate)
Benten-do
Keisei Ueno
Ueno-eki (Station)
Shitamachi Fuzoku Shiryokan
Genku-ji
Banryo-ji
Asakusa Kannon (Senso-ji)
Taiko-kan (Drum Museum)
Tokyo Higashi Hongan.ji
Kaminarimon
ASAKUSA
Shitaya-jinja
Korakuen (Amusement Garden)
KOISHIKAWA-KORAKUEN
Tokyo Domu (Tokyo Dome)
Yushima Tenjin
Okachimachi
UENO
OKACHIMACHI
Kanda Myojin
Torigoe-jinja
Yushima Seido
AKIHABARA
Ochanomizu
Meiji Daigaku Kokogaku Hakubutsukan (Archaeological Museum of Meiji University)
Meiji University
Nikolai-do (Cathedral)
Transportation Museum
Akihabara
SUMIDA-KU
Reconstruction Memorial Hall
Ryogoku Public Hall
Kokugikan (Sumo Arena)
Edo Tokyo Museum
Ryogoku
RYOGOKU
Nippon Bodukan
KITANOMARU KOEN
Science Museum
KANDA
Kanda
Kokuritsu Kindai Bijutsukan (Mus. of Modern Art)
Chidorigafuchi Military Cemetery
KOKYO HIGASHI GYOEN
Otemon
Communications Museum
Bank of Japan
OTEMACHI
Palace Hotel
Currency Museum
NIHOMBASHI
Kokyo (Imperial Palace)
Marunouchi Building
Tokyo-eki (Station)
Tekko Building
Nihom-bashi
Royal Park Hotel
Nakamura Gakuen
Fukagawa Edo Museum
Niju-bashi
NIJU-BASHI
KOKYO GAIEN
MARUNOUCHI
YAESU
Yamatane Museum
TCAT (Tokyo City Air Terminal)
KIYOSUMI TEIEN
Tokyo International Forum
Metropolitan Police Departement H. Q.
KOTO-KU
HIBIYA KOEN
Yurakucho-eki (Station)
Hotel Seiyo Ginza
Ginza Church
CHUO-KU
Hojo-in
Min. of Finance
Imperial Hotel
Sony Building
GINZA
Ginza 4-chome
Min. of Int. Trade & Ind.
MINATO
Tomioka Hachimangu
ETCHJIMA KOEN
Kabuki-za
TSUKUDA
BOTAN
Atago-jinja
Shimbashi
Shimbashi Enbujo
Nishi Hongan-ji
Sumiyoshi-jinja
Seishoji
Shiodome City Centre
SHIMBASHI
TSUKIJI
Tsukiji Fish Market
TSUKISHIMA
HAMA RIKYU TIEU
Shiba-Daijingu
SHIBA RIKYU TEIEU
Odaiba, Bayside
Sumida-gawa
Harumi-bashi
Toyosu

東郷記念館
DANCE
ギター・ベース
当ビル3F
PARIS KID'S
フォンタナ
PARIS KID'S
20% OFF
¥700
竹下通り
番広
地下

TOKYO

Vying with Mexico City as the world's largest city, the Tokyo metropolitan area and its 30 million people exist in the former capital of the shoguns – and in an earthquake zone

Map on pages 134–5

Japan has always been a country of villages. If Tokyo is Japan's biggest village – and it is by far at over 620 sq. km (240 sq. miles) and 12 million people in central Tokyo alone – then one can easily reduce Tokyo itself into a gathering of smaller villages anchored around major railway stations. Indeed, these stations are helpful for understanding Tokyo's layout, which doesn't have a central urban core.

Most of Tokyo's smaller "villages" lie on a circular rail line called Yamanote-sen, or Yamanote Line. There are 29 stations on the Yamanote and it takes about an hour to make the complete loop, actually an oval in shape. Look at the layout of the Yamanote-sen, and of the placement of the stations along the way, and orientation in Tokyo becomes so much easier. The important stations on the line are Tokyo, Ueno, Shinjuku and Shibuya. In the centre of the oval defined by the Yamanote-sen, a bit off-centre to the east, are the grounds of what once was the Edo castle. The Imperial Palace has replaced the castle, but the old symmetry of the castle defences – moats and gates – are still evident today. In all cases, most of Tokyo is accessible by one station or another, by one train or subway line, or many. Use them. They're fast, cheap and utilitarian. Just stay off the trains during rush-hour for obvious reasons. Or walk. Only then do the many of Tokyo's villages feel connected, giving a sense of the big village, of Tokyo itself.

LEFT: Harajuku's Takeshita-dori. **BELOW:** back alley in Shinjuku.

Imperial Palace

In the centre of Tokyo is the **Imperial Palace**, or **Kokyo** ❶, a functional palace where the emperor and his family reside. Much of the grounds – including the palace itself – are closed to the public and secluded behind massive stone walls, old trees and Edo-Period moats. Exceptions are the Emperor's birthday, 23 December (9.30am–4pm), and 2 January (9.30am–3pm).

Most of the 110-hectare (270-acre) palace complex is forested or given over to private gardens and small ponds. The Showa emperor (Hirohito), who reigned from 1926 until 1989, was a skilled biologist and much of the inner garden area is a nature preserve.

Kokyo Gaien ❷, the palace's outer garden to the southeast, is an expansive area of green and impeccably sculpted pine trees planted in 1889. A large, gravel-covered area leads to the famous postcard scene of **Niju-bashi** ❸, a distinctive bridge across an inner moat and one of the most widely recognised landmarks in Japan. Tourists come here by the bus-load for a group portrait in front of the bridge *(bashi)* and moat. Niju-bashi is both elegant and a functional entrance – the main gate – into the palace grounds. On the two days in the year when the palace is open to the public, visitors are allowed to cross Niju-bashi and stand near the imperial residence to receive greetings from the emperor. Behind is **Fushimi-yagura**, a lookout turret of the original Edo castle. Parts of the outer grounds were unpleasant places in 1945 immediately after the Showa emperor (Hirohito) announced Japan's surrender on the radio. Numerous loyal soldiers, refusing to admit defeat or surrender to the Allies, disembowelled themselves outside the palace.

Tokyo was the world's largest city with over 1 million people in the 17th century. Following World War II, the population was around 3 million. By 1970 it had reached 9 million.

Visitors are also permitted in the **Kokyo Higashi Gyoen** ❹ (Tues–Thur, Sat–Sun 9am–4pm, Mar–Oct until 4.30pm), the East Imperial Garden of the palace, which can be entered through Ote-mon, Hirakawa-mon and Kitahanebashi-mon, three of the eight gates *(mon)* into the palace grounds. Inside are remains of the defences of Edo-jo, the shogunate's castle *(jo)*, and the foundations of the castle's *donjon*, the primary lookout tower of the shogun's residence.

The castle itself, Edo-jo, was constructed of granite and basaltic rocks quarried at Izu Peninsula, a hundred kilometres south. Several thousand boats made the two-week roundtrip carrying immense stones. Off-loaded near Kanda to the north, the stones were dragged on sleds – often with seaweed laid underneath for lubrication – by oxen and men provided by the shogun's warlords, always eager to impress the shogun. Half a century later, around 1640, the Edo castle was completed. But less than two decades later, it was reduced to ashes in a fire.

Of the original 21 defensive guard towers, or *yagura*, three still stand, including Fushimi-yagura near Niju-bashi. Unfortunately, today nothing substantial remains of the old Edo castle itself, except for the three turrets and the *donjon* foundations, not to mention the moats and gates. Nor are there surviving visual representations of the castle.

The Meiji emperor chose the shogunal castle site to be the new imperial res-

BELOW: Niju-bashi and Fushimi-yagura.

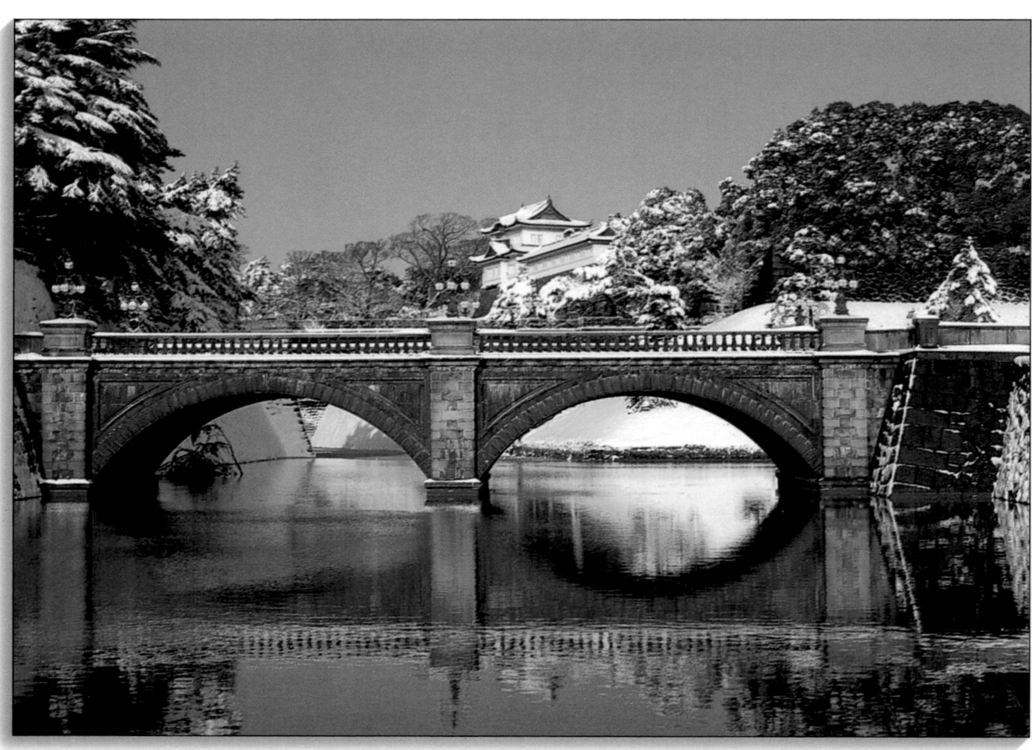

idence and moved there in 1869 from Kyoto, the city that had been the imperial capital for more than a millennium. The new Imperial Palace was completed in 1889 of exquisitely designed wood, and the city was renamed Tokyo, or Eastern Capital. The palace has remained the residence of Japan's emperors since. (In 1945, the 1889 Meiji palace was destroyed in Allied bombing raids.)

At the northern part of the old castle grounds in **Kitanomaru-koen** is the **Kokuritsu Kindai Bijutsukan** ❺ (National Museum of Modern Art; Tues–Sun 10am–5pm, Fri until 8pm; admission fee). The modern building displays examples of Japan's contemporary artists, many of whom studied in Europe in the 20th century, in well-presented galleries. In the northern corner of Kitanomaru-koen is the octagonal martial-arts hall known as the **Nippon Budokan**. Built to host Olympic judo events in 1964, its gold topknot a gesture to the hairstyles of sumo wrestlers, the building is also used as a rock-concert venue.

Yasukuni shrine

West from Kitanomaru-koen, Yasukuni-dori leads to **Yasukuni-jinja** ❻. What is said to be Japan's largest *torii* – eight storeys high, made of high-tension steel plates and weighing 100 tons – boldly announces the shrine. Its entrance nipping the northern tip of the Imperial Palace grounds, this Shinto shrine is Japan's most controversial. Proponents say it honours those who died for Japan and the emperor; opponents say it glorifies Japanese aggression and honours convicted war criminals. Pinched between the two extremes are politicians, who must decide whether or not to attend annual ceremonies at the shrine. When a prime minister does visit, governments throughout Asia respond in vocal disapproval.

The souls of more than 2½ million Japanese soldiers killed between 1868

Map on pages 134–5

The 16-petal chrysanthemum, adopted as a symbol of the Imperial household by the Emperor Gotoba in the 13th century, still appears as a design motif for clothing, sword blades, banners and official documents connected with Japanese royalty: those who sit on or near the "Chrysanthemum Throne".

BELOW: robot dog for sale.

JAPAN'S LOLITA COMPLEX

You see both groups on the rush-hour trains: tired blue-suited middle-aged men reading newspapers with baseball scores on one page and adverts for sex clubs on the other, and chattering groups of high-school girls wearing sailor uniforms, white socks and carrying an assortment of electronic toys. It's not unusual for the men to cast an eye at the girls, who are in increasing numbers catering to the men's fantasy. In Japanese it's called *enjo kosai*, or paid dating, loosely translating as the oldest profession.

Many Japanese men seem obsessed with high-school girls. Animated TV programmes, adult comic books, weekly tabloid magazines and sports newspapers – all display ads for cute girls in school uniforms and photos of "AV girls", or porn actresses. Television advertising directed towards men often features schoolgirls.

A couple of years ago, the Tokyo government issued a report that said one-fourth of high-school girls in Tokyo had called a telephone-dating club at least once. In every major city, public telephone booths are covered with stickers advertising teenage dates. Today, however, it is tougher for *enjo kosai*. Police have cracked down on telephone dating clubs, which had started recruiting junior high-school girls.

(the shrine was founded in 1869) and World War II are enshrined at Yasukuni (lit. peaceful country). In the shrine's archives, the names, dates and places of death for each soldier are recorded. The **Yushukan** (War Memorial Museum; daily 9am–5pm; admission fee; www.yasukuni.or.jp), part of Yasukuni-jinja, includes samurai armour and a rocket-propelled kamikaze winged bomb.

Yasukuni-jinja's torii *is made of steel.*

Tokyo Station

Directly east from the Imperial Palace and Kokyo Gaien is the **Marunouchi** district, once an inlet of Tokyo Bay, its waters extending almost up to where the Palace Hotel now sits. Atop this land-fill of Marunouchi – meaning "inside the wall" of the Edo castle fortifications – an exclusive residential area for Tokugawa samurai lords was created in the early 17th century. Known as Daimyo Koji, or the Little Lanes of the Great Lords, Marunouchi served not only as a buffer between the shogun's castle and the outside world of commoners but also permitted the shogun to keep an eye on his provincial warlords, whom he required to live in Edo on a rotating basis. Today it is filled with corporate headquarters and government offices.

A wide boulevard slices through these corporate buildings from the grounds of the Imperial Palace to **Tokyo-eki** ❼ (Tokyo Station). While not Japan's busiest station – Shinjuku is the possessor of that honour – Tokyo Station is nonetheless sizeable with 19 platforms side by side, including the terminus for the *shinkansen* or bullet train. Deep beneath the station are additional platforms for more trains and JR lines. The Marunouchi side of the station is fronted by the original station, built in 1914 of red brick in a European style. Air raids in 1945 damaged the station, taking off the top floors; renovations, finished in

Below: soldiers killed in the name of the emperor are enshrined at Yasukuni-jinja.

1947, left it somewhat lower. Inside the concourse is the **Tokyo Station Gallery** (Tues–Fri 10am–7pm, Sat–Sun until 6pm; admission fee).

The redbrick facade of the station is surrounded by a grove of recently constructed skyscrapers. The reconstructed and extended **Marunouchi Building**, one of Tokyo's new mini-city complexes, immediately catches the eye. Its gourmet food basement and four shopping levels attract large numbers of Japanese tourists from the countryside. The views of the palace grounds from the 35th and 36th floors are worth the extra cost of a window table.

Ginza and Nihombashi

Extending from the **Yaesu** central exit is Yaesu-dori, which intersects the major arteries of Chuo-dori and Showa-dori, running south to Ginza and north to Ueno. On the corner of Yaesu and Chuo-dori, the **Bridgestone Museum of Art** (Tues–Sat 10am–8pm, Sun until 6pm; admission fee) houses an important collection of European paintings. Highlighting the Impressionists and later artists like Picasso and Van Gogh, it also includes the work of Meiji-era Japanese painters.

Immediately south of Tokyo Station is the **Tokyo International Forum ❽**, an echoing complex of concert and exhibition halls. Adjacent, in the Kotsu Kaikan Building, is the **Tourist Information Centre** (daily 9am–5pm, telephone-only service on 1 Jan; tel: 03 3201 3331). If you are expecting to travel in Japan, visit this centre for extensive information, whether walking tours through Tokyo or lodging in Okinawa. The staff speak English. South again are elevated train tracks extending from **Yurakucho-eki ❾** (Yurakucho Station), constructed in 1910; the *shinkansen* and Yamanote-sen trains snake along the overhead tracks.

In 1921, prime minister Hara Takashi was assassinated at Tokyo Station, and in 1930, also at Tokyo Station, an assassination attempt was made on prime minister Hamaguchi. He was wounded and died a year later.

BELOW: Tokyo station.

When considering a place to eat or drink in Ginza, take care in choosing. Prices can be astronomical. On the other hand, beneath the elevated train tracks of nearby Yurakucho are many cheap stands and shops offering *yakitori* and cold beer.

An elevated expressway over Harumi-dori defines the boundary between Ginza and Yurakucho. Towering on the opposite side of the expressway are the tall, curving exteriors of the Seibu and Hankyu department stores, anchored at the ground by a musical clock and a hard-to-miss (or ignore) police box.

Of all places in Japan, **Ginza** has perhaps the greatest name recognition in the world after Tokyo and Kyoto. During the super-heated bubble economy of the late 1980s, land in Ginza was valuable, and became the most expensive real estate in the world.

Ginza derives its name from *gin*, or silver. Japan once used three different coinage systems, each based upon silver, gold and copper. Tokugawa Ieyasu decided to simplify the system to only silver. In 1612, he relocated the official mint from the countryside to Ginza. Two centuries later, the mint was once again shifted, to Nihombashi, but the name of Ginza stayed.

Shopping diversions

The Mitsukoshi store anchors **Ginza 4-chome ❿**, where Chuo-dori intersects Harumi-dori, the second main avenue *(dori)*. (Most Tokyo districts are subdivided into *chome*; Ginza has eight.) Chuo-dori, sometimes called Ginza-dori, is one of two main arteries through Ginza and extends northwards to the east of Tokyo Station and into Nihombashi. A few blocks past the flyover separating Ginza from Nihombashi and Yaesu is a monument to the original site of Ginza. Further on, numerous fashionable boutiques, galleries and immense department stores – including Matsuya (Ginza's largest) and Mitsukoshi (founded in 1673, with the current Ginza store dating from 1930) – line the wide avenue. Ginza's potential for shopping abounds.

BELOW: the main Ginza crossing at twilight.

A popular meeting place is the **Sony Building** ⓫ (daily 11am–7pm). Its several floors are filled with the latest technical innovations and gadgetry.

Along Hibiya-dori is the towering **Imperial Hotel** ⓬ (Teikoku Hoteru). The first Imperial Hotel opened in 1890. Its modest structure was later replaced by a wonderful Frank Lloyd Wright design; the day after it opened to the public in 1923, the Great Kanto Earthquake hit Tokyo. The hotel was one of the few buildings to escape destruction. The Wright building was replaced by the modern structure in 1970. Across from the Imperial Hotel, **Hibiya-koen** ⓭ (Hibiya Park) was Japan's first European-style plaza, opened in 1903. It quickly became a popular venue for rallies and demonstrations against rises in rice prices during the early 1900s.

Kabuki-za.

Along Harumi-dori

Harumi-dori extends from Hibiya-koen back down through Ginza 4-chome and Tsukiji and across the Sumida-gawa, Tokyo's barely accessible river (*gawa* or *kawa*). Down Harumi-dori, just past Showa-dori is the **Kabuki-za** ⓮ (Kabuki Theatre), founded in 1889. The present cream-coloured building with its traditional roof and grand entrance dates from 1949. Highly stylised *kabuki* melodramas are performed here twice daily.

Closer towards the Sumida-gawa is **Tsukiji** ⓯ and its wholesale fish market *(chuo oroshiuri ichiba)*, where merchants arrive long before dawn to select the best of the day's fresh catch. Other produce is also auctioned here and there is a storage refrigerator large enough to chill ten days' food supply for the entire city. *Tsukiji* means, simply, "built land". As with Marunouchi, another landfill area near the Imperial Palace, the newly created land provided space for samurai estates, although of lower ranking than Marunouchi. In the mid-1800s, a part of

BELOW: the landmark Wako Department store.

Tsukiji was set aside for foreigners and a hotel was constructed which later burned to the ground.

Returning north to the Yaesu side of Tokyo Station, Chuo-dori crosses Nihombashi-gawa over **Nihom-bashi** ⓰ (Nihon Bridge). The ugly elevated Shuto Expressway directly above was erected for the 1964 Tokyo Olympics. Both the concrete-lined river and expressway diminish the significance of the original 1603 arched wooden bridge that was the centre of Edo-Period Tokyo and the zero point for the five main roads leading out of Edo to the rest of Japan. The present stone bridge dates from 1911. Just one block southwest of the bridge is the altogether more pleasant **Tako no Hakubutsukan** (Kite Museum; Mon–Sat 11am–5pm; admission fee). Over 2,000 kites cover the walls and ceiling, many displaying Japanese motifs: manga characters, images from famous woodblock prints, armour-bearing warriors and depictions of Mount Fuji.

Woodblock print of Nihom-bashi during the Edo Period.

On the eastern periphery of Nihombashi, towards the Sumida-gawa, the **Tokyo City Air Terminal** ⓱ (TCAT) is a downtown check-in facility for flights departing the international airport at Narita. Not only can airline and baggage check-in be done here, but clearance of immigration, too. A nonstop limousine bus service *(see Travel Tips, page 355)* goes to Narita.

Kanda

If there is a book, however old and in whatever language, that seems unattainable, it can be found in **Kanda** ⓲, especially around Jimbocho Station. There are stores specialising in art books, second-hand books, comic books – in English, French, German, and Russian. The bookshops have been in Kanda since the 1880s, nearly as long as the nearby universities. Many of the early book printers

Below: fish market at Tsukiji.

established their shops in Kanda, followed later by several of the most famous publishers in Japan. A short walk north past Ochanomizu Station and across the Kanda River, are two important shrines. **Kanda Myojin**, a vividly coloured and decorated shrine dedicated to the rebel general Taira no Masakado, is a lively venue for Shinto-style weddings, rituals, cultural performances and one of the city's main festivals, the Kanda Matsuri. Continue up the slope to **Yushima Tenjin**, the city's foremost shrine of learning, a place much frequented by students supplicating the shrine's tutelary spirit for favourable exam results. The grounds of the shrine are a popular spot for plum-blossom viewing in mid-February.

Haneda Airport, located south of Tokyo, handles most of the capital's domestic flights.

Akihabara

The neighbourhood of **Akihabara** ⓳ epitomises the old Edo tradition of merchants or craftsmen of a particular commodity congregating together. Indeed, Akihabara is singularly devoted to the sales of all things electrical and electronic with hundreds of shops vying for attention in a compact area around Chuo-dori.

West of Akihabara but in walking contingency with the Kanda-Jimbocho book quarter, the district of Ochanomizu is transected by the Kanda River. A minute to the north of the waterway is **Yushima Seido**, an intriguing former academy and one of the few Confucian temples left in Japan. Ochanomizu's association with religion and learning, now obscured by a prevalence of ski shops and stores selling musical instruments, can be sensed two blocks south of the temple, with the appearance of **Nikolai-do** ⓴ (Nikolai Cathedral), a Russian Orthodox church, designed by British architect Josiah Conder in 1891. The building lost the top of its dome in the 1923 earthquake, but this has been replaced with a smaller one. Look out for the cathedral's beautiful stained-glass windows.

BELOW: shopping in Akihabara.

THE HEAT ISLAND

With the advance of global warming, Tokyo is developing some climatic features that give new meaning to the expression "concrete jungle".

Parakeets and hemp palm trees, normally associated with tropical zones like Hainan Island in southern China, are now commonplace in a city where the number of "tropical nights", defined by temperatures that fail to drop below 25°C (77°F), are increasing every year. Tokyo's tropical temperatures, averaging 2–3 degrees higher than surrounding areas, are no longer confined to the summer either, inching into late-spring and early-autumn days.

More roof-top greenery, the use of moisture-retaining building materials, experiments in creating grass car parks and water-retaining road materials are underway, but before any progress is made, expect more sultry tropical nights and days.

Meiji University has several academic buildings along Ochanomizu's main street, as well as the superb **Meiji Daigaku Kokogaku Hakubutsukan** (Archaeological Museum of Meiji University; Mon–Fri 10am–4.30pm, Sat till 12.30pm; admission free), housing a collection of objects found on digs around Japan sponsored by the university's archaeological faculty.

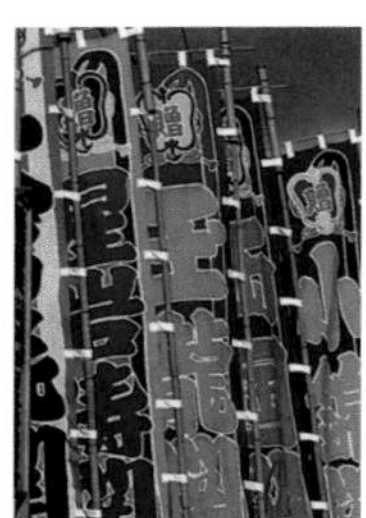

Banners outside the Kokugikan with the names of tournament sumo wrestlers.

Green and pleasant

Heading west along the river or taking the overground Sobu Line one station on, the Suidobashi district leads to a popular amusement area catering to all tastes. Most visible of these is the **Korakuen Amusement Park** and **La Qua**, sharing the same grounds. Among the highlights of the combined theme parks are a free-fall parachute ride and a highly original roller coaster that passes over the rooftops and between the buildings here, offering at the same time a bird's-eye view of the city. Next to Korakuen is the **Tokyo Domu** 21 (Tokyo Dome, also called the Big Egg), a venue used primarily for the Yomiuri Giants baseball matches, but also for major rock concerts, exhibitions and trade shows.

Easily approached by following directions in English and Japanese, the **Koishikawa Korakuen**, one of the city's finest Edo Period stroll gardens, stands in the shadow of the dome. The oldest garden in Tokyo, it was intended for amusement as much as aesthetic contemplation, incorporating scenes from the Chinese classics as well as miniaturised Japanese landscapes.

Another generous expanse of green in this congested part of the city, the **Koishikawa Shokubutsu-en** (Koishikawa Botanical Garden), lies to the north, easily accessed from Hakusan Station on the Mita Line and within the

BELOW: Koishikawa Botanical Gardens.

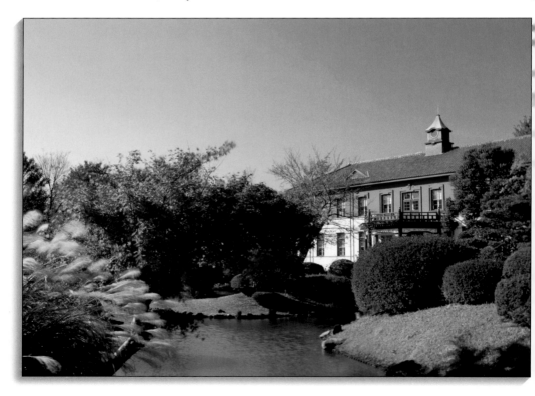

same Bunkyo Ward area. This research garden passed into the hands of the Tokyo University faculty in 1877 and over 100 species of herbs are grown here, amid trees and ponds.

Map on pages 134–5

Sumo world

East of Akihabara and on the other side of the Sumida-gawa, the area known as **Ryogoku** is the site of Tokyo's sumo arena, **Kokugikan** ㉒. A lot of very large men live in Ryogoku – it is the home of many of the sumo *beya*, or stables, as the training centres/dormitories for the *rikishi* (wrestlers) are called.

Behind the Kokugikan is the **Edo Tokyo Museum** ㉓ (Tues–Sun 9.30am–5.30pm, Sat until 6pm; admission fee), a spectacular hall that encompasses a massive reconstruction of a part of *shitamachi* Edo from the 19th century. It is like walking onto the set of a samurai drama; there is even a life-like dog relieving himself by the guard tower. Every 20 minutes, the lighting cycles through night and day. There are intricately constructed models of villages and a life-size reconstruction of Nihom-bashi, the Edo-Period bridge. It is one of the finest museums in Japan, well-planned and meticulously thought out. Two other notable sights are located within this area east of the Sumida River. Directly south along Kiyosumi Avenue, a few blocks in from the river, the intimate human scale of the exhibits and reconstructed buildings at the **Fukagawa Edo Museum** (daily 9.30am–5pm, closed second and fourth Mon each month; admission fee) is appealing after the massive Tokyo-Edo Museum. Opposite the museum, the **Kiyosumi Teien** is a distinctive and very spacious Edo Period garden replete with a central pond set with miniature islands.

BELOW: Edo Tokyo Museum.

TIP

In late autumn and winter, the paths around Shinobazu Pond provide an earthy setting in which to sample oden (fish cakes, fried tofu and vegetables in broth). Served from carts with seating around hot cauldrons, these warming snacks are best washed down with with beer or sake.

BELOW: Asakusa Kannon Temple (Senso-ji).

Around Ueno

North of Tokyo Station and Akihabara, exactly eight minutes on the Yamanote train, is **Ueno-eki** ㉔ (Ueno Station). It was once the commoner's part of town, in what was called Shitamachi. Nowadays there's an aspect of urban life around Ueno not typically noticeable in Japan – the homeless men who camp out in Ueno-koen.

West of the station, **Ueno-koen** (Ueno Park) is Tokyo's most distinctly park-like park: sprawling grounds with trees, flocks of scrounging pigeons, monuments and statues, homeless Japanese, a zoo, a big pond with lilies and waterfowl, and national museums. It's not quite as tidy and pristine as one might expect in Japan.

In the spring, Ueno-koen is cherished amongst Japanese for its blossoming cherry trees. The idea of blossom-viewing – *hanami*, a tradition extending back centuries – seems aesthetically appealing; in fact, it is often a drunken and crowded party with few serene moments.

The **Tosho-gu** ㉕, a shrine adjacent to a five-storeyed pagoda, was established in 1627 (the present buildings date from a 1651 renovation) by a warlord on his own estate to honour the first Tokugawa shogunate, Tokugawa Ieyasu. The path to Tosho-gu (lit. Illuminator of the East) is lined with dozens of large, symbolic stone or copper free-standing lanterns, all donated by warlords from throughout the land to cultivate a little merit with the shogun. Although not as embellished as it was in the Edo Period, the main shrine building is still a magnificent, ornate building. The outer hall features murals painted by the famous Edo artist Kano Tanyu. Also interesting is the Chinese-style Kara-mon, a gate decorated with dragons that are meant to be ascending to and descending from heaven. It's said that the dragons slither over to the park's pond, Shinobazu-no-ike, under the cover of night to drink the water.

Shinobazu-no-ike (Shinobazu Pond) was once an inlet and is now a pond *(ike)* dense with lotus plants. A small peninsula juts into the pond with a Buddhist temple to Benten – goddess of mercy – perched on the end. A promenade follows the pond's 2-km (1¼-mile) circumference. The **Shitamachi Fuzoku Shiryokan** ㉖ (Shitamachi Museum; Tues–Sun 9.30am–4.30pm; admission fee), near the pond at the park's south entrance, is a hands-on exhibit of Edo commoners' daily life in Shitamachi, as this part of Edo Tokyo was known.

The **Kokuritsu Seiyo Bijutsukan** ㉗ (National Museum of Western Art; Tues–Sun 9.30am–5pm; Fri until 8pm; admission fee) has a collection of nearly 1,000 pieces, ranging from the Renaissance to the contemporary and including Gauguin, Rubens and Jackson Pollock, not to mention several sculptures by Rodin and a sizeable collection of 19th-century French art. The **Tokyo Kokuritsu Hakubutsukan** ㉘ (Tokyo National Museum; (Tues–Sun 9.30am–5.30, Fri until 8pm, Nov Sat–Sun until 6pm); admission fee) offers a superbly displayed collection of Asian art and archaeology. The main hall holding the extensive Japanese collection dates from 1937. Arching over the outside entrance to the museum grounds is an immense samurai-estate gate.

A 10-minute walk north of the museum following the walls of Kan'ei-ji, a temple established to symbolically protect the inauspicious northern entry point into Edo, takes you to **Yanaka**, a charming old quarter of winding lanes, temples, traditional shops, bathhouses, small art galleries, old wooden houses, and a leafy, moss-covered cemetery full of time-eroded Buddhist statuary. West of Ueno is the most prestigious of Japanese universities, **Tokyo Daigaku** (Tokyo

Map on pages 134–5

Tokyo Daigaku, or Tokyo University.

BELOW: Tokyo National Museum.

University), founded by Imperial decree in the 1870s. The campus, more popularly known as Todai, was built on the estate of the powerful Maeda feudal lords after being transplanted from Kanda in the 1880s.

Schoolgirls posing at Senso-ji's south gate, Kaminari-mon.

Asakusa

From the mid-1800s until World War II, **Asakusa** was a cultural nucleus of theatre and literature, and of cuisine and the sensual delights. The area's cultural and social flowering began with exile – first with the banishment to Asakusa of the Yoshiwara, or the licensed prostitution district in the 1600s, and then later with that of theatre, especially *kabuki*, in the 1800s.

The people of Asakusa were known as Edokko, or people of Edo. Asakusa dripped with *iki*, a sense of style and urbane polish, and with *inase*, or gallantry. It was the place to be seen in Edo Tokyo, reaching its heyday in the 1800s.

Anchoring Asakusa was **Senso-ji**, or **Asakusa Kannon** ㉙, perhaps the oldest Buddhist temple in the region and a draw for people from around Japan who brought with them spending money to make Asakusa prosper.

Old places always start with a legend. Asakusa's legend has it that Senso-ji was founded in AD 628 when two fishermen netted a small statue of Kannon, the deity of mercy. A temple was built by the village leader to house it.

The south entrance to the temple, on Asakusa-dori, is a large gate called Kaminari-mon, or Thunder Gate. Here begins Nakamise-dori (lit. inside the shops), where two rows of red buildings funnel temple-goers northwards through a souvenir arcade before spilling out onto the temple grounds. The interactive **Taiko-kan** (Drum Museum; Wed–Sun 10am–5pm, last entry 4.30pm; admission fee), with dozens of different kinds of Japanese and other

Below: summer fireworks on the Sumida.

Bridges Worth Crossing

How grateful I feel/As I step crisply over/The frost on the bridge – Basho. When Shin Ohashi, or New Great Bridge, was completed in the capital of Edo in 1693, the great poet Matsuo Basho, was sufficiently elated to compose the above haiku. Like many Edo period writers and artists, Basho was a great admirer of the new bridges that were springing up across the capital.

Tokyo's Sumida River provides the setting for what is, perhaps, one of the most interesting concentrations of bridges in Japan. Each bridge has its own identity and if the woodblock prints and gazetteers of the time are to be believed, major bridges provided common, unlicensed space for all manner of activities, from full-moon viewing, freak shows and archery (read "prostitution") tents, to the shackling and public display of criminals.

The painted girders and bolts of the older bridges that have survived earthquakes, intense volumes of traffic and the hell-fire of war, are reassuringly durable presences amidst the accelerated confusion of today's city. Sakurabashi, the last bridge of note, is an example of how such structures can have a benevolent effect on the environment. In 1985, river-facing Sumida and Taito wards constructed the bridge exclusively for the use of pedestrians.

drums, sits at the intersection of Kaminaridori and Kokusaidori, above a shop selling Buddhist and Shinto paraphernalia.

A few blocks north of the museum, the Nimi Building, topped with a giant chef's head and hat, comes into view. This announces the entrance to **Kappabashi Dogugai** (Kappabashi Kitchenware Town), where restaurant and kitchen equipment are sold wholesale. Of main interest to foreign visitors are Kappabashi's plastic food samples of the type seen on display in restaurant windows, such us sushi platters, and plates of spaghetti with a fork suspended in the air.

In the other direction, east of Senso-ji, is the **Sumida-gawa** (Sumida River), which empties into Tokyo Bay. The exit for the Ginza Line, Tokyo's first subway line that opened in 1927, surfaces near the Azuma-bashi (Azuma Bridge). Just north of the bridge is **Sumida-koen**, a park intended to open up the river that passes through the old core of Tokyo. Although the Sumida was a well-used river during the Edo Period and into the early 1900s, as its commercial importance faded with industrialisation, it became inaccessible and hidden behind concrete. But as the Japanese began travelling during the 1970s and 1980s, they returned with memories of romantic urban rivers in Europe. Only since the mid-1980s have efforts started to bring the Sumida back into the lives of Tokyo's residents.

Roppongi and Minato

In the lower middle of the oval defined by the Yamanote-sen and just to the southwest of the Imperial Palace is an area favoured by Tokyo's expatriate community: **Minato-ku**, a Tokyo ward *(ku)* made up of Minamiaoyama, Akasaka, Roppongi, Nishiazabu and Hiroo. The area is peppered with embassies and high-priced expatriate (and company-subsidised) housing – US$10,000 a month

Roppongi Crossing is now one of the world's busiest junctions. However, during the Allied occupation, it was, as Robert Whiting says in his book Tokyo Underworld, *occupied by "a police box, a small bookstore, and two vacant lots. At night, the surrounding side streets were so deserted that residents spoke of seeing ghosts".*

BELOW: a night out.

Tower of Ark Hills, looking west towards Roppongi.

rent is not unusual – and liberally spiced with nightclubs and restaurants.

Up on a hill, **Roppongi** 30 is the heart of the area's social life, nightlife and courting life. It crawls with both foreigners and Japanese on the prowl for the opposite sex. Its main avenues are bright and loud, the back alleys lined with themed drinking establishments meant to nurture nostalgia or homesickness in strangers in a strange land. But don't confuse the activity here with the blatant sex trade of Shinjuku's Kabukicho. In Roppongi, it's only upscale food and drinks garnished with probing smiles.

Roppongi means "six trees". There may have been six trees here, perhaps pine, at one time. Another possibility for the name are the six samurai lords who had estates here during the Edo Period.

East of Roppongi along the road towards the Imperial Palace, the **Ark Hills** complex of offices, apartments and stores is the work of Mori Taikichiro. Riding the real-estate boom of the 1970s and 1980s, he advocated urban redevelopment and replaced some of the claustrophobic neighbourhoods of Tokyo with modern complexes. At his death in 1993, he owned more than 80 buildings in central Tokyo and was considered the world's richest private citizen.

Pressing west along Roppongi-dori from the main crossing, the gigantic **Roppongi Hills** is another Mori Corporation project, one of the most publicised in Japan. Towering and brash, the 16-hectare (40-acre) site, with its restaurants, nine-screen cinema, public amphitheatre, apartments, and over 200 shops and interconnecting walkways, is undeniably impressive. A first-rate modern gallery, the Mori Art Museum, was run by Englishman David Elliott from 2001–2006, Elliot's appointment signaled the declared aim of Roppongi Hills to be an international space. Superb views of the city can be had from the gallery's observation deck.

Check the horizon to the south, towards the area known as Shiba: the red-and-white **Tokyo Tower** 31 (daily 9am–10pm, last entry 9.30pm; admission fee) juts skyward, looking industrial and out of place. Finished in 1958, its primary purpose was to broadcast television signals. Subsequent lyrical allusions to the Eiffel Tower or urban elegance were fabrications of creative writing. It's an ugly projection into the skyline – 333 metres (1,093 ft) – but views from the observation deck at 250 metres (820 ft) are excellent.

BELOW: Tokyo Tower from across Tokyo Bay.

Tokyo Bayside

Tokyo-wan (Tokyo Bay) has shrunk over the centuries due to extensive landfill. The shoguns did it for the housing of their samurai, while politicians have done it in the past decades for glory and political favour. **Odaiba** island is extremely popular with young people who flock to shopping and amusement treats like **Decks Tokyo Beach**; **Joyopolis**, a virtual-reality emporium; **Palette Town**, a leisure centre that includes a giant wheel; **Venus Fort**, a bizarre indoor shopping street with over 160 shops under an artificial sky that changes from sunny, to grey, to violet and stormy depending on the time of day and whims of its programmers.

The island has become an experimental zone for architects. One of the most outstanding designs is the highly visible **Fuji TV Building** 32, a Kenzo Tange design, whose titanium-clad surfaces are connected by "sky corridors" and girders. The blue arch of the **Telecom Centre** is another chunk of post-modernism, but one that pales against the extraordinary **Tokyo Big Sight** ㉝. Consisting of four inverted pyramids standing on a narrow base that seems to defy gravity by supporting large atriums and an eighth-floor Observation Italian restaurant, this is a sight to behold.

A curious addition to the island's futuristic structures is the **Oedo Onsen Monogatari** ㉞ (daily 11am–9am, last entry 7am; admission fee), a traditional hot-spring bath designed along theme-park lines, just a short walk from the **Museum of the Future** (aka Museum of Emerging Science and Innovation; Wed–Mon 10am–5pm), with its robot-led tours of Japanese hi-tech designs.

A good view of the island and its futuristic constructions can be seen from a monorail that leaves Shimbashi Station for the artificial islands over the **Rainbow Bridge**. Odaiba can be reached on the driverless Yurikamome Line from Shimbashi Station.

While you are in the Shimbashi area, stroll over to the highly visible **Shiodome City Centre** ㉟, another of Tokyo's new mini-cities. Skyscraper office blocks loom, but a set of indoor malls and an outdoor pizza parlour at the rear of the complex make for a pleasant, up-market place to dine, shop or drop by for a cocktail in superlatively modern surroundings that have attracted the trendy, after-work office set.

Ebisu, Shibuya and Harajuku

One stop south of Shibuya on the Yamanote Line, the expanded and redesigned south side of Ebisu Station is now home to **Yebisu Garden Place**, an enormous shopping, restaurant, hotel, office and entertainment complex that has become

TIP

To see Japanese consumerism at its most diverse, visit Shibuya's Tokyu Hands store. Imagine something and you'll find it here – whether pots and pans, expensive leather goods, lapidary items, furniture, or traditional Japanese tools for woodworking.

BELOW: Shibuya's main junction.

one of Tokyo's most fashionable new districts. Located on the site of the old Yebisu Beer Brewery, the **Beer Museum** (Tues–Sun 10am–6pm, last entry 5pm; admission free) traces the history, brewing methods and merchandising of beer around the world. On the eastern side of the plaza is the important **Tokyo-to Shashin Bijutsukan** (Tokyo Metropolitan Photography Museum), the city's foremost exhibition space for photography and video art (Tues–Sun 10am–6pm, Thur–Fri till 8pm; admission fee).

Emperor Meiji was a strong supporter of adopting Western ideas and technology. He wore Western clothing and enjoyed Western food. He also composed nearly 100,000 poems in traditional style and ordered the annexation of Korea in 1910.

Although many resident foreigners might nominate Roppongi to the east, **Shibuya** is one of the trendiest commercial neighbourhoods in the whole of Tokyo. Roppongi caters to foreigners and has done so with style for decades. Shibuya, on the other hand, caters to Japanese youth with lots of money to spend and style to flaunt. Shibuya was a rural but bustling stop along one of the great highways built during the Tokugawa years and leading from Edo Tokyo. Later, mulberry (for an abortive attempt at silk production) and tea fields surrounded Shibuya's first railway station, which opened in 1885. Several private rail lines opened in the subsequent years, each with its own station. Finally, all the stations were consolidated at the current site of **Shibuya-eki** ㊱ (Shibuya Station) in 1920. The most popular exit of Shibuya Station, opening to the northwest, is named after a dog. Outside of that entrance you will find a statue erected in 1964 of the said dog, an Akita named Hachiko. This is a favourite spot to rendezvous.

Beyond Shibuya Station

Beyond the Hachiko entrance is an immense intersection. Looking straight ahead, note the tall, cylindrical Shibuya 109 building, a good reference for orientation. The crowded road to its right leads up a gentle hill to Tokyu department store, and adjacent to it, the **Bunkamura**, a performance hall built during the roaring 1980s. Something is always going on inside – art, music, theatre – and the interior spaces are pleasantly cool on a hot day.

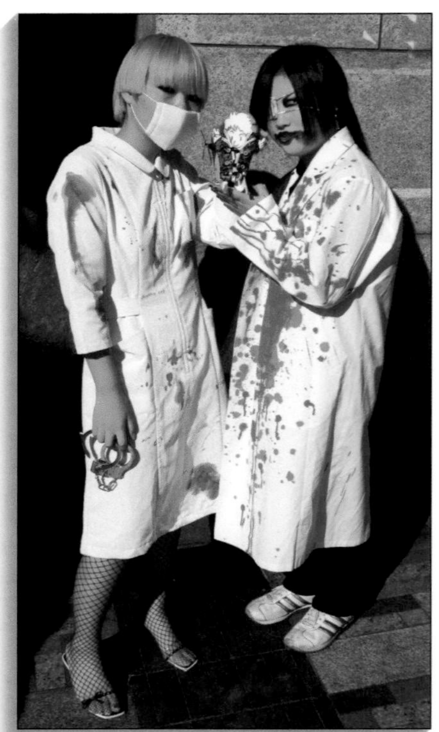

Below: living art in Yoyogi-koen.

At the top of the hill to the left is the huge **NHK Broadcast Centre** ㊲, a 23-storey building with two dozen TV and radio studios. NHK is the government-run, viewer-subsidised television and radio broadcaster. Open to the public inside the centre is the **NHK Studio Park**, a well-designed introduction to television broadcasting with a number of interactive exhibits. Overhead observation windows look down upon sets for the ever-popular samurai dramas, which rarely seem to be in production during visitor hours.

Nearby **Yoyogi-koen** ㊳ served as the Olympic Village during the 1964 summer games. Previously, the area was a barracks called Washington Heights for the US Army. Everything was eventually torn down, but rather than erecting something new, the site was turned into a park. It now includes a wild bird park and playground. Yoyogi gained notoriety for some of the worst free music in town and for its punks and Elvis clones. Wannabe rock groups gave weekend "concerts" on a closed-off street, all playing at the same time and hoping to establish a following of adolescent girls that would cascade into Japan-wide popularity. The city government finally put an end to the well-planned spontaneity.

Meiji shrine

Yoyogi-koen is an extension of one of Japan's most famous Shinto shrines, **Meiji-jingu** ㊴. The shrine deifies Emperor Meiji and Empress Shoken. (Their remains, however, are in Kyoto.) The emperor was restored to rule in the 1868 Meiji Restoration when the Tokugawa shogunate collapsed. The emperor died in 1912 and the empress two years later. The original shrine, built in 1920, was destroyed during World War II; the current shrine buildings were reconstructed in 1958. The shrine itself is constructed of Japanese cypress.

The shrine's grounds cover 70 hectares (175 acres) and were a favourite retreat of the emperor. The long walk to the shrine passes through a tunnel of trees and beneath three large *torii* gates, said to include one of the largest wooden gates in Japan: 12 metres (40 ft) high with pillars more than a metre in diameter. Cypress wood over 1,700 years old from Taiwan was used for the gate.

The entrance to Meiji-jingu is near **Harajuku-eki** ㊵ (Harajuku Station), architecturally interesting for a Japanese railway station. Leading from the station are a number of hip and groovy avenues. For some reason, probably its proximity to once-outrageous Yoyogi-koen, narrow Takeshita-dori, a small side street between the station and Meiji-dori, has become a teeny-bopper avenue of shops. It lacks breathing room on weekends *(see picture on page 136)*.

More room is found instead on the wide and upscale **Omotesando** ㊶, an avenue running from the southern end of Harajuku Station. Omote-sando has a European feel about it from the expansiveness of the boulevard (at least for Japan) to the zelkovea trees that line it. The 12-storey concrete and glass shopping and residential complex, **Omotesando Hills**, was designed by Osaka-born Tadao Ando; it features high profile stores and restaurants.

Map on pages 134–5

TIP

Gropers and perverts known as *chikan* are common on Tokyo rush-hour trains, targeting mostly Japanese females. The good news is that women are striking back as there is a sharp rise in the number of prosecutions of wayward males.

BELOW: Meiji shrine and cycling past the Bank of Japan HQ.

Set back from the busy intersection straddled by Omotesando Station, the **Nezu Bijutsukan** (Nezu Institute of Fine Arts) is an oasis of tranquillity hidden behind a sandstone wall. There are fine examples of Chinese bronzes, ceramic and lacquerware, calligraphy, textiles and Chinese and Japanese paintings. The museum is currently closed for renovation until 2009. More alluring to some is the museum's delightful garden, a densely wooded landscape with a teahouse overlooking a small iris pond.

Kabukicho is a notorious hangout for yakuza. *Many of the "hostess" bars catering to Japanese men employ women from Thailand and the Philippines, often as indentured labour.*

Shinjuku

After building Edo castle and settling down, Tokugawa Ieyasu had the **Shinjuku** area surveyed at the urging of some entrepreneurs. He then established a guard post – near today's Shinjuku 2-chome – along the Koshu Kaido, a road that led west into the mountains. Shinjuku (lit. new lodging) quickly became one of the largest urban towns in Edo, filled with shopkeepers, wholesale distributors, inns and teahouses. Shinjuku was also known for the male sensual delights, with "serving girls" working at 50 "inns". Unlike those in Asakusa, the women of Shinjuku worked without licenses and were generally considered downscale.

Nowadays, it is said by the Japanese that **Shinjuku-eki** ㊷ (Shinjuku Station) is the world's busiest railway station. It is certainly a furiously busy place – approaching 3 million people daily – and congested, and if one is unfamiliar with the station, patience can melt within minutes.

Shinjuku Station is one of the most important stations in Japan, a major transfer point for both metropolitan and regional trains and for subways. As with most large urban stations in Japan, there are multitudinous shops and restaurants filling every unused space in the multi-level labyrinth above and below ground. There are also four massive department stores within Shinjuku Station itself, two of which have their own private rail tracks leading from Shinjuku: Keio, with a line that opened in 1915, and Odakyu, its line beginning in 1927.

If you find the four department stores within the station uninspiring, leave by the station's east entrance onto Shinjuku-dori, where there are more department stores and thousands of shops, and tens of thousands of people. This entrance of Shinjuku Station is a popular meeting spot. A small open plaza tempts the idle to linger, especially when there is something to watch on the immense outside television screen at Studio Alta.

This side of the station is a superb rambling area, which one can do for hours with little purpose. Many of those who have a purpose enter **Kabukicho** ㊸, north of Yasukuni-dori. After World War II, residents of this area sought to establish a sophisticated entertainment area of cinemas and dance halls, and perhaps most importantly, a *kabuki* theatre. Hence, Kabukicho (*cho* means "ward" or "district"). But somewhat optimistically, the naming of the neighbourhood preceded construction of a *kabuki* theatre, which was never built. The cinemas were, however, and for many years Tokyo's best cinema-viewing was in Kabukicho; European films were very popular during the 1960s, especially with intellectuals and political radicals. Eventually they moved elsewhere, leaving Kabukicho to the *yakuza*. Kabukicho is

BELOW: neon lights in the Shinjuku district.

famous nowadays for its sexual entertainment, which tends towards voyeurism rather than participation. Also on the east side of Shinjuku but light years away in mood is **Shinjuku Gyoen** (Shinjuku Imperial Garden; Tues–Sun 9am–4.30pm; admission fee), a popular cherry blossom viewing venue in the spring that is divided into Japanese, French and English sections.

For more stately pursuits, follow Yasukuni-dori under the tracks to the west side of Shinjuku. (You could also exit the station directly to avoid the east side altogether.) Of most immediate interest are the numerous tall buildings on this side. Much of Tokyo is composed of either alluvial soil or landfill, both of which are geologically unstable foundations. Given the shakiness of Tokyo's land, not to mention the experience of several devastating earthquakes, tall buildings in Tokyo have been limited. But Shinjuku sits atop rather solid ground, giving architects the confidence to build what they claim are earthquake-proof buildings that utilise sophisticated techniques for stress dissipation and structure stabilisation.

Map on pages 134–5

An old-fashioned and highly atmospheric row of tiny bars, yakitori, *noodle and other cheap restaurants vie for space along Shomben Yokocho, just to the left of the underpass that connects East and West Shinjuku.*

Tokyo's skyline

The twin towers of the **Tokyo Metropolitan Government Office** ❹❹ were conceived and started at the beginning of the so-called bubble economy in the 1980s. They were intended to make a statement that Tokyo was now one of the world's great and most powerful cities. Around 13,000 city employees fill the buildings each day.

At the top of both towers, on the 45th floors at 202 metres (660 ft), expansive observation galleries with cafeterias offer Tokyo's finest views (north observatory Mon–Fri 9.30am–11pm, south observatory until 5.30pm if north observatory closed; free). This section of Shinjuku lying west of the railway tracks supports a number of other impressive skyscrapers, the nearby NS and Sumitomo buildings, and the Shinjuku Park Tower among them. The NTT InterCommunication Centre, an interactive, hi-tech site with an internet café and electronic library, is housed inside the impressive, 54-floor **Tokyo Opera City**, another Kenzo Tange design. Shinjuku's newest shopping experience, the massive **Takashimaya Times Square**, is a short stroll from here near the station's south exit. This futuristic shopping complex includes a branch of Tokyu Hands (the large home department store), Joyopolis and an IMAX theatre.

BELOW: towers of Tokyo Metropolitan Government Office.

"Little Asia"

If the streets of Kabukicho seem luridly exotic, **Shin Okubo**, a few minutes' walk directly north, is engagingly exotic. The haunt of bar hostesses, drug dealers and pimps, "Little Asia", as it is known, is also home to Koreans, Thais, Filipinos, Chinese and even Russians, a lively mix of people, cultures and beliefs that is visible in the extraordinary range of restaurants, mini-markets, churches and shrines along Shin Okubo's main strip and back lanes. With its distinctly urban, working-class cosmopolitan character, one wonders if Shin Okubo is a world apart from the capital, or the prototype for a new Tokyo. ❑

JAPAN'S TRAINS TURN TRAVEL INTO AN ART

The shinkansen, *which means "new trunk line", is a technological symbol of Japan to the world, but it's not the only train plying the islands*

The French have made a gallant effort to redefine what it is to have a fast train. But the Japanese simply do it better, and have been doing it longer – since 1959, when construction of the Tokaido *shinkansen*, or bullet train, began. Five years later, service on the Tokaido Line began between Tokyo and Osaka with 60 trains daily. And while the French TGV-A set the record for the fastest conventional train at 515 kmh (322 mph), that was just the once. The fastest regularly scheduled train between two station stops is the JR500-series *Nozomi (see top-centre photo)* between Osaka and Fukuoka at over 300 kmh (185 mph).

The Japanese live by the train and play by the train, literally and figuratively. The highest real-estate values are found near the railway station in any city, and entire mini-cities sprout near most stations. A train will take you nearly anywhere in the islands – to the remotest cape or valley.

For the Japanese, train travel is a life experience in itself in which the journey can be more important than the destination. Families will board the train and go on outings anywhere, and a carriage can take on the atmosphere of a social club. Some will even charter a special train with *tatami*-mat carriages and go nowhere in particular, just party in locomotive style.

The Japanese like to have the biggest, smallest or fastest thing in the world. The latest prototype bullet train, the new Fastech 360Z, currently under development, is designed to travel at a top speed of 360 kmh (223 mph).

▷ **WAITING** Except during rush hour, queues are well-behaved and lacking in any overt excitement.

△ **TAKE ME, I'M YOURS** Since Japan National Railways was broken into five regional lines in 1987, each line has tried to outdo the others with innovative and unusual designs.

▷ **HIGH-BROW ADVERTS** With a captive audience, often with nowhere to look but up, Japan's periodicals promote their latest weekly and monthly offerings from the rafters.

△ **NEVER LATE OR SLOW**
Shinkansen like the JR500-series above, Japan's fastest train, have an annual schedule deviation of 36 seconds, inclusive of the typhoon season and winter.

▽ **RAIL LUNCH**
Express trains offer food and beer, while local stations offer *ekiben*, a version of the *bento* box lunch made of local ingredients and packaging.

◁ **MAY I ASSIST, SIR?**
Not every train requires white-gloved wranglers, but they'll be found in Tokyo's busy stations – like Shinjuku – during the rush-hour crush.

A PRIMER OF AMAZING FACTS

According to Japan Railways (JR), on any given day there are 8,600 people – drivers, train staff, controllers, and maintenance engineers – involved in operating the Tokaido *shinkansen* line between Tokyo and Osaka. Each train carries 6.2 tons of water for drinking and flushing toilets, and each 16-car train carrying 1,300 passengers is 400 metres (1,300 ft) long.

Each 16-car train also requires 40 motors generating 12 megawatts to move it through the 66 tunnels that the *shinkansen* uses between Tokyo and Osaka. The longest of these is 8 km (5 miles) long. On the other hand, the shortest tunnel is but 30 metres (100 ft) long.

When the *shinkansen* is travelling at 270 kph (170 mph), it will take a little over 5 km (3 miles) to come to a complete stop. The strengthened glass in the windscreen of the *shinkansen* is 22 mm (0.9 inch) thick, while the passenger windows are triple-glazed, with two outer layers of hardened glass and a 5-mm (0.2-inch) thick inner pane separated from the outer panes by an air gap. It's a hardy train, indeed.

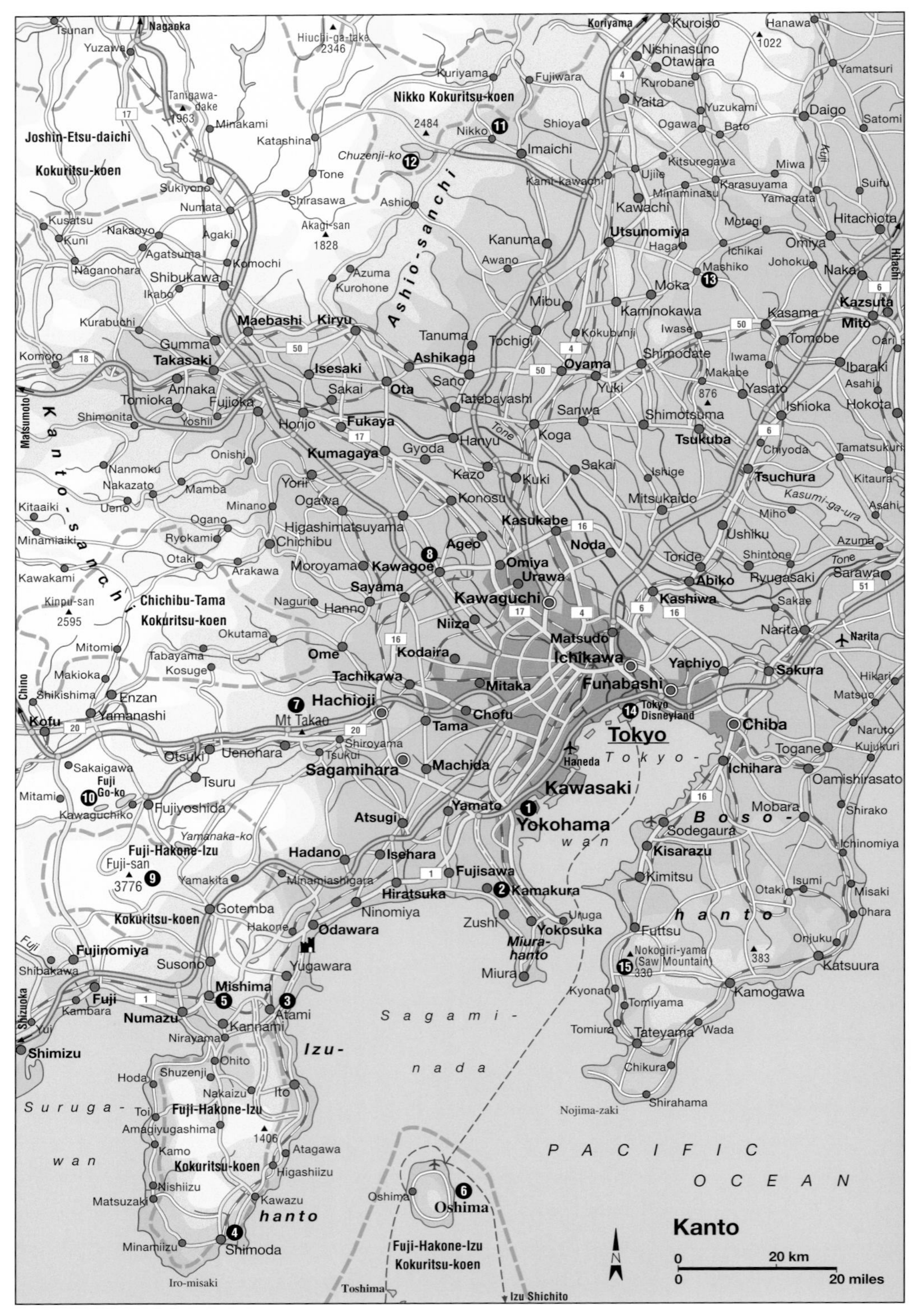
Kanto
Tsunan
Nagaoka
Yuzawa
Hiuchi-ga-take
2346
Koriyama
Kuroiso
Hanawa
1022
Tanigawa-dake
1963
Kuriyama
Fujiwara
Nishinasuno
Otawara
Kurobane
Yamatsuri
Nikko Kokuritsu-koen
Yaita
Yuzukami
Daigo
Satomi
Joshin-Etsu-daichi
Kokuritsu-koen
Minakami
Katashina
2484
Nikko
Shioya
Ogawa
Bato
Chuzenji-ko
Imaichi
Kitsuregawa
Miwa
Tone
Kami-kawachi
Ujiie
Karasuyama
Suifu
Sukiyono
Ashio-sanchi
Minaminasu
Yamagata
Numata
Shirasawa
Ashio
Kawachi
Hitachiota
Kusatsu
Nakaoyo
Agaki
Akagi-san
1828
Utsunomiya
Motegi
Kuni
Kanuma
Haga
Ichikai
Omiya
Agatsuma
Komochi
Awano
Johoku
Naka
Naganohara
Azuma
Mashiko
Hitachi
Shibukawa
Kurohone
Moka
Ikabo
Mibu
Kaminokawa
Kazsuta
Kurabuchi
Maebashi
Kiryu
Kasama
Mito
Tanuma
Kokubunji
Iwase
Tomobe
Gumma
Tochigi
Shimodate
Oari
Komoro
Takasaki
Ashikaga
Oyama
Iwama
Ibaraki
Annaka
Isesaki
Sano
Yuki
Makabe
Asahi
Tomioka
Fujioka
Sakai
Ota
Tatebayashi
876
Yasato
Hokota
Matsumoto
Shimonita
Yoshii
Honjo
Fukaya
Sanwa
Shimotsuma
Ishioka
Kanto-sanchi
Tone
Koga
Tsukuba
Onishi
Kumagaya
Gyoda
Hanyu
Chiyoda
Tamatsukuri
Nanmoku
Sakai
Nakazato
Mamba
Yorii
Kazo
Kuki
Ishige
Tsuchura
Kitaura
Kitaaiki
Ueno
Minano
Ogawa
Konosu
Mitsukaido
Kasumi-ga-ura
Asahi
Ogano
Kasukabe
Miho
Minamiaiki
Ryokami
Higashimatsuyama
Noda
Ushiku
Azuma
Chichibu
Ageo
Toride
Shintone
Tone
Otaki
Arakawa
Moroyama
Kawagoe
Omiya
Abiko
Ryugasaki
Sarawa
Kawakami
Urawa
Sayama
Kashiwa
Kinpu-san
2595
Chichibu-Tama
Kokuritsu-koen
Naguri
Hanno
Kawaguchi
Sakae
Niiza
Narita
Okutama
Matsudo
Narita
Mitomi
Ome
Kodaira
Ichikawa
Tabayama
Kosuge
Yachiyo
Makioka
Tachikawa
Sakura
Hikari
Funabashi
Matsuo
Shikishima
Enzan
Mitaka
Chino
Hachioji
Tokyo Disneyland
Yamanashi
Chofu
Kofu
Mt Takao
Tama
Chiba
Naruto
Tokyo
Shiroyama
Kujukuri
Otsuki
Uenohara
Tsukui
Togane
Haneda
Tokyo-
Sakaigawa
Sagamihara
Machida
Ichihara
Oamishirasato
Fuji Go-ko
Tsuru
Kawasaki
Mitami
Fujiyoshida
Kawaguchiko
Yamato
Mobara
Boso-
Shirako
Yokohama
Atsugi
Sodegaura
Yamanaka-ko
wan
Ichinomiya
Fuji-Hakone-Izu
Hadano
Isehara
Kisarazu
Fuji-san
3776
Yamakita
Fujisawa
Minamiashigara
Kimitsu
Isumi
Misaki
Hiratsuka
Kamakura
Otaki
Gotemba
Ninomiya
hanto
Ohara
Kokuritsu-koen
Hakone
Zushi
Uruga
Odawara
Yokosuka
Futtsu
Onjuku
Fuji
Miura-hanto
Nokogiri-yama (Saw Mountain)
330
383
Fujinomiya
Susono
Shibakawa
Yugawara
Miura
Katsuura
Mishima
Kyonan
Kamogawa
Fuji
Kambara
Numazu
Atami
Tomiyama
Shizuoka
Yui
Kannami
Sagami-nada
Tomiura
Wada
Nirayama
Tateyama
Shimizu
Izu-
Ohito
Chikura
Hoda
Shuzenji
Nakaizu
Ito
Shirahama
Suruga-wan
Toi
Fuji-Hakone-Izu
Nojima-zaki
Amagiyugashima
1406
Kamo
Atagawa
PACIFIC OCEAN
Kokuritsu-koen
Higashiizu
Nishiizu
Oshima
Oshima
Matsuzaki
Kawazu
hanto
Minamiizu
Shimoda
Fuji-Hakone-Izu
Kokuritsu-koen
Iro-misaki
Toshima
Izu Shichito
N
0 20 km
0 20 miles

OUT OF TOKYO

Trains make day trips from Tokyo easy. To the south are Yokohama, Kamakura and the Izu Peninsula, west, Mount Takao; and to the north, the historical sights of Kawagoe

Map on page 162

The very sound of **Yokohama** ❶ is somehow exotic. And although the city today is both an integral part of the Greater Tokyo area and a major urban centre in its own right, Yokohama has a distinctive personality and even a mystique, much of it stemming from its vital role as one of the greatest international seaports of the Far East.

When Commodore Matthew Perry and his armada arrived in 1853, Yokohama was just a poor fishing village next to a smelly swamp. Under the terms of a treaty negotiated in 1858 by the first US envoy to Japan, Townsend Harris, the port of Kanagawa, located on the Tokaido (the East Sea Road between Edo Tokyo and Kyoto), was to be opened to foreign settlement. But given its proximity to the important Tokaido, the shogunate reconsidered and built an artificial island on the mud flats of Yokohama instead for the foreigners.

That attempt to segregate the "red-haired barbarians" proved fortuitous for all concerned, since Yokohama's superb natural harbour helped international trade to flourish. The wild, early days of the predominantly male community centred around such recreational facilities as Dirty Village, the incomparable Gankiro Teahouse, and the local race track. Periodic attacks by sword-wielding, xenophobic samurai added to the lively atmosphere.

PRECEDING PAGES: atop Mt Fuji.
BELOW: Yokohama's modern port.

Eventually, foreign garrisons were brought in and the merchants could live in a more sedate environment. Honcho-dori became the centre of commercial activities, and the street is still lined with banks and office buildings. With a population of more than 3 million, Yokohama is second in size only to Tokyo.

Happily, however, many of those places worthy of exploring are concentrated in a relatively small area and can be covered for the most part by foot. Another aspect that makes Yokohama – only a 30-minute train ride from Tokyo – alluring is that its broad, relatively uncrowded streets (except on weekends) and laidback atmosphere provide a perfect antidote to Tokyo's claustrophobia and frantic pace.

Central Yokohama

Start a walking tour of central Yokohama at **Sakuragicho-eki** (Sakuragicho Station), which is the terminus for the Toyoko Line originating at Tokyo's Shibuya Station. Sakuragicho was also the last stop on Japan's first railroad, which began service to Shimbashi in Tokyo in 1872. Central Yokohama is now dominated by the massive **Minato Mirai 21** (MM21) shopping and leisure complex, between Sakuragicho Station and the ocean. Trumpeted as the last great Japanese mega-complex to be constructed before the millennium (and after the economic meltdown in the

Steamship berthed at Yokohama, 1930s.

1990s), its 190 sq. km (75 sq. miles) is dominated by the 73-storey **Landmark Tower**, Japan's tallest building at 296 metres (970 ft) and having one of the highest observatory decks (daily 10am–9pm; admission fee) – on the 69th floor – in Japan. Other buildings of note are the Yokohama Grand InterContinental Hotel, strikingly designed to resemble a sail, and the **Maritime Museum** (Tues–Sun 10am–5pm; admission fee). The *Nippon Maru*, a traditional sailing ship, is anchored nearby. The **Yokohama Museum of Art** (open Fri–Wed 10am–6pm; admission fee) has an excellent collection of 19th- and 20th-century paintings and modernist sculptures.

What is claimed to be the world's largest Ferris wheel, known as Cosmo Clock 21, stands on Shinko-cho, a reclaimed island that has become one of the city's newest sights. Also here is the red-brick Akarenga shopping and entertainment complex.

Southeast side

On the southeast side of the Oka-gawa, a stream that bisects Yokohama from Sakuragicho Station, is an area of old government buildings, banks and the like. Further on is a tree-lined street with red-brick pavements: Bashamichi-dori (Street of Horse Carriages). Here is the **Kanagawa Prefectural Historical Museum**. The building, built in 1904, was formerly the head office of a bank. As one of the best surviving examples of the city's old commercial architecture, it has been designated a so-called Important Cultural Property by the national government.

In the same neighbourhood are the stately Yokohama Banker's Club and on the right, four blocks down, the lovely red-brick Yokohama Port Opening Memorial Hall, which miraculously survived the Great Kanto Earthquake of 1923 and the bombings of World War II. Also in the area are numerous offices for the prefectural government. This district is sometimes called the Bund and its oldest buildings have a distinctly European look, something shared with buildings along the Bund in Shanghai, built about the same time.

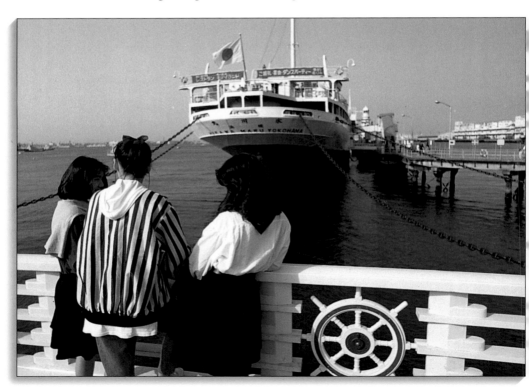

BELOW: the harbour from Yamashita Park.

The **Yokohama Archives of History**, on the site of the former British consulate, houses a museum with various exhibits about Yokohama's fascinating history and a reading room with related audio-visual materials. Across the boulevard is the **Silk Centre**, with a delightful museum on the history of that mysterious fabric; at one time, Yokohama owed its prosperity primarily to silk, in which the local Indian community was intimately involved.

Yamashita-koen (Yamashita Park) is well worth a visit for the people-watching. On a clear summer night, a rock band is liable to be wailing away on a temporary stage several hundred feet offshore. The former passenger liner and hospital ship *Hikawa Maru* is permanently moored here and can be visited. Conveniently, there is a beer garden on deck, and boat tours of the harbour leave from next to the ship. Further down the same road is the New Grand Hotel, which, although slightly down at the heel, is still a civic institution and the best spot for a break over coffee and cake. Next to it is the somewhat garish 106-metre (348-ft) **Marine Tower** and a doll museum.

The aquarium at **Yokohama Hakkeijima Sea Paradise** is very popular. Aquariums abound in Japan, and this is one of the finest in the country. Nearby are a 1.2-km (¾-mile) long roller coaster and the Blue Fall – a 107-metre (350 ft), 125-kph (80 mph) chair-drop that claims to be the highest in the world.

Chinatown

No visit to Yokohama would be complete without a meal in **Chukagai**, Yokohama's Chinatown. This dozen or so blocks is the largest Chinatown in Japan and is nearly as old as the port. The area within its five old gates accounts for 90 percent of the former foreign settlement. Chinatown also takes pride in the

Map on page 162

Rebuilt in 1927, the Hotel New Grand played host to many famous guests, including Babe Ruth, Charlie Chaplin, General MacArthur, and the writer Osaragi Jiro who wrote many of his novels here in Room 318.

BELOW: Marine Tower, Yokohama.

PERRY'S ARRIVAL

More than two centuries of isolation evaporated in 1853 when Matthew Perry, a US naval officer, sailed an expedition of four ships into Uraga, near Yokosuka. His sole mission was to force Japan into trade and diplomacy with the US, which then became an equal with Britain, France and Russia in East Asia.

He refused demands to leave and insisted that he be received. Mindful of China's recent defeat in the Opium Wars, the Japanese agreed as a stall for time while improving their defences. In 1854 Perry reappeared in Tokyo Bay with nine ships to conclude a first treaty, which included a US consul in Japan and trade rights. Other countries demanded treaties, which the shogun realised he could not refuse. This weakness helped the collapse of the shogunate system. Perry later advocated a network of Pacific bases, but the US Government waited over 50 years before doing so.

historical role it had in providing staunch support to Sun Yat-sen when he was here in exile trying to rally support for revolution on the Chinese mainland.

On days when a baseball game is on at nearby Yokohama Stadium, the area is visited by more than 200,000 people, the majority intent on dining at one of the approximately 150 local restaurants. Most also sneak in at least a peak at the exotic shops selling imported Chinese sweets and sundries from elsewhere in Asia. There are also many herbal medicine and teashops. Although in most Chinatowns, from San Francisco to London, restaurants prepare food for Chinese tastes, in Yokohama everything is adjusted to Japanese taste buds, with a tad of French influence. (Top chefs recruited from Hong Kong and Taiwan have to be deprogrammed to prepare Chinese food in Japan.)

Back in the old days, the waterfront Bund often stood in contrast to the **Bluff**, or **Yamate Heights**, where the leading foreign merchants lived in palatial homes. Nanmon-dori in Chinatown was the central street that ran through the international settlement and connected the two. It became a local tradition – known as Zondag, from the Dutch word for Sunday – that on every Sunday the flags of the many nations represented there were flown and brass bands marched down the road. There is a foreign cemetery *(gaijin bochi)* where around 4,200 foreigners from 40 countries are buried. The adjacent Yamate Museum, with quaint displays on the life of early foreign residents, sits near where one of Japan's earliest breweries was located.

Yokohama and Kamakura are easily accessible from Tokyo Station on the same train, the Yokosuka Line. Yokohama is exactly 30 minutes from Tokyo, Kamakura just 1 hour.

Motomachi, a popular shopping street just below the Bluff and slightly inland from Yamashita-koen, means "original town". This is somewhat of a misnomer because the area was developed long after Yokohama itself was established. Still, Motomachi, adjacent as it was to the foreign district (now Chinatown), has played an important role in the city's history by serving the needs of foreign vessels and their crews visiting the port. Motomachi's legacy of "foreignness" led to its revival in the 1960s and 1970s. However, the focus of fashion in Yokohama has shifted to Isezaki-cho, south of Kannai Station, and to the big department stores around Yokohama Station. A short bus ride south of the Yamate will bring you to the contiguous Negishi district and the **Sankeien Garden** (daily 9am–4.30pm; admission fee). This classic Japanese garden was built by a prosperous silk merchant in 1906 and incorporates into its spacious grounds and lakeside area several teahouses, a three-storey pagoda and the restored Rinshunkaku, a villa built by the shogun Tokugawa Yoshinobu.

BELOW: the city's Chinatown.

Kamakura

Cradled in a spectacular natural amphitheatre, **Kamakura** ❷ is surrounded on three sides by wooded mountains and on the fourth by the blue Pacific. From 1192, when Minamoto Yoritomo made it the headquarters of the first shogunate, until 1333, when imperial forces breached its seven "impregnable" passes and annihilated the defenders – Kamakura was the de-facto political and cultural capital of Japan. During those years, the military administration based here built impressive temples and commissioned notable works of art, a great deal of it Zen-influenced. Despite the endemic violence of Japan's middle ages, most survived and can be viewed today.

It is a pity that the majority of visitors spend only a day or two in Kamakura, since it is best appreciated leisurely with visits to famous historical sites – there are 65 Buddhist temples and 19 Shinto shrines – interspersed with walks through the quiet, surrounding hills. Kamakura is only an hour from Tokyo Station and 30 minutes from Yokohama on the JR Yokosuka Line. For that reason, much of it resembles an open-air madhouse on weekends, a time when it is highly recommended for the traveller to be elsewhere.

Visitors customarily begin their sightseeing from **Kamakura-eki** Ⓐ (Kamakura Station). In addition to the main rail line, there is a private electric-trolley line, the delightful Enoden (Enoshima Dentetsu). The Enoden, which began operations in 1902, plies a meandering route with some wonderful views between Kamakura and Fujisawa, with 13 stops in between. For about half its 10 km (6 mile) length, the carriages run along the ocean. When the trains are not crowded, the conductors allow surfers to bring their boards aboard. Unfortunately, the delightful old carriages have been replaced with modern ones. If time permits, take the Enoden the entire length.

Maps on pages 162 & 168

Among Sankeien's Important Cultural Properties is the villa of its creator, Hara Tomitaro. The buildings, connected by corridors, form a ganko-gata, *or "flight of geese" pattern. Hara called his residence the Kakushokaku, the "Palace of the Flying Crane".*

Great Buddha

Hop off the Enoden at Hase, the station closest to the **Daibutsu** Ⓑ (Great Buddha). A road leads to the statue. In the hills to the left and along the way are **Goryo-jinja** (next to the Enoden tracks), which holds a unique festival every 18 September with humorous characters sporting macabre masks; **Hase-dera**, a temple with a 9-metre (30 ft), 11-headed Hase Kannon statue, along with thousands of small *jiso* statues decked out in colourful bibs and bonnets and dedicated to lost babies (mostly due to abortion) and **Kosoku-ji**, a temple known for its collection associated with the priest Nichiren. On a knoll to the right of the approach to the Buddha is the 1,200-year-old **Amanawa Myojin**. Dedicated to the Sun Goddess, Amaterasu Omikami, the shrine offers majestic views.

Even first-time visitors to Japan have no doubt seen photos of Daibutsu, the Great Buddha. But if not, there's little chance of missing the colossus. At 11 metres (40 ft) in height – minus the pedestal – and weighing 93 tons, this representation of the compassionate Amida is unlikely to get lost in crowds posing for pictures below. The features of the statue were purposely designed out of proportion when it was cast in 1252 so that the proper proportions come together when one is standing 4 to 5 metres (15 ft) in front of the statue. For a fee, crawl around inside the statue. Astonishingly, the Great Buddha has survived the onslaughts of earthquakes, typhoons and tsunamis, like the one in 1495 that ripped away the wooden building that once enclosed it.

On the east side of Kamakura Station is **Wakamiya-oji** Ⓒ, a broad boulevard that begins at the beach and heads inland under three massive *torii* archways to the Tsurugaoka Hachiman-gu. Parallel to Wakamiya-oji is **Kamachi-dori**, Kamakura's modest

BELOW: Daibutsu.

answer to the Ginza and with little elbow room on weekends. The area abounds with all kinds of trendy shops and eating places, and many of the Japanese-style restaurants here and elsewhere in the city have incorporated Zen principles of cooking.

Along Kamachi-dori and especially on some of the side alleys, craft shops encourage serious browsing. Kamakura is most famous for *Kamakura-bori* (lacquerware), which originated in the area in the 13th century for the production of utensils used in religious ceremonies. Unlike the traditional Chinese lacquerware from which it drew its inspiration, the first step in *Kamakura-bori* is to carve the design and then apply the lacquer. Like fine wine, *Kamakura-bori* improves with age, taking on richer and subtler hues and lustres.

On weekends during the summer, Kamakura is elbow to elbow with people. Unless crowds bring you joy, you will have little fun trying to shop and sightsee.

Province of temples

The area due east of Kamakura Station, on the other side of Wakamiya-oji, is largely the province of temples of the Nichiren sect. Although most foreigners have heard of Zen, few know much about Nichiren (1222–82) and his teachings, despite the fact that the iconoclast priest founded the only true Japanese Buddhist sect. Nichiren was an imposing personality who in his lifetime was nearly executed, exiled twice, and set upon by mobs on more than one occasion, and who continues to generate feelings of both respect and disdain centuries after his death. Nichiren's importance in political (as opposed to religious) history lies in his prediction of the Mongol invasion as divine punishment for the failure of the authorities to accept his arguments. The irascible Nichiren seems to have been quite put out that the Mongols did not actually conquer the country.

The temples of **Myohon-ji** **D**, **Hongaku-ji**, **Chosho-ji**, **Myoho-ji** and

BELOW: bamboo grove in Kamakura.

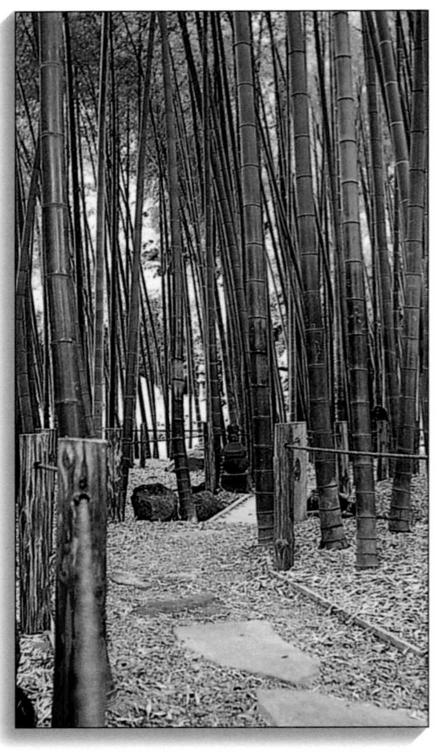

Ankokuron-ji are all Nichiren temples and are worth a visit. The Myohon-ji, for example, although only 10 minutes from the station, seems a world apart.

At the top end of Wakamiya-oji, the approach into **Tsurugaoka Hachiman-gu** **E** crosses a steep, red, half-moon bridge that separates the Gempei Ponds. The name Gempei refers to the Minamoto (Genji) and Taira (Heike) clans, which fought to the end in the samurai power struggle known as the Gempei War. The three islands on the right – the Genji side – signify the Chinese character for birth, symbolising the victory of Yoritomo and his followers, while the four in the Heike Pond stand for the death of the rival Taira. Yoritomo's indomitable wife, Masako, who ironically was of Taira blood, apparently built the pond to rub in her husband's victory over the ill-fated heirs of Taira.

Behind the Heike Pond is the Kanagawa Prefectural Museum of Modern Art, and a little past the Genji Pond is the modern and disaster-proof **Kokuhokan** (National Treasure Hall; open Tues–Sun 9am–4pm; admission fee). Each month the Kokuhokan teasingly changes the limited displays of the 2,000 treasures from the temples of Kamakura. Still, whatever is being shown at any given moment should be stimulating for those interested in Buddhist art.

Continuing up towards the main shrine, cross a 25-metre (80-ft) dirt track, along which every 16 September mounted archers gallop and unloosen their arrows at targets in the ancient samurai ritual of *yabusame*. Next is an open area below the steps to the *hongu*, or shrine hall. Here is the red stage upon which Shizuka, Yoritomo's paramour, danced defiantly at the order of his vengeful older half-brother, using the occasion to sing the praises of her lover. The pregnant girl's courage sent Yoritomo into a furious and vengeful rage, and although he spared her life, he executed her son.

Zen and Nichiren forms of Buddhism reflect the removal of boundaries between Buddhism and Shinto, with Shinto the realm of daily life and Buddhism of the afterlife.

BELOW: main temple building at Hachiman-gu.

Minamoto Yoritomo.

Just past the stage on the left of the steps is a huge gingko tree measuring 8 metres (26 ft) around and reputed to be 1,000 years old. It was near here, in 1219, that Yoritomo's second son, Sanetomo, at 26 years old already an accomplished poet, was assassinated by his own nephew. Thus came to an end Yoritomo's line; thereafter, the shogunate was controlled by Masako's family, the Hojo, through a regency.

Tsurugaoka Hachiman-gu's prominence on the top of Stork Mountain and the shrine's dedication to Hachiman, the god of war and tutelary deity of the Minamoto, made it the central point of reference for the numerous offices of the military government situated below. Actually, the shrine was founded way back in 1063 by one of Yoritomo's ancestors. Yoritomo's very unpretentious tomb is to be found off to the right of the shrine near a hill. It is an austere grave befitting a samurai, unlike the monstrous mausoleums for the Tokugawa shoguns at Nikko, which look as if they were built for mafioso dons. Before exploring the hills north of the Tsurugaoka Hachiman-gu, **Hokuku-ji Temple**, a 10-minute walk, offers a closer retreat. Follow the road that runs east of the main entrance to the Hachiman-gu until you see signs on the right, pointing you across the river to the temple. Hokoku-ji's main draw is its tranquil bamboo forest where visitors can repair to a tea pavilion for a bowl of thick, green *matcha*, the brew used in the tea ceremony.

Two isolated temples of great interest and few crowds are the **Kakuon-ji**, back in the hills behind Yoritomo's tomb, and the **Zuisen-ji**, considerably to the east. The former was founded in 1296. Its Buddha hall, dating to 1354, houses a beautiful Yakushi Nyorai flanked by guardians representing the sun and moon, as well as a shrine to the Black Jizo, whose indelible colour results from its constantly being scorched by the flames of hell in its efforts to save souls. Access to this temple is strictly controlled. Zuisen-ji has a Zen rock-and-water garden designed by its founder, the monk Muso Kokushi.

BELOW: in the hills above Kamakura.

Another spot to visit that is not so far off the beaten track, but which is nevertheless largely missed by the tourist packs, is so-called **Harakiri Cave**, a 20-minute walk to the northeast of Kamakura Station past the shallow, meandering Nameri-gawa. In 1333, in what was then a temple called Tosho-ji, the last Kamakura regent, who had been scorned for his patronage of dog fights, died by his own hand while surrounded by more than 800 of his cornered followers.

North of Tsurugaoka Hachiman-gu is **Kencho-ji** Ⓕ, established in 1253 and perhaps Kamakura's most significant Zen temple. Before fires in the 1300s and 1400s razed the temple, Kencho-ji had 49 sub-temples. To the right of the main gate, San-mon, is the temple's bell *(bonsho)*, cast in 1255 and inscribed by the temple's first abbot, a priest from China. The large juniper trees beyond the main gate are said to have been planted by the Chinese priest.

To the north is the station at **Kita Kamakura** (North Kamakura), the first stop beyond Kamakura towards Tokyo. East of the station is **Engaku-ji** Ⓖ, which dates from the late 13th century and was intended for the souls of those killed during the unsuccessful Mongol invasion the previous year. After the main gate and on the right are steps to a 2.5-metre (8-ft) high bell cast in 1301, the largest temple bell in Kamakura. The bell's sound, it is said, guides souls that have been spared by the king of hell back to earth and the living. Engaku-ji's Butsu-den dates from 1964 and has been rebuilt many times over the centuries after fires and earthquakes.

Not far from Engaku-ji and on the main road across the tracks between Kita Kamakura and central Kamakura is **Tokei-ji** ⓗ, which can be seen from Engaku-ji's bell tower. Begun in the 1280s as a nunnery, Tokei-ji became noted as a refuge for abused wives. Women who found sanctuary here worked as lay helpers for three years, during which time they were safe from husbands. At the end of the three years, the women were released from marriage. While you are here, cross the tracks opposite the nunnery for a look at the **Kamakura Old Pottery Museum** (Tues–Sun 10am–5pm; admission fee). A five-minute walk south along the main road takes you to **Jochi-ji Temple**. Founded in 1283, it is one of Kamakura's top Zen temples, although much of it was destroyed in the great 1923 earthquake.

Enoshima

The wooded islet of **Enoshima** ⓘ (Bay Island) has many attractions in any weather and is easily reached either from Shinjuku in Tokyo on the private Odayku Line (a pleasant 75-minute ride), or from Kamakura on the quaint and rattling Enoden electric railway. As always, avoid weekends and holidays.

The island, about 2 km (1 mile) in circumference, is a wooded hill surrounded by rocky beaches and cliffs. But these days it hardly deserves the name of island: the 600-metre (2,000-ft) long Benten Bridge, which connects Enoshima to the bright lights of the resort town of Katase, has gradually turned into a major

The hills above Kamakura are laced with hiking trails good for an hour or a day of rambling. To find them, just follow a Japanese seemingly dressed for a hike in the Swiss Alps

BELOW: *jizo* images at a temple.

causeway. The usually crowded beaches of Shichirigahama and Miami stretch far to the east and west. Still, access on foot or by car is simple, and there is plenty of parking space at the foot of the hill. Just beyond where the causeway meets the island is the yacht harbour, constructed for the Summer Olympics in 1964.

Not only are there appropriate clothes and tools for every activity in Japan, but there are definite times when sports can, and cannot, be undertaken. The first of September is the end of summer and thus the end of ocean swimming, even if summer's heat still lingers.

The ascent of the hill begins at the end of Benten Bridge along a narrow street crammed with restaurants and souvenir shops. This narrow street leads up to the start of a series of covered escalators, which make the upward progress simple. First stop is the charming **Enoshima-jinja**, built in 1182 and dedicated to Benten, the goddess of fortune. Her naked statue used to reside in a cave on the far side, but fears for her safety led to a place in the shrine itself.

On top are tropical plants, greenhouses, miniature trains, and restaurants and patios providing views of the ocean. An observation tower, 50 metres (160 ft) high and accessible by lift, gives more exposed views.

The more spiritually minded might like to visit the famous **Ryuko-ji**, a temple near the station that features a fine pagoda, albeit one of the 20th century. The temple is dedicated to Nichiren, founder of the only genuinely Japanese sect of Buddhism. It was here that Nichiren was saved from execution by a timely stroke of lightning that hit the uplifted blade of the executioner's sword.

Izu Peninsula

Extending into the Pacific between Sagami and Sugura bays is **Izu-hanto** (Izu Peninsula), 60 km (40 miles) long and 30 km (20 miles) wide and where countless bays, beaches, and *onsen* (hot springs) meld with a very inviting climate to give Izu its reputation as a resort for all seasons. Seafood is excellent here, too. Trains run only along the eastern coast, however.

BELOW: beach at Enoshima.

Eastern Izu begins at **Atami** ❸, a hot spring dating back more than 1,000 years. During the Edo Period, the shogun had its waters brought to the Edo palace so he could enjoy a relaxing bath. Today, Atami is a lively and even bawdy town offering reasonably sophisticated nightlife. Access from both Tokyo and Osaka is easy via the *shinkansen*. The **MOA Museum of Art** (Fri–Wed 9.30am–4pm; admission fee), located above the train station, has a fine collection of *ukiyo-e* (woodblock prints), ceramics and lacquer works, many of which have been designated as National Treasures and Important Cultural Properties by the national government.

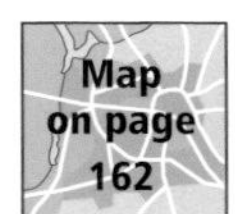
Map on page 162

Kabuki actors and people connected with the entertainment world often pray before the Hadaka (Naked) Benten statue on Enoshima. Besides being one of the Seven Lucky Gods, she is also patroness of beauty, music and the arts.

Those travellers who have read James Clavell's *Shogun* may recognise **Ito**, south of Atami on the eastern coast of Izu-hanto, as the temporary abode of the shipwrecked Englishman who ingratiated himself into Japanese affairs. Today it is a popular hot-spring resort, punctuated by the Kawana resort complex in the south part of the city. The **Ikeda Museum of 20th-Century Art** (Thur–Tues 9am–5pm; admission fee) offers some 600 paintings and sculptures by Matisse, Picasso, Chagall, Dalí and other masters. South is another hot-spring outpost, **Atagawa**, noted for **Atagawa Banana-Wanien** (Banana and Crocodile Park).

Shimoda ❹ is a somewhat sleepy resort city at the southern terminus of the railway line. A fine view of **Iro-misaki** (Cape Iro) to the south can be had from the top of **Nesugata-yama**, three minutes by cable car from Shimoda Station. The view includes volcanically active Oshima, an island to the east and part of Metropolitan Tokyo.

The first US consul general to Japan, Townsend Harris, was based here, arriving in 1856. This was the first permanent foreign consulate in Japan, chosen by the shogun in part for its remoteness and thus its distance from centres of power. A monument in **Shimoda-koen** (Shimoda Park) commemorates the occasion. The friendship treaty between Japan and the US was signed at **Ryosen-ji** in 1854.

Central Izu is the cultural heart of the peninsula. The **Taisha-jinja** in **Mishima** ❺ is revered as Izu's first shrine; its treasure hall keeps documents of the first Kamakura shogun as well as swords and other artefacts. The Egawa house in **Nirayama** is the oldest private dwelling in Japan. **Shuzen-ji**, along the Katsura-gawa, sprang up around a temple founded by the monk Kobo Daishi; this quiet hot-spring town became a favourite hideaway for Japan's great literary talents such as Natsume Soseki, Nobel prizewinner Kawabata Yasunari, and Kido Okamoto.

The west coast is less visited by tourists and has no train service. Still, resort towns such as **Toi** reputedly have the best hot springs in this part of the country.

Izu Shichito

Time permitting, overnight trips can be made to the ruggedly beautiful **Izu Shichito** (Izu Seven Islands), a group of mostly volcanic islands accessible only by boat or air. **Oshima** ❻ is the largest and closest. It is also the most touristy, with good deep-sea fishing, snorkelling, surfing, hot springs and an active volcano, Mt Mihara. Each island has something different to recommend it. **Niijima** is popular with young people during the summer, and has curious saltwater hot-

BELOW: the rocky coastline at sunset.

spring pools at the edge of the sea. **Toshima** is the smallest, with a warm microclimate that supports camellia flowers; **Shikinejima** is a tranquil islet known for its hot springs; **Kozushima** is said to be the finest island for fishing; **Mikurajima** is the most unspoilt. Visitors to **Miyakejima** must wear gas masks to protect against the toxic gas still being produced by Mt Oyana, which erupted in July 2000. The furthest flung and most exotic of the islands is **Hachijojima**, 70 minutes by plane, 11 hours by ferry. It is known for its semi-tropical flora and fruits, and locals produce an exquisite silk fabric known as *ki-hachijo*.

In the middle of May, Shimoda celebrates the Kurofune Matsuri (Black Ship Festival) in commemoration of Perry's landing with ceremonies, parades, and, of course, spectacular fireworks.

Mount Takao

If you have a hankering to do some nature hiking within the boundaries of Greater Tokyo, **Mt Takao ❼**, easily accessed on the Keio Line from Shinjuku Station, is the obvious choice. Seven trails wind up the mountain, three of them from just outside the Takao-san-guchi railway station. No. 1 trail is the most popular route up, though some visitors prefer to take the cable car or chairlift, and then walk down via trail No. 6, a forest walk that includes a stream and freezing cold waterfall popular with religious ascetics. The ascent takes you through a monkey park alive with Japanese macaques, to the summit and the gloriously vivid colours of **Yakuo-in**, a temple founded in the 8th century. Mt Takao is something of a pilgrimage spot for botanists, its slopes and trails covered in wild as well as cultivated flowers.

Kawagoe

Kawagoe ❽, a former castle town of dark wood, plaster and tile godowns (called *kurazukuri*), and ageing temples, prospered as a supplier of goods to Edo during the Tokugawa Period, hence its sobriquet "Little Edo".

It's a 15-minute walk from Kawagoe Station to reach the historical core of the town. **Ichiban-gai** is Kawagoe's most famous street and the one with the largest concentration of *kurazukuri*.

Across the street from the **Hattori Minzoku Shiryokan**, a privately run folk museum with pamphlets and maps in English (Tues–Sun 11am–5pm), is **Yamawa**, a beautiful ceramic store housed in a street corner godown. Its stylish café serves green tea and sweet potato delicacies.

One block up from the Hattori Folk Museum, down a lane to the right is the **Toki no Kane**, a wooden tower that has become the most photographed image of Kawagoe. The current structure was built after a fire broke out in 1893. Two blocks up across the street, the narrow lane on the left is **Kashi-ya Yokocho** (Confectioners' Row). Souvenirs and trinkets have been added to shops selling old-fashioned sweets and purple, sweet-potato ice cream.

Little remains of Kawagoe Castle, but the exquisite **Honmaru-goten Palace**, with its beautifully painted screens and archaeological artefacts, more than makes up for that. A 10-minute walk south takes you to **Kita-in**, an important Buddhist temple-museum with a traditional Japanese garden. Kita-in's main crowd-puller are the **Gohyaku Rakan** stones, 540 statues depicting disciples of the Buddha in different, highly realistic, sometimes humorous poses and expressions. ❑

Below: the wooden bell tower at Kawagoe.

Fuji and Hakone

The region around **Fuji-san** ❾ (Mt Fuji but never Mt Fuji-san) has been the inspiration for the works of many of Japan's most celebrated writers, poets and artists. It would be hard to find a mountain more highly praised for its beauty than Fuji-san or a lake more often photographed than Hakone's **Ashi-ko**. Most of the region is designated a "national park", but due to Japan's rather weak laws protecting and restricting commercial exploitation of such assets, one can often consider a national park to be a "nature" amusement park.

Sweeping up from the Pacific to form a nearly perfect symmetrical cone 3,776 metres (12,388 ft) above sea level, the elegantly shaped Fuji-san watches over Japan. Fuji's last eruption in 1707 covered Edo-Period Tokyo, some 100 km (60 miles) away, with ash. Like many natural monuments held to be sacred and imbued with a living spirit, Fuji-san was off-limits to women for many centuries. It was not until 1867, when an Englishwoman boldly scaled the mountain, that there is any record of a woman climbing the peak. Today, half of the 400,000 annual hikers are women.

Although climbers are known to set out to challenge the mountain throughout the year, the "official" climbing season for Fuji-san begins on 1 July and ends on 31 August. The mountain huts and services found along the trails to Fuji's peak are open only then. Expect thick crowds and a distinctly commercial atmosphere, not only around the facilities but along the entire trail to the top.

For those who wish to see the rising sun from Fuji's peak, start in the afternoon, stay overnight (forget sleeping – it's noisy) at one of the cabins near the top, and make the remaining climb while the sky is still dark. The other option is to climb through the night. The trails are well travelled and hard to miss.

Fuji Go-ko ❿ (Fuji Five Lakes) skirts the northern base of Fuji-san as a year-round resort, probably more than most visitors seeking Japan's sacred mountain would expect or want. From east to west, the lakes are Yamanaka, Kawaguchi, Sai, Shoji and Motosu. (A *-ko* added to the end of these names signifies "lake".)

Yamanaka-ko, which is the largest in the group, and the picturesque Kawaguchi-ko are the most frequented of the five, but some of the best spots are hidden near the smaller and more secluded Motosu-ko, Shoji-ko and Sai-ko. Some recommended visits include the Narusawa Ice Cave and Fugaku Wind Cave, both formed by the volcanic activities of one of Fuji's early eruptions.

Hakone is set against the backdrop of Fuji-san and has long been a popular place for rest and recreation. Hakone's 16 hot springs are nestled in a shallow ravine where the Hayakawa and Sukumo rivers flow together. The inns here have natural mineral baths. If you are on a daytrip, the Tenzan public bath provides a hot-spring treat for just a few hundred yen. Miyanoshita is the oldest and the most thriving of the spa towns.

Note: The area around Mt Fuji is probably the most popular in Japan. As such, it can be highly commercial and very crowded. ❑

RIGHT: the unmistakable sight of Japan's sacred mountain capped with snow.

NIKKO

Known as much for its autumn splendour as for its Buddhist temples embellished with carvings and details, Nikko is less than two hours away from the claustrophobia of metropolitan Tokyo

After learning that the main attraction at Nikko, a temple called Tosho-gu, comprises 42 structures and that 29 of these are embellished with some sort of carving – 5,147 in all, according to a six-year-long survey concluded in 1991 – more than a few travellers begin to realise that they've allotted too little time for Nikko.

The small city of **Nikko** ⓫ itself is of little interest, serving merely as a commercial anchor to the splendours that decorate the nearby hillsides and plateau across the river to the west from the main railway stations. The Tobu train arrives exactly (and a watch can be set by it) 101 minutes after departing Tokyo's Ueno Station, a fact that the railway's advertising department has made a catchphrase for years.

How this region – once a several-day trek from the shogunate's capital in Edo (present-day Tokyo) – was chosen as the site of Tokugawa Ieyasu's mausoleum is a story in itself. True, Nikko forms a sort of crown at the northern perimeter of the great Kanto Plain, of which Edo was the centre. However, Ieyasu was from Kansai, not Kanto, and he had established his capital in Kanto primarily to distance himself from the imperial forces in Kansai's Kyoto, forces he had vanquished to seize power in the first place.

Still, Ieyasu's grandson Iemitsu (1604–51) set in motion the process that turned this once out-of-the-way region into Tokugawa territory about 20 years after Ieyasu's death. In fact, Iemitsu himself and his successor Ietsuna – and the Tokugawa shoguns and princes for the next 250 years – made at least three annual pilgrimages to the site to pay tribute to the founder of the dynasty that kept Japan and its people isolated from the outside world.

BELOW: old print of Tosho-gu's pagoda.

Through the gates

Ironically, however, given the Tokugawa aversion to things from outside Japan, many of the 5,000-odd carvings at **Tosho-gu** depict things foreign. The facade of the main shrine, for example, features carvings of three Chinese men, said to represent important figures of that country who, having turned down their chances to be kings or emperors, became folk heroes. Perhaps the carvings are meant to convey the fallacy that Ieyasu came to power only after the Toyotomi emperor had voluntarily abdicated in his favour.

Most ironic of all – and most hypocritical, considering its importance in the annals of Japanese art – is the famous, not to say fabulous, **Yomei-mon**, the gate beyond which only the highest-ranking samurai could pass into the inner sanctum of the shrine, and then only after laying aside their swords. This gate is a masterpiece. Technically, it is a 12-column, two-storey structure with hip-gable ends on right and left, and with cusped gables on four sides. This description, while accurate, is somewhat misleading, however. Even though its *keyaki*-wood columns are painted white to make it appear larger, the gate is quite small. Nearly every surface of the gate is adorned with delicate carvings of every sort – children at play, clouds, tree peonies, pines, bamboo, Japanese apricots, phoenixes, pheasants, cranes, wild ducks and other waterfowl, turtles, elephants, rabbits, a couple of furry tigers, Chinese lions, and the traditional symbols of regal power, dragons.

A large, white dragon (one of 92 in and around the shrine) is the main feature of the central beam in front of the second storey of this fanciful structure, and two drawings of dragons appear on the ceiling of the porticos. The drawing nearer the entrance is known as *nobori-ryu* or ascending dragon, while the other is *kudari-ryu* or descending dragon.

Building at Tosho-gu.

Keep in mind that although it is designated a National Treasure and is considered an example of the heights of Japanese art, Yomei-mon's (and many of the other treasures at Nikko) nameless artisans were of Korean, not Japanese, origin. This is no small matter, given the sense of racial and cultural superiority that the Japanese tend to claim over Koreans.

What lies beyond this gate? Another gate, of course: **Kara-mon** (Chinese Gate), also a National Treasure. It is smaller than the Yomei-mon (at about 3 by 2 metres overall) and is also laden with carvings – dragons (ascending and descending, and lounging around), apricots, bamboo, tree peonies, and more.

The ceiling has a carved figure of a fairy playing a harp, while on the ridge of the front gable is a bronze figure of a *tsutsuga*, which like quite a few other

BELOW: Tosho-gu's inner courtyard.

carvings and castings in the shrine precincts is not quite a real animal, but rather one created from hearsay and ancient myth and mixed with a healthy (Korean, perhaps) imagination.

To help get your bearings, the Kara-mon is the last barrier to pass through before reaching the entrance to the *haiden* (oratory) and the *honden* (main hall), which is the place most visitors remember as they are requested to remove shoes. An official guidebook describes *haiden* and *honden* as the "chief edifices of the shrine". Chief they are, but interesting they are not – at least not to the casual visitor who, not knowing what to look for, tends to shuffle along with the crowd and then returns to the shoe lockers without a pause.

Explaining Shinto's lack of ethical codes: "It is because the Japanese were truly moral in their practice that they require no theory of morals."
– MOTO-ORI NORINAGA (1730–1801)

Unfortunately, many of the key elements inside are partially or entirely hidden from the view achieved by this method. Confused (and no doubt somewhat bored) after their shuffle through the "chief edifices", most visitors exit, redon their shoes and spend the next 10 minutes or so looking for the famous **Nemuri-neko**, or carving of the Sleeping Cat. Some never find it at all and make their way back down the hillside feeling somewhat cheated. To make sure this doesn't happen to you, do not follow the logical path back toward the Yomei-mon. Instead, turn left (right if facing the *haiden/honden* complex) until you are back on the terrace between Yomei-mon and Kara-mon. Next, advance straight ahead (paying the small fee charged at a makeshift entrance to the Oku no In, or Inner Precincts) and into the open-sided, red-lacquered corridor that skirts the foot of the steep hillside, atop of which is the actual Tokugawa tomb. Nemuri-neko, a painted relief carving, is over the gateway.

This small grey cat, well-enough executed and rather cute but otherwise unremarkable, is said to symbolise tranquillity. The fact that it is asleep is taken to

BELOW: storage casks of sake at Nikko temple.

mean that all "harmful mice" have been sent packing and the shrine is therefore safe. The carved sparrows behind the dozing cat presumably aren't a threat.

Shogunate tomb

While here, climb the 200-odd stone steps to the top of the hill and the Tokugawa tomb, called **Hoto**, wherein it is said are the remains of Tokugawa Ieyasu. Some spectacular views of rooftops and the surrounding terrain are had from here. On the way past Tosho-gu, through the Yomei-mon to the main entrance and beyond, be sure to stop by the **Yakushido**, one of the few places in these sacred Shinto surroundings with a Buddhist atmosphere. It's off to the right. Here, too, remove shoes. The attraction of this building (it is not exactly a Buddhist temple) is the huge *naku-ryu*, or crying dragon, drawing on the ceiling. It seems that when people stood under the original – drawn in India ink by Kano Yasunobu (1613–85) – and clapped their hands as in prayer, the dragon was heard to utter a long, agonised groan. What this was meant to signify is not recorded and perhaps we will never know, because in 1961 a fire destroyed the building – and the original drawing along with it.

Among the other sights to take note of as one leaves the shrine are the sutra library, which boasts nearly 7,000 volumes of the Buddhist sutras in a large, revolving bookcase that was invented by the Chinese. Its other treasures include numerous stone, bronze and iron lanterns presented by the *daimyo* paying their respects to the shogunate and a pair of stone *tobikoe no shishi* (leaping lions) as the main pillars of the stone balustrade.

The bronze candelabrum, bronze lantern and large revolving lantern were presented by the government of the Netherlands to Japan in 1636. The revolv-

¥1,000 discount tickets providing admission to the Tosho-gu, Futarasan shrine and Rinno-ji temple, are available at the desk in front of the Rinno-ji Treasure House.

BELOW: images in stone of the shogun's samurai.

ing lantern in front of the drum tower is adorned with the three-leaf crests of the Tokugawa clan, but they are placed upside down, perhaps, as an official guidebook to the sutra library explains, "by mistake".

The 19th-century traveller Isabella Bird wrote of a visit to Nikko, "To pass from court to court is to pass from splendour to splendour; one is almost glad to feel that this is the last, and that the strain on one's capacity for admiration is nearly over."

Here, also, are the sacred storehouses on the sides of the middle court. The upper one shows two elephants carved in relief, as well as the *mikoshi-gura* (sacred palanquin house), the repository for the sacred portable shrines used in the annual festival, and the *kagura-den* (sacred dance stage). The flower basket in the gilded panel at the right corner was probably inspired by a basket used by early Dutch traders; it is the only carving in the precincts that shows Western artistic influences.

Beyond the 40-metre (130-ft) high five-storey pagoda, its first storey decorated with the 12 signs of the Chinese zodiac, and just before reaching the 9-metre (30-ft) tall **Omote-mon** (Front Gate), with its large images of the two deva kings, there is what may be the most famous carvings of all – not just in Nikko, but in all the world. Just under the eaves of the royal stables building, which is the only unlacquered structure in the shrine precincts, are the **Three Monkeys**: hear no evil, speak no evil, see no evil. Small carvings they are, despite their fame, but so too are all 5,000-plus carvings at Tosho-gu.

Just a short stroll down the broad avenue leading from the Thousand Steps (there are only 10) entrance to Tosho-gu is the **Tosho-gu Homotsu-kan** (Tosho-gu Treasure House; daily 8.30am–5pm, Oct–Mar 9am–4pm; admission fee), a small museum housing various ancient articles, including carvings, from Tosho-gu and other places around Nikko. During peak tourist seasons, a number of kiosks will set up in the small adjoining park, Koyoen, to sell beverages and food, lending a commercial flair to the area.

BELOW: one of Nikko's bridges.

Continue west along the wide avenue for a few minutes to reach **Futarasan-jinja**, on the right side and away from Tosho-gu. Futarasan-jinja enshrines the three primary Shinto deities: Okuninushi no Mikoto, his consort Tagorihime no Mikoto, and their son Ajisukitakahikone no Mikoto. All three are revered for having helped to create and then make prosperous the Japanese islands.

Within the grounds is a large bronze lantern called **Bake-doro** (Goblin Lantern), which is said to have once taken on the shape of a goblin so frightening that a samurai attacked it one night, leaving "sword scratches" that are still visible to this day.

Amongst the world's major religions, Shinto is unique, with a supreme being, the Sun Goddess or Amaterasu Omikami, that is female.

Beyond Tosho-gu

Further afield but still within the general area of Tosho-gu are several other places of interest. One is the **Hon-gu**, established in 767 by the priest Shodo and one of the oldest shrines in Nikko. The present buildings date back only to the end of the 17th century, when the shrine was rebuilt after being destroyed by fire. Just behind it is **Shihonryu-ji**, also founded by Shodo. In fact, it is not a Shinto shrine but rather a Buddhist temple. It also was destroyed by fire and the present three-storey pagoda was erected in its place at the end of the 17th century. The pagoda and the image of the thousand-hand Kannon inside are the temple's main attractions.

Then there is **Rinno-ji**, a temple of the Tendai sect of Buddhism. Its significant claim is the fact that General Ulysses S. Grant, the 18th president of the United States and a hero of the American Civil War, stayed here during his eight-day sojourn to Japan and Nikko in 1879. It was one of Grant's few trips outside of North America. Actually, the temple has more than Grant-slept-here

BELOW: the lake at Chuzenji.

going for it. In its spirit hall are the tablets of its long line of abbots, all drawn from the imperial family. In another building, built in 1648 and still the largest in Nikko, are three quite amazing Buddhist statues, all measuring 8 metres (26 ft) in height and worked in gilded wood. The Bato Kannon, on the left, has the figure of a horse's head on its forehead and is the deity for animal protection.

With queues of up to one hour for some of the popular attractions, Disneyland can be a tiresome place. Most salaried workers in Japan get paid on the 25th of the month. Crowds at the Magic Kingdom are noticeably thinner in the week before that date.

In the forests and into the hills

The lush forests of Nikko are filled with ancient trees. The majority are *suji*, or Japanese cedar. When veiled in mist, one might think they have stood here since the beginning of time, or at the very least are part of a primeval virgin forest. They don't go back quite that far, but they are nevertheless very old, especially those trees in the Tosho-gu precincts proper and along the many kilometres of avenues and roads within and leading to Nikko. These cedars were planted as seedlings, one by one, from year to year, under the direction of a man named Matsudaira Masatsuna (1576–1648).

Matsudaira, so the story goes, was the *daimyo* of Kawagoe and one of the two persons honoured by edict of the shogun to supervise the construction of Tosho-gu. The extent of the man's personal wealth is not recorded nor how much of it was spent, in addition to the budget he was given by the Tokugawa shogun, in planting these trees.

However, it can be assumed that he wasn't very well off to begin with. When his turn to present a grand offering to the shrine came – as all the other *daimyo* were obliged to do – Matsudaira was broke. What could he do as an offering, he wondered. Around 1631, several years before the shrine itself was finished, he began to transplant cedar seedlings – plentiful in the surrounding mountains (which he owned) – into strategic positions around the shrine grounds and along the seemingly endless roads. It took him 20 years and an estimated 25,000 seedlings. Today, these trees are what in part define Nikko and its surroundings for travellers. The beneficence continues. The trees and the banks along the avenues are protected as Natural Treasures and Places of Historical Importance under Japanese law.

BELOW: fishing on Chuzenji-ko.

Thanks to the numbers of visitors who flock to Nikko and the region's fine scenery, the area abounds with other diversions. Unfortunately, getting around without a vehicle is a problem. If money permits, rent a car (not cheap). If time permits, take a taxi or a bus (this will take longer) up the famed I-Ro-Ha switchback road to **Chuzenji-ko** ⓬, a large and quite picturesque lake due west of Nikko. From there, savour the altitude of 1,270 metres (4,170 ft), clear air and lakeside scenery. A sightseeing boat leaves the pier, just across the road from the bus stop, for a one-hour tour of the lake. Its heavily wooded shores are lined with hotels, inns, campsites, and other tourist wonders. Five minutes walk in the opposite direction is the observatory of the 100-metre (320-ft) high **Kegon Falls** (Kegon no Taki); a lift descends right to the bottom of the gorge (open daily) where a platform allows views of the thundering falls. If you choose not to stay overnight at the lake, try one of the several *onsen* on the picturesque Kinu-gawa, closer to Nikko itself.

Also in the area of the Kinu-gawa is **Nikko Edo-mura**, a theme park. The not-so-cheap entrance fee entitles one to stroll around the extensive grounds on streets that look like a movie set of the old Edo days. There is a "real" *ninja* show, a mock trial in a magistrate's court, and many other attractions. It is great entertainment and an enjoyable way to learn about the old days of pre-Meiji Japan.

Mashiko

Synonymous with a rustic, earthenware ceramic, the village of **Mashiko** ⓭, just 30 km (20 miles) southeast of Nikko, is a living pottery village, with some 300 working kilns scattered among the surrounding paddy fields. Mashiko is easily accessed by *shinkansen*, a 50-minute ride from Tokyo to Utsunomiya Station, where buses can be boarded for the one-hour ride to the village.

Although Mashiko has been a craft village for over a millennium, its name was made in the 1930s when renowned potter Hamada Shoji built a kiln here, later to be joined by English ceramicist Bernard Leach. Hamada's house and kiln, located in the **Togei Messe** (Tues–Sun 9.30am–5pm, winter till 4pm) complex, have been lovingly restored. Several tourist information booths located in Utsunomiya Station provide leaflets and maps in English. A lively village with dozens of ceramic shops and stalls, Mashiko stages regular pottery fairs and festivals.

Hamada Shoji has been a great influence to potters all over the world. His glazing techniques are greatly copied and admired; temmoku *iron glaze, rice-husk ash glaze, and* kaki *persimmon glaze have become his trademarks.*

Disneyland and Chiba

Besides Narita Airport, what brings most visitors east to Chiba Prefecture today is **Tokyo Disneyland** ⓮ (daily; hours vary with the season; admission fee;

BELOW: Minnie and friends at Tokyo Disneyland.

Map on page 162

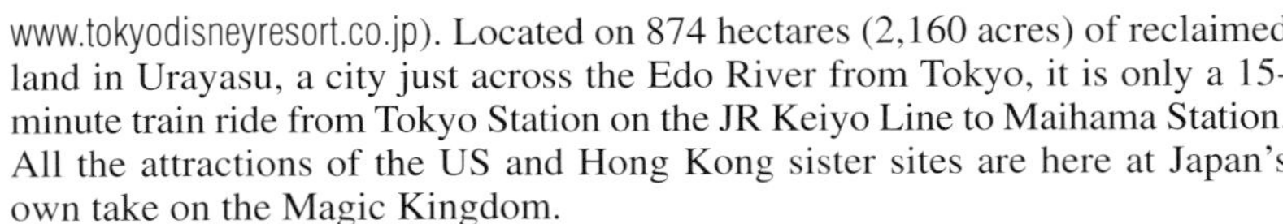

www.tokyodisneyresort.co.jp). Located on 874 hectares (2,160 acres) of reclaimed land in Urayasu, a city just across the Edo River from Tokyo, it is only a 15-minute train ride from Tokyo Station on the JR Keiyo Line to Maihama Station. All the attractions of the US and Hong Kong sister sites are here at Japan's own take on the Magic Kingdom.

Adjacent is a newer, contingent complex, the very popular **DisneySea Park** which offers attractions designed along aquatic themes and legends. You may want to spend a whole day at each park *(see page 380)*. Directly and indirectly, Tokyo Disneyland is responsible for 96,000 jobs – its total economic impact on par with Japan's camera industry.

Descend a long flight of steps from Nokogiri-yama and visit Japan's largest figure of the Buddha, the Yakushi Nyorai. The base to the tip of the giant lotus bud that stands behind the statue's head measures an impressive 31 metres (100 ft).

Around Narita

Most people are in a hurry to leave Narita Airport (officially known as the New Tokyo International Airport), which is a shame as the area has much to offer. First and foremost is Shinsho-ji, usually referred to simply as **Narita-san**. A 15-minute walk from JR Narita or Keisei stations, this temple, said to date back to AD 940, is one of the most important in the entire Kanto region, drawing 12 million visitors a year, worshippers and sightseers alike, especially during the first three days of the New Year. It is the headquarters of the Shingon sect of esoteric Buddhism. The three-storey pagoda in front of the Great Main Hall is the original 18th century building and is richly decorated with golden dragons' heads. A large garden with rivers and ornamental ponds is adjacent to the temple. Narita-san is also well known for its drive-in chapel at the side of the complex that welcomes drivers – and their vehicles – to be blessed by a priest and, for a fee, to be adorned with lucky amulets to protect against accidents.

Below: Narita-san temple.
Right: autumn colours in Nikko.

For a digest of Japanese social history, the **Kokuritsu Rekishi Minzoku Hakubutsukan** (National Museum of Japanese History; Tues–Sun, Mar–Sept 9.30am–5pm, Oct–Feb 9.30am–4.30pm; admission fee) in the former castle town of **Sakura**, is a short hop from the airport on the Keisei and JR Sobu lines. The comprehensive museum is set within the extensive landscaped grounds.

Nokogiri-yama ⓯ (Saw Mountain) is located along the southwestern coastal region of Chiba's Boso Peninsula. It was known for its Boshu-seki stone from the 14th to the 18th century. The sites of the quarries left jagged edges resembling a saw, hence its name. The foot of Nokogiri-yama is a short walk from Hamakanaya Station on the JR Uchibo Line.

A cable car (daily 9am–4pm) takes visitors halfway up the mountain, a number of steep flights of steps providing enough physical effort to enforce the sensation of being a pilgrim, at least for the day. The top of the mountain affords a fine panorama of Tokyo Bay and Mount Fuji. On exceptionally clear days (Sundays and national holidays are good bets), far away Suruga Bay in Shizuoka Prefecture can also be glimpsed.

The holy mountain has quite an illustrious history with enough sights to please everyone, including a 33-metre (110-ft) Kannon, Goddess of Mercy, carved into the rockface near the top of the mountain, and a cluster of 1,553 stone statues of *rakan* (disciples of the Buddha). ❑

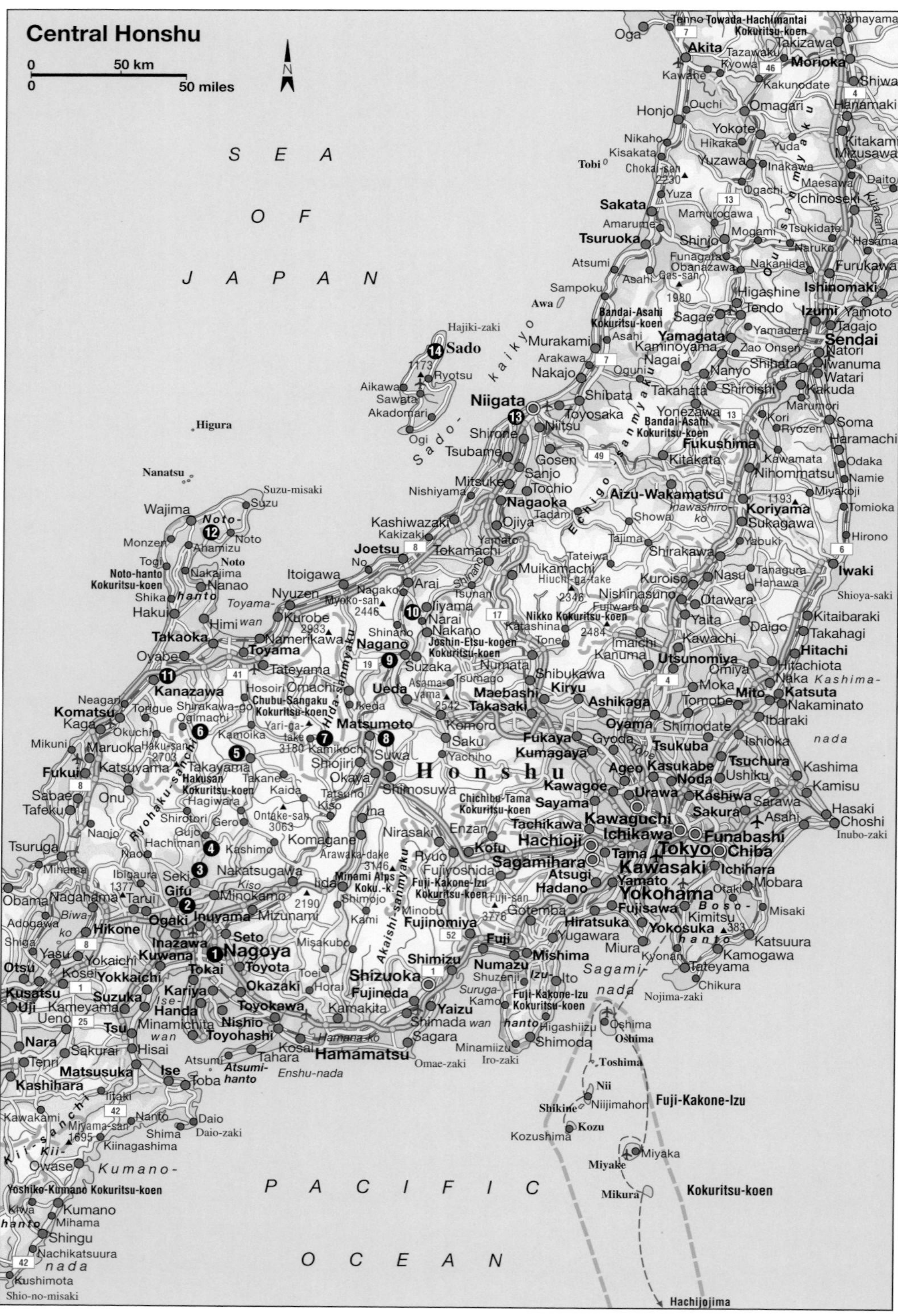

Central Honshu
0 50 km
0 50 miles
N
SEA OF JAPAN
PACIFIC OCEAN
Honshu
Oga
Tenno
Towada-Hachimantai Kokuritsu-koen
Tamayama
Akita
Tazawako
Takizawa
Morioka
Kawabe
Kyowa
Kakunodate
Shiwa
Honjo
Ouchi
Omagari
Hanamaki
Yokote
Nikaho
Hikaka
Yuda
Kitakami
Mizusawa
Kisakata
Tobi
Chokai-san
2230
Yuzawa
Inakawa
Maesawa
Daito
Yuza
Ogachi
Ichinoseki
Sakata
Mamurogawa
Amarume
Mogami
Tsukidate
Tsuruoka
Shinjo
Naruko
Hasama
Funagata
Obanazawa
Nakaniida
Furukawa
Atsumi
Asahi
Gas-san
1980
Sampoku
Higashine
Ishinomaki
Awa
Tendo
Izumi
Yamoto
Bandai-Asahi Kokuritsu-koen
Sagae
Yamadera
Tagajo
Asahi
Yamagata
Sendai
Murakami
Kaminoyama
Zao Onsen
Natori
Arakawa
Nagai
Iwanuma
Nakajo
Oguni
Nanyo
Shibata
Watari
Shiroishi
Kakuda
Shibata
Takahata
Marumori
Niigata
Toyosaka
Yonezawa
Kori
Soma
Bandai-Asahi Kokuritsu-koen
Ryozen
Haramachi
Niitsu
Shirone
Fukushima
Tsubame
Gosen
Kitakata
Kawamata
Odaka
Sanjo
Nihommatsu
Namie
Mitsuke
Tochio
Miyakoji
Nishiyama
Nagaoka
Aizu-Wakamatsu
1193
Tomioka
Tadami
Inawashiro-ko
Koriyama
Ojiya
Showa
Sukagawa
Kashiwazaki
Hirono
Kakizaki
Yamato
Tajima
Yabuki
Joetsu
Tokamachi
Tateiwa
Shirakawa
No
Shinano
Muikamachi
Tanagura
Iwaki
Itoigawa
Arai
Hiuchi-ga-take
Kuroiso
Nasu
Hanawa
Nyuzen
Nagako
2346
Nishinasuno
Shioya-saki
Myoko-san
Iiyama
Tsunan
Fujiwara
Otawara
Kurobe
2446
Narai
Nikko Kokuritsu-koen
Yaita
Kitaibaraki
2933
Nakano
Katashina
2484
Daigo
Takahagi
Namerikawa
Shinano
Tone
Imaichi
Kawachi
Toyama
Nagano
Joshin-Etsu-kogen Kokuritsu-koen
Kanuma
Utsunomiya
Hitachi
Tateyama
Suzaka
Numata
Omiya
Hitachiota
Ueda
Asama-yama
Tsumago
Shibukawa
Kiryu
Moka
Naka
Kashima-nada
Mito
Katsuta
Hosoiri
Omachi
2542
Maebashi
Ashikaga
Tomobe
Nakaminato
Chubu-Sangaku Kokuritsu-koen
Ikeda
Takasaki
Hida-sanmyaku
Matsumoto
Komoro
Oyama
Shimodate
Ibaraki
Yari-ga-take
3180
Kamikochi
Saku
Fukaya
Gyoda
Tsukuba
Ishioka
Suwa
Yachiho
Kumagaya
Shiojiri
Ageo
Kasukabe
Tsuchura
Kashima
Okaya
Noda
Ushiku
Kamisu
Shimosuwa
Chichibu-Tama Kokuritsu-koen
Kawagoe
Urawa
Kashiwa
Sawara
Tatsuno
Sayama
Sakura
Hasaki
Kiso
Ina
Asahi
Choshi
Ontake-san
3063
Enzan
Tachikawa
Kawaguchi
Inubo-zaki
Nirasaki
Hachioji
Ichikawa
Funabashi
Komagane
Kofu
Tama
Tokyo
Chiba
Arawaka-dake
3146
Ryuo
Sagamihara
Kawasaki
Ichihara
Iida
Fujiyoshida
Atsugi
Yamato
Mobara
Minami Alps Koku.-k.
Fuji-Kakone-Izu Kokuritsu-koen
Hadano
Yokohama
Otaki
Akaishi-sanmyaku
Fuji-san
3776
Gotemba
Fujisawa
Boso-hanto
Misaki
2190
Shimojo
Minobu
Hiratsuka
Kimitsu
Kami
Fujinomiya
Yokosuka
383
Katsuura
Yugawara
Miura
Fuji
Mishima
Kyonan
Kamogawa
Shimizu
Numazu
Tateyama
Shizuoka
Shuzenji
Izu-hanto
Ito
Sagami-nada
Chikura
Fujineda
Suruga-wan
Kamo
Fuji-Kakone-Izu Kokuritsu-koen
Nojima-zaki
Yaizu
Higashiizu
Oshima
Shimada
Shimoda
Sagara
Minamiizu
Iro-zaki
Omae-zaki
Toshima
Nii
Shikine
Niijimahon
Fuji-Kakone-Izu
Kozu
Kozushima
Miyaka
Miyake
Mikura
Kokuritsu-koen
Hachijojima
Hajiki-zaki
Sado
Sado-kaikyo
1173
Ryotsu
Aikawa
Sawata
Akadomari
Ogi
Higura
Nanatsu
Suzu-misaki
Suzu
Wajima
Noto-hanto
Noto
Monzen
Anamizu
Togi
Noto
Nakajima
Noto-hanto Kokuritsu-koen
Nanao
Shika
Toyama-wan
Hakui
Himi
Takaoka
Oyabe
Kanazawa
Neagari
Komatsu
Torigue
Shirakawa-go
Kaga
Ogimachi
Okuchi
Kamioka
Mikuni
Maruoka
Haku-san
2703
Fukui
Katsuyama
Takayama
Takane
Hakusan Kokuritsu-koen
Ryohaku-sanchi
Kaida
Sabae
Ono
Hagiwara
Tafeku
Shirotori
Gero
Nanjo
Hachiman
Tsuruga
Nao
Kashimo
Mihama
Ibigaura
Seki
Nakatsugawa
1377
Gifu
Tarui
Minokamo
Obama
Nagahama
Biwa-ko
Ogaki
Inuyama
Mizunami
Adogawa
Hikone
Seto
Shiga
Inazawa
Misakubo
Yasu
Nagoya
Kuwana
Toyota
Yokaichi
Otsu
Tokai
Kosei
Yokkaichi
Toei
Horai
Okazaki
Kusatsu
Suzuka
Kariya
Uji
Kameyama
Ise-wan
Handa
Toyokawa
Kamakita
Ueno
Nishio
Minamichita
Toyohashi
Hamana-ko
Nara
Sakurai
Hisai
Kosai
Tahara
Hamamatsu
Tenri
Atsumi
Atsumi-hanto
Enshu-nada
Matsusuka
Ise
Toba
Kashihara
Iitaki
Kawakami
Nanto
Daio
Miyama-san
Shima
Daio-zaki
1695
Kii-sanchi
Kii-hanto
Kiinagashima
Owase
Kumano-nada
Yoshiko-Kumano Kokuritsu-koen
Kiwa
Kumano
Mihama
Shingu
Nachikatsuura
Kushimota
Shio-no-misaki

CENTRAL HONSHU

Map on page 186

Central Honshu offers an industrialised Pacific coastline, lofty hot springs and skiing in the so-called Japan Alps, and a rugged and often isolated coast along the Sea of Japan

Known for its flat, white *kishimen* noodles, its pickles known as *moriguchi-zuke*, and its confection called *uiro*, **Nagoya** ❶ is better recognised as a centre of industry, producing construction materials and automobiles. Nagoya is located almost precisely in the centre of Japan along the old Tokaido highway and is a major transport hub to and from other cities, including Tokyo and Osaka. Japan's fourth-largest city with a little over 2 million people, Nagoya is primarily an industrial city with just a few sights for the traveller.

Nagoya was originally planned by the shogun Tokugawa Ieyasu to be a castle town. He built **Nagoya-jo** (Nagoya Castle; daily 9am–4.30pm; admission fee) in 1612 for his ninth son, Yoshinao, but the town didn't really develop into a powerful presence. Much later, Nagoya had to be redesigned and reconstructed after suffering extensive air-raid damage in 1945. The castle, rebuilt in 1959 and now functioning as a cultural and historical museum, is considered Nagoya's primary attraction. The museum displays treasures of the Tokugawa family.

Nagoya's **Atsuta-jingu** is second only to the Ise-jingu, in Mie Prefecture, in its importance to the emperor of Japan and Shintoism. One of the imperial family's three sacred treasures, the Kusanagi sword *(kusanagi no tsurugi)*, is kept here. (The other two sacred treasures, the jewel and mirror, are kept at the Imperial Palace in Tokyo and at Ise, respectively.) All three treasures are said to have been given to the imperial family by the sun goddess Amaterasu Omikami. None are viewable by the public. Hundreds of ancient trees thrive amidst ancient artefacts, including the 600-year-old Nijugocho-bashi, a bridge made of 25 blocks of stone. The shrine's festival is in June.

BELOW: making ornamentation for a new shrine.

There are museums all over Nagoya, ranging from the treasure-laden **Tokugawa Art Museum** (open Tues–Sun 10am–5pm; admission fee), displaying heirlooms of the Owari-Tokugawa family, to the **Aichi Bijutsukan** (Fine Arts Museum), which often displays the works of Japan's up-and-coming artists. Visitors may participate in a quiet tea ceremony at the Tokugawa Art Museum, where once a year the exquisite but fragile scroll of the *Genji Monogatari*, or *Tale of Genji* is on view. East of the station in the entertainment and shopping district of Sakae, the **Design Museum** (Wed–Mon 11am–8pm; admission fee), on the fourth floor of the Nadya Park Design Centre Building, has a fascinating collection of commercial products and hi-tech objects.

Outside of Nagoya

Some 25 km (15½ miles) north of Nagoya is **Inuyama**, site of Japan's oldest castle (built in the mid-1400s). Standing in its original state above the Kiso-gawa, it has been owned by the same family since the 1600s. A little east of the castle, in the grounds of the Meitetsu Inuyama Hotel, is the exquisite **Uraku-en** (daily 9am–5pm, Dec–Feb till 4pm; admission fee) a lush garden replete with traditional teahouses. Near Inuyama is **Meiji-mura** (Meiji Village; daily 9.30am–5pm, Nov–Feb till 4pm, Dec–Feb closed Mon; admission fee), with 60 Meiji-era buildings collected from around Japan and reassembled here. Of special note is Frank Lloyd Wright's original Imperial Hotel, built in Tokyo and moved here when the new hotel was built. Every March, one of Japan's strangest festivals occurs not far from Inuyama, at a little shrine – **Tagata-jingu** – dedicated to phalluses. A huge and anatomically correct phallus is carried through the streets, and crowds of men and especially women try to touch it, hoping to enhance their fertility.

Kanto cats.

Further north of Nagoya, **Gifu** ❷ has a modern clothing industry. But for Japanese tourists, Gifu is undoubtedly better-known for its 200-year history of cormorant fishing *(uaki)* on the three rivers – the Kiso, Ibi and Nagara – that cut through the city. Today, *uaki* is distinctly a tourist attraction with the collared birds doing their thing at night, illuminated by small fires suspended in iron baskets from the front of the boats. Gifu's highly respected craftsmen add another touch of tradition to the city, especially its lantern and umbrella makers.

Gifu's castle commands an impressive view from the top of Kinka-zan (Golden Flower Mountain). It was built about seven centuries ago, has suffered numerous razings, and was rebuilt in 1956. A three-minute gondola ride to the foot of the mountain arrives at Gifu-koen (Gifu Park) and the Museum of History and the Nawa Insect Museum. The latter contains various bugs, butterflies and spiders – some of which are uncomfortably large – from around the world.

BELOW: harvesting of rice is by both machine and hand.

Finally, no summary of the Nagoya region would be complete without mention of **Seki ❸**, a sword-forging village a bit east of Gifu and the site of the Battle of Sekigahara, waged in the early 17th century between the forces of Tokugawa Ieyasu and Toyotomi Hideyori. The battle was a significant turning point in Japanese history and a catalyst for a complete shift in the archipelago's power structure. Although Tokugawa was outnumbered nearly two to one, his warriors slaughtered more than a third of the enemy troops to put Tokugawa on the shogun's throne, which he and his descendants held for the next 250-odd years. Today, only an unassuming stone marks the spot of Tokugawa's heroic triumph.

Gujo Hachiman

Writer and long-distance walker Alan Booth was quick to sense something special when he wrote about **Gujo Hachiman ❹** in his classic travelogue *Looking for the Lost*: "What I was in fact approaching was a town of a kind I'd dreamed of finding when I'd first arrived in Japan almost 20 years before, a town so extraordinary that, when I went out to stroll around it that evening, I almost forgot to limp."

Gujo sits at the confluence of the very clean and beautiful Nagara and Yoshino rivers, their *ayu* (sweetfish) rich waters popular with fishermen. The town sits in a mountain valley that long ago was a way station on an important trade route that led to the Sea of Japan. An imposing fortress once stood here. Built as a symbol of the town's former importance, the current castle, dating from 1934, replaced the original. It's a stiff walk to the pinnacle, but the views from the top are commanding. This is the best place to appreciate the shape of the town, which, as all the local travel information will tell you, resembles a fish.

Hashimoto-cho, an old merchant area, remains the commercial heart of the

If Caucasian or black, expect to be stared at, pointed at or talked about. When trying to talk with locals, know that the resulting giggles are not mocking, but indicative of embarrassment.

BELOW: a macaca monkey sitting in a hot spring.

town. Look behind the modern facades here and you will discover buildings, which, in some cases, have stood here for centuries. The physical fabric of the town is as appealing as the setting, consisting of dark, stained-wood homes and shops, white plastered buildings, wooden bridges, steep walls constructed from boulders, and narrow stone-paved lanes. Museums, galleries and attractive shops selling local products like Tsumugi textiles can be found along these lanes.

Fish and running water are the ever-present themes of this town, the latter a source in the summer months of contests in which young men, and these days also women, jump from a 7-metre (23-ft) high bridge into the deep, fast-flowing waters of the Nagara River. Raised above the river, a sunken stone basin proclaims that you have reached Sogisui, a natural spring. Although the English translation written on a marker reads "The Fountain of Youth", a closer rendering would be "water of the local god". An invitation to drink deeply of these waters is an invocation to good health and longevity.

Because of the 1998 Olympics, Nagano now has a bullet train line direct from Tokyo, making crowds more dense.

Takayama to the coast

High in the mountains is **Takayama ❺**, luring travellers with *onsen* (hot springs), hikes, tennis courts and other activities. Originally established in the 1500s as a castle town for the Kanamori family, Takayama retains an old charm nurtured by its *ryokan* (traditional inns), sake breweries and craft shops. **Takayama-jinya** (Administrative House; daily 8.45am–5pm, Nov–Feb till 4.30pm; admission fee) dates from the early 1600s; current buildings are early 19th-century reconstructions. Displays include a torture chamber.

In the centre of Takayama is Sanmachi Suji, with three streets lined by museums, traditional shops, sake breweries, and countless spots to eat. In the summer months it can be yet another tourist madhouse. Museums abound, but the not-to-miss museum is **Hida Minzoku-mura** (Hida Folk Village; daily 8.30am–5pm; admission fee), an open-air assembly of traditional houses that was collected from around the Takayama region and reassembled here. Artisans demonstrate regional folk crafts. The town is especially famous within Japan for two festivals: one in mid-April called Sanno *matsuri* (festival) with a procession of *yatai* (floats), and the Hachiman *matsuri* in October.

BELOW: early-morning fruit seller.

Shirakawa-go and Gokayama

A safe haven for the defeated Taira clan, the regions of Shirakawa-go and Gokayama were once so secluded that during the later Edo Period Lord Maeda secretly produced gunpowder here. Until a road was constructed in 1925, villages here, set among thickly forested mountain valleys, were virtually inaccessible. Not so these days, especially after the area's designation in 1995 as a UNESCO World Heritage Site, a mixed blessing guaranteeing the preservation of the region's unique architectural heritage, while inviting a blight of tourism on its fragile eco-structure. The beauty of the valleys and their distinctive A-frame thatched houses somehow manages to transcend the crowds.

The largest collection of steeply angled *gassho-zukuri* houses are concentrated in the village of **Ogimachi ❻**, easily accessed these days by buses from Takayama or Kanazawa. Hike up to an observation spot 10 minutes north of the main bus terminal for sweeping views of the valley and houses. **Wada-ke** (daily 9am–5pm; admission fee), the first notable structure walking back in the direction of the main village, is one of several museums. This one is a former family residence, once occupied by the Wada family, replete with household items and an impressive lacquer ware collection.

A little south, **Myozen-ji Temple Museum** (daily 9am–5pm; admission fee) is a large building even by local standards. The great beams of its five storeys, once used by monks and priests as living quarters, are blackened from smoke from the first-floor open hearth used for cooking and to provide warmth. An adjacent thatched temple and bell tower add to the mood.

Although it has a rather contrived feel, the **Gassho-zukuri Folklore Park** (Fri–Wed 8.30am–5pm; admission fee), a showcase collection of farmhouses relocated here after a dam on the nearby Sho-kawa threatened their existence, is well worth seeing. The open-air museum has 25 farmhouses and puts on demonstrations of weaving, carving and other handicrafts. Despite its World Heritage designation, Ogimachi, like all the villages here, is a working farming community. To get a sense of life here, an overnight stay in one of the *gassho-zukuri*, many now serving as guesthouses, is highly recommended.

Some 10 km (6 miles) from Ogimachi, the hamlet of **Suganuma** consists of just 14 houses, 10 of which are *gassho-zukuri*. Despite its diminutive scale, it has two interesting museums, the **Gokayama Minzoku-kan** and the **Ensho-no-Yakata**, the first displaying household items from daily life, the second highlighting the clandestine production of gunpowder.

Some 8 km (5 miles) north, **Ainokura** is another gem of rural architecture and life.

Map on page 186

Ogimachi is best known for its extraordinary, month-long Gujo Odori, or "Gujo Dance". Held at the height of the O-Ban, the August Festival of the Dead, in which the spirits of the departed are said to return, the entire town seems to erupt in a fever of all-night dancing.

EAVES DROP

The name for Shirakawa-go's unique style of farmhouses, known as *gassho-zukuri*, or "praying hands," comes from the sharp "A" shape of their wooden frames, designed to withstand deep snowdrifts in the winter months.

Gently soaring structures, the roofs alone can reach a depth of 9 metres (30 ft). Constructed without nails, the wooden beams, tightly secured with rope, are a tribute to the traditional skills of Japanese carpenters. The smoke from *irori* open-hearth fires rises through the buildings, blackening rope and wood with soot, but also preserving them and killing off termites and thatch bugs.

With the development of sericulture in the late 1800s, the upper floors under the eaves were used to raise silkworms. Up to 30 people could inhabit one house, parents and their immediate family sleeping in a private room, servants and unmarried sons sharing an entire floor or two.

As privacy was virtually impossible in such circumstances, couples would retreat to the nearest wood or glade for snatched moments of intimacy, a practice that manifested itself nine months after the end of winter, with a noticeable rise in the birth rate.

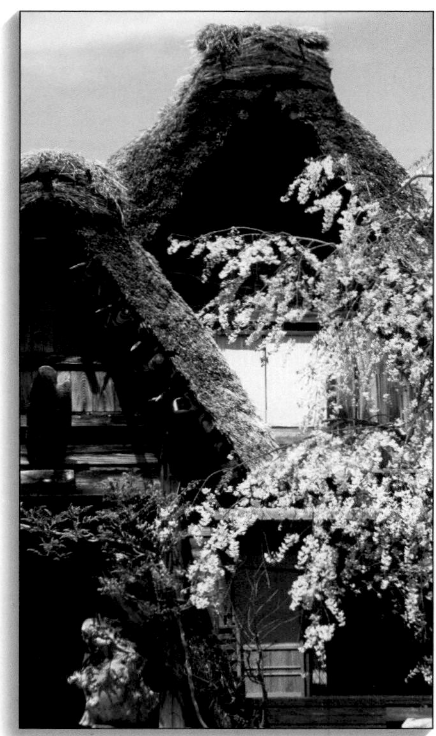

BELOW: thatched roofs at Shirakawa-go.

Walter Weston (1861–1940), an English clergyman, made mountain climbing in the "Japanese Alps" a popular sport. His appreciation of Japanese tradition and his love of nature can be read in his four volumes of work, including Mountaineering and Exploring in the Japanese Alps *(1896).*

Though requiring a 30-minute uphill hike from the village of Shimonashi, the village attracts a good number of visitors. The **Ainokura Minzoku-kan** (daily 8.30am–5pm) has interesting displays of local crafts, including handmade toys and paper, but it's the spectacular location of the village and endless meandering hiking trails leading from it across densely forested mountains, that visitors come for.

Kamikochi

In his novel *The House of Nire*, Kita Morio writes, "In the already fading light the linked peaks of the Alps were solid and harsh, all ranged there in the early dusk like a huge folding screen." One of the most ravishing panels of that folding screen, snow-dusted or gilded with sunlight according to the season, is Mount Hotaka and the high valley of **Kamikochi** ❼ at its feet.

The valley is a part of the **Chubu-Sangaku National Park** in the region of Nagano Prefecture known as Azumi. You know you have reached the area of Kamikochi when you begin to see cameo images of mountain peaks reflected in the ponds of the Azusa river basin.

The unsettling paradox of visiting a rural area crowded out with nature lovers can be avoided by visiting Kamikochi on a summer weekday, in early October, or in the spring shortly after the opening of the mountain road, which is unusable from 5 November to 30 April.

Most walkers set off from the bus terminal in the village, crossing the fast currents of the Azusa River by way of Kappa Bridge. The origin of this strange name (in Japanese folklore, *kappa* are malignant water sprites known in their worst tantrums of violence to tear a victim's bowels out through the anus) can only be guessed at.

BELOW: Nagoya Castle in spring.

After negotiating the bridge, trekkers usually pay brief homage at the Weston Memorial, which has a plaque dedicated to the Englishman who pioneered mountain climbing here at the turn of the 20th century. Trekkers then strike out on anything between a half-day and a full two-day-three-night circuit of a region many seasoned walkers regard as some of the finest hiking trails in Japan.

Matsumoto ❽ is popular in summer with Japanese heading off into the mountains on bikes and on foot. In the 14th century it was the castle town of the Ogasawara clan. **Matsumoto-jo** is an excellent example of a Japanese castle with its original donjon, dating from late 1590s. Three turrets and six floors are punctuated with fine historical displays and a nice view at the top. Adjacent to the castle is **Nihon Minzoku Shiryokan** (Japan Folkcraft Museum), with displays of regional artefacts and crafts, as well as flora and fauna.

Venue of the 1998 Winter Olympics, **Nagano** ❾ is a moderately sized city of half a million people and was established in the Kamakura Period as a temple town. That temple, Zenko-ji, dates from the 7th century and was the site for Ikko Sanzon, the first Buddha image in Japan. Northeast of Nagano, in Obuse, is the **Hokusai-kan** (Hokusai Museum; daily 9–5pm, Nov–Mar till 4.30 pm; admission fee), with a decent collection of Hokusai's *ukiyo-e*, or woodblock prints.

Map on page 186

Matsumoto was the home of Dr Suzuki Shin'ichi, the famous music teacher who encouraged children to play by his method. He believed that if taught a musical instrument properly, every child would be capable of high musical achievements.

Kiso Valley

Taking the Chuo Line southwest of Matsumoto you soon enter the Kiso Valley region between the Northern and Central Alps. The valley once formed part of the Nakasendo, one of the five key highways linking Edo with central Honshu. Despite vigorously promoted tourism, the region still manages to convey a sense of pre-industrial Japan.

The most affluent of the 11 post towns along the valley, **Narai** ❿ and its 1-km (½-mile) long main street boast some of the best-preserved wooden buildings in the valley. Look out for the exquisite lattice-work called *renji-goshi*, as fine as filigree. **Nakamura-tei** (daily 9am–4.30pm; admission fee), a former comb merchant's shop, is now a museum where you can pick up a pamphlet on local architecture. A second museum, the **Narakawa Folklore Museum** (daily 9am–5pm; Dec–Mar till 4pm; admission fee), houses a fine collection of local wares and lacquer. Unlike the other post towns along the valley, this one permits traffic to pass along its main street. Depending on your point of view, this spoils the town or confirms that it is a living, working community rather than a historical showcase.

Time permitting, a half-day stopover in **Kiso Fukushima**, a sleepy, far less touristy post town south of Narai, provides a nice respite from the crowds. Inns line the Narai-gawa. **Sumiyoshi-jinja**, an ancient shrine on a slope above the town, has an unusual sand and gravel garden designed by the modern landscape master Mirei Shigemori.

Following the Chuo Line south, **Tsumago** is a beautiful, well-appointed town whose carefully preserved buildings bespeak the efforts of the local community to restore and save their heritage. All high-tension wires and TV aerials have been eviscerated from the scene, improving it no doubt, but giving the impression of a

BELOW: a game of *bochi* is very therapeutic.

carefully managed open-air museum. It is still a beauty and well worth an overnight stay, if only to see the superb **Okuya Kyodokan** (daily 9am–4.45pm; admission fee), a folk museum located inside a spacious villa and former inn. The museum provides an excellent introduction to the town, with a large display of local products and daily items, as well as a fascinating photo display on the town before and after its restoration. Ask at the **tourist information office** (daily 8.30am–5pm) about a useful local service that arranges to have your luggage sent forward for you to your next accommodation in Magome, freeing you to follow the lovely 8-km (5-mile) hiking trail between the two towns.

The name of the southernmost post town of Magome means "horse basket". Travellers to the town would have to leave their horses there before encountering the mountainous trek to Magome Pass.

Where Tsumago is tucked into the valley, **Magome** clings to the side of a hill offering terrific views of nearby Mount Ena. The town suffered a series of fires, the worst in 1895, so it is not as old as the other towns, but its stone paths, wood and plaster buildings, many now serving as shops and inns, have a weathered quality that makes them feel older. Shimazaki Toson, a Meiji Period author, is the town's pride and joy. The **Toson Kinenkan** (daily 8.30am–4.45pm, Nov–Mar till 4.15pm; admission fee), a museum housed in a former inn, traces the writer's life through displays of original works and personal effects.

Sea of Japan coast

On the coast of the Sea of Japan, **Kanazawa** ⓫ came under the rule of the Maeda clan in the 16th century, a stewardship that lasted nearly three centuries and which supported a vigorous artistic effort. Lacking military or industrial targets, Kanazawa was spared bombing during World War II. Today, samurai houses in the Nagamachi area line twisting streets. **Kenroku-en** (Kenroku Garden; daily 7am–6pm, Oct–Feb 8am–4.30pm; admission fee) is considered one

Below: samurai houses in Nagamachi.

Map on page 186

of Japan's top gardens and has its heritage in an ancient Chinese garden from the Song dynasty. Feverishly crowded, the garden is not for the contemplative. Consider instead an excursion out onto **Noto-hanto** ⓬ (Noto Peninsula), which jabs out into the Sea of Japan like a crooked finger. The sedate eastern coast, encircling a bay, is moderately developed for tourism. The western coast, sculpted by the vigorous winds and currents of the Sea of Japan, is rocky and rustic. Noto's main town, **Wajima**, is noted for *Wajima-nuri*, a type of lacquerware. Wajima is also known for its morning market *(asa-ichi)*, which can take on a tourist-focused mood at times but is still worth a visit. North along the coast is **Niigata** ⓭ in the centre of Japan's Yukiguni, or Snow Country, of which novelist Kawabata Yasunari wrote in his 1947 novel *Yukiguni*. Except as a transit point, there is little in Niigata for foreign travellers.

Sado-jima

Two hours from Niigata by ferry, **Sado-jima** ⓮ was first an island of exile in the 13th century and later, during the Edo Period, a prison colony. Japan's fifth-largest (1,900 sq. km/850 sq. mile) island, Sado is mountainous and wonderfully accommodating in summer, but winters can be brutal. Sado is probably most famous for the Kodo drummers, from a village near **Ogi**. In August is the Earth Celebration, three days of world music – from Africa to Japan to Europe – and dance. Workshops are also offered, but if you are planning to go, transport and accommodation must be arranged well in advance. The island is associated in many Japanese minds with old, salt-encrusted temples, the clear bathing waters of its west coast, the old goldmine of **Sado Kinzan**, and *okesa*, Sado's haunting music of exile. ❑

BELOW: Kotoji stone lantern in Kenroku-en garden.

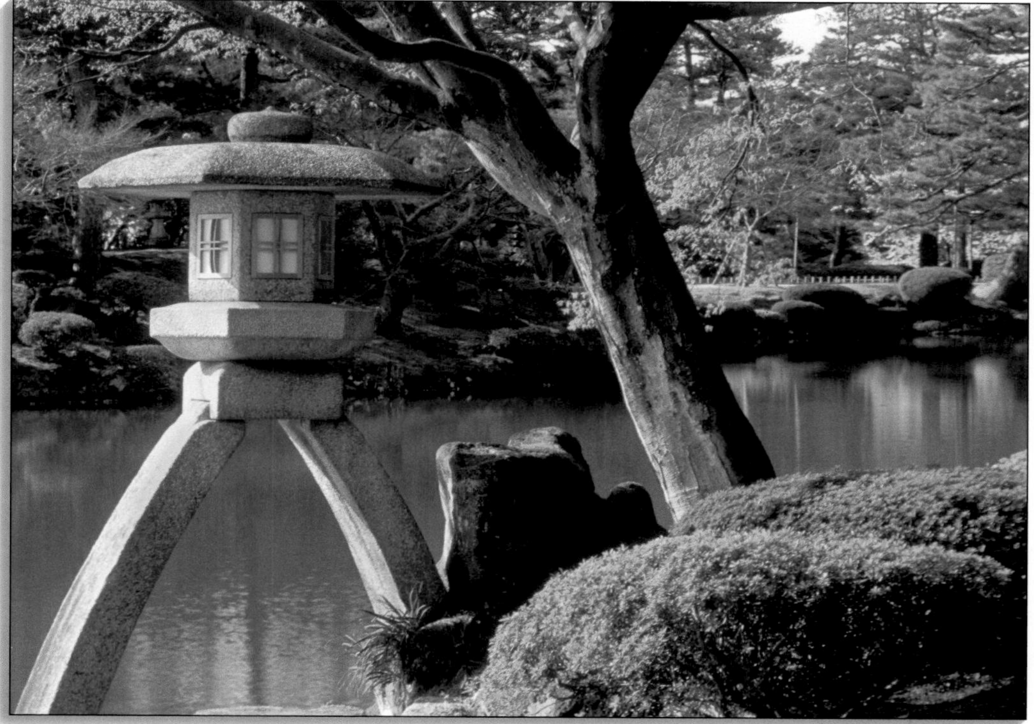

THE NORTH

Most Japanese regard the northern extents of Tohoku and Hokkaido as the ends of the earth, however close they are

"I might as well be going to the ends of the earth." That's how Basho, Japan's great 17th-century haiku poet, put it on the eve of his departure into the north in 1689. Back then, when Basho decided to prowl the back country, the roads were narrow and minimal, or non-existent. Today, Sendai, Tohoku's predominant city and north of Tokyo along the Pacific coast, is only two hours from Tokyo via *shinkansen*. Moreover, it is often mentioned as a new site for Japan's capital, should it be decided that Tokyo is just too big and too expensive and too congested.

Even the large island of Hokkaido, forcibly settled during the Meiji Restoration in the late 19th century, is but nine hours from Tokyo by train or two hours by plane. (In fact, the Tokyo–Sapporo air corridor is one of the world's busiest.)

The north has always been perceived as remote and strange, existing outside the normal sphere of Japanese life. Even imagining that such a place as Hokkaido exists, for example, is a romantic effort, as it is so different from the rest of Japan, rather like Alaska is to the contiguous US. But perhaps this is not so much a matter of distance as of psychology – there is a seemingly limitless amount of open space and nature untouched by people.

Undoubtedly, the northern mountains have a lot of to do with perceptions of remoteness. There are mountains everywhere in Japan, but those in the north tend to be bigger, more imposing and, from late autumn to mid-spring, not especially accommodating.

Then, too, the people of the north bear some responsibility. Tohoku was originally settled by itinerant warlords and soldiers who constructed castle fortresses to keep out potentially unfriendly neighbours, mostly from the south. These castle towns developed into insular communities with their own unique lifestyle, crafts, cottage industries and language. The famous *Tohoku-ben*, still spoken by many people here, is actually a series of subdialects with numerous variations. For people from elsewhere in Japan, it is a foreign language requiring, literally, a dictionary.

It is perhaps no longer an easy matter to find ourselves – as Basho was able to do – alone in some idyllic spot. Yet it is possible, and for the adventurous at heart (for a little while anyway), to lose oneself in the mysterious back country of the north. ❑

PRECEDING PAGES: farmland in southern Hokkaido.
LEFT: morning walk by a hot spring in Shiretoko Peninsula.

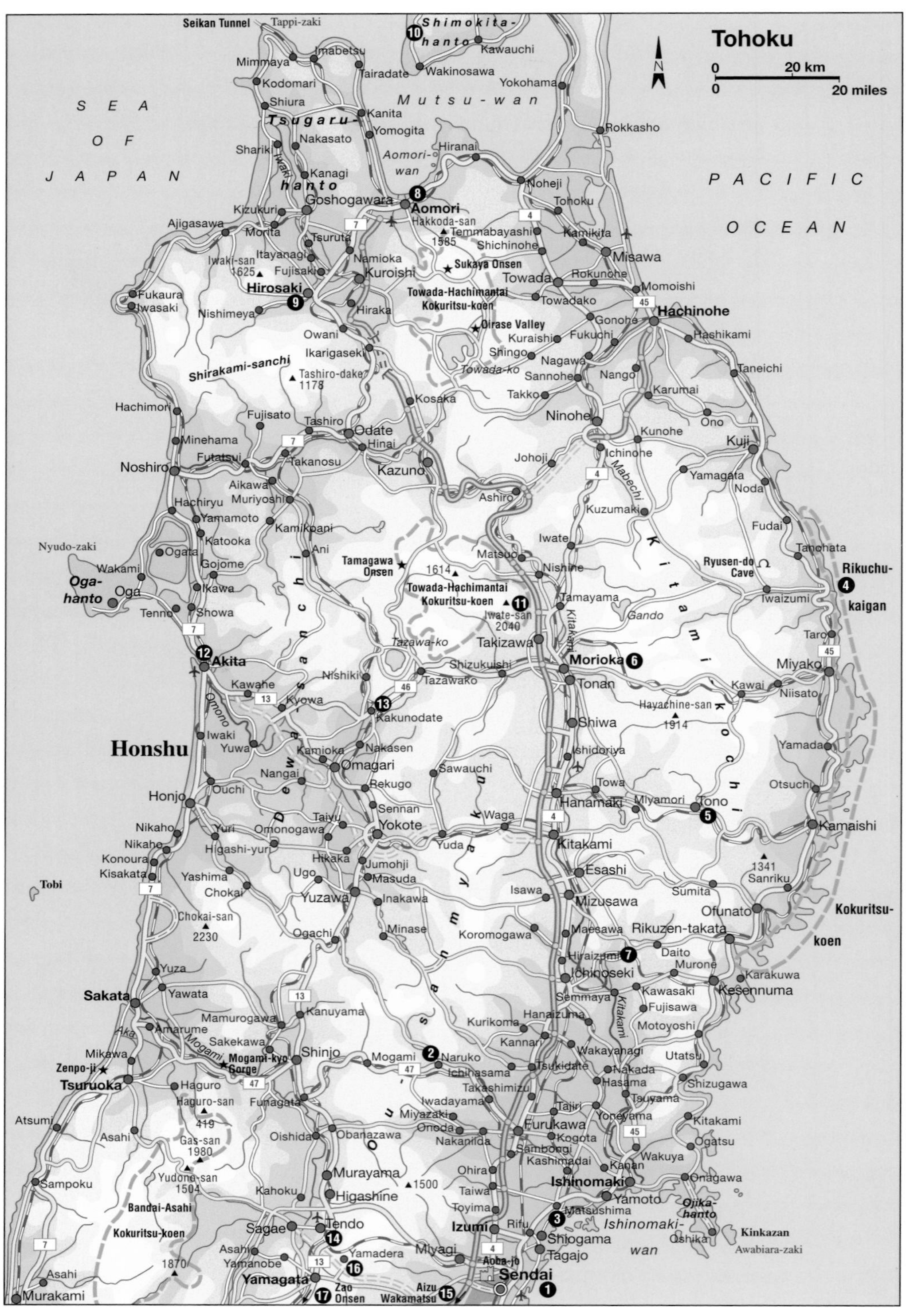
Tohoku
0
20 km
0
20 miles
N
SEA OF JAPAN
PACIFIC OCEAN
Seikan Tunnel
Tappi-zaki
Shimokita-hanto
Kawauchi
Mimmaya
Imabetsu
Tairadate
Wakinosawa
Yokohama
Kodomari
Mutsu-wan
Shiura
Kanita
Tsugaru-hanto
Yomogita
Rokkasho
Shariki
Nakasato
Hiranai
Iwaki
Aomori-wan
Kanagi
Noheji
Goshogawara
Aomori
Tohoku
Kizukuri
Hakkoda-san 1585
Ajigasawa
Morita
Temmabayashi
Kamikita
Tsuruta
Shichinohe
Itayanagi
Namioka
Misawa
Iwaki-san 1625
Fujisaki
Sukaya Onsen
Kuroishi
Towada
Rokunohe
Momoishi
Fukaura
Hirosaki
Towada-Hachimantai Kokuritsu-koen
Towadako
Iwasaki
Nishimeya
Hiraka
Gonohe
Hachinohe
Oirase Valley
Owani
Kuraishi
Fukuchi
Hashikami
Ikarigaseki
Shingo
Nagawa
Shirakami-sanchi
Tashiro-dake 1178
Towada-ko
Sannohe
Nango
Taneichi
Takko
Karumai
Hachimori
Kosaka
Ninohe
Ono
Fujisato
Tashiro
Kunohe
Kuji
Minehama
Odate
Hinai
Ichinohe
Futatsui
Takanosu
Johoji
Noshiro
Kazuno
Mabechi
Yamagata
Aikawa
Noda
Muriyoshi
Ashiro
Hachiryu
Kuzumaki
Yamamoto
Kamikoani
Fudai
Katooka
Iwate
Nyudo-zaki
Ogata
Ani
Tanohata
Matsuo
Gojome
Tamagawa Onsen
1614
Nishine
Ryusen-do Cave
Rikuchu-kaigan
Wakami
Oga-hanto
Oga
Ikawa
Towada-Hachimantai Kokuritsu-koen
Tamayama
Iwaizumi
Tenno
Showa
Iwate-san 2040
Kitakami
Gando
Kitakami-kochi
Taro
Akita
Tazawa-ko
Takizawa
Morioka
Shizukuishi
Miyako
Nishiki
Tazawako
Kawai
Kawabe
Kyowa
Tonan
Niisato
Hayachine-san 1914
Omono
Kakunodate
Dewa-sanchi
Shiwa
Iwaki
Honshu
Yuwa
Kamioka
Nakasen
Yamada
Ishidoriya
Omagari
Nangai
Sawauchi
Ouchi
Rekugo
Towa
Otsuchi
Honjo
Hanamaki
Miyamori
Tono
Sennan
Waga
Nikaho
Yuri
Taiyu
Omonogawa
Yokote
Kamaishi
Ou-sammyaku
Nikaho
Higashi-yuri
Yuda
Kitakami
Konoura
Hiraka
Jumohji
1341
Kisakata
Esashi
Tobi
Yashima
Ugo
Masuda
Sanriku
Chokai
Isawa
Sumita
Yuzawa
Inakawa
Mizusawa
Ofunato
Kokuritsu-koen
Chokai-san 2230
Ogachi
Minase
Koromogawa
Maesawa
Rikuzen-takata
Hiraizumi
Daito
Yuza
Murone
Ichinoseki
Karakuwa
Sakata
Yawata
Kesennuma
Semmaya
Kawasaki
Kanuyama
Fujisawa
Mamurogawa
Kurikoma
Hanaizumi
Motoyoshi
Aka
Amarume
Kannari
Sakekawa
Mikawa
Mogami
Mogami-kyo Gorge
Shinjo
Mogami
Naruko
Wakayanagi
Utatsu
Zenpo-ji
Tsukidate
Nakada
Ichihasama
Tsuruoka
Haguro
Hasama
Shizugawa
Takashimizu
Haguro-san 419
Funagata
Iwadayama
Tajiri
Toyama
Atsumi
Miyazaki
Yoneyama
Kitakami
Onoda
Furukawa
Asahi
Oishida
Obanazawa
Nakaniida
Kogota
Ogatsu
Gas-san 1980
Sambongi
Kashimadai
Wakuya
Yudono-san 1504
Murayama
Ohira
Kanan
Onagawa
Sampoku
Kahoku
1500
Taiwa
Ishinomaki
Higashine
Yamoto
Ojika-hanto
Bandai-Asahi Kokuritsu-koen
Toyima
Matsushima
Sagae
Tendo
Rifu
Izumi
Ishinomaki-wan
Kinkazan
Shiogama
Oshika
Asahi
Yamanobe
Yamadera
Miyagi
Tagajo
Awabiara-zaki
1870
Aoba-jo
Asahi
Yamagata
Sendai
Zao Onsen
Aizu Wakamatsu
Murakami
1
2
3
4
5
6
7
8
9
10
11
12
13
14
15
16
17
4
7
13
45
46
47

TOHOKU

Its dialect is as thick as the winter snows that blow in over the Sea of Japan from Siberia. Tohoku's hold on northern Honshu makes it seem another world to Japan's urban majority

Map on page 200

Perhaps as a way of explaining and coping with the difficult realities of weather and topography, the northern portion of Honshu known as Tohoku remains filled with myths – clever foxes who turn into beautiful women and lure unsuspecting men to their doom, green-headed river creatures who snatch small children venturing too close to the water, and devils and ghosts in great abundance.

By Japanese standards, the Tohoku region is sparsely populated, with 10 million people in an area just under 67,000 sq. km (26,000 sq. miles). This northern part of Honshu comprises six prefectures: Aomori, Akita, Iwate, Miyagi, Yamagata and Fukushima. Its climate is comparable to New England in the United States, with the possible exception of the month of August when certain parts of southern Tohoku slyly pretend they are on the equator. (In fact, the city of Yamagata holds the record for the highest recorded temperature in Japan: 41°C or 104°F, in 1933.)

Long known for its natural beauty, rugged mountains, sometimes incomprehensible dialects, innumerable hot springs, and its harsh winters, especially on the Sea of Japan side that gets the brunt of Siberian storms, Tohoku was once known as Michinoku (lit. interior or narrow road). The name was not as benign as it seems, for it implied a place rather uncivilised and lacking in culture. In the old days, a barrier wall was constructed at Shirakawa, in southern Fukushima, to separate the civilised world of the south from the barbarians in the north. Although the name was eventually changed to the innocent *tohoku* (lit. northeast), the region's image of cultural immaturity lingers for many urban Japanese to the south.

There is a certain irony in this, since it is generally agreed that Tohoku is perhaps the last bastion of traditional Japanese culture. To a large degree, Tohoku has escaped the rapid modernisation that the rest of Japan has undergone since the end of World War II. In the north it is still possible to discover farms growing rice by methods used hundreds of years ago, tiny fishing villages nestled into cliffs overlooking unspoiled sea coasts, isolated hot-spring inns, and a people whose open friendliness is unstinting even as their dialect remains an exclusive mystery. No longer unknown, Tohoku is a place of spectacular beauty and a must-see for adventurous visitors.

BELOW: friendly smile while tending cultivated flowers.

Sendai

The largest city in Tohoku and on the eastern coast, **Sendai** ❶ was originally called Sentaijo after the Thousand Buddha Statue Temple that once graced the top of Aoba-yama, the wooded hilltop park. The name was changed to Sendai, or Thousand Generations, by the Date clan during their reign of the area, possibly in the mistaken belief that they would reign supreme for that long.

Sendai is today a cosmopolitan city of approximately 910,000 people, the capital of Miyagi Prefecture, and the pre-eminent city of the entire Tohoku region. Sendai is the logical jumping-off point for exploring the rest of Tohoku. It is known as the Green City and the City of Trees, and visitors arriving on the *shinkansen* from treeless urban points south will understand why. From **Sendai-eki** (Sendai Station), considered one of the most beautiful train stations in Japan, the main boulevards running east and west are all tree-lined.

South of Sendai, the traditional paper-making centre of Shiroishi produces washi, *a thick hand-made paper created from mulberry. Sendai craft shops sell dyed sheets of this durable paper, once used for clothing, in the form of wallets, hats and doorway curtains.*

Those wide, European-style avenues are a pleasure along which to stroll. If so inclined, the entire downtown area is small enough to cover in an hour or so of leisurely walking. From Sendai's tallest building, the **SS-30 Building** with its 30 floors, one can relax in numerous top-floor restaurants that offer an excellent view of mountains to the north and west, the Pacific Ocean to the east, and the city below. A 10-minute walk west up Aoba-dori from Sendai Station is **Ichiban-cho**, Sendai's main shopping arcade. Parts of it are covered in skylights and all of it is vehicle-free. Evenings suggest a walk a little further to Kokobuncho-dori, Sendai's main after-hours strip where there are the usual (and seemingly endless) Japanese-style bars, nightclubs, discos, karaoke boxes and other entertainment.

Just beneath the surface, the traditional ways of Tohoku remain in Sendai. The visitor can still watch artisans and craftsmen making knives, *tatami* flooring, and the famed *kayaki tansu* or chests in the traditional shops tucked into the shadows of much larger and more modern architecture.

Sendai didn't come into its own until Date Masamune, the great one-eyed

BELOW: harvest before the first winter snow.

warlord of the north, moved to his newly constructed castle on Aoba-yama. Both **Aoba-jo** (Aoba Castle) and the Date family collapsed during the Meiji era, but the walls of Aoba-jo remain. In addition, a small museum, souvenir shop, shrine and statue of the great Masamune himself now occupy the grounds. Looking northward and down from the castle grounds, one can see the Hirose-gawa, unpolluted and thus unusual in Japan. Edible trout still swim downstream.

Map on page 200

Zuihoden, the burial site of Date Masamune, sits atop Kyogamine-yama. There are several cemeteries along the way up, as well as a beautiful Rinzai Zen temple, **Zuiho-ji**. Above the temple are steps leading to the mausoleum at the very top, and nearby are the tombs of samurai who committed ritual suicide when Masamune died. There is also an exhibition room displaying pictures taken when the mausoleum was opened during restoration, necessitated by bomb attacks near the end of World War II.

Osaki Hachiman-jinja was originally built in 1100 and later moved to its present location by Date Masamune. Dedicated to the god of war or of archery, this shrine is one of Japan's national treasures. Walk up the 100 or so steps to the top – reportedly the count is never the same twice. Follow the stone-paved path lined with enormous cedar trees to the shrine, picturesquely set back in a small forest. It is done in Momoyama style with gold, black lacquer and bright colours.

There are several more modern attractions worth a look, especially in **Aobayama-koen** (Green Hill Park), including **Shiritsu Hakubutsukan** (Sendai Municipal Museum; daily 9am–4.45pm; admission fee) and a prefectural fine-art museum. The municipal museum is interesting architecturally, with an extensive and permanent exhibition of the area's history. There is also a children's

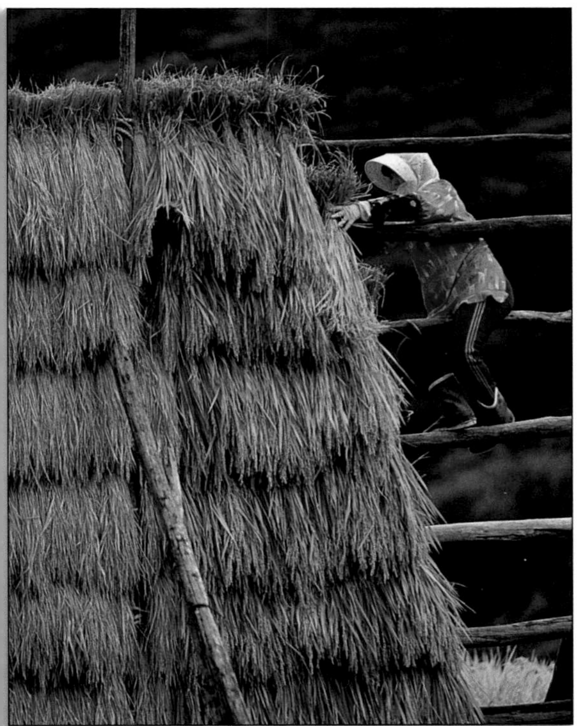

BELOW: the drying of rice is a small-scale operation.

THE POETRY OF BASHO

Matsuo Basho, the pseudonym of Matsuo Munefusa (born 1644), is considered to be the greatest of Japan's haiku poets. Basho took the 17-syllable haiku form and enriched it with descriptive simplicity and contrast. Frequently used to describe Basho's poetry is *sabi* – the love of the old, faded and unobtrusive. In 1679 Basho wrote his first verse:

On a withered branch
A crow has alighted:
Nightfall in autumn.

A samurai for a local feudal lord, Basho moved to the capital city of Edo (now Tokyo) after his lord's death. In 1684, Basho made the first of many journeys through the islands, to Tohoku and written of in *Oku no Hosomichi (The Narrow Road to the Deep North)*, considered by many to be one of the most beautiful works in Japanese literature.

section where everything on display can be touched. The prefectural fine-art museum has a sculpture wing with an outdoor sculpture garden.

If you have the time and the energy, consider the **Tohoku University Botanical Garden**, a place to cool off on a hot summer afternoon as well as to observe owls, bats and the region's flora and fauna. The observatory here is a relatively good place for star- and planet-viewing if you don't mind waiting in line. Finally, there's Kotsu-koen, a "traffic park" for children complete with roads, red lights, busy intersections and train tracks. Kids can cruise around in pedal-powered cars and get a taste for what real life is like on Japan's claustrophobic roads.

The captain of a tourist boat prepares to get underway on Matsushima Bay.

On the northern outskirts of Sendai, near Kitayama Station and a delightful place for a mountain stroll, are two Zen temples, **Rinno-ji** and **Shifuku-ji**. Both date from the 15th century and were destroyed then rebuilt many times over the years. They offer beautiful Zen-inspired gardens, with azaleas and irises in the spring, brilliant foliage in autumn, and dazzling winter scenes.

Matsushima

A short ride to the northwest of Sendai is **Naruko** ❷, Tohoku's most popular *onsen (*hot-spring). Once a sacred site to honour the gods of the hot springs, Naruko is known for its medicinal waters (the treatment of nervous tension is a speciality here) and the production of wooden *kokeshi* dolls, with ball-shaped heads and limbless cylindrical bodies. Now produced in many regions, *kokeshi* originated in Tohoku as a winter industry.

BELOW: tourist cruise boat in Matsushima Bay.

Just north of Sendai is **Matsushima** ❸, considered by Japanese to be one of the three officially designated most-beautiful spots *(Nihon-sankei)* in Japan. (The others are on Miyazu Bay, north of Kyoto, and Miyajima, near Hiroshima.)

Be warned: such a banner guarantees crowds, tackiness and considerable noise, and Matsushima is just that. Still, the bay is filled with beautiful pine-covered islets of all shapes and sizes, and a fleet of boats cruises the islands, sometimes in the form of ridiculous peacocks and other gimmicks. The poet Basho couldn't get enough of this place, nonetheless, declaring his arrival in Matsushima as the happiest moment of his life. While here, try the *sasa-kamaboko* (moulded fish paste) and the squid-on-a-stick.

Northward along the coast

Continuing north along the coast, the fishing port of **Ishinomaki** is noted for seafood. Try the *hoya* (sea squirt) in vinegar sauce. Ferries from Ishinomaki skirt around **Ojika-hanto** to **Kinkazan** (Gold Flower Mountain), a once-mysterious place of bamboo groves, dense forest, and roaming wild deer and monkeys.

At the northeast tip of Miyagi and on the coast is the city of **Kesennuma** and its variety of shark dishes. Beyond Kesennuma begins Iwate Prefecture's famed **Rikuchu-kaigan Kokuritsu-koen** ❹ (Rikuchu-kaigan National Park, commonly known as **Sanriku**), 200 km (125 miles) of fantastic coastline, fishing villages and beautiful sandy beaches. Jodogahama (Paradise Beach) was named by a visiting priest long ago who assumed that this was as close to heaven-on-earth as he would ever get.

Midway up Sanriku and inland over the mountains is the town of **Tono** ❺, offering a perfectly preserved glimpse into feudal Japan. No modern trappings here. Farming is still done the old-fashioned way; note the *magariya* or traditional L-shaped farmhouses. The long side of the structure is for people, the short side for animals and ghosts. Do not go too near the rivers here – this is

The Japanese word furosato, *meaning native home, carries a nostalgic, rural connotation: thatch-roofed farmhouses, mossy waterwheels, homemade pickles and ripening paddies. For the Japanese, even those who have never visited the area, the Tono Basin is their collective* furosato.

BELOW: morning walk, Matsushima.

where the legendary *kappa* resides beneath the waters, waiting to pull people and horses under. (The traditional way to defeat a *kappa*, if encountered, is to bow in greeting, forcing the kappa to return the bow and thus drain the depression atop its head of the *kappa's* life-giving fluid, water.)

Just to the southeast and at the base of Iwate-san is **Morioka** ❻, Iwate's capital and self-proclaimed as famous for its competitions for eating *wanko soba*. Other than that, it's rather unremarkable.

Temple in winter on Haguro-san.

Hiraizumi

But further south is the town of **Hiraizumi** ❼, near Miyagi Prefecture. Exiting the station here, it's hard to believe that this ordinary-looking town once rivalled Kyoto in its cultural splendours. But that was 850 years ago. Having said that, some remarkable remnants from that age have survived from its glory days as the domain of the powerful Fujiwara clan.

The Fujiwara's ploughed their wealth into building projects of great splendour. Sadly, only two remain out of 40, but they are well worth the visit. **Chuson-ji** (daily 8.30am–4.30pm; admission fee) was founded by a Tendai priest in 850, then later rebuilt in the Heian Period style, one of a handful of buildings to have survived from that period. The temple's two great treasures are the **Konjiki-do**, an astonishing structure covered almost entirely in gold leaf, the main altar inlaid with mother-of-pearl, lacquer and gilded copper.

A second construction, built in 1108, is the **Kyozo**, a sutra hall with an octagonal dais decorated with inlaid motifs. The newly built **Sankozo** is a Treasure Hall housing valuable sutras in gold ink on indigo paper, a famous thousand-armed Kannon statue, and Fujiwara items, including lacquerware and swords.

BELOW: torii gates at Chuson-ji and musical festivities.

Many people visit Hiraizumi to experience the wonderful **Motsu-ji** (daily 8.30am–4.30pm; admission fee), a 12th-century garden also known as the Jodo-teien, and one of the few remaining Heian Period landscapes in Japan. The garden, with a central pond and scatterings of ancient foundation stones for a temple that once stood here, is alive with flowers in every season.

Map on page 200

Aomori

Capital of Aomori Prefecture, the city of **Aomori** ❽ is a logical departure point for both Hokkaido and Towada-Hachimantai National Park to the south. **Hirosaki** ❾, an hour's ride southwest from Aomori, is an old castle town with the most elegant (some say most difficult) regional dialect in Tohoku, as well as what Japanese chauvinists claim are Japan's most beautiful women. It is also noted for retaining a bit of the old samurai-era atmosphere. To the southeast are the Hakkodo Mountains, running down the middle of Aomori Prefecture to the river valley of Oirase. Before entering this spectacular valley of steep cliffs, churning rapids and waterfalls, spend a night at **Sukaya Onsen**. The waters here are thought to be curative and the location is rustic and traditional.

The highlight of the gardens of Motsu-ji is in late June and beginning of July when over 30,000 irises are in full bloom.

North lies Aomori Prefecture and the **Shimokita-hanto** ❿ (Shimokita Peninsula). The world's northernmost community of wild monkeys can be found here, as well as the ominous **Osore-zan**, 870 metres (2,870 ft) high. With its bubbling, multi-coloured mud pits and clinging sulphur clouds, Osore's translation of "dread" or "terror" seems apt.

Towada-Hachimantai Kokuritsu-koen (Towada-Hachimantai National Park) covers a vast area, touching the borders of three prefectures – Aomori, Akita and Iwate. The onsen at **Tamagawa**, on the Akita side of Hachimantai

BELOW: the *namahage* festival at New Year.

Plateau, has hot, acidic and slightly radioactive water, considered to be one of the best springs in the area. Excluding Hokkaido, this is Japan's last area of untamed wilderness with several volcanoes, including **Iwate-san** ⓫, 2,040 metres high (6,700 ft) and considered the Fuji-san of the north, with its bubbling mud pools, steam geysers and scenic splendour. South of **Towada-ko**, Iwate-san is one of eight active volcanoes in the Tohoku region.

TIP

While in the vicinity, you might consider spending time in Bandai Kogen, a mountain area punctuated with beech trees, wetlands and almost 300 lakes. The jewel of these highlands is Bandai-san, a 1,819-metre (5,970-ft) mountain next to Lake Inawashiro.

West from Hachimantai is Akita Prefecture, home of **Tazawa-ko** (reportedly Japan's deepest lake) and the spectacular **Oga-hanto**, home of the *namahage*, or the devils of the new year. These horrible creatures burst into local homes on 3 January each year and are not appeased until fed large quantities of sake and rice cakes. **Akita** ⓬ is another little city with nothing to distinguish it, save perhaps its winters. **Kakunodate** ⓭, however, is noted for having preserved several samurai houses and streets, some lined with luscious cherry trees.

South of Akita, the prefecture of **Yamagata** is rustic and traditional. The **Dewa San-zan** (Three Mountains of Dewa) are Yamagata's three holy mountains, where ascetic mountain priests called *yamabushi* still perform sacred rituals. Join the other pilgrims and walk the 2,446 steps to the summit of **Haguro-san**. Afterwards, travel down the Mogami-gawa on a flat-bottomed boat while the boatman sings of the area's legends. Towards the inland highlands is **Tendo** ⓮, an *onsen* town famous for its craftsmen who make *shogi* chess pieces.

Aizu-Wakamatsu

Further south, in Tohoku's most southerly prefecture of Fukushima, the castle town of **Aizu Wakamatsu** ⓯, with its feudal history, pleasant parks and gardens, is also a centre for folk arts, ceramic and lacquerware making. Having

BELOW: a calm day on Lake Inawashiro.

opposed the overthrow of the Tokugawa shogunate in 1868, and witnessed the deaths of 20 teenage samurais who committed suicide rather than surrender to the new imperial forces, Aizu's historical credentials are unassailable.

The bullet train from Tokyo Ueno Station to Koriyama eats up the miles, but the slower run from Tokyo's Asakusa Station on either the Tobu or Aizu lines is by far the more scenic route. If you are planning to stay overnight in Aizu, this route offers the option of stopping off at Nikko for the day.

Aizu's sights are spread out, so bus or bicycle are the best way around. A good place to orientate yourself is **Iimori-yama**, a hilltop affording excellent views in all directions. The peak can be reached via a steep staircase or care of an escalator (Mar–Nov daily 8am–5pm; admission fee). Japanese tourists come here mainly to pay homage to the **Byakkotai graves**. The Byakkotai (White Tigers) were the young warriors who committed ritual disembowelment after being severed from their main force and failing to get to the safety of the Tsurugu castle, which they mistakenly thought was burning. Feelings are divided on whether this was the knee-jerk reaction of a culture of violence, or a noble gesture, but all agree on the tragic waste of life, the "heroes" aged 16 and 17.

Two km (1 mile) south of the hill, **Buke-yashiki** (Apr–Nov daily 8.30am–5pm; admission fee), is a skilful reproduction of samurai houses and, along with one or two original buildings, provides insights into the living conditions of the samurai class. Another 2 km (1 mile) west, **Oyaku-en** (daily 8.30am–5pm; closed first week of July/Dec; admission fee) is a tranquil Japanese garden set in the grounds of a former village owned by the local Matsudaira clan. A pond and stroll garden, it is also known as a medicinal garden, one that still cultivates some 300 types of herbs, many of which are available at the gar-

Map on page 200

BELOW: Oyaku-en medicinal garden and Tsuruga-jo.

den shop. Teahouses always seem to have the best views of gardens. Repair to the small *tatami*-floored rooms here, where you will be served *matcha*, a traditional frothy green tea with a small Japanese confection.

Castle keep

A 15-minute walk from the garden, Aizu's warrior past is to the fore at **Tsuruga-jo** (daily 8.30am–5pm, last admission 4.30pm, closed first week of July/Dec; admission fee), the town's reconstructed castle keep. The walls and moats of this great castle are original, the manicured park setting an afterthought. A good one though, especially in spring when over 1,000 cherry trees burst into bloom, the white walls of the keep contrasting with the blue skies and pink blossom, an image reproduced on thousands of calendars. The dramatic castle exterior and views from the upper floors are more interesting than the lacklustre interiors and museum of local history.

The views of the temple and valley below from the Godai-do (the red pavilion where sutras are stored) are the best to be had from Yamadera.

If you are interested in Japan's best-known poison, sake, a popular warrior tipple, a five-minute walk north takes you to the **Aizu Sake Historical Museum** (mid-Mar–mid-Dec daily 8.30am–5pm, mid-Dec–mid-Mar 9am–4.30pm); admission fee), where the process is explained in vivid photos and displays. The museum is housed in a beautiful, 350-year old wooden building. The souvenir shop here is almost as entertaining as the museum itself.

Yamadera

The pride and joy of Yamagata is the awesome temple complex of Risshaku-ji, better known as **Yamadera** ⓰. It was founded in 860 by a Zen priest. Perched on the side of a mountain, its 40 or so temple buildings, connected by paths leading through ancient cedar forest, are a fantastic sight even for those who may by now feel templed-out. The main hall, **Kompon Chudo**, dates from the 14th century, other structures from the 16th century. At the top of the 1,015 steps you'll need to ascend to reach it is **Okuno-in**, the holy of holies for the pilgrims who offer up prayers here. Descending the hillside, you'll come across a statue of the poet Basho, whose famous work, *The Narrow Road to the Deep North*, includes a haiku written while visiting Yamadera: *"How still it is! Stinging into the stones, The locust's trill."*

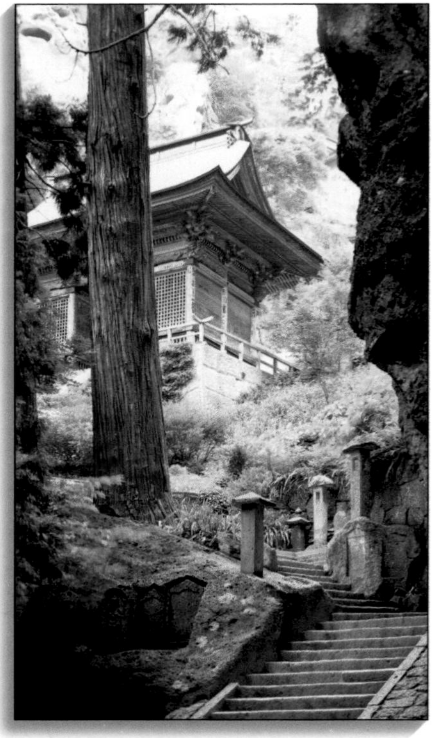

BELOW: steps to Yamadera.
RIGHT: fishing boats, Matsushima.

Zao Onsen

Some 20 km (12 miles) southeast of Yamagata city, **Zao Onsen** ⓱ is one of the largest ski resorts in Tohoku. The main focus of Zao Quasi National Park, there are runs to choose from, as well as night skiing during the months of December to late March. The Zangesaka and Juhyogen courses are the most interesting, passing groups of snow monsters. Siberian winds whip up the snow into frozen droplets that coat fir trees along the slopes, turning them into weird and wonderful ice sculptures.

Zao Onsen, as the name suggests, is also an all-year hot-spring resort. There's nothing quite like tackling the hiking trails or ski slopes during the daytime, then having a pre-dinner soak in a mountain hot spring while contemplating the next step of your trip. ❑

HOKKAIDO

The northern island of Hokkaido holds a special place in the Japanese imagination, conjuring up images of wild lands and misty mountains amidst a romanticism of possibilities

Maps on pages 214 & 216

Hokkaido has been part of the Japanese nation only since it was settled in the 19th century as an example of Meiji Restoration development. Nowadays, Hokkaido is to many Japanese as Alaska is to Americans: the northern extents with a romantic sense of frontier, where summers are short and winters exceedingly cold, and where the people are just a little bit different for living there in the first place. Japan's northern island is where the temples and castles of the southern islands give way to mountains, forests and farms. One will find the residents here more direct and friendlier than their southern counterparts and, due to the Meiji-era Westernisation, quite sophisticated. Hokkaido is also home to Japan's last indigenous people, the Ainu, who are of Caucasian ancestry and with no genetic connection to today's Japanese. With a population of only 20,000, the Ainu are today a phantom culture with a forgotten language, looked upon by Japanese as a sightseeing curiosity and whose main occupation – besides fishing and farming – is dressing up and posing for photographs at tourist sites. A brutal statement, but unfortunately true.

Hokkaido has the feeling of remoteness, but this is mostly psychological. The Tokyo–Sapporo air corridor is one of the busiest in the world, and Hokkaido offers the standard overdeveloped and tacky tourist traps and loudspeaker-enhanced "scenic" places so common throughout Japan. But Hokkaido can also be high adventure in the rustic north, with some of Japan's most undeveloped areas. Its climate parallels Quebec and Finland, and in winter icebergs scrape its shores. In summer, hills and fields are riotous with wildflowers and filled with dairy cows.

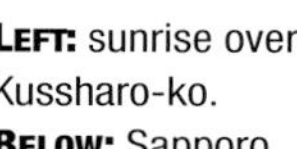

LEFT: sunrise over Kussharo-ko.
BELOW: Sapporo.

Sapporo

In southwest Hokkaido, **Sapporo** ❶ is the island's capital and its largest city with 1.7 million people. It is an immensely liveable city, especially by Japanese standards. Streets are laid out in a grid, making navigation easy and useful addresses a reality, and they are also wider than most of those in Japan.

The city is anchored by **Odori-koen** Ⓐ (Odori Park), running east and west through the centre and perhaps one of Japan's liveliest, most charming boulevards. In the first week of February, this broad avenue is the venue for Sapporo's world-famous Snow Festival. Snow statues and ice sculptures made by corporate, professional and amateur teams are decidedly complex and often quite large. In summer, beer gardens spring up on the grassy areas and people linger outdoors long into the night.

Amongst the Japanese, a must-see is **Tokei-dai** Ⓑ (Clock Tower), an architecturally undistinguished

The little stream that flows through Sapporo has been made in a dead straight line… the trees have been planted exact distances apart. The city viewed from Sapporo Tower is a clear contradiction of the distaste for symmetry that Japanese aesthetics are held to embody.

– The Roads to Sata
Alan Booth

structure built in the late 1870s and not really worth going out of one's way to see. Directly east of Odori-koen a couple of blocks is the **TV Tower** Ⓒ, with a decent viewing platform 90 metres (295 ft) above the ground.

Just northwest of **Sapporo-eki** Ⓓ (Sapporo Station), itself a few blocks north of Odori-koen, is Hokkaido University. The university operates the nearby **Botanical Garden** Ⓔ, which contains over 5,000 examples of Hokkaido's flora. Within its grounds is **Batchelor Kinenkan** (Batchelor Memorial Museum; daily 9am–4pm; admission fee), a museum with an excellent collection of Ainu artefacts and named after an Englishman who spent decades researching the Ainu of Japan. Rev. John Batchelor was a 19th-century minister who studied the indigenous people of both Hokkaido and Siberia. The collection of Ainu artefacts he left behind is probably the best in Japan.

To the east a couple of kilometres is the **Sapporo Brewery** Ⓕ and Beer Garden, built on the site of the original brewery. Sapporo was Japan's first beer brewery, dating from the mid-1870s.

Two blocks south of Odori-koen is **Tanuki-koji**, a vibrant strip of restaurants and shops. The market of Nijo serves every dining and household need for locals and purveys souvenirs in abundance for eager first-time visitors. Finally, a couple more blocks south is **Susukino** Ⓖ, Sapporo's nightlife and strip-joint district of "soaplands" (full-body massages lubricated by soap).

West of Sapporo is **Otaru** ❷, once a fishing and trading centre and where many of the buildings are an eclectic blend of Western and 19th-century Japanese influences. Otaru is the gateway to the **Shakotan-hanto**, a peninsular microcosm of Hokkaido with its rugged coastlines, abundant campsites, ski areas, boating and fishing in the Sea of Japan, and glorious sunsets from the capes

Below: a small exhibit in Sapporo's snow festival.

Maps on pages 214 & 216

(misaki) of Shakotan and Kamui. This area's proximity to Sapporo makes sight-seeing hectic at times, especially on holidays and weekends. One of the island's most rewarding attractions is the **Historical Village of Hokkaido** (Tues–Sun 9.30am–4pm; admission fee), an open-air museum set in parkland, displaying over 60 historical buildings from the 19th and early 20th centuries. The village is a fascinating re-creation of life in the early pioneering years of the island.

To the south of Sapporo

The **Shikotsu-Toya Kokuritsu-koen** (Shikotsu-Toya National Park) is Hokkaido's most accessible national park and thus highly commercial and often crowded. Closest to Sapporo is **Shikotsu-ko** ❸, a huge caldera lake. Shikotsu-Kohan, a fishing village, provides lodgings and tour boats of the lake, and there are numerous youth hostels and campsites in the area.

Toya-ko ❹, south of Shikotsu, is a round caldera lake with a large island smack in the centre. Tour boats visit its islands, where the view of **Yotei-zan**, at 1,893 metres (6,200 ft), to the north is best. Climbers can attack Yotei or three other peaks: Eniwa, Fuppushi and Tarumae. The latter, on the south shore of Shikotsu-ko and rising 1,040 metres (3,400 ft), is a volcano that still steams and fumes; it is probably the best climb. The route to Tarumae from Shikotsu-ko passes through the eerie beauty of Koke no Domon (Moss Gorge). The resort areas around Toya-ko are boisterous in summer, with fireworks during the August festival season. There are many *ryokan* in the area, with hot-spring baths *(onsen)* having lake views. The "must-see" here is **Showa Shin-zan**, a small volcano just south that emerged unannounced from the earth in 1944. **Usu-zan** ❺, Showa Shin-zan's parent volcano, stands nearby. A cable car runs

BELOW: views of the smouldering Showa Shin-zan from the cable car on Usu-zan.

from near Showa Shin-zan up Usu-zan. At the top are the remains of trees destroyed when Usu-zan blew up in 1977, wreaking havoc on the resort. An even more devastating eruption occurred in 2000, destroying much of the area's tourist infrastructure. See it on film in the **Volcano Science Museum** (daily 9am–5pm; admission fee).

The best route from Toya-ko east to the tourist hot spring of **Noboribetsu** ❻ is by bus through gorgeous Orofure Pass. Noboribetsu's notable sight and activity is at the Dai-Ichi Takimoto-kan Hotel, where 40 indoor, sex-segregated hot-spring baths, once of wood but now of marble, can hold 1,000 bathers simultaneously. There is nothing else like it. (If you give the *onsen* a try, expect to be stared at. You are something foreign in the water.)

There are two festivals in August at Noboribetsu, recommended only if you love crowds. For a gourmet treat, in season ask for *kegani koramushi*, or small freshwater crabs. While here, tour the volcanic Jigoku-dani (Hell Gorge) and go up to the summit of Shihorei.

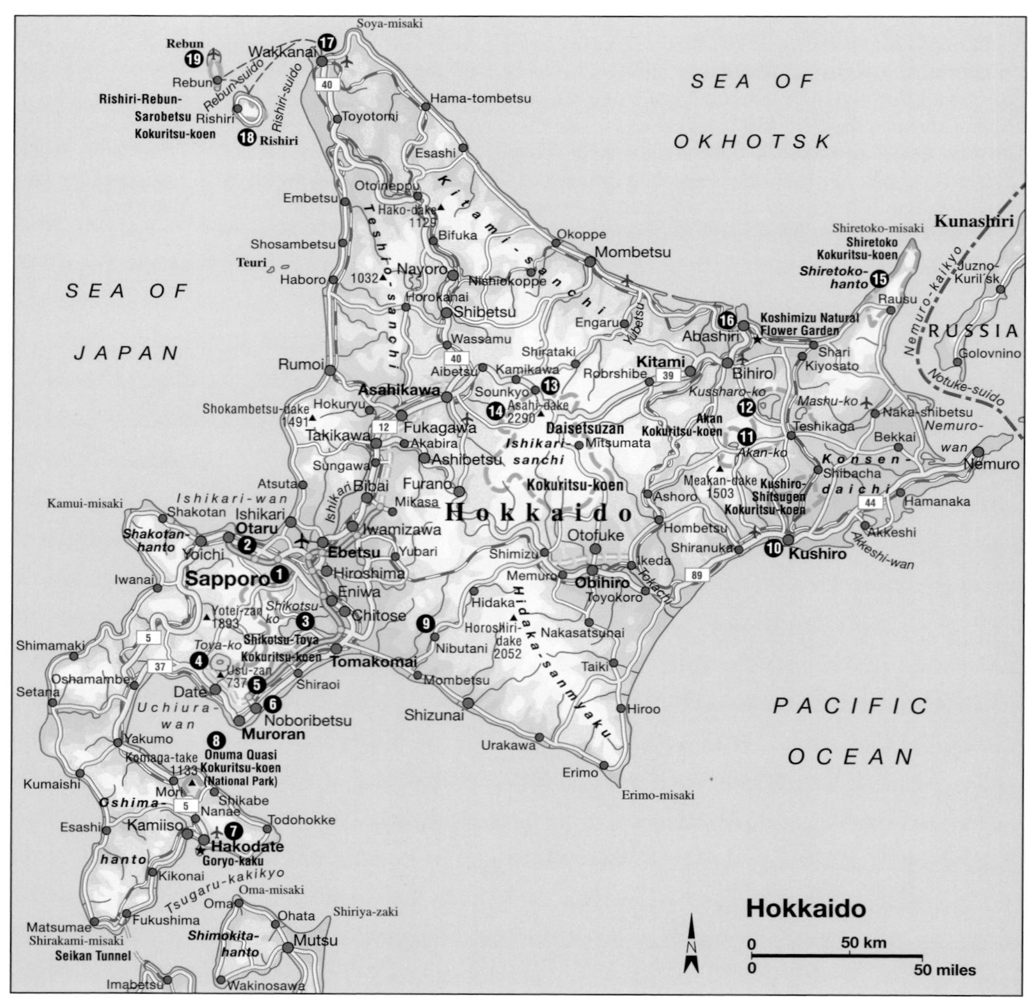

Hakodate

At the southern tip of Hokkaido and just across the Tsugaru Strait from Aomori and Honshu's northern tip is **Hakodate** ❼. Known for its rather wicked weather, Hakodate also offers one of the most romantic views from atop **Hakodate-yama**. A cable car climbs to its 334-metre (1,100 ft) summit.

Hakodate is Hokkaido's historic city, with Japanese settlers arriving from the south as early as the 13th century. Russians followed in the mid-1700s. At the base of Hakodate-yama is **Motomachi**, a foreign enclave since the 1850s. In fact, Hakodate was one of three Japanese cities (including Yokohama and Nagasaki) opened to the West after Perry's opening of the country in the 1850s. Northeast of Motomachi is **Goryo-kaku**, a star-shaped fort (a typical Russian design) where loyalists of the collapsing Tokugawa shogunate lost the final battle against the Meiji imperial army in 1869. For an intriguing perspective on the ethnic and commercial routes into Hokkaido, see the city's premier museum, the **Hakodate City Museum of Northern Peoples** (daily 9am–7pm; admission fee).The museum has a incomparable collection of Ainu artefacts, Chinese and Siberian costumes.

The Seikan Tunnel is the world's longest underwater tunnel (53.9 km/33½ miles) and links Honshu with Hokkaido, which are separated by the Tsugaru Strait.

Whereas Sapporo is a night city, Hakodate is at heart a morning city. Don't miss the fish market at dawn, when the squid fleet and the crab trappers return to port. Use the tram system, dating from 1913, to explore. For dinner, have Japan's freshest seafood. Crab and salmon are abundant and delicious; a unique salmon stew *(shake nabe)* called *sanpei-jiru* is truly remarkable. *Ika somen* – thinly sliced, noodle-like strips of raw squid – is the city's speciality.

Onuma Quasi National Park

Some 20 km (12 miles) north of Hakodate, **Onuma Quasi National Park** ❽ is easily reached in about 40 minutes by local train, making it the perfect day trip or overnight stay. Rated as some of the most stunning scenery in Japan, the park consists of three marshy lakes: Onuma, Junsai-numa and Konuma, and a 1,133-metre (3,700-ft) peak, **Komaga-take**, a dormant volcano.

Onuma, the largest, is generally considered to be the most beautiful of the three lakes. The view across the lily-covered lake to the soaring peak of the volcano in summer is certainly mightily impressive. The lake has over 100 islets, joined by walking bridges. Exploring the lakes on foot, or circuiting them by bicycle is a good way to avoid the tour groups who are usually shepherded into boats for cruises. Hikers can enjoy stunning views of the lakes and surrounding countryside by taking one of the two 2½-hour walking trails up the volcano.

Nibutani

Inland from Hokkaido's southern coast, some 50 km (30 miles) east of Tomakomai port, **Nibutani** ❾ is an authentic Ainu village with a number of interesting, tastefully displayed exhibits and archival material.

There are two museums of special interest, the most outstanding being the **Kayano Shigeru Ainu Memorial Museum** (Apr–Nov daily 9am–5pm; admission

BELOW: Ainu posing with tourists.

fee), where you'll find a first-rate photo exhibition on Ainu fishing techniques, etchings showing Ainu hunting, daily items, a giant stuffed salmon and a preserved emperor fish, and a number of Ainu huts with craftsmen inside engaged in making traditional artefacts.

Eggs cooked on a steam vent on Io-san for sale to tourists.

A visit to the **Nibutani Ainu Culture Museum** (daily 9am–4.30pm; admission fee) will complete your education on the Ainu heritage. Original Ainu huts stand outside, in stark contrast to the modern concrete and glass museum building. Embroidered traditional costumes, exhibits on the religious life of the Ainu people, and videos of dances and rituals provide a highly visual entrée into Ainu life and culture.

Kushiro and Akan National Park

To the east of Sapporo along the southern coast is the port city of **Kushiro ⑩**, where ultramodern architecture contrasts with one of Japan's most congenial dockside scenes that include a recent shopping and restaurant development called Fisherman's Wharf. Amongst the Japanese, Kushiro is noted mostly for the migrating red-crested cranes that put on elaborate and well-attended mating displays in the fields outside the city. Further east, Nemuro-hanto and the marshlands that stretch north from Kushiro along the eastern coastline are a recluse's paradise.

North of Kushiro in the centre of Hokkaido are the virgin forests, volcanoes and caldera lakes that draw tens of thousands of visitors every year to 900-sq.-km (350-sq.-mile) **Akan Kokuritsu-koen** (Akan National Park), whose best staging point is Kushiro. Tour buses dominate this park, which makes a car or a bicycle a plus. Ainu are abundant in Akan National Park; they dance

BELOW: egg seller near the steam vents of Io-san.

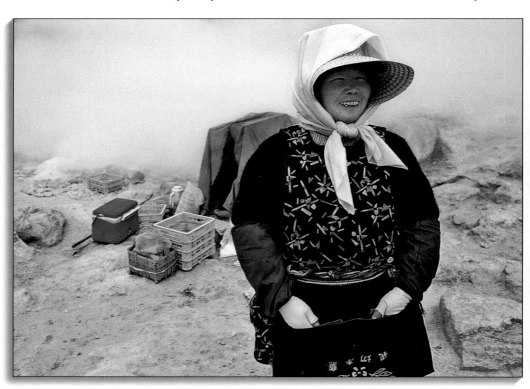

and sing on schedule when the tour buses arrive. The smiles evaporate when the tourists leave. Within the park, **Akan-ko** ⓫ is famous with the Japanese for *marimo* – odd, green algae balls also known as God's Fairies that will either delight or bore you. **Akan Kohan**, the main town, has 10 *ryokan* and the park has half a dozen youth hostels and plenty of campsites. Two volcanic peaks, Oakan-dake and Meakan-dake, tempt climbers; Meakan is the preferred jaunt, partly because an *onsen* awaits the weary climber. North of Akan Kohan, Bokke has bubbling, hot mud.

The bus ride between Akan-ko and Mashu-ko to the northeast features wonderful views at **Sogakudai** overlooking Meakan and Oakan. Mashu-ko is a landmark and is called Devil's Lake by the Ainu. Its 200-metre (650-ft) high cliffs towering over misty waters have often served as leaps of death for lovers.

Less touristy is **Kussharo-ko** ⓬, at 80 sq. km (30 sq. miles) the largest inland lake in Hokkaido and home to "Kusshi", Japan's very own "Nessie", of whom there have been several alleged sightings. Three congenial *onsen* surround Kussharo: Kawayu, Wakoto and Sunayu, where hot sands provide a welcome novelty. **Io-san**, or Mount Sulphur, steams and reeks impressively and is worth a visit despite the commercialisation. **Bihoro**, a pass above Kussharo's west shore, has breathtaking vistas.

Daisetsuzan National Park

Wilder and colder than Akan and Shikotsu-Toya, **Daisetsuzan Kokuritsu-koen** (Daisetsuzan National Park) is the largest national park in Japan with 230,900 hectares (570,500 acres). Directly in the centre of Hokkaido and to the west of Akan, the climate is nearly always cool, even in summer. This is a landscape of

Because of American agricultural experts brought to Hokkaido in the early 20th century, farms look rather similar to those in Iowa or Vermont. Likewise, Hokkaido's urban streets have a broad American look and are spacious by Japanese standards.

BELOW: farm with an American look.

volcanic peaks and steep highlands, magnificent gorges, carpets of alpine wildflowers, and sightings of the park's rich wildlife, including deer, fox, bears and exotic birds. In the park, there are several good youth hostels and campsites.

The opening of Japan by the arrival of Perry not only forced the country from its 250-year isolation, but eventually resulted in the collapse of the shogun and the return of the imperial line to power.

Start at **Sounkyo** ⓭, a tourist village near the gorges of Sounkyo (Gorges Reaching to the Clouds), with chiselled walls of volcanic rock punctuated by feathery waterfalls and more than 100 metres (300 ft) high. From Sounkyo, one of the park's two cable cars ends near the peak of Kuro, a jumping-off point for good hiking. The goal is Hokkaido's highest peak, **Asahi-dake** ⓮, 2,290 metres (7,500 ft) high. Along the way, hikers come across vast tracts of creeping pine and virgin forests, timberline barrens, small lakes and side trails, volcanic vents, flower-covered hillsides, patches of year-round snow – and the inevitable pesky mosquitos. Among the best festivals in Hokkaido are Sounkyo's Kyokoku Himatsuri, the Ainu Fire Festival in late June, and Sounkyo's Ice Festival in winter.

Shiretoko peninsula

Rich in land and marine ecosystems, a key region for salmon, sea mammals, migratory birds, woods of silver birch and resinous pine, home to deer and one of the world's largest concentrations of brown bear, it is not surprising that the outstanding biodiversity of the **Shiretoko** ⓯ region should have been listed as a UNESCO World Heritage Site in 2005.

Jutting out into the Sea of Okhotsk, this lonely, 70-km (43-mile) long peninsula is one of the wildest and most remote regions in Japan, a fact that is reflected in its name, *Shiretoko* translating from the Ainu language as "the end of the earth". Hardly any roads transect the half of the peninsula now designated as the **Shiretoko National Park**, an expanse of virgin forest, volcanic

BELOW: bathing at Kamuiwakka Falls, Shiretoko National Park.

Map on page 216

peaks, waterfalls and hot springs. In midwinter, the waters off the northern coast of the peninsula are frozen solid with ice pack. Most visits to the region are sensibly made in the months between June and September, although the frozen winter months have a crystalline beauty of their own.

Utoro, a bland spa town and fishing port, is the southeastern entrance and the area's main resort, with some useful amenities for an overnight stay. Though the town can be eschewed during the daytime, the lovely hot spring at **Iwaobetsu**, near Rausu-dake, the area's highest peak, is worth a half-day soak. Further up the coast, the **Shiretoko Shizen Centre** (mid-Apr–mid-Oct 8.am–5.40pm, mid–Oct–mid-Apr 9am–4pm; admission fee), has useful introduction material and film footage on the area, but the region's main attraction lies some 9 km (6 miles) north of here. On the eastern side of the peninsula is **Rausu**, a fishing and onsen village.

Forest paths and lakes

Shiretoko Go-ko, an area of forest paths and five exquisite lakes, is connected by wooden walkways. An observation point near the parking lot provides panoramic views across the lakes and forest towards the sea. Note that there are only four buses a day from Utoru to the lake. With a car or taxi, you can follow a dirt road up the peninsula to a stunningly located warm-water river and a series of waterfalls and hot springs collectively known as **Kamuiwakka-no-taki**. You can rent a pair of surprisingly comfortable straw sandals for the slippery hike up to the bathing pools.

From Shiretoko's high ground visitors can gaze across the Nemuro Straits towards Kunashiri, an island faithfully marked on all Japanese maps as part of

BELOW: inside Abashiri Prison Museum.

their nation. Since World War II, however, this and other islands in the Northern Territories have been held by the Soviet Union, then Russia, the source of a long-running dispute that periodically sours relations between the two countries. Kunashiri, easily visible on a clear day, is a mere 25 km (16 miles) away.

Buddhist tomb on the island of Rishiri.

Along the northern coast

The best route away from the Shiretoko is west along the northern coast through the village of Shari and towards **Abashiri** ⑯, with its interesting but quirky prison museum, pleasant walks along Tofutsu-ko, and the wildflower gardens. The **Abashiri Prison Museum** (daily 8am–6pm; admission fee) shows the preserved prison structures, including the minimalist cells that are barely adequate for this harsh climate. Japanese films about the *yakuza (see page 232)* often feature the notorious Abashiri Prison. Also in Abashiri is a fine museum that displays the plants and animals of Shiretoko-hanto, along with excavated prehistoric artefacts. Best of all, Abashiri is at the beginning of Hokkaido's easiest long-distance bicycle route, a trip along the island's northern coast alongside the Sea of Okhotsk, which is popular with youths on summer holiday.

Wakkanai ⑰ lies at the northernmost tip of Hokkaido. In spring, the break-up of the ice pack to the north of Wakkanai is a mainstay of national television news. Wakkanai itself is undistinguished, although increasingly street and store signs in Russian suggest its popularity with Russians. In fact, the Russian island of Sakhalin is often visible to the north. Wakkanai is also a port for the export of older Japanese cars to Russia, where there is a thriving market for them, and it is the terminus for ferry services to some of the remote northern islands, including Rishiri and Rebun. Of course, in winter the ice pack can thwart travel by sea to these two small northwestern islands.

BELOW: east or west on Rishiri.
RIGHT: waterfall at Tennin-kyo.

Rishiri and Rebun

The volcanic islands of **Rishiri** ⑱ and **Rebun** ⑲, part of the **Rishiri-Rebun-Sarobetsu Kokuritsu-koen** (Rishiri-Rebun-Sarobetsu National Park), are just west of Wakkanai, from where the ferry to the islands departs. Before boarding the ferry, visit the alpine wildflower reserve at **Sarobetsu**, a rainbow of colour as far as the eye can see, especially in July. This is one of Hokkaido's real wonders. Rishiri and Rebun themselves offer various delights for the cyclist, hiker, camper and fisherman. It's possible to lodge at a *minshuku* (home-style inn) on either island and get up early in the morning with your host to go fishing in the Sea of Japan.

Hiking is excellent. Rishiri offers the best hiking with a climb up Rishiri-san, poking upwards to 1,720 metres (5,620 ft) above sea level, like Neptune's elbow. On Rebun, which is comparatively flat, hike from Sukotan-misaki to Momiwa, or cycle from Kabuka to Funadomori to make the most of the rewarding coastline scenery. Joining a youth hostel group is good insurance against getting lost.

Staying on these northern islands is an adventure. There is a hotel, the Kitaguni Grand, but staying in a hostel (there are three on Rishiri and one on Rebun) or a *minshuku* is a more down-to-earth choice and offers visitors a more authentic local experience. ❑

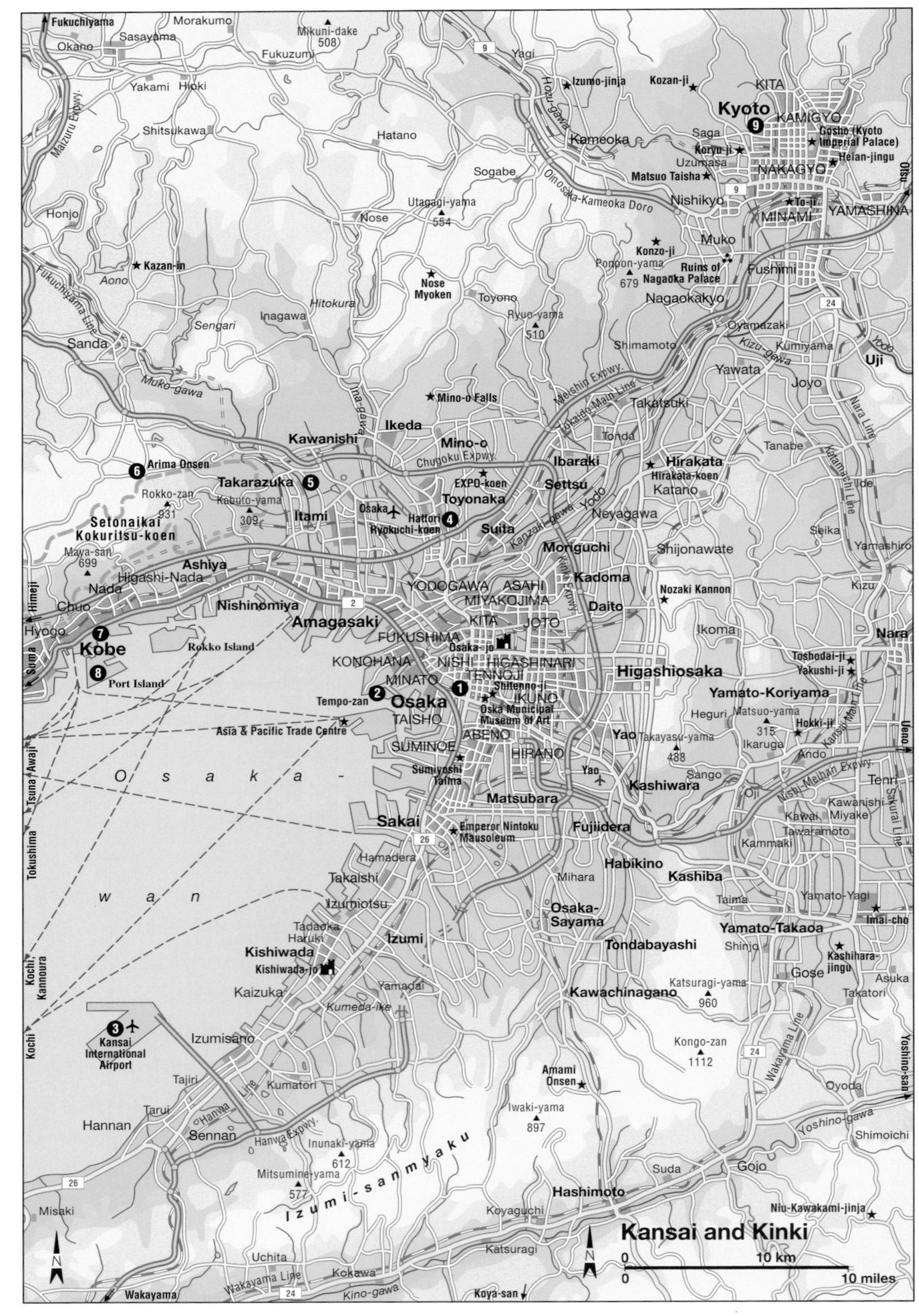
Kansai and Kinki
Kyoto
Osaka
Kobe
Nara
Osaka-wan
Izumi-sanmyaku
1 Osaka-jo
2 Tempo-zan
3 Kansai International Airport
4 Hattori Ryokuchi-koen
5 Takarazuka
6 Arima Onsen
7 Kobe
8 Port Island
9 Kyoto
Fukuchiyama
Sasayama
Morakumo
Mikuni-dake 508
Yagi
Izumo-jinja
Kozan-ji
Kameoka
Koryu-ji
Gosho (Kyoto Imperial Palace)
Heian-jingu
Matsuo Taisha
To-ji
Kazan-in
Nose Myoken
Konzo-ji
Ruins of Nagaoka Palace
Mino-o Falls
Setonaikai Kokuritsu-koen
Rokko Island
Asia & Pacific Trade Centre
Shitenno-ji
Oska Municipal Museum of Art
Sumiyoshi Taisha
Emperor Nintoku Mausoleum
Kishiwada-jo
Nozaki Kannon
Toshodai-ji
Yakushi-ji
Hokki-ji
Imai-cho
Kashihara-jingu
Amami Onsen
Niu-Kawakami-jinja
Koya-san
Wakayama
Himeji
Tokushima
Kochi
Yoshino-san
Otsu
Ueno
10 km
10 miles

THE KANSAI REGION

In contrast with the Kanto to the north, the Kansai vibrates with entrepreneurial intensity and historical importance

The old Tokaido (Eastern Sea Road) that connected the ancient capital at Kyoto with the seat of the feudal shogunate at Kamakura (and later, with Edo Tokyo) has all but disappeared. But it was along that much-travelled highway, at a point where it passed through the Hakone hills, that the Kamakura *bakufu* set up a heavily armed outpost in the 13th century to stifle threats by the western warlords and imperial loyalists. It is from this post that the regions to the west got their name: *Kansai,* or Western Barrier.

In the Kamakura days, virtually all lands west and south of those barriers – including the Nagoya and Gifu regions (covered in the Central Honshu chapter) – were considered to be in the Kansai. Later, around or just before the beginning of the Edo Period, the definition narrowed to include only the Kyoto, Nara, Osaka and Kobe areas.

Naturally, persons native to the Kansai feel an intense rivalry with other parts of the country, particularly the Kanto region, home of Tokyo. Although much of the Kansai region is still agricultural, declaring that one is from Kansai doesn't evoke a backwater image. In fact, despite their snickers at the Osaka dialect and at the rather sophomoric sense of humour to be found in Kansai, those in Tokyo must yield to the renown and respect of the entrepreneurial skills of people from Osaka and Kobe. Indeed, the great commercial and industrial complexes of Osaka and Kobe are the centres of Japan's international commerce. Moreover, there is the unquestionable urban sophistication of ancient Kyoto, which, after all, was the nation's powerful premier city for well over 1,000 years.

Osaka is a street-smart city, a place where the successful person has read the signals and kept an eye out for both opportunities and problems. For what it's worth, Osaka is the centre of the *yakuza*, the organised crime activity in Japan. But it is also the base of Japan's most innovative electronics manufacturer, Matsushita, and is a leader – together with Nagoya in Chubu – in the development of robotic production techniques.

Whether the traveller chooses the hills of Kobe, the hustle of Osaka, the antiquities of Kyoto, or the sublime of Nara, the Kansai region probably offers more to the first-time visitor than does that megalopolis 500 km (300 miles) to the north, Tokyo. ❑

PRECEDING PAGES: Kyoto's Kiyomizu-dera in winter.

an
HIROTA
ヒロタ
シュークリーム
KIRIN
PLAZA OSAKA

OSAKA AND KOBE

Tokyo may be where the bureaucrat and banker confer, but Osaka is where the entrepreneur and marketer huddle, making it Japan's centre of commerce with a gritty straightforwardness

Kansai shakes and hustles. You can see it in the restless crowds on the streets and packed in the subways. Osaka especially is an entrepreneurial city where lost time means lost opportunities and lost profits. This merchants' entrepôt thrives, as it has for centuries, on the manipulation of the *soroban* (abacus), which many here claim has a language all its own and that in Japan only Osakans understand.

Commerical conduit

Some Japanese look askance at **Osaka ❶**, as if it belonged to another somewhat unrelated part of the hemisphere. Its humour is different and a bit more rollicking than Tokyo. Greetings are to the point: *Mokarimakka?* Making much money? Even the language and intonation have a gritty, home-cooked flavour, raising eyebrows of disdain in sophisticated and bureaucratic Tokyo. Osaka is known for the character of its people: straightforward, business-savvy jay-walkers who know how to eat well. While sophisticated Kyotoites are said to spend their money on clothes, Osakans prefer to dispose of their hard-earned yen on culinary exploits.

Osaka goes by all sorts of nicknames – so many that they would put even an enthusiastic civic promoter to sleep. Among them are the City of Water, for its numerous rivers and one-time canals, and City of a Thousand Bridges, for the nearly 1,000 *bashi* that span the waterways. But all the waterways and bridges have only served one purpose: moving goods and material in and out of Osaka, Japan's commercial trading centre to the world.

Osaka's business connection is documented as far back as the 4th century, when Emperor Nintoku made Naniwa (Osaka) his capital. His business acumen was considerable for a politician; for example, he astutely decided to rebate all taxes to local businesses for three years after he was informed of an impending recession. His ploy worked rather well and the Osaka business ethic was conceived, as was the unique language of its merchants, *akinai kotoba*.

The city's stellar port and river connection to the capital in Kyoto played a central role in its economic and cultural development. Merchants from around the country (and from China and Korea) flooded the city. Osaka grew in strength and economic power, culminating with the shogunate of legendary Toyotomi Hideyoshi (1536–98), who chose Osaka as his seat of government, built himself a fine castle, and then turned the city into Japan's foremost commercial and industrial centre.

For the next 270 years, Osaka was the "kitchen of Japan" with raw materials pouring in and high-quality finished products flowing out. Kyoto and fledgling

LEFT: Kirin Plaza Building, in Osaka's Dotonbori.
BELOW: bar reading material.

Edo (present-day Tokyo) were consumers, Osaka the provider. When the capital and commercial centre moved to Tokyo, Osaka was – and remains – where the coin-of-the-realm is minted. And even though the aerial bombings of World War II nearly destroyed Osaka (unlike nearby Kyoto, spared the wrath of American air raids for its cultural, historic and religious landmarks), the city quickly returned to its commercial prominence and hustle.

Tokyo, of course, is Japan's economic and political engine, but Osaka remains an industrial, money-making dynamo with a gross national product greater than that of Canada. While Tokyo looks toward New York and London, Osaka casts its gaze towards the Asian mainland.

Domestic flights to Osaka arrive at the older airport near the city centre, while international flights use the newer Kansai International Airport, in Osaka Bay.

Contemporary Osaka

Osaka has an extensive, user-friendly subway and circular train line that makes exploring the city painless. Flanking Chuo-ku (Central District) are two sides of the Osakan coin: one half centres on Umeda, in Kita-ku (North District), the northern area around Osaka Station, while the other side is Minami-ku (South District), the southern part of the city in and around Namba Station. While only 10 minutes apart by subway, they are worlds apart in mind and manner. Umeda is Osaka's newer face where most of the city's skyscrapers, offices, hotels and shopping centres are sprouting. Minami, the unpretentious side of the city, is claimed to be the real Osaka. Most Osakans will say that Umeda is where one works, but Minami is where the Osakan heart beats. It's also where the say-what-you-mean *Osaka-ben* (Osaka dialect) is spoken with pride.

Most trains (except the *shinkansen*, or bullet train) arrive at the **Osaka-eki** Ⓐ (Osaka Station) complex in Umeda, so it is from here that a tour of the city

BELOW: an Osaka shopping centre.

might start. At Osaka Station, three train lines (JR, Hankyu and Hanshin lines) meet with Osaka's three main north–south subway lines. Like most train stations in Japan, Osaka Station offers an underground shopping mall, perhaps one of the largest of its kind in the world. Meandering corridors connect station exits and entrances with department stores, hotels, hundreds of shops and boutiques, and uncountable places to eat. The main areas of the shopping mall cover over 3 hectares (7.4 acres). San-Ban-Gai, located directly under the Hankyu Umeda part of the station, has another collection of shops and restaurants.

From the Shin (New) Hankyu Hotel, cross under the railway tracks west to the twin towers of the futuristic **Umeda Sky Building**, where the 41st-floor observation deck (daily 10am–10pm; admission fee) offers panoramic views of the city; in the basement is a 1960s retro-style restaurant food court.

Back up on the street from the station complex is Midosuji, Osaka's main north–south boulevard. South from Umeda is **Nakano-shima** Ⓑ (Nakano Island); this narrow island between the canals of Dojima-gawa and Tosabori-gawa is the centre of city government and home to many major Osaka companies. A footpath runs most of the way around Nakano-shima; sightseeing boats to tour the canals can be picked up nearby.

From Midosuji, follow the path on Nakano-shima east along the river, passing in front of Osaka City Hall, library, and the quaint, red-brick public hall. Across from the public hall is the superb **Toyo Togei-kan** Ⓒ (Museum of Oriental Ceramics; Tues–Sun 9.30am–4.30pm; admission fee), housing the famous Ataka collection of Chinese and Korean porcelain, one of the best collections in the world with over 1,000 pieces. East of the museum is **Nakanoshima-koen** Ⓓ (Nakanoshima Park), with a rose garden and willow-draped paths.

Osaka has made several contributions to Japan's culture over the centuries, such as the poet Matsuo Basho (1644–94). The puppetry of bunraku, with its two-thirds life-size puppets, also originated in Osaka.

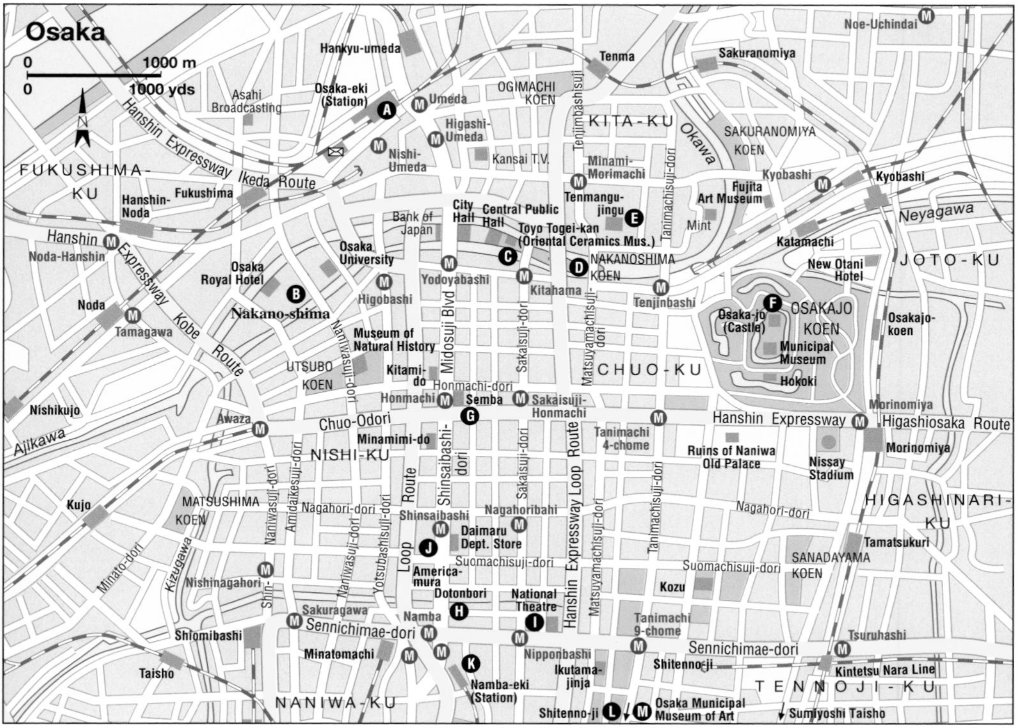

Osaka

Gambling spawned the name "yakuza". In an old card game, points came from the last digit of the hand's total. A hand of 20 (the sum of 8, 9 and 3 and the worst possible) has a score of zero. The hand 8-9-3 is pronounced ya-ku-sa and means "good for nothing" and, by extension, "outcast".

The hard-to-miss Osaka Castle rising to the east is reached by following the footpath to the eastern end of Nakano-shima, then up the spiral ramp onto Tenjin-bashi. Walk north across the bridge, then right at the police box. A short jaunt ends at the entrance of **Sakuranomiya-koen** (Cherry Garden). A few blocks north of this point sits funky **Tenmangu-jingu** Ⓔ, dedicated to the god of learning. Sakuranomiya-koen has extensive trails lined with cherry trees. If lucky enough to be here during the second week in April, you'll get a good look at Japan's national flower, the cherry blossom, in full bloom. In the evenings, uncountable numbers of Osakans will be at their merriest – and most uninhibited – while drinking and singing under the trees at lively *hanami* (flower-viewing) parties.

Follow the footpath about a kilometre along the river past the Osaka Mint, then take the footbridge (Kawasaki-bashi) over the river to the castle straight ahead. Up and then down through an underpass and up onto an overpass eventually leads to it. (You can also take a taxi from Nakano-shima.)

Osaka Castle

Osaka-jo Ⓕ (Osaka Castle) is the most-visited site in the city *(see picture on pages 236–37)*. The magnificent castle on the hill is an ode to everything that was great in the past and even of future possibilities. Unfortunately for the romantic and the historian, it is not the original castle, but rather a replica. The main donjon, towering above the expansive gardens and stone walls, is a 1931 concrete replica of the original that was built by Toyotomi Hideyoshi in 1585. With the conscripted help of all the feudal lords of the nation and the labour of tens of thousands, the massive structure was completed in just three years. It was destroyed 30 years later by Tokugawa Ieyasa and then again rebuilt. Much of the

BELOW: *yakuza* member sharing his fine tattoos.

YAKUZA

Yakuza (organised crime) origins date to the 1600s, when the unemployed samurai sometimes dressed in odd clothing and carrying longswords terrorised people for leisure. Later, men called *bakuto* were hired by the shogun to gamble with labourers paid by the government so as to reclaim some of the substantial wages. The *bakuto* introduced the custom of *yubitsume* (severing the top joint of the little finger), as an act of apology to the boss, and tattooing.

The most notorious of the *yakuza* organisations is the Yamaguchi-gumi, which originated in Osaka in the 1920s.

The *yakuza* have established alliances with Chinese Triads, Italian and US Mafia in the US and Italy, drug cartels, and others. Legitimate businesses mask their criminal activities; it is estimated that *yakuza* have funnelled well over US$10 billion into legitimate investments in the US and Europe.

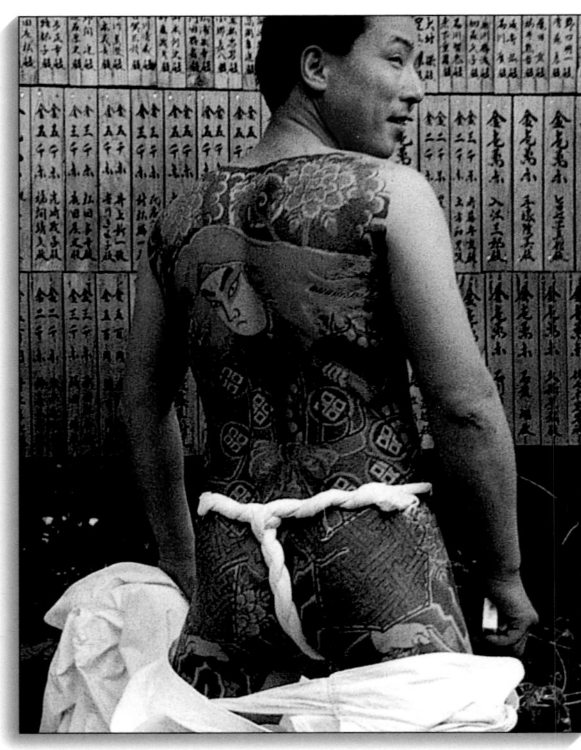

original grounds, moats and walls still stand. Extensive restoration work to the castle building, which houses an impressive multi-storey museum, was completed in 1997. The view from the top floor is impressive.

Adjacent to the castle is the **Osaka Business Park**, worth a visit to see what the future of Osaka may be like. Planners aim to make this one of Osaka's main centres. Already it sports a slew of state-of-the-art skyscrapers, theatres, shopping centres, restaurants and the New Otani Hotel.

South of Nakano-shima, head south on Midosuji under the ginkgo trees. Japan's thriving pharmaceutical industry started in Osaka with the import of Chinese herbal remedies, and most of Japan's drug companies still have their headquarters here along Doshomachi, just off Midosuji. Tucked away in a corner sits the pharmaceutical shrine of Sukuna-Hikona. It's a tiny little place that blossoms in importance entirely out of proportion to its size once a year in November, when the Shinno Matsuri is held. The festival commemorates the discovery that ground tiger bones, among other things, combat malaria.

South on Midosuji is the district of Honmachi, where Midosuji and Honmachi boulevards cross. Just north of the crossing is **Semba** **G**, the apparel wholesale area of Osaka. Most large wholesalers have outgrown their Semba origins, but some 800 small wholesalers still operate in the Semba Centre Building, a two-storey structure entirely under a 930-metre (3,000-ft) long expanse of elevated highway. Many of Osaka's most venerated businesses got their start in Semba, and some Japanese say that there is no one as astute in business as a Semba-trained businessman manipulating a *soroban* faster than a calculator.

Follow Midosuji south until the next major crossing, Nagahori. The first landmark to look for is the **Sony Tower**, at the mouth of Osaka's premier covered

The house was built in the old Osaka style... An earthen passage led from the entrance through to the rear. In the rooms, lighted even at noon by but a dim light from the courtyard, hemlock pillars, rubbed to a fine polish, gave off a soft glow.

– THE MAKIOKA SISTERS
TANIZAKI JUNICHIRO

BELOW: Nakano-shima.

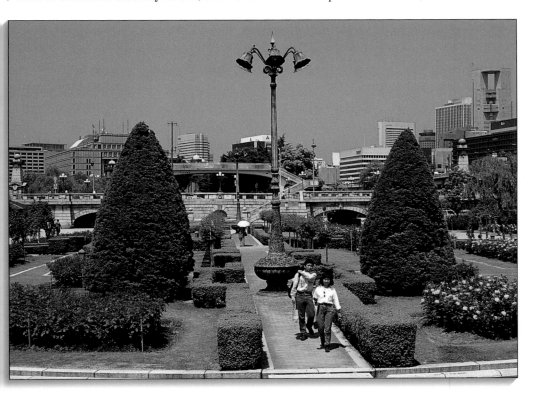

Late at night Japan's urban areas are often punctuated by the shriek of racing motorcycles with no silencers, driven by bosozuku ("speed tribes"), who are renegade youth intent on disrupting the norms of society.

shopping street, Shinsaibashi-suji, which extends south towards Namba Station. Here are ancient little shops sitting in apparent ignorance of the outrageously fancy boutique plazas towering on either side.

South on Shinsaibashi is one of the most fascinating stretches in Osaka. In the **Dotonbori** **H** amusement quarter, neon lights illuminate giant moving crabs, prawns and octopuses that adorn the facades of neighbourhood seafood restaurants. For Japanese tourists, it's de rigueur to stop and pose with *kuidaore*, a mechanical drum-beating clown more famous locally than Ronald McDonald and Colonel Sanders combined (and both of them are quite famous in Japan).

At the Dotonbori Canal, Shinsaibashi ends and Ebisusuji begins. Here, Shin Takamatsu's son et lumière **Kirin Plaza Building**, architecturally akin to something out of the movie *Blade Runner*, stands on the north bank of the canal. Venture about halfway across the **Ebisu-bashi**, a bridge across the canal, and squeeze in along the stone railing. Then sit tight for one of the best nonstop people-watching parades in the country.

There is more to Dotonbori than just the passing crowds, however. For hundreds of years, this was the theatrical heart of Japan with six *kabuki* theatres, five *bunraku* playhouses, and a myriad of other halls where the great storytellers and comics of Osaka performed. Today, most of the old theatres have been replaced by cinemas, among which the elegant old **Shochiku-za** is an architectural link to the golden age of black-and-white films. The venerable **Naka-za**, with its *kabuki* and *geisha* dances, and the vaudevillian Kado-za are still active, but they are the last of the legitimate theatres left in Dotonbori. Several years ago, the Bunraku Puppet Theatre moved from its old Asahi-za home to the **National Theatre** **I**, a few blocks to the east.

Below: canal along Dotonbori.

Heading south

Just south of Naka-za, the alley named Hozenji Yokocho is lined with scores of traditional Osaka eating and drinking establishments. (Some can be quite expensive, so confirm prices before ordering.) Continue down the alley to **Hozen-ji**, one of the most visited and venerated temples in Osaka. Local businessmen come to pray for good business, young couples to ask for happy futures and older people to pray for good health. A very serviceable temple.

For a glimpse of a more modern Japan, stroll through **America-mura** **J** (America Village) tucked into the narrow streets on the west side of Midosuji. This potpourri of Americana done Japanese-style is where stylish youth are out en masse to see and be seen. The area is filled with used-clothing boutiques and makeshift flea markets, where vintage Levis can fetch thousands of dollars.

South is the wide boulevard of Sennichimae-dori. Cross it and walk east a block to Printemps (pronounced *plantam*) department store. Turn right and enter the Sennichimae shopping arcade, a typical blue-collar area of *pachinko* parlours, cinemas and cheap restaurants. The arcade leads to one of Osaka's most famous wholesale areas, Doguyasuji, an entire market devoted to kitchen and restaurant supplies. As is the case in most Japanese cities, certain streets and neighbourhoods in Osaka are noted for a particular commodity: Matchamachi, or Toy Town; Nipponbashi, or Den-Den Town, for computers and electric appliances; Tachibana-dori for furniture; Hakimonodonya-gai for Japanese-style footwear and umbrellas; and Itachibori for tools.

From Doguyasuji, it's just two blocks to **Namba-eki** **K** (Namba Station), where there is nothing too remarkable save the vast underground shopping arcade of Namba City and Rainbow Town. Three main subway lines connect at Namba Station, also the terminus for both the Kintetsu and Nankai railways serving Nara, Wakayama and points south.

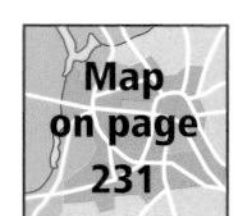
Map on page 231

Osaka is where the fun is: it has the best entertainment districts in Japan, the most lively youth neighborhood, the most charismatic geisha madams and the most colorful gangsters. It also has a monopoly on humor...

– LOST JAPAN
ALEX KERR

BELOW: a *pachinko* (pinball) parlour keeps everyone happy.

Temples

Founded in 593 by Prince Shotoku, **Shitenno-ji Temple** **L** is the oldest Buddhist temple in Japan, though none of its original structures has survived. The current complex, a heartless concrete reconstruction 2 km (1½ miles) southeast of Namba, has at least kept to the original layout, and there is a touch of genuine antiquity in the *torii* gate at the main entrance, dating from the 13th century.

It's a lively, well-patronised site, however, and on festival days swells with the faithful. Its **Treasure House** (Tues–Sun 8.30am–4pm; admission fee), encased in a modern white building, has a small collection of Buddhist art, a wonderful display of sumptuous costumes and mandalas used in court dance.

It's a short walk south, via **Isshin-ji**, a smaller but well-supported temple with a mischievous display of half-naked dancing girls on the entrance gate, to the **Osaka Municipal Museum of Art** **M** (Tues–Sun 9.30am–4.30pm; entrance fee). The museum houses a fine collection of ancient Japanese Jomon pottery, Edo-Period and Chinese art.

Contiguous with the museum is **Tennoji-koen** (Tues–Sun 9.30am–5pm; admission fee), with a modern conservatory stuffed with hothouse plants and trees. Integral to the park is **Keitakuen**, a moderately interesting Japanese garden bequeathed by Baron Sumitomo, a member of the giant trading company of the same name.

Some 5 km (3 miles) south on the Hankai Tram Line, **Sumiyoshi Taisha**, with a pedigree dating to 211, is Osaka's most prestigious shrine. Of special interest is the style of architecture, known as *sumiyoshi zukuri*, a Shinto design with its exposed logs and finials and a thatched roof. The brilliant red building is immediately recognisable after you cross the drum-shaped Sori-hashi bridge.

Kansai International Airport in Osaka Bay.

Osaka Bay

In the far west of Osaka along **Osaka-wan** (Osaka Bay), **Tempo-zan Harbour Village** ❷ makes an excellent place to explore for a half day. The highlight of this waterfront development is the excellent and enormous **Kaiyukan Aquarium** (daily 10am–8pm; admission fee), where visitors can get a close-up glimpse of giant whale sharks and immense spider crabs. Other attractions nearby include the **Suntory Museum** (Tues–Sun 10.30am–7.30pm; admission fee) with galleries and an IMAX cinema. At 112 metres (368 ft) high and difficult to miss, the world's largest Ferris wheel looms nearby. Osaka's newest and brashest addition to its western waterfront is the **Universal Studios Japan** (www.universalstudios.com/usji; admission fee) theme park. Water taxis and a shuttle train whisk visitors to the park where simulated rides include the special effects found on the re-created sets of *Jaws*, *Jurassic Park*, and, for a more sobering experience, the city's extraordinary **Liberty Osaka** (Tues–Sun 10am–5pm; admission fee), 2 km (1 mile) west of the studios. It is a human rights museum which takes a frank and disturbing look at some of the skeletons in Japan's own cupboard.

BELOW: Kaiyukan Aquarium.

Seemingly afloat in Osaka Bay, **Kansai International Airport** ❸ opened in the late 1990s as an alternative to Tokyo's overextended Narita. On an artificial island and away from developed areas, the airport allows flights 24 hours daily, whereas Narita is closed late at night.

For those without time to explore the age-old traditional architecture in the Japanese countryside, consider a trip to **Hattori Ryokuchi-koen** ❹, north of central Osaka and near the old international airport. Here is an open-air museum of old Japanese-style farmhouses displaying nine different styles of *minka* farmhouses with thatched roofs.

Beyond Osaka and Kobe

Theatre lovers and the culturally adventurous might want to make the trek (about 30 minutes from Osaka's Umeda Station or Kobe's Sannomiya Station) out to **Takarazuka** ❺, where high-stepping women have been staging flashy musical extravaganzas for nearly 90 years. Back in 1910, Takarazuka was a small town at the end of the then newly opened Hankyu rail line. In order to attract passengers, the train company built a resort and put together an all-female performing company. There are 400 performers divided into four casts, two performing simultaneously here and in Tokyo, while the other two troupes rehearse.

To the west, scalding hot springs *(onsen)* await weary hikers north of scenic, 930-metre (3,000-ft) high **Rokko-zan** in the town of **Arima** ❻. Reached by bus and cable car from Rokko Station, this ancient spa boasts all the usual hot-springs amenities plus is the home of nationally recognised basket-makers.

One bargain in town is the public Arima Onsen Kaikan, where for a few hundred yen one can bathe in the same curative waters offered at the much costlier

Maps on pages 226 & 231

The female actors of a Takarazuka play the male parts. Lead performers are well known and have a devoted following of female fans who throng to Tokyo's Takarazuka Theatre, across from the Imperial Hotel.

BELOW: Tempo-zan Harbour Village.

inns. Arima's waters are said to soothe all human ailments except love – an irony since the town has done much to nurture that particular affliction.

Kobe

The Korean War in the early 1950s pulled Japan from economic depression. UN forces used Japan's ports, including Kobe, as staging areas and Japanese suppliers provided most of the goods and services.

The Chinese *kanji* characters for Kobe translate as "god's door". But **Kobe** ❼, 30 km (20 miles) east of Osaka, is more like a doorsill – a long and narrow ledge squeezed between the coastal mountains and Osaka Bay. Although lacking in fantastic attractions for travellers – and so usually overlooked – Kobe is one of the most liveable and attractive cities in Japan, perched on hills overlooking a harbour.

In 1995, Kobe was jolted by the horrific Great Hanshin Earthquake that killed over 6,000 people in the Kobe area. Entire neighbourhoods, especially in the western sections of the city, were flattened when Japanese-style homes – wooden post-and-beam frames with heavy tiled roofs – collapsed and burned in the resulting fires. Buildings and elevated roads, mostly of contemporary concrete construction, collapsed spectacularly. Transport routes were severely damaged, including Kobe's container-port facilities, which are on landfill.

The earthquake wreaked havoc beyond anyone's belief and the government's inept emergency response was equally astounding. Dire predictions that Kobe would take several years to rebuild proved true; it was not until the summer of 1998 that the last of the tens of thousands of displaced residents were finally able to resettle into homes after four years in temporary housing. Today, for the most part, Kobe has returned to normal.

Those arriving in Kobe by *shinkansen* will disembark at **Shin Kobe-eki** (New Kobe Station; regular trains from Osaka and Kyoto stop at Sannomiya-eki). A

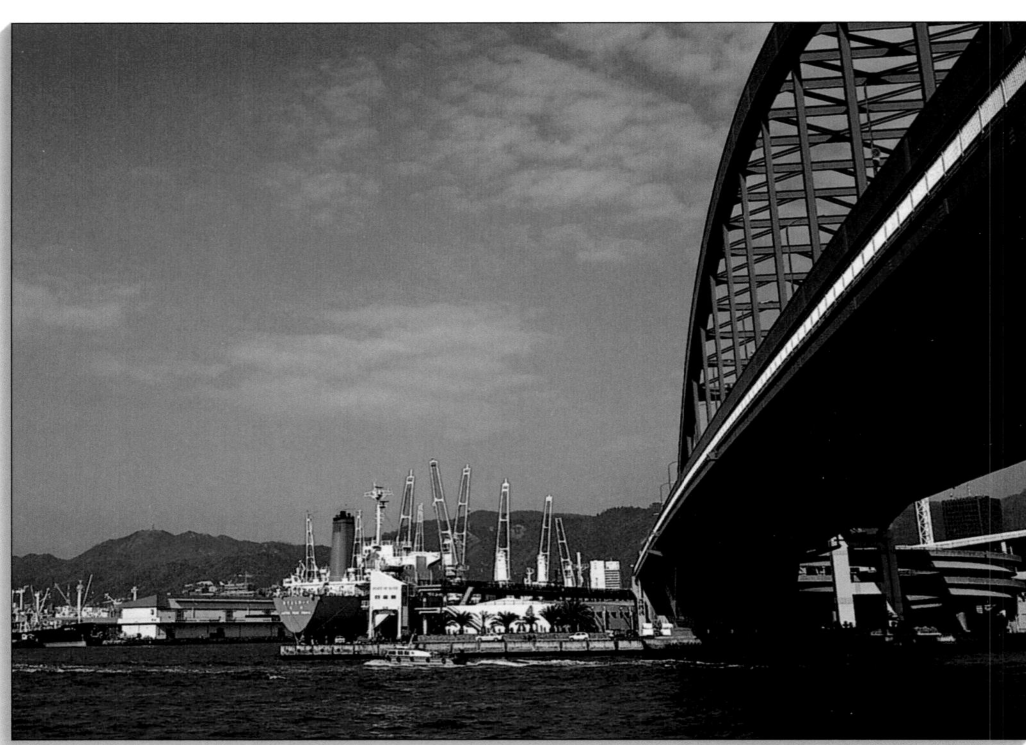

Below: Kobe's port facilities.

few blocks to the west and still on high ground, **Kitano-cho** is where rich foreign traders once staked out impressive residences at the turn of the 20th century, their growing influence freeing them from the foreign ghetto originally allocated near the wharves. Presenting a fanciful potpourri of European and American architectural styles, several of these *ijinkan* – foreign residences now sharing the hill with trendy boutiques and restaurants – are open to the public. Westerners tend to find the interiors unexceptional, but standouts include the impeccably restored Kazamidori and the Choueke House, which offer an intimate glimpse into the lifestyle of long-time foreign residents.

While exploring the neighbourhood, try to locate the Muslim mosque, Jewish synagogue, the Catholic, Baptist and Russian Orthodox churches, and the Jain temple, all within a few blocks of one another in a unique assemblage for an Asian city this size.

The cardinal point on the Kobe compass is **Sannomiya**, where **Sannomiya-eki** (Sannomiya Station) is embraced by this popular shopping and entertainment district. Extending west from Sannomiya, parallel shopping arcades extend to Motomachi-eki (Motomachi Station) and beyond. The arcade directly beneath the overhead tracks is the remnant of a black market that surfaced amid the post-World War II rubble and today is a bonus for bargain-hunters seeking second-hand or imitation goods.

South of Motomachi Station and just west of the elegant Daimaru department store look for the dragon gate announcing **Nankinmachi**, which is Kobe's two-block-long Chinatown. Although not of the standard and calibre of Chinatowns elsewhere in the world, this small but vibrant enclave surpasses anything that can be seen in the historic ports of Yokohama and Nagasaki.

Map on page 226

BELOW: shipping on the Inland Sea.

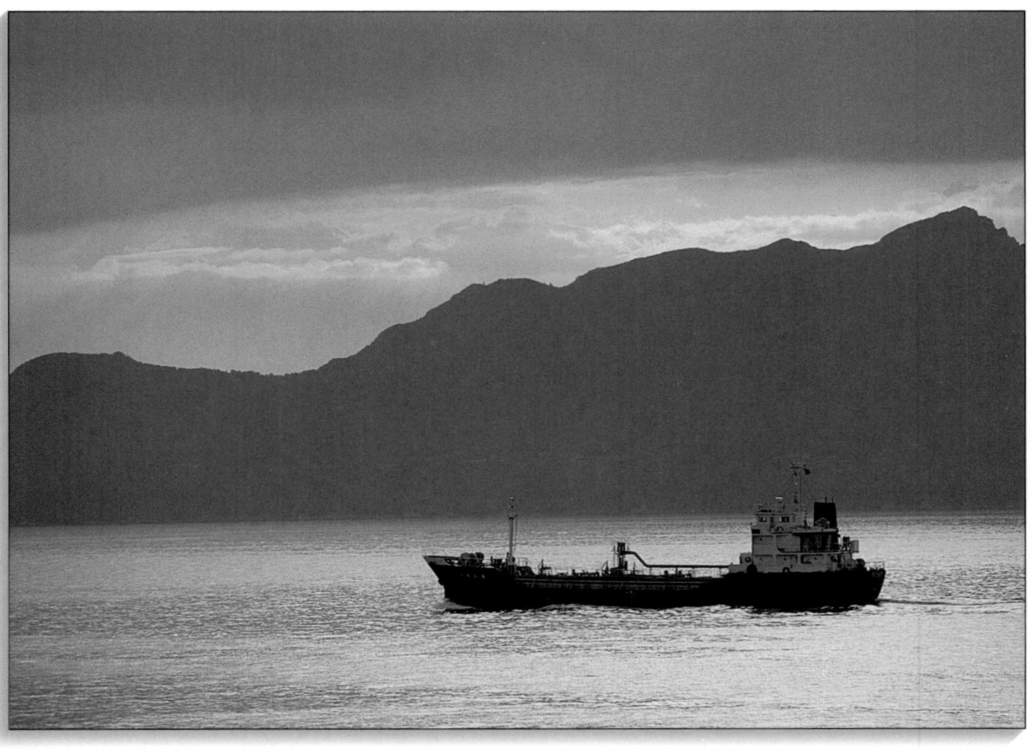

Map on page 226

From Chinatown, it's a short walk south to **Meriken Hatoba** and the waterfront. The surrounding redeveloped wharf frontage is the site of an informative and strikingly designed maritime museum. A visit here should also include a ride to the top of adjacent Port Tower and the 45-minute harbour cruise.

Port Island

Offshore is the hard-to-ignore **Port Island** ❽, also its Japanese name. In a feat of near science fiction and biblical dimensions, Kobe has "recycled" its surplus mountains to build up from the sea floor two of the world's largest artificial islands. This massive undertaking was to confirm Kobe as a prime trading port. The *Portliner* monorail from Sannomiya Station provides a convenient elevated loop ride around Port Island. Here – and on neighbouring **Rokko Island** (hard-hit by the earthquake) and also reachable by a monorail from JR Sumiyoshi Station – visitors can get a first-hand look at the future of container vessels. The island's new, high-tech **Fashion Museum** (Mon–Sat 11am–5.30pm Fri 11am–7.30pm; admission fee) is housed in a futuristic building as arresting as the exhibitions themselves. The centre of the island has a hotel, sports and convention facilities, plus an amusement park and sea-view apartments for 20,000 residents. Port Island is also where the jet-boat shuttle from **Kobe City Air Terminal** (KCAT) departs for the 30-minute ride to the Kansai International Airport.

Port Island is a good point from which to gaze back at Kobe, especially at night when it becomes a flickering tiara augmented by two insignia on the mountainside. One symbol is an anchor and the other a pair of interlocking fans representing the unification of Hyogo Prefecture and Kobe. It was due to the fan-shaped perfection of the harbours that the trading port flourished back in AD 700.

BELOW: "Fish Dance", a sculpture in Kobe.

For an intriguing look at the cultural side of foreign trade, drop in at the nearby **Kobe Municipal Museum** (open Tues–Sun 10am–4.30pm; admission fee), housed in a former bank. This small, admirable museum focuses on Japan's early encounters with the West and features a rare collection of *namban* ("southern barbarian") art, works inspired by contacts with the first Portuguese and Spanish traders who arrived here during the 16th and 17th centuries. The nearby **Kobe Phoenix Plaza**, an exhibition space that documents the 1995 earthquake and its aftermath, has been a surprising success, proving that no matter how traumatic the effects, the Japanese are still fascinated by the violent potential of their archipelago.

Finally, down the coast from Sannomiya at the southern end of Kobe is one of the largest beaches in western Japan, **Suma**, where there is Aqualife Park with a large aquarium and a dolphin show. From the vantage point of Suma's beach, the Akashi Kaikyo Ohashi, claimed to be the world's longest suspension bridge, can be seen connecting Japan's main island of Honshu to Shikoku via the large island of Awaji.

Kobe and Osaka are at the eastern end of **Seto Naikai**, or the **Inland Sea**. This protected 9,500-sq.-km (3,700-sq.-mile) body of water is encircled by western Honshu, Shikoku and Kyushu. Numerous ferries from all major cities on the Inland Sea offer an interesting and relaxing mode of travel. ❑

Earthquakes

Japan is highly prone to earthquakes. There are minor shakes recorded on seismological instruments almost every day, and bigger ones that startle people from their sleep, rattle dishes and knock objects off shelves occur several times a year. From time to time over the centuries, a major quake has hit the Tokyo area, causing heavy damage and leading to huge loss of life.

The reason for the earthquakes is that the Japanese archipelago is at a place where three moving segments of the earth's crust – the Pacific Plate, the Philippine Plate and the Eurasian Plate – come into violent contact. This explains Japan's volcanic activity and its many hot springs.

The Philippine Plate is the prime culprit, sliding in under central Honshu in a northeastern direction at about 3 cm (1¼ in) a year. The movement, in turn, puts stress on the primary fault that affects Tokyo and other earthquake-prone regions. Add to this a nest of faults spread widely under the islands, sometimes as deep as 100 km (60 miles).

In Tokyo, the danger from earthquakes is made worse because much of the city is on unconsolidated alluvial soil and on landfill. This is a very poor foundation, which makes buildings tremble and oscillate more than they would on solid ground. Much of the waterfront damage during the 1995 Kobe earthquake was because of landfill liquification. Much of the remaining damage was due to fire from burst gas mains.

A major tremor whiplashes the Tokyo area every 60 or 70 years on average, and the last one, the Great Kanto Earthquake – a 7.9-magnitude jolt on the Richter scale – took place in 1923. At that time, most of the central part of the city was levelled and totally destroyed by fire and over 100,000 people were killed. Close to Ryogoku Station, 40,000 people were incinerated when a fire tornado swept across an open area where they had sought safety.

Some experts say that Tokyo is now much safer than it was in 1923. Buildings, bridges and elevated highways are reinforced and built according to the latest techniques. In addition, much of the city is been made fireproof. There are also shelters and elaborate plans to provide help should the worst happen. But the 1995 Kobe earthquake has shattered just about every one of those assurances. In Kobe, earthquake-proof structures collapsed like jelly. Rescue and relief plans proved unworkable, and government response, both on the local and national levels, was inept and embarrassingly inadequate. Nearly 6,000 people died.

Is Japan – and the world's largest metropolitan area, Tokyo – prepared? Given the experience of the 1995 Kobe quake, the preparations and assumptions for a Tokyo-area earthquake have had to be reassessed.

Tokyo is the world's most populated city, with extensive underground networks of subways and gas lines, and above ground, glass-covered buildings and flimsily constructed residences. Tens of thousands of people will probably die in a Kobe-strength quake. Many experts, Japanese and foreign, doubt that government plans are sufficient. ❑

RIGHT: assessing the damage from the Kobe earthquake, 1995.

KIMONOS FOR ALL SEASONS AND STYLES

Adopted from ancient Chinese court attire, the Japanese kimono today is mostly a ceremonial dress of exquisite textures and appeal

Western dress is the norm amongst today's Japanese, and few wear traditional attire except on special occasions such as weddings or festivals. But when a busy street of suited businessmen and trendy schoolgirls is punctuated by the colours and elegance of a kimono, Japan momentarily reverts to another time and place.

Contrary to expectations, the kimono did not originate in Japan. Like many things "distinctly" Japanese, the kimono has its roots in China – the Chinese court. During the Nara Period (710–784), the Japanese imperial court adopted the Chinese-style *p'ao*, a long, kimono-like gown brilliant with colours and embellishment; kimono styles used by Japanese women during this time were similar to the *p'ao* garments of women in Tang-dynasty China. Indeed, the Heian-era court dress worn by Japan's emperor and empress today during special occasions displays Chinese characteristics unchanged since the 12th century.

As did most things adopted by the Japanese over the centuries, the kimono underwent changes that eventually made it distinctly Japanese. During the Muromachi Period (1338–1573), for example, women introduced the *obi,* a narrow sash, and adapted the kimono sleeves to fit Japanese climate and styles.

▽ **KIMONO EVOLUTION**
The kimono adopted Chinese styles while taking on distinctly Japanese lines, whether for ceremony (as with these kimono), theatre or fashion.

△ **OBI ACCESSORIES**
The *obi* (sash) – often ornate and made of embroidered silk – today is about 25 cm (10 in) wide and 3.7 m (12 ft) long.

▽ **SHICHI-GO-SAN**
In November, shrines are filled with girls of 3 and 7 and boys of 5 wearing kimono, often hired.

▽ **HEAVY GATHERINGS**
Although said to be comfortable, and certainly attractive, elaborate kimonos can be heavy to wear.

◁ **DIFFERENCES**
While the basic kimono design is consistent, regional and ceremonial differences abound.

△ **TYING THE KNOT**
The traditional Shinto marriage requires complicated kimono for both man and woman.

▽ **EVOLVING DESIGNS**
While conservative kimono are common, Japan's youth often demand something a little more funky.

◁ **YUKATA**
Sumo wrestlers wearing *yukata,* a summer kimono of cotton with stencil-dyed patterns.

▷ **RITUAL**
Three-year-old girls at a shrine for blessing.

THE OBI: SIMPLE AND EXQUISITE

Once a simple and narrow sash introduced by Muromachi-Period women, the *obi* has evolved into one of the most beautiful – and complicated – aspects of the kimono today.

The *obi*'s need came about when the Japanese made changes to the adopted Chinese-court *p'ao.* A short-sleeved form of kimono *(kosode)* began to be worn as an outer garment, constrained by the *obi*. Later, the *obi* took on increased importance when women of the feudal estates wore an elaborate and exquisite outer kimono called *uchikake*. As centuries passed, only married women wore the *kosode*, while unmarried women wore the long-sleeved *furisode*.

The wider and more embellished silk seen today developed in the early 1700s during the Edo Period. This *obi* can be tied in a number of ways and may be embellished with *netsuke*, beautifully carved images used to cinch cords and fasten the details of the woman's *obi*.

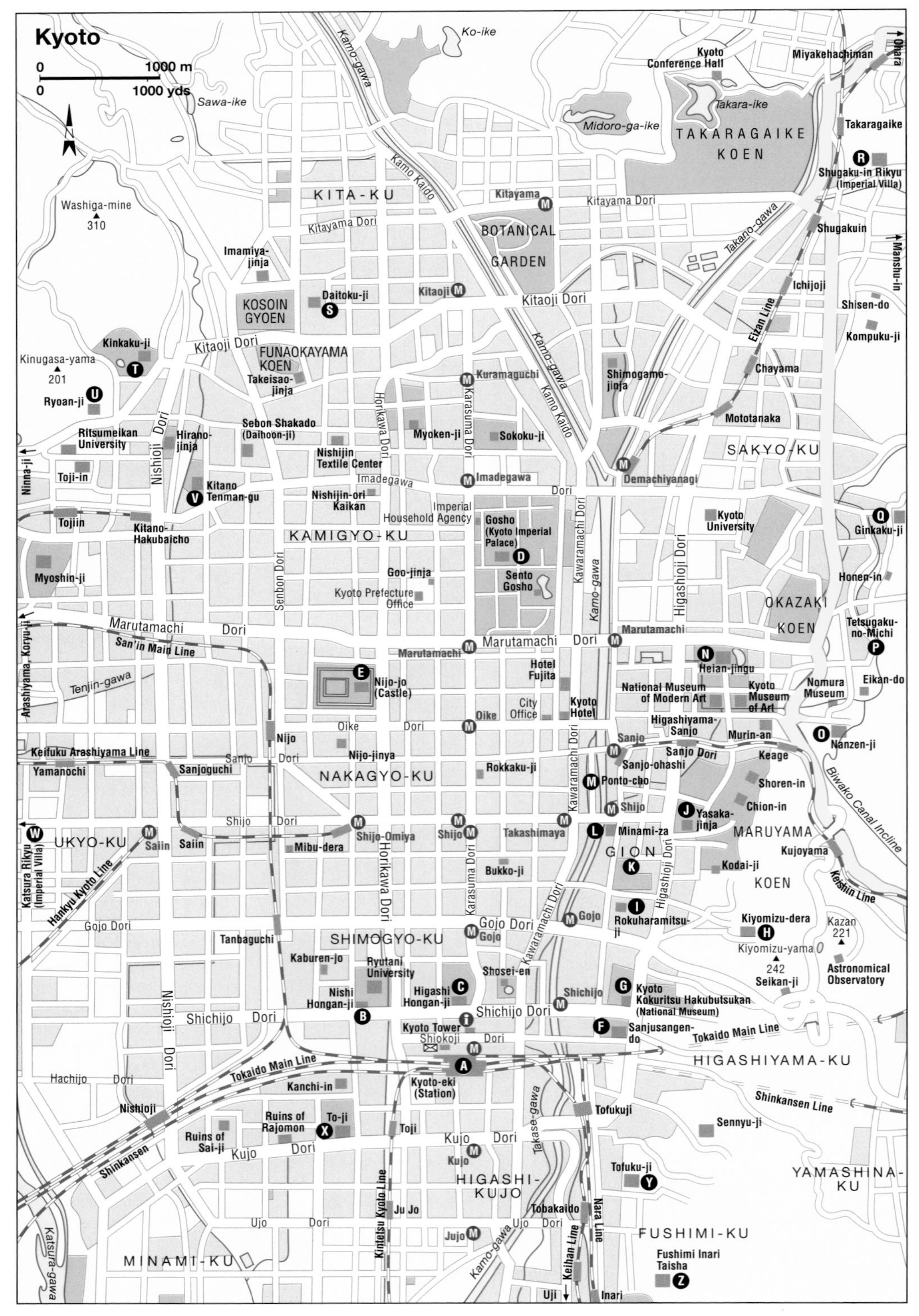
Kyoto
0 1000 m
0 1000 yds
Ko-ike
Kamo-gawa
Sawa-ike
Kyoto Conference Hall
Miyakehachiman
Ohara
Takara-ike
Midoro-ga-ike
TAKARAGAIKE KOEN
Takaragaike
Shugaku-in Rikyu (Imperial Villa)
Kamo Kaido
KITA-KU
Kitayama
Kitayama Dori
Washiga-mine 310
Kitayama Dori
BOTANICAL GARDEN
Shugakuin
Takano-gawa
Manshu-in
Imamiya-jinja
Daitoku-ji
Kitaoji
Kitaoji Dori
Ichijoji
Shisen-do
KOSOIN GYOEN
Eizan Line
Kompuku-ji
Kinkaku-ji
Kitaoji Dori
FUNAOKAYAMA KOEN
Kinugasa-yama 201
Takeisao-jinja
Kuramaguchi
Shimogamo-jinja
Chayama
Ryoan-ji
Horikawa Dori
Karasuma Dori
Kamo-gawa
Kamo Kaido
Mototanaka
Ritsumeikan University
Hirano-jinja
Sebon Shakado (Daihoon-ji)
Myoken-ji
Sokoku-ji
SAKYO-KU
Ninna-ji
Nishioji Dori
Nishijin Textile Center
Toji-in
Imadegawa
Imadegawa
Demachiyanagi
Kitano Tenman-gu
Nishijin-ori Kaikan
Dori
Imperial Household Agency
Gosho (Kyoto Imperial Palace)
Kawaramachi Dori
Kyoto University
Ginkaku-ji
Tojiin
Kitano-Hakubaicho
KAMIGYO-KU
Higashioji Dori
Myoshin-ji
Senbon Dori
Goo-jinja
Sento Gosho
Kamo-gawa
Honen-in
Kyoto Prefecture Office
OKAZAKI KOEN
Arashiyama, Koryu-ji
Marutamachi Dori
Marutamachi
Tetsugaku-no-Michi
San'in Main Line
Marutamachi Dori
Marutamachi
Heian-jingu
Tenjin-gawa
Nijo-jo (Castle)
Hotel Fujita
National Museum of Modern Art
Kyoto Museum of Art
Nomura Museum
Eikan-do
City Office
Kyoto Hotel
Oike
Oike Dori
Higashiyama-Sanjo
Murin-an
Nijo
Sanjo
Nanzen-ji
Keifuku Arashiyama Line
Sanjo Dori
Nijo-jinya
Sanjo Dori
Keage
Yamanochi
Sanjoguchi
Sanjo-ohashi
Rokkaku-ji
Kawaramachi Dori
Shoren-in
NAKAGYO-KU
Ponto-cho
Biwako Canal Incline
Shijo
Chion-in
Shijo Dori
Yasaka-jinja
Shijo
Takashimaya
MARUYAMA
Katsura Rikyu (Imperial Villa)
UKYO-KU
Saiin
Saiin
Shijo-Omiya
Minami-za
Mibu-dera
Kujoyama
GION
Higashioji Dori
Kodai-ji
Hankyu Kyoto Line
Bukko-ji
KOEN
Keishin Line
Horikawa Dori
Karasuma Dori
Kawaramachi Dori
Gojo Dori
Gojo
Rokuharamitsu-ji
Kiyomizu-dera
Kazan 221
Gojo Dori
Gojo
Tanbaguchi
SHIMOGYO-KU
Kiyomizu-yama 242
Kaburen-jo
Ryutani University
Shosei-en
Seikan-ji
Astronomical Observatory
Nishi Hongan-ji
Higashi Hongan-ji
Shichijo
Kyoto Kokuritsu Hakubutsukan (National Museum)
Nishioji Dori
Shichijo Dori
Shichijo Dori
Kyoto Tower
Sanjusangen-do
Shiokoji Dori
Tokaido Main Line
HIGASHIYAMA-KU
Tokaido Main Line
Hachijo Dori
Kanchi-in
Kyoto-eki (Station)
Shinkansen Line
Nishioji
Ruins of Rajomon
To-ji
Toji
Takase-gawa
Tofukuji
Sennyu-ji
Ruins of Sai-ji
Kujo Dori
Kujo Dori
Kujo
Shinkansen
Tofuku-ji
YAMASHINA-KU
Kintetsu Kyoto Line
Ju Jo
HIGASHI-KUJO
Tobakaido
Nara Line
Uji Dori
Uji Dori
Jujo
Kamo-gawa
Keihan Line
FUSHIMI-KU
Katsura-gawa
MINAMI-KU
Fushimi Inari Taisha
Uji
Inari

KYOTO

Spared destruction by the Americans during World War II, today the former imperial capital and modern city retains pockets of Japan's elegant spiritual and architectural past

Map on page 226

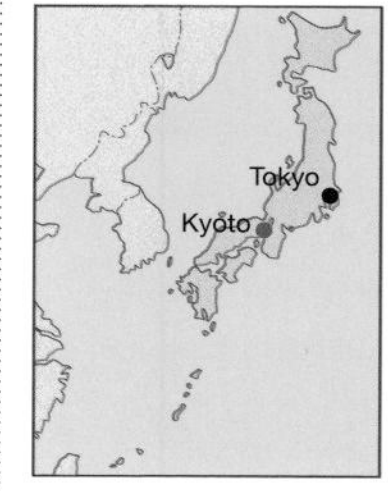

Tokyo might have the national government and Osaka the entrepreneurial savvy, but **Kyoto** ❾ defines traditional Japan and possesses an ingrained aristocratic bloodline, punctuated by a history unrivalled by any other Japanese city. As the country's artistic and cultural repository, Kyoto ranks with Athens, Cairo and Beijing as a living museum. Still, don't expect a quiet, idyllic place. Kyoto is Japan's fifth-largest city, with a population of 1½ million. Kyoto is a large metropolis, crowded and noisy and, like most other Japanese cities, lacking aesthetic appeal in its modern contours. Even the temples can feel claustrophobic with busloads of tourists and students doing the rounds.

Rapid post-war modernisation saw tens of thousands of old traditional houses lining Kyoto's narrow back streets razed to the ground in favour of modern, convenient living spaces. These old houses – splendid *kyo-machiya* – were of simplistic wooden facades and dancing rectilinear patterns; sliding paper doors; window slats in clay walls; lattices, trellises, benches, and hanging blinds of reeds and bamboo; and the *inuyarai*, or curved bamboo fences, that protruded out from the houses to protect against street traffic and dogs.

Home to 17 United Nations World Heritage Sites, Kyoto sits in a gradually sloping basin enclosed by a horseshoe of mountains on three sides, open southward to the Nara plains, between the rivers Katsura-gawa to the west and Kamo-gawa to the east, and the Kitayama Mountains that stretch north to the Japan Sea.

Early April is when the cherry blossoms bloom, and by May, everything else has blossomed in ritual radiance. The rains of June offer a misty contrast to venerable temples and shrines, and also help to thin the crowds. The sticky heat *(mushi atsui)* of summer is cooled by breezes off the surrounding mountains, making the long July and August evenings some of the best. September and October deliver near-perfect temperatures for walking along Kyoto's temple paths. The autumn colours break out in earthy reds and oranges in November, making it one of the most popular times to visit.

The frigid, festive air of December and January is contagious all over town, while a light dusting of snow in February and March can cast Kyoto into a Zen-like state. Be aware that, at all the best times to visit Kyoto, most of Japan is doing likewise.

BELOW: costumes from a *jidai matsuri* (historical festival).

Beginnings

For nearly 1,100 years, from AD 794 until 1868, Kyoto was home to the emperor, and thus was capital of the nation. Japan's first permanent capital was established in Nara in 710, but by 784, the intrigues of power-hungry Buddhist priests forced Emperor Kammu to move the capital to Nagaoka, a nearby suburb of present-day Kyoto.

Ten years later, in 794, Kammu relocated the capital again to the village of Uda, renaming it Heian-kyo – the Capital of Peace. It wasn't until 988 that the use of *kyoto* (capital) began to appear in official records. A century later, Kyoto was the city's proper name.

Shrines are always Shinto, and temples are always Buddhist. The suffixes of -jinja, -jingu *and* -gu *denote a shrine, while* -tera, -dera, -in, *and* -ji *denote a temple. However, a shrine may also have a Buddhist temple within its grounds, and a temple may have a shrine.*

The arrival of Buddhism in Japan in the 6th century brought great Chinese influence to the archipelago, reaching its peak of cultural flowering during the Heian Period (794–1185). Heian-kyo was built to a scale model of the Chinese Tang dynasty's (618–906) capital of Chang'an (now Xi'an), in China. Heian-kyo extended in a grid pattern still in evidence today for 5.2 km (3.2 miles) from north to south and 4.4 km (2.7 miles) east to west. Walls with 18 gates and a double moat surrounded the city. And because of earlier and persistent trouble with priests in Nara, Buddhist temples were forbidden inside the capital, explaining in part why many of Kyoto's most venerated temples are isolated in the hills surrounding the city.

Frequently levelled by earthquakes, floods, fires and wars over the centuries, the buildings of Kyoto have been moved, rebuilt and enlarged, and now represent a mosaic of historical periods. As a result, a scant few structures in Kyoto predate 1600, though many temples and shrines faithfully reproduce the earlier styles. It is commonly understood that a decision by the Americans not to bomb Kyoto during World War II – its historical heritage was considered too valuable – assured that these ancient structures stand today. Kyoto today offers some 1,600 Buddhist temples, 400 Shinto shrines, dozens of museums, two imperial villas, a palace, castle, and thousands of arts and crafts shops.

BELOW: Kyoto's mix of architecture.

Around Kyoto Station

Most people first encounter Kyoto from inside the gargantuan **Kyoto-eki** Ⓐ (Kyoto Station), less than three hours from Tokyo by *shinkansen*. Construction of this futuristic 16-storey building, completed in 1997, created one of the hottest controversies in Kyoto's 1200-year history. Preservationists, environmentalists, and much of the city's population were opposed to its construction, especially for the sheer size of the complex, its obstruction of the mountain skyline, and its modern-glass structure lacking semblance to traditional architecture.

Exiting the station, the horrific sight of Any City, Japan, greets the visitor. The station area, and tragically much of central Kyoto, displays the characterless, cluttered sprawl of all Japanese cities. But fortunately, amid the thoughtless creations that increasingly plague the city are a vast treasure of sights behind fading imperial walls, down narrow lanes, and amid the surrounding hills.

Directly north of Kyoto Station are two notable temples, Nishi (West) Hongan-ji and Higashi (East) Hongan-ji. As was the case with many of Kyoto's historical treasures, Japan's great unifier, Toyotomi Hideyoshi (1536–98), was responsible for establishing **Nishi Hongan-ji** Ⓑ. In 1591, Toyotomi brought the Jodo-shinshu Buddhist sect to the temple's current location. Its Chinese influences are many and historians sometimes consider it the best example of Buddhist architecture still around. The *hondo*, or main hall, was rebuilt in 1760 after fire destroyed it. The founder's hall – *daishido* – contains a self-carved effigy of the sect's founder. Cremated after his death, his ashes were mixed with lacquer and then applied to the effigy. The study hall *(shoin)* contains a number of rooms named for their decorations: Wild Geese Chamber, Sparrow Chamber and Chrysanthemum Chamber.

With some 40 universities, Kyoto is the educational centre of western Japan. A decline in student numbers, however, has been brought on by a lack of campus expansion funds; unable to afford more land in the city, many campuses are moving to rural areas.

BELOW: Kyoto's main train station obscures the city's horizon.

To the east, **Higashi Hongan-ji** Ⓒ was established in 1603 when the first Tokugawa shogun, wary of the Jodo-shinshu monks' power at nearby Nishi Hongan-ji, attempted to thwart their influence by establishing an offshoot of the sect. Only the main hall and founder's hall are open to the public. The present buildings were erected in 1895 after fire destroyed the predecessors. When these current structures were being built, female devotees cut and donated their hair, which was woven into 50 ropes used during construction; some of the ropes are on display between the main temple buildings. Just two blocks east, the temple's tranquil **Kikoku-tei** (open daily 9am–3.30pm) is a garden sanctuary of water, rocks and moss.

The record-holder for the archery competition at Sanjusangen-do shot 13,000 arrows during a 24-hour period in the late 1600s; just over 8,000 of the arrows hit the target.

Central Kyoto

Due west on the other side of the Kamo-gawa, the **Gosho** Ⓓ (Kyoto Imperial Palace) remains the emperor's residence in Kyoto and thus under the control of the Imperial Household Agency, which dictates every nuance and moment of the imperial family's life. Originally built as a second palace for the emperor, the Kyoto Imperial Palace was used as a primary residence from 1331 until 1868, when Tokyo became the new residence with the fall of the shogunate and with the Meiji restoration of the imperial system. The palace has gone through many restorations over the centuries; the current buildings were constructed in the mid-1800s. Shishinden (the Enthronement Hall), standing with its sweeping cedar roof before a silent stone courtyard, is an impressive emblem of imperial rule. It was constructed in the *shinden* style, where all buildings are connected by covered walkways or galleries. The court town that once surrounded the hall is now **Kyoto Gyoen**, the public Kyoto Imperial Park.

BELOW: tour group on the march.

From the palace, a few blocks west is **Nishijin**, the weaver's quarter. The **Nishijin Textile Centre** has excellent displays of working looms and woven goods. After browsing the centre, walk through the narrow side streets – the ancient crafts of weaving and dyeing are still practised in the old wooden buildings.

South is **Nijo-jo** Ⓔ, a castle begun in 1569 by the warlord Oda Nobunaga and finished by Tokugawa Ieyasu, ally to Oda Nobunaga, to demonstrate his military dominance over the city. In 1867, it served as the seat of government from where Emperor Meiji abolished the shogunate. Rectangular in shape, the castle's magnificent stone walls and gorgeous gold-leafed audience halls reflect the power of the Edo-Period shoguns. The linking corridors of the castle's Ninomaru Palace feature "nightingale" (creaking) floors to warn of intruders. The garden is a grand example of a lord's strolling garden.

Just south of the castle is **Nijo Jinya**, originally the home of a wealthy merchant and later used as an inn by visiting *daimyo*. The old manor house is full of trap doors, secret passageways and hidden rooms.

Eastern Kyoto

Just east of Kyoto Station and across the Kamo-gawa, **Sanjusangen-do** Ⓕ (Sanjusangen Hall, also called Rengeo-in) was last rebuilt in 1266. The temple houses 33 *(sanju-san)* alcoves nestled between 33 pillars under a 60-metre (200-ft) long roof. Inside is a 1,000-handed Kannon, the *bodhisattva* of mercy and compassion, and her 1,000 disciples. Each of their faces is different; Japanese look for the face that resembles their own – or that of a relative – to whom to make an offering. A famed archery festival, first started in 1606, takes place at the temple on 15 January.

Originally, the northeast wall of the Gosho was left incomplete, reflecting a belief that this direction brings misfortune. Beds are never laid out with the head facing this direction, nor are houses built with entrances at this inauspicious angle.

BELOW: the hall at Sanjusangen-do.

TIP

Antique lovers should not miss Shinmonzen-dori, a few blocks north of Shijo-dori in the Gion. Dozens of shops sell screens, scrolls, *ukiyo-e* prints, Imari porcelain, lacquer, and bronzes from China, Korea and of course Japan.

On the opposite side of Shichijo-dori to the north is the **Kyoto Kokuritsu Hakubutsukan** Ⓖ (Kyoto National Museum; Tues–Sun 9am–4.30pm; admission fee), founded in 1897 and exhibiting artefacts of history, art and crafts. Several other temples are east of the museum. Up the Kiyomizu-zaka, a slope on the east side of Higashioji-dori, is **Kiyomizu-dera** Ⓗ *(see photo on pages 224–25).* The temple's main hall *(hondo)* sits perched out over the mountainside on massive wooden pilings. The verandah, or *butai* (dancing stage), juts out over the valley floor overlooking the city below. A popular Japanese proverb equates taking any big chance in life to jumping off the elevated stage at Kiyomizu. Founded in 788, Kiyomizu-dera predates Kyoto and is dedicated to the 11-faced Kannon. The two 3.6-metre (12-ft) tall deva kings *(nio)* guarding the front gate speak the whole of Buddhist wisdom: the right one has lips pursed in the first letter of the Sanskrit alphabet, *a*, while the one on the left mouths *om*, the last letter. Behind the main hall with its dancing stage is Jishu, one of the most popular Shinto shrines in the country, and where the god of love and good marriage resides. (Most Buddhist temples in Japan also house some sort of Shinto shrine.) Don't trip over the "blind stones" *(mekura-ishi)* or the people walking between them with their eyes closed. The belief is that if one can negotiate the 20 metres (60 ft) between the stones with their eyes closed, silently repeating the name of their loved one, love and marriage are assured.

Steps lead down from Kiyomizu's main hall to **Otowa-no-taki**, a waterfall where visitors sip water from a spring said to have many health benefits, if not sheer divine power for the true believer. A short walk leads up the other side of the valley to a small pagoda with a view encompassing the entire hillside.

From Kiyomizu, return down the slope and follow a flight of stone steps

BELOW: a *maiko* in kimono, Gion.

THE WATER CITY

"Even in my sleep/ I hear the sound of water/Flowing beneath my pillow" – Yoshi Osamu. Of all Japanese cities, Kyoto, with its rivers, commercial canals, irrigation channels, artesian wells and garden ponds is perhaps, the most aquatic of Japan's inland urban centres, though in such a discreet way that you would hardly notice.

At one time there were literally thousands of wells in Kyoto. Wells were, and still are to some degree, an integral part of Kyoto life. They acquired a social function in the community, becoming focal points for informal gatherings. This practice among the townspeople of Kyoto gave birth to the expression *"Ido bata kaigi"* – literally, "to have a meeting around a well". Some private houses, if they are old enough, will still have them.

Glasses of water are often placed along with rice cakes and other delectables, in front of the stone figure of Jizo, a popular Buddhist saint found at roadsides or junctions. Fountains at the gates of Shinto shrines and strips of dyed cloth being fastened in the current of the Kamo River are constant reminders of the everyday importance of water.

Stroll anywhere in Kyoto and you are rarely beyond its presence. Water continues to be one of the main leitmotifs defining the character of the old imperial city.

down to Sannen-zaka, a street meaning "three-year slope". It is said that any pilgrim who trips or stumbles along this slope will have three years of bad luck. Today, the cobbled lane is less superstitiously known as Teapot Lane for all of the pottery shops lining its path. Continue to the charming Ninen-zaka, or "two-year slope". The restaurants near here are good for *soba* or *udon* noodles.

Back across Higashioji-dori sits **Rokuharamitsu-ji** Ⓘ, one of Kyoto's gems. At the rear of the main hall, built in 1363, is a museum with two fine Kamakura-Period (1185–1333) sculptures: Taira-no Kiyomori, of the Heike clan, and Kuya, founder of the temple. The eyes of Kiyomori, presaging the tragic destruction of his clan, sum up the anguish often seen in Kamakura-Period art. Kuya, who popularised the chanting of the lotus sutra, is shown reciting magic syllables, each of which becomes Amida, the saviour.

The many hostess-staffed "snack" bars in Gion are a pricey diversion in which an hour or two can easily cost US$500.

North are the brilliant-orange buildings of **Yasaka-jinja** Ⓙ, affectionately called Gion-san after the adjoining Gion pleasure quarter. One of the tallest granite *torii* in Japan at 9 metres (30 ft) in height marks the portal to the shrine. From the shrine's back gate, one enters adjoining Maruyama-koen. The park is known for its beautiful garden and magnificent cherry blossoms in early April. Two interesting temples sit just beyond: **Chion-in** and **Shoren-in**.

Geisha district

East of the Kamo-gawa in central Kyoto, **Gion** Ⓚ is Kyoto's famous pleasure-quarter or geisha district, today an uncanny blend of traditional and grotesque modern architecture. In Kyoto, geisha are known as *maiko* and *geiko*, not geisha. The word geisha in old Kyoto referred to male entertainers dressed as women; in Tokyo and Osaka, however, it came to mean women. *Maiko* debut at about

BELOW: a *maiko* making her way down a Kyoto alley.

TIP

Around the corner from Murin-an, International Community House is an excellent visitor resource, with a reading library, events and bulletin board, a giant TV with continuous CNN broadcasting, and a coffee shop.

16 years old and wear distinctive long trailing *obi*. At about 21, they may advance to the ranks of *geiko*, with their highly ornate kimono.

Along Gion's narrow streets, one will rarely see *geiko*, but there's a good chance to catch sight of a *maiko* hurrying to entertain a guest. The teahouses in the quarter are in the style of Kyoto's old *machiya* townhouses, but with added delicate touches such as the orange-pink plastered walls *(ichirikijaya)*. The best place to see the houses is along the alleyways that splinter off Hamani-koji, south of Shijo-dori. Just north of here is Gion Shimbashi, another well-preserved neighbourhood of old wooden buildings. At the intersection of Shijo-dori and the Kamo-gawa, **Minami-za Ⓛ**, built in the early 1600s, is the oldest theatre in Japan and is still used for *kabuki* performances.

Imperial drama

For the height of imperial drama, try a *noh* play, which developed in Kyoto in the 14th century. Rooted in *sarugaku* (ballad operas), the lyrical and melodramatic form became known as *sarugaku no noh*, later shortened to *noh*. A classical presentation includes five plays with several humorous interludes *(kyogen)*. Most presentations today show only two plays and two interludes. *Noh* greatly departs from Western ideas of drama by abandoning realism in favour of symbolism.

Noh developed in Kyoto as one of Japan's original art forms, along with *kabuki* and *bunraku* (puppet theatre). *Kabuki* (*ka-bu-ki*, or singing-dancing-performing) was the last purely Japanese art form to flourish, developing during the Edo Period as a commoner's entertainment. Originally dancing shows performed by women, *kabuki* turned to men as performers when the shogun declared the form immoral and forbidden to women. It has more

BELOW: Heian-jingu.

Map on page 244

variety and greater dynamic force than *noh* and appeals to a wider audience.

Other areas for traditional nightlife include traffic-free **Ponto-cho** Ⓜ along the west bank of Kamo-gawa and just across from Gion. The narrow street is lined with interesting bars, restaurants and *tayu* (top-ranked courtesan) houses. Kawaramachi is another busy shopping, eating and entertainment neighbourhood, also located beyond the Kamo's west bank. An excellent spot to dine in summer are the restaurants along Kamo-gawa, between Shijo and Sanjo streets.

Cross over Sanjo-dori and continue north to **Okazaki-koen**. This park holds museums, halls, a library and zoo. The best of the lot is the highly informative, visually stimulating **Fureaikan** (Tues–Sun 10am–6pm), a museum of traditional crafts housed in the basement of the Miyako Messe building.

Ginkaku-ji.

Heian-jingu

An arching 24-metre (80-ft) high *torii* leads from Okazaki-koen to the vermilion-coloured gate of **Heian-jingu** Ⓝ, more of an architectural study than a Shinto centre. The shrine, dedicated to Kyoto's first and last emperors, is a replica of the original Imperial Palace built in 794 and last destroyed by fire in 1227. The shrine was erected in 1895 to commemorate Kyoto's 1,100th anniversary and displays architecture of the Heian Period, when Chinese influence was at its zenith. Shinto shrines took on Buddhist temple features during this period, when the plain wooden structures were first painted.

Passing through the shrine's massive gate, it's hard to imagine that the shrine is but a two-thirds scale version of the original palace. The expansive, white-pebble courtyard leads the eye to the Daigoku-den, or main hall, where government business was conducted. The Blue Dragon and White Tiger pagodas

BELOW: purification at Heian-jingu.

dominate the view to the east and west. To the left of the main hall is the entrance to the garden, designed in the spirit of the Heian Period for the pleasures of walking and boating. Mirror ponds, dragon stepping stones, and a Chinese-style bridge are some of the beguiling features.

The temple was fairly deep in the northern hills… Genji climbed the hill behind the temple and looked off towards the city.

'Like a painting,' he said. 'People who live in such a place can hardly want to be anywhere else.'

– THE TALE OF THE GENJI
MURASAKI SKIKIBU

Tranquil shrines

From Heian-jingu walk southeast to **Murin-an**, a 19th-century landscaped villa designed by the celebrated gardener Ogawa Jihei. The grass-covered grounds of this secluded garden, with its azalea-lined stream, incorporate an unspoilt view of Higashiyama. From the garden it is a short walk east to **Nanzen-ji** **O**, which was originally the residence of 26-year-old Emperor Kameyama (1249–1305) after his abdication in 1274. Nanzen-ji sits nestled in a pine grove at the foot of Daimonji-yama and is part of the Rinzai school of Zen Buddhism, Zen's largest and best-known school. It's also one of Kyoto's most important Zen temples. The complex consists of the main temple and 12 sub-temples, of which only four are regularly open to the public.

Nanzen-ji provides an example of the Zen's belief in the relationship between all things. The pine grove influences the architecture, art influences the garden, and taken together they all influence the observer. The temple reflects the Chinese style *(kara-yo)* that arrived in Japan along with Zen. This style, evolving through the Ashikaga Period (1338–1573), achieved a near-perfect balance between the lordly Chinese style and the lightness of the native Japanese style. Exploring the two buildings of the abbots' quarters – Daiho-jo and Shoho-jo – reveals how garden architecture and landscape painting interrelate. The quarters are full of famous paintings, like *Tiger in the Bamboo Grove*, and the sur-

BELOW: taking shelter from the rain.

rounding gardens are renowned as some of the best in Japan. Here, the gardens are for sitting and contemplation, not strolling.

From Nanzen-ji, follow **Tetsugaku no Michi** Ⓟ, or the Philosopher's Walk, north past the Nomura Museum, Eikan-do temple, and the intriguing hillside temple of Honen-in. The walk, named for the strolling path of Japanese philosopher Nishida Kitaro (1870–1945), snakes about 2 km (1 mile) along the bank of a narrow canal to Ginkaku-ji. The quiet path – save for the crowds of tourists at times – is noted for its spring cherry blossoms and autumn foliage.

The walk ends at the Silver Pavilion, or **Ginkaku-ji** Ⓠ. The Ashikaga-era shogun who erected it in 1489 died before its completion and contrarily it remains without silver. However, its exquisite pavilion and Zen garden are not disappointing. The first floor of the pavilion was a residence and displays the Japanese *shinden* style. The second floor served as the altar room and shows a Chinese Buddhist style. The mound of white stones *(Kogetsu-dai)* in the garden was designed to reflect moonlight onto the garden. The quaint tearoom in the northeastern section of the pavilion is touted as the oldest in Japan.

A 20-minute walk directly north of the Silver Temple is **Kompuku-ji**, the first of three exquisite gardens. A dry landscape arrangement with a steep bank of azaleas, this temple is affiliated with the Rinzai school of Zen, but also has literary associations with Basho and Buson, two of Japan's greatest haiku masters. The narrow, bamboo entrance to **Shisen-do**, a rustic hermitage with an adjacent stone garden bordered by azaleas, maples and persimmon, is a short walk from here. Northeast on foot takes you to the tranquil precincts of **Manshu-in**, a hillside Tendai sect temple that dates from 1656.

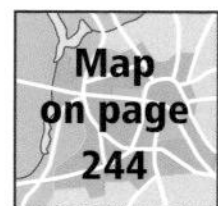
Map on page 244

Temple signs are generally explicit.

BELOW: one of Kyoto's strolling gardens.

To the northeast

In the northern foothills, the **Shugaku-in Rikyu** Ⓡ (Shugaku-in Imperial Villa) was built in 1659 as an emperor's retreat. The imperial villa at Shugaku-in seems pure fantasy compared to Katsura Imperial Villa. It consists of three large, separate gardens and villas. In Rakushiken (Middle Villa) stands a cedar door with carp painted on both sides. It is said that the carp would escape each night to swim in the villa's pond. Not until golden nets were painted over them, in the 18th century, did they stay put. (Shugaku-in requires permission from the Imperial Household Agency before visiting.)

Hiei-zan, an 850-metre (2,800-ft) high mountain northeast of Shugaku-in Imperial Villa, has long held historic and religious importance to Kyoto. Here, **Enryaku-ji** was founded to protect the new capital from evil northeast spirits. Apparently this exalted mission gave the temple's monks an inflated sense of importance. Over the decades, they became aggressive friars of the martial arts and swept into Kyoto on destructive raids. Their not-so-monastic rumbles were quenched by warlord Oda Nobunaga, who destroyed the temple in 1571. Today, there are three pagodas and 100 sub-temples, some offering accommodation and making Hiei-zan one of the area's most accessible hiking areas.

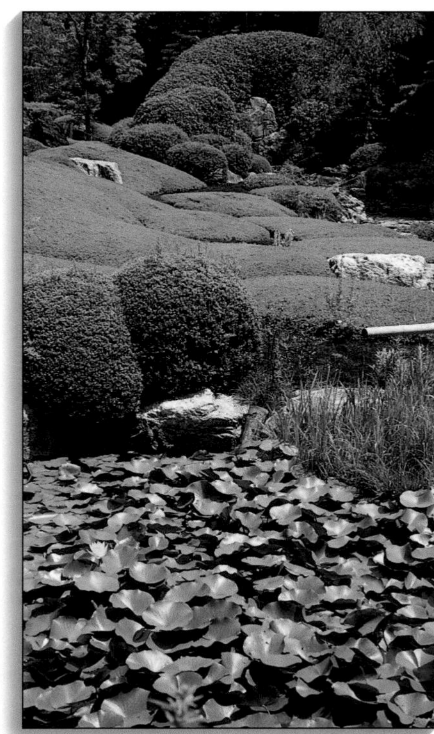

To the northwest and west

To the north and west of the city centre, skirting the foothills, are three renowned Zen temples that should not be missed. Established as a small monastery in 1315, the present buildings of **Daitoku-ji** S were built after 1468 when one of the several fires in its history burned down the temple. It is the holy of holies, where Zen married art. The great Zen calligrapher Ikkyu (d. 1481), painter Soga Dasoku (d. 1483), and founders of the tea ceremony Murata Juko (d. 1502) and Sen-no Rikyu (d. 1591) all came from Daitoku-ji. The great warlord Oda Nobunaga is buried here. Although a brutal warrior, Nobunaga was fundamental to the 16th-century unification of Japan and was a leading patron of the arts.

Original structure of Kinkaku-ji in the early 1900s. It was destroyed by arson in 1950.

Some eight of Daitoku-ji's 22 subsidiary temples are open to the public. The three best-known are Daisen, Zuiho and Koto. In Daisen-in is Kyoto's second most famous – maybe the best – Zen garden. Unlike the abstractions of other gardens, the Daisen garden more closely resembles the ink-wash paintings of Zen art.

The Daitoku complex has been criticised for its commercialism, but it is still worth the visit. This is also one of the best places to sample authentic Zen temple food, just like the monks eat.

Walk west along Kitaoji-dori past Funaokayama-koen to the best-known temple in Kyoto, if not all Japan: **Kinkaku-ji** T, or the Golden Pavilion. It's a replica built in 1955 of a 15th-century structure and last re-covered in gold-leaf in 1987. Each of the pavilion's three storeys reflects a different architectural style. The first floor is of the palace style, the second floor of the samurai-house style, while the third floor reveals the Zen-temple style. The large pond in front of the pavilion and surrounding grounds make it a perfect setting.

Below: Kinkaku-ji.

The original temple was burned down in 1950 by a man who entered the Buddhist priesthood after being seduced by the pavilion's beauty. Thinking that his sense of aesthetics might approach perfection if he burned down the very object that had enchanted him in the first place, he did exactly that. The author and right-wing nationalist Mishima Yukio fictionalised the burning episode in his 1956 book, *Kinkakuji*.

Further west, visit **Ryoan-ji** Ⓤ, or Temple of the Peaceful Dragon, early in the day before the peace is shattered by the busloads of tourists and students. Here is the most famous Zen rock garden (*karesansui*, or dry landscape) in the world and one of Kyoto's main tourist attractions. The 16th-century garden is an abstract of an ink-wash painting executed in rock and stone. The sense of infinite space is said to lift the mind into a Zen state.

A little past Ryoan-ji to the west, **Ninna-ji**'s formidable gate with its fierce-looking *nio* guardians is one of the best in Japan. Returning east, **Myoshin-ji** was founded in 1337 on the site of an imperial villa. Cast in 698, Japan's oldest bell hangs here. Tenth-century **Kitano Tenman-gu** Ⓥ is one of Kyoto's most earthy shrines and hosts a popular antiques market on the 25th of each month. Its restrained wooden architecture enshrines Sugawara Michizane, a 9th-century scholar and statesman. Small wooden votives, or *ema* – with a picture of a horse on one side and a wish or prayer (most for success in school exams) written on the other side – hang in the courtyard. The shrine also celebrates the first calligraphy of the year, when schoolchildren offer their writings to the shrine. The present shrine structure was built in 1607. Tenman-gu is known for its splendid plum trees that bloom in the snows of February, and for the geisha who serve tea under the flowering trees.

Ninna-ji is famous for a locally cultivated type of cherry tree called Omuro cherry. This low-branching temple treasure blooms later than the usual cherry trees in Kyoto.

BELOW: figuring out life at Ryoan-ji.

Uzamasa district

The **Uzumasa district** south of Ryoan-ji features two strikingly different sights: a temple of immense antiquity and cultural clout, and a cheesy but fun film studio.

Koryu-ji (daily 9am–5pm; entrance fee) traces its roots to 622, when either Prince Shotoku or Hata no Kawakatsu, an important family of Korean lineage, founded the temple. It's a disputed point, but one that need not delay you in seeking out the treasures of this unique temple. The first building of note, the **Kodo** (Lecture Hall), is one of the oldest constructions in Kyoto, dating from 1165. The statues inside are even older, most dating from the 7th and 8th centuries. Impressive as they are, these are overshadowed by the collection housed in the contemporary **Reiho-kan** (Treasure House). The two most outstanding statues here are the image of Prince Shotoku at the age of 16, and Miroku Bosatsu, or Future Buddha.

For a more dramatic but decidedly lighter view of history, repair to the nearby **Toei Uzumasa Eiga-mura** (daily Mar–Nov 9.30–4pm, Dec–Feb 9am–5pm; closed 26 Dec–31 Dec; admission fee), a commercial studio renowned for churning out *chambara*-style, sword and Zen-flavoured samurai films and now, TV dramas. Outdoor studio sets are open to the public, and there are often rehearsals and shots going on in the indoor studios. Out in the western hills, **Arashiyama** was once the playground of Heian aristocrats. Today it is punctuated by temples. Cross over the Hozu-gawa on picturesque Togetsu Bridge to the shop-lined promenade along the river. Just beyond sits **Jikishian**, a refuge temple for women.

One of Japan's most famous strolling gardens lies inside **Katsura Rikyu** **W** (Katsura Imperial Villa), due west of Kyoto Station on the west side of Katsura-gawa. Its garden features a number of splendid teahouses overlook-

Both Japanese and foreign visitors need special permission to visit one of the imperial villas. Bring your passport to the Imperial Household Agency office at the Kyoto Imperial Palace early on the day you wish to visit.

BELOW: garden at Katsura Rikyu.

ing a large central pond. Katsura, with its severe refinement, has exercised more influence on contemporary architecture than perhaps any other building in the whole of Japan.

South of Kyoto Station

Just south of Kyoto Station, **To-ji** **X** boasts one of the nation's enduring postcard images: the five-storey Goju-no-to pagoda. Rebuilt in 1644, and standing at 55 metres (180 ft), it is Japan's tallest pagoda. The temple itself was established in 796 and today draws large crowds to its flea markets. Built next to the old city's south gate, To-ji became Japan's main Buddhist temple. Its main hall *(kondo)* reflects Buddhist traditions from India, China and Japan.

To the east up against the hills, **Tofuku-ji** **Y** contains Japan's oldest and most important Zen-style gate, from the 15th century. Yet its 25 subsidiary temples are rarely visited and the grounds are usually quiet. Walk through the abbot's quarters *(hojo)* to the platform over the ravine looking down on Tsuten Bridge – it's one of the most delightful views in Kyoto. During the last week of November, don't miss the festival of old brushes and pens where writers and painters cast their old tools into a sacred fire.

A few blocks south of Tofuku-ji is where tunnel-like paths of hundreds of bright-red *torii* tempt walkers. Actually, there are over 10,000 *torii* covering the paths of **Fushimi Inari Taisha** **Z** – the fox shrine founded in the 9th century in honour of the fox that farmers believe is the messenger of the harvest god. Walk the full 4-km (2½-mile) course. Fushimi is renowned for its high-quality sake, and its famous brewery, Gakkien, is housed in an original Edo-period warehouse where visitors can sample products. ❑

Farmers have always associated the presence of foxes with abundance. There are over 40,000 Inari shrines throughout Japan, the deity is especially popular among the business community. Fushimi Inari is the head shrine.

BELOW: *torii* of Fushimi Inari Taisha, and Amida, twin temple carving at Arashiyama.

まい
八坂庚
八坂

AROUND KYOTO

Just beyond Kyoto's hilly boundaries is the cradle of its ancient agricultural life. Some surprising cultural highlights nestle in the midst of this rustic scenery.

Map on page 264

Who would expect to find ancient Buddhist statuary and a paradise garden in a mist-filled valley less than an hour from Kyoto Station, or to enter a futuristic art gallery, concealed in the side of a mountain? Equally impressive is Hikone Castle, one of only a handful of original fortresses to have survived. In ancient times, retinues of powerful lords and shoguns would make way for Uji's yearly procession of wooden chests, carrying Japan's most valuable green tea harvest. The brew still ranks as the very best, but the journey now to Uji can be made in just 30 minutes.

Ohara

A pleasant 50-minute bus ride through the northeastern suburbs of Kyoto crosses a fertile valley plain into the village of **Ohara ❶**. The area has a strong association with ancient Kyoto aristocracy: emperors, empresses, imperial kin and consorts who repaired here for respite and refuge. Retired aristocracy, peasants, high priests and monks co-existed in a simple but rarified atmosphere. Ohara has long been associated with the Buddhist faith. The legacy of beauty, calm and tradition clearly appeals to the handful of textile artists, potters and writers who have settled in Ohara.

An insight into the way that ordinary people lived in this naturally well-endowed area can be glimpsed in the **Ohara Kyodokan** (daily 9.30am–5pm; admission fee), a 19th-century farmhouse that has been turned into a folk museum. The wooden household utensils, farming tools and furniture convey the sense of a basic, but not uncomfortable existence.

Temple district

Ohara attracts a steady trickle of visitors, though most remain within the main temple district. A lane leading east from the main road winds up a hill beside a stream towards **Sanzen-in** (daily 8.30am–4.30pm, Dec–Feb until 4pm; admission fee), Ohara's most important temple. Tubs of pickles, mountain vegetables, rice dumplings and a local speciality called *shiso-cha* (beefsteak-leaf tea), are sold along the way. The tea, which is slightly salty, supposedly contains flecks of gold.

Sanzen-in, like all the sacred sites here, is a subtemple of Kyoto's grand Enryaku-ji. Soft, flower-filled gardens, maples and massed hydrangea bushes replace the towering cedar forests that characterise the surroundings of the parent temple, blending in perfectly with the natural curvature of hill, forest line and mountain. Sanzen-in, standing in moss-covered grounds shaded by towering cryptomeria, is one of the great iconic images of cultural Japan.

LEFT: a geisha grins for the camera.
BELOW: Raigo-in.

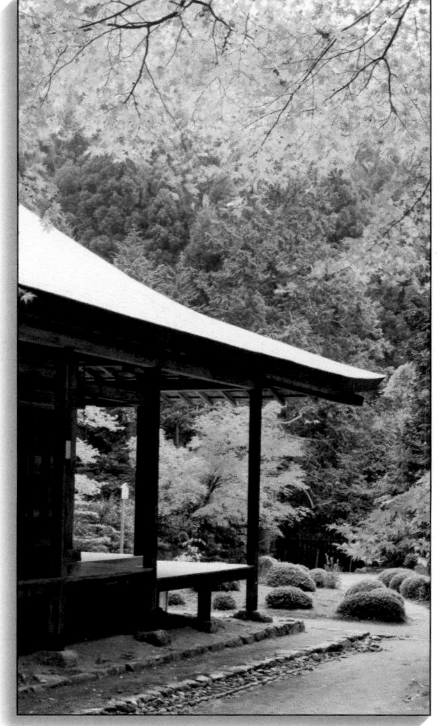

Sanzen-in is an amalgam of buildings, some ancient, others more recently restored. Genshin, the retired abbot of Enryaku-ji temple in Kyoto, had the first Amida Hall built here in 985. The hall looks out over the garden, designed to evoke the unearthly beauty of the Pure Land sect. A statue of Amida, carved by Genshin himself with an intricate arabesque halo, is enshrined here.

The Shuheki-en Garden (Garden that Gathers Green), located at Sanzen-in, is to the south and east of the Kyaku-den, or reception hall. It was created by the tea ceremony master, Kanamori Sowa (1584–1656).

Natural surroundings

More earthly delights are laid out in the gardens above the temple where rhododendrons and bush clover make way for a newer hydrangea garden created by a former abbot of Sanzen-in. The earth is acidic on the hillside here, so the flowers are a watercolour-blue. The hydrangea, all three thousand bushes, are best seen during the June rainy season. A gravel path above Sanzen-in leads to **Raigo-in**, a temple located in a seldom visited clearing in the forest. The main hall is still used for the study of *shomyo* chanting.

According to local legend, you are not supposed to hear Otonashi-no-Take (Soundless Falls), but if you continue up the same road a gentle splashing sound will soon be detected. The cascade is located amidst maple trees, cedar and clumps of wisteria. You cross a wooden bridge over a second river, the shallow, fast-flowing Ritsugawa, to reach the front lawn of **Shorin-in** (daily 9am–5pm; admission fee), a temple often overlooked by visitors. An appealingly under-maintained garden, its main hall, a nicely weathered wooden building, dates from the 1770s.

Nearby **Hosen-in** (daily 9am–5pm; admission fee) is distinguished by a magnificent 700-year-old pine at its entrance. The unusual form looks vaguely familiar, turning out to be clipped into the resemblance of Fuji-san. The inner crane and turtle garden is framed like a painting or horizontal scroll by the pillars of the *tatami* room visitors sit within to contemplate the scene while sipping green tea served with a delicate Japanese confection. **Jakko-in** (Mar–Nov 9am–5pm, Dec–Feb 9am–4.30pm; admission fee), built as a funerary temple for the emperor Yumei in 594, lies across the fields along a lane lined with old houses and shops selling yet more varieties of pickles and local products. The original structure was destroyed in an arson attack a few years ago and is now being rebuilt. The temple is associated with the renowned *Tales of the Heike*, where it is described as a nunnery inhabited by the empress Kenreimon-in. The compact garden here bears a remarkable resemblance to its description in the book.

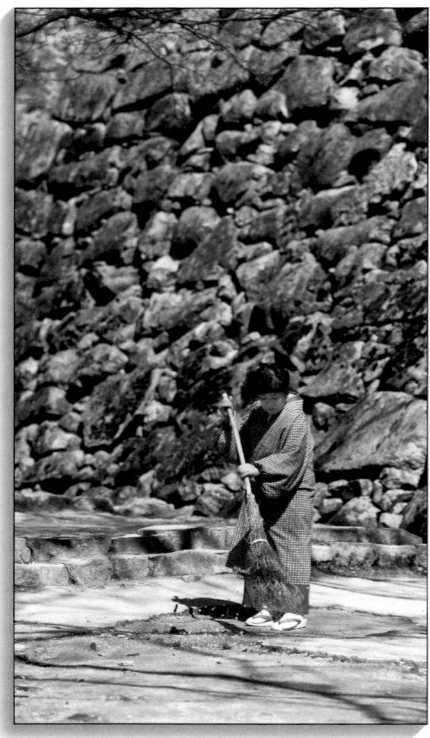

BELOW: sweeping the path to Hikone Castle.

If your thirst for solitude needs further quenching, a 40-minute walk north of Jakko-in leads to **Amida-ji** (daily 9am–4.30pm; admission fee) temple in Kochitani (the Valley of Ancient Knowledge). A large Chinese-style gate marks the entrance to the route, a further 20-minute walk through an eerily still maple forest. There are no restaurants, shops or souvenir outlets here, the faded colours, uneven floors and the musty air of wooden halls and corridors of the buildings adding to the ancient mystique of the valley.

Hikone

A little over one hour from Kyoto on the JR Tokaido Line, **Hikone ❷**, the second-largest city in Shiga Prefecture, and one attractively situated on the shores of Lake Biwa,

Map on page 264

manages to still feel like the provincial castle town it once was. The tourist office to the left of Hikone Station has helpful literature and the excellent English-language *Street Map & Guide to Hikone*.

Hikone Castle (daily 8.30am–5pm; admission fee), the centrepiece of the town, dates from 1622, when local lords, the Ii family, had it constructed. One of Japan's last original castles, it is also considered one of its finest. In keeping with the Japanese military's love of the cherry blossom, over 1,000 trees surround the castle. From the third storey there is a splendid view of the town and lake. Your castle admission ticket also allows you to enter nearby **Genkyu-en**, once the Ii clan's private garden. The Chinese-influenced design, completed in 1677, is best appreciated from the raised teahouse, where for ¥500 you will be served powdered green tea *(matcha)* with a traditional sweet.

For an even quieter setting, consult your map to find **Ryotan-ji** (daily 9am–5pm; admission fee), a 17th-century temple to the south of the station that has two superb gardens, one the pond variety, the other a well composed Zen garden. Look out for the pond garden's rock turtle island.

Museum in the mountain

Art and architecture dovetail at the extraordinary **Miho Museum** ❸ (opens for only some months in the year; www.miho.or.jp/english). The I.M. Pei design is located near the town of Shigraki-no-Sato, inside a mountain in the lush green landscape of Shiga Prefecture. It is an unusual concept, a museum run by "new religion" leader Koyama Mihoko and her daughter Hiroko to promote their belief that spiritual completion comes through a fusing of art and nature. The result is stunning: as the electric shuttle bus emerges from a tunnel, transecting a giddy

BELOW: the interior of the Miho Museum.

bridge over a deep valley, you disappear on the other side through a screen of tetrahedrons into the opposite mountain and the James Bond-like inner vault of the museum proper. The roof is an enormous glass and steel contruction and the museum is divided into two wings. The north wing displays exquisite Japanese art objects, from Buddhist relics to ceramic and hanging scrolls, and the south wing contains art treasures from the great world civilizations, including Egypt, Assyria and ancient China.

Although it is not impossible to get to the Miho Museum by public transport, it is much easier to join a guided tour organised by JTB Sunrise Tours directly from Kyoto and Osaka (tel: 075-341 1413; www.jtb.co.jp; email: itdw_sunrise@jtb.jp).

Byodo-in

About 10 km (6 miles) south of Fushimi Inari Taisha, on the way to Nara and in the town of **Uji**, is one of Japan's most famous buildings, **Byodo-in** ❹ (daily 8.30am–5.30pm; admission fee).

Uji was a popular country retreat for aristocrats, and elegant retirement estates were built here. For members of the Heian Period imperial court in Kyoto, Uji, now reached in just 30 minutes by rail, must have felt a world away. From their well-situated villas, the nobility could enjoy watching the gentle range of green hills that stand as a backdrop to the majestic Uji River, the home even now of herons and sweetfish. One of these villas was owned by Fujiwara Michinaga, the emperor's chief advisor. A closer glimpse of this era is found in Murasaki Shikibu's (a lady-in-waiting at the court) 11th-century narrative, *The Tale of Genji*, the world's first full-length novel. "He was obliged to move to Uji where fortunately he still possessed a small estate… after a time he began once more to take an interest in flowers and autumn woods, and would even spend hour after hour simply watching the river flow." Some years after Shikibu's work was completed, Yorimichi, the son of Fujiwara, converted the villa into a temple dedi-

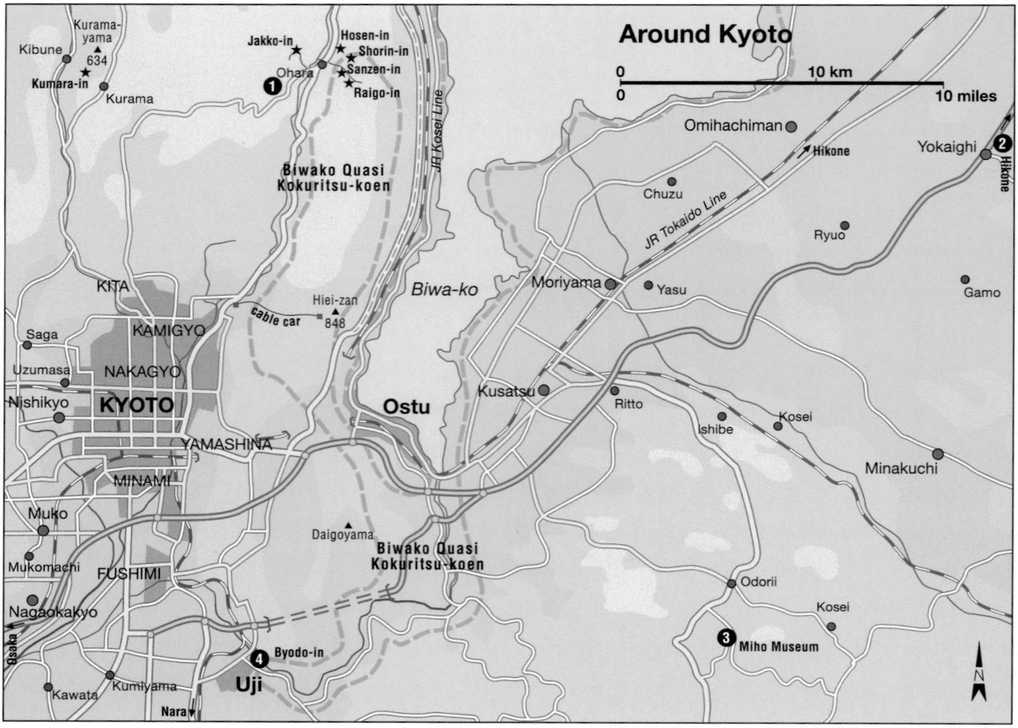

Around Kyoto

cated to Amida, the Buddha of the Western Paradise. The centrepiece of the project was the Amida Hall, commonly known as the Phoenix Hall, and the entire ensemble is known as Byodo-in. Amazingly, the building has survived centuries of weather, fire, earthquakes and years of neglect. In December 1994 it was declared a UNESCO World Heritage Site.

The best view of the perfectly balanced main building and its ornamental wings, seemingly floating on the surface of the water, can be had from across the pond that surrounds the complex, an image that appears on the reverse side of the ¥10 coin. When the doors to the hall are open, a gilded statue of Amida, floating on a bed of lotuses, is visible within. Some of the more valuable or vulnerable objects in the hall, such as wall murals, wooden statues and the original temple bell, have been preserved and are housed in the recently built **Homotsu-kan** (Treasure Hall; daily 9am–4pm; admission fee) situated on a hill behind the Phoenix Hall.

Riverbank

Besides Byodo-in, Uji has several other features of interest, not least of which is the river itself and its series of bridges, islands, shrines and teahouses lining its banks. The journey into Uji's past begins at the "Bridge of Floating Dreams", the modern version of the original 7th-century structure that spans the river. A narrow shopping street runs from here to Byodo-in. The first thing you will sense here is the smell of roasting tea. Fragrant *uji-cha* was first planted in the 13th century. Uji green tea is now regarded as the finest in Japan. On summer evenings, demonstrations of cormorant fishing take place along the river, adding to the magic of fireworks, poetry readings and other events. ❑

Map on page 264

Lotuses, the symbol of Buddhism, are planted throughout the gardens at Byodo-in, their purple and white flowers at their best on an early summer morning.

BELOW: carp at Byodo-in come up for air.

NARA

Map on page 270

Japan's capital in the 8th century, Nara later escaped the civil wars that shook the country. A repository of ancient treasures, it embodies Chinese, Korean and even Middle Eastern styles

The ancient site of **Nara** belongs to an era before Zen gardens and tea ceremony, before Japan became Japan. Buddhist thought from India and arts from as far as Greece and Turkey flowed east along the Silk Road and Nara was the last stop. Preserved here long after extinction in their home countries are the finest examples of Tang dynasty architecture from China, early Korean religious sculpture, and treasures from Iran.

Japan had its capital at Nara from AD 710 to 784, after which the government moved to Kyoto and the Nara area lost political importance. This was Nara's great blessing. As a result, it avoided the wars that destroyed other ancient capitals of China, Korea and Japan.

Nara Buddhism represented an early exuberant form of Buddhist thought, rich in symbolism. Everywhere in Nara are *mandala*, the diagrams or arrangements representing cosmic truth. Represented at the centre is the essence of the main god. Expanding outward in circles or squares are other gods exerting their powers to help the centre. *Mandala* can be represented in the arrangement of statues on an altar to the layout of temple buildings. Every placement and gesture has meaning. For example, two guardian figures flank the gates to large temples. One has his mouth open, the other closed. These symbolise the sounds *a* and *om*, the first and last letters of the Sanskrit alphabet. Being first and last, they encompass all and hence have magical power to protect against evil.

Hand gestures, clothing and implements are significant. Most ornate are the *mandorla*, or halos, in which can be seen the intercultural impact of the Silk Road. The halos originated in Indian Buddhism and travelled east to Japan and west to Europe, where they were adopted by Christianity. The flames in the halos signify divine light.

Statues with great power were hidden from the public and became the so-called secret Buddhas, shown only on rare occasions. For instance, the Kuze Kannon of Horyu-ji was hidden from the public for a thousand years before seeing the light of day in the late 19th century. Many statues are still only shown in the spring or autumn or on religious holidays.

Many Nara masterpieces owe their beauty to the technique of dry lacquer, in which the contours of the figure are moulded out of a paste of lacquer applied over a central core. The use of a soft plastic material, rather than carving, allows for great subtlety of expression. While the origins of using lacquer are rather obscure, the technique of lacquer in its most basic form is found throughout Asia, including China, Korea, Thailand and Burma.

LEFT: lanterns at Kasuga Taisha. **BELOW:** statues are rich with meaning.

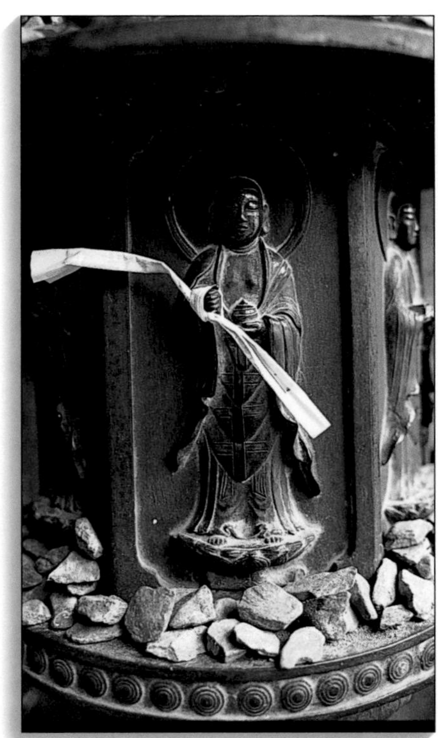

Old Nara

Old Nara, much larger than the city today, followed the traditional model of Chinese imperial cities: a sacred square with streets radiating from the central palace in a grid pattern. During the centuries of neglect after 784, the palaces of Nara disappeared, but the temples and shrines on the northeastern edge of the city survived. This corner of the city is now a public park, **Nara-koen** (Nara Park). Tame deer, sacred to the shrine of Kasuga Taisha, are its symbol.

A temple to the east of **Nara-eki** Ⓐ (Nara Station) is **Kofuku-ji** Ⓑ, on the western side of Nara-koen. The patrons of Kofuku-ji were the Fujiwara clan, who gained power in the mid-7th century and succeeded in dominating the government for the next 500 years. Even after the capital moved to Kyoto, the Fujiwara continued to support Kofuku-ji as the family temple. Kofuku-ji is known for its two pagodas. The five-storey pagoda, built in 1426, is a copy of an original dating from 730 and is the second-tallest pagoda in Japan; the three-storey pagoda dates from 1114.

Scent of
chrysanthemums,
And in Nara
All the ancient
Buddhas.

– BASHO
17TH CENTURY

The attached **Kokuhokan** (Treasure House; Tues–Sun 9am–5pm; admission fee) – a dreary, concrete building – offers the best introduction to Japanese sculpture available. Most famous is the set of guardians (734) with sweet, child-like faces moulded out of dry lacquer. Of these, the six-armed Ashura is one of the best-loved statues in Japan. In addition, the museum displays a cast bronze head of Yakushi Nyorai, practically Egyptian in its abstract simplicity, and massive heads of temple guardians originally from statues that must have been 15–20 metres (50–65 ft) high. Nara developed in an age before Japan became the land of the miniature. The buildings and statues aimed to exceed even the grandeur of Imperial China.

BELOW: tame deer at Nara-koen.

Map on page 270

From Kofuku-ji, cross the street east to **Kokuritsu Hakubutsukan** Ⓒ (National Museum; Apr–Sept Tues–Fri, Sat–Sun 9.30am–6pm, Oct–Mar Tues–Sun 9.30–5pm; admission fee). The most interesting part of the museum is the East Gallery. At the end of October and the beginning of November, the normally stored treasures of Todai-ji are displayed to the public. Regular displays include an array of Buddha images from past centuries and archaeological artefacts excavated from ancient tombs.

To the north across Nara-koen's central avenue is **Todai-ji** Ⓓ, founded in 743 and the most important temple in Nara. Walk north towards the temple and **Nandai-mon**, a gate dating from 1199. With its 18 pillars and elaborate roof construction, it is one of the outstanding monuments of the Kamakura Period. Inside the gate stand great wooden statues, called *nio*, who guard the entrance to Todai-ji. They were carved in around the 13th century.

Straight ahead is Todai-ji, with the **Daibutsu-den** (Hall of the Great Buddha). Enshrining a monumental bronze image of Vairocana, the Cosmic Buddha, the hall was meant to proclaim the power of the imperial state. It was destroyed numerous times by fire; the present building dates from 1706. Although only two-thirds of its original size, Daibutsu-den is said to be the largest wooden structure in the world. The present building is not entirely a first-rate piece of architecture (note the pillars made of bound timbers, rather than single beams such as those of Nandaimon). Still, the interior retains a sense of the medieval grandeur that was Nara.

The Buddha has been greatly altered in later restorations, but the petals of the lotus upon which the Buddha sits retain original engravings in fine lines showing Shaka (the historical Buddha) as one of 110 billion avatars of Vairocana. The bronze statue is 16 metres (55 ft) tall and weighs 500 tons. Like the statuary

BELOW: Todai-ji and its figure of Kokuzo Bosatsu.

found in the nearby Sangatsu-do and Kaidan-in, it shows off Tempyo Period (729–764) art and craftsmanship. To the east of Daibutsu-den is a road lined with picturesque stone lanterns leading up the hill to two temples. **Sangatsu-do** Ⓔ (March Hall), built in 746, contains a large central statue of Fukukenjaku Kannon (the god of compassion) radiating light beams and surrounded by a *mandala* arrangement of attendants and guardian beings. Next door is **Nigatsu-do** (February Hall), the perfect place for a final view of the park. Raised high over the city, this pyramidal building was frequently burned and rebuilt, most recently in 1669. Every 13 March since its founding in 752, the emperor sends an emissary at midnight with water symbolising the coming of spring. The arrival of the water is the occasion for a fire festival, with monks carrying burning pine running around the verandah and spinning sparks into the night. The building is closed to the public.

The area south of Sarusawa Pond is an excellent place to find *ryokan*, traditonal Japanese inns. Note that rates tend to go up on the weekends and in the peak spring and autumn seasons.

Kasuga Taisha Ⓕ was originally built in AD 710, but its buildings have been reconstructed numerous times following the Shinto tradition that sacred structures be thoroughly rebuilt at intervals, often every 20 years, as is also the case with the shrines at Ise. Kasuga Taisha's treasure house is a modern structure housing the shrine's artefacts.

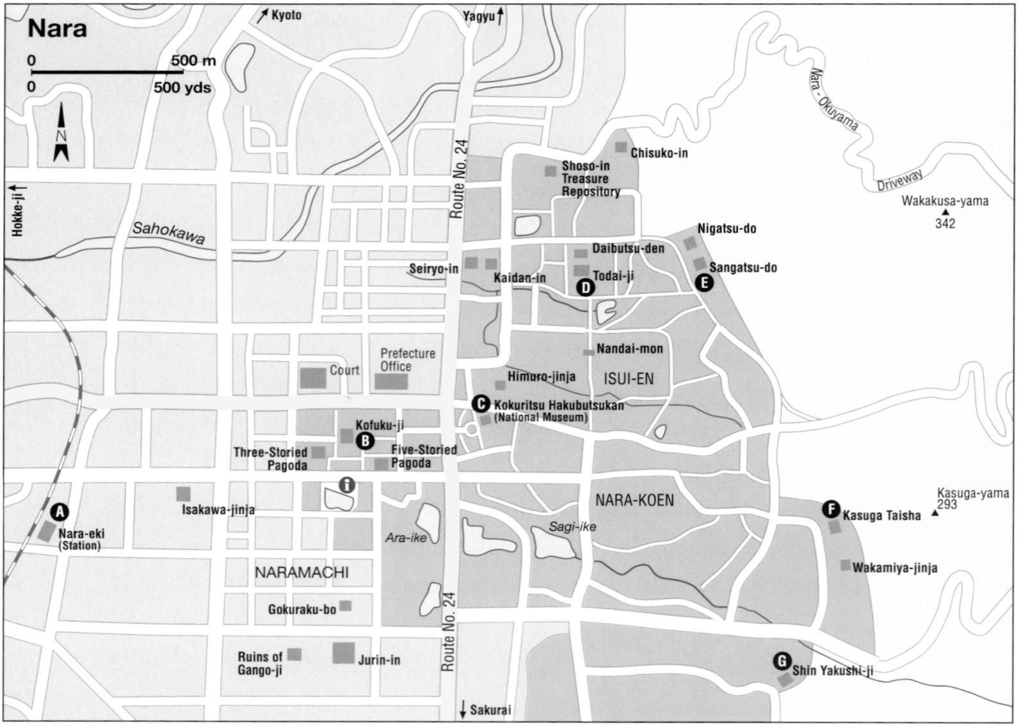

The city of Nara contains numerous other temples of historical importance. The most interesting temple outside Nara-koen is **Shin Yakushi-ji** Ⓖ, built in 747 to the southeast. This, along with Sangatsu-do, is one of the few original Nara buildings. The central figure of Yakushi Nyorai (Healer) grants aid to those suffering from ailments of the eyes and ears. Most unusual is the set of 12 clay guardian images still standing intact. Shin Yakushi-ji, tucked away among crowded streets in a forgotten part of town, is a favourite. Just a few steps west of the temple is the Nara City Museum of Photography, with a splendid collection of images of Nara by the late Irie Taikichi and others.

Northwest

The best place to begin here is **Hannya-ji**, the Temple of Wisdom. Surrounded by a garden of wildflowers, it has great charm. In the garden is a Kamakura-era gate with elegant upturned gables and a 13-storey Heian-era stone pagoda. The temple houses a Kamakura statue of Monju, the god of wisdom. Monju rides on his sacred lion, carrying in his hand the sword to cut through ignorance. About 2 km (1¼ miles) from Nara-koen, it was the centre of the ancient city. Of the palace nothing survives but a large field with circular clipped hedges showing where the pillars used to stand. Just east of the palace field is **Hokke-ji**, a nunnery known for its 8th-century statue of Kannon.

The statue of Kannon at Hokke-ji is one of the secret Buddhas, on view only from 30 March to 7 April, 6 to 8 June, and 25 October to 8 November each year.

North of Hokke-ji are imperial tomb mounds surrounded by moats, and beyond them to the northwest is **Akishino-dera**, patron temple of the arts. The original temple was founded in 775, but the present hall dates from the Kamakura Period. Inside is Gigeiten, god of the arts and a favourite of Nara cognoscenti. The head is original Nara, with the delicacy of expression typical of dry lacquer. The body, a recreation from the Kamakura Period, has the S-curve of Chinese sculpture.

Southwest

The southwestern temples are a major destination for travellers. The first temple from Nara-koen is **Toshodai-ji**, founded by the Chinese monk Ganjin in 751. The roof of the *kondo* (main hall) is the finest surviving example of Tang dynasty architecture. Note the inward-curving fish tails on the roof, unique to

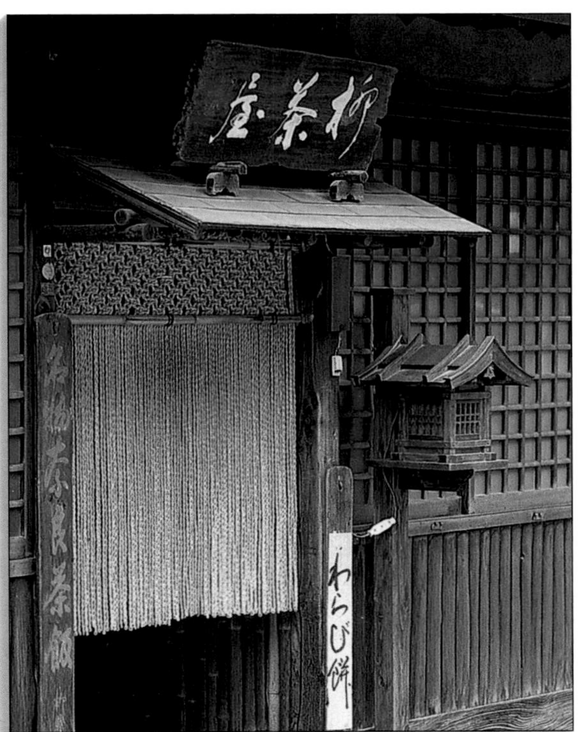

BELOW: entrance to traditional teashop.

DIALECTICAL ROOTS

Japanese ranks ninth worldwide in number of speakers. Since the mid-20th century following World War II, no nation other than Japan has used Japanese as a language.

The origins of Japanese are not known with any certainty. A strong hypothesis connects Japanese to Korean, with the introduction through Kyushu over 2,000 years ago of a language of southern Korea, along with the cultivation of rice.

Dialects abound in this archipelago punctuated by mountain peaks and deep valleys, not to mention the islands themselves. Some dialects – those of Kyushu and Tohoku come to mind – are nearly unintelligible to most Japanese people. Even the differences between Tokyo and Osaka (known for its earthier language) are pronounced. *Kyotsu-go*, or "common language" and based on the Tokyo/Kanto dialect, linguistically unifies the islands.

The finest workmen from Paekche in Korea were used to construct the Horyu-ji. They were careful to align the buildings with the North Star, a strict requisite of continental Buddhist architecture.

Nara. **Yakushi-ji** is a 10-minute walk due south from Toshodai-ji. All of the original buildings have been destroyed by fires except the eastern pagoda, originally built in 698 and rebuilt 718. This is constructed of a harmonious arrangement of three roofs, with smaller roofs underneath creating the illusion of six storeys. Unfortunately, the complex as a whole lacks the Nara charm due to modern reconstructions of the western pagoda (1981) and the main hall (1976). The main hall houses an original triad (considerably restored) of Yakushi flanked by Nikko, Light of the Sun, and Gakko, Light of the Moon.

Horyu-ji

The goal of most travellers in this area is **Horyu-ji**, which has the oldest wooden buildings in the world. Horyu-ji was founded in 607 by Prince Shotoku, the pivotal figure who established Chinese culture in Japan. The temple is something of a time capsule preserving hundreds of art works from the 7th and 8th centuries. Horyu-ji is divided into two wings. Most visitors start from the western cloister. The main gate, dating from 1438, leads to an avenue lined by earthen walls characteristic of Horyu-ji. Note the wood-grain patterns created by pressing the walls with boards, thought to make the walls earthquake resistant. At the end of the avenue is **Chu-mon** (Middle Gate). The pillars of the gate (dating from 607, rebuilt circa 670) are famous for their entasis (outward curvature), a feature of Greek architecture that travelled to Japan via the Silk Road.

Inside the western cloister are the pagoda and *kondo* (main hall), built circa 670. The *kondo* houses a rare group of bronzes dating from 620 in Wei style. They are distinguished by elongated faces, the "archaic smile" and the abstract, almost art-deco lines of the falling drapery and the flames of the *mandorla*. In

Below: procession of Buddha images in Nara.

the centre is the Shaka Triad (Sakyamuni, the historical Buddha, with attendants). To the right is Yakushi and to the left is Amida, the Buddha of Paradise. Guardians, standing on demons, are Japan's oldest "Four Heavenly Kings."

One of the pleasures of Horyu-ji is the walk out through the cloister, an old example of a Chinese form that influenced temples and palaces throughout eastern Asia. Outside the cloister, walk east to the two concrete buildings of the museum, **Daihozod-en** (Great Treasure House). These buildings are even uglier than the museum of Kofuku-ji, but the treasures inside are important. Among the displays in the museum: the Kudara Kannon from Korea; the portable shrine of Lady Tachibana; and the Hyakuman pagodas, which contain strips of paper printed with short prayers. Published in 764 in an edition of 1 million, they are the world's oldest printed material.

From the museum there is a walk bordered by temples and earthen walls to the eastern cloister. In the centre is an octagonal building of Chinese inspiration, surmounted by a flaming jewel and known as the **Yumedono**, Hall of Dreams. Built around 740, it commemorates a dream of Prince Shotoku in which an angel appeared to him while he was copying the sutras. The Yumedono contains a secret Buddha, the Kuze Kannon, that is only on view in the spring and autumn. Behind the eastern cloister is **Chugu-ji**, a nunnery housing a wooden statue of Miroku, god of the future and the supreme statue of Nara. Possibly of Korean workmanship, it dates from the early 7th century. Although Miroku is enshrined in a drab concrete building, this is an ideal place to stop, rest and meditate for a while.

Slightly removed from the Horyu-ji complex are the two temples of **Hokki-ji** and **Horin-ji**, around 1 km (½ mile) north of Chugu-ji. Hokki-ji contains a three-storey pagoda built in 706. Horin-ji was rebuilt only in 1975.

The Kuze Kannon, dedicated in the year 737, remained a hibutsu, *or hidden image, until American art professor Ernest Fenellosa was given permission in 1884 to unravel the statue from 90 metres (295 ft) of white cloth.*

BELOW: roof lines of Taima-dera.

South Yamato and Asuka

Taima-dera and **Shakko-ji** are known for their thousands of varieties of peonies. Taima-dera contains two Nara Period pagodas and a "secret" *mandala* painting (an Edo Period copy is on view). On 14 May each year parishioners don masks of the Buddhas and parade through the grounds in a unique display of walking sculpture.

Asuka, the capital before Nara from 552 to 645, was the first city to have avenues on the Chinese grid pattern and large Buddhist temples. It was here that Prince Shotoku introduced Chinese law and philosophy. And it was here that the poems of the *Manyoshu*, Japan's first anthology of poetry, were written. Today, there is only a village of farmhouses and rice paddies, but the ruins conjure up an idea of the past. In Asuka, two burial mounds open to the public contain Japan's only known tomb murals. Excavated in 1972, they are displayed in a modern building often crowded with visitors. More evocative is the inner chamber of a 7th-century tumulus. The earthen covering has disappeared, leaving 75-ton boulders exposed. **Tachibana-dera** stands at the site of Prince Shotoku's birthplace. Most of the temple's buildings date from the Edo Period, but the pleasant country surroundings exude something of old Asuka. Most important of the area's temples is **Asuka-dera**, enshrining the Great Buddha of Asuka, a bronze image of Shaka and Japan's oldest large-scale Buddhist statue.

Northern hills

The northern and eastern hills are convenient for relaxing afternoon drives out of Nara, notably the Nara Okuyama road, starting from behind Todai-ji. The jewel of the northern hills is **Joruri-ji**, one of the few surviving Heian temples. Joruri-ji, established in 1179, is a miniature Buddhist paradise. In the centre is a pond symbolising the lake of heaven. To the right is the Western Paradise and the temple of Nine Amida. During the year, the rays of the sun sweep across the temple lighting each Buddha image in turn. In a direct line across the pond is a pagoda with a statue of Yakushi, Lord of the Eastern Paradise. About one kilometre's walk into the hills are the **Tono-o Sekibutsu**, stone carvings dating from the Kamakura Period. Buddhas cut into the rock – in an abstract, even crude style, and covered with lichens – are called *magaibutsu* and have a magical aura about them. The hills of Nara contain hundreds of such carvings.

BELOW: cherry blossom in Nara.

Eastern mountains

Soon after leaving Sakurai, at the southeastern end of the Yamato Plain, the road begins to climb into verdant hills. The first stop is **Hase-dera**, known for its peony festival in the last week of April. A covered stairway of 399 steps hung with lanterns leads up to the main hall, which enshrines Japan's largest wooden statue, an 11-headed Kannon carved in 1538. A half hour's drive to the east leads to the village of Ono. Turn south on the winding road along the Muro-gawa. Across the river is the **Miroku Magaibutsu** cut into the cliff face. This is the largest hillside carving in Japan, dating from 1207.

Out of Nara

It's an easy run directly south of Nara to **Imai-cho**, where the old quarter of the town is a 10-minute stroll from Yagi-nishiguchi Station. A thriving merchant town since the 17th century, over 500 traditional wood and plaster houses have survived, a half dozen or so of which are open to the public. Imai-cho's merit is that most of the houses are occupied, making the town feel like a living entity rather than a stagey museum set. A single ticket admits you to all the *machiya* as these residences are known. The most interesting is the **Imanashi Jyutaku** (daily 10am–5pm), dating from 1650. Another notable building and Important Cultural Property is the Kawai Residence, which still functions as a private home and sake brewery.

The village of **Yoshino**, a quiet getaway at most times, is awash with visitors during the spring cherry blossom season when an astonishing 100,000 trees, are in bloom. Grown at different elevations on the slopes of **Yoshino-san**, the earliest to bloom are at the bottom, the last at the top, an effect that stretches the viewing season to a full month.

It's an easy enough ascent from Yoshino Station to the village, which sits on the side of the mountain, but there is also a convenient cable car. Before following the trails through the cherry trees, spare some time for the nicely appointed temples and shrines along and off the main street. **Kimpusen-ji** temple, with its fierce guardian statues and a main hall, said to be the second largest wooden building in Japan, is a designated National Treasure.

Chikurin-in, a beautifully designed and finished temple, operates primarily as an up-market Japanese inn, but has a fetching and quite famous stroll garden, said to have been partly designed by the tea master Sen no Rikyu. The

The graceful buildings of Kongobu-ji temple at Koya-san are worth seeing for their religious and secular treasures, including screen paintings by the respected Kano school of artists. There is also an impressive stone garden here called the Banryu-tei, which you can contemplate from the verandah.

BELOW: try some fresh sweets.

garden uses Yoshino-san to great effect as borrowed scenery. To get to Yoshino take the Kintetsu Nara Line, changing onto the Kintetsu Yoshino Line at Kashihara-jingu-mae.

Koya-san

With 117 temples concealed within the green and mysterious canopies of cryptomeria trees and moss, a night spent at a *shukubo*, or temple lodging, on **Koya-san** is one of those quintessentially Japanese experiences not to be had with more conventional sights. Although easily accessed on the Hashimoto and Nankai lines from Nara to the terminus at Gokurakubashi Station and the cable car up to the mountain, Koya-san still manages to seem remote and isolated. The mountain became a major religious centre in 816, when the celebrated priest Kobo Daishi set up a temple here. Today it is a retreat, meditation centre and place of Buddhist study for trainee priests and monks.

The Reihokan Museum (daily 8am–5pm; closed 20 Dec–4 Jan; admission fee) at Koya-san has a first-rate collection of priceless Buddhist art.

Koya-san can be explored at random, but Ichinohashi, the entrance to **Okuno-in** cemetery, is a good starting point. A veritable city of the dead, moss-covered tombstones mark the resting place of everyone from commoners to members of the imperial family to Kobo Daishi himself. Followers of the priest believe that when he ascends to meet the Buddha, those buried near him will also rise to glory, hence the jam of tombs. Kobo Daishi's mausoleum at the far end of the cemetery, the most sacred spot on Koya-san, is located behind the Lantern Hall, where thousands of lights are kept burning. On the other side of the small town that serves all Koya-san's needs is the central religious compound known as the **Garan**, and also the symbol of the mountain, a two-storey vermilion pagoda called the **Daito**, or Great Stupa. ❑

BELOW: temple banners flap in the breeze at Koya-san.

The Shrines of Ise

While not part of the Kansai district, Ise and its shrines, east from Nara and Kyoto, perhaps best exemplify the nature and purpose of the Japanese Shinto belief. An excursion to Ise can be enlightening, but know beforehand that visitors are not allowed into the shrines' compounds under any circumstances.

No one can say exactly how long the two main shrines of what are collectively called the Grand Shrines of Ise have existed. Historical evidence suggests that **Naiku**, or the Inner Shrine, has been in place since around the 4th century, and **Geku**, or the Outer Shrine, since the late 5th century.

At Ise, the venerable cypress-wood *(hinoki)* shrine buildings stand today in perfect condition – almost new and mocking the ravages of time. The secret of the fine condition of these most sacred of Shinto shrines is *sengu*, or shrine removal, performed at Ise every 20 years over the past 13 centuries, the latest and 61st *sengu* taking place in 1993. *Sengu* consists of the razing of the two main buildings of both shrines, along with 14 smaller auxiliary structures. In the *sengu*, before the existing structures are destroyed, new shrine buildings of identical scale and materials are erected on adjacent foundations set aside for that purpose. Then Japan's largest and most important festival, Jingu Shikinen Sengu, begins as the deities of the respective shrines are invited to pass from the old into the new structures. Later, the old structures are torn down and sections of the timbers sent to Shinto shrines throughout Japan.

Why this work? First, the 20-year period can be viewed as a transition point. In human life, it is a line of demarcation between generations. Thus, *sengu* perpetuates an appreciation and an awareness of the cultural and religious significance of the shrines from age to age. Two decades is also perhaps the most logical period in terms of passing on from generation to generation the technological expertise needed for the reconstruction.

Geku is dedicated to Toyouke no Omikami, the goddess of agriculture. The grounds of Geku cover about 90 hectares (220 acres). A thatched gateway stands at the outermost of the three formidable fences, which is as far as anyone except imperial personages, envoys and shrine officials get to Shoden, the main hall. The clean, simple lines of the building are the very essence of Japanese architecture, showing nary a trace of the often bolder Chinese and Korean influences that dominate shrines elsewhere in Japan.

Naiku is a few kilometres from Geku. Here, as in the Outer Shrine, the object of attention is enclosed in a series of fences and can be viewed only from the front of a thatched-roof gate in the outermost fence.

Naiku is said to contain the *yata no kagami* (sacred mirror), which, along with a sword and a jewel, constitute the Three Sacred Treasures of the Japanese imperial throne. Mythology says that the mirror was handed by Amaterasu Omikami to her grandson when he descended from heaven to reign on earth. She gave him the gift of rice agriculture and a blessing for Japan. ❑

RIGHT: bundled ceremonial rice stalks at Ise Shrine.

THE SOUTH

Southern Japan includes western Honshu and two main islands, Kyushu and Shikoku, along with Okinawa

Here we should mention that what we refer to as "south" is called "western" Japan by the Japanese. Still, this part of the archipelago extends south*ward*. Chugoku, Shikoku and Kyushu are exceedingly different yet have one element in common: Seto Naikai, or the Inland Sea. All three regions also face the open ocean, and as a result, each area has widely varying climates and local qualities. In fact, beyond geography and the fact they are all in Japan, these regions sometimes bear little or no resemblance to each other.

That section of Honshu from, say, Himeji down the coast along the Inland Sea to Hiroshima is markedly different from the Sea of Japan side. Likewise, Shikoku, though the smallest of Japan's four main islands, could as well be in a different hemisphere from the one occupied by the islands of Okinawa. As for Kyushu – well, there are those who believe that this large island, particularly the southern part, is a nation unto itself and who cite the long tradition of fierce independence stemming from the Satsuma clans, not to mention Kyushu's thick dialect, as proof.

Even in the most populous and industrial cities of Kyushu, or even in large and well-developed cities like Honshu's Okayama and Hiroshima, the pace is mellow, if not downright sleepy, compared with Tokyo and Osaka. Not all is idyllic down this way, however. The southern parts lie in the path of seasonal typhoons and thus are regularly given good soakings by torrential rains riding up from the Philippines and Taiwan. Moreover, there are more active volcanoes on Kyushu than on any other Japanese island. Among the more notable are Sakura-jima, near Kagoshima; Aso-san (with the world's largest-diameter caldera) and Unzen-dake, which violently blew up in 1991.

Volcanoes have given the archipelago an unlimited variety of ceramic-quality clays, along with natural chemicals for glazes. Kyushu and parts of Chugoku are noted for their hearty pottery, an art with a considerable amount of Korean influence.

Shikoku, Chugoku and Kyushu are large enough to keep travellers occupied for quite some time. Smaller gems await even further south, however. Like pearls upon the ocean, islands drip away from Kyushu's southern tip and stretch down to within 200 km (125 miles) of Taiwan. This string of islands, Nansai-shoto, is over 1,200 km (750 miles) in length. Best known by foreigners is Okinawa for its historical importance in World War II and also for its cultural uniqueness. There are numerous other islands, each significantly distinct from its neighbours and all worthy of exploration. ❑

PRECEDING PAGES: cherry trees in blossom at Himeji Castle.
LEFT: an island amongst bigger islands of the Seto Naikai, or Inland Sea.

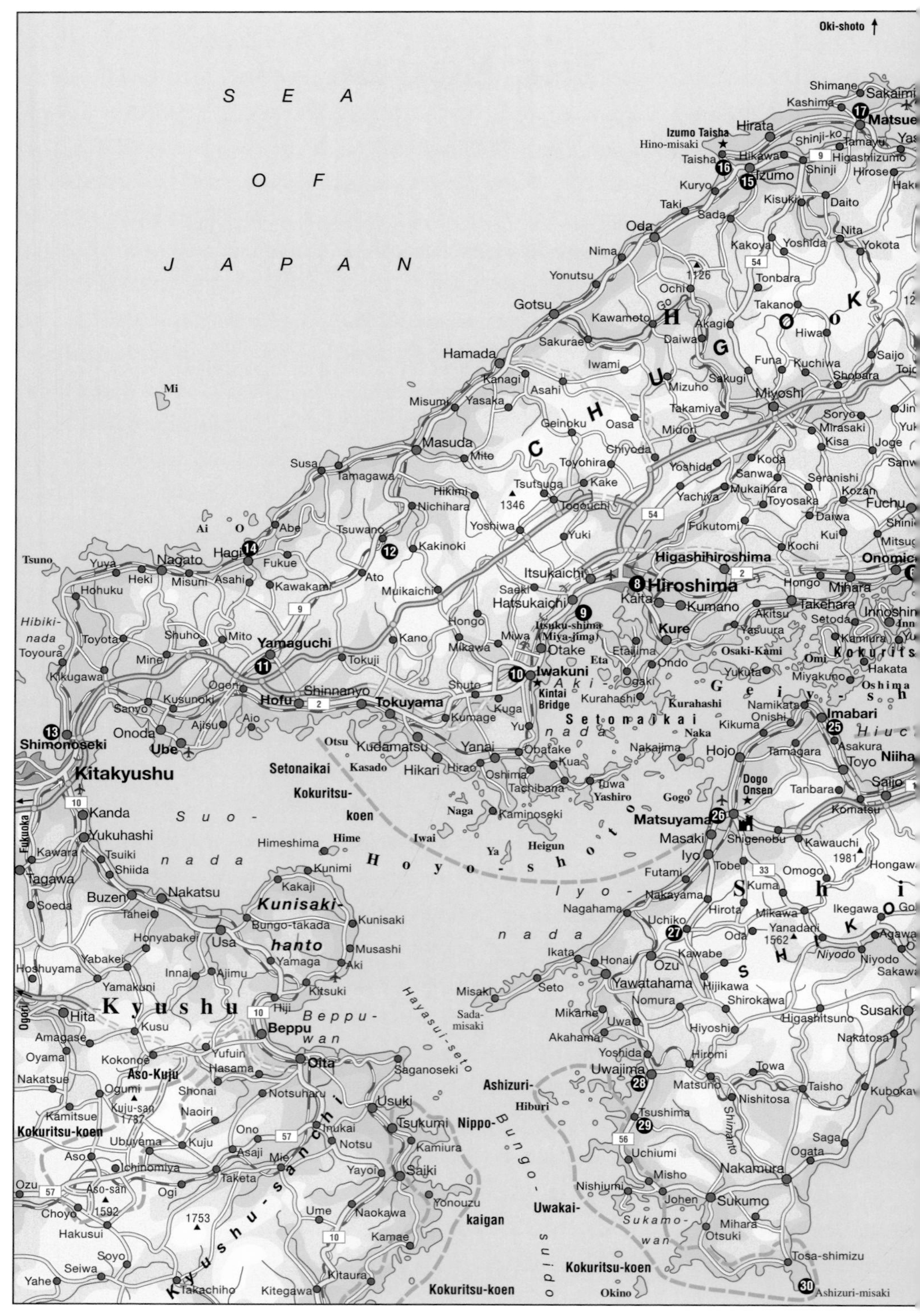
Oki-shoto
SEA OF JAPAN
Shimane
Sakaiminato
Kashima
Matsue
Izumo Taisha
Hino-misaki
Hirata
Shinji-ko
Tamayu
Taisha
Hikawa
Higashiizumo
Izumo
Shinji
Hirose
Kuryo
Kisuki
Daito
Taki
Sada
Oda
Nita
Nima
Kakoya
Yoshida
Yokota
1126
Yonutsu
Ochi
Tonbara
Gotsu
Takano
Kawamoto
CHUGOKU
Akagi
Daiwa
Hiwa
Sakurae
Hamada
Iwami
Funa
Kuchiwa
Saijo
Kanagi
Sakugi
Shobara
Asahi
Mizuho
Miyoshi
Misumi
Yasaka
Takamiya
Soryo
Geinoku
Oasa
Midori
Mirasaki
Masuda
Mito
Chiyoda
Kisa
Joge
Susa
Toyohira
Koda
Tamagawa
Yoshida
Sanwa
Seranishi
Tsutsuga
Kake
Hikimi
Mukaihara
Kozan
Nichihara
1346
Togouchi
Yachiyo
Toyosaka
Fuchu
Abe
Yoshiwa
Daiwa
Ai
O
Tsuwano
Yuki
Fukutomi
Kui
Hagi
Kakinoki
Kochi
Tsuno
Yuya
Nagato
Fukue
Itsukaichi
Higashihiroshima
Onomichi
Heki
Misumi
Asahi
Ato
Hiroshima
Hongo
Mihara
Hohuku
Kawakami
Muikaichi
Saeki
Kaita
Takehara
Hatsukaichi
Kumano
Hibiki-nada
Akitsu
Setoda
Innoshima
Hongo
Itsuku-shima (Miya-jima)
Kure
Toyota
Shuho
Mito
Yasuura
Toyoura
Yamaguchi
Kano
Miwa
Mikawa
Otake
Etajima
Osaki-Kami
Kamiura
Mine
Tokuji
Omi
Kokuritsu
Eta
Ondo
Hakata
Kikugawa
Iwakuni
Yukuta
Miyakubo
Ogori
Shinnanyo
Shuto
Aki-nada
Ogaki
Oshima
Kusunoki
Hofu
Tokuyama
Kintai Bridge
Kurahashi
Geiyo-shoto
Sanyo
Kuga
Namikata
Kumage
Setonaikai
Onishi
Imabari
Aio
Ajisu
Kikuma
Shimonoseki
Onoda
Yu
Naka
Ube
Otsu
Kudamatsu
Yanai
Obatake
Nakajima
Hojo
Tamagara
Asakura
Niihama
Kitakyushu
Setonaikai Kokuritsu-koen
Kasado
Hikari
Hirao
Kua
Toyo
Oshima
Towa
Dogo Onsen
Tanbara
Saijo
Tachibana
Yashiro
Gogo
Komatsu
Fukuoka
Kanda
Naga
Kaminoseki
Matsuyama
Yukuhashi
Suo-nada
Iwai
Masaki
Shigenobu
Kawauchi
Kawara
Himeshima
Hime
Ya
Heigun
Iyo
1981
Tsuiki
Hoyo-shoto
Tobe
Hongawa
Shiida
Kunimi
Futami
Omogo
Tagawa
Kakaji
Iyo-nada
Kuma
SHIKOKU
Soeda
Buzen
Nakatsu
Kunisaki-hanto
Nakayama
Nagahama
Hirota
Mikawa
Ikegawa
Tahei
Kunisaki
Uchiko
Yanadani
1562
Honyabakei
Usa
Bungo-takada
Oda
Agawa
Musashi
Ikata
Kawabe
Niiyodo
Yabakei
Yamaga
Honai
Ozu
Niyodo
Hoshuyama
Innai
Ajimu
Aki
Sakawa
Yamakuni
Kitsuki
Hayasui-seto
Misaki
Seto
Yawatahama
Hijikawa
Kyushu
Hiji
Nomura
Shirokawa
Ogori
Hita
Beppu-wan
Sada-misaki
Mikame
Higashitsuno
Susaki
Kusu
Beppu
Uwa
Amagase
Akahama
Hiyoshi
Nakatosa
Oyama
Kokonoe
Yufuin
Oita
Yoshida
Hiromi
Hasama
Saganoseki
Uwajima
Towa
Nakatsue
Aso-Kuju
Ogumi
Shonai
Ashizuri-
Matsuno
Taisho
Kuju-san
1787
Notsuharu
Hiburi
Nishitosa
Kuboka
Naoiri
Usuki
Tsushima
Shimanto
Kamitsue
Kokuritsu-koen
Tsukumi
Nippo-
Bungo-suido
Ono
Inukai
Ubuyama
Kuju
Asaji
Notsu
Saga
Aso
Mie
Kamiura
Uchiumi
Ogata
Ichinomiya
Kyushu-sanchi
Yayoi
Misho
Ozu
Aso-san
Taketa
Saiki
Nishiumi
Nakamura
1592
Ogi
Choyo
Johen
Sukumo
Yonouzu
Ume
Naokawa
kaigan
Uwakai-
Hakusui
1753
Sukamo-wan
Mihara
Otsuki
Kamae
Soyo
Tosa-shimizu
Seiwa
Kitaura
Kokuritsu-koen
Yahe
Takachiho
Kitegawa
Kokuritsu-koen
Okino
Ashizuri-misaki
Mi
2
9
10
33
54
56
57

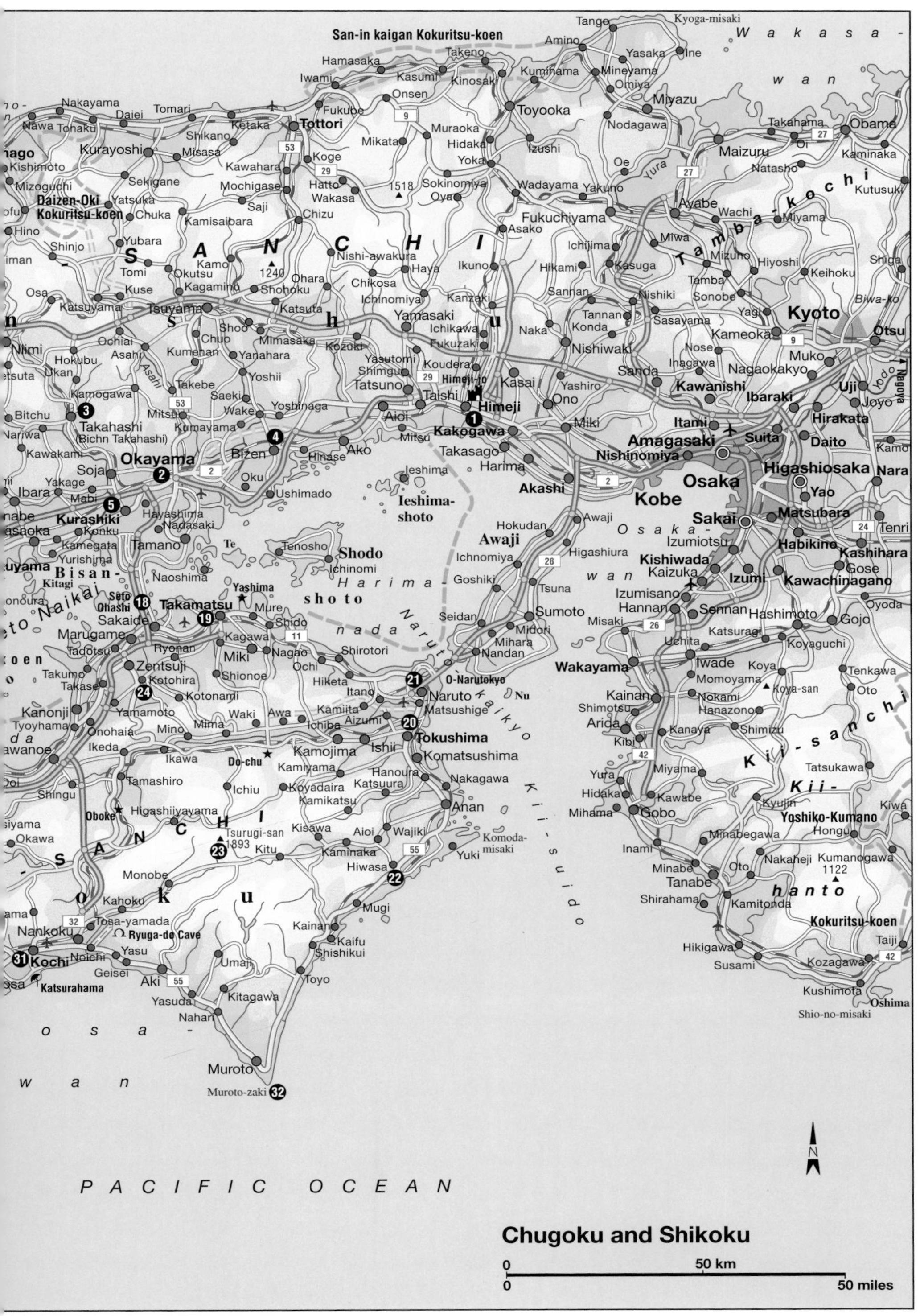

Chugoku and Shikoku

CHUGOKU

While we might consider this portion of Honshu and the adjacent island of Shikoku as southern Japan, the Japanese call the area western Japan. In fact, it's southwest

Map on pages 282–3

Most travellers would look at a map of Japan's main island of Honshu and consider Chugoku to be the southern part. The Japanese, however, consider it to be the western part. In fact, of course, it is southwest. Compass directions aside, the Chugoku region spreads over the bottom third of Honshu, bounded by **Seto Naikai** (Inland Sea) to the south and the Sea of Japan to the north. Not many foreign travellers get to Chugoku other than to its main cities of Okayama and Hiroshima. The region includes the prefectures of Okayama, Hiroshima, Yamaguchi, Shimane and Tottori, and it offers some splendid views of rustic Japan, especially along the Sea of Japan coast.

Seto Naikai, or the Inland Sea of Seto, is a 9,500-sq.-km (3,700-sq.-mile) body of water surrounded by Kyushu, Shikoku and the western extent of Honshu. Over 1,000 small islands pepper the sea. Osaka, Kobe and Hiroshima are all on the sea's coast. Although often industrialised these days, the sea still retains some exquisite vistas, enough for the area to have been designated Japan's first national park in 1934.

LEFT: tending to cherry trees. **BELOW:** Himeji-jo.

Himeji

At the upper end of Chugoku, the industrial city of **Himeji** ❶ is dominated by the marvellous snow-white castle that seems to hover above the town. Variously called the White Egret or Heron Castle, **Himeji-jo** (Himeji Castle; daily 5am–6pm, Sept–May until 4pm; admission fee) is a 15-minute stroll from the *shinkansen* station along a road lined with modern sculptures. Resting resplendent on the banks of the Senba-gawa, the castle of Himeji is the largest and most elegant of the dozen existing medieval castles in Japan. Although the city was extensively bombed during World War II, the castle emerged unscathed and has been maintained in pristine condition.

The site occupied by the castle has been fortified since 1333, and an actual castle was built here in 1580 by Toyotomi Hideyoshi. In 1681, Ikeda Terumasa, Tokugawa Ieyasu's son-in-law, rebuilt and expanded the castle to its present form. Castles in this period served both as military strongholds and as administrative centres. Terumasa's design, with financial help from the shogunate, elegantly merged martial necessity and artistic form on a scale previously unknown in Japan.

The castle's construction was a Herculean task requiring 400 tons of wood, 75,000 tiles weighing a total of 3,000 tons, and a huge number of large stones. These stones weren't easy to come by and tales of their procurement live on in the ramparts. Ancient

A Japanese castle in its original state such as Himeji-jo is rare, as most were either burned to the ground during feudal wars or in World War II.

stone coffins mined from nearby tombs can be seen in one part of the precinct. The contribution of a millstone, from a woman living in the town below the castle, is still remembered today.

The castle was never tested in battle, but walking up past the succession of defensive lines – three concentric moats surrounding high, curved ramparts punctuated by gates and watchtowers with arrow slits and gun ports – it seems an impregnable bastion. Roads within the castle grounds twist and turn, the better to confuse hostile forces if the outer defences were breached, and the uppermost floors of the castle contain hidden places where troops could continue to shoot at the enemy until the bitter end *(see picture on pages 278–79)*.

Himeji-jo is a hillock (as distinct from a mountain or flatland) castle atop a 45-metre (150-ft) hill. There are spectacular views from the main donjon, which rises 30 metres (100 ft) from the castle grounds. *Shachihoko*, huge ornamental fish that were strategically placed on the roof as charms to ward off fire, can be seen close up from the top floor; some now support lightning rods.

An attractive angle on Himeji-jo in any season is from the grounds of the surprisingly quiet **Himeji Koko-en** (daily 9am–4.30pm, May–Aug till 5.30pm; admission fee), located next to the castle moat. Built just a few years ago on the site of old samurai residences, Koko-en is a beautiful composite of nine separate Edo-style gardens with a teahouse and pools with carp. You can buy a combined ticket to the castle and gardens.

The **Hyogo-kenritsu Rekishi Hakubutsukan** (Hyogo Prefecture History Museum; Tues–Sun 10am–4.30pm; admission fee) nearby to the north contains informative displays about Japanese castles, including the most magnificent of them all, Himeji.

BELOW: a quiet, aquatic corner of Korakuen Garden.

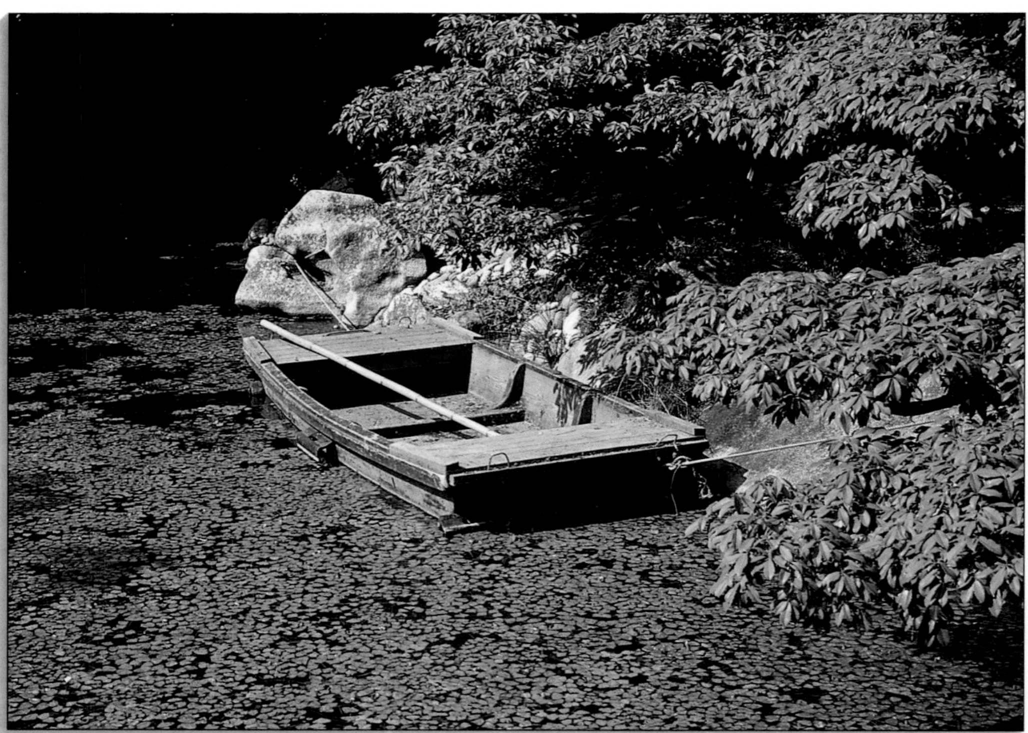

Okayama

The rapidly growing city of **Okayama** ❷ has once again asserted itself as the region's most dynamic metropolis. For this reason it often finds itself playing host to visiting foreigners, mostly on business and not for sightseeing. Okayama's most notable attraction, the **Koraku-en** (Koraku Garden) was originally laid out in 1686 for the warlord Ikeda. Located on an island in the Asahi-gawa across from **Okayama-jo** (Okayama or Crow Castle because of its black exterior), Koraku-en is unusual for its large grassy areas and the cultivation of such crops as rice and wheat. Tea is also grown and harvested here and tea-houses are scattered throughout the fine strolling garden.

Other sights in Okayama include the **Orient Museum** (Tues–Sun 9am–5pm; admission fee), with exhibits tracing the impact of Near Eastern civilisation on Japan; the **Okayama Prefectural Museum of Art** (Tues–Sun 9am–5pm; admission fee); and the **Yumeji Art Museum** (Tues–Sun 9am–5pm; admission fee), with works by Yumeji Takehisa.

Takahashi

Takahashi ❸ is one of those towns it is easy to overlook. Its railway station, 40 km (25 miles) northwest and just under one hour from Okayama on the JR Hakubi Line, is quiet and undistinguished, though the journey itself, hugging the attractive, well-contoured Takahashi-gawa, is attractive. The shallow, winding river is well stocked with *ayu* (sweetfish), a local speciality found on the menus of most of the town's traditional restaurants or, sprinkled with salt and smoked over a charcoal brazier, served from roadside stalls.

Takahashi enjoys a modest celebrity among travellers and cognoscenti of curious and obscure places. A provincial town with mountain and valley setting, Takahashi's cultural credentials, however, are unimpeachable. And most of its sights are conveniently located within walking distance of that uninspiring station.

Picking up a local map at the information office (Mon–Fri 8am–6pm; Sat 8.30am–5pm) at the bus terminus beside the station, make your way to **Raikyu-ji**, a Zen temple whose date of origin is disputed, but about which most historians concur that a rebuilding took place under the orders of the shogun Ankoku in 1339. However illustrious the temple and its collection of hanging scrolls and sutras may be, it is its magnificent garden that sets the site apart.

Created by Kobori Enshu, a member of the local nobility who would go on to become one of the foremost designers of gardens in Japanese landscape history, the small but dynamic balanced asymmetry of the garden is classified as a *karesansui* (dry landscape) type. Enshu finished the garden, also known as "Tsurukame Garden" on account of its crane- and turtle- shaped islands (signifying longevity), in 1609. Mount Atago can be glimpsed in the distance beyond the garden proper, forming the classic "borrowed view" frequently incorporated into such designs.

If Raikyu-ji represents Takahashi's spiritual and artistic heritage, **Takahashi-jo**, the town's castle, stands for its martial traditions. This well-appointed

Map on pages 282–3

Iron tracks and worn stone are part of Okayama's endearingly aged streetcar system. Called chin chin densha *in Japanese – a euphonic rendering of the sound made by the starting bell – Okayama has a system that is both efficient, cheap and well supported.*

BELOW: a basket of freshly caught sweetfish.

fortress, constructed on the peak of Gagyuzan-san is, at 430 metres (1,400 ft), Japan's highest castle, something of a tourist draw for the town. Adding to elevation as a formidable defence, the lower and mid levels of the mountain were further fortified with samurai villas and farmhouses designed to act as a second line of defence in the event (tested on several occasions) of attack. Interestingly enough, many of the homes here in the district of **Ishibiya-cho**, grand constructions sitting on raised ground above stone walls and foundations, are still occupied by the descendants of Takahashi's old samurai families.

Meiji- and Taisho- era wooden buildings and private estates face the Kouyagawa as it runs through the centre of Takahashi, their Japanese features mixing effortlessly with the Occidental experimentation in architecture associated with the time. The Takahashi church and the wooden Takahashi Elementary School, now serving, along with the **Buke-yashiki-kan Samurai House** (daily 9am–5pm; admission fee) in Ishibiya-cho as local history museums, are good examples of this blending. This and the **Local History Museum** (daily 9am–5pm; admission fee) house items closely associated with this period of contact with the West, expressing Japan's fascination with Western science, design, and the new technology that would lead to the transformation of Japan from a feudal backwater to an advanced nation. Exhibits include an old Morse code set, a symbol and harbinger of modernity, period clocks, and a microscope. There are also local exhibits pre-dating this period, and a fine collection of black-and-white photos of the town.

Bizen ❹, about 45 minutes by train east along the coast from Okayama, is famous for its unglazed, coarse pottery that is frequently enhanced by kiln "accidents", such as a stray leaf or a bit of straw sticking to the side of a pot that leaves an interesting pattern after firing. There are more than 100 kilns in Imbe, the 700-year-old pottery-making section of Bizen, along with several museums including the Bizen Togei Bijutsukan (Ceramics Museum) and Fujiwara Kei Kinenkan gallery.

TIP

Kurashiki is about the only city in Japan to escape the ravages of wrecking balls, World War II bombings and urban development. The town attracts millions of visitors annually, so avoid weekends and of course holidays. Most of its museums are closed on Mondays.

BELOW: a night out in the old district of Kurashiki.

Kurashiki

West of Okayama, **Kurashiki** ❺ is a textile-producing city containing the pearl of Japanese tourist attractions: an arts district that brings world-class Japanese and international art and traditional crafts together in an exquisite setting. Some 13.5 hectares (33 acres) of 300-year-old rice warehouses, Meiji-era factories, and the homes of samurai and wealthy merchant families have been elegantly preserved and converted into museums, craft shops and art galleries. Kurashiki is for walkers, with most of the attractions within a block or two of the central canal. The streets and alleys bordering on this central canal look much as they did during the town's cultural and economic zenith in the 18th century. Automobiles are not allowed to disturb the atmosphere of its preserved quarter.

The tourist centre here provides maps, information and a cheerful place to rest weary feet. Better still, Kurashiki is patrolled by Sato Yasuzo, a charming and mildly off-beat retired English teacher whose main pleasure in life is befriending foreign tourists ("It is my serendipity to meet you here today") and showing them the hidden corners of his home town. Sato is a fount of information and able to point out the dolphin sculptures placed on roofs as a talisman against fire, obscure shops selling traditional wedding accoutrements, off-duty geisha, locations where major documentaries and period films were shot, and a score of other fascinating minutiae. He expects no recompense for his informal guided tours and probably does more to promote this part of Japan than any single member of the National Tourism Organisation.

During the Edo Period, Kurashiki was a central collection and storage site for the shogun's taxes and tribute – paid in rice – from communities throughout western Honshu, Seto Naikai and Shikoku. Numerous stone rice warehouses *(kura)* are clustered around willow-lined canals, thus giving the town its name. Their striking designs employ black tiles deeply set in bright-white mortar, capped by roofs of black tile. Stone bridges, arched so that barges piled high with sacks of rice from the hinterland could pass below them, span the waterways. Kurashiki's preservation was largely the work of Ohara Magosaburo, the wealthy scion of Kurashiki's leading family. The Ohara family's textile mills were the primary source of employment in Kurashiki during the Meiji Period, by which time rice levies had been replaced by cash taxes, thus making the city's huge rice warehouses redundant.

Ohara Magosaburo built the nation's first museum of Western art in 1930, the **Ohara Museum of Art** (Tues–Sun 9am–5pm; admission fee), and stocked it with works by El Greco, Monet, Matisse, Renoir, Gauguin and Picasso. The neo-classical building remains the city's centrepiece, although new galleries have proliferated around it over the years. The restored *kura* next to the main gallery are likely to be of more interest to visitors already familiar with European art as

Devotees of Japanese kitsch will adore the Kurashiki Tivoli Park just north of the station. A miniaturised Copenhagen funfair decked out in the colours of a Viennese musical box, this theme park has to be seen to be believed.

BELOW: pearl farms.

they contain Japanese folk art and a fine collection of ancient Chinese art. Other rooms are devoted to the works of the great *mingei* (Japanese folk art) potters such as Hamada Shoji, Kawai Kanjiro and Tomimoto Kenkichi.

Many of Kurashiki's warehouses-turned-art-houses are devoted to preserving and revitalising *mingei*. Among the most interesting is the **Japanese Folk Toy Museum** (daily 9am–5pm; admission fee). The first floor is packed with traditional Japanese toys, dolls and kites, while a collection of toys from around the world can be seen on the second floor. The adjacent toy store is as interesting as the museum. Next door, the **Kurashiki Mingei-kan** (Museum of Folk Craft; Tues–Sun 9am–4.15pm; admission fee) displays about 4,000 simple, handmade objects that are or were used in everyday life. The building that houses this museum was remodelled from four two-storey wooden rice granaries.

The Seto Ohashi Memorial Museum of Bridges in Kurashiki.

Visitors can learn about the daily life of one of Kurashiki's leading families at the **Ohashi House** (Tues–Sun 9am–5pm; admission fee), constructed in 1796 for a merchant family. Of samurai status, the house is much larger than typical merchant houses of that time. Note the unusual roof tiles. Ivy Square, an arts complex created out of the red-brick textile factories that brought about the Ohara family fortune, houses the Kurabo Memorial Hall, with displays on the textile industry as well as scores of shops and restaurants.

Leaving the canal area, weary travellers might stop for a drink at the Kurashiki Kokusai Hotel, designed by Kurashiki native Shizutaro Urabe, before heading for the city's more distant attractions. These include the **Seto Ohashi Memorial Museum of Bridges** (the building is shaped like an arched *taiko* bridge), and **Washu-zan**, a hill with tremendous views of the great bridge itself, Seto Ohashi, as well as the Inland Sea, Seto Naikai.

BELOW: red-carpet tour bus.

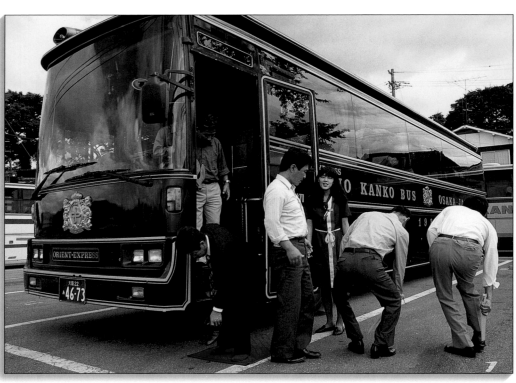

Map on pages 282–3

A nondescript city on the northern shore of the Inland Sea, **Onomichi** ❻ was an important commercial port 800 years ago. Wealthy merchants flocked to the city during the Edo Period, building 81 temples on the steep slopes overlooking the sea to celebrate their prosperity. With the coming of the railroad in the late 19th century, however, commerce literally passed the city by. Because of its relative lack of importance, American bombers also passed by Onomichi, and when the *shinkansen* route was mapped, Onomichi was passed over again. As a result of its slide into relative obscurity, the city has retained much of its pre-Meiji heritage. Some 25 of the old temples remain, the most interesting being the 1,100-year-old **Senko-ji**, which is best reached via the tram. From here, walk down the hill towards town taking in as many temples as you can stand.

Tomonoura

Some 14 km (9 miles) south of the JR *shinkansen* stop at Fukuyama, a 30-minute bus ride from outside the station takes you to the delightful fishing port of **Tomonoura** ❼. In this well-preserved but working town at the very extremity of the Numakuma Peninsula, southern enough for garden cacti, one may savour the smell of the sea, squawking gulls, the sight of kites wheeling over temple roofs. And fleeting images of history. The warrior Masashige passed through here on his way to Kyushu, as did the Empress Jingu.

Succoured, as it always has been by the sea, Tomonoura has not entirely escaped Japan's post-war uglification programme, as some of its cement installations testify. The town seems to have had its last flirt with concrete in the 1980s, however, and then mercifully left it at that.

BELOW: fish hang out to dry in Tomonoura.

The waters here are abundant in sea bream, a local speciality. You'll also see octopus, caught on lines rather than in pots or nets, being hauled from the water just below the sea walls, gleaming and full of life. The raised bund along the port also provides space for women to set up stalls under temporary plastic roofing, where the local catch is displayed and tasty fare sold. Shrimps are sold directly from their drying frames, from street stalls, or from the doorways and entrance halls of private homes, conveying the largely accurate impression that most of the inhabitants of this village are engaged in one way or another with the sea.

The sea bream netting methods can be glimpsed in simulated form in the models and photographs at the **Tomonoura Museum of History**. From the museum grounds, a commanding view of grey, undulating ceramic roofs, their eaves interlocking, suggests a community that is also tightly knit. Donald Richie, a profoundly attentive traveller, described the town at the end of the 1960s as having "the casual look of most towns where progress has been late in arriving. It is a crosswork of little streets like those in Italian mountain villages."

Tagashima-jo, the ruins of an old castle that once stood on the headland above the harbour, and its adjacent temple, Empuku-ji, offer another angle on the town. Here you can glimpse the harbour to the west, and **Benten-jima**, a tiny island, to the east. Of Indian provenance, the goddess Benten is a sensuous figure, now firmly inducted into the Shinto pantheon and serving as the patroness of music, the arts and beauty.

Half the enjoyment of this little town where it is still possible to lose your bearings, is to explore its labyrinth of lanes and stone alleys, noting the old wooden houses, ship's chandlers, and the bijoux gardens that can be glimpsed behind timeworn fences. One area of streets near the harbour contains the **Shichikyo-ochi Ruins**, a misleading name for what is in fact a graceful ensemble of wood and plaster sake breweries and warehouses dating from the mid-18th to 19th century.

Mushroom cloud over Hiroshima about an hour after the atomic blast.

Despite its diminutive scale, there are several temples of note in Tomonoura. **Io-ji** was supposedly founded by Kobo Daishi, a priest who, if only half the temples that claim a connection are true, must have been one of Buddhism's most itinerant pilgrims. **Fukuzen-ji**, a reception hall located near the ferry terminus and once used to receive Korean missions, inspired flights of calligraphy from envoys such as the man of letters I-pan-o, who were overcome with the beauty of the view. Only slightly disfigured by small concrete installations and power lines, it remains largely intact.

Hiroshima

One moment – 8.15am, 6 August 1945 – irrevocably changed world history. An atomic flash signalled the instant destruction of **Hiroshima** ❽, the eventual loss of over 200,000 lives, and forever linked the city's name with nuclear holocaust and mass killings. The immediate and lasting impact on Hiroshima gives concrete reality to the horrors of atomic and nuclear war. Unlike

BLACK RAIN

It was like a white magnesium flash... We first thought to escape to the parade grounds, but we couldn't because there was a huge sheet of fire in front of us... Hiroshima was completely enveloped in flames. We felt terribly hot and could not breathe well at all. After a while, a whirlpool of fire approached us from the south. It was like a big tornado of fire spreading over the full width of the street. Whenever the fire touched, wherever the fire touched, it burned... The whirlpool of fire that was covering the entire street approached us... After a while, it began to rain. The fire and the smoke made us so thirsty... As it began to rain, people opened their mouths and turned their faces towards the sky and tried to drink the rain... It was a black rain with big drops.

Takakura Akiko
300 m (1,000 ft) from ground zero

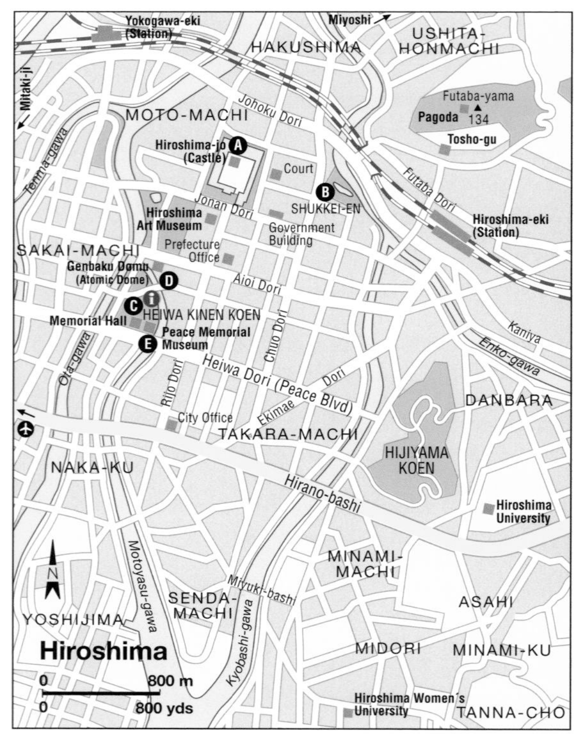

Nagasaki, the second city to have received such an attack but which doesn't dwell much on past history, there seem to be reminders of Hiroshima's atomic bombing around virtually every corner in the city.

Amazingly, Hiroshima's people quickly rebuilt a vibrant city from the ashes, making it larger and more prosperous than the old one and leaving a few carefully chosen scars to memorialise its abiding atomic legacy. A shining example of the city's metamorphosis is the Mazda automobile factory, where the humans appear to play second fiddle to the computers and robots that put entire cars together in a matter of hours, on a single production line that snakes remorselessly around the factory floor.

Hiroshima was chosen for the first atomic-bomb attack because of its military importance. The city was one of Japan's most vital military depots and industrial areas (a fact that goes unmentioned in the atomic bomb museum). However, Hiroshima's military significance predates World War II by several hundred years. Troops were staged here in preparation for the invasion of Korea in 1582. A castle incorporating the latest construction and defensive techniques was built here seven years later by the Mori clan. It rested on pilings driven into reclaimed swampland, and the outer moats were built above the level of the surrounding land so that their walls could be breached, flooding the plain where siege troops would likely mass. The castle was an important bastion of the Tokugawa shogun's forces, a western outpost facing the often hostile Choshu and Satsuma clans.

In the 19th century, **Hiroshima-jo** Ⓐ (Hiroshima Castle; daily 9am–6pm, Dec–Feb until 5pm) was occupied by the emperor during the occupation of Manchuria. The castle also served as an important Japanese Army headquar-

Maps on pages 282 & 292

TIP

The best way to see Hiroshima is from a tram. As other Japanese cities tore up their tram lines after World War II, their cars were sent to Hiroshima; the city has acquired an eclectic collection of tram cars, many dating back to the 1940s.

BELOW: Genbaku Domu, Hiroshima.

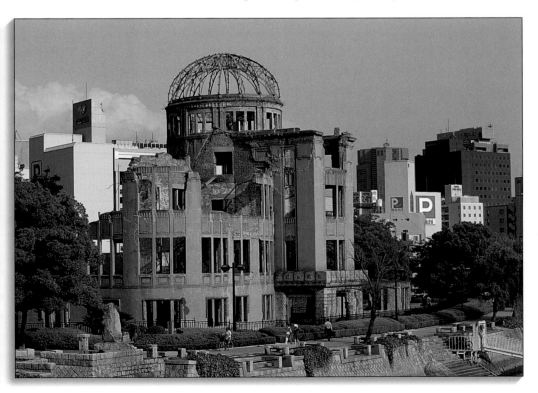

ters during World War II and was completely destroyed by the atomic bomb. Reconstructed in 1958, the castle contains an excellent museum.

A few blocks east of the castle, **Shukkei-en** **B** (Shukkei Garden) was built on the banks of the Kyobashi-gawa in 1620 in emulation of a famous Chinese lake. Early spring brings cherry blossoms to the garden, while azaleas bloom a little later, and multicoloured carp inhabit the garden's central pond throughout the year.

Industrial Promotion Hall before the atomic bombing.

The **Heiwa Kinen-koen** **C** (Peace Memorial Park), southwest of the castle and wedged between the rivers of Motoyasu and Ota, is adjacent to the **Genbaku Domu** **D** (Atomic Dome), which marks ground zero of Hiroshima's atomic explosion. At its maximum intensity, the temperature approached that on the sun's surface and almost everything within sight was vapourised instantly. The famous building with the carefully maintained skeletal dome once housed the Industrial Promotion Hall and was one of the few surviving vertical structures. Today the park has a serene air; men old enough to remember the explosion sit meditatively on benches, the sonorous tones of the Peace Bell echo through the trees, and the solemnity is varied only by the exuberance of children who dash about with clipboards in hand for their school projects and then stand silent in prayer before the many shrines.

Tange Kenzo designed the heart of the park complex, which comprises the **Peace Memorial Museum** **E** (daily Mar–Nov 8.30am–6pm, Aug until 7pm, Dec–Feb until 5pm; admission fee), Peace Memorial Hall, the Cenotaph and Peace Flame. The museum contains graphic portrayals of the bombing. Although the museum is filled with powerful images of terrible suffering, it certainly is not the hall of horrors one might expect. A visit to the museum is an emotional experience, even though it has been accused of failing to place the bombing in historical perspective, mainly as a result of right-wing nationalist opposition. The museum seems to suggest that the bomb fell on Hiroshima, figuratively as well as literally, out of the blue. There is little suggestion of Japan's brutal war record, and the suffering meted out on other peoples. However, given the enormity of the attack against the innocent civilians of the city, this is perhaps excusable.

BELOW: Genbaku Domu through the Cenotaph.

The **Cenotaph**'s inverted U-shape reflects the design of the thatched-roof houses of Japanese antiquity. It contains a stone chest with the names of the victims of the atomic bombing and bears an inscription, "Sleep in peace: the error will not be repeated". The **Peace Flame** and Atomic Dome can be seen through it. The statue of the children killed by the bombing is dedicated to Sasaki Sadako, who died of leukemia caused by radiation when she was just 12 years old. She believed that if she could fold 1,000 paper cranes – a symbol of happiness and longevity for Japanese – she would be cured. Despite her illness, she managed to complete folding 1,000 cranes. As she did not get better, she started on a second thousand. She had reached some 1,500 when she finally died in 1955, 10 years after the atomic bomb exploded. Her spirited actions inspired an outpouring of national feeling and her classmates completed the second thousand paper cranes. Today, schoolchildren from all over the country bring paper cranes by the tens of thousands to lay around Sadako's memorial, a tribute that is simultaneously heart-rending, beautiful, and a terrible condemnation of militarism.

Many visitors ring the Peace Bell before crossing the Motoyasu-gawa to the dome. Colourful rowing boats can be rented by the hour near the **Heiwa Ohashi** (Peace Bridge), offering a more cheerful perspective on Hiroshima. Sightseeing cruises depart from the nearby pier.

Half an hour away and northwest of central Hiroshima, **Mitaki-ji** is set in a lush forest with three waterfalls. Buddhas adorn the hillsides, and a fierce, life-size baby-killing devil statue of wood hangs out on the temple's porch. A friendly dog often welcomes visitors to the teahouse, which is decorated with a colourful collection of masks and kites. The walk from the central train station to the temple grounds passes a group of graves belonging to many unknown atomic-bomb victims.

Miyajima

Though it is formally called **Itsuku-shima** (Strict Island), this major Hiroshima-area tourist attraction is better known as **Miyajima** ❾, the Island of Shrines. To find the spirit and splendour of Miyajima, one of the country's holiest sites, visitors must make their way through herds of tame deer and the litter left by thousands of tourists. Most of the island is covered with uninhabited virgin forest. A good way to see it is from the 1.6-km (1-mile) long cable car that runs over Momijidani-koen to the top of Misen.

The large crimson *torii* (shrine gate), rising out of the sea in front of the **Itsukushima-jinga**, is probably the most familiar Japanese cultural icon and representative of Shintoism. But this *torii*, which is plastered on nearly every

Maps on pages 282 & 292

A Shinto shrine always has a torii, *or pi-shaped gate, in front of it.* Torii *come in various colours and designs, but the function is always the same: dividing the shrine's sacred grounds from secular areas beyond.*

BELOW: famous *torii* of Miyajima.

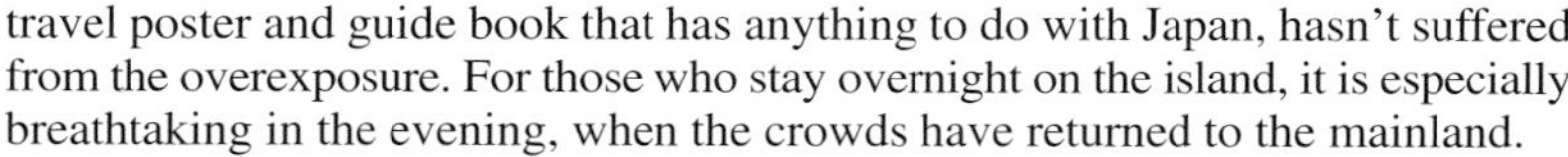

travel poster and guide book that has anything to do with Japan, hasn't suffered from the overexposure. For those who stay overnight on the island, it is especially breathtaking in the evening, when the crowds have returned to the mainland.

The current gate was built in 1874, but a similar *torii* has lured visitors for seven centuries. The island's spiritual roots are much older, however. The first shrine, honouring Amaterasu's three daughters – goddesses of the sea – was built in the 6th century. To maintain the island's "purity", births and deaths have been prohibited on Miyajima from the earliest times. The entire island of Miyajima was dedicated as a sanctuary by Taira no Kiyomori, who ordered the Itsukushima-jinga completely rebuilt in 1168.

That trees, at least Japanese trees, have souls, cannot seem an unnatural fancy to one who has seen the blossoming of the umenoki *and the* sakuranoki. *This is a popular belief in Izumo and elsewhere.*
– *In A Japanese Garden*
Lafcadio Hearn

Itsukushima-jinga itself rests on stilts and seems to float like a giant ship when the tide comes in. Costumes and masks used in the *bugaku*-dance festival (first week of January) and the *noh* plays, performed in mid-April, are on display in the Asazaya (morning prayer room), which is reached via a bridge. Next to Itsuku-shima, one of the oldest *noh* theatres in Japan, built in 1568, also seems to float a few inches above the sea. A nearby building contains hundreds of government-designated National Treasures and Important Cultural Objects, including illuminated sutras made by the Taira clan in the 1160s.

A five-storey pagoda, built in 1407, and the hall of **Senjokaku** (A Thousand Mats) are at the top of a hill behind Itsukushima-jinga. Senjokaku, built in 1587, is the great warlord Toyotomi Hideyoshi's contribution to Miyajima. The island has a number of noteworthy *matsuri* like its February **Oyster Festival** and a pine torch parade in December. The best of these utilise the island and shrine's stunning setting. Look out for the 16 June Kangensai with its traditional music and boat parade, and on 14 August, the **Hanabi Matsuri**, a huge firework display in front of the shrine.

Below: banners representing carp on Boys' Day.

To the west

Iwakuni ❿, 44 km (27 miles) west of Hiroshima, is on both the *shinkansen* and JR San-yo Line. The stations are located to the west and east of the central area where most of the sights are. Each has a useful tourist information office with handouts in English. A third tourist information office (daily 9.30am–5pm) is conveniently located in the old samurai district.

Iwakuni's premier sight is, without question, **Kintai-kyo**, the Brocade Sash Bridge, a graceful span that undulates between five steep arches, a popular image with tourist promoters and directors of TV samurai dramas looking for instant image bites. The original bridge, built in 1673, was destroyed in a flood in 1950. Rebuilt a few years later, the present construction is almost indistinguishable from the original. There's a small toll charge to cross the bridge.

On the far side of the bridge, **Kikko-koen**, a pleasant parkland area, includes the surviving residences of an old samurai district and a ruined moat that once served a castle, **Iwakuni-jo**. The castle was relocated into a more commanding and picturesque spot when it was rebuilt in 1960. There's a cable car to take you to the top of the hill, but the walk is hardly strenuous.

If you happen to be in Iwakuni during the summer months from June to August, you can, for a fee, board a night boat to observe *ukai*, a visually exciting, traditional method of fishing using cormorants and baskets of burning flames that light up the river surfaces.

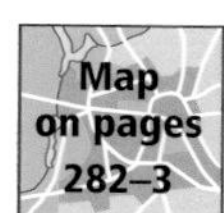

Yamaguchi

The bullet train does not number the provincial city of **Yamaguchi** ⓫ among its stops, sparing it both excessive development and crowds of visitors. Just 30 minutes on the JR Yamaguchi Line from Ogori, the city's best-known form of transport is a 1937 locomotive, one of the few in Japan to remain in regular service. Operating on weekends and holidays from late March through November, the gleaming steam engine, called the **SL Yamaguchi-go**, runs between the castle town of Tsuwano and Ogori.

During the Sengoku era (1467–1573), Japan's century of anarchy, much of the cultural and political life of the country shifted to the relative security of Yamaguchi. Many literati, noblemen and their retinues sought refuge here, bringing with them the sensibilities and tastes of the imperial capital, Kyoto. Several of Yamaguchi's easily sought-out temples and shrines date from this period.

Japan's first Christian missionary, the Basque priest Francis Xavier, stayed in Yamaguchi for two months trying, without much success, to convert the locals. Xavier and his mission are still remembered with affection in Yamaguchi, though, where there is a gleaming **St Francis Xavier Memorial Cathedral**. A strikingly modern structure, a pyramid of silver and egg-shell white, it is crowned with metallic towers, sculptures and a brace of suspended bells. Its stained-glass windows and coloured jars of burning candles create the effect of a slightly dimmed café-gallery.

Were the Yamaguchi Post Office to be looking for an image to place on a commemorative stamp of their prefectural capital, they would no doubt choose the city's magisterial five-storey pagoda, built in the grounds of the **Ruriko-ji** temple. Made from Japanese cypress, each roof a fraction steeper than the one below it, the pagoda, typical of the Muromachi-era Zen Kyoto style, is strikingly situated beside an ornamental pond graced by bushes and topiary, the effect only slightly marred by a tape recording giving an account of the history of the building.

Serene scene

A kilometre (½ mile) or so northeast of the pagoda, the **Sesshu-tei**, named after its designer, the master painter and priest Sesshu, is a Zen-inspired garden, a combination of dry landscape and moss, an arrangement of stones, rocks, lawn and lily-pad pond, best viewed in its intended entirety from the broad wooden verandah at the rear of the temple, from where the garden resembles a horizontal scroll.

Transected by the only moderately busy Route 9, it is possible to preserve some of the serenity of Seishu's garden by following a path along the **Ichinosaka-gawa** as it makes a sinuous course back to the town centre. Crossed by pedestrian bridges, the banks of the stream, a place of water reeds and azaleas, is a popular walk in springtime when its cherry trees are in full blossom, while in the summer there are swarms of fireflies.

BELOW: scaring the crows.

Tsuwano

Easily accessed from either Yamaguchi city or Hagi, **Tsuwano** ⓬ is one of the best-preserved medieval towns in Japan, and another of its "Little Kyotos". Its exquisite samurai and merchant houses, temples and museums are located in a narrow, photogenic ravine. An extraordinary 80,000 colourful carp live in shallow streams and culverts that run between the main road, Tonomachi-dori, and the walls of the samurai residences. The fish were stocked as a food resource in case of a siege and the streams would provide ready water in the event of fire.

The tourist information centre (daily 9am–5pm) near the station has a very decent English guidebook to the town. The centre is a good starting point to explore the old district of Tonomachi, beginning with the **Katsushika Hokusai Museum of Art** (daily 9.30–5pm; admission fee), which has an exquisite collection of woodblock prints, paintings and illustrations by Hokusai Katsushika, arguably the 19th century's foremost Japanese artist.

Following Tonomachi-dori southeast of the museum, the spire of Tsuwano's 1931 **Catholic Church** are visible. It's a modest sight, but worth a few minutes to view the stained-glass windows. A moderately interesting folk museum stands nearby on the banks of the Tsuwano-gawa. The building, known as the **Yorokan**, once served as a school for young samurai.

Continuing down the main road, cross a bridge over the river to the rather pretentiously named **Musee de Morijuku** (daily 9am–5pm; admission fee), housing work by mainly local artists. The museum building, a beautifully restored farmhouse with a very accomplished series of sand and gravel gardens, upstages the collection itself.

Two shrines of interest lie a few minutes to the west. **Yasaka-jinga** and **Taikodani Inari-jinga**, an Inari fox shrine with a tunnel of bright red *torii* gates wending its way uphill to the main shrine and its colourful Shinto paraphernalia.

Climb or take the cable car from here up to the site of **Tsuwano-jo**, another hilltop castle with the best views of the town. The original castle was built in 1295 as a bulwark against a possible Mongol attack, a very real threat at that time. Ironically, it was the Meiji era's passion for reckless modernisation, and dismantling feudal castles, which reduced Tsuwano-jo to a ruin.

Crossing back over the river to the southeast end of town, the last sight of note, especially for those interested in Japanese literature, is the combined **Mori Ogai Kyutaku & Mori Ogai Memorial Museum** (daily 9am–5pm; admission fee). A major novelist and essayist of the Meiji Period, Mori was born in Tsuwano in 1862. The house and museum, containing original manuscripts and personal effects, is very evocative of the period. Several of Ogai's works, including the novels *The Wild Geese* and *Vita Sexualis*, are available in English.

Shimonoseki

At the western limit of Honshu, **Shimonoseki** ⓭ is the gateway to Kyushu and to Korea as well, with *shinkansen* (bullet train) service to Hakata Station in Fukuoka and daily overnight ferries to Pusan, South

Yasaka-jinga is best known for its Sagi-Mai, *a heron dance performed on 20 and 27 July by men dressed in plumes and heron-beaked headdresses. It is a little similar to a spring and autumn event performed by women at Asakusa's Senso-ji shrine in Tokyo.*

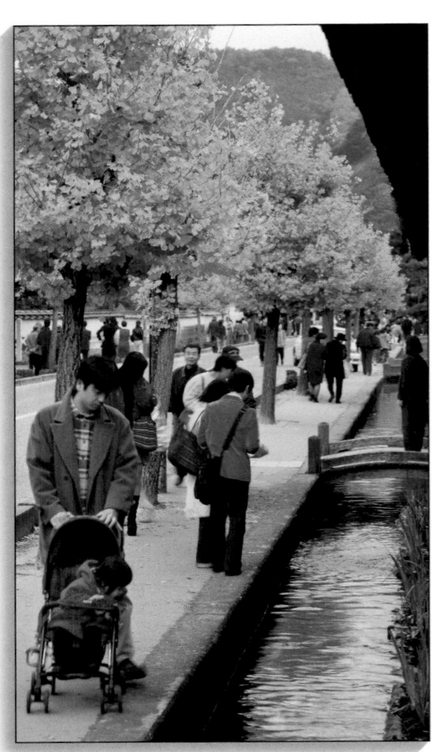

BELOW: watching the fish go by in Tonomachi-dori.

Korea. There isn't much reason to linger here, but one of the largest aquariums in Asia, the **Shimonoseki Suizokukan**, and the shrine of Akamon may be of interest to those waiting for a boat to Korea.

Shimonoseki has been an important port over many centuries, although today it is less so. The area was also the site of some of Japan's most important sea battles. History and literature students will recall that the final scenes of *Tale of the Heike* were set here. It is where the exiled empress dowager hurled herself and the infant emperor into the swirling tides. Several spots in the area claim to be the actual location, but, in fact, any would do, as the cliffs are high and the waters do swirl frighteningly as the Sea of Japan meets Seto Naikai.

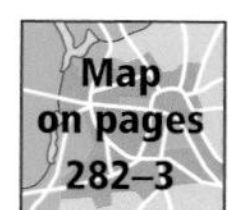
Map on pages 282–3

Although noted for its historical and artistic qualities, remember that, like Kyoto, Hagi is also a modern city with the clutter and commercialism of any other city.

Honshu's northern coast

From Shimonoseki, the coastal road loops back around east along the northern coast of Honshu and the Sea of Japan. Samurai footsteps echo through the narrow streets in the heart of **Hagi ⓮**, and indeed the whole town resounds to the beat of historical events that have shaped Japan as it is today. If there is one reason to journey to this part of the coast, it is here in Hagi – a place that is as picturesque as it is fascinating.

Many of the statesmen who played significant parts in the Meiji Restoration came from here, Korean potters brought their art and flourished in Hagi, and it is the site of some of the earliest steps taken in glass-making.

Start where Hagi itself started, at the castle site at the foot of **Shizuki-san**. Built on the orders of Terumoto Mori in 1604, who then presided over the area that is now Yamaguchi Prefecture, the castle stood until 1874 when it was pulled down to express allegiance to the new Meiji government, which had returned the emperor to power. Parts of the walls and the former dungeon remain today, and there's a Japanese teahouse in the adjacent gardens.

From here, head to the Asa Mori clan residence, the largest of the surviving samurai houses that arose in Hagi beyond the castle walls, or, just a few steps away beyond a natural, grassy sea wall, **Kikugahama beach**, a sandy curve with clean water for a pleasant swim. The streets of the castle town, or Jokamachi, were divided into three sections: one for lower-ranking samurai, a second for rich politicians, and the third for merchants. Wandering its lanes – particularly Edoya, Iseya and Kikuya – every turn reveals another pocket of days gone by. The son of a doctor and one of the Meiji Restoration's dynamos, Kido Takayoshi, grew up in a house on Edoya. Another prominent Restoration figure, Takasugi Shinsaku, lived on Kikuya and was cured of smallpox by Dr Aoki Shusuke, another inhabitant of Edoya. All their residences are on view to the public. After the Meiji Restoration, a number of *natsu mikan* (orange or tangerine) trees were planted in Hagi, mainly to provide some relief to the unemployed samurai. Many trees dot the Horiuchi (inner moat) district, and in May and June the scent of the blossoms is almost intoxicating.

Hagi's other great influence on Japan is its pottery, ranked the second most beautiful in the country after that of Kyoto. At first glance it can appear deceptively

BELOW: shrine preparations.

Hagi pottery came to Japan in the wake of the warlord Hideyoshi Toyotomyi's invasion of Korea in the 16th century. Two Korean potters were brought with the returning armies to practise their craft. Today there are some 100 kilns scattered about the city.

BELOW: Izumo Taisha shrine. **RIGHT:** casting concrete barriers to prevent coastal erosion.

simple and rustic, but closer examination reveals subdued colours and classical features, especially in the glazing that is exceptionally clear and vivid.

Lesser known is Hagi's glass, introduced around 1860 as the Edo Period drew to a close and using European techniques. After a century-long hiatus, the old techniques are now being used again to make Hagi glass.

Eastward along the coast

Further on along the coast, **Shimane** and its modest peninsula consists of three ancient districts: Izumo, Iwami, and the islands of Oki-shoto. It is one of the longest-inhabited areas of Japan and offers special insights into the cultural heritage of the nation. **Izumo** ⓯ covers the eastern part of the prefecture and is known as the mythical province where the history of Japan began. Several shrines, temples and ancient buildings can be seen around the prefecture, including the **Taisha** ⓰, the oldest Shinto shrine in the country. Dedicated to the spirit god of marriage, it is paid particular heed by couples.

Shinji-ko sits at the eastern end of the prefecture. The lake's 45-km (30-mile) long coastline offers beautiful sights throughout the year, and sunset over the lake is one of the finest evening scenes in Japan. At the eastern end of the lake sits **Matsue-jo**. Often called Plover Castle because of its shape, the castle was built in 1611 by Yoshiharu Horio, a samurai general. It is the only remaining castle in the Izumo area and very little has been done to modernise it, so the feeling inside is truly authentic. Across the castle moat to the north lies Shiominawate, an area where ranking samurai once lived.

Matsue ⓱ was also the home of a renowned writer and observer of Japan, Lafcadio Hearn (1850–1904). Greek-born Hearn was raised in the US and went to Japan in 1891 as a *Harper's* magazine reporter. In his many years in Japan, he wrote numerous works, including *Kwaidan: Stories and Studies of Strange Things*; *Shadowings, Japan: An Attempt at Interpretation*; *Bushido: The Soul of Japan*; and *A Daughter of the Samurai*. Although written over a century ago his observations carry well over time. Along with Matsue's other cultural credentials such as its samurai dwellings, history museum and the interesting Karakoro Art Studio with its exhibits of local crafts, is the **Lafcadio Hearn Memorial Museum** (daily 8.30am–5pm, Apr–Sept until 6.30pm; admission fee). Hearn's great-grandson Bon Koizumi is the curator. Also in Matsue is the ancient shrine of **Kamosu**. Its unique architectural style, *taisha-zukuri*, is the oldest architectural style in Japan.

The islands of **Oki-shoto** sit between 40 and 80 km (25–50 miles) off Shimane-hanto. The old province surrounds some 180 islands and islets in the Sea of Japan. The islands, once a dumping grounds for convicts, sit inside the Daisen-Oki National Park. A unique sight on the islands are the bullfights, in which two bulls lock horns and push away. Bullfighting was originally devised in the 1200s to entertain Emperor Go-Daigo while he was in exile. Temples, shrines, rugged coasts and great fishing mark this area off the beaten path. ❑

SHIKOKU

Until 1988, the only way to reach Japan's fourth-largest island was by air or water. It's an island of rugged terrain and open exposure to Pacific typhoons, and its people are fiercely independent

Map on pages 282–3

The least-developed and rarely visited of Japan's four main islands, Shikoku's attractions (and drawbacks) are attendant on its relative isolation. The island can provide a more "Japanese" experience than either Honshu or Kyushu. Its people are less familiar with foreigners and its atmosphere has been less influenced by the homogenising aspects of modern culture. It is also more diffused. Places likely to be of interest to travellers are relatively far apart and more difficult to get to than on more widely travelled pathways.

Shikoku's separate identity is not as isolated as before. The smallest of Japan's main islands, it was the last to be linked by bridge with Honshu, the largest and most populated of Japan's islands. In 1988 the completion of the **Seto Ohashi** 18 gave Shikoku a ground transport link to the rest of Japan. The bridge carries both road vehicles and trains from Honshu, near Kurashiki, to Sakaide on Shikoku *(see picture on page 51)*.

The Seto Ohashi is actually a series of six bridges using five small islands as stepping-stones across **Seto Naikai** (Inland Sea). At 12.3 km (7½ miles) in length, it is one of the longer double-deck bridges in the world, carrying four lanes of traffic above dual rail tracks. First suggested by a prefectural assembly man in 1889, officials were finally persuaded of its logic in the late 1960s. Construction was set to begin in 1973 but was postponed in the aftermath of the first oil crisis of the 1970s. Construction finally began in 1978 and, after nearly 10 years of work and expenditure exceeding some US$1 billion, the first cars and trains finally rolled across in 1988. The extremely high tolls, around US$50, have left the bridge underused. Still, it is a popular attraction for Japanese tourists, but unless you are a bridge engineer or civil engineer, just use it to get to Shikoku or else take one of the ferries from Osaka or Kobe.

The most numerous and distinctive visitors to Shikoku today – arriving by plane as often as not – are *ohenrosan* – devout Buddhist pilgrims making the rounds of the 88 holy temples and shrines established on Shikoku by the priest Kobo Daishi some 1,200 years ago. In the feudal period, it was common for white-robed pilgrims carrying staffs to complete the circuit on foot, a feat requiring more than two months. Today's similarly adorned pilgrims usually make the rounds in two weeks or less via air-conditioned buses.

Shikoku is split into northern and southern sections by steep, rugged mountains. The relatively dry northern part, facing the Seto Naikai, is more industrialised. The south is wilder, warmer and wetter. The weather is most favourable in early spring and at the beginning of the autumn.

PRECEDING PAGES: planting *igusa* for *tatami* mats. **LEFT:** Cape Ashizuri. **BELOW:** 88-temple pilgrim en route.

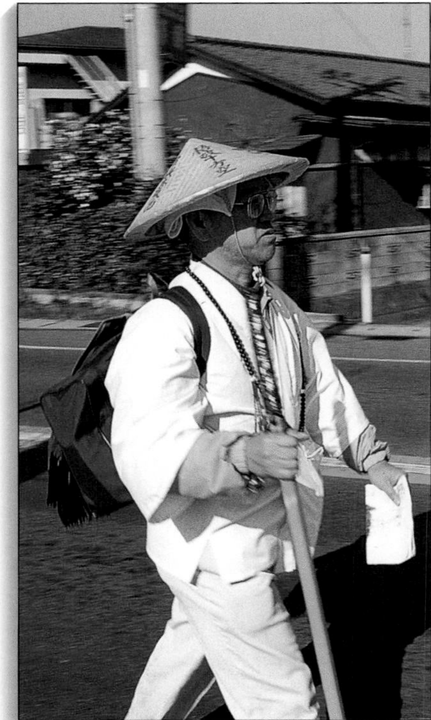

Takamatsu

The capital of Kagawa Prefecture, **Takamatsu** ⓳ is the main railway terminal and ferry port in eastern Shikoku. **Ritsurin-koen** (Ritsurin Park) contains one of the finest traditional gardens in Japan with 54 hectares (133 acres) of ponds, hills, pine forests and a botanical garden. One of the garden's best rewards is a cup of tea at the beautiful Kikugetsutei teahouse. The **Sanuki Mingeikan** (Folk Art Museum), near the entrance of the park, displays comprehensive collections of crafts from Shikoku and throughout Japan. However, the region's most popular craft are the distinctive *sanuki-udon* noodles, served daily at thousands of *udon* restaurants throughout the area.

Hotel key drop.

A few kilometres east by train from the centre of Takamatsu is **Yashima**. It was one of the seemingly countless battlefields of the Gempei War (1180–85) between the Minamoto and Taira clans. The architectural embodiments of Shikoku's past – an open-air *kabuki* theatre, a vine suspension bridge, thatch-roofed farmhouses, and a variety of other traditional buildings – have been collected and preserved in **Shikoku-mura** (Shikoku Village). This tiny part of Shikoku island was itself once an island; now a narrow strip connects it to the mainland. It juts out into Seto Naikai and provides extensive views, particularly from Yashima's lofty temple on the hill. In addition to the temple's beautiful garden is its Treasure House, stuffed with interesting relics and local art and craft objects.

Eastern Shikoku

BELOW: Seto Naikai, or the Inland Sea, near Takamatsu.

Tokushima Prefecture faces Osaka Bay and the Pacific Ocean along the western end of Shikoku. In ancient times, Tokushima was known as Awa no Kuni – Millet Country. Today, most of the prefecture's traditional arts still use the

Chinese characters for Awa no Kuni. The Awa Odori – the summer "crazy dance" festival – is held in mid-August and is perhaps the most humorous of Japanese festivals, with residents and tourists joining in processional dances and contests for the "biggest fool of all". Another home-grown entertainment are puppet shows featuring giant puppets accompanied by *shamisen* and performed by farmers between growing seasons.

The garden of the old castle of **Tokushima** ⓴ is set against the backdrop of forest-covered Shiro-yama. The garden consists of a traditional landscaped area with a fountain. Over a quarter of the 88 Kobo Daishi temples are in the immediate vicinity of Tokushima. The city has several old, fire-resistant *godown* (warehouses) used by merchants to store their goods in earlier times. The *godown* line both sides of the once-prosperous and busy main highway through the centre of Tokushima.

About 20 km (12 miles) to the north, **Naruto** ㉑ faces the **Naruto-kaikyo** (Naruto Straits), where the **O-Narutokyo** (Great Naruto Bridge) connects Tokushima with Awaji-shima and is one of the longer suspension bridges in Asia. The attraction to travellers is not the bridge, however, but rather the countless whirlpools, some as large as 20 metres (60 ft) in diameter, that swirl in the Naruto Straits flowing beneath the bridge. The whirlpools are largest in the spring and autumn, when tides reach a speed of 20 km an hour (12 mph). Sightseeing boats chug right up to the whirlpools during peak tourism season.

The 100-km (60-mile) long coastline of Tokushima Prefecture holds some of the best beaches in Japan. Along the centre of the coast, **Komoda-misaki** (Cape Komoda) stretches out into the Pacific. The peninsula is noted for its luxuriant subtropical flora. The offshore reefs, washed by the warm Japan Current, are the

Map on pages 282–3

The nearest is almost black, those farther away a dark gray, the ones behind them purplish, until – islands piled like low thunderheads – the farthest pale into a watered blue…

– THE INLAND SEA
DONALD RICHIE

BELOW: canal through a rural Shikoku village.

site of some of the best surf-fishing in Japan. The area is also noted as an egg-laying location for giant loggerhead turtles. In **Hiwasa** ㉒ to the south is a sea-turtle museum. Also in Hiwasa is **Yakuo-ji**, a temple known to ward off evil. Men and women in their *yakudoshi* (unlucky years) visit here to ask for divine help by placing a one-yen coin on each step as they climb up to the temple. The grounds of Yakuo-ji, the 23rd temple on the great Shikoku pilgrimage and famous for its series of paintings of the miseries of the Buddhist hell, affords fine views of Hiwasa harbour.

The new generation.

Tsurugi-san ㉓ (1,893 metres/6,200 ft) dominates the interior of eastern Shikoku and is one of the main peaks of Shikoku. In contrast to its name – meaning "sword" – the crest of the mountain slopes gently. A lift brings visitors up to near the summit, followed by a 40-minute hike to the peak. A lodging house, skiing area, and old shrines make Tsurugi a major recreation area.

South of Tsurugi-san, the gorge of **Konose** lies deep in the mountains at the source of the Naka-gawa. It is a site of magnificent natural beauty, and in autumn, red and yellow foliage covers the surrounding mountains.

To the west of Tsurugi-san is the gorge at **Oboke**, formed by the upper reaches of the Yoshino-gawa. The site is noted for towering cliffs and giant rocks polished like marble from the cascading waters. Spring and autumn are the best times to visit the gorge, which is visited by bus-loads of tourists. The Iya Valley, with its hot springs, river rafting, and the much-photographed **Oku Iya Kazura-bashi**, a pair of unique vine bridges, are a little east of Oboke.

The valley along Yoshino-gawa, north of Tsurugi-san and running due west from Tokushima, holds most of the area's main attractions. The valley is full of ancient temples, shrines, museums and cultural sites. The area is also

BELOW: vegetable drying while waiting out a political campaign.

Map on pages 282–3

peppered with *ai yashiki* (indigo-dyeing plants); *awa*-style indigo dyeing has flourished as the main industry of Tokushima for centuries.

About 30 km (20 miles) up the Yoshino-gawa from Tokushima is **Do-chu** (Earthen Pillars). The strangely shaped pillars were formed over millions of years as the result of soil erosion. Nearby are the historic streets of Udatsu and the Awagami traditional paper factory. The entire valley is served by the JR Yoshinogawa rail line from Tokushima.

Southwest of Takamatsu, **Kotohira** ㉔ is home to one of the most famous and popular shrines in Japan, **Kotohira-gu** (also called Konpira-san). Dedicated to Okuninushi no Mikoto, the guardian of seafarers, the shrine has lured sailors and fishermen seeking propitious sailing since the shrine's inception in the 11th century. In recent years, their numbers have been swelled by the 4 million tourists arriving each year. The main shrine is at the end of a long, steep path lined with stone lanterns. A trip to the top of the 785 stairs and back takes at least an hour.

The **Kanamaru-za**, restored to its original early 19th-century condition, is the oldest existing *kabuki* theatre in Japan. Its stage, resonating with the fading echoes of thousands of performances, is exciting to visit even when empty. In the third week of April, the nation's best *kabuki* actors bring it alive. The revolving section is turned by strong men pushing the 150-year-old mechanism under the stage, and the audience is seated on cushions on *tatami*.

Western Shikoku

Facing Seto Naikai along Shikoku's northeastern shore, Ehime Prefecture was described as early as AD 712 in the *Kojiki*, Japan's first chronicle of historical events and legends. Ehime has many historical places, hot springs and festivals.

BELOW: harvesting cultivated pearls.

Several castles dot the Ehime landscape. In **Imabari** ㉕ is **Imabari-jo**. It is a rare coastal castle built in 1604 by Takatora Todo. The massive walls and moats, filled by water from the sea, let its masters fight attacks by land or sea.

Ancient temples and shrines are another attraction of Ehime Prefecture. **Oyamazumi-jinja**, on **Omi-shima**, has been worshipped since ancient times as the central shrine of all village shrines in Japan. It is a shrine to the gods of the sea and of soldiers; many old camphor trees give the shrine a solemn atmosphere. **Ishite-ji**, the 51st temple on Shikoku's 88-temple pilgrimage, was built by the decree of Emperor Shomu in 728. It was restored by the great priest Kobo in the early 9th century. Its treasure hall holds some 300 important historical articles.

Matsuyama-jo, which stands in the middle of the city of **Matsuyama** ㉖ and with a slightly incongruous baseball park and athletic stadium at its base, has had a chequered history. It was completed in 1603, burnt down but was rebuilt on a slightly smaller scale in 1642, struck by lightning and razed to the ground in 1784, and then not fully rebuilt until 1854. The present-day edifice is a result of restoration work completed in 1986, so it's not exactly an original, but the cable-car ride up to it is fun and this is a good place to get your bearings.

Away to the west near **Dogo-koen** stands the **Dogo Onsen Honkan**. People in Matsuyama have been coming to Dogo for more than a century, taking off their shoes at the entrance to the rambling three-storey castle affair topped with a white heron and leaving their clothes and cares behind as they wallow in the glory of the alkaline hot spas. It is thought that they've been doing so for as long as 3,000 years – Dogo Onsen is reckoned to be the oldest hot spring in use in Japan. It was first mentioned in the *Kojiki*, and in the *Manyoshu*, the country's first anthology started in the 5th century.

Remember that in the Japanese *onsen* or hot spring no clothes are worn (though a small hand towel offers modesty), and one should thoroughly wash and rinse before entering the water, used only for soaking.

Below: ship in the Inland Sea.

One can get a basic soak in **Kamin-yu** (Water of the Gods) for a few hundred yen, but that would be like going to a Michelin-star restaurant and merely nibbling on the breadsticks. Pay the full price and head up Dogo's precipitous stairways to **Tamano-yu** (Water of the Spirits). Language is not a problem as smiling ladies point the way to a private *tatami* room where you can leave clothes in a locker, don a *yukata*, and head for the bath itself.

Males and females go their separate ways at this point, but as in all *onsen*, soap and thoroughly rinse off first, sitting on a little wooden stool and dousing your body from a wooden bucket. Then – bliss is the only word for it – it's time to lower yourself inch by inch into the waters (hot but not scalding) and let the body gradually adjust. It's a tingling cleanliness that washes over you, that penetrates beneath the skin, and that drowsily wafts over the mind. After 10 or 20 minutes, heave yourself out, dry off, and climb back up to the *tatami* room. The maid will pull out your sitting pillows and serve tea and marzipan balls. The balcony looks out over tiled roofs and trees, and laughter and the contented buzz of conversation drifts over from adjoining rooms.

Japan's countless hot springs are indicative of the islands' continuing volcanism.

Japanese poets and novelists have long sung of the joys of this *onsen*, but as the drum booms gently from the *shinrokaku* room on the third floor to mark the passing hours, time and the other vagaries scarcely seem relevant any more.

One of Ehime's more interesting historical sites is the *kabuki* theatre in **Uchiko** ㉗. This full-scale *kabuki* theatre was built in 1916 in the Irimoya-zukuri style, its tiled roof typical of the housing style of the 1800s. Its restoration in 1985 preserved the old-style drum tower on the top floor, a rotating stage, an elevated passageway and box seats.

Uwajima-jo was built in 1595 by Takatora Todo. The castle's three-storied tower stands atop an 80-metre (260-ft) hill overlooking the city of **Uwajima** ㉘, noted throughout Japan for bullfights. Curious libertines drawn to Uwajima by tales of **Taga-jinja** (and its sex museum) should be aware that many of the more tantalising exhibits within this shrine are locked away in glass cases and there is little interpretation in English, although, of course, most of the items on display – from lurid photos to well-proportioned fertility sculptures – are self-explanatory.

To the south in **Tsushima** ㉙ is a strolling garden, **Nanrakuen-koen**, covering more than 15 hectares (37 acres) and the largest on Shikoku. Developed in 1985, the garden has four theme areas: mountains, villages, towns and the sea. Some 30,000 irises, which bloom in early May, cover most of the gardens. Near Nanrakuen-koen is a gorge, **Nametoko**, carved out by the Shimanto-gawa, which is reported to be the last clear river in Japan. The gorge runs through Ashizuri-Uwakai National Park.

Ehime Prefecture is also noted for its many and varied festivals: the Ikazaki Kite Festival in May displays Ehime's 300-year history of kite-making; the Saijo Festival in October features 80 moveable shrines; the Niihama Drum Festival in October includes a competition between 33 massive drums, or *taiko*. Other festivals include bullfights, samba (yes) competitions and the Matsuyama Spring Festival in April.

BELOW: fishing boat leaving Uwajima.

Southern Shikoku

Two large capes frame Kochi prefecture. On the far western side of Kochi lies **Ashizuri-misaki** ㉚. This cape is noted for towering marble cliffs and Japan's first underwater park. In early spring, camellia cover the cape in a dazzling red carpet of blossoms.

The prefecture of Kochi broadly encircles the wide **Tosa-wan** (Tosa Bay), with its capital of **Kochi** ㉛ facing the south on a flat plain. Kochi is best known for the role its leading families played in forging the alliance between the Satsuma and Choshu clans and the ensuing imperial Meiji Restoration of 1868. Its most renowned citizen from this period is Sakamoto Ryoma. Sakamoto – from a half-merchant, half-samurai family – left the class system and set up a trading company in Nagasaki.

While there, he helped establish a network of anti-Tokugawa samurai but was assassinated in Kyoto in 1867 – just a year before the overthrow of the shogun and restoration of the emperor to legitimate rule. He is remembered in the museum at **Kochi-jo** (Kochi Castle), an elegant castle built in the 17th century and rebuilt in the 18th. A market is held every Sunday on the road leading to the Ote gate of Kochi-jo. The market is popular with local residents, with as many as 700 small stalls selling vegetables, antiques, plants and just about everything else imaginable. The market runs for about a kilometre along both sides of the road. A statue of Sakamoto Ryoma graces the beach at **Katsurahama**, more famous as one of the few locations in Japan where dog-fighting is legal. This beautiful beach is a popular spot for admiring the moon. Katsurahama-koen is nearby, and there are many places of interest such as a shell museum, dog-fighting centre and aquarium.

Below: aqua-farming is heavily practised. **Right:** harvest of *mikan* on a steep coastal hill.

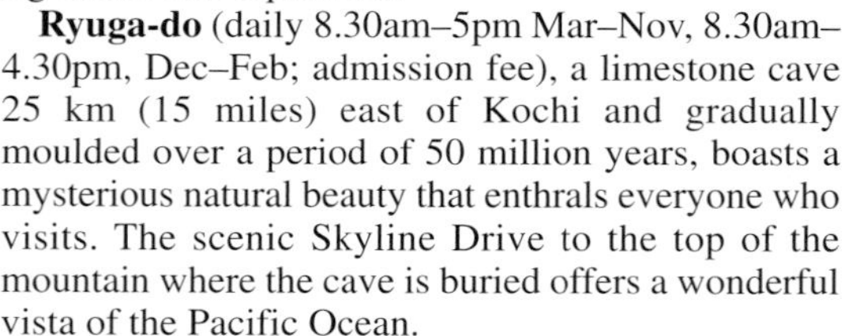

Ryuga-do (daily 8.30am–5pm Mar–Nov, 8.30am–4.30pm, Dec–Feb; admission fee), a limestone cave 25 km (15 miles) east of Kochi and gradually moulded over a period of 50 million years, boasts a mysterious natural beauty that enthrals everyone who visits. The scenic Skyline Drive to the top of the mountain where the cave is buried offers a wonderful vista of the Pacific Ocean.

A few kilometres west of Kochi, in **Ino**, is a fabulous paper museum. Ino has a long history of paper-making, and Kochi paper is famous throughout Japan. (For a place to be viable in Japan's domestic tourism industry, it must be "famous" for something, for anything.) In the museum, visitors can try their hand at paper-making in addition to observing the paper-making process. Near Kochi sits the Nishijima Fruit Farm. Its 11 huge hothouses, each measuring 70 metres (230 ft) in length and 45 metres (150 ft) in width, cover the spacious grounds. The temperature within each hothouse is maintained at 25°C (77°F). Sample the delicious Kochi melons here year-round.

On the far eastern side of Kochi from Ashizuri-misaki, **Muroto-zaki** ㉜ points out southward into the Pacific Ocean. The cape is warm year-round and at its tip the towering waves of the Pacific have eroded the rocks and reefs into strange shapes. The area is also noted for its connection with the venerable Kobo Daishi, founder of the Shingon sect of Buddhism. ❑

YAMAHA

UNDERCURRENTS OF LIFE AND RITUAL

At the core of Japanese life is the ancient, animist belief of Shinto, which informs daily life in basic ways, enriched by introduced Buddhism.

An outsider may perceive a certain fog enveloping the Japanese beliefs in gods and afterlife and in the metaphysical concerns of life. Buddhism and Shinto coexist, and on occasion appear to meld together. Unlike believers in a monotheistic system, Japanese are more willing to accept a world that has a lot of grey areas with few absolutes, in which compromise and tolerance of thought is essential. It is not uncommon to find Shinto shrines and Buddhist temples sharing the same sacred grounds, each tending to specific needs but complementing one another as a whole.

Shinto doesn't exist as doctrine, but rather as an integral undercurrent to one's daily life. Shinto is Japan's indigenous religion, but the term Shinto did not appear in any Japanese literature until the 6th century, and in fact the label came into existence only as a way to distinguish it from Buddhism, introduced from mainland Asia. Nor were there visual images of Shinto deities – *kami* – until the imagery of Buddhism established itself in the archipelago. Over the centuries, Daoism and Confucianism also influenced Shinto.

Ancient Shinto was polytheistic, maybe even pantheistic, and people believed *kami* existed not only in nature, but also in abstract ideas such as creation, growth and human judgement.

▷ **COEXISTING WITH BUDDHISM**
Buddhist priests, such as these Zen priests at a Kyoto temple, have no qualms in sharing the metaphysical with Shinto priests.

△ **GIFTS TO THE GODS**
Offerings at a small shrine in Okinawa; some of the most sacred sites are simple and lack grand structures.

△ **GOOD HARVEST WISH**
As in ancient times, prayers and imagery of good rice harvests often punctuate festivals in Japan.

△ **MORNING PRAYERS**
Shinto priests at morning prayers. The sacred image is often kept from view, seen only by the head priest.

▽ **VANISHING POINT**
Torii – dividing the secular world from Shinto shrines – make an unusual tunnel at Fushimi Inari, Kyoto.

△ **QUICK PRAYER**
There are no weekly holy days. Rather, the Japanese attend a shrine or temple when the need arises.

◁ **SHRINE IMAGERY**
The rope, white paper, and other symbols announce a sacred site as of Shinto importance.

▷ **SADO**
Tea ceremonies – symbolic of Japanese ways – are mostly Zen Buddhist influenced.

A LIFE OF SHINTO BLESSINGS

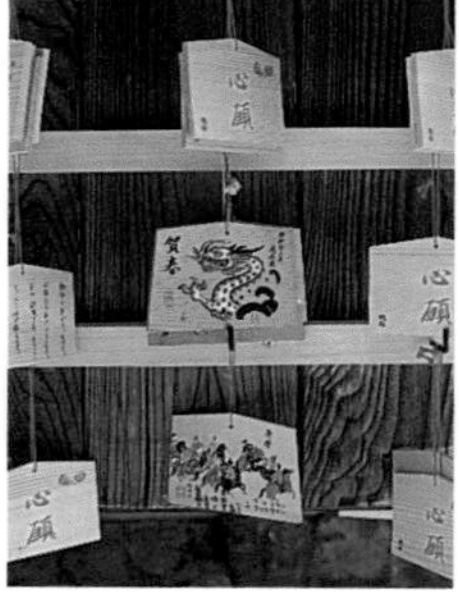

Traditions of Shinto (and of Buddhism, too) are the traditions of Japan itself. They pepper the daily lives of the Japanese, who perform them as routines of life when the urge or need arises.

The small votives *(ema)* above are hung at shrines to seek good luck in exams or other secular rituals. Infants are brought to the shrine 30 to 100 days after birth to initiate the child as a new believer. Children dressed in kimono attend *shichi-go-san* (seven-five-three) on 15 November every year. Girls of three and seven years old and boys of five years old visit the shrine to thank the *kami* for their life so far and to pray for good health. In January, 20-year-olds return to the shrine marking their becoming adults. When they are married, it is usually a Shinto ceremony (although a separate Western-style ceremony is increasingly common). Death, however, is usually a time of Buddhist ritual and family remembrance.

山形屋

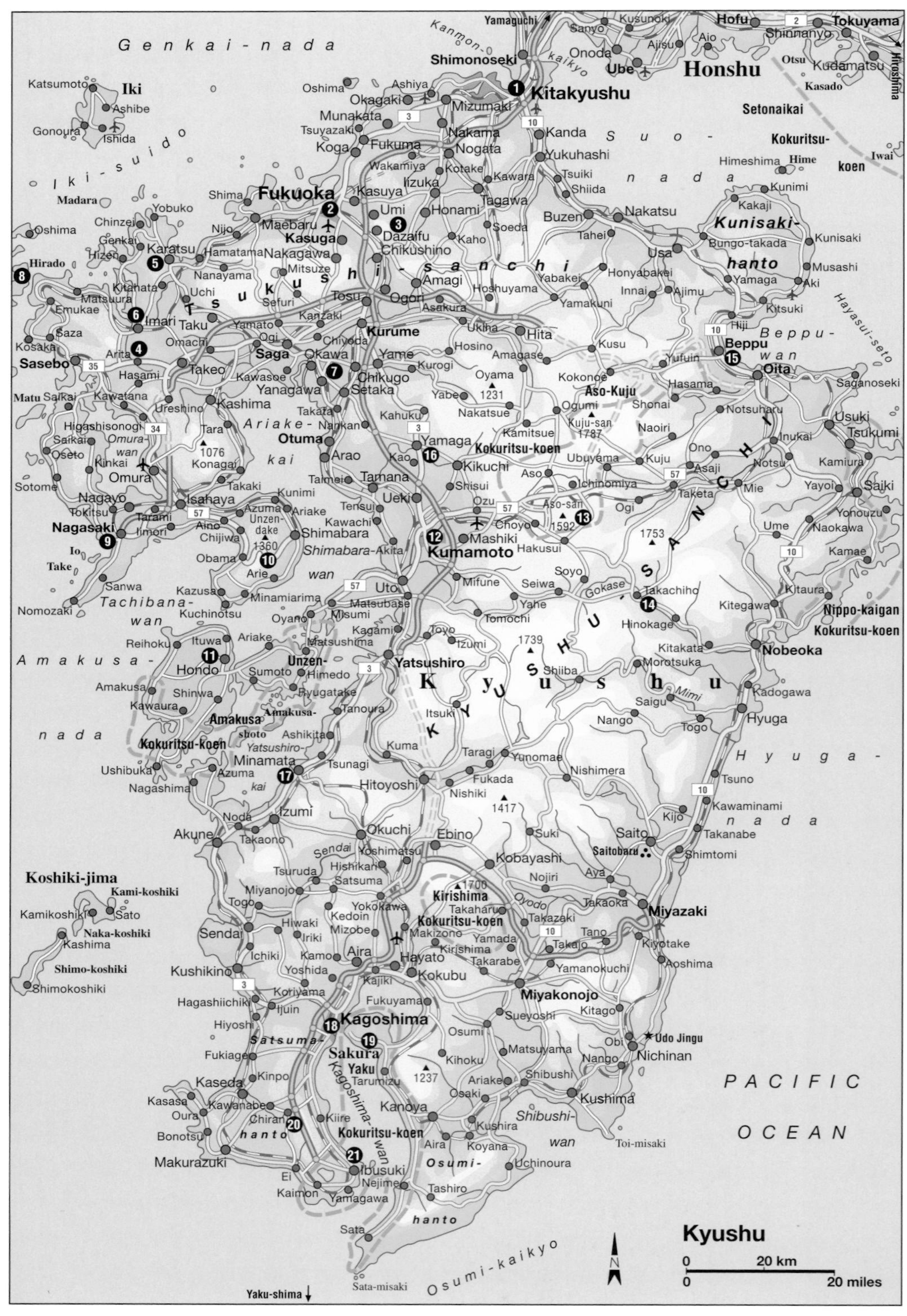
Genkai-nada
Iki
Katsumoto
Ashibe
Gonoura
Ishida
Iki-suido
Madara
Oshima
Hirado
Kanmon-kaikyo
Yamaguchi
Shimonoseki
Kitakyushu
Sanyo
Kusunoki
Hofu
Tokuyama
Shinnanyo
Aio
Ajisu
Onoda
Ube
Honshu
Otsu
Kudamatsu
Kasado
Hiroshima
Setonaikai
Kokuritsu-koen
Iwai
Himeshima
Hime
Suo-nada
Oshima
Okagaki
Ashiya
Munakata
Mizumaki
Tsuyazaki
Nakama
Koga
Fukuma
Nogata
Kanda
Yukuhashi
Wakamiya
Kotake
Iizuka
Kawara
Tsuiki
Shiida
Kasuya
Fukuoka
Shima
Umi
Honami
Tagawa
Buzen
Nakatsu
Kunimi
Kakaji
Kunisaki-hanto
Kunisaki
Bungo-takada
Musashi
Yamaga
Aki
Soeda
Tahei
Usa
Yobuko
Chinzei
Genkai
Hizen
Karatsu
Nijo
Maebaru
Kasuga
Dazaifu
Chikushino
Kaho
Hamatama
Nakagawa
Mitsuze
Tsukushi-sanchi
Yabakei
Honyabakei
Nanayama
Amagi
Inai
Ajimu
Kitahata
Matsuura
Uchi
Sefuri
Tosu
Ogori
Hoshuyama
Yamakuni
Kitsuki
Emukae
Asakura
Kanzaki
Imari
Taku
Yamato
Ukiha
Hita
Hiji
Beppu-wan
Beppu
Hayasui-seto
Saza
Kosaka
Ogi
Kurume
Chiyoda
Omachi
Hosino
Kusu
Yufuin
Oita
Sasebo
Arita
Saga
Okawa
Yame
Amagase
Kurogi
Hasami
Takeo
Kawasoe
Yanagawa
Chikugo
Oyama
1231
Kokonoe
Hasama
Saganoseki
Matu
Saikai
Kawatana
Setaka
Yabe
Aso-Kuju
Ureshino
Kashima
Nakatsue
Ogumi
Shonai
Notsuharu
Higashisonogi
Omura-wan
Ariake-kai
Takata
Kuju-san
1787
Usuki
Saikai
Tara
Nankan
Kahuku
Kamitsue
Naoiri
Inukai
Tsukumi
Oseto
1076
Otuma
Yamaga
Kokuritsu-koen
Ono
Kinkai
Konagai
Arao
Kao
Ubuyama
Kuju
Kamiura
Omura
Kikuchi
Asaji
Notsu
Sotome
Takaki
Tamana
Shisui
Aso
Ichinomiya
Mie
Yayoi
Saiki
Nagayo
Isahaya
Kunimi
Taimei
Ueki
Ozu
Aso-san
1592
Taketa
Ogi
Tokitsu
Tarami
Azuma
Ariake
Tensui
Yonouzu
Nagasaki
Aino
Unzen-dake
Kawachi
Choyo
1753
Ume
Naokawa
Iimori
Chijiwa
1360
Shimabara
Kumamoto
Mashiki
Io
Take
Obama
Shimabara-wan
Akita
Hakusui
Kamae
Arie
Soyo
Sanwa
Kazusa
Mifune
Seiwa
Gokase
Takachiho
Kitaura
Nomozaki
Tachibana-wan
Kuchinotsu
Minamiarima
Uto
Matsubase
Yahe
Nippo-kaigan
Kokuritsu-koen
Oyano
Misumi
Tomochi
Kitegawa
Hinokage
Reihoku
Ituwa
Ariake
Matsushima
Kagami
Toyo
Izumi
1739
Kitakata
Nobeoka
Amakusa-nada
Hondo
Unzen-Himedo
Yatsushiro
Morotsuka
Sumoto
Kyushu
Kyushu-sanchi
Shiiba
Mimi
Amakusa
Shinwa
Ryugatake
Saigu
Kadogawa
Kawaura
Amakusa Amakusa-shoto
Tanoura
Itsuki
Nango
Togo
Hyuga
Ashikita
Kokuritsu-koen
Yatsushiro-kai
Kuma
Ushibuka
Minamata
Tsunagi
Taragi
Yunomae
Hyuga-nada
Azuma
Nishimera
Tsuno
Nagashima
Hitoyoshi
Fukada
Nishiki
1417
Kawaminami
Noda
Izumi
Kijo
Takanabe
Akune
Takaono
Okuchi
Ebino
Suki
Saito
Sendai
Yoshimatsu
Saitobaru
Shimtomi
Tsuruda
Hishikari
Kobayashi
Koshiki-jima
Kami-koshiki
Satsuma
Nojiri
Aya
Miyanojo
1700
Kirishima
Oyodo
Kamikoshiki
Sato
Togo
Yokokawa
Takaharu
Takaoka
Miyazaki
Kedoin
Kokuritsu-koen
Takazaki
Naka-koshiki
Kashima
Sendai
Hiwaki
Mizobe
Makizono
Tano
Iriki
Yamada
Kiyotake
Shimo-koshiki
Ichiki
Kamo
Aira
Hayato
Kirishima
Takajo
Takarabe
Aoshima
Kushikino
Yoshida
Kokubu
Yamanokuchi
Shimokoshiki
Kajiki
Hagashiichiki
Koriyama
Fukuyama
Miyakonojo
Ijuin
Sueyoshi
Kitago
Kagoshima
Hiyoshi
Osumi
Udo Jingu
Satsuma-hanto
Sakura
Kihoku
Matsuyama
Obi
Fukiage
Nango
Nichinan
Yaku
Kinpo
Kagoshima-wan
1237
Kaseda
Tarumizu
Ariake
Shibushi
PACIFIC OCEAN
Osaki
Kasasa
Kushima
Kawanabe
Kanoya
Oura
Chiran
Kiire
Kushira
Shibushi-wan
Bonotsu
Toi-misaki
Kokuritsu-koen
Aira
Koyana
Makurazuki
Uchinoura
Ibusuki
Osumi-hanto
Ei
Nejime
Kaimon
Tashiro
Yamagawa
Sata
Kyushu
Osumi-kaikyo
0 20 km
0 20 miles
Sata-misaki
Yaku-shima
N

KYUSHU

An erupting volcano next to a large city, Kagoshima, and the history of a port city, Nagasaki, are unique to Kyushu, as are some of Japan's most independently minded leaders

Map on page 318

Kyushu is far to the south and, it seems at times, almost forgotten by the rest of Japan. But Kyushu has always been in the vanguard of development and change. Kyushu is where the Yamato tribe – and thus the Japanese people – first took root in what was to become their homeland. It was Kyushu that withstood the onslaught of the Mongols from the mainland. It is also from where the Japanese first struck out on foreign conquest – the invasion of Korea in 1594 – and where ancient Chinese and Korean culture entered the archipelago as foundations for Japanese art and philosophy. In later years, it was one of the few places where Westerners had a foothold in the xenophobic islands.

Any traveller coming from the north usually enters Kyushu at **Kitakyushu ❶**, considered by some as a city in search of a soul – it is an amalgamation of five cities (Moji, Kokura, Yawata, Tobata and Wakamatsu) with a combined population of over a million. The civic marriage was arranged by Tokyo bureaucrats in 1963, but it has yet to be consummated by a blending of culture or politics. It is a lacklustre city with little of interest for travellers. Kitakyushu is linked to Shimonoseki on Honshu by a bridge across the Kanmon Strait. Immense steel mills (now an endangered species) and factories were built here to take advantage of the region's rich coal deposits.

PRECEDING PAGES: Kagoshima and Sakura-jima.
BELOW: unhappy three-year-old at temple blessing.

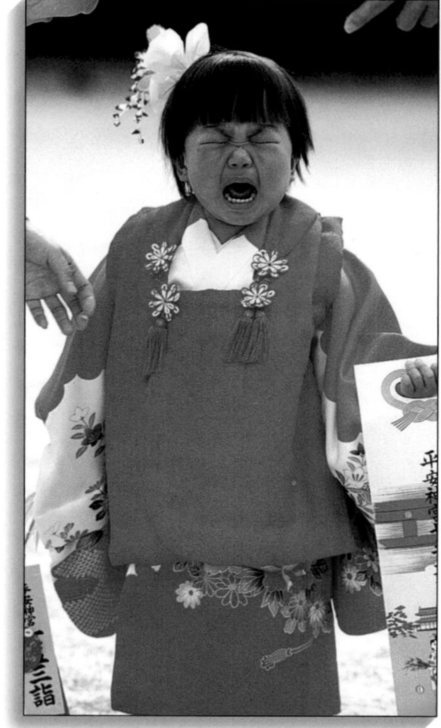

Fukuoka

Northern Kyushu has a long history of overseas influence. In the 13th century it was targeted by foreign invaders, but other "imports" have been of a more peaceful nature. **Fukuoka ❷** is reportedly where both tea and Buddhism were introduced to Japan, and Korean captives brought back here were responsible for starting up a sizeable pottery industry. Today, with a population of 1.2 million, Fukuoka competes with Kitakyushu as the largest city on Kyushu.

The city remains an important hub in regional trade and commerce, but while shopping and hotel complexes such as the glistening Canal City dominate the skyline, Fukuoka still retains a lot of charm at ground level. Canals crisscross the central urban area and in the evenings and on weekends small stalls selling snacks and alcohol are set up on the paths beside the water, each an oasis of relaxation and merriment for the hordes of harried *sararimen* ("salarymen") wending their way home from work.

Fukuoka's history has not always been benign. During the Nara and Heian periods, the area was the principal Japanese port for trade with China and Korea, but in 1274 a reconnaissance force of some 30,000 Mongols landed near Fukuoka after annihilating garrisons on the islands of Tsushima and Iki, just to the

Hakata Yamagasa takes place in the first half of July; seven enormous floats are displayed around the city for a fortnight. On the 15th, groups of brawny men race the floats, which each weigh a ton, through the streets in a hilarious tumult of noise, excitement and general frenzy.

north of Kyushu in the Korea Strait. The invaders enjoyed similar success on Kyushu, but the death of their commander, along with serious storms that threatened their ships, forced them to retreat. Seven years later, in 1281, Kublai Khan dispatched another Mongol expeditionary force of 150,000 troops, the largest amphibious assault recorded in history prior to World War II. Backed by a ferocious armoury of catapults and cannons, the Mongols gradually wore down the tenacious Japanese resistance, but when they were on the brink of victory after 53 days of fighting, a terrific typhoon – *kami-kaze* (lit. divine wind) – sent most of the invading fleet to the bottom of the sea. Remnants of the defensive wall built to repel the Mongols can still be seen on the outskirts of Fukuoka, although nowadays they are rather unimpressive.

Relics of Fukuoka's most famous visitors are preserved 2 km (1¼ miles) northeast of Hakata Station at the **Genko Kinekan** (Mongol Invasion Memorial Hall), along with a statue of Nichiren, who was among the mystics taking credit for the fortuitous kamikaze storm that sank the Mongol fleet.

Modern Fukuoka traces its roots to 1601, when a castle was built on the west side of the **Naka-gawa** in what is today Ohori Park and the town that grew up around the castle took the same name of Fukuoka. Only the castle's walls survive nowadays, but they provide an excellent view over the city. Hakata, a town for merchants who enjoyed a less important status than the ruling samurai, was built on the other side of the river. Hakata-ku has been a ward within Fukuoka since 1889, but the name remains – **Hakata-eki** (Hakata Station), the southern terminus of the *shinkansen* line; Hakata clay dolls; and the popular Hakata Yamagasa festival are all named after the merchant city. In its role as the crossroads between Japan and China, Fukuoka was the place where Zen Buddhism first touched the

CANAL DREAMS

Fukuoka's modernity and willingness to experiment is exemplified by the Canal City shopping and entertainment complex. Canal City was created by California architect Jon Jerde who also designed Universal Studio's cartoon-like City Walk, and the giant Mall of America. Opened in 1996, it was the first mall of its kind in Kyushu to mix shopping and leisure activities in one unified space. Curvaceous walls, like opera or window balconies, with overhanging plants, overlook an artificial canal, or "spouting walkway", with outdoor retail booths and a performance space. Sleek cafés, restaurants, and a number of import clothing stores are represented here along with a 13-theatre AMC mega-movieplex. Canal City's exploding fountains, in keeping with the city's thoughtful planning and administrative ethos, uses rain and waste water, which is treated within the complex.

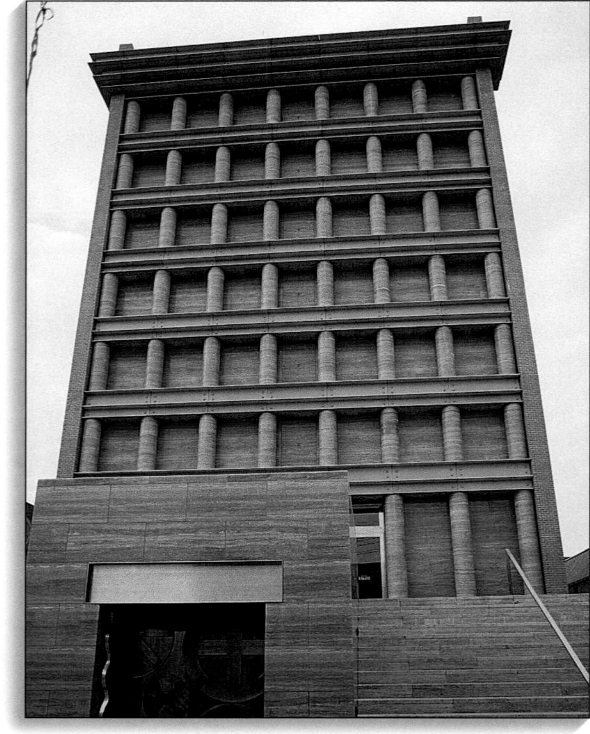

BELOW: modern architecture.

archipelago's shores. Located northwest of Hakata Station near Mikasa-gawa, **Shofuku-ji** is the oldest Zen temple in Japan, founded in 1195 by Eisai after years of study in China. Sadly, much of the temple suffered bomb damage during World War II and the current complex is only a fraction of its former self. Eisai is also credited with bringing the first tea seeds into the country.

The **Sumiyoshi-jinja**, the oldest extant Shinto shrine on Kyushu, was built in 1623. South of Shofuku-ji and due west of the train station, it sits atop a hill that provides an excellent city view. A museum, Hakata Machiya Furusato-kan, chronicling the history of the city, is located on a street running almost opposite **Kushida-jinga** in the central district of Nakasu, the city's most important shrine.

All in all, Fukuoka today is still very much open to outside influence and sees itself as the cultural crossroads of this part of Asia. The downtown **ACROS Centre**, easily recognisable for its imaginative stepped-garden exterior, stages international opera, ballet, symphony orchestras and popular musical extravaganzas, as well as more traditional Japanese performances.

Two other significant structures overlook life in the city. A mammoth seaside stadium, **Hawks Town**, whose retractable dome is the first of its kind in Japan, is home to the local baseball team as well as a hotel and shopping mall. And a little further along the coast above Momochi-koen stands the 234-metre (768-ft) **Fukuoka Tower** (daily 9.30am–9.30pm, Oct–Mar until 9pm; admission fee), with two observation towers that provide stunning views over the surrounding area.

Other points of interest in Fukuoka include **Fukuoka-shi Bijutsukan**, a museum housing a collection of Japanese art, and **Ohori-koen** (Ohori Park), a pleasant park harbouring the remains of **Fukuoka-jo** (Fukuoka Castle) and reconstructions of its turret and gates.

Fukuoka International Association, located on the eighth floor of the ims Building in Tenjin, is an excellent information centre with noticeboards, events calendars, brochures and newspapers in English.

BELOW: the roof of the Fukuoka Dome at the Hawks Town shopping and leisure centre.

Forty minutes from Fukuoka and inland to the southeast, **Dazaifu** ❸ is home to **Tenman-gu**, a shrine built in 1591 to commemorate the poet-scholar Sugawara Michizane, who died in AD 903 after being unjustly exiled from the court in Kyoto. Successive mishaps befell Kyoto, supposedly because of Sugawara's banishment. As a result, he gradually came to be acknowledged as Tenman, a deity of culture and scholars.

Much of the pottery and ceramics found in western Honshu and Kyushu is defined by both an elegance and a rustic simplicity.

Nowadays, students of all ages tramp over the bright-orange shrine's arched bridge to beseech his help in passing school examinations, which can make or break careers and lives in Japan. Sections of defensive walls built after the first Mongol invasion can still be seen on the road to Dazaifu.

Dazaifu offers a lot more than just a simple pilgrimage to Tenman-gu and its commercial offerings. Rather than bearing left at the end of the approach road to the shrine, turn right and, tucked into a small lane you will come across a stark Zen garden fronting the grounds of **Komyo Zen-ji** temple. Remove your shoes to enter its dimly lit wooden corridors where Buddhist art and other treasures lurk in the unlit rooms that the temple's trickle of visitors file passed. You have to look twice, surprising yourself with a small camphor statue, Korean bowl or earth-coloured tea cup, objects that have been sitting in the shadows for centuries. The rear walkways provide a slightly elevated view of another rock, gravel and moss garden below.

The **Kanzeon-ji** temple, with its rare ordination stage and great bell, is a 15-minute walk from here. Its Treasure House contains a number of highly prized statues, some of the figures masked, including an unusual horse-headed Kannon. A short walk further on, near a small museum to the site, are the remains of the Tofuro, or City Tower, a look-out post used during the Yamato Period when

Below: sumo lessons for kids; Fukuoka is host to an annual sumo tournament.

rebellious tribes like the Kumaso in southern Kyushu threatened the realm. There are several axially arranged foundation stones here of former administrative buildings.

Dazaifu's heady blend of religion, historical relics and academia dissolve in the curative waters of **Futsukaichi Onsen**, just 3 km (2 miles) south. Although this is the closest spa town to Fukuoka, Kyushu's largest city, it rarely gets crowded even on weekends. There are three hot springs here, conveniently lumped together. The perfect place to nurse out the days' aches and pains.

Ceramic cities

When Ri Simpei, an ordinary Korean potter, first chanced upon *kaolin* clay – the essential ingredient for producing fine porcelain – in **Arita** ❹, 50 km (30 miles) west of Fukuoka around the turn of the 17th century, he probably had little notion of the ramifications of his discovery.

Shoes are never worn in the house or school but are kept near the entrance.

Nearly 400 years later, Arita and its neighbours **Karatsu** ❺ and **Imari** ❻ are the hub of a thriving pottery industry. The delicate craftsmanship and brightly coloured glazes that are the hallmarks of pottery from this region are prized all over Japan, and further afield, too. Simpei and the other potters who were brought over from Korea as prisoners of the Nabeshima *daimyo* were kept under close guard so their trade secrets did not slip out.

To understand something about those times, the **Nabeshima Hanyo-koen** at Okawachiyama (a short bus ride from Imari) portrays the sort of techniques and living conditions in which Simpei and his fellow workers lived. There are plenty of working potteries in the area as well, but **Kyushu Toji Bunkakan** (Kyushu Ceramic Museum) in Arita is the best place to view the full range of

BELOW: Kyushu farms are small and family-owned.

Kyushu pottery. Imaizumi Imaemon and Sakaida Kakiemon are celebrated workshops with galleries and shops open to the public.

Karatsu is also highly regarded for its stoneware. Several galleries and workshops, including the Nakazato Taroemon and the Ryuta kilns, are open to visitors. The Hikiyama Tenijo museum exhibits 19th-century Karatsu *kun-chi* festival floats, which are paraded through the town every November. **Saga**, a pottery town in its own right, is a excellent base from which to explore the three principal ceramic centres of Arita, Imari and Karatsu.

Kyushu cuisine is no less feisty than its inhabitants, typical preparations being slices of sashimi *horse meat, grilled sparrow, and* karashi renkon*, deep-fried lotus root stuffed with miso and mustard, washed down with* shochu*, a potato-based firewater.*

For a breath of ocean air, take a stroll or hire a bike to explore the pine groves of **Niji-no-Matsubara**, which stretch along the beach found at Matsuragate.

Yanagawa

Like Kyoto, **Yanagawa** ❼ on the southern island of Kyushu, under an hour on the Nishitetsu Omuta Line from Fukuoka station, is a water city. The angularity of Yanagawa's grid of canals contrasts intriguingly with the winding lanes of the old town that transects it. An aerial view would no doubt reveal something like an octopus on a chequerboard.

Yanagawa was founded by the Kamachi clan in the 16th century. Its water sources however, are far older, dating back to the Yayoi Period when an area of damp lowland existed near the mouth of several rivers that funnelled into the nearby Ariake Sea. Canals were dug to drain the land and improve its agricultural prospects. The canals remain more or less intact, covering a total length of 470 km (290 miles). Twelve percent, in fact, of the town's surface area is water.

It's a comfortable place to stroll through, though many visitors elect to view the town, its willow-lined canals flowing by old samurai villas, luxuriating back

BELOW: Canal City shopping complex in Fukuoka.

Map on page 318

gardens and old brick storehouses, from the comfort of a canal barge. The vessels are propelled by boatmen who, like Oxbridge punters, use poles to propel the barges along the currentless waterways. During winter months the boats install quilts with heaters placed underneath.

Mihashira-jinga in Takehatake Park is the town's spiritual centre and is a fine example of a building that has acquired a patina of age. The present park, full of pine and cherry trees, was used as a riding ground during the feudal era. Like the old town with its low and squat appearance, the shrine, full of worn, uneven flagstones, stained green with time, and a magnificent wooden entrance, has a minimally maintained air, making it look far older than the date given for its founding.

Eating baked and steamed *unagi no seiromushi*, rice and eel steamed with a sauce made from sugar and soy, with a finely sliced omelette on top, is part of the Yanagawa experience. The fish is said to increase a person's stamina and virility, especially during the dog days of summer. At lunch time the whole town seems to smell of baked eel, as charcoal-coloured smoke billows out into the street from vents at the side of restaurants. In winter, visitors can sample duck. *Yanagawa nabe*, small fish cooked with local vegetables and egg in an earthenware pot, is another local speciality.

Hirado

Continuing west from Imari for another 40 km (25 miles), the focus shifts to Japan's early Christians. The first foreign settlement in Japan was established by Dutch traders on **Hirado-shima** ❽ (Hirado Island) in 1550, although the one-time island is now connected to the mainland by a bridge. The Francis Xavier Memorial Chapel consecrates the Spanish saint's visit to Hirado after he

LEFT: fishy festival float.
BELOW: boating on the canals at Yanagawa.

was expelled from Kagoshima in southern Kyushu. European activity here ended when the Dutch were forced to move to Dejima, in Nagasaki Harbour, in 1641. But secretive Christians maintained a version of the faith here for centuries afterwards, often under the threat of imprisonment and death. This bit of historical lore has provided the basis for a thriving domestic tourist industry here, with "real" icons for sale.

Fugu*, or blowfish, is the local speciality and is reputed to be especially good in winter. If prepared incorrectly, deadly toxins can poison the diner.*

Nagasaki

Like Hiroshima, **Nagasaki** ❾ is a name automatically associated with the atomic bomb that brought World War II to its terrible and tumultuous climax. It is particularly ironic that this most terrible manifestation of Western technology should have been detonated in a city that was one of the first to open up to the outside world and where foreign inventions and ways were once eagerly adopted.

The path was not always smooth, of course, and many early Christian converts were brutally executed and foreign residents were expelled from time to time. But Nagasaki was one of the first Japanese cities to take a serious interest in Western medicine. It was here, too, that the first railway and modern shipyard in Japan were established.

Now home to more than half a million people, Nagasaki clings to steep hills wrapped around a very active deep-water harbour, competing with Kobe for designation as Japan's San Francisco. Like San Francisco, it has a lively Chinatown and a continuing spirit of receptiveness to novel ideas. One of the most interesting cities in Japan, travellers on a restricted time budget should allow for two days or more to explore Nagasaki and its surroundings.

BELOW: tram ride in Nagasaki.

Maps on pages 318 & 326

Nagasaki's harbour has played a prominent role in Japan's relations with the outside world. Dutch traders initiated the first sustained European presence here, on an island in the harbour that also acted as a conduit for most of the early Christian missionaries. The port at Nagasaki was established in 1571 to serve Portuguese traders. A decade later, Omura Sumitada, a local *daimyo* who had grown rich on trade with the foreigners, turned over partial administration of the port to the Jesuit missionaries who followed in the merchants' wake.

A generation later, fearing that the Christians and their converts would subvert his authority, the shogun Toyotomi Hideyoshi banned Christianity. He ordered six Spanish priests and 20 Japanese Christians, including two teenage boys, to be rounded up in Kyoto and Osaka. They were brought to Nagasaki and crucified in 1597 as a warning to Japan's largest Christian community. A memorial constructed in 1962 and museum (daily 9am–5pm; admission fee) stands in **Nishizaka-koen** (Nishizaka Park) on the spot of the crucifixions, near **Nagasaki-eki** Ⓐ (Nagasaki Station) at the north end of downtown.

TIP

Like Fukuoka, also on Kyushu, Nagasaki is thought by many foreigners to be one of Japan's most pleasant large cities.

Christianity was utterly and viciously suppressed following the Christian-led Shimbara Rebellion of 40,000 peasants south of Nagasaki in 1637. As a result, Japan's sole officially sanctioned contact with Europeans for the next two centuries was through a settlement on **Dejima** Ⓑ, in Nagasaki Harbour and south of the present-day Nagasaki Station. The artificial island – now part of the mainland – was built for Portuguese traders but it was occupied by the Dutch after the Portuguese were banished in 1638. Its occupants were confined to a small, walled area and contact with Japanese was limited to a small circle of officials, traders, prostitutes and, in the later years, scholars.

As no other Europeans were permitted in Japan until 1854, whatever news of European technology and culture that filtered into Japan came through this settlement. The **Shiryokan** (Dejima Museum; Tues–Sun 9am–5pm; free) near the site preserves relics of the settlement.

Like the Dutch, Nagasaki's Chinese, mostly from Fujian along China's southern coast, were officially confined to a walled ghetto but restrictions on their movements were not as strictly enforced. The Chinese in Nagasaki left the only pure Chinese architecture to be found in Japan, along with one of the three Chinatowns remaining in Japan. (The others are in Yokohama and Kobe.) The narrow and winding streets of **Shinchimachi** are filled with Chinese restaurants catering to tourists, as there are very few Chinese remaining in Nagasaki.

Two popular "Chinese" dishes in Japan, *saraudon* and *champpon*, were invented in Shinchimachi. Like most of the foreign food served in Japan, they bear only a passing resemblance to the original but they are still quite palatable. On the subject of food, the other "foreign" delicacy that survives in Nagasaki is the *kasutera* or sponge cake that is supposedly baked to an old Portuguese recipe and sold (in exquisitely wrapped packages) in bakeries around town.

The Chinese community was granted permission to build its own temples. Teramachi (Temple Town) contains two of the oldest Chinese temples in Japan, as well as numerous Japanese Buddhist temples and

BELOW: the entrance to Chinatown.

graveyards. **Kofuku-ji** **C**, founded in 1620, was built on the edge of the original Chinatown in the northeast part of town. The Chinese quarters burned down in 1698; the current Shinchimachi occupies land designated for Chinese merchants following the fire. Centrally located, **Sofuku-ji** **D** is a bright, elaborate Ming-style temple and is in better condition than most Ming-era temples in China. The Masodo (Hall of the Bodhisattva) contains an image of the goddess of the seas, flanked by fierce guardians reputed to have thousand-mile vision. Nagasaki's premier shrine, **Suwa-jinja**, is a 10-minute walk east. Points of interest include a graceful main hall, a curious collection of guardian lions and an imposing horse statue, and the shrine's dynamic festival, the Kunchi Matsuri.

Replicas of the bombs dropped on Hiroshima and Nagasaki.

Within walking distance of the temples, the **Nakashima-gawa** (Nakashima River) is spanned by a picturesque range of bridges. The best known and most photographed is **Megane-bashi** **E**, whose English translation of Spectacles Bridge becomes apparent when there is enough water in the river to ensure a good reflection. The original bridge was the oldest stone arch bridge in Japan, built in 1634 by a priest from Kofuku-ji. However, a flood in 1962 destroyed it and the present structure is a carbon-copy restoration.

True to its traditional receptiveness to new ideas, Nagasaki embarked on an aggressive modernisation campaign in the latter part of the 19th century. Thomas Glover, a Scotsman, was one of the first and most significant of the European traders who arrived soon after Commodore Matthew Perry's Black Ships reopened the country. Glover helped Nagasaki achieve many Japanese firsts: the first railway, the first mint, and the first printing press with moveable type were all built in Nagasaki as a result of his efforts. He was also very active in supporting the rebels who defeated the shogun's forces – mainly through a profitable line in gun-running – and re-established the emperor's rule in 1868 in the Meiji Restoration. There is considerable controversy over whether Glover's marriage to a geisha did, as many guidebooks assert, inspire Puccini's opera *Madame Butterfly*. Glover also built the first Western-style mansion in Japan.

BELOW: traditional dress at the Okunchi Festival.

At the southern end of the city, **Glover-en** **F** (Glover Gardens; daily Mar–mid-July, mid-Oct–Nov 8am–6pm, mid-July–mid-Oct until 9.30pm, Dec–Feb 8.30am–5pm; admission fee) contains this mansion, built in 1863, and several other early Meiji-era, Western-style houses – elegant mixtures of Japanese and European architecture plus the inevitable statues of Puccini and his tragic Japanese heroine. It is amusing to wander around the grounds today, which now have vending machines, covered escalators and recorded announcements, and speculate that these are technological innovations of which Glover himself would have approved.

If your trip does not coincide with the annual Okunchi Festival in early October, when Chinese-style dragon dances and parades are held in the vicinity of Suwa-jinja, a trip to the **Kunchi Shiryokan** (Kunchi Museum) near Glover Garden will at least give a visitor some idea of the floats and costumes involved.

Nearby in the same neighbourhood is **Oura Tenshu-do** (Oura Catholic Church), said to be the oldest Gothic-style structure in Japan. Completed in 1865, it is dedicated to the 26 Christian martyrs who were crucified in the 16th century and has some fine examples of stained glass. Signposts point along a paved footpath east of the church to an interesting enclave of foreign influence, the **Dutch Slopes**. Flagstone roads and old brick walls pass well-preserved Western-style houses, some of which, including museums of local history and photography, are open to the public.

The highly conspicuous **Koshi-byo**, a red and orange lacquered Confucian temple (daily 8.30am–5pm; admission fee), lies close by the slopes. The treasures within its sanctuary are sumptuous.

Oranda-zaka (Dutch slopes) is a hilly area where Western merchants, notably from the Netherlands, settled in the late 19th century.

A city remembers

A simple stone obelisk stands at the epicentre ("hypocentre" in Japan) of the atomic blast that devastated much of Nagasaki on the morning of 9 August 1945. The plutonium bomb, which was nearly twice as powerful as the uranium bomb dropped earlier over Hiroshima, landed about 3 km (2 miles) off course over **Urakami**, a Christian village just to the north of downtown. (The Mitsubishi Heavy Industry shipyard, on the west side of the port and the first modern shipbuilding facility in Japan, was the intended target; the pilot's vision was hampered by poor visibility.)

Urakami Roman Catholic Church, the largest Christian church in Japan, stood a few hundred metres from the epicentre; it was rebuilt in 1958. Headless statues of saints scorched in the blast remain as mute witnesses to the tragedy. A similarly poignant memorial is the small hut used by Dr Takashi Nagai, who struggled to treat bomb victims as best he could until he himself succumbed to radiation sickness in 1951.

The **Atomic Bomb Museum** Ⓖ (daily 8.30am–5.30pm; admission fee) at the

BELOW: Sofuku-ji.

International Culture Hall contains photos, relics and poignant details of the blast and its 150,000 victims. Simple objects – a melted bottle, the charred remains of a kimono – as well as photos of victims provide stark evidence of the bomb's destructive powers.

Kumamoto residents have a reputation for being stubborn and moody. Easy to anger and offend, but generous to a fault, this combustible mix is summed up in a local word, mokkosu, *which roughly translates as "feisty".*

As important as its displays are, the museum fails to provide historical context or background to the bombing. Arguments for and against this revolve around whether it is appropriate to include Japan's appalling war record, and thereby attribute partial blame for the bombing to the Japanese, or whether this undoubted atrocity against humanity should be allowed to stand for itself.

Heiwa-koen Ⓗ (Peace Park) is dominated by the Peace Statue – a man with right hand pointing to the sky (signalling the threat from the atomic bomb) and left hand extended (symbolising world peace). The Peace Fountain, on the south side of the park, was built in remembrance of the bomb victims who died crying for water. Heiwa-koen was built on the site of a former jail, whose occupants and warders were all killed in the blast. On the other side of the harbour, the cable car climbing the 332-metre (1,089 ft) peak of **Inasa-yama** Ⓘ provides fantastic vistas of the harbour and surrounding hills, especially at night. Further south is the Mitsubishi shipyard, intended target for the atomic bomb.

An hour out of Nagasaki stands **Huis Ten Bosch**, one of the most graceful theme parks in Japan with many replicas of Dutch buildings and windmills, canals and clogs galore. Theme park is perhaps an understatement, as Huis Ten Bosch has been carefully constructed on environmentally friendly lines and stands as a modern-day testimony of the area's close links with the Dutch. There is something particularly Japanese about the place in the way that the replicas are built to look precisely like the originals, even to the point of making the Amsterdam canal houses lean out at an angle over the water. Once through the pricey gate most attractions are free, and it's as much fun to watch the Japanese tourists dressing up in traditional Dutch clothing for photos.

BELOW: Peace Statue in the park.

Shimabara Peninsula

The most scenic route between Nagasaki and Kumamoto takes travellers through Shimbara Peninsula and the Amakusa Islands on a combination of buses and ferries. Down the peninsula, roughly midway between Nagasaki and Kumamoto, is **Unzen-dake** ⑩, whose *jigoku* (hell) pits of boiling mud and coloured mineral waters are less dramatic but less commercialised than those in Beppu, on the east coast of Kyushu. In the 17th century, Christians who refused to renounce their faith were thrown into these *jigoku*. The town is named after the 1,360-metre (4,460-ft) high volcano Unzen-dake, on the peninsula and in **Unzen-Amakusa Kokuritsu-koen** (Unzen-Amakusa National Park). Unzen erupted in 1991, causing considerable death and damage. **Shimabara-jo** (Shimabara Castle), destroyed in a 1637 Christian rebellion, was reconstructed in 1964. The castle houses a museum displaying the *fumi-e* Christian images, which suspected believers were forced to walk upon. **Amakusa-shoto** (Amakusa Islands), about 70 islands in all, lie between Unzen and Kumamoto. The Kirishitankan in **Hondo** ⑪ is a museum with relics of the Amakusa Christians.

Kumamoto

Maps on pages 318 & 326

Although it isn't a popular tourist destination, **Kumamoto** ⓬ is an interesting and dynamic provincial capital. This city of half a million people is best known for its 17th-century castle, 350-year-old **Suizenji-koen** (Suizenji Park), and its horse-meat sashimi. Kumamoto also has the most successful technical research park (adjacent to the airport) in Japan. Kumamoto Prefecture has a sister-state relationship with the American state of Montana, due more to the power and influence of the former American ambassador to Japan, Mike Mansfield, a Montanan, than to any similarity between the two places.

Kumamoto-jo (Kumamoto Castle) was built in 1607 by Kato Kiyomasa. Unfortunately, the castle's 49 towers were made of wood and most were incinerated in an 1877 siege. The restored donjon, housing a museum as well as original turrets, moats and stone palisades, evoke the grandeur of what was one of Japan's most impressive castles.

Honmyo-ji, a Nichiren temple housing Kato's tomb, can be seen from the castle's towers. A cup of tea can be enjoyed in the basement of the **Kumamoto Traditional Crafts Centre** (Tues–Sun 9am–5pm; admission fee) across the street from the castle. The first floor features a colourful collection of toys, tools, jewellery and ceramics produced by Kumamoto craftsmen. The museum is part of the prefecture's efforts to sustain traditional crafts, largely abandoned after World War II. Suizenji-koen, designed in 1632 and south of the modern city, contains landscaped models of Mount Fuji.

The Kyushu Kokusai Kanko Bus has regular departures for **Aso-Kuju Kokuritsu-koen** (Aso-Kuju National Park), but the JR Hohi Line switchback train from Kumamoto to Aso affords great views.

BELOW: Aso's main caldera.

Blood Pond Hell.

Signposts along the roads welcome visitors to *Hi-no-Kuni*, the "Land of Fire". The generic **Mt Aso** ⓭ is actually a series of five volcanic cones, its massive caldera stretching to a circumference of 128 km (80 miles). Of the five peaks Daikanbo, at 936 metres (3,070 ft), is the highest. Nakadake, emitting sulphurous fumes and high-temperature gases that occasionally bring hiking above the basin to an abrupt halt, is an active volcano, which last erupted in 1979. The ideal way to explore the area beyond the main road connecting the caldera with the town would be by bicycle – a steep ride up, a blissful one down – or time permitting, on foot.

Once in the caldera, a striking shape materialises on the right-hand side of the road. This is the grass-covered hill known as **Komezuka**, the name meaning "inverted rice-bowl". Equally suggestive of the ziggurat or burial mound of some ancient nature cult, it is a configuration of great beauty.

Buses en route for **Nakadate**, the massive, highly active crater which is for many the highlight of an Aso trip, stop a little further on at Kusasenri-ga-Hama, a circular plain that was originally a minor crater. A large pond at its centre serves as a watering hole for cattle and horses. The **Aso Volcano Museum**, with its 170-degree multi-screens relaying images of the crater and its catchment area is also here. All this subterranean activity means superb hot springs, most found in the caldera itself, though there are *onsen* retreats tucked away in the highlands nearby as well.

East of Kumamoto and on the other side of Aso, the shrine at **Takachiho** ⓮ is where the *iwato kagura*, a sacred dance, is performed for tourists every night. **Takachiho-kyo** (Takachiho Gorge), featuring 80-metre (260-ft) cliffs, is another one of the many spots where the sun goddess Amaterasu is said to have emerged from her cave to create the islands and people of the archipelago. A cave near the shrine at Iwato is touted as the very one.

BELOW: sand-bath therapy at Beppu.

Hot springs

If seeking to go to hell and then come back, head for **Beppu** ⓯ on the northeastern coast of Kyushu. The resort town is famous – and thus highly commercialised – for its *jigoku*, or variously coloured ponds of water and mud that steam and boil, as well as its hot springs. A popular destination for Japanese tourists, Beppu is gaudy and rather tacky and a far cry from the serene elegance of Japanese travel posters. Besides the hype, there are other hells, more than can be experienced in a lifetime, including: Blood Pond Hell, a vermillion-coloured boiling pond; Sea Hell, a boiling mud pond 120 metres (400 ft) deep; and Mountain Hell, a mud pond in the hills complete with statues of gorillas. All these are far too hot for bathing, but in the many *onsen* inns, comfortable hot-sand and hot-mud baths are available.

A more serene and sophisticated hot-spring resort, **Yufuin**, less than an hour from Beppu, is known for its galleries, elegant country inns, fashionable guesthouses, and the beautiful morning mists that rise from the warm, thermal waters of **Lake Kinrin**. Bicycles can be rented for a circuit of the lake, hiking trails taken up nearby Mt Yufu or through the woods.

The Usuki Sekibutsu, a collection of more than 60 stone Buddhas, is all that remains of the **Mangetsu-ji**,

once an important temple. The stone images are some of the most exquisite and mysterious Buddhist images in Japan.

Descending Kyushu's rugged east coast, the pleasant provincial city of **Miyazaki**, with its locally grown mangos, palm-lined streets and indoor water theme park called Seagaia, or Ocean Dome, is a convenient stopover on the way to the Nichinan coast that stretches south of the city. The delightfully rural Nichinan Line train follows the shore, taking a slightly inland route.

Aoshima, a seaside resort with plenty of action and animation of the modern kind at its beaches, cafés, hotels and amusement arcades, is the most popular stop on the line. Patronised by sun-worshippers and weekend surfers, Aoshima's main draw is its tiny subtropical island of the same name, surrounded by great platforms of "devil's washboard" – eroded rock formations with row upon row of shallow pools and indented octopus-shaped rings sunk into long furrows of basalt – which disappear at high tide.

30 km (18 miles) south of Aoshima is the vermilion coloured shrine of Udo Jingu. It occupies an unusual setting in the mouth of a cave beside the ocean.

Castle town

The crowds rarely make it as far as the old samurai town of **Obi**, a few stops slightly inland on the Nichinan Line. A few discerning Japanese, a quiet trickle of visitors (virtually no foreigners as yet), file in and out of its gardens and samurai villas, though you will often find yourself left alone. Not that Obi is completely unaffected by mainstream tourism. There is even a man (only one mind), who will pull you around the historic core of the town in a *jinrikshaw* (rickshaw), telling you local stories and legends.

At the core of the old quarter, 15 minutes on foot from Obi Station, Otemon-dori, a ramrod straight avenue lined with old houses, plaster storerooms and

BELOW: girls in uniform.

stone and clay walls topped with ceramic tiles leads to the superbly restored Ote-mon, or main gate, the entrance to the Obi castle grounds.

Destroyed in 1870, only its walls, carefully reconstructed in the original style using joinery rather than nails, and a whitewashed history museum, remain. Up a further flight of steps in the castle precincts, the Edo Period **Matsu-no-Maru**, the residence of Lord Ito's most senior wife, is a faithful replica of the original, replete with women's quarters, reception rooms and the Gozaemon, a beautifully stark tea ceremony room.

Obi was once a thriving merchant centre. The main road through the castle town has several fine examples of whitewashed merchant houses dating from the Edo to early Showa periods, some now serving as stores and museums.

The wooden gate to the **Yoshokan**, former residence of the Ito clan, is just to the left of the Ote-mon. Obi's most graceful samurai residence, this airy construction was built for the family's chief retainer and then requisitioned for their own use after feudal holdings were abolished in the Meiji era. All the rooms in the Yoshokan face south in conformity with tradition and the rules of geomancy. Each chamber overlooks a fine dry landscape garden with the ultimate *shakkei*, or "borrowed view", in the form of Mount Atago.

Proceeding south, **Ishinami Beach** is one of the finest stretches of unspoiled white sand along the Nichinan coast. **Kojima**, at the southern end of the cove, is inhabited by wild monkeys. A cluster of rustic farmhouses, doubling in the summer months as *minshuku*, lay within a short stroll of the beach. **Toi Misaki**, a scenic but over-developed cape marred by tacky hotels and other resort facilities, marks the southern tip of this extraordinary, time-worn coast.

The recently restored Edo-style **Yachiyo-za**, in **Yamaga** ⓰ and 50 minutes by bus from Kumamoto, is one of 10 *kabuki* theatres in Japan and well worth a visit. Built in 1910, it is a mixture of traditional Japanese and imported innovations, including a revolving stage and concealed trap doors. Patrons sit on *tatami*, warming themselves with a *hibachi* in winter. Around the corner, a lantern museum displays hundreds of handmade lantern headdresses.

Below: all in a day's fishing.

The bay near **Minamata** ⓱, in the southern part of Kumamoto Prefecture, is a monument to the excesses of industry. A severely debilitating and often fatal ailment known as Minamata disease was traced to shellfish and other products taken from its waters, into which industries had been discharging mercury and other wastes for decades. Legislation hurriedly passed by the Diet soon after the disease's discovery in the 1970s now constitutes the basis of Japan's still-weak pollution controls. Nevertheless, litigation regarding the responsibility for the mercury dumping was dragged out until the mid-1990s, with no entity admitting responsibility. Minamata Bay itself is being reclaimed and turned into an ecological park.

Kagoshima

This prefecture in the far south of Kyushu consists of two peninsulas, Satsuma and Osumi, that encircle **Kagoshima-wan** (Kagoshima Bay) and also a chain of islands stretching south towards Okinawa. A distinct, rapid-fire dialect is spoken here – and in much of Kyushu – and the speech of older people, lacking the homogenising influences of national TV and radio, is almost incomprehensible to other Japanese. **Kagoshima** ⓲, on the interior side of Satsuma-hanto and the southernmost metropolis in Kyushu, is situated on large Kagoshima Bay. It is famous for being Japan's most polluted city. The pollution comes from **Sakura-jima** ⓳ (Cherry Island), the very active volcano east across the bay and rising 1,120 metres (3,670 ft) directly above the water *(see pictures on pages 284-85 and 320–21)*. The mountain has erupted more than 5,000 times since 1955, sending clouds of ash and often large boulders raining down on Kagoshima. (Umbrellas are used as much for ash as for rain.) More than half a million people live within 10 km (6 miles) of Sakura-jima's crater. No other major city is as precariously positioned; Naples, Kagoshima's sister city, is twice as far from Vesuvius. Sakura-jima itself can be reached via a short ferry ride from Kagoshima or by road around the periphery of the bay. As the name indicates, it was once an island but an eruption in 1914 spilled some 3 billion tons of lava down its southeast flank and joined the island to the peninsula. There are dramatic views from the **Yogan Tenbodai** on the southeast side of Sakura-jima. Extra-large *daikon* (Japanese radishes) grow in the rich volcanic soil, along with kumquats, summer oranges and other fruits.

Map on page 318

Satsuma clans

Aside from the ash and sometimes polluted air of Kagoshima, the city itself is delightful and retains the spirit of the once-powerful Satsuma clans, from whom the area takes its name. The Satsumas were ruled by the Shimazu *daimyo*, among the most dynamic of the Japanese hereditary rulers, for seven centuries. The Shimazu's distance from Edo Tokyo bred a fierce independence here in southern Kyushu. The Shimazu were open to new ideas from abroad. They welcomed Francis Xavier to Kagoshima, the first Japanese city he visited, in 1549. Returning from Japan's ill-fated invasion of the Korean peninsula in the early 17th century, the Shimazu brought captive Korean potters to Kagoshima, where they developed satsuma-ware.

Despite their receptiveness to outsiders, the Satsuma clans opposed the Edo shogunate's capitulation to European demands that Japan open its ports to trade. Demonstrating resistance to the shogun's edicts, Shimazu retainers killed an Englishman near Edo in 1862. The British retaliated the following year by sending a squadron of ships to bombard Kagoshima. To the British sailors' surprise, the lords of Satsuma admired this demonstration of modern naval power. They welcomed Her Majesty's officers to the still-smoking city and purchased some of their ships. In 1866, the Satsuma clan joined with the rival Choshu clan in a successful military coup against the shogun, which restored imperial rule with the Meiji Restoration in 1868. (Close relations between the Japanese and British navies lasted until the 1920s, and Satsuma clansmen dominated Japan's navy until World War II.)

Satsuma-ware and the more rustic Kuro-Satsuma pottery can be purchased in **Naeshirogawa**, a village that was settled by Korean potters in the 1600s. In addition to pottery, Kagoshima is known for *kiriko* cut glass.

Iso-koen, containing a garden laid out in 1661, provides excellent views of Sakura-jima. Just outside the

BELOW: special-occasion footwear.

Map on page 318

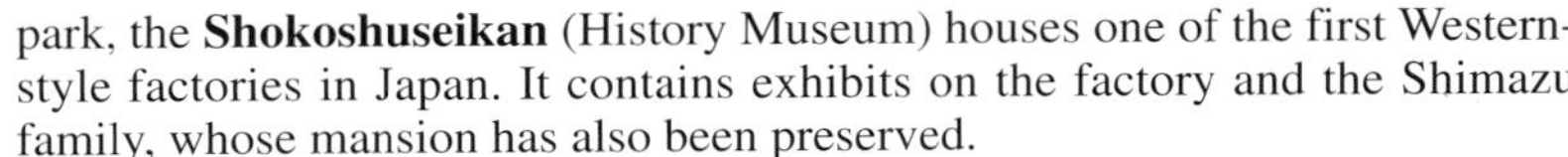

park, the **Shokoshuseikan** (History Museum) houses one of the first Western-style factories in Japan. It contains exhibits on the factory and the Shimazu family, whose mansion has also been preserved.

The cemetery of Nanshu holds the remains of Saigo Takamori (1827–77), who led the forces that defeated the shogun. Saigo later perished after leading the 1877 rebellion against the Meiji regime he had created. Saigo made his last stand at the hill called Shiroyama. With defeat inevitable, he had a loyal follower decapitate him. He was buried at Jyokomyo-ji.

Buses leave Kagoshima on the hour from 9am for the 50-minute ride to **Chiran** ⓴, a charming samurai town set in a pastoral landscape of striking warmth, a concentration of green volcanic peaks, tea plantations and white stucco-faced houses.

Chiran is best known for its miniature Edo Period gardens, six of which are open to the public. Background scenery, such as mountains, forest and hills are used as part of the garden. The top of the hedges are clipped into angles to match the outline of the hills.

The *tokko-tai*, better known in the West as kamikaze pilots, flew from Chiran and other bases in southern Kyushu, on the first leg of their one-way missions. Visitors should view the **Tokko Heiwa Kaikan** (daily 9am–5pm; admission fee), or Peace Museum for Kamikaze Pilots, a 3 or 4-km (2–3-mile) taxi or bus ride into the hills north of town. A rather splendid plane, superior to the hastily refurbished trainers most flew, greets visitors to the open space beside the museum. The museum's centrepiece, its **Peace Hall**, was completed in 1975. Its collection, though chilling, is more sentimental than gruesome, with drawers full of uniforms, flying gear and adolescent mascots, its walls and cabinets bristling with letters and photos. In one image, a pilot tightens the rising-sun *hachimaki* bandanna of a comrade, a symbol of samurai valour and pre-battle composure, around the head of a doomed but smiling youth.

Ibusuki ㉑ is a spa town southwest of Kagoshima with hot-sand baths near **Kaimon-dake**, a 900-metre (3,000-ft) high volcano looking much like Fuji.

BELOW: taking the sands at Ibusuki. **RIGHT:** waterfall on the island of Yaku-shima.

Japan's ambitious space programme, if small by American, Chinese, French and Russian standards, operates a launch pad at **Uchinoura**, on Osumi-hanto to the east of Kagoshima. Most launches, however, are now made from Tanega-shima, an island south of Kagoshima and near another island, Yaku-shima.

Yaku-shima

A circular island 1,000 km (600 miles) south of Tokyo and 135 km (80 miles) from Kagoshima, **Yaku-shima** is a naturalist's fantasy, declared a UN World Heritage Site in 1993 for its flora. There is the rare Yaku-shima rhododendron, and the *Yaku-sugi* cedar trees that are over 1,000 years old. (Youthful cedar trees less than 1,000 years old are *ko-sugi.*) Existing at 700 to 1,500 metres on the slopes of some of Yaku-shima's 40 peaks that are higher than 1,000 metres (600 ft), the cedar trees are like elderly sages amidst the dense foliage. The largest cedar is said to be the world's biggest, with a circumference of 43 metres (141 ft) at its roots, a trunk circumference of 16.4 metres (54 ft) and a height of 25 metres (80 ft). The Japanese also claim that it is the oldest in the world at 7,200 years, but there is some dispute about this.

Waterfalls and lush hiking trails lace this ancient volcanic island that is nearly 30 km (20 miles) in diameter. Two small towns with accommodation are home to most of the island's 14,000 people. ❑

メガネの山下
どらえもん
香港飯

OKINAWA

Once an independent kingdom called Ryukyu, Okinawa is a world of its own. Bloodied by World War II, tropical Okinawa is today Japan's domestic resort escape

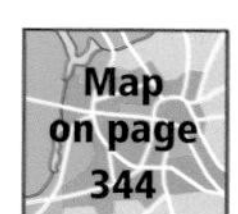

Extending for 1,200 km (600 miles) southwest from Kyushu, the 70-plus islands of the Ryukyus, or **Nansei-shoto**, stretch across the ocean to within 200 km (125 miles) of Taiwan. For centuries, the Okinawans minded their own business and accommodated themselves to outsiders. But during the age of imperialism in the late 19th century, their independence fell prey to the ambitions of powerful neighbours.

Ryukyu is the Japanese pronunciation of the Chinese name Liugiu, which is what the Ming dynasty Chinese called the islands. Taken over by Japan, which then long ignored the islands like a faraway province, Okinawa was the final beachhead for a planned Allied invasion of the Japanese archipelago in World War II. The battle for Okinawa was bloody for both sides and for the Okinawan civilians. Placed under American control by the UN following the end of World War II, the islands reverted to Japanese sovereignty in 1972. Now, all islands north of the main island of Okinawa are part of Kyushu, and the main island and islands to the south are in Okinawa Prefecture.

PRECEDING PAGES: protective *shisa*. **LEFT:** Naha. **BELOW:** Okinawan beach resort.

Okinawa sits in a subtropical belt, blessed with average temperatures of around 23°C (73°F). A short rainy season blankets the area in heavy rains during May and June. Spring and autumn are enjoyable, typhoons in September and October notwithstanding.

There are exquisite white-sand beaches, azure waters, and some unusual flora and fauna. Okinawa is, along with Guam, Japan's backyard resort escape. But Okinawa has the highest unemployment rate in Japan and an average annual income half that of Tokyo. Yet, its gentle, friendly people give no hint of Tokyo-envy nor of the incredible suffering that Okinawans have known through times of war – and even during times of peace. Okinawans are proud of their heritage and will often remind travellers that they are not Japanese. A fine and relaxing manner in which to gauge the differences between Okinawa and the rest of Japan is a visit to a local pub: no disco or ubiquitous karaoke found in big-city clubs elsewhere in Japan; rather, listen to the frequently plaintive sounds of the *sanshin*, the three-stringed, snakeskin-covered Okinawan banjo known elsewhere as the *shamisen*. Traditional Okinawan dance and theatre differ considerably from their Japanese counterparts.

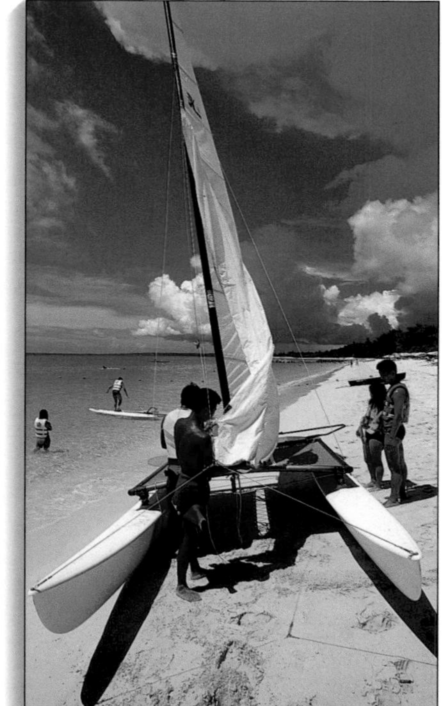

The area was under pressure from the government in the late 1990s to rehouse an American miltary base, with generous financial rewards offered in return. To persuade Okinawa to agree to this move, the government elected it the site of the July 2000 G7 summit.

Okinawans are quite proud of their exquisite textiles, which are typically hand-woven from linen and silk and feature beautiful designs created with painted-on dyes. The designs traditionally differed by area, and the *bingata* stencil-dyed fabric, originally made exclusively for aristocrats, is the most highly prized of the fabrics.

Naha

Shisa *images are placed atop buildings for protection from evil demons.*

The centre of Okinawa's tourism is the city of **Naha ❶**, and Naha's centre of tourist activity is Kokusai-dori (International Road), which is a jangle of typical Japanese urban architecture – cluttered and without aesthetic appeal – and crowds of walkers and swarms of vehicles. Yet only a short distance away are typically Okinawan neighbourhoods. **Naminou-gu**, a small Confucian shrine, and the **Gokoku-ji**, a temple that was once considered a national religious centre, are along the waterfront not far from the central post office and just north of an old pleasure quarter that retains its fair share of bars, cabarets and steak houses.

Okinawan crafts are a delight. Active since 1617, the **Tsuboya** pottery district, off Himeyuri-dori and southeast of Kokusai-dori, houses two dozen kilns that make everything from the *kara-kara* flasks once carried by country gentlemen to the fearsome *shisa* figures that guard dwellings. Tsuboya's pottery history began in the early 1600s when a Korean potter was forced to settle here after being taken prisoner. Pottery made in Tsuboya bears 17th-century Korean characteristics, as is also the case in Kyushu. The recently built **Tsuboya Ceramic Museum** (Tues–Sun 10am–6pm; admission fee), with pottery displays and models of reconstructed local buildings, is an excellent introduction to the history of the area.

Naha is the perfect spot for first experiments with Okinawan cuisine. Now familiar with the sashimi, *unagi, yakisoba* and other delicacies of central Japan,

BELOW: Naha Port.

travellers might brave *mimiga* (sliced pig ears with vinegar), *ashite-bichi* (stewed pig legs), *rafutei* (pork simmered in miso, sugar, rice wine and soy sauce), *goya champuru* (stir-fried meat and melon), or one of the many kinds of local *somen* noodles. *Awamori*, the local distilled rice brew served with ice and water, packs a wallop that puts all else to shame.

Map on page 344

Shuri

The first castle on **Shuri**, west of downtown on a hill overlooking Naha and the oceans beyond, was established in 1237. Under the second Sho dynasty, established in 1469 by King Sho En, Shuri became a mighty palace and temple complex. Shuri remained the political and cultural centre of the Ryukyus until 1879, when the last Okinawan king, Sho Tai, was forced to abdicate by the Meiji government in Tokyo. During the 82-day battle of Okinawa in 1945, when the Japanese Army chose Okinawa as the last stand against the Allies before an anticipated invasion of the main Japanese islands, **Shuri-jo** (Shuri Castle) was the headquarters of the Japanese forces. It was destroyed in the fighting. Pre-war accounts describe a marvel on a par in architectural and artistic interest with Kyoto, Nara and Nikko. Much of the castle's stonework has now been rebuilt.

Nearby, **Ryutan-koen** is an expansive park barely able to absorb the hordes of tour buses or the clusters of on-going groups posing for photographs with classically attired Okinawan women in front of **Shuri no Mon**, the traditional gate to the castle grounds. The **Tama-udon**, minutes from the gate, contains the bodies of Sho En and other members of his family. The much improved nearby **Okinawa Prefectural Museum** (Tues–Sun 9am–5pm; admission fee), presents a good digest of Okinawa's rich history and culture.

Hibiscus, a form of Chinese rose used, among other things, to decorate Buddhist altars and to beautify graves, is found throughout Okinawa. The wood of the deigo *tree, whose red flower is the official bloom of Okinawa, is the source of high-quality lacquerware.*

BELOW: tourists at Shuri, and a main gate to Shuri-jo.

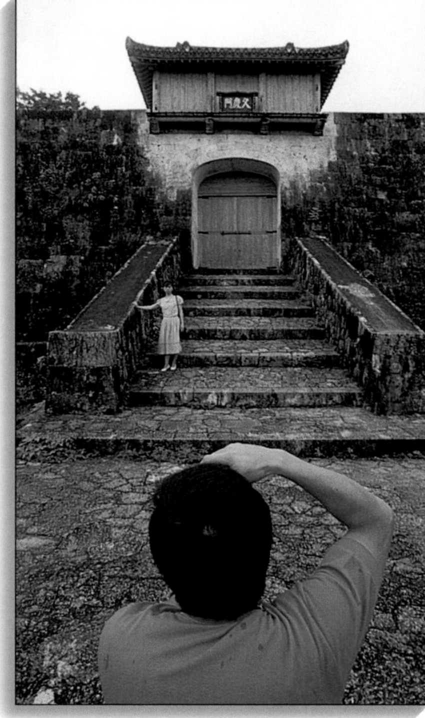

South of Naha

Southern Okinawa is noted for caves. The most famous caves are the tunnel labyrinths at **Romogusuku**, near the Naha airport and the last headquarters of the Imperial Navy. The military commanders refused to surrender as the Allies pounded the island's south with naval bombardments; over 4,000 Japanese men committed suicide. Reminders and memorials of the bloodiest battle of the Pacific war that cost the lives of 13,000 Americans, 110,000 Japanese, and 140,000 Okinawan civilians (one-eighth of the population) are numerous throughout the south of the island.

The islands of Okinawa were under US control from 1945 until 1972, when they were returned to Japan. Today, most of the US military's presence in Japan is on Okinawa.

The coastal highway south past the international airport leads to **Itoman** ❷, claimed to be the home of some of the most fearless sailors in the world. Itoman's mid-August tug-of-war with intertwined "male" and "female" ropes draws crowds from afar. Several heavily promoted and developed caverns pepper the southern coastline, including **Hakugin-do**, a cavern with a shrine dedicated to the guardian deity of Itoman.

The story of **Himeyuri no To** (Lily of the Valley Tower) is famous: it involves a deep pit where a group of high-school girls and their teachers committed suicide – rather than endure the possibility of capture by Americans – after singing their school song. **Mabuniga-oka**, on a promontory overlooking the ocean, is the site of the last resistance of the Japanese Army.

Gyokusen-do ❸ is said to be East Asia's largest cave. Only about one-fifth of it is open to the public; unfortunately, in this part visitors have broken off most of the stalactites and stalagmites, and the cave's floor has been pockmarked by footprints. Near the entrance to the caves is the **Habu-koen** (Snake Park), where there are displays of fights between mongooses and habu snakes, whose venom is strong enough to fell a horse. The park is now part of the newly created **Gyokusendo Kingdom Village** (daily 9am–5pm; admission fee). Built over an impressive network of caves, the village displays an extensive collection on local culture, arts and crafts.

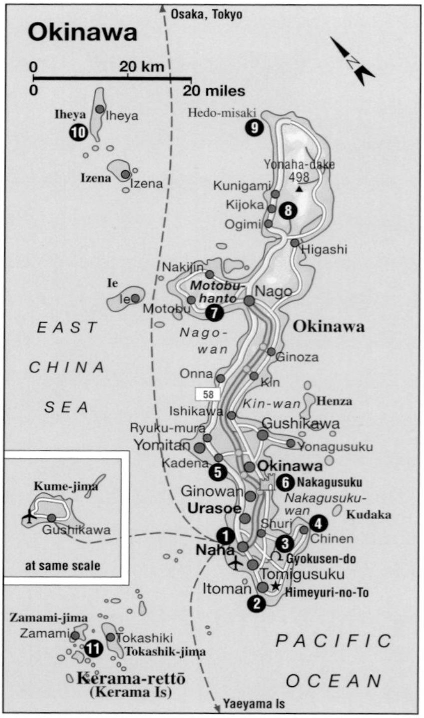

A 5-km (3-mile) ferry ride from **Chinen** ❹ on Okinawa's southeast coast brings visitors to small and flat **Kudaka-jima**, the so-called island of the gods. This is where the great ancestress of the Ryukyuan people, Amamikiyo, is said to have descended from heaven and bestowed on them the five grains. The people of these isolated, storm-swept islands came to believe that their fate rested in the hands of the gods, and an arcane priestess cult still thrives. Covered with sugar cane and *fukugi* trees, Kudaka-jima, which has a resident population of about 300 people, is usually somnolent. But in mid-November every 12th year, the five-day Izaiho Festival is held, in which local women serve collectively as *noro*, or priestesses, to perform rites and communicate with the gods. Like other *utaki*, or sacred places throughout Okinawa, visitors often remark that the sounds of the sea, wind and the singing birds seem strangely louder here.

Central and northern Okinawa

The central portions of Okinawa are largely occupied by controversial US military bases, most important of which is the air base at **Kadena** ❺. In the 1990s, Oki-

nawans vocally sent the message that they wanted some of their land returned; many of the bases are on private land, which the central Japanese Government has mandated. Some of the American military presence is slowly being shifted away from Okinawa.

Outside Kadena, offerings are sleazy and garish, but there are good beaches in the area. The ruins of the castle at **Nakagusuku** ❻, built in the 15th century, are the largest in Okinawa. The Nakamura home in Nakagusuku offers an inspection of how an 18th-century gentry family lived.

Back on the west coast, the main road north of Naha, towards Moon Bay, passes **Ryukyu-mura** (daily 8.30am–5.30pm; admission fee), a theme park that has preserved some genuine traditional farmhouses and other tangible features of Okinawan culture. Despite the souvenir-dominated entrance and exit areas, the "village" is an intriguing digest that includes displays of Okinawan crafts like textile weaving and dyeing, Eisa dancing, and performances on the *san-shin*. Okinawan dishes and sweets made from the local brown sugar are readily available.

American influence over Okinawa.

Jutting out from the west coast about two-thirds of the way to the northern tip of Okinawa, **Motobu-hanto** ❼ (Motobu Peninsula) was the site of an ocean exposition in the 1970s. Most of the tourist-focused offerings are on the exposition's former site, Exposition Memorial Park, including several exhibitions about Okinawan culture and the ocean. The restored ruins of **Nakijin-jo** (Nakijin Castle), on the peninsula's northern tip, are a fine place to watch a sunset *(see picture on page 349)*. Offshore, tiny **Ie-jima** is where a famous US war correspondent, Ernie Pile, was killed in World War II.

A visit to the far north of Okinawa, or *yanbaru*, will reward the adventurous with rugged hills, beaches and secluded fishing villages, along with some of the

BELOW: waters designed for scuba diving and pictures.

friendliest people anywhere. In the village of **Kijoka** ❽, one can watch the various steps required to produce the plantain-fibre textile *bashofu*. The view at **Hedo-misaki** ❾, the cape at the northern tip of the island, is stunning. But don't go wandering off in the bush in *yanbaru*, as this is *habu* – the deadly poisonous snake found in Okinawa – country.

One of the Ryukyu's sacred islands is **Iheya-jima** ❿, to the northeast of Okinawa. According to Okinawan legend, King Jimmu Tenno began his conquest of Japan from here. Moreover, a huge cave on the island, referred to as the "Hiding Place", is said to be the very cave where the sun goddess Amaterasu hid herself until the other deities could coax her out, thereby restoring light to the world.

Outer islands

The best way to experience the Ryukyuan way of life is to visit the outer islands, or *saki-shima*, reached by ferry or air from Naha. **Kume-jima**, 3 hours by ferry from Naha's main harbour, has several fine traditional homes in Nakazato.

The **Kerama Islands** ⓫ are only 35 km (20 miles) west of Naha, and the coral reefs in the surrounding waters provide excellent scuba-diving. A favourite diving and beach spot, **Zamami-jima** is a largely unspoiled island with its own dialect and customs. The **tourist information office** (daily 8.30am–5.30pm) in the harbour has a good map in English of the island. Zamami is a major centre for whale watching. It may surprise foreigners to learn that a good many Japanese are just as concerned as they are about preserving whales. The tourist office includes the Whale-Watching Association, which runs two-hour boat trips daily at 10.30am.

BELOW: resort on Miyako.

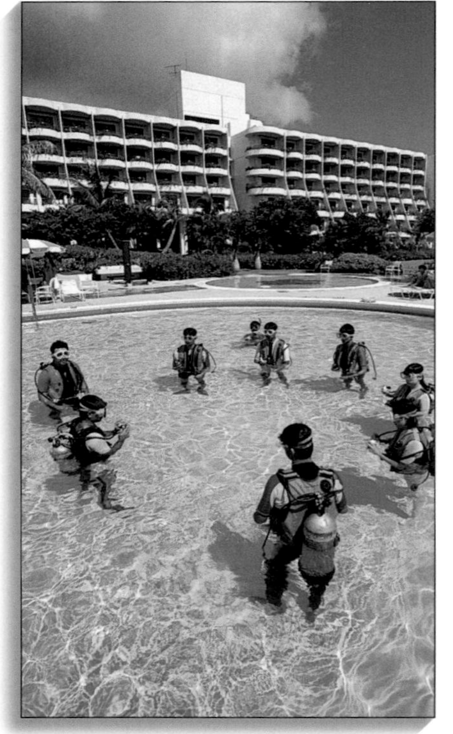

Further afield is the Miyako group of eight islands. **Miyako-jima** ⓬, the main island, is an hour by air or 10 hours by boat from Naha. At its port of **Hirara** are the *o-honoyama* (tax stones). After the samurai of Satsuma (now Kagoshima) on Kyushu invaded the Ryukyu kingdom in 1609, it became in everything but name a tributary to that fief's lord, even though the country also continued to pay tribute to the Ming dynasty in China. At the time, all children on Miyako-jima were paraded once a year before the *ninto-zeiseki*. Those taller than the stone had to pay the tax or else were shipped off to work as forced labour. This system was abolished in 1918. Miyako-jima earned a place in Japanese school books when five local fishermen spotted the Czarist fleet steaming towards Japan during the Russo-Japanese War (1904–05). The timely warning allowed the Imperial Navy, under Admiral Togo Shigenori, to surprise and annihilate the Russians in the Battle of Tsushima Straits. Nearby **Irabu**, an island that can be reached by boat from Hirara, offers attractive scenery and fine diving.

Yaeyama islands

The narrator of Kushi Fusako's short story *Memoirs of a Declining Ryukyuan Woman*, observes "We always seem to be at the tail end of history, dragged along roads already ruined by others." Efforts to stamp out traditional Okinawan customs by the mainland Japanese Government were only partially successful in the

Yaeyama Islands, where the indigenous beliefs of these parts, the animism and shamanistic practices that pre-dated the Japanese acquisition of the islands, survive. Further from Tokyo than Taipei, the Yaeyamas assimilated both Chinese and Japanese influences. These remote islanders have also been influenced by Southeast Asians, allowing for other, more exotic influences to creep in. Being out of the mainstream has benefited these islands in a number of other ways. The Yaeyamas were fortunate enough to be left comparatively unaffected by Japanese colonial policies of the last century and to have emerged unscathed from the pitched battles of World War II, and the effects of the subsequent American Occupation of Okinawa, which only ended in 1972.

Maps on pages 344 & 347

An undersea earthquake occurred near Ishigaki Island in 1776, resulting in a massive tsunami. In 1924, underwater volcanic activity in the oceanic area north of Iriomote Island caused the sea to boil for several days.

Ishigaki

Ishigaki-jima ⓭ is the main island of the Yaeyama chain and its administrative centre. Its name signifies "stone walls", a derivation from the local dialect *"Ishiagira"*, meaning "a place of many stones". Its airport and harbour serve the other outlying islands in the group. Ishigaki offers visitors more creature comforts than are normally found on the other islands, and a larger number of conventional sights, but also makes an excellent base from which to explore islands whose names and locations are unfamiliar even to many Japanese people.

Ishigaki's island feel is intensified by the roadside presence of colourful dugout canoes, more suggestive of Polynesia than Japan. Samples of the region's unique culture can be seen at the **Yaeyama Museum** (Tues–Sun 9am–4.30pm; admission fee), where good examples of ancient Panori ceramics, old Yaeyama-*jofu* textiles and more canoes can be found. Also of interest in the town itself is the beautifully preserved **Miyara Donchi** (daily except Tues 9am–5pm), the ancestral home of the Matsushige family. Modelled on aristocratic buildings at the royal capital of Shuri in Naha, it is the only such house left in Okinawa. Built in 1819, its stone garden, made from pitted coral in the Chinese manner, and sprouting with myriad tropical plants, sets it far apart from mainland Japanese dry landscape arrangements.

The white beaches, clear blue waters, coral and tropical fish are ideal for snorkelling and diving. A bus ride from the port, protected **Shiraho-no-umi** on the southeast coast boasts the world's largest blue coral reef. Heading north along the western shore, the **Yaeyama Minzoku-en** (daily 9am–6pm; admission fee), a theme park in a lovely setting on a hill above Nagura Bay, has well-preserved Okinawan buildings, gardens and an exhibition on the history of the islands' weaving styles. The island is of considerable ecological importance. **Kabira Bay** on the north shore is unquestionably the island's most spectacular

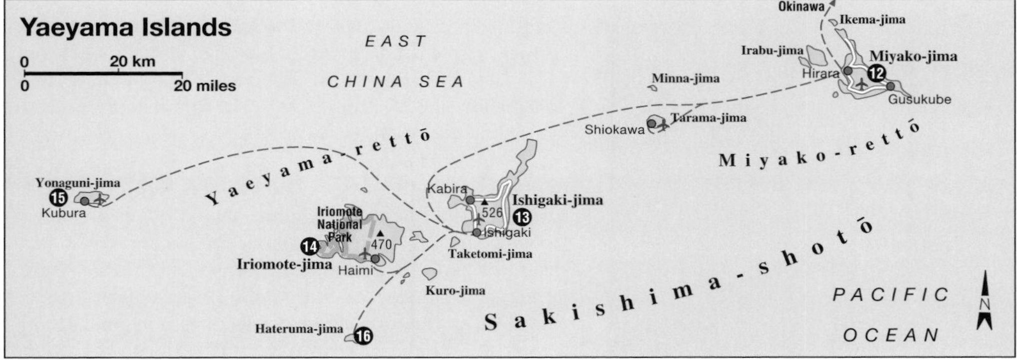

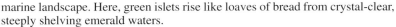

Iriomote is noted for its rare flora and fauna. The Irimote wildcat, a nocturnal feline, was discovered in 1965 and is endemic to the island. Other rare species include the atlas moth, the yellow-margined box turtle and the crested serpent eagle.

marine landscape. Here, green islets rise like loaves of bread from crystal-clear, steeply shelving emerald waters.

Although **Taketomi-jima** can be reached by ferry in just 12 minutes from Ishigaki's port, it remains a time capsule among these southern seas, the hospitality of its 400 or so inhabitants a measure of how well it has retained its identity. The name Taketomi signifies "prosperous bamboo", stands of which can be seen at the roadsides or in the centre of this island, whose circumference stretches to little more than 9 km (5½ miles). These days the island is noted for its sumptuous flowers and plant life. Bougainvillea and hibiscus, traditionally used in this part of Okinawa to decorate graves and Buddhist altars, spill over walls made from volcanic rock, built as a defence against the furious typhoons that strike the islands from late September to early October.

Kondoi Misaki, the island's finest beach, located along the southwestern shore, is known for its star-shaped sand grains, actually the remains of tiny, fossilised sea creatures. Taketomi is also famous as the source of *minsa*, an indigo fabric often used as a belt for a women's kimono. *Minsa* is only produced on Taketomi. Strips of the material can be seen drying on the stone walls of the village, or at the **Mingei-kan**, a weaving centre where you can observe women at work on the fabrics.

A ferry also goes to the large island of **Iriomote ⓮**, which is no doubt the most unusual island in the Japanese archipelago – a touch of New Guinea in Japan. Except for the towns of Ohara in the southeast and Funaura in the north, the island is mostly tropical rain forest. Thankfully, development on the island has been limited to only one resort, although others have been proposed. River trips along the broad, Amazonian-like **Urauchi-gawa** on Iriomote island include trekking through the jungle to a series of natural waterfalls.

Yonaguni-jima ⓯, a forested island with some of the chain's most spectacular diving and snorkelling offerings, is now accessible by plane. Yonaguni is Okinawa's most westerly island, a mere 125 km (78 miles) from Taiwan.

Southernmost point

It is worth making the sometimes choppy, 50-minute crossing from Ishigaki port to **Hateruma-jima ⓰**, a rustic island out on a limb among the southern Yaeyamas, a place where empty roads lead not to hotels and shops, but to an infinity of sea and sky. The name "Hateruma" means "the end of the coral", an indication that this is Japan's southernmost island, it's last landmass. Local maps to the island's **Southernmost Point Monument**, a cement and rock affair stuck on top of a bluff above the cliffs, read "Beyond here, the Philippines." Renting a bicycle for the day nicely matches the rhythm and pace of this small, 6-km (4-mile) long island.

Ghostly banyan trees, *fukugi* and Indian almond trees dot the island. Among the island flowers are bamboo orchids, hibiscus and plumeria. Taking root in the sand of Hateruma's superb **Nishi-no-Hama**, or West Beach, are pineapple-like *pandanus* trees. For divers, underwater Hateruma is a glorious filigree of coral, stone holes, rock arches and deep blue silhouettes. ❑

BELOW: Southernmost Point Monument, Hateruma. **RIGHT:** Nakijin Castle.

INSIGHT GUIDES

TRAVEL TIPS

JAPAN

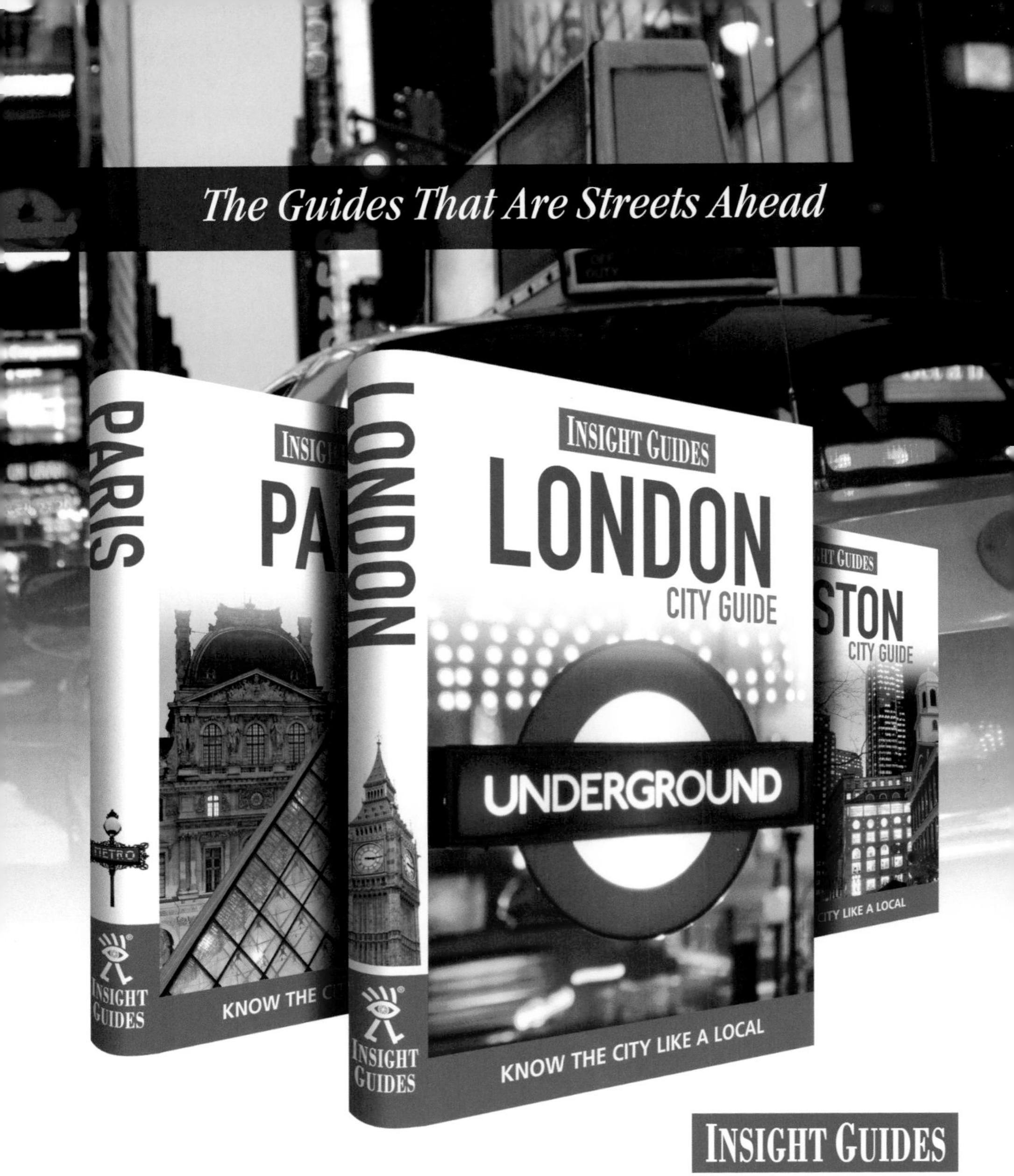

TRAVEL TIPS

TRANSPORT

GETTING THERE AND GETTING AROUND

GETTING THERE

By Air

Tokyo, the main gateway to Japan, is served by two main airports: **New Tokyo International Airport** (Narita), 66 km (41 miles) east of the city, and **Tokyo International Airport** (Haneda), 15 km (9 miles) to the south of the city centre. The airports are usually simply referred to as Narita and Haneda.

All international flights to Tokyo arrive at Narita, except those on China Airlines (from Taiwan), which flies into Haneda.

Narita Airport

Although it is a little inconveniently located, Narita airport's services have vastly improved since its renewal and extension. It has two terminals and two runways. Both terminals have currency-exchange counters, ATMs, restaurants and cafés, internet facilities, post offices and health clinics, and a range of shops including duty-free. Terminal 2 has a children's playroom, day rooms for taking a nap, and showers.
General info: 0476-32-2802; www.narita-airport.jp/en
Flight info: 0476-34-8000
Tourist info: 0476-30-3383 (Terminal 1); 0476-34-6251 (Terminal 2).

Haneda Airport

Haneda (www.tokyo-airport-bldg.co.jp) is Tokyo's main hub for domestic flights. Both domestic airlines – Japan Air Lines (JAL) and All Nippon Airways (ANA) – operate flights throughout Japan from Haneda.

The only international flights using Haneda are those to and from Taiwan. The international terminal is located well away from the main domestic terminals and is connected by a regular shuttle bus.

While Haneda does not have international business centres, its two domestic terminals are well designed, with Japanese, Western and Chinese restaurants, cafés, shops, a post office, information desks and a book store.
Airport info: 03-5757-8111

Osaka-Kansai Airport

Kansai International Airport (www.kansai-airport.or.jp/english) serves the entire Kansai region, especially Osaka, Kyoto and Kobe. Airport facilities are good, city transport rapid and efficient.

Nagoya Airport

This international airport (www.nagoya-airport-bldg.co.jp/index-e.html) is handily located between Tokyo and Osaka. Flight routes include those to and from the USA, Australia, Canada, and Asian destinations like Singapore, Thailand and Hong Kong.

Flying from the UK and the US

The four big-name airlines serving Tokyo from the UK are British Airways, JAL, ANA and Virgin Atlantic. Flying time direct from London is between 11–13 hours.

Coming from the US or Canada, you are spoilt for choice. Besides JAL and ANA, among the better-known airlines are Delta, United Airlines, Northwest, American Airlines and Continental. Flying time from the US west coast is 12–13 hours; from the east coast it is 18–20 hours, including stopovers, though there are now some non-stop flights such as from New York.

Tokyo is an increasingly important transport hub for direct flights from major destinations like Beijing, Shanghai, Hong Kong, Bangkok and further afield from Singapore, Bali and Sydney.

While fares vary between airlines, April, August and December tend to be the most expensive times to fly to Japan from the UK or US as they coincide with the country's Golden Week, O-Bon and Christmas-New Year holidays. Flying a few days either side of these peak periods can result in huge savings.

Fukuoka Airport

Western Japan's main arrival and departure point from overseas, this international airport mainly provides flights to Asian destinations, and also a regular Honolulu service.

Key Airlines

American Airlines
3-1-1 Marunouuchi, Chiyoda-ku
Tel: 03-3248-2011
www.aa.com
British Airways
1-16-4 Toranomon, Minato-ku
Tel: 03-3593-8811
www.ba.com
Qantas Airways
1-16-4 Toranomon, Minato-ku
Tel: 03-3593-7000
www.qantas.com.au
Singapore Airlines
1-10-1 Yurakucho, Chiyoda-ku
Tel: 03-3213-3431
www.singaporeair.com
United Airlines
3-1-1 Marunouchi, Chiyoda-ku
Tel: 0120-11-4466
www.ual.com
Virgin Atlantic Airways
5-2-1 Minami-Aoyama, Minato-ku
Tel: 03-3499-8811
www.virgin-atlantic.com

Naha Airport

The main gateway to Okinawa, Naha international airport's main destinations are Hong Kong, Shanghai, Taipei and Seoul.

Niigata Airport

The main international airport in northern Japan, Niigata provides useful links to Harbin, Shanghai, Xian, Guam and other Asian airports.

More Gateways

A number of smaller airports, including those in Nagasaki, Kumamoto, Kagoshima and Sapporo, may be worth checking out for their connections to and from Asian destinations in South Korea, Hong Kong, Shanghai and other East Asian destinations.

Other Departure Points

JAL and Qantas have daily flights to Japan, including Sapporo, a popular winter ski package now. Cheaper airlines with regular schedules from **Australian cities** are Malaysian Airlines, Cathay Pacific and the Indonesian carrier Garuda. JAL, ANA, Air Canada, and a number of US airlines like Delta and United offer flights between Vancouver and Toronto in **Canada**. Air New Zealand, Thai International, Qantas and Malaysian Airlines are the main companies flying out of Auckland, **New Zealand**. There are innumerable flights from the main cities of **Continental Europe**, such as Paris, Frankfurt, Rome and Amsterdam. Cathay Pacific, JAL, ANA and Air China are the main airlines serving Hong Kong and China, but there are cheaper carriers also. Singapore Airlines, Thai Airways International, JAL and ANA are among many companies serving South East Asia destinations such as Bangkok, Singapore, Ho Chi Minh City and Jakarta.

By Sea

Although few people arrive by sea, the slow approach to this speed-defined city would certainly be a novelty. Japan's ferry services are quite extensive, at least in their connections with South Korea, China and Taiwan.

There is a regular boat service between South Korea's port of Pusan and Shimonoseki in Japan. A hydrofoil also travels between Pusan and Hakata in Japan.

Ferries from China (Shanghai and Tanggu) arrive in Osaka and Kobe respectively, from where passengers travel either by rail or air to Tokyo.

The weekly ferries that ply between Keelung and Kaohsiung in Taiwan stop off in the Okinawan islands of Ishigaki and Miyako before arriving in Nara.

GETTING AROUND

On Arrival

From Narita Airport

A taxi to downtown Tokyo from Narita costs between ¥20,000 and ¥30,000, depending on destination and traffic. Most people prefer either the bus or train as it is cheaper. Either way, it's 2–3 hours by road.

Bus: a regular limousine bus service (www.limousinebus.co.jp) runs between Narita and TCAT (Tokyo City Air Terminal) in central Tokyo, to Tokyo and Shinjuku stations, and to most major hotels in Tokyo. Tickets (around ¥3,000) are bought at the airport after clearing immigration and customs. There are several routes depending on destination. Buses are boarded outside the terminal at the kerb, and will accept any amount of luggage at no extra charge. The buses leave every 20 minutes, taking 2 to 3 hours to arrive at central hotels. There are also buses to Yokohama and Haneda, the domestic airport.

Trains: there are two train alternatives into Tokyo: Japan Railways (JR) Narita Express (www.jreast.co.jp) and the Keisei Skyliner (www.keisei.co.jp). Both are twice as fast as taxi or bus, but not as convenient, as once at a station, you'll have to make arrangements for transport around the city. Be aware also that, while the city's train system is all-encompassing, carrying luggage through train and subway is a feat of considerable effort with long hikes and Fuji-like climbs. If you have more than one piece of luggage, don't even think about getting around or reaching your hotel by either overhead train or subway, especially during the hot and humid summer months. Instead, consider the limousine bus or the baggage delivery service available at the airport *(see below)*.

In terms of connections, the Narita Express is more convenient, stopping at JR stations in Chiba, Tokyo (Station), Shinjuku, Ikebukuro, Yokohama and Ofuna. The Skyliner stops just at Ueno Station and nearby Nippori. Both take about the same time to reach Tokyo – an hour – and neither has restrictions on luggage.

The Narita Express costs approximately ¥3,000 for standard class and tickets can be bought up to a month in advance at travel agents, Floor B1 of the airport or at the station before boarding. The Keisei Skyliner costs around ¥2,000 and tickets can also be bought in advance or at the station.

The Skyliner is far more comfortable than the Narita Express. Narita Express's seats are small with almost no leg room: usually you sit facing another seat, knee to knee, in groups of four. For the arriving traveller trying to shake jet lag, or exhausted from last-minute sightseeing before leaving Japan, this arrangement leaves a lot to be desired, especially for the price and especially when the train is overcrowded. (JR permits standing passengers when trains are full, making them even fuller.)

The Skyliner, on the other hand, is never overbooked or crowded, and the seats are quite comfortable, with lots of leg room. This is far and away the better deal, both in price and in comfort. If you are not carrying a lot of luggage, a connection can be made at Ueno Station to JR trains or the subway system. Or you could take a taxi.

Domestic air connections: if making a domestic air connection, you must take the taxi, bus or train into Tokyo and make the connection at Haneda Airport. No domestic flights are made out of Narita. The limousine bus will take you directly from Narita to Haneda, as will a very expensive taxi ride.

Baggage delivery: most residents of Japan take advantage of Japan's fast and reliable delivery network. After clearing immigration and customs, take your luggage to the ABC counter in the main terminal. Often a queue indicates the counter. For about ¥1,500 per bag, ABC will deliver the luggage by the following day wherever you are.

From Haneda Airport

If you are coming into Haneda Airport, then a taxi to the town centre will cost about ¥5,000 to ¥6,000 and takes about 30–40 minutes. Provided your luggage is light, you can take the Monorail to Hamamatsucho Station on the JR Yamanote Line. The trip takes about 17 minutes.

From Kansai Airport

The Kansai International Airport (KIX) has replaced Osaka Airport (Itami) as the international air terminus for the Kansai region. It was also intended to relieve the overcrowding at Narita Airport, which has restricted operating hours. However, some domestic flights still fly from Itami, possibly necessitating an inconvenient connection from international to domestic flights. The second largest and the first 24-hour-operation airport in Japan, Kansai International Airport opened in 1994. It is located southeast of Osaka Bay, 5 km (8 miles) off the coast and about 60 km (37 miles) from JR Shin-Osaka Station for *shinkansen* (bullet train) connections. KIX, constructed on an artificial island in Osaka Bay and one of the world's most expensive airports – ¥2,600 departure tax – is architecturally impressive and extremely functional. All international and domestic connections at KIX are made at the same terminal in a matter of minutes. Make sure to confirm that domestic flight connections are from KIX and not Itami-Osaka Airport. Despite being on an island, getting to and from KIX is relatively easy: two railways, two expressways, some 10 limousine bus lines, and four high-speed ferries connect the island to every point in the Kansai.

For travel information, the **Kansai Tourist Information Centre** is located in the arrival lobby (1st Floor) and is open daily 9am–9pm. For handling currency exchange, there are 10 banks at the airport, with one or more open 6am–11pm. Japan Rail Passes can be validated either at the JR West Information Counter in the International Arrivals Lobby (1st Floor, open daily 8am–9pm), at the TIS-Travel Service Centre (open daily 10am–6pm), or at the green-coloured Midori-no-madoguchi Reservations Ticket Office (open daily 5.30am–midnight) at JR Kansai Airport Station.

Japan Rail Pass

Japan's rail services are unsurpassed in the world. Extremely efficient, they go nearly everywhere, even to the remotest neck of the woods.

Foreign travellers intending to travel in Japan should consider the Japan Rail Pass. The pass allows for virtually unlimited travel on the national JR network, including the *shinkansen*, or bullet trains. Passes must be purchased outside Japan, and you must be travelling in Japan under the visa entry status of "temporary visitor".

Once in Japan, the pass must initially be validated at a JR Travel Centre (which are everywhere in Japan). Once it is validated, reservations can be made at any so-called Green Window *(midori no madoguchi)* at major stations.

While trains are not especially cheap in Japan (long-distance fares equal air fares), the pass is a great deal. A 7-day pass costs around ¥30,000 – less than the round-trip fare from Narita Airport to Kyoto via Tokyo.

	Standard	**First-class**
7-day:	¥30,000	¥40,000
14-day:	¥50,000	¥65,000
21-day:	¥60,000	¥80,000

Prices are approximate. Children aged 6 to 11 travel at half of the above prices.

To/From Osaka

Train: JR (Japan Railways) Haruka Express, with reserved seating, runs between KIX and Osaka's Tennoji Station (29 min) and Shin Osaka Station (45 min), where you catch the *shinkansen*, or bullet train. The JR Kuko-Kaisoku connects KIX with Osaka's Tennoji Station (45 min) and Namba Station's Osaka City Air Terminal (O-CAT), which offers express baggage check-in (60 min). **JR train information**: tel: 0724-56-6242.

Nankai Railroad also connects KIX with Osaka's Namba Station. Three trains make the run. For Nankai train information tel: 0724-56-6203.

Bus: there are a number of de-luxe buses between KIX and various Osaka hotels and rail stations. For bus information call Keihan Bus Co. tel: 0724-55-2500.

Ferry: two high-speed ferries connect KIX with Osaka's Tenpozan port (40 min). For ferry information tel: 06-575-1321.

To/From Kyoto

Train: JR Haruka Express, reserved seats, connects Kyoto Station with KIX (75 min). For JR train information tel: 075-351-4004.

Bus: a Keihan bus leaves from Uji, south of Kyoto, for KIX and takes about 2 hours. For Keihan bus information call tel: 0724-55-2500.

To/From Nara

Bus: a bus runs from KIX to Nara JR Station (95 min). For bus information call Keihan Bus Co. tel: 0724-55-2500.

To/From Kobe

Bus: connect by bus from KIX to Kobe's Sannomiya Station (90 min). For bus information, call Keihan Bus Co. Tel: 0724-55-2500.

Ferry: the Kobe Jet Shuttle is the best and fastest way to get to or from Kobe. The Jet Shuttle runs between KIX and the Kobe City Air Terminal (K-CAT) on Port Island (30 min), where a free bus service is provided to Kobe's Sannomiya Station. For Jet Shuttle information tel: 078-306-2411.

To/From Southern Islands

Ferries: two high-speed ferries connect KIX with Awaji and Shikoku islands. To Tsuna and Sumoto on Awaji Island (40 min), for information tel: 0799-24-3333. To Tokushima on Shikoku Island (82 min), for information tel: 06-575-2101.

From Fukuoka

Domestic flights connect to most cities (Tokyo 1 hour 40 minutes and Osaka 1 hour). International flights connect to Australia, China, Guam, Honolulu, Indonesia, Korea, Malaysia, New Zealand, Philippines, Singapore, Taiwan and Thailand.

From Hiroshima

40 minutes from town and linked by regular bus services. Domestic flights connect to most cities (Tokyo 1 hour 20 minutes and Osaka 45 minutes). International flights connect to China, Hong Kong, Korea and Singapore.

From Nagasaki

One hour or more from town and linked by regular bus services. Domestic flights connect to most cities (Tokyo 2 hours and Osaka 1 hour). International flights connect to China and Korea.

From Okinawa

15 minutes from Naha and linked by regular bus services. Domestic flights connect to most cities (Tokyo 3 hours and Osaka 2 hours). International flights connect to Guam, Hong Kong, Korea and Taiwan.

From Sapporo

30 minutes from town and linked by regular bus services. Domestic flights connect to most cities (Tokyo 2 hours and Osaka 3 hours). International flights connect to Australia, Guam, Hong Kong, Honolulu and Korea.

From Sendai

25 minutes from town and linked by regular bus services. Domestic flights connect to most cities (Tokyo 45 minutes and Osaka 1 hour 30 minutes). International flights connect to China, Guam, Hong Kong, Honolulu, Korea and Singapore.

Public Transport

Rail

JR Train Information, in English, information only, no reservations, weekdays 10am–6pm. Tel: 03-3423-0111.

Japan has one of the most efficient and extensive rail networks in the world. Rail service is provided by **Japan Railways (JR)** and several regional private lines. The trains on important routes run every few minutes. High-speed trains – such as JR's **shinkansen**, sometimes called the bullet train and which travels at speeds of up to 275 kph (170 mph) – offer a good alternative to air and long-distance bus travel. Between Tokyo and Kyoto, travel times and prices are similar for both air and shinkansen. The train, however, is from city centre to city centre; plane, from airport to airport.

Subway systems in Japan are clean, safe, and convenient. They are faster than congested road transport. However, they are notorious for being crowded, especially during morning and evening rush hours.

All subway stations post timetables. Regular service is Monday to Saturday. The Sunday and holiday timetable has slightly fewer trains. Trains run until just after midnight, so be sure to check the time of the last train. All stations have a route map with fares for each stop near the ticket machines, but not always in English. Your present location is shown with a red mark.

The fares are regulated on a station-to-station basis, so if you cannot determine the fare required, just purchase the cheapest ticket available. You can pay the difference, if needed, at the exit gate upon arrival at your destination.

A child's ticket is half fare. Most ticket machines now accept ¥1,000 notes in addition to coins. There is often a single machine at the end of the row that will also accept ¥5,000 and ¥10,000 bills. There is usually a machine that gives change or sells prepaid cards nearby.

Savings can be made by buying a ***teiki*** (train pass), valid for one, three or six months. Major subway and overland train stations issue passes. Another way to save on train fares is to buy a ***kaisuken***, a series of 11 tickets between two destinations for the price of 10.

Station arrivals are announced in Japanese inside the trains but these are often difficult to understand. There is usually a map of the stops on the line and connecting lines above the train doors, usually written in both Japanese and English.

Timetables and subway system maps in Japanese can be obtained at most stations, and in English at major train and subway stations.

Discount Tickets

In the major cities, there are special tickets that allow unlimited travel for one day and are good value. They can be purchased at ticket windows and sometimes at special ticket machines, often marked in English.

Tokyo

Nine of Tokyo's 13 subway lines (now collectively known as the Tokyo Metro), are run by the Rapid Transportation Authority (Teito), the remaining four by the Tokyo Municipal Authority (Toei)

Tokyo Free Kippu: one-day pass for JR trains and Toei trains and buses. All may be used as often as you want (except JR express trains). Approx. ¥1,500.

Tokunai Free Kippu: unlimited-use, one-day pass in Tokyo for use only on JR trains (except JR express trains) running within the 23 wards of Tokyo. Approx. ¥800.

Toei Economy Pass: unlimited-use, one-day pass for Toei trains, buses and subway trains within Tokyo on any day within a 6-month period. Approx. ¥700.

Tokyo Combination Ticket: unlimited use of all JR, metro and bus lines in the Tokyo area. Pass offices (see the triangle symbol on metro maps), are located at major stations. Approx ¥1580.

Kyoto

Unlimited-use, one-day bus and subway train ticket that can be used on all city buses and subway trains in the Kyoto area. Approx. ¥1,200; 2 days, ¥2,000.

Osaka

Unlimited-use, one-day pass for buses and subway trains. Approx. ¥900.

JR Train Discounts

If you have not purchased a Japan Rail Pass or don't qualify, JR offers a number of special fare discounts. Amongst them:

Discount round-trip: a 20 percent discount to destinations more than 600 km (370 miles) one-way.

Shuyuken tickets: excursion tickets with a saving of around 20 percent for direct travel between a starting point and a designated area in which unlimited travel can be made. Valid on all JR trains and bus lines.

Package tours: discount lodging as well as discounted rail and bus travel. Packages may be purchased at JR travel centres, at a Green Window *(midori no madoguchi)* or leading travel agents.

Orange Card: a prepaid card with discounts for travel on JR trains. Cards come in several denominations and are used to buy JR tickets from vending machines for distances of less than 100 km (60 miles).

Full Moon Green Pass: senior-citizen discount for couples whose total age is over 88 years. Good for a Green Car (first-class) and B-type sleeping car berth on any JR line except the JR bus line. Prices start at ¥80,000 for 5 days.

Seishun 18 Kippu: a coupon for five days' travel, each section used for one day's unlimited train travel. Good for ordinary JR trains, rapid JR trains, and the JR ferryboat between Miyajimaguchi and Miyajima Island. Passengers may get on and off as many times as wanted at any JR station and at the JR ferry terminal within the same date. Price is approx. ¥12,000 both for adults and children. It may be shared by several people, provided they travel together and do not split the coupon.

Taxis

Taxis are the most comfortable way of getting around, but also the most expensive. The basic fare in Tokyo is ¥650 for the flag drop. A short trip can easily run to ¥3,000 to ¥5,000. No tipping is expected or required. Taxis are readily available on almost every street corner, major hotel and railway station. A red light in the front window is illuminated if the taxi is available.

- *Don't touch the door when getting in or out of a taxi.* The doors on taxis are operated by the driver with a remote lever. Get out, walk away and forget the door.
- Most taxi drivers speak only Japanese, so it can be helpful to have your destination written in Japanese.
- Don't be surprised if an available taxi ignores you late at night; the driver is looking for a *sarariman* – and a nice, tidy fare – on his way back to the suburbs.

Private Transport

Driving in Japan is a headache. Roads are narrow and crowded, signs confusing, rental cars and petrol expensive. Motorway and bridge tolls are very costly. If at all possible, consider flying or, better, taking the train.

ACCOMMODATION

HOTELS, YOUTH HOSTELS AND TRADITIONAL INNS *(RYOKAN)*

Hotels

There are hotels everywhere, but unfortunately few of them are up to international standards. Those that are reflect it in their price. However, convenience is a very dear commodity here, so often you are paying for the location more than the service or luxury. Below is a brief listing of major hotels in alphabetical order. Please note that the rankings are according to prices of single or twin rooms. Bear in mind that in Japan there is a per-person rate for rooms. So if you are sharing a room with another person, the rate will double, treble for three, and so on. In most hotels and all *ryokan* (Japanese-style inns), you are provided with a *yukata* robe, toothbrush, razor, shower cap, etc.

Many hotels offer only twin beds, which are the most popular arrangement in Japan. Smoking rooms may have a thick stench of stale smoke.

Finally, hotel rooms are quite compact. Even a ¥20,000 room in a de-luxe hotel can be snug. So-called business hotels (favoured by many Japanese business travellers), generally found in the moderate and budget categories (and a few in the expensive category), have rooms that are not just snug, but cramped. As a rule, smaller hotels have fewer amenities, including no room service. If you are not intending to luxuriate all day in your room though, these can be good bases for exploring destinations.

Western-style hotels offer rooms whose rates may vary from ¥8,000 to ¥30,000. There are hotels which also provide Japanese-style guest rooms and landscaped gardens. Others have restaurants serving Continental food as well as local *sukiyaki*, *sushi* and *tempura*. Most of these hotels provide direct limousine bus connections to the nearest international airports.

Ryokan (Japanese-style inns) exude an atmosphere of traditional Japanese living and a stay will be a rewarding experience. They charge an average of ¥9,000 per person, depending on the type of bath facilities offered. The rates at a truly elegant *ryokan* can rise far higher.

There are about 80,000 *ryokan* in Japan, of which 2,000 are members of the Japan Ryokan Association (JRA) (www.ryokan.or.jp), who ensure that a high standard of service is maintained. Guests sleep in rooms covered with *tatami* (straw) mats, on *futon*. The baths are sometimes communal, though there are usually separate baths for men and women. Morning and evening meals are served in the guest's room.

Minshuku are small, family-run bed-and-breakfast lodgings operated within private homes, without the frills (toiletries and *yukata* gowns, etc). Guests are expected to fold up their *futon* bedding and tidy it away for the day. A stay in a *minshuku* will give you a more intimate experience of Japanese home life. Rates are from ¥5,000 up. The Japan National Tourist Organisation (JNTO) lists some 230 *minshuku* for overseas visitors (log on to www.japantravelinfo.com).

International Tourism Centre of Japan (ITCJ), part of the JNTO, has listings of around 700 small, usually family-run hotels all over the country. They have reservation offices at most tourist information centres. Log on to their website at www. itcj.or.jp.

Japanese Inn Group (www.jpinn.com) offers the foreign traveller recommendations and bookings for traditional Japanese inns, usually with traditional *tatami* floors, *futon* bedding, *yukata*, and *furo*, the Japanese-style bath. The Japanese Inn Group consists of about 90 reasonable *ryokan*, hotels, *minshuku* and pensions located throughout Japan. Most member facilities are small, family-run Japanese-style accommodation with a home-town atmosphere and affordable rates (per person between ¥4,000–6,000), with meals extra.
Head office: c/o Asakusa Ryokan, 1-31-11 NIshi-Asakusa, Taito-ku, Tokyo 111-0032. Tel: 03-3822-2251, fax: 03-3822-2252.
Kyoto office: c/o Hiraiwa Ryokan, 314 Hayao-ho, Kaminokuchi-agaru, Ninomiya-cho-dori, Shimogyo-ku, Kyoto 600. Tel: 075-351-6748, fax: 075-351-6969.
Japan Minshuku Centre Booking Office, B1, Tokyo Kotsu Kaikan Bldg, 2-10-1, Yurakucho, Tokyo. Tel: 03-3216-6556 (English spoken), www.minshuku.co.jp. Mon–Sat 10am–6pm. Average cost: ¥6,000–¥13,000 per person with two meals. Reservation by phone is not accepted. Reservation for high tourist season (July–August, 29 April–5 May, 25 December–4 January, weekends) can only be accepted for more than two persons per room.

Capsule Hotels

Capsule hotels, conveniently located near key stations, provide Apollo spacecraft-style compactness as a last resort for the drunk, stranded or merely inquisitive. Capsule cells come complete with TV, air conditioning, a radio and alarm. Complexes have showers, bath, sauna and restaurants. The majority are for men only.

ACCOMMODATION LISTINGS

TOKYO

Akasaka Tokyu Hotel
2-14-3 Nagatacho, Chiyoda-ku
Tel: 03-3580-2311
www.tokyuhotels.co.jp
One of the most conveniently located hotels in Akasaka; it is just minutes away from all the action. ¥¥

ANA Intercontinental Tokyo
1-12-33 Akasaka, Minato-ku
Tel: 03-3505-1111
www.anaintercontinental-tokyo.jp
An exquisite hotel in the heart of Ark Hills, a popular office and shopping complex. Down the hill from Roppongi. Convenient for business and fun. ¥¥¥

Asakusa View Hotel
3-17-1 Nishi-Akakusa, Taito-ku
Tel: 03-3842-2117
www.viewhotels.co.jp/asakusa/
Ideal location for sightseeing. Traditional Japanese rooms are available on the 6th floor. Superb views of the river from the 28th-floor bar. ¥¥

Asia Center of Japan Hotel
8-10-32, Akasaka, Minato-ku
Tel: 03-3402-6111
www.asiacenter.or.jp
Rooms in the newer wing are better than the older ones, but may be difficult to secure as this is one of the most popular low-budget travel lodgings in the city. Just a few minutes from Nogizaka Station. ¥

Hyatt Regency Tokyo
2-7-2 Nishi Shinjuku, Shinjuku-ku
Tel: 03-3348-1234
http://tokyo.century.hyatt.com
One of the buildings amidst all the skyscrapers of Shinjuku. Japanese-style Hyatt service and accommodation. Health facilities and disco. ¥¥¥¥

Crowne Plaza Metropolitan
1-6-1 Nishi-Ikebukuro, Toshima-ku
Tel: 03-3980-1111
www.ichotelsgroup.com
Three minutes from Ikebukuro Station's west exit. Ikebukuro's finest hotel. ¥¥¥

Diamond Hotel
25 Ichibancho, Chiyoda-ku
Tel: 03-3263-2211
Just a few minutes from Hanzomon Station. Nice quiet area. ¥¥¥

Fairmont Hotel
2-1-17 Kudan Minami, Chiyoda-ku
Tel: 03-3262-1151
Fax: 03-3264-2476
Old British style. About 6 minutes from Kudanshita Station, right in front of the Imperial Palace moat. ¥¥

Ginza Nikko Hotel
8-4-21 Ginza, Chuo-ku
Tel: 03-3571-4911
www.jalhotels.com
About four minutes from Shimbashi Station. ¥¥

Haneda Tokyu Hotel
2-8-6 Haneda Kuko, Ota-ku
Tel: 03-3747-0311
www.tokyuhotels.co.jp
Right inside Haneda Airport. Guests walk out of the entrance straight into the check-in areas, restaurants and shops. ¥¥

Hilltop Hotel
1-1 Surugadai, Kanda, Chiyoda-ku
Tel: 03-3293-2311
www.yamanoue-hotel.co.jp
This very pleasant hotel near Ochanomizu Station is an old favourite of writers and artists. Excellent food and service. ¥¥

Hilton Tokyo
6-6-2 Nishi Shinjuku, Shinjuku-ku
Tel: 03-3344-5111
www.hilton.com
Set in a central grove of Shinjuku skyscrapers the Hilton Tokyo follows in the tradition of the Hilton chain. Facilities include spacious contemporary guest rooms, several restaurants and bars, top-notch fitness club, tennis court and pool. ¥¥¥¥

Hilton Tokyo
6-6-2 Nishi-Shinjuku, Shinjuku-ku
Tel: 03-3344-5111
www.hilton.com
The largest Hilton in Asia . ¥¥¥¥

Hotel Ibis
7-14-4 Roppongi, Minato-ku
Tel: 03-3403-4411
Fax: 03-3479 0609
Trendy decor and located where a lot of the action can be found. ¥¥

Hotel New Otani
4-1 Kioicho, Chiyoda-ku
Tel: 03-3265-1111
www.newotani.co.jp
The largest hotel in Asia. Health facilities, with 1,533 rooms, a 400-year-old Japanese garden, and very good location. ¥¥¥¥

Hotel New Koyo
2-26-13, Nihonzutsumi, Taito-ku
Tel: 03-3873-0343
www.newkoyo.jp
Clean Japanese and Western rooms in Tokyo's day labourer district. This may be Tokyo's best deal. ¥

Hotel Okura
2-10-4 Toranomon, Minato-ku
Tel: 03-3582-0111
http://tokyo.okura.com
Long-established hotel, defining itself as one of the finest in the world. Health facilities, excellent restaurants and executive salon. ¥¥¥¥

Hotel Villa Fontaine Nihombashi
1-7-6, Nihombashi Honcho, Chuo-ku
Tel: 03-3242-3370
Surprisingly affordable hotel with smart rooms. Located near Mitsukoshi-mae Station on the Ginza and Hanzomon lines. ¥

Imperial Hotel
1-1-1 Uchisaiwai-cho, Chiyoda-ku
Tel: 03-3504-1111
www.imperialhotel.co.jp
First built in 1890, with a new tower completed in 1983. Pool, shopping arcade, several excellent restaurants. Convenient to government offices and Ginza. ¥¥¥¥

Keihin Hotel
4-10-20, Takanawa, Minato-ku.
Tel: 03-3449-5711
www.keihin-hotel.co.jp
Just opposite Shinagawa Station, this small, old-style hotel has mostly Western rooms, though a few Japanese rooms are available on request. Rooms and bathrooms are on the small side, but small seems to be the theme, something reflected also in the attractive room rates. ¥¥

Keio Plaza Hotel
2-2-1 Nishi Shinjuku, Shinjuku-ku
Tel: 03-3344-0111
wwwkeioplaza.com.
A 45-storey skyscraper on the west side of Shinjuku. Near the Tokyo Metropolitan Government Office towers. Health facilities and executive salon. ¥¥¥

Kimi Ryokan
2-36-8, Ikebukuro, Toshima-ku
Tel: 03-3971-3766
www.kimi-ryokan.jp
Helpful English-speaking staff in very clean, inexpensive *ryokan*. Very popular, so book well in advance. ¥

Marroad Inn Akasaka
6-15-17, Akasaka, Minato-ku.
Tel: 03-3585-7611
www.toto-motors.co.jp/marroad/akasaka
A small business hotel offering plain but serviceable rooms with the obligatory desk and TV. Helpful staff and a very decent Chinese restaurant that offers a cheap, three-course dinner. ¥¥

Marunouchi Hotel
1-6-3, Marunouchi, Chiyoda-ku.
Tel: 03-3217-1111
www.marunouchi-hotel.co.jp
Close by the Marunouchi exit of Tokyo Station, this recently renovated hotel was first established in 1924. A sophisticated small hotel whose lobby and corridors are decorated with antiques. French, Japanese and Chinese restaurants, and a snug bar. ¥¥

New Takanawa Prince Hotel
3-13-1 Takanawa, Minato-ku
Tel: 03-3442-1111
www.princehotels.co.jp/newtakanawa-e
Addition to the Takanawa Prince. All of the rooms have private balconies. Pool (summer only). ¥¥

Palace Hotel
1-1-1 Marunouchi, Chiyoda-ku
Tel: 03-3211-5211
www.palacehotel.co.jp/english

PRICE CATEGORIES

Price categories are for a double room without breakfast and taxes:
¥ = Under ¥10,000
¥¥ = ¥10–20,000
¥¥¥ = ¥20–30,000
¥¥¥¥ = Over ¥30,000

Old but quiet and peaceful surroundings overlooking the Imperial Palace moats and gardens. **¥¥¥¥**

Richmond Hotel
3-5-14, Mejiro, Toshima-ku.
Tel: 03-3565-4111
www.richmondhotel.co.jp
A comfortable and cosy hotel in a fashionable part of town just 1 minute down Mejiro-dori from the station of the same name. Comfortable, European-style furnished rooms, sophisticated restaurant and top-notch service. **¥¥**

Roppongi Prince Hotel
3-2-7 Roppongi, Minato-ku
Tel: 03-3587-1111
Close to Roppongi Station. Outdoor heated pool with jacuzzi. **¥¥¥**

Royal Park Hotel
2-1-1 Nihombashi, Kakigaracho, Chuo-ku
Tel: 03-3667-1111
http://rph.co.jp/english.
Next door to the Tokyo City Air Terminal. Indoor swimming pool, fitness club, Japanese garden and executive floors. Convenient for many different areas. **¥¥¥¥**

Ryokan Shigetsu
1-31-11, Asakusa, Taito-ku
Tel: 03-3843-2345
www.shigetsu.com
This surprising, elegant *ryokan* offers comfort and good amenities along a lane just off busy Nakamise-dori. Both Japanese- and Western-style en-suite rooms. Excellent restaurant and Japanese bath. **¥**

Sakura Hotel
2-21-4, Kanda-Jimbocho, Chiyoda-ku
Tel: 03-3261-3939
www.sakura-hotel.co.jp
Close to Exit A6 of Jimbocho Station, the Sakura is a surprisingly good deal given its central location. All rooms are non-smoking. **¥**

Shibuya City Hotel
1-1 Maruyamacho, Shibuya
Tel: 03-5489-1010
Seven minutes from Shibuya station, this friendly boutique hotel is well placed for the shopping, nightlife and arts venues of the area. **¥**

Sawanoya Ryokan
2-3-11 Yanaka, Taito-ku
Tel: 03-3822-2251
www.tctv.ne.jp/members/sawanoya
In the old quarter of Yanaka, small but comfortable rooms in a *ryokan* run by a friendly, English-speaking couple. **¥**

Shibuya Excel Hotel Tokyu
1-12-2 Dogenzaka, Shibuya-ku
Tel: 03-5457-0109
www.tokyuhotels.co.jp
Right in the thick of Shibuya, the hotel is situated in part of the Mark City shopping complex attached to the station. **¥¥**

Shibuya Tobu Hotel
3-1, Udagawa-cho, Shibuya-ku
Tel: 03-3476-0111
Fax: 03-5489 1030
A cute little hotel situated along Koen-dori near NHK. Within about 10 minutes of Shibuya Station. Tastefully decorated, contemporary-style rooms, a small restaurant, and very personal service from the bi-lingual staff. **¥¥**

Tokyo Bay Ariake Washington Hotel
3-1-28 Ariake, Koto-ku
Tel: 03-5564-0111
www.wh-rsv.com
The same comfortable facilities as the other hotels in this chain, the Washington is popular with visitors to exhibitions at the nearby Tokyo Big Sight. **¥¥**

Tokyo Prince Hotel
3-3-1 Shibakoen, Minato-ku
Tel: 03-3432-1111
www.princehotelsjapan.com
Another of the Prince chain. Located next to Zojo-ji temple. Pleasant outdoor garden restaurant, which is very popular in summer. Pool (summer only). **¥¥¥**

Westin Hotel Tokyo
1-4-1 Mita, Meguro-ku
Tel: 03-5423-7000
www.westin.com/tokyo
Conveniently near the Yebisu Garden Place shopping and restaurant complex. Refined and comfortable. **¥¥¥¥**

Central Honshu

Nagoya

Fitness Hotel 330 Nagoya
3-25-6 Meieki, Nakamura-ku.
Tel: 052-562-0330
Fax: 052-562-0331
Don't be put off by the name of this business hotel. A relaxing set-up conveniently located for JR Nagoya Station. Nicely decorated rooms with TV, en-suite baths and tea makers. **¥**

Nagoya Hilton
1-3-3 Sakae, Naka-ku
Tel: 052-212-1111
www.hilton.com
All the facilities and comforts you would expect from this expensive brand-name chain. **¥¥¥**

Nagoya Rolen Hotel
1-8-40 Sakae, Naka-ku
Tel: 052-211-4581
www.rolenhotel.co.jp/main.htm
Handily located between Nagoya JR Station and the district of Sakae, this business hotel offers comfortable rooms run by an English-speaking staff. **¥**

Ryokan Meiryu
2-4-21, Kamimaezu, Naka-ku
Tel: 052-331-8686
www.jpinn.com/inn/7-1.html
A budget *ryokan*, whose comfortable *tatami* mat rooms have both TV and air conditioning. **¥**

THE NORTH

Tohoku

Sendai

Dormy Inn
2-10-17, Cho, Aoba-ku
Tel: 022-715-7077
Small but pleasant rooms with en-suite bathrooms and satellite TV. Just a minute's walk from Hirose-dori subway station. **¥**

Hotel Metropolitan
1-1-1 Chuo, Aoba-ku.
Tel: 022-268-2525
www.s-metro.stbl.co.jp
Prestigious hotel located right next to Sendai Station. Japanese and Western rooms, choice of three restaurants, gym and pool. **¥¥**

Intercity Hotel
2-9-4, Hon-cho, Aoba-ku
Tel: 022-222-4647
Comfortable, well-priced rooms in friendly hotel just opposite the Dormy Inn. **¥¥**

Aomori

Grand Hotel
1-1-23 Shin-machi
Tel: 0177-23-1011
www.j-hotel.or.jp
Ask for a room with a sea view in this cosy, well-managed hotel. **¥¥**

Hotel Aomori
1-1-23 Tsutsumi-Machi
Tel: 0177-775-4141
Fax: 0177-773-5201
Large, reasonably priced, 17-storey hotel with good restaurant. **¥¥**

Hotel JAL City
2-4-12, Yasukata
Tel: 0177-32-2580
Fax: 0177-35-2584
A cheerful, modern hotel in a central location, five minutes from the station. Rooms with contemporary styling. **¥¥**

Washington Hotel
2-1-26, Honcho
Tel: 0177-75-7111
www.wh-rsv.com
Part of the dependable Washington chain, this recently built hotel on the eastern side of town is convenient for the airport limousine. **¥¥**

Lake Towada

Towada Prince Hotel
Okawatai, Towadako, Kosaka-machi
Tel: 0176-75-3111
Fax: 0176-75-3110
www.princehotels.co.jp/towada-e
A low-rise hotel on the edge of the lake with good views from the lounge, dining room and guest rooms. **¥¥**

Yamagata

ANA Castle Hotel
4-2-7 Toka Machi
Tel: 0236-31-3311
Fax: 0236-31-3373
www.anahotels.com
Large, luxury hotel 10 minutes' walk from the station.

Metropolitan Yamagata Hotel
1-1-1 Kasumi-cho
Tel: 0236-990-0039
Fax: 0236-628-1166
Four-star hotel with three restaurants, multilingual staff and conference facilities. ¥¥¥

Yamagata Grand Hotel
1-7-42 Honcho
Tel: 0236-41-2611
Fax: 0236-41-2621
The restaurant offers both Western and Japanese food. ¥¥

Yamashiroya Ryokan
Tel: 0236-22-3007
A few minutes north of the station, a block south of the city museum, basic but perfectly clean and cheap traditional-style inn. ¥

Morioka

Hotel Ace
2-11-35 Chuo-dori
Tel: 0196-654-3811
North of Odori, a clean and welcoming business hotel. Some English spoken by staff. ¥

Hotel Ruiz
Saien-dori.
Tel: 0196-625-2611
A popular, well-run business hotel located just opposite Morioka Station. ¥

Kumagai Ryokan
Tel: 0196-651-3020
South of Saien-dori, just across the river from the station, a friendly, low-budget inn with English-speaking owners. ¥

Morioka Grand Hotel
1-10 Atagoshita
Tel: 0196-25-2111
Fax: 0196-22-4804
Hotel with superb views overlooking Mount Atago and both French and Japanese restaurants. ¥¥

Hokkaido

Sapporo

Hotel New Budget Sapporo
Minami 3, Nishi 6.
Tel: 011-261-4953
Fax: 011-261-4960
Conveniently located near Susukino Station, a clean, modern business hotel with non-smoking floors. Rates include a continental breakfast. ¥

Hotel New Otani Sapporo
1-1 Nishi 2-W, Chuo-Ku
Tel: 011-222-1111
Fax: 011-222-5521
Top-end hotel close by the JR station and Odori-koen. Café and restaurants are recommended. ¥¥¥

Keio Plaza Hotel Sapporo
7-2 Nishi Kita 5
Tel: 011-271-0111
Fax: 011-221-5450
www.keioplaza-sapporo.co.jp
Located close to the Botanic Gardens and the university, this hotel includes a health club amongst its facilities. ¥¥¥

Hotel New Otani Sapporo
1-1 Nishi 2-W, Chuo-Ku
Tel: 011-222-1111
Fax: 011-222-1111

Marks Inn Sapporo
Nishi 3, Minami 8
Tel: 011-512-5001
An affordable, well located business hotel with the unusual option of semi-double rooms at a decent rate for two people, including a simple breakfast. ¥

Nakamuraya Ryokan
Nishi 7, Kita 3
Tel: 011-241-2111
www.nakamura-ya.com
A spacious, traditional Japanese inn within a modern building two minutes east of the Ainu Museum. ¥¥

Safro Spa
Minami 6, Nishi 5
Tel: 011-531-2233
Email: info@safro.org
Formerly known as the Hokuo Club, this extraordinary capsule hotel offers luxury facilities such as heated swimming pool, sauna, a small cinema and individual baths. Men and women welcome. ¥

Hakodate

Auberge Kokian
13-2 Suehiro-cho
Tel: 0138-26-5753
An elegant, recently renovated old house now serving as a small hotel. Rather expensive, but the rates include breakfast and dinner. ¥¥¥

Hakodate Harbourview Hotel
5-10 Otemachi
Tel: 0138-22-0111
A small but well-appointed hotel with a surprisingly wide range of restaurants.

Hakodate Kokusai Hotel
5-10 Otemachi
Tel: 0138-23-5151
Fax: 0138-23-0239
Located in the western area overlooking Hakodate Bay. ¥¥¥

Hotel Hakodate Royal
16-9 Omori-cho
Tel: 0138-26-8181
Fax: 0138-27-4397
www.hakodate.or.jp/hotel/royal
In the centre of the city, this modern hotel has three restaurants, a sushi bar and great night views of city from its balcony bar. ¥¥

Pension Hakodate-Mura
16-12 Suehiro-cho
Tel: 0138-22-8105
Atmospheric wooden building in the historical Motomachi area, near the waterfront. ¥

Kushiro City

Fukuiso
30-16 Wakamatsu-cho
Tel: 0154-23-5858
Dirt-cheap *minshuku* five minutes from the station. Small *tatami* rooms with TV and air conditioning. ¥

Kushiro Pacific Hotel
2-6 Sakaecho
Tel: 0154-24-8811
Fax: 0154-23-9192

Kushiro Royal Inn
14-9-2, Kurogane-cho
Tel: 0154-31-2121
Close by the station, this is probably the city's most convenient hotel. Moderate rates include breakfast. ¥¥

KANSAI

Ise

Ise City Hotel & Annex
On the main road near the station
Tel: 0596-22-5100
Fax: 0596-22-5101
Reasonably priced, cheerful and well-serviced business hotel with English-speaking staff. The annexe rooms are a little more expensive. ¥

Hoshide-kan
Just before the main junction, in the old Kawasaki district
Tel: 0596-28-2377
A ramshackle but likeable *ryokan* that offers excellent vegetarian dishes in the attached restaurant. ¥

Yamada-kan
Opposite Ise-shi Station
Tel: 0596-28-2532
Japanese-style rooms in a traditional *ryokan*. Shared bathrooms typical of the cheaper *ryokan*. Very handy for the station. ¥

Kobe

Green Hill Hotel Urban
2-5-16, Kanno, Chuo-ku
Tel: 078-222-1221
Fax: 078-242-1194
www.ghn.jp
Smartened up after the earthquake, this small hotel is good value with breakfast thrown in, and is near Shin Kobe Station. ¥

Hotel Tor Road
3-1-19, Nakayamate-dori
Tel: 078-391-6691
Fax: 078-391-6570
A moderately priced hotel with above-average sized rooms. Free breakfast is served in the café-restaurant. ¥¥

Kobe Meriken Park Oriental Hotel
5-6 Hatoba-cho
Tel: 078-325-8111
www.meriken-oh.co.jp
A high-end hotel on the harbour, but a surprisingly good deal given the location and first-rate facilities. The sea views from the balcony alone are worth a stay here. ¥¥¥

Hotel Okura Kobe
2-1 Hatoba-cho
Tel: 078-333-0111

PRICE CATEGORIES

Price categories are for a double room without breakfast and taxes:
¥ = Under ¥10,000
¥¥ = ¥10–20,000
¥¥¥ = ¥20–30,000
¥¥¥¥ = Over ¥30,000

www.kobe.hotelokura.co.jp/english/overview
All the usual facilities you would expect from this luxury, world-class hotel located beside the Port Tower. Tasteful interiors, and both indoor and outdoor swimming pools. ¥¥¥¥

Shin-Kobe Oriental Hotel
1-7-14 Kitano-cho
Tel: 078-291-1121
www.orientalhotel.co.jp
Located in a towering building beside Shin-Kobe Station, this luxury hotel has fine views, an unusually large choice of restaurants, and an adjacent shopping mall. ¥¥¥¥

Kyoto (Central)

Hiiragiya
Fuyacho-Anekoji-aguru, Nakagyo-ku
Tel: 075-221-1136
www.hiiragiya.co.jp
A well-known and timeless *ryokan*, dating from the mid-19th century. Expensive, but a Kyoto experience. ¥¥¥¥

Hotel Oaks
Nishinotoin Shiijo, Shimogyo-ku
Tel: 075-371-0941
www.h-oaks.co.jp
Part of a chain of reasonably priced business hotels, the smallish rooms are well fitted out, and there are both Japanese and Western-style restaurants to choose from. ¥

Kinmata
407 Gokomachi Shiijo-agaru, Nakagyo-ku
Tel: 075-221-1039
This venerable *ryokan*, built in 1801, is famous for its *kaiseki ryori* dishes, but there is much more: exquisite service, a cedar-wood bath, and traditional garden. Worth the steep fee. ¥¥¥¥

Kyoto Brighton Hotel
Nakadachiuri, Shinmachi-dori, Kamigyo-ku
Tel: 075-441-4411
www.brightonhotels.co.jp/kyoto-e
Graceful, well decorated rooms in an up-market hotel near the Imperial Palace. Easy access to sightseeing areas from nearby Imadegawa subway station. ¥¥¥¥

Sun Hotel
Kawaramachi Sanjo-sagaru, Nakagyo-ku
Tel: 075-241-3351
Fax: 075-241-0616
A standard but exceptionally well-appointed business hotel in the centre of downtown Kyoto, with a decent Italian restaurant. English spoken. ¥

Kyoto (Station Area)

Crossroads
45-14 Ebisu Banda-cho, Shimogyo-ku
Tel: 075-354-3066
Fax: 075-354-3022
www.rose.sannet.ne.jp/c-inn/
Worth the brisk 15-minute walk west of Kyoto Station and the Nishi-honganji temple to reach this friendly, traditional inn. English spoken. ¥

El Inn
13 Higashi-sannooucho, Higashikujo
Tel: 075-672-1100
Fax: 075-672-9988
Just 1 minute from the south exit of Kyoto Station, this business hotel offers competitive rates for their small but comfortable en-suite rooms. English spoken. ¥

Kyoto 2 Tower Hotel
Higashinotoin Shichijo-sagaru, Shimogyo-ku
Tel: 075-361-3261
Fax: 075-351-6281
www.kyoto-tower.co.jp
Nicely decorated and equipped en-suite rooms, and helpful English-speaking staff, this business hotel is just a few steps from the Kyoto Tower side of the station. ¥

Matsuba-ya Ryokan
Kamijuzumachi Higashinotoin nishi-iru, Shimogyo-ku
Tel: 075-351-3727
www.matsubayainn.com/index.htm
Cosy but highly efficiently run *ryokan* dating back to the Meiji era. All rooms are Japanese style and the bathing communal. ¥–¥¥

Tour Club
362 Momiji-cho Kitakoji-agaru, Higashi-Nakasuji-dori, Shimogyo-ku
Tel: 075-353-6968
www.kyotojp.com
Kyoto's most popular backpacker lodging, with both dorm and en-suite rooms. Hostel facilities include internet access and cheap bicycle rentals. ¥

Kyoto (East)

Kiyomizu Sanso
3-341 Kiyomizu, Higashiyama-ku
Tel: 075-561-6109
Reservations are mandatory for this century-old inn as they only have four rooms. A homely establishment off the Sannen-zaka slope; the food is family-style Kyoto cuisine. ¥¥

Three Sisters Inn
Kurodani-mae, Okazaki, Sakyo-ku
Tel: 075-761-6336
Fax: 075-761-6338
The three Yamada sisters who have been running this inn for as long as anyone can remember offer beautiful rooms in an atmospheric area near the Heian shrine. English spoken. ¥

Westin Miyako Hotel
Sanjo Keage, Higashiyama-ku
Tel: 075-771-7111
www.westinmiyako-kyoto.com
A top-quality hotel a short walk from Nanzenji temple, the Miyako's landscaped gardens, tasteful rooms and fine restaurants, suggest graceful living. ¥¥¥

Kyoto (North)

Aoi-so Inn
16-8, Karasuma Shimei, Kita-ku
Tel: 075-431-0788.
A cheap and popular guest house whose rooms are built around the core of a traditional Kyoto courtyard house. Shared toilets and coin-operated showers. The owner speaks English and Spanish. Close to Kurumaguchi subway station. ¥

Myoren-ji
Teranouchi Omiya Higashi-iru, Kamigyo-ku
Tel: 075-451-3527
A friendly *shukubo* (temple lodgings) run by the friendly wife of the head priest. Spacious, *tatami* rooms and an important stone garden. Tickets, soap and towels are issued for bathing at the nearby public bath. ¥

Tani House
8 Daitokuji-cho, Murasakino, Kita-ku
Tel: 075-492-5489
Fax: 075-493-6419
http://kansaiconnect.com/members/tani
Just east of the great Daitoju-ji temple, the shared or private rooms here are basic but adequate. Cheap and cheerful, with good deals on bicycle rentals. ¥

Utano Youth Hostel
29 Nakayama-cho, Uzumasa, Ukyo-ku
Tel: 075-462-2288
http://web.kyoto-inet.or.jp/org/utano-yh
A large youth hostel run by friendly English-speaking staff. Not far from the Ryoan-ji temple and garden. The breakfast buffet is a good start to the day. A rather early 10.30pm curfew though. ¥

Osaka

Hearton Hotel
3-3-55 Umeda
Tel: 06-6342-1111
www.hearton.co.jp/english
Close by JR Osaka Station, rooms fill up quickly in this newish business hotel. Well-designed rooms come with cable TV, bath and refrigerator. ¥¥

Imperial Hotel Osaka
1-8-50 Temmabashi
Tel: 06-6881-1111
www.imperialhotel.co.jp
A sibling of the more famous Tokyo Imperial, but no less swish. Custom-designed rooms overlooking the Okawa River, with a range of novelty touches and first-rate restaurants. ¥¥¥¥

Hotel Nikko Osaka
1-3-3 Nishi-Shinsaibashi
Tel: 06-6244-1281
www.hno.co.jp/english/index_e.html
A world-class hotel with rates to match its sumptuous rooms, restaurants and bars. Located in one of Osaka's liveliest entertainment districts. ¥¥¥¥

Osaka Shiritsu Nagai Youth Hostel
1-1 Nagai-koen
Tel: 06-6699-5631
www.osaka-yha.com
A well-run hostel offering both dorm and private rooms at competitive rates. English-speaking staff. ¥

Sunrise Inn
925 Naka-Kaizuka-shi
Tel: 06-32-3711
Close to Kaizuka Station, this mid-range hotel has decent-sized rooms and a first-rate restaurant that

offers the chance to try out local cuisine at affordable prices. ¥¥

Nara

Hotel Fujita
47-1 Sanjo-cho
Tel: 0742-23-8111
www.fujita-nara.com
A well-maintained and efficient business hotel right on central Sanjo-dori. Comfortable en-suite rooms at reasonable rates. ¥

Nara Hotel
Nara Deer Park
1096 Takahata-cho, Nara-shi, Nara-ken
Tel: 0742-26-3300
www.hotels.westjr.co.jp/nara
This still remains Nara's top hotel choice, and the location, within a Meiji period building with its own landscaped gardens abutting Nara Park, is hard to beat. ¥¥¥

Ryokan Matsumae
28-1 Higashi-Terabyashi-cho
Tel: 0742-22-3686
Fax: 0742-26-3927
www.h3.dion.ne.jp
A friendly *ryokan* in the old quarter of town, there is a choice of rooms with bath or communal bathing. Close to Nara Park. ¥

Superhotel JR Nara Ekimae
500-1 Sanjo-dori
Tel: 0742-20-9000
Fax: 0742-20-9008
Excellent value for a hotel that is right opposite the station. The hotel, part of a popular chain, is relatively new, so the rooms and facilities are in very good shape. ¥¥

THE SOUTH

Chugoku

Okayama

Hotel Granvia
1-5 Ekimoto-cho
Tel: 086-234-7000
Fax: 086-234-7099
Email: front-dp@granvia-oka.co.jp
Right beside the station, this Western-style hotel is one of the top options in Okayama. Bright and cheerful rooms and a couple of souvenir shops for last-minute purchases. ¥¥

Matsunoki
19-1 Ekimoto-cho
Tel: 086-253-4111
Fax: 086-253-4110
www.tiki.ne.jp/~matunoki
A mid-range hotel with both Western and Japanese-style rooms. A four-minute walk west of the station. Good value. ¥¥

Okayama New Station Hotel
18-9 Ekimoto-cho
Tel: 086-253-6655
Fax: 086-254-2583
The rates are cheap at this standard but well-managed little business hotel. Like the Matsunoki, this one is conveniently located on the west side of the station. ¥

Kurashiki

Kurashiki Ivy Square Hotel
7-2 Honmachi
Tel: 086-422-0011
Fax: 086-424-0515
Located in the atmospheric Bikan quarter, this reasonably priced hotel occupies a converted warehouse and factory complex. ¥¥

Minshuku Kamoi
1-24 Honmachi
Tel: 086-422-4898
Fax: 086-427-7615
Although the style of this *minshuku* is traditional, the building itself is modern. A pleasant location near Tsurugata-yama park, the owners prefer guests to commit to the room and meals package, which is good value here. ¥

Ryokan Kurashiki
4-1 Honmachi
Tel: 086-422-0730
Fax: 086-422-0990
Located in the heart of the historic Bikan district, the pain of the bill here is mollified by exquisite service and beautifully decorated suites. ¥¥¥

Hiroshima

ANA Hotel
7-20 Nakamachi, Naka-ku
Tel: 082-241-1111
www.anahotels.com/eng/hotels/hij
The ever-reliable chain of luxury hotels is just a few minutes' walk from the Peace Park. A nicely landscaped garden, swimming pool, and a good selection of restaurants guarantee a comfortable stay. ¥¥¥¥

Dormy Inn Hiroshima
3-28 Komachi, Naka-ku
Tel: 082-240-1177
A mid-range hotel in a convenient location for the central sights. One unusual feature for a moderate lodging like this is the hot spring and sauna available to guests. ¥¥

Hiroshima Kokusai Hotel
3-13 Tatemachi, Naka-ku
Tel: 082-248-2323
www.kokusai.gr.jp/room/index-english.html
Standard mid-range hotel with a revolving restaurant and fine city views. ¥¥

Hotel Sunroute
3-3-1 Otemachi, Naka-ku
Tel: 082-249-3600
www.sunroute.jp
Just a few minutes' walk east of the Peace Park, this business hotel is good value, with above-average room sizes, and a Japanese and Italian restaurant. ¥

Hagi

Hokumon Yashiki
210 Horiuchi
Tel: 0838-22-7521
Fax: 0838-25-8144
Hagi's most famous, and expensive, *ryokan* lives up to its reputation, with tastefully designed Japanese rooms and graceful, kimono-clad maids. Close to the castle ruins. ¥¥¥

Hotel Orange
370-48 Hijiwara
Tel: 0838-25-5880
Fax: 0838-25-7690
An unassuming but good-value business hotel on the Matsumoto River, handily located just opposite the station. ¥

Tomitaya
Hashimoto-cho
Tel: 0838-22-0025
Fax: 0838-25-8232
A modern *ryokan* in traditional style, the pleasant rooms and excellent food are a more reasonably priced alternative to the Hokumon Yashiki. ¥¥

Shikoku

Takamatsu

ANA Clement Takamatsu
1-1 Hamnocho
Tel: 0878-811-1111
www.anaclement.com
Arguably Takamatsu's premier accommodation, the ANA certainly has the best views across the Inland Sea. Several bars and restaurants to choose from. ¥¥¥

Ebisutei
13-13 Nishinomaru-cho
Tel: 0878-821-4112
Basic but friendly, family-run *ryokan*, with small, meticulously kept rooms. ¥

Takamatsu Terminal Hotel
10-17 Nishinomaru-cho
Tel: 0878-822-3731
www.webterminal.co.jp
Handy for the station, castle ruins and buses down to Ritsurin-koen, this standard business hotel is good value, the rooms above-average size. Some English spoken. ¥

Matsuyama

Hotel Heiwa
3-1-34 Heiwa-dori
Tel: 0899-921-3515
Fax: 0899-921-3520
This friendly business hotel just north of the castle is good value. TV, tea- and coffee-making set, air conditioning and en-suite bathrooms. ¥

Matsuyama ANA Hotel
3-2-1 Ichiban-cho
Tel: 0899-933-5511
Fax: 0899-921-6053
The ANA chain again claims top hotel spot for its luxurious rooms

PRICE CATEGORIES

Price categories are for a double room without breakfast and taxes:
¥ = Under ¥10,000
¥¥ = ¥10–20,000
¥¥¥ = ¥20–30,000
¥¥¥¥ = Over ¥30,000

overlooking the castle. Several restaurants and a small shopping arcade add to the diversity. ¥¥¥¥

Dogo Kan
7-26 Dogo Tako-cho
Tel: 0899-941-7777
The quintessential Matsuyama experience is a night here at its world-famous *onsen*. It's also the town's most expensive accommodation. ¥¥¥¥

Kochi

Hotel No. 1 Kochi
16-8 Nijodai-cho
Tel: 0888-873-3333
Fax: 0888-875-9999
A very reasonable deal for a business hotel with some interesting and innovative features, such as a women-only floor, and a rooftop hot spring for bathing. ¥

Joseikan
2-5-34 Kamimachi
Tel: 0888-875-0111
Fax: 0888-8824-0557
A *ryokan* in the traditional style. The cuisine, rooms and graceful service explain the sobering bill you will be discreetly handed at the end of your stay. ¥¥¥

New Hankyu Kochi
4-2–50 Honmachi
Tel: 0888-873-1111
www.hotel.newhankyu.co.jp/kochi-e/index.html
Considering this is Kochi's premier Western-style hotel, with a swimming pool, fitness centre and several restaurants, the prices here are surprisingly reasonable. ¥¥

Kyushu

Fukuoka

Canal City Fukuoka Washington Hotel
1-2-20 Sumiyoshi
Tel: 092-282-8800
Fax: 092-282-0757
Spacious rooms with TV, fridge and en-suite bath at this upmarket business hotel chain. ¥¥

Grand Hyatt Fukuoka
1-2-882 Sumiyoshi
Tel: 092-282-1234
Fax: 092-282-2817
www.grandhyattfukuoka.com
Sitting right in the middle of Canal City, this is one of the best-appointed hotels in Fukuoka. Befitting its reputation as the premier hotel in town, the rooms are suitably large and tastefully designed. The bathrooms are luxurious. ¥¥¥¥

Maruko Inn
3-30-25 Hakata-eki mae
Tel: 092-475-2680
Fax: 092-475-2680
A comfortable, friendly mid-range business hotel not far from Hakata station. A good deal. ¥

Hotel New Simple
1-23-11 Hakata-eki mae
Tel: 092-411-4311
Fax: 092-411-431
Hard to beat the rates here, though the rooms are spartan and the bathing communal. A handy location near the Gion subway station. ¥

Nagasaki

Holiday Inn
6-24 Doza-machi
Tel: 0958-8828-1234
Fax: 0958-828-0178
A surprisingly elegant, well-furnished and designed hotel for the moderate rates they charge. ¥¥

Hotel New Nagasaki
14-5 Daikoku-machi
Tel: 0958-826-8000
Fax: 0958-823-2000
Nagasaki's grandest hotel is just outside the station. Step past the marble lobby to restaurants, bars, a fitness centre, a shopping arcade, and spacious, well fitted-out rooms. ¥¥¥

Minshuku Tanpopo
21-7 Hoei-cho
Tel: 0958-861-6230
Fax: 0958-8864-0032
A competitively priced *minshuku*, 10 minutes equidistant from the Peace Park and the Matsuyama tram stop. ¥

Nagasaki Grand Hotel
5-3 Manzai-machi
Tel: 0958-823-1234
Fax: 0958-822-1793
Easy access to Glover Park, the downtown area and station, make this a viable option, and the rates for well-equipped, en-suite rooms are attractive. ¥¥

Kumamoto

Kajita
1-2-7 Shin-machi
Tel: 096-353-1546
Email: kajita@titan.ocn.ne.jp
Close to the castle walls, this friendly, well-priced *minshuku* has nice *tatami* rooms and optional, but recommended meals. If you phone from the station, the owners will pick you up. ¥

Maruko Hotel
11-10 Kamitori-cho
Tel: 096-353-1241
Fax: 096-353-1217
A modern hotel in the Japanese style, the helpful staff at the Maruko speak English. Well-maintained rooms, and a Japanese bath on the 6th floor. ¥¥

New Otani
1-13-1 Kasuga
Tel: 096-326-1111
Fax: 096-326-0800
www.newotani.co.jp
An upmarket hotel at affordable rates, the Otani buzzes with efficiency. A good selection of restaurants and shops. Located close to Kumamoto Station. ¥¥¥

Kagoshima

Nakazono Ryokan
1-18 Yasui-cho
Tel: 0992-226-5125
This friendly and cosy *ryokan* is a very good deal considering its central location. The owner is a mine of information on the city. ¥

Nanshukan
19-17 Higashi-Sengoku-cho
Tel: 0992-226-8188
Fax: 0992-226-9383
Beside Chuo Park, a good location and price for medium-sized rooms in a moderately priced business hotel. ¥

Tokyu Inn
5-1 Chuo-cho
Tel: 0992-256-0109
Fax: 0992-253-3692
www.tokyuhotels.co.jp/en
A short stroll from Nishi-Kagoshima Station, the rooms in this well-kept business hotel come equippped with TV, fridge, phone and bath. ¥¥

Young Inn Kagoshima
16-23 Izumi-cho
Tel: 0992-223-1116
Fax: 0992-225-1509
One of the cheapest options, the rooms in this guesthouse are simple, the bathing and toilets communal. ¥

Okinawa

Naha

Naha Dai-ichi Hotel
2-2-7 Kume
Tel: 098-868-0111
Fax: 098-868-0555
A short walk from the Kencho-mae monorail stop and Kokusai-dori. Rates include a very decent self-service breakfast. ¥

Nansei Kanko Hotel
3-13-23 Makishi.
Tel: 098-862-7144
A cheerful-looking moderately priced hotel located at the north end of Kokusai-dori. ¥¥

Toyoko Inn Naha Izumisaki Kosaten
2-1-20 Kume
Tel: 098-951-1045
www.toyoko-inn.com
Located at the convenient south end of Kokusai-dori, this is great value for a mid-range hotel close to the shops, entertainment areas and monorail. ¥¥

Ishigaki

Club Med Kabira
Kabira Bay
Tel: 0980-84-4600
www.clubmed.com
This is the smartest beach resort on the island. Expensive, but worth it for the superb location on Kabira Bay. ¥¥¥¥

Hotel Miyahira
Misaki-cho
Tel: 0980-82-6111
Well-equipped Western-style rooms in a slightly upmarket hotel close to the all-important ferry and bus terminals. ¥¥

Guesthouse Rakutenya
291 Okawa
Tel/fax: 0980-83-8713
Two old, architecturally interesting wooden buildings in the Okinawan style, Rakutenya is just a stroll from Ishigaki port. Book early as the rates are attractively low. ¥¥

PRICE CATEGORIES

Price categories are for a double room without breakfast and taxes:
¥ = Under ¥10,000
¥¥ = ¥10–20,000
¥¥¥ = ¥20–30,000
¥¥¥¥ = Over ¥30,000

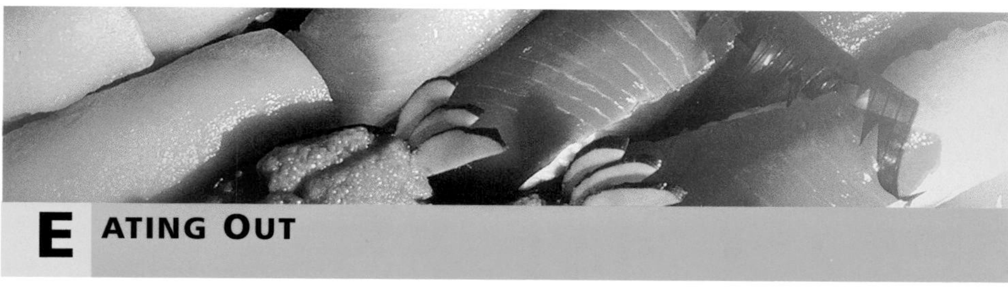

EATING OUT

RECOMMENDED RESTAURANTS, CAFES & BARS

Japan is an eater's paradise, and the diversity of possibilities would fill a separate Insight Guide. For a broad-brush survey of Japanese cuisine, see the *Food and Drink* chapter on pages 117–21. But since you've come so far, be bold and try anything that you come across, and stay away from the Western fast-food joints, which are appearing all over Japan.

There are many, many restaurants in Japan – alleys are lined with them – but many places opened up during the heady bubble economy, supported in large part by businessmen with expense accounts often devoted to food and entertainment. Even the lowliest of businessman and eatery found themselves mutually benefitting from the overheated economy.

If the media is to be believed, the recession that followed is now over and the economy is rebounding. One positive outcome of that prolonged recession, though, at least from the point of view of travellers and the fully employed Japanese, has been the cut-throat competitiveness of the food sector throughout Japan, particularly with set lunch offerings. Bargain deals in all kinds of restaurants, even in expensive areas like Tokyo's Ginza, are still the norm.

Green Tea Versatility

Said to be extremely healthy, the bitter, acerbic edge characteristic of Japanese green tea, or *matcha*, is an acquired taste. By-products of green tea are *matcha*-flavoured biscuits, incense aromas, *ochazuke*, hot green teas poured over rice, matchalatte coffee and milkshakes, chewing gum and green tea ice-cream. Häagen Dazs even has a version of this specially for the Japanese market.

The easiest places to sample *matcha* are at international hotels and in the teahouses of well-known traditional Japanese gardens.

Eating Etiquette

Good table manners, Japanese-style, go a long way. Here are a few tips: The wet towel *(oshibori)* you receive to freshen up at the beginning of the meal should be neatly rolled up when you've finished, and don't use it on anything except your hands.

It is bad manners to wave your chopsticks around, to use them to point at someone, to stick them upright in your rice (an allusion to death) or to pull dishes forward. If you have a communally shared bowl of food, then turn your chopsticks around and use the reverse points to pick up the food.

Japanese-style soups *(suimono)* and noodles in broth (except *ramen*) are sipped straight from the bowl. Whereas it is altogether acceptable form in Japan to slurp noodle dishes there is no need to slurp soups. Sip them directly from the bowl without a spoon, as this is the best way to savour their delicate flavour.

For dishes that are dipped in sauce, such as *tempura* and *sashimi*, hold the sauce dish with one hand and dip the food into it with the chopsticks. Soy sauce should not be splashed onto a dish. Rather, pour into the small soy sauce dish, only a little at a time and sparingly.

You will never see Japanese eating and walking at the same time. They buy the food or snack, then find a place to properly sit and completely finish it.

Economical Eating

Increasingly, Japanese are buying meals at convenience stores like 7-Eleven. The competition between convenience stores is stiff, so the food is made fresh daily, is excellent quality and represents really good value for money. Look out especially for "lunch set specials" which can be as cheap as ¥650. Fast-food joints have sets for as little as ¥350.

Family restaurants like Denny's, Cocos and Volks often have a free coffee refill service after the first cup. Tipping is almost non-existent in Japan, which helps offset costs.

What to Eat

The list below is roughly divided into sections. Please note that unless otherwise stated, the cost is for dinner and does not include drinks. However, most restaurants, regardless of their dinner prices, have special lunch menus with prices beginning at around ¥800. The closing times stated are, in most cases, for last orders. Translations of the dishes are given in the Language section (page 392).

In general, don't expect to escape from most decent restaurants for less than ¥3,000 per person, excluding drinks. On average, a night on the upscale side of town can run from ¥10,000 to ¥15,000. If you're on a budget, stick to medium-range restaurants, street stands and convenience stores.

The traveller need only walk down any street in any town or city and find more possibilities for eating than one can sample in a year. Plastic food in display cases or photographic menus make decisions both easier and more difficult – too many choices. Look, sniff, and enter.

RESTAURANT LISTINGS

TOKYO

Japanese

Akasaka Tofu-ie
Sanyo Akasaka Bldg, 1F, 3-5-2 Akasaka, Minato-ku
Tel: 03-3582-1028
Open daily 11.30am–11.30pm
Some of the tofu lunch sets are entirely vegetarian, though this is not an organic restaurant by any means. Fermented tofu and sesame tofu are among the best of the range of incredibly fresh bean curd on offer. **¥¥**

Chanko Kawasaki
2-13-1 Ryogoku, Sumida-ku
Tel: 03-3631-2529
Open daily 11.30am–2.30pm, 5–11pm
This 1937 restaurant specialises in *chanko-nabe*, a stew served to sumo wrestlers. Fish, chicken and vegetables are boiled in a pot along with tofu, titbits and side dishes that change seasonally. **¥¥**

Chibo
Yebisu Garden Place Tower, 38F, 4-20-3 Ebisu, Shibuya-ku
Tel: 03-5424-1011
Open daily 11.30am–3pm, 5–11pm
Okonomiyaki in a trendy Yebisu Garden setting with superb views across the bay. Additions to the original formula include French cheeses and asparagus stuffing. English-language menu. **¥¥**

Fukuzushi
5-7-8 Roppongi, Minato-ku
Tel: 03-3402-4116
Open 5.30–11pm; holidays 5–10pm; closed Sun.
A sushi shop with an English-language menu. Offers tuna, mackerel and cod and the less familiar delights of conger eel, shad and grouper. **¥¥¥**

Gesshinkyo
4-24-12 Jingumae, Shibuya-ku
Tel: 03-3796-6575
Open daily 6–10pm
Traditional vegetarian cuisine using up to 40 different kinds of vegetables in each meal. Appreciate the artistry of this living Zen food in traditional, totally no-smoking surroundings. **¥¥¥**

Hayashi
1-12 Nihombashi-Muromachi, Chuo-ku
Tel: 03-3241-5367
Open Mon–Sat 11am–9pm
Expensive but sublime; the *tempura* here is in a league of its own. The seafood and vegetable morsels are closer to the light, non-fatty variety found in the elegant restaurants and inns of Kyoto. **¥¥¥¥**

Ikebukuro Gyoza Stadium
Namco Namja Town 2F, Sunshine City, 3-1-1 Higashi-Ikebukuro, Toshima-ku
Telephone Sunshine City Information Center on 03-3989-3331.
Gyoza are meat- and vegetable-stuffed dumplings fried and served with rice, pickles and other trimmings. The main mall of Namja Town features 22 *gyoza* restaurants. Although the *gyoza* are only ¥300 each, you could easliy run up quite a bill while sampling these tasty treats. **¥¥**

Kanda Yabu Soba
2-10 Kanda-Sudacho, Chiyoda-ku
Tel: 03-3251-0287
Open 11.30am–7pm; closed Mon
An institution in Tokyo eating circles, classic Edo-style hand-made buckwheat noodles in traditional surroundings. Soba choices come in hot soup or with a cold soy-based dip. Go early at lunchtime as the lines start to form on the stroke of noon. **¥**

Keika Kumamoto Ramen
3-7-2 Shinjuku, Shinjuku-ku
Tel: 03-3354-4501
Open daily 11am–10.45pm
Much featured on TV, this noodle shop specialises in the pork broth-based ramen called *tonkotsu*, which is a staple of Kyushu that's suddenly become the thing to eat. The *chashumen* noodles are superb. Long lines at lunchtime. **¥**

Little Okinawa
8-7-10 Ginza, Chuo-ku
Tel: 03-3572-2930
Open Mon–Sat 5pm–3am
Southern cuisine in a friendly, "little" setting. Strong on noodles, pork, bitter, stir-fried gourds, and *awamori*, a firebrand spirit unique to these islands. The atmosphere is the second-best thing to jumping on a flight to Okinawa. **¥¥**

Maisen
4-8-5 Jingumae, Shibuya-ku
Tel: 03-3470-0071
Open daily 11am–10pm
The best of a *tonkatsu* chain, this one is situated in a converted bathhouse. Tell-tale signs include tall ceilings and two carp ponds. All the roast pork, chicken and oyster sets are delicious and can be ordered from the English-language menu along with a glass of icy draught beer. **¥¥**

Nambantei
4-5-6 Roppongi, Minato-ku
Tel: 03-3402-0606
Open daily 5–11pm
Tasty *yakitori* broiled over charcoal in relaxed, faux-rustic surroundings. English-language menu available. **¥¥**

Shin Hinomoto
2-4-4 Yurakucho, Chiyoda-ku
Tel: 03-3214-8021
Open 5pm–midnight; closed Sun and holidays
Noisy, friendly *izaka-ya* (pub) built under the railway tracks serving fresh fish at very reasonable prices. Tables spill out onto the street where the aroma of char-broiled skewers of chicken *yakitori* and the promise of ice-cold lager draw the customers in. **¥**

Sushi-bun
Chuo Shijo Bldg, No.8, 5-2-1, Tsukiji, Chuo-ku
Tel: 03-35541-3860
Open 5.30am–2.30pm; closed Sun
www.sushibun.com
Located in Tsukiji market, the temple of fish markets, regarded by many as the best sushi at the best prices, Sushi-bun opens early for the local traders. Squeeze around the counter for set platters. First come, first served. English-language menu. **¥¥**

Zakuro
3-8-2 Nihombashi, Chuo-ku
Tel: 03-3271-3791
Open daily 11am–10pm
A favourite dinner spot among businessmen, who come here for quality Kobe steak. Also serves *sukiyaki, shabu-shabu and tempura*. Fresh seasonal vegetables are used in the Japanese manner. Dining in private rooms or at a tempura bar. Branches in Ginza and Akasaka. **¥¥¥**

Australian

Salt
5F Shin-Marunouchi Building 1-5-1 Marunouchi, Chiyoda-ku
Tel: 03-5288-7828
Open daily 11am–3.30pm
Aussie celebrity chef Luke Mangan's venture features fabulous seafood matched with a fine cellar of Aussie wines in a sleek setting. **¥¥¥¥**

Chinese & Korean

Fumin
B1, 5-7-17 Minami-Aoyama, Minato-ku
Tel: 03-3498-4466
Open daily 11.30am–2.30pm, 5–11pm
Ever-popular Chinese home-cooking in a fashionable part of town. Fumin attracts long lines but it's worth the wait for the large helpings of wonderfully seasoned and aromatic dishes, and house

PRICE CATEGORIES

Prices for three-course dinner per person without drinks and taxes:
¥ = Under ¥2,000
¥¥ = ¥2,000–3,000
¥¥¥ = ¥3,000–5,000
¥¥¥¥ = Over ¥5,000

specialities like the spring onion *wanton*. ¥¥¥

Hong Kong Garden
4-5-2 Nishi-Azabu, Minato-ku
Tel: 03-3486-3711
Open daily 11.30am–4pm, 5.30–10.30pm
A massive gastro-dome recreating for Tokyoites the flavour of dining in the former crown colony. Seating for up to 800 persons. The trolley-borne dim sum is arguably the best in Tokyo, the cuisine largely steamed and stir-fried Cantonese, with hints of other regions. English-language menu. ¥¥¥¥

Kankoku Shokudo
1-12-3 Okubo, 3F, Shinjuku-ku
Tel: 03-3208-0209
Open daily 9am–4am
Cheap, savoury Korean dishes at a restaurant located close to Tokyo's "Little Asia" district of Shin-Okubo. Lashings of *kimchi* pickles, spicy seaweed, savoury side dishes and assorted barbecue dishes grilled on individual hot plates that are the main fare in this lively eatery. ¥

Mugyodon
Sangyo Bldg, 2F, 2-17-74 Akasaka, Minato-ku
Tel: 03-3586-6478
Open 5pm–midnight
Authentic Korean cuisine with no softening of the food for Japanese palettes. All the usual options like *sukiyaki* (one-pot meal) and fiery side dishes of *kimchee*. A very friendly, informal place which means it's very popular and often crowded out. ¥¥

Ethnic

Angkor Wat
1-38-13 Yoyogi, Shibuya-ku
Tel: 03-3370-3019
Open 11am–2pm, 5–11pm. Sun and holidays 5–11pm
Cheap, crowded, and as persistently authentic, right down to the spices, as any Cambodian street market stall. Perky Cambodian waitresses serve chicken and green-mango salads, rice and pork dishes, and fiery side dishes in a plain dining hall full of atmosphere. ¥

Café Rendevous
Yanagiya Bldg, 2-18-6 Takadanobaba, Shinjuku-ku
Tel: 03-5285-0128
This tiny, hole-in-the-wall eatery in a basement in Tokyo's Little Myanmar district offers a surprisingly authentic menu featuring pungent dishes like *mohinga*, a savoury stew with fermented fish sauce, *tofu-joh*, a yellow lentil curd, and *lape-toh*, green-tea salad. ¥¥

Hyakunincho Yataimura
2-20-25 Hyakunin-cho, Shinjuku-ku
Tel: 03-5386-3320
Open 5pm–4am, Sun 5pm–2am
Street food from half a dozen Asian countries under one very low-budget roof. Wander from stall to stall making up a combination meal from the Indonesian, Thai, Korean and other cuisines represented here. ¥

Oh' Calcutta
26-9, Ota Bldg, B1, Shibuya-ku
Tel: 03-3780-2315
Open daily 11am–11pm
Located in a basement along Shibuya's main youth street, Center-gai, mouth-watering northern and southern Indian dishes. Generous lunch buffet for just ¥1050. ¥¥

American & Fusion

Farm Grill
Ginza Nine Bldg #3, 8-5 Ginza, Chuo-ku
Tel: 03-5568-6156
Open daily 11am–11pm
Grills, barbecues and rotisserie chicken in a spacious dining room at great prices. You could be in Kansas. Local and American beers. Good wine list too. ¥¥

Las Chicas
5-47-6 Jingumae, Shibuya-ku
Tel: 03-3407-6865
Open daily 11am–11pm
A design centre, exhibition space and art salon, with restaurants and bars, run by a bilingual staff, offering a Western-Continental-Asian mix that includes Thai sauces with jacket potato and sour cream, homemade breads and original salads. Tasty cocktails and Australian wines at the bars. ¥¥

New York Grill
Park Hyatt Hotel, 3-7-1-2 Nishi-Shinjuku, Shinjuku-ku
Tel: 03-5322-1234
Open daily 11.30am–2.30pm, 5.30–10pm
Spectacular sky view setting in the glass-fronted apex of Shinjuku's superb Park Hyatt Hotel. The massive Sunday brunches, with sirloin steaks and lobster ceviche top most people's favourite lists, and cocktails at the New York Bar are an institution for the expat community. ¥¥¥¥

Olives
West Walk Roppongi Hills, 5F, 6-10-1, Roppongi, Minato-ku
Tel: 03-5413-99571
Open daily 11.30am–3.30pm, 6–11.30pm
Roppongi Hills is the setting for a new restaurant run by American chef Todd English. The very best of fusion cuisine, with European and American concepts blended with Japanese. The steaks and risottos are otherworldly. If you have room, try the superb chocolate cake duo. ¥¥¥¥

Spago
5-7-8 Roppongi, Minato-ku
Tel: 03-3423-4025
Open daily 11.30am–2pm, 6–10pm
Fresh, simple food in the California style, with touches of Japanese cuisine and an open West Coast feel to the main dining room. Spago's sommelier can advise on wine and sake choices. ¥¥¥

French

Aux Bacchanales
1-6 Jingumae, Shibuya-ku
Tel: 03-5474-0076
Open daily 5.30pm–midnight restaurant; 10am–midnight (café)
The best street-side café in town, a place to see and be seen in the Parisian manner. Plus a casual restaurant serving great bourgeois brasserie and bistro fare. A wide menu with plenty of cheap red wines to choose from. ¥¥

Chez Matsuo
1-23-15 Shoto, Shibuya-ku
Tel: 03-3485-0566
Open daily noon–3pm, 6–11pm
Top-end French cooking in one of the most elite residential areas of Tokyo. Soak up the atmosphere of privilege in an exclusive 1920s ivy-covered villa with leafy garden views. The duck, stewed fig in red wine, and rack of lamb are sublime. ¥¥¥¥

Tête à Tête
2-3-9 Yotsuya, Shinjuku-ku
Tel: 03-3356-1048
Open 11.45am–2pm, 5.45–9.45pm; closed Sun and holidays
Along with the Aux Bacchanales chain, this is one of the most consistent of the numerous no-frills French bistros that Tokyo is blessed with. A wide selection of both urban and rustic French country dishes in a relaxing atmosphere. ¥

Indian

Nataraj
B1F Sanwa-Aoyama Building
2-22-19 Minami-Aoyama
MInato-ku
Tel: 03-5474-0510
Open Mon–Fri 11.30am–3pm, 5.30–11pm, Sat–Sun 11.30am–11pm
Tokyo's foremost Indian vegetarian restaurant serves grills and curries from the tandoor oven. Spice levels are mild but can be raised. ¥¥¥

Italian

Enoteca Pinchiorri
Kore Bldg, 7F, 5-8-20 Ginza, Chuo-ku
Tel: 03-3289-8081
Open 11.30am–8.30pm
Run by a couple with a similar set up in Florence, Tokyo's best Florentine restaurant is well known for its wine list. Award-winning food and wine in a sophisticated atmosphere in the heart of Ginza. ¥¥¥¥

Il Pinolo
Heiwado Bld, 1-8-7 Higashi-Azabu, Minato-ku
Tel: 03-3505-6860
Open 11.30am–3pm, 5.30–10.30pm; closed Sun
Innovative Tuscan cuisine presented in a casual setting, with a pleasant

terrace for the summer months. Homemade pastas, plenty of herbs and olive oil make this an authentic Italian eating experience. ¥¥¥

Vegetarian

Bodaiju
4-3-14 Bukkyo Dedo Center Bldg, 2-3F, Shiba, Minato-ku
Tel: 03-3456-3257
Open daily 11.30am–2pm, 5–10pm
The name means bodhi tree, the one the Buddha sat under awaiting enlightenment. Creative Chinese vegetarian food with a filling and nutritious set lunch ¥

Café 8
4-27-15, Time & Style Galleria, 3F, Minami-Aoyama, Minato-ku
Tel: 03-5464-3207
Open daily except Wed 11am–1pm, Fri and Sat 11am–3pm
An 8-minute walk from Omotesando Station, this completely vegetarian restaurant offers inexpensive à la carte dishes and sets starting at a mere ¥800. ¥

Crayon House
3-8-15 Kita-Aoyama, Minato-ku
Tel: 03-3406-6409
Open 11am–10pm
Two organic restaurants in the basement of a children's bookshop. The first, Hiroba, is French, with a nicely priced buffet lunch; the second, Home, is Japanese, offering whole rice and buns, a veggie main dish, fruit and organic tea. ¥¥

Daigo
2-4-2 Atago, Minato-ku
Tel: 03-3431-0811
Open daily noon–3pm, 5–9pm
Vegetarian banquets of great delicacy are served in rooms that look out onto the tranquil garden. ¥¥¥¥

Pure Café
5-5-21 Minami-Aoyama
Tel: Minato-ku
Tel: 03-5466-2611
Open daily 8.30am–10.30pm
Self-service all-day café serving light, additive-free and (almost) entirely vegan meals. Opens early for those looking for a healthy breakfast with organic coffee. ¥

Cafés

Ben's Café
1-29-21 Takabanobaba, Shinjuku-ku
Tel: 03-3202-2445
Open daily 11.30am–midnight
www.benscafe.com
Artsy, New York-style café with a very tasty selection of cakes. ¥

Café Paulista
Nagasaki Centre, 1F, 8-9-16 Ginza, Chuo-ku
Tel: 03-3572-6160
Open daily 8.30am–10.30pm
The coffee In this venerable Ginza café is brewed from beans imported from Brazil. The prices are affordable and choosing the snacks and cake sets allow you to feel comfortable staying longer. ¥

Gab
R. Bldg, 1F, 32-8 Uragawa-cho, Shibuya-ku
Tel: 03-3770-1345
Open 11–4am, Mon 11am–midnight
"Gab" as in chatting away, is a New York-style open-fronted café with a lively mix of locals and expats. The hamburger and pasta lunches are nicely prepared. ¥

Gallery éf
2-19-18 Kaminarimon, Taito-ku
Tel: 03-3841-0442
Open Wed–Mon 11am–7pm, lunch 11.30am–2pm.
The back of the café is the gallery entrance. Good homemade cakes. ¥

NAGOYA

Kawaiya
31 Iida-machi, Higashi-ku
Tel: 052-931-0474
Open 11am–2.30pm, 5–7.30pm, closed Sun
Tasty flat *kishimen* noodles, a local speciality, some varieties with grated *daikon* radish and shrimp toppings. Great value: from ¥600. ¥

Torigin
1F, Miyaki Bldg, 3-14-22 Nishiki, Naka-ku
Tel: 052-951-1184
Open 5–11pm, 2nd and 3rd Sun
A Nagoya-style *yakitori* eatery featuring, as the name suggests (*tori* means chicken), barbecued chicken-on-a-stick. There are over 30 varieties on the menu, all served with rice or noodles. ¥¥

Tiger Café
1-9-22 Higashi-sakura
Tel: 052-971-1031
Open daily 11am–3pm, Sun 11am–midnight
Friendly French cafe serving light meals, pastries and coffee. ¥¥

SENDAI

Date Yashiki
3-4 Kokubun-cho, Aoba-ku
Tel: 022-261-2071
Open daily 5–8.30pm
A steamed rice specialist. Try the flavoursome *gomoku*, where the salmon and crab are steamed on the rice. ¥¥

Sendai Kaki Toku
4-9-1 Ichibancho, Aoba-ku
Tel: 022-222-0785
Open daily 11am–2pm, 5–9pm
Japan is a great place for fried, stewed and tofu-mixed oyster. This place has it all, including fresh oysters served with vinegar or a twist of Japanese citrus. Cheaper options of rice and tempura. ¥¥¥

Saboten
28F SS30 Bldg 4-6 Chuo
Open daily 11.30am–10pm
Good-value cafe-style restaurant at the top of Sendai's tallest building. Various set meals. ¥¥

SAPPORO

21 Club
25F, Hotel Arthur, Minami 10-jo, Nishi 6
Tel: 011-561-1000
Open 11.30am–3pm, 5–9.30pm
A very fashionable *teppanyaki* restaurant with panoramic views over the city, and sky-high prices to match. ¥¥¥¥

Sapporo Beer Garden
Kita 7, Higashi 9
Tel: 011-742-1531
Open 11.30am–9pm
Seating up to 3,000 people, the set meal here entitles you to as much barbecued lamb as you can eat within a 100-minute limit. There is an outdoor seating area for cooling off in the summer. ¥¥

Yagumo
B2, Plaza Bldg, Odori 4-chome
Tel: 011-231-0789
Open 10.30am–8.30pm
A traditional noodle and soba shop, decorated with folk art and agrarian objects. ¥

Kitanofuji
Suskino Plaza Bldg, Minami 7, Nishi 4
Tel: 011-512-5484
Open 4–11pm
Serves *chanko nabe*, the famous hearty stews of sumo wrestlers. There is a large sumo ring in the centre of the restaurant. ¥¥

OSAKA

Daikoku
2-2-7 Dotonbori, Chuo-ku
Tel: 06-211-1101
Open 11.30am–3pm, 5–8pm; closed Sun.
Point to the pictures on the menu or the other customers' plates to order grilled fish, and *kayaku gohan*, fried tofu on steamed rice. A popular restaurant for all ages, it's been in business for over 100 years. **¥¥**

Mimiu Honten
4-6-18 Hirano-cho, Chuo-ku
Tel: 06-231-5770
Open 11.30am–9.30pm; closed Sun.
If you have the *udon suki*, which you should as this is the place that popularised it, the bill can run quite high. It's worth trying this delicious mixture of *udon*, clams, seasonal vegetables, chicken and shrimp at least once though. **¥¥¥¥**

Otoya
5F, Itoya Bldg, 1-6-21 Sonezaki, Shinchi, Kita-ku
Tel: 06-341-2891
Open 5pm–1am; closed Sun
A cheap eatery that offers a taste of Osaka's best-known concoction, *okonomiyaki*, sometimes called Japanese pizza. The mix includes octopus, shrimp, pork and vegetables. **¥**

Takoume
1-1-8 Dotonbori, Chuo-ku
Tel: 06-211-0321
Open 5–10pm; closed Sun
This small, 150-year old restaurant is a time slip in this otherwise modern district. Enjoy its atmosphere while it lasts. The speciality here is *oden*, a soup of radish, sausage, fishcakes, squid and much more. A hearty winter dish when washed down with beer or hot sake. **¥¥**

Yotaro Honten
2-3-14 Koraibashi, Chuo-ku
Tel: 06-231-5561
Open 11.30am–2pm, 4.30–8pm; closed Sun
Sea bream never tasted as good and fresh as it does here, where it is cooked in a clay pot on a bed of rice. An almost biblical simplicity reigns in this modest *tai gohan*. **¥¥**

KOBE

Las Ramblas
B1, KDD Kobe Bldg, 83 Kyomachi, Chuo-ku
Tel: 078-393-0730
Open 11.30am–2pm, 5.30–8.30pm; closed Mon
Good-value paella and tapas, served along with a decent selection of Iberian wines and sherry in this chic Spanish bar. **¥¥**

Marrakesh
1-20-15 Nakayamate, basement of Maison de Yamate
Tel: 078-241-3440
Open 5–11pm, Sat & Sun noon–2pm, 5–11pm; closed Mon
The mint teas, sultana-encrusted couscous, tajine stews and Moroccan flat bread make a change from Japanese food. Nice decor reminiscent of North African interiors. **¥¥¥**

Okagawa
1-5-0 Kitano-cho
Tel: 078-222-3511
Open daily 11am–2pm, 5–9pm
A trendy, contemporary atmosphere serving the top end of Japanese cuisine: *kaiseki, shabu-shabu* and *sukiyaki*. **¥¥¥¥**

Sanda-ya
Kitano-zaka
Tel: 078-222-0567
Open daily 11.30am–8.30pm
Kobe is synonymous with beef, its own special, marbled, rather expensive variety. Here it's moderately priced but tasty, served along with rice, *miso* soup and vegetables. **¥¥**

KYOTO

Hinadori
Kitsuji-dori, 9 Somon-cho, Kinugasa, Kita-ku
Tel: 075-467-1855
Open 11.30am–3pm, 5–9pm. Closed Thur
A relaxed French bistro with good-value set lunches and à la carte dinner choices. In the atmospheric Kinkaku-ji temple district. **¥¥**

Ikkyu-an
Opposite the south gate of Kodai-ji temple, Kodai-ji Minamimon-mae, Higashiyama-ku
Tel: 075-561-1901
Open noon–6.30pm; closed Tues
Although it doesn't come cheap, the experience of eating *fucha ryori*, Zen vegetarian dishes served in the Chinese manner, is an exquisite rarity. **¥¥¥¥**

Kushihachi
33-1 Kami Hakubai, Hakubai-cho, Kitano
Tel: 075-461-8888
Open daily 5–11pm
A lively chain restaurant serving *kushiage* food: grilled meat titbits served on sticks. A popular and lively venue. This type of food goes well with sake or beer. **¥¥**

Masago
Ryoton Zushi-machi, Sanjo-sagaru, Koromodana-dori, Nakagyo-ku
Tel: 075-221-0211
Open daily 11am–2pm, 5–8.30pm
Located in the elegant former abode of a tea-ceremony master, *kaiseki* dinners are served in a converted storehouse overlooking a lovely Japanese garden. **¥¥¥¥**

Okutan
86 Fukuchi-machi, Nanzen-ji, Sakyo-ku
Tel: 075-771-8709
Open 11.30am–2pm, 5–8pm; closed Tues
Delicious tofu pots, rice, pickles, *tempura* and grated mountain potato add up to quite a blow-out. **¥¥¥**

Taam Sabaai
2F Kiyosumi Bldg, 51-6 Minamishiba-cho, Shimogamo.
Tel: 075-781-7758
Open daily 11.30am–1.30pm, 5.30–9.30pm
Relaxed and friendly atmosphere and genuine Thai cuisine. Run by a couple from Chiang Mai who have incorporated some northern touches into their dishes. **¥¥¥**

Tempura Yoshikawa Inn
Tominojoki, south of Oike-dori, Nakagyo-ku
Tel: 075-221-5544
Open 11am–2pm, 5–8.30pm; closed Mon
Kyoto-style *tempura* is light and delicate compared to the Tokyo variety. This traditional inn-cum-restaurant serves some of the best in town, in a teahouse setting. They also have private rooms for evening *kaiseki* dinners overlooking a private classical garden. Great atmosphere. **¥¥¥**

Tsuruya Yoshinobu
Intersection of Horiikawa and Imadegawa-dori, Horikawa Imadegawa, Kamigyo-ku
Tel: 075-441-0105
Open daily 9.30am–5.30pm
A Japanese confectioners that has been in business since the early 19th century. The sweets are made on the second floor, where the decoration process can be watched. Japanese *wagashi* (tea ceremony-style sweets) are served with a bowl of brothy green tea in the tea salon. **¥**

PRICE CATEGORIES

Prices for three-course dinner per person without drinks and taxes:
¥ = Under ¥2,000
¥¥ = ¥2,000–3,000
¥¥¥ = ¥3,000–5,000
¥¥¥¥ = Over ¥5,000

NARA

Kan
731 Todaiiji-machi
Tel: 0742-22-0602
Open Thur–Tues 11.30am–7.30pm
Located in the southern section of Nara Park, this inexpensive *soba* noodle shop specialises in *kan teishoku*, a satisfying, good-value set lunch or dinner that includes noodles, *tempura*, vegetables, rice and salad. ¥¥

Yanagichaya
48 Todaiiji-machi
Tel: 0742-22-7560
Open 11.30am–5pm; closed Mon
Well known for its *chameshi* – rice cooked in green tea with tofu – the vegetarian kitchen cues are taken from nearby Kofuku-ji Temple, where the monks prepare a similar repast. Yanagichaya also serves *kaiseki* set dinners, which must be reserved in advance. ¥¥¥

Yoshikawa Tei
1F, San-Fukumuru Bldg, 17 Hanashiba-cho
Tel: 0742-23-7675
Open 11.30am–2pm, 5.30–8.30pm; closed Mon
A miniscule restaurant with about six tables. The chefs do well in preparing near-authentic French bistro-style dishes. ¥¥

Asuka
1 Shonami-cho
Open Tues–Sun 11.30am–8pm
Tel: 0742-26-4308
Smart, reasonably priced tempura restaurant. ¥¥

OKAYAMA

Azumazushi
3-1-48 Omote-machi
Tel: 086-231-0158
Open 11am–2pm, 5–9pm; closed Wed
Okayama is famed for its fresh seafood dishes, many of which are mixed with vegetables and vinegared rice. The classic dish to order is *barazushi*. For an introduction to the region's fish dishes, ask for the *azuma teishoku*, the restaurant's own assortment of fish. ¥¥

Maganedo
1-8-2 Uchisange
Tel: 086-222-6116
Open 11am–7pm; closed Sun
A former sweetshop dating back to the 1920s, whose owners switched to handmade *soba*. A nice rustic setting to try *inaka soba* – country soba – the house choice. ¥

Matsunoke-tei
20-1 Ekimoto-machi
Tel: 086-253-55410
Open 11am–10pm; closed Sun
A classy but moderately priced *kaiseki* restaurant that also offers some *shabu-shabu* selections. ¥¥¥¥

HIROSHIMA

Kanawa
On the Motoyasu River, a boat moored near the grounds of the Peace Park
Tel: 082-241-7416
Open 11am–2pm, 5–10pm; closed first and second Sun of month
Oysters are the great Hiroshima speciality, cultivated out on the bay on rafts. Every variety of serving method, from fried, steamed, marinated, raw, baked or in stews and soups. This floating restaurant has been here for nearly 40 years. ¥¥¥¥

Okonomimura
5-13 Shin Tenchi
Tel: 082-241-8758
Open daily 11.30am–midnight
After Osaka, Hiroshima is the main contender for Japan's best *okonomiyaki*, a pancake covered in seafood, meat, vegetables and lashings of sauces. The "mura" of the title means village, suggesting, with its 20-plus stalls to choose from, something like a Singaporean hawker centre. ¥

Suishin Restaurant
Tate-machi
Tel: 082-247-4411
A tiny but well-regarded sushi restaurant with all the usual choices. Specialises in *kamameshi* (rice casserole). These are augmented with oysters and, if you dare, blowfish. ¥¥¥¥

TAKAMATSU

Nicho
7-7 Hyakuma-cho
Tel: 087-851-7166
Open 11.30am–2pm, 5–9pm; closed Sun
A renowned *kaiseki* restaurant located in a traditional wooden house along a street of similarly elegant residences. Meals are served in individual private rooms. ¥¥¥¥

Wara-no-ie
91 Naka-machi, Yashima
Tel: 087-843-3115
Open daily 10am–7pm
Excellent value for *udon* noodles, simple sushi preparations and *tempura*, all in a converted thatch-roofed inn. ¥

Tenkatsu
7-8 Hyogo-machi
Tel: 087-821-5380
Open Mon–Fri 11am–2pm, Sat–Sun 11am–9pm
Well-renowned *tempura* and sushi restaurant. Sit at the counter that surrounds a sunken tank, filled with fish. Good-value set evening meals. ¥

FUKUOKA

Shin Miura
21-12 Sekijo-machi
Tel: 092-291-0821
Open noon–10pm
Shin Miura, located in a 100-year-old building, is *the* place to sample *mizutaki*, a sashimi chicken dish in which the poultry is slightly braised in soy, spring onion dipping sauce and vinegar. The main course includes a thick chicken and vegetable broth. ¥¥¥¥

Ume-no-hana
4-6-7 Nakasa
Tel: 092-262-3777
Open daily 11am–3pm, 5pm–2am
Popular restaurant offering light vegetarian and tofu dishes. ¥¥

Hard Rock Café Fukuoka
2-2-1 Jigyohama, Chuo-ko
Tel: 092-832-5050
Open Sun–Thur 11.30am–11pm, Fri & Sat 11.30am–3am
The usual rock'n'roll memorabilia lines the walls here in Fukuoka. Chicken wings, fajitas, nachos, burgers, steaks and ribs galore. ¥

NAGASAKI

Ichiriki
Suwa-machi
Tel: 0958-24-0226
Open daily noon–2pm, 5–7.30pm
Located along Teramachi Street, this atmospheric restaurant is known for a typical Nagasaki dish called *shippoku*, a combination of Japanese, Chinese and Western food made from stewed pork, sashimi, vegetables and soup. **¥¥¥¥¥**

Kouzanrou
12-2 Shinchi
Tel: 0958-24-5000
Open daily 11.30am–9pm
Befitting a port city with its own Chinatown, Chinese restaurants are a common feature. Kouzanrou's menu is extensive, from the humble *champon* noodle to the more elaborate, spicy Sichuanese fare. **¥¥¥**

Yosso
8-9 Hamacho
Tel: 0958-21-0001
Open daily 11am–8pm
Established in 1866, Yosso's speciality is *chawan mushi*, a warm egg-custard preparation that includes vegetables and small amounts of chicken. Also serves *chawan mushi teshoku*, which includes shrimp and eel steamed over rice. **¥¥**

KUMAMOTO

Goryohachi
1F, 12-8 Icho kaikan, Hanabatake-machi
Tel: 096-352-5751
The good folk of Kumamoto certainly like their food strong. Local dishes at moderate rates include *ba sashi* (raw horsemeat), Kumamoto-style sashimi, and side plates of *karashi renkon*, lotus root covered in mustard. **¥¥¥**

Okumura
1-8-8 Shin-machi
Tel: 096-352-88101
Open daily 11.30am–3pm, 5–10pm
A classic *kaiseki* restaurant, replete with all the tasteful design trappings and graceful service associated with this upper end of the eating scale. **¥¥¥¥**

Sando
1-9 Sutorimu Choanji, Suido-machi
Tel: 096-324-3571
Open 11am–2pm, 5–9pm; closed Tues
A straightforward no-frills steak house, serving locally raised beef as well as abalone. **¥¥¥¥**

Shankar
7-11 Kamitori-cho
Open daily 10.30am–11pm
Good-value Indian restaurant. **¥¥**

KAGOSHIMA

Gonbe-e
8-12 Higashi Sengoku-machi
Tel: 099-222-3867
Open 5–11pm; closed Sun
A small restaurant run by a friendly woman; the main fare here is homemade tofu. *Yu-dofu* is cooked at your table and served with a dipping sauce made from *yuzu* – Japanese citrus. **¥¥**

Kurobuta
6-17 Higashi Sengoku-cho
Tel: 099-224-8729
Open 11.30am–3pm, 5.30–10pm; closed Mon
Only select Kagoshima pork is used in the preparation of Kurobuta's *tonkatsu* dishes. The deep-fried pork cutlets are served in the traditional way with shredded cabbage and rice. **¥¥**

Satsuma
27-30 Chuo-machi
Tel: 099-252-2661
Open 11am–3pm, 5–11pm; closed Mon
The speciality here is *tonkotsu*, Kyushu-style noodles simmered in miso, *shochu* sauce and brown sugar. Garlic, vegetable and pork slices are added to the broth. **¥**

NAHA

Ayajo
3-25-13 Kumochi
Tel: 098-8861-7741
Open daily 5–10pm
A good introduction to the cuisine of the islands, dishes are served on the local Tsuboi earthenware, to the strains of Okinawan music. **¥¥¥**

Yunangi
3-3-3 Kumochi
Tel: 098-867-3765
Open daily noon–3pm, 5.30–10.30pm
Titbits of Okinawan food like bitter melon served with tofu and slices of ham are secondary to Yunangi's main function as a superb venue for testing *awamori*, the island's stronger version of sake. Set in a country-style restaurant. **¥¥**

ISHIGAKI

Iso
9 Okawa, opposite the harbour, behind the post office
Tel: 0980-82-7721
Open daily 11am–10.30pm
A good place to sample Yaeyama cuisine such as julienned pig's ear, goat stew and various intestinal soups, as well as more conventional dishes like pork stewed in ginger. **¥¥**

Yunta
9-2 Misaki-cho
Tel: 0980-82-7118
Open daily 11am–2pm, 5–10pm
One of the best spots on the island to try fresh fish. The set lunches are particularly good value. Diners tend to opt for the sushi and *sashimi* offerings in the evening. Perfect with a glass or two of fiery *awamori*. **¥¥**

Maru Hachi Soba
402-2 Tonoshiro
Sit at tables or on *tatami* mats. This is the place to go for a noodle experience. Pay a little bit more for noodles with pickles and rice. **¥**

La Vie
1-2-6 Hamazaki-cho
Tel: 0980-83-3402
European stylish restaurant with good set lunches. **¥¥**

PRICE CATEGORIES

Prices for three-course dinner per person without drinks and taxes:
¥ = Under ¥2,000
¥¥ = ¥2,000–3,000
¥¥¥ = ¥3,000–5,000
¥¥¥¥ = Over ¥5,000

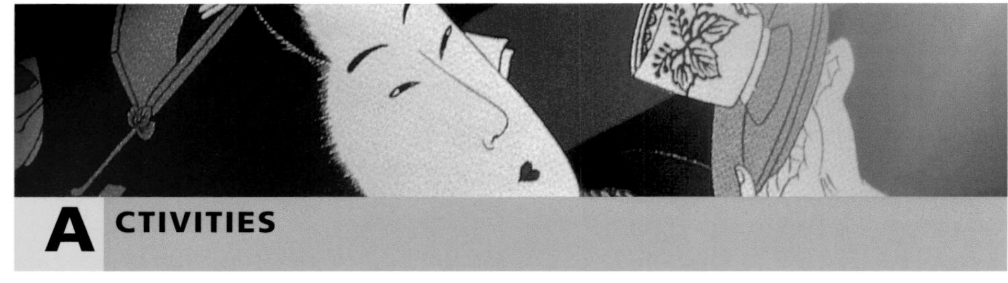

ACTIVITIES

THE ARTS, NIGHTLIFE, FESTIVALS, SHOPPING, SPORTS, SIGHTSEEING TOURS AND CHILDREN'S ACTIVITIES

THE ARTS

Traditional Theatre

Tokyo

National Theatre
4-1 Hayabusa-cho, Chiyoda-ku
Tel: 03-3265-7411 (enquiries), 03-3230-300 (reservations)
English-language summaries are included in programmes and headphone translations provided for the plots. Matinees begin at noon; evening performances from 4.40pm. When *kabuki* is not running, *bunraku* takes over.

Kabuki Theatre (Kabuki-za)
4-12-15 Ginza, Chuo-ku
Tel: 03-3541-3131 (information), 03-5565-6000 (tickets)

National Noh Theatre
4-18-1 Sendagaya, Shibuya-ku
Tel: 03-3423-1331
Only performed about once a week during the afternoon, so check beforehand. Japanese only.

Imperial Theatre
3-1-1 Marunouchi, Chiyoda-ku
Tel: 03-3213-7221
Classic plays, both old and contemporary.

Meiji Theatre (Meiji-za)
2-31-1 Nihonbashi-Hamacho, Chuo-ku
Tel: 03-3660-3939
Mainstream modern plays and samurai dramas. Japanese only.

Shimbashi Embujo
6-12-2 Ginza, Chuo-ku
Tel: 03-3541-2600
Low-brow sword and sorcery samurai dramas.

Other Cities

Gion Kobu Kaburenjo
1F Yasaka Kaikan, Kyoto, beside Gion Corner. Along a pedestrian lane between Shijo-dori and Higashioji-dori
Tel: 075-752-0225
Also known as Gion Corner, a daily digest of Japan's performing arts. Very touristy, but worth it if you don't have time for the real thing.

Kanze Kaikan
Niomon-dori, Kyoto
Tel: 075-771-6114
Noh and Kyogen performances in Kyoto's main venue for this high-performance art.

Minami-za
Corner of Kawabata-dori and Shijo-dori in Gion, Kyoto
Tel: 075-561-1155
Kyoto's long-established Kabuki theatre. December is the highlight, with a festival featuring all the big names in *kabuki*.

National Bunraku Theatre
Three-minute walk from Exit 7 of Nipponbashi Station on the Kintetsu or Sakaisuji subway lines, Osaka.
Tel: 06-6212-2531
Osaka's great puppet traditions performed in the months of Jan, Apr and June–Aug only.

Osaka Noh Hall
A short walk east of Hankyu Umeda Station
Tel: 06-6373-1726
A full programme of Noh dramas, including some free Saturday morning performances.

Osaka Shochiku-za
Dotombori Arcade
Tel: 06-6214-2211
Kabuki in a beautifully restored theatre beside Dotombori canal.

Other Theatres

Tokyo

Art Sphere
2-3-16 Higashi-Shinagawa, Shinagawa-ku
Tel: 03-5460-9999
An interesting location on Tennozu Isle for the latest in contemporary dance.

Session House
158 Yaraicho, Shinjuku-ku
Tel: 03-3266-0461
Experimental venue for Japanese and foreign solo dancers.

Tokyo Cynics
The Fiddler, Tajima Bldg B1F, 2-1-2 Takadanobaba, Shinjuku-ku
Tel: 03-3204-2698
Lunatic antics, skits and satire from a group of English-speaking comedians.

Concert Venues

Tokyo

Bunkamura Orchard Hall
2-24-1 Dogenzaka, Shibuya-ku 150
Tel: 03-3477-9150

Casals Hall
1-6 Kanda Surugadai, Chiyoda-ku
Tel: 03-3294-1229

Suntory Hall
1-13-1 Akasaka, Minato-ku
Tel: 03-3584-3100

Tokyo Opera City
3-2-2 Nishi-Shinjuku, Shinjuku-ku
Tel: 03-5353-0770

NIGHTLIFE

Rock & Pop

Japan has a vibrant live music scene with its own homegrown brand of music called J Pop. Top international acts, from the Beatles to Coldplay have performed in Japan, the world's second-largest music market. Besides concert halls and rock venues around the country like Tokyo Dome, Yokohama Stadium and Fukuoka Dome, domestic and foreign rock bands appear in clubs called "live houses".

Rock & Pop Venues

Tokyo

Akasaka Blitz
TBS Square, 5-3-6 Akasaka, Minato-ku
Tel: 03-5571-3088
Nippon Bukokan
2-1 Kitanomaru-koen, Chiyoda-ku
Tel: 03-3216-0781
Tokyo Dome (Big Egg)
1-1 Koraku, Bunkyo-ku
Tel: 03-5800-9999
Tokyo International Forum
3-5-1 Marunouchi, Chiyoda-ku
Tel: 03-5221-9000

Jazz & Live Music

Tokyo

Blue Note Tokyo
6-3-16 Minami-Aoyama, Minato-ku
Tel: 03-5485-0088
A sophisticated venue for top international acts. Despite the expensive entrance and drinks charges, the place is always full.
Body & Soul
B1, 6-13-9 Minami-Aoyama
Tel: 03-5466-3348
Good wine and cocktails to the sound of jazz.
Club Quattro
Parco Quattro, 5F, 32-13, Udagawa-cho, Shibuya-ku
Tel: 03-3477-8750
International rock bands play this club, which is up on the 5th floor of Parco department store.

Fukuoka

Blue Note
2-7-6 Tenjin
Tel: 092-715-6666
Followers of jazz will enjoy this sophisticated club in Fukuoka, a sister branch of the Tokyo one.
The Voodoo Lounge
3F, Tenjin Centre Building, 3-2-13 Tenjin
Tel: 92-432-4662
Trendy venue with live bands every night. Also sports TV.

Kyoto

Taku Taku
Tominokoji Bukkoji-sagaru
Tel: 075-351-1321
Appreciative audiences for live blues and rock. Modest cover charge includes one drink.

Okinawa

Chakra
Kokusai-dori
Tel: 098-869-0283
Traditional and Okinawan pop along Naha's Kokusai-dori. Open 7pm–2am.
Hinotama Holle
2-1-35 Higawa
Tel: 098-831-6101
Hip-hop, Latin and well-known local bands.

Osaka

Bears
B1 Shin-Nihon Namba Bldg, 3-14-5 Namba-naka
06-6649-5564
New, alternative live music. Moderate entrance fee.
Osaka Blue Note
B1 Ax Bldg, 2-3-21 Sonezaki-Shinchi
Tel: 06-6342-7722
Expensive but legendary jazz club; also hosts soul and R&B performers.

Clubs

Tokyo is the obvious venue for the club scene, though other cities around the country are trying to recreate the same atmosphere on a more modest scale. Japanese youth are very savvy about the newest movements in music, should you get into conversation with them.

Tokyo

Ageha
2-2-10 Shin-Kiba
Koto-ku
Tel: 03-5534-1515
Agheha is the name that bayside venue Studio Coast adopts at weekends when it becomes Tokyo's biggest dance club, with three separate dance rooms and a poolside bar. Hundreds of clubbers bus in from Shibuya for massive hip-hop, house, techno and trance parties.
Club Asia
1-8 Maruyama-cho
Shibuya-ku
Tel: 03-5458-5963
Multi-level dance floors and bars make this an interesting design venue. Phone before if possible, as they have quite a few private events.
Fai
B2F, 5-10-1 Minami-Aoyama, Minato-ku
Tel: 03-3486-4910
A wide range of sounds from the turntables here, but with definite 1970s and 80s leanings.
Lexington Queen
Third Goto Bldg, B1F, 3-13-14, Roppongi, Minato-ku
Tel: 03-3401-1661
This huge disco is the place where all the foreign celebs get taken while in town. Great fun.
Yellow
Cesaurius Nishi-Azabu Bldg, 1-10-11 Nishi Azabu, Minato-ku
Tel: 03-3476-0690
Strong on techno, new music and Brazilian jazz; also serves as a venue for parties and fashion events.
Velfarre
7-14-22 Roppongi, Minato-ku
Tel: 03-3402-8000
Supposedly the biggest disco in Asia; with a 2,000-person capacity. Several bars and a revolving stage. A good mix of locals and *gaijin*.

Hiroshima

Jacara
5F, Shatore No.3 Building, 13-13 Ginzan-cho, Naka-ku.
DJs play an eclectic mix of music at this friendly dance club.

Kyoto

Sekai
B1-B2 Imagium Building, Shijo Kawaramachi-agaru, Higashi-iru
Tel: 075-223-2965
Hip-hop, reggae and house music venue that hosts some quite big-name DJs. Usually warms up around 9pm.

Osaka

Underlounge
B1 634 Building, 2-7-11 Nishi-Shinsaibashi
Tel: 06-6214-3322
Japanese and overseas guest DJs play house, hip-hop and techno on the finest sound equipment.

Comedy

Tokyo

Punchline Comedy Club
Pizza Express
3F, 4-30-3 Jingumae
Shibuya-ku
Tel: 03-5775-3894.
The Tokyo branch of comedy entrepreneur John Moorhead's pan-Asian comedy club hosts top stand-up comedians from around the world.
Suehiro-tei
3-6-12 Shinjuku
Shinjuku-ku
Tel: 03-3351-2974
This atmospheric Japanese-style theatre features regular performances of *rakugoh*, Japan's art of comedic story-telling, as well as magic and origami paper-cutting. No English translation.

Bars & Pubs

Tokyo

Agave
7-15-10, Clover Bldg, B15, Roppongi, Minato-ku.
Tel: 03-3497-0229.
A Mexican and Latin inclination in the decor, music and astonishing selection of tequilas. Mojitos and

Tokyo *Sake* Spots

Akaoni
2-15-3, Sangenjaya
Setagaya-ku
Tel: 03-3410-9918
Open daily 5.30–11.30pm.
Serves fresh *sashimi* with a choice of over 100 different sakes.
Sakana-tei
2-23-15, Dogenzaka
Shibuya-ku
Tel: 03-3780-1313
Open Mon–Sat 5.30pm–1am.
Small and reasonably priced, this large selection of sake comes with optional side dishes.
Sake Plaza
1-1-21 Nishi-Shinbashi
Minato-ku
Tel: 03-3519-2091
Open Mon–Fri 10am–6pm.
The best place to start, with over 1,000 brands on offer, and daily sake tasting. Has an extensive library with books and videos on the subject.
Sake no Ana
3-5-8, Rangetsu Bldg., B1F, Ginza, Chuo-ku
Tel: 03-3567-1133
Open Mon–Sat 5.30pm–1am.
Sake representing every prefecture in Japan. A little expensive.
Sasagin
1-32-15, Yoyogi-Uehara, Shibuya-ku
Tel: 03-5454-3715
Open Mon–Sat 5–11.30pm
Roughly 80 brands of excellent-quality sake are available along with excellent food and titbits in this elegant and very ambient location.

daiquiris, and the other rum and pineapple stingers suggest strong Caribbean leanings.
Geronimo
7-14-10, 2F, Roppongi, Minato-ku.
Tel: 03-3478-7449.
Open 11–1am.
A short stroll from Exit 4 of Roppongi Station, this is a very popular shot bar for both expats and local business people. Gets quite crowded during happy hour (6–8pm).
Old Imperial Bar
1-1-1, Uchhisaiwai-cho, Hibiya, Chiiyoda-ku.
Tel: 03-3504-1111.
Open 10am–midnight.
A legendary bar in the Imperial Hotel. Part of the building has been preserved from the original Lloyd Wright design that was lost in the 1960s. Everyone from Igor Stravinsky to Tom Wolfe has patronised this bar.
The Aldgate
World Bldg, B1, 12-9 Udagawa-cho, Shibuya-ku.
Tel: 03-34662-2983.
Open 5pm–2am.
A home from home for London Eastenders. Besides the usual fish 'n' chips, the Aldgate has vegetarian dishes. Claims to have the world's best collection of British rock CDs. Features all the big football matches on TV.
The Dubliners' Irish Pub
Shinagawa Mitsubishi Bldg, Grand Passage, B1F, 2-16-3 Kounan, Minato-ku.
Tel: 03-6718-2834.
Open 11.30am–11pm.
Authentic pub grub in the form of fish 'n' chips, Irish stew and cottage pie. Guinness, Kilkenny and more on tap. Also a decent cocktail bar. Live music. Branches in Nishi-Azabu, Shinjuku, Shibuya.
The Pink Cow
Villa Moderna, B1, 1-3-18, Shibuya, Shibuya-ku.
Tel: 03-3406-5597.
Open 11am–midnight.
Beloved of the art, fashion and media crowd, the Pink Cow offers a good range of wine, beers, cocktails as well as food. Drinking is often accompanied by special events like poetry readings, jazz recitals, book launches and art exhibitions.

Fukuoka

Happy Cock
9F, 2-1-51 Daimyo
Very popular bar, serving a nice range of dishes from Thai and Mexican to pizzas.
Off Broadway
2F, Tenjin Centre Building, 3-2-13 Tenjin
In the heart of the lively Tenjin district, a popular bar whose house music is mostly Latin and reggae.

Hiroshima

El Barco & Barco Tropical
3F, Sanwa Building 2, Yagembori 7-9
Latin mood music and tropical cocktails set the scene for this relaxed bar.
Molly Malone
4F, Teigeki Building, Chuo-dori
Excellent Irish pub fare and beer. A sociable place to meet up with locals and expats.

Kagoshima

Taiheiyo Biru-kan
Izumi-cho
Down by the harbour, this old storehouse is the perfect venue for this micro-brewery and beer restaurant.

Kyoto

Cock-a-hoop
7F, Empire Building, Kiyamachi Sanjo-agaru.
Tel: 075-221 4939
A friendly and cheap bar with lots of Latin sounds. Attractive riverside location.
Hub
71, Daikoku-cho, Kawaramachi Sanjo-sagaru.
Tel: 075-212 9027
A British pub chain, which, besides the usual range of ales, has a nifty selection of cocktails.
Tadg's Irish Pub & Restaurant
2F Oto Bldg, Keihan Shijo Station, Exit 8.
Tel: 075-525 0680
Good reliable pub food and booze in a relaxed atmosphere.

Okinawa

Helios
Matsuo, Kokusai-dori.
Tel: 098-863 7227
A small bar specialising in local micro-brews.

Osaka

Canopy
IM Excellence Building, 1-11-20, Sonezaki-Shinchi.
Tel: 06-6341 0339
Near Higashi-Umeda Station, a friendly mix of Japanese and foreigners patronise this cheap and popular bar.

Sapporo

Habana
Minami 3, Nishi 5,3F
Live Latin music, salsa parties and spicy food.
King Xhmu
Minami 7, Nishi 4
Rather expensive entrance charge includes two drinks. Techno music mostly.
Miss Jamaica
Minami 3, Nishi 6
A cool Caribbean bar featuring reggae, rum and tequila at affordable prices.

FESTIVALS

Festivals, or *matsuri*, seem to be happening at any given time somewhere in Tokyo, and indeed have been an important part of Japanese life for hun dreds of years. Many of the festivals have their roots in the long history of Japan's agricultural society. In today's ever modernising Japan, they are one of the few occasions when the Japanese can dress up and relive the past. Below is a short list of the main national holidays and the most important festivals. For information on forthcoming events going on during any particular week or month, please consult the Tourist Information Centre *(see page 390)* or any of the tourist publications.

January

The first ***sumo*** tournament of the year, ***Hatsu-basho***, is held for 15 days at Tokyo's **Kokugikan** in mid-January. **Shujin-no-hi** (Adults' Day), falls on the second Monday of January, when 20-year olds visit shrines in their finest kimonos.

February

On the 3rd is ***Setsubun***, the traditional bean-throwing ceremony that is meant to purify the home of evil. Roasted beans are scattered from the inside of the house to the outside while people shout, "*Oni wa soto*" (Devils, go out!), and from the outside of the home to the inside while "*Fuku wa uchi*" (good luck, come in) is shouted. The same ceremony is also held at temples and shrines. **Plum Viewing** festivals begin in early to late February. The most famous viewing spot in Tokyo, Yushima Tenjin shrine, holds *ikebana* and tea-ceremony displays at this time. Sapporo's famous **Yuki Matsuri** (Snow Festival) on the 5th–11th, features giant statues sculpted from snow and ice.

March

On the 3rd is ***Hina Matsuri*** (Girls' Day), a festival for little girls. Small *Hina* dolls, representing imperial court figures, are decorated and displayed at home and in several public places. *Yamabushi* mountain monks perform the **Fire-Walking Ceremony** in mid-March at the foot of Mount Takao outside Tokyo. Spectators can test their mettle by walking barefoot across the smouldering coals of the fires. Many shrines throughout Japan have their **Daruma Fairs** on 3–4 March, selling red, white and black dolls of the famous Zen monk. One of the two empty eyes should be painted in upon undertaking a new, difficult task, the other filled in upon its successful completion.

April

From early to mid-April is ***O-hanami*** (cherry-blossom viewing), one of the important spring rites. People love to turn out and picnic, drink *sake* and sing songs under the pink blossoms. Kyoto has a multitude of blossom-viewing parties, the most famous being at Daigo-ji. On the 8th is ***Hana Matsuri*** (Birthday of Buddha), when commemorative services are held at various temples such as Gokoku-ji, Senso-ji, Zojo-ji and Hommon-ji. A colourful display of horseback archery is put on by men dressed in medieval costumes during the **Yabusame Festival** in Sumida Park in mid-April. Acrobatic marionettes balance on towering festival floats as they are carried across the bridges of the town in the **Takayama Festival** from 14–15 April.

May

In mid May, the ***Natsu-basho*** (summer ***sumo*** tournament) is held for 15 days at the Kokugikan in Tokyo. On the 3rd Saturday and Sunday, the ***Sanja Matsuri*** is held. This is one of the big Edo festivals honouring the three fishermen who found the image of Kannon in the river. Tokyo's **Asakusa-jinja Senso-ji** temple is a great place to go at this time to see the dancing, music and many portable shrines. In mid-May the huge **Kanda Festival**, one of Tokyo's most important *matsuri*, is held every other year. Processions and floats and portable shrines parade through this downtown area. A fine historical costume parade takes place in Kyoto during the 15 May **Aoi Matsuri** (Hollyhock Festival).

June

The summer rains blanket Kyoto from mid-June to mid-July. **Kifune-jinja**, dedicated to the god of water, celebrates the season in a vibrant water festival. Torchlight performances of *noh* plays are held 1–2 June at the Heian Shrine. On the second Sunday is ***Torigoe Jinja Taisai***, a night-time festival, when the biggest and heaviest portable shrine in Tokyo is carried through the streets by lantern light. It all happens at the Torigoe Shrine. From the 10th to the 16th is ***Sanno Sai***, another big Edo festival featuring a *gyoretsu* (people parading in traditional costumes) on Saturday at the Hie Shrine. June is the season for **iris viewing**, one of the best locations being the Iris Garden in the grounds of the Meiji shrine in Tokyo.

July

From the 6th to the 8th is the ***Asagao Ichi*** (Morning Glory Fair) in Tokyo, when over one hundred merchants set up stalls selling the morning flower at Iriya Kishibojin. On the 7th is the ***Tanabata Matsuri***, a festival celebrating the only day of the year when, according to the legend, the Weaver Princess (Vega) and her lover the Cowherder (Altair) can cross the Milky Way to meet. People write their wishes on coloured paper, hang them on bamboo branches, and then float them down a river the next day. Also in Tokyo, on

Traditional Tea Ceremony (in English)

Nothing expresses Japanese formality and emphasis on social protocol more effectively than the tea ceremony. Although tea drinking appeared early in Japanese history, it was not until the 12th century that the special strain of the tea bush and the technique of making powdered green tea *(matcha)* were brought from China. Making the tea is not the challenge; it is making it in the right spirit that consumes a lifetime of effort. Implements and procedures have value only towards a higher objective – the ability to show sublime hospitality. Experience it for yourself.

Chado Kaikan, 3-39-17 Takadanobaba, Shinjuku-ku, Tokyo. Tel: 03-3361-2446. 15-minute walk from Takadanobaba Station or take a bus for Otakibashi-Shako to Takadanobaba 4-chome stop. Open Mon–Thur 10.30am–2.30pm. Closed on holidays. Fee, 1-hour. Advanced reservation is required.

Imperial Hotel (Toko-an), 1-1-1 Uchisaiwai-cho, Chiyoda-ku, Tokyo. (4F, the Main Wing). Tel: 03-3504-1111, ext.5858. Near Hibiya Station on Hibiya, Chiyoda, or Toei Mita Line. Open Mon–Sat 10am–4pm. Fee, 20-minute participation periods. Advanced reservation is required.

Kenkyusha Nihongo Centre, 1-2 Kagurazaka, Shinjuku-ku, Tokyo. Tel: 03-5261-8940. 5-minute walk from the west exit of Lidabashi Station on JR Sobu Line, or the B-3 exit of Iidabashi Station on Yurakucho or Tozai Line. Open Mon 6–8pm, Fri 2–4pm or 6–8pm. Fee, 2-hour participation periods. Advanced reservation is required.

Urasenke Tea School, Urasenke Foundation Chado Research Centre. Tel: 075-431-6474. e-mail: info@urasenke.or.jp. Information on events.

the 9th and 10th is the ***Hozuki Ichi*** (Ground Cherry Fair) at Senso-ji from early morning to midnight. A visit to this temple on the 10th is meant to be equal to 46,000 visits at other times. On the last Saturday of July, the ***Sumida-gawa Hanabi Taikai*** (Sumida River Fireworks) is held. This is the biggest fireworks display in Tokyo, and the best places to watch the display are between the Kototoi and Shirahige bridges, or at the Komagata Bridge. Fukuoka's pride and joy, its **Hakata Yamagasa**, takes place 1–15 July, an event that sees colourful portable shrines carried through the streets. Kyoto's grandest event, the 17 July **Gion Matsuri**, features massive floats hung with fine silks and paper lanterns.

August

Late July/early August hosts a more contemporary event that is fast becoming a tradition: international and local acts gather for the huge, three-day **Fuji Rock Festival** in Naeba. Between the 13th and the 16th is the ***Obon*** festival, when people return to their hometowns to clean up graves and offer prayers to the souls of departed ancestors. The traditional ***Bon Odori*** folk dances are held all over around this time. The best known, running for almost two months, is in Gujo Hachiman. The largest single turnout of dancers is in Tokushima. Both Aomori and Hirosaki hold **Nebuta and Neputa Matsuri** from 1–7 August. Giant paper figures are lit up from inside like lanterns. The most renowned Bon-Odori summer dances are held in Tokushima during its **Awa Odori**.

September

Mid-September is the time for moon-viewing, with many events across Kyoto. Osawa Pond has been known since Heian times as one of Japan's three great moon-viewing sites.

October

From mid to late October is chrysanthemum-viewing time, and there are flower displays dotted around the cities. Nagasaki's **Okunchi Matsuri**, from 7–9 October, is an interesting blend of Chinese, European and Shinto, with dragon dances and floats representing Dutch galleons. Kyoto's **Jidai Matsuri**, on 22 October, is a splendid, quietly dignified costume parade.

November

The 15th is ***Shichi-Go-San*** (Seven-Five-Three), a ceremony for 5-year-old boys and 3- and 7-year-old girls. The children usually dress up in *kimono* and hakama *(loose trousers)* and are taken to visit a shrine.

December

Kaomise (face-showing) is Kyoto's gala *kabuki* performance at Minami-za, when the actors reveal their real faces. 7th–8th, Senbon Shaka-do celebrates the day of Buddha's enlightenment with a **radish-boiling ceremony** to help ward off evil. The 14th is ***Gishi Sai***, a memorial service for the famous 47 Ronin who, on this day in 1702, avenged the death of their master and later committed ritual suicide. They are buried at the Sengaku-ji in Tokyo, where the service is held. On the 31st at the stroke of midnight, every temple bell in the country begins to toll. The bells toll 108 times, for the 108 evil human passions. This is called ***Joya no Kane***, and the general public are allowed to strike the bells at various temples.

SHOPPING

Japan is a very expensive place to shop, but there are still bargains to be had if you seek them out. The high quality of Japanese products is well known, and there are some items that can only be bought in Japan. Certain areas promote only particular kinds of merchandise, which means that some domestic travel is involved for the serious shopper. Following is a guide to the main shopping attractions in the cities and other areas throughout Japan.

In and Around Tokyo

Akihabara: the electronic jungle of the world featuring hundreds of discount stores.
Aoyama: high-class fashion boutiques.
Asakusa: traditional Japanese toys, souvenirs, workmen's clothes, etc.
Daikanyama: a newish addition to Tokyo's fashion scene, with many boutiques targeting the 20–30s age group.
Ginza: the most expensive shopping centre. Several major department stores are located here, such as Hankyu, Matsuya, Matsuzakaya, Mitsukoshi, Printemps, Seibu and Wako, and exclusive boutiques. Also some traditional Japanese goods stores.
Harajuku: another fashion area, though mostly geared to the young, which makes shopping relatively cheap. Several antiques shops, and Kiddyland for the kids.
Hibiya: mostly antiques shops, jewellery shops, and art galleries.
Kanda and **Jimbocho**: many second-hand bookstores.
Naka Meguro: one of the latest fashion towns. Affordable clothing; very trendy.
Nihombashi: a good place to pick up traditional craft work. Two of Japan's oldest department stores, Mitsukoshi and Takashi-maya are located here.
Roppongi: several antiques shops in the area, the Axis design building which features interior design as its main theme, and Seibu's Wave building which specialises in audio-visual equipment.
Shibuya: a good place to start with, Shibuya has a little bit of everything. Tokyu Hands is a must to visit; probably the most complete do-it-yourself department store in the world. Also here are the Seibu, Tokyu and Marui departments stores, the Parco "fashion buildings" besides the hundreds of small boutiques geared to young shoppers.
Shimokitazawa: popular with Tokyo youth, Shimokita is a Mecca for art cafés, avant-garde theatre, and small shops selling dead stock, hand-me-downs and grungy student ware.
Shinjuku: several big camera and electronic discount stores such as Yodobashi and Sakuraya. Also, Isetan and Marui department stores.
Ueno: Ameyoko is good for cheap food, cosmetics, clothing and toys. One of the few open markets in Tokyo. The shops in the back streets sell traditional Japanese goods.

Antiques

In most of the shops listed here, the staff speak English and are helpful. Watch out for badly restored pieces that have been given a quick coat of glossy lacquer and are sold like new.
Antique Gallery Kikori, Hanae Mori Building, B1, 3-6-1 Kita Aoyama, Minato-ku. Tel: 03-3407-9363. Small but interesting selection of *tansu* and other items.
Antique Gallery Meguro, Stork Building, 2nd Fl, 2-24-18 Kamiosaki, Shinagawa-ku. Tel: 03-3493-1971. Antiques market of sorts covering 740 sq. metres (885 sq. yards) that houses several small antiques shops.
Edo Antiques, 2-21-12 Akasaka, Minato-ku. Tel: 03-3584-5280. Large selection of *tansu* and *hibachi.*
Fuji-Torii, 6-1-10 Jingumae, Shinjuku-ku. Tel: 03-3400-2777. High-quality store specialising in screens and Imari porcelain.
Japan Old Folkcraft and Antique Centre (Tokyo Komingu Kotto-kan), 3-9-5 Minami Ikebukuro, Toshima-ku.

Tel: 03-3980-8228. 35 dealers covering 600 sq. metres (718 sq. yards) and displaying various antique items.
Oriental Bazaar, 5-9-13 Jingumae, Shibuya-ku. Tel: 03-3400-3933. Apart from antiques, this is also a nice place to browse and pick up traditional Japanese toys, paper *(washi)*, kimono, etc.

Bookshops

There are bookshops all over Tokyo, and it is quite acceptable to browse through the books and magazines in the shop without having to buy them. In spite of the large number of bookstores, there are relatively few that specialise in English books. Below is a list of the major shops in Tokyo that stock foreign books and books on Japan. Besides these places, you can also get foreign newspapers and magazines in most hotels.
Aoyama Book Centre. Tel: 03-3479-0479. Open daily 10–5.30am; Sun and holidays 10am–10pm. One minute from Roppongi Station (Hibiya Line).
Book 1st, 33-5 Udagawa-cho, Shibuya-ku. Tel: 03-3770-1023. Over 1,300 magazine titles on the 1st floor of this new bookstore, with English books are stocked on the 3rd floor.
Good Day Books, 3F, 1-11-2, Eisu, Sibuya-ku. Tel: 03-5421-0957. Tokyo's largest and best-used bookstore; some new books also.
Kinokuniya, 3-17-7 Shinjuku, Shinjuku-ku. Tel: 03-3354-0131. Open 10am–7pm. Closed 3rd Wed of each month. Foreign books on the 6th floor. Very popular.
Kitazawa Shoten, 2-5-3 Kanda Jimbocho, Chiyoda-ku. Tel: 03-3263-0011. Open 10am–6pm. Closed Sun. Second-hand books on the 2nd floor, and English literature on the 1st floor.
Libro (Ikebukuro Branch), 1-28-1 Minami Ikebukuro, Toshima-ku (Seibu Dept. sma bif, B2F). Tel: 03-5992-8800. Open daily 10am–8pm, except Tues.
Manga no Mori, 12-10, Udagawa-cho, Shibuya-ku. Tel: 03-5489-0257; www.manganomori.net. Top manga collection, with just about every post-war Japanese character featured. Other branches in Shinjuku and Higashi Ikebukuro. Open daily 11am–9pm.
Maruzen, 2-3-10 Nihombashi, Chuo-ku. Tel: 03-3272-7211. Open 10am–6pm. Closed Sun. Foreign books on the 3rd floor. Very popular.
Sanseido Books, Kanda-Jimbocho, Ciyoda-ku. Tel: 03-3233-3312. Good all-round store.
Tower Records Shibuya, 1-22-14 Jinnan, Shibuya-ku. Tel: 03-3496-3661. Interesting alternative selection of books, with extensive foreign magazines and papers.
Yaesu Book Centre, 2-5-1 Yaesu, Chuo-ku. Tel: 03-3281-1811. Large selection of general books. Located next to Tokyo Station; there's another store in Yebisu Garden Place.
Yurindo Landmark Plaza Store, Landmark Plaza, 5F, 2-2-1-2 Minato-Mirai, Nishi-ku, Yokohama. Tel: 04-5222-55000. Open 11am–8pm.

Ceramics

Besides workshops, department stores are the best places for Japanese ceramics offered at reasonable prices. On back streets, small shops also sell ceramics but prices are higher.
Iseryu Shoten, 3-8-2 Ningyocho, Nihombashi, Chuo-ku. Tel: 03-3661-4820. Closed Sundays and holidays.
Saga Toen, 2-13-13 Nishi Azabu, Minato-ku. Tel: 03-3400-3682.
Tachikichi & Co. Ltd, 6-13 Ginza, Chuo-ku. Tel: 03-3571-2924.

Department Stores

Daimaru, 1-9-1 Marunouchi, Chiyoda-ku. Tel: 03-3212-8011. Closed Thur.
Isetan, 3-14-1 Shinjuku, Shinjuku-ku. Tel: 03-3352-1111. Closed Wed.
Marui, 3-30-16 Shinjuku, Shinjuku-ku. Tel: 03-3354-0101. Open 10.30am–7.30pm.
Matsuya, 3-6-1 Ginza, Chuo-ku. Tel: 03-3567-1211.
Matsuzakaya, 3-29-5 Ueno, Taito-ku. Tel: 03-3832-1111.
Mitsukoshi, 1-7-4 Muromachi, Nihom-bashi, Chuo-ku. Tel: 03-3241-3311. Closed Mon.
Printemps, 3-2-1 Ginza, Chuo-ku. Tel: 03-3567-0077. 10am–7pm. Closed Wed.
Seibu (Main Store), 1-28-1 Minami Ikebukuro, Toshima-ku. Tel: 03-3981-0111. Closed Thur.
Takashimaya, 2-4-1 Nihombashi, Chuo-ku. Tel: 03-3211-4111. Closed Wed.
Tokyu, 2-24-1 Dogenzaka, Shibuya-ku. Tel: 03-3477-3111. Closed Thur.

Electronics & Cameras

Bic Camera, 1-11-7, Higashi-Ikebukuro, Toshima-ku. Tel: 03-988-0002. Large chain with stores all over Tokyo. Open daily 10am–8pm.
Laox, 1-2-9, Soto-Kanda, Chiyoda-ku. Tel: 03-3255-9041. Massive discount chain store with English-speaking staff. Open daily 10am–7.30pm.
Sakuraya Camera, 3-17-2, Shinjuku, Shinjuku-ku. Tel: 03-3354-3636. Giant retailer with similar price range and selection as Yodobashi Camera. Open daily 10am–8pm.

Flea Markets

An alternative to department-store shopping, flea markets, often located in shrine or temple compounds, offer a colourful experience.
Arai Yakushi Temple, Arai Yakushi-mae Station on the Seibu Shinjuku Line in Tokyo. Every second Sunday.
Hanazono Shrine Antiques Market, 5-17-3, Shinjuku, Shinjuku-ku, Tokyo. Tel: 03-3200-3093. On the edge of Kabukicho, a popular market running from 7am–5pm every Sunday.
Heiwajima Kotto Fair, 6-1-1, Heiwajima, Heiwajima Tokyo Ryutsu Building, Center, 2F, Tokyo. Tel: 03-3980-8228. A giant, three-day flea market and antiques fair held five times a year. Phone to confirm schedule.
Nogi Shrine Flea Market, 8-11-27, Akasaka, Minato-ku, Tokyo. Tel: 03-3478-3001. Pleasant shrine location for this once-monthly market. Second Sunday of month, 5am–4pm.
Setagaya Boro-Ichi, Boro Ichi-Dori Street, Setagaya. Near Setagaya station. Tel: 03-3411-6663. Tokyo's best-known flea market, a huge affair dating back to the 1570s. Held 15–16 Jan and 15–16 Dec.
Togo Shrine Flea Market, 1-5-3, Jingumae, Shibuya-ku. Tel: 03-3403-3591. Held in shrine precincts, a huge market every first, fourth and fifth Sunday, weather permitting. Open 4am–3pm.
To-ji. The famous wooden pagoda of this temple south of Kyoto Station hosts the city's best Sunday-morning flea market.

Softmap, 3-14-10, Kami-Kanda, Chiyoda-ku. Tel: 03-5609-6597 Akihabara's premier computer discount store. New and used PCs and Macs. Open daily 10.30am–8pm, until 7pm Sun.

Japanese Paper (Washi)

Haibara, 2-7-6 Nihombashi, Chuo-ku. Tel: 03-3272-3801. Closed Sun and holidays.
Isetatsu, 2-18-9 Yanaka, Taito-ku. Tel: 03-3823-1453.
Kurodaya, 1-2-5 Asakusa, Taito-ku. Tel: 03-3844-751. Closed Mon.
Kyukyodo, 5-7-4 Ginza, Chuo-ku. Tel: 03-3571-4429.
Ozu Shoten, 2-6-3 Nihombashi Honcho, Chuo-ku. Tel: 03-3663-8788. Closed Sun.

Tsutsumo Factory, 137-15, Udagawacho, Shibuya-ku. Tel: 03-5478-1330. *Tsutsumo* means "to wrap" in Japanese. Traditional and modern designs in wrapping paper. Also has nice cards, some in thick, *washi* paper.

Kimonos (antique)

These shops specialise in antique kimono, *obi*, traditional blue and white textiles, *furoshiki*, *hanten*, etc. Prices from ¥1,000 up.

Flea markets also sell them, and you can usually pick up very beautiful old kimono and *obi* in good condition.

Hayashi Kimono, International Arcade, 1-7 Uchisaiwaicho, Chiyoda-ku. Tel: 03-3581-3591.
Ikeda, 5-22-11 Shiroganedai, Minato-ku. Tel: 03-3445-1269. Closed Sun.
Konjaku Nishimura, Hanae Mori Building, B1, 3-6-1 Kita Aoyama, Minato-ku. Tel: 03-3498-1759. Closed Thur.

Fans (Sensu)

Bunsendo, 1-30 Asakusa, Taito-ku. Tel: 03-841-0088. Open 10am–7pm. On a lane to the left of Nakamise, the shop-lined approach to the great Senso-ji temple has an exquisite collection of traditional fans.
Kyosendo, 2-4-3, Nihonbashi, Ningyocho, Chuo-ku. Tel: 03-3669-0046. Open Mon–Sat 10am–7pm. Located in Tokyo's business centre, a tiny world of aesthetic sensibilities can be found in this famous shop.
Wan'ya Shoten, 3–9, Kanda-Jimbocho, Chiyoda-ku. Tel: 03-3263-6771. Open daily 9.30am–5.30pm. Also specialises in Noh masks. There is a second branch in the Ginza.

Fashion Boutiques & Buildings

Japan cuts a very high profile when it comes to fashion, importing the best and creating its own world-respected designs. Multi-storey fashion buildings, each floor crammed with boutiques and outlets, are a unique feature of Japanese cities.

109, 2-29-1, Dogenzaka, Shibuya-ku. Tel: 03-3477-5111. Unmissable, silo-shaped silver building, the 109 is a Mecca of Shibuya chic.
Bell Commons, 2-14-6, Kita Aoyama, Minato-ku. Tel: 03-475-8111. Well-established fashion building with other attractions like cafés and galleries installed.
Comme Ça Store, 3-26-6, Shinjuku, Shinjuku-ku. Tel: 03-5367-5551. Popular Shinjuku store that opens until 9pm.
Final Home, 15-1, Udagawa-cho, Shibuya-ku. Tel: 03-3477-5922. Provocative clothing for modern urbanites.
Laforet Harajuku, 1-11-6, Jingumae, Shibuya-ku. Tel: 03-3475-0411. Major fashion building housing about 100 boutiques. Strictly for the young.
Parco, 15-1, Udagawa-cho, Shibuya-ku. Tel: 03-3464-5111. Many branches of this department store in Japan offering a wide selection of smart and stylish clothing.
Uniqlo, 6-10-8, Jingumae, Shibuya-ku. Tel: 03-5468-7313. Fashionable discount chain with branches all over.
Yohji Yamamoto, 5-3-6, Minami Aoyama, Minato-ku. Tel: 03-3409-6006. Classy designer store with prices to match.

Lacquerware (Shikki)

Bushi, Axis Building, B1 5-17-1 Roppongi, Minato-ku. Tel: 03-3587-0317. Closed Mon.
Heiando, 3-10-11 Nihombashi, Chuo-ku. Tel: 03-3272-2871. Closed Sun and public holidays.
Inachu Japan, 1-5-2 Akasaka, Minato-ku. Tel: 03-3582-4451.
Kuroeya, Kuroeya Kokubu Building, 2nd Floor, 1-2-6 Nihombashi, Chuo-ku. Tel: 03-3271-3356. Closed Sat, Sun and public holidays.

Musical Instruments

Bachi Ei Gakkiten *(Shamisen)*, 2-10-11 Ningyocho, Nihombashi, Chuo-ku. Tel: 03-3666-7263. Closed Sun and holidays.
Kikuya Shamisen Ten *(Shamisen)*, 3-45-11 Yushima, Bunkyo-ku. Tel: 03-3831-4733. Closed Sun and holidays.
Tsurukawa Gakki Honten *(Koto)*, 1-12-11 Kyobashi, Chuo-ku. Tel: 03-3561-1872. Closed Sun and holidays.
Ishida Biwa Ten *(Biwa)*, 3-8-4 Toranomon, Minato-ku. Tel: 03-3431-6548. Closed Sun and holidays.
Miyamoto Unosuke Shoten *(drums)*, 6-1-15 Asakusa, Taito-ku. Tel: 03-3874-4131. Closed Sun and public holidays.

Paper Lanterns

Hanato, 2-25-6 Asakusa, Taito-ku. Tel: 03-3841-6411. Open 10am–9pm. Closed 2nd and 4th Tuesdays.
Kashiwaya, 2-3-13 Shintomi, Chuo-ku. Tel: 03-3551-1362. Closed Sun.

Umbrellas (Kasa)

Hasegawa Hakimonoten, 2-4-4 Ueno, Taito-ku. Tel: 03-3831-3933. Closed Sun.
Iidaya, 1-31-1 Asakusa, Taito-ku. Tel: 03-3841-3644.

Woodblock Print (Ukiyo-e)

Asakusa Okuramae Shobo, 3-10-12 Kuramae, Taito-ku. Tel: 03-3866-5894. Closed Sun, but will stay open for appointments. Specialist on books and prints on *Edo* and sumo.
Hara Shobo, 2-3 Jimbocho, Kanda, Chiyoda-ku. Tel: 03-3261-7444. All types of prints old and new, from the highest quality to a "bargain drawer". English is spoken here.
Matsushita Associates, Inc., 6-3-12 Minami Aoyama, Shibuya-ku. Tel: 03-3407-4966. Closed Sun.
Oya Shobo, 1-1 Kanda, Jimbocho, Chiyoda-ku. Tel: 03-3291-0062. Closed Sun.
Sakai Kokodo Gallery, 1-2-14 Yurakucho, Chiyoda-ku. Tel: 03-3591-4678.

Outside Tokyo

Within Tohoku

Matsushima
Shiogama Suisan Nakaoroshi Ichiban: morning market.
Owariya, in front of Suigen-ji: wind bells.
Aomori
Murata Kogei-sha, Shinmachi Dori: local crafts.
Morioka
Kyabatake, near Minami Ohashi on the Kitagami River, open daily from 5am: morning market.
Zaimoku-cho, every Saturday, April–Nov 3–9pm: night market
Iwachu, Nanbu Tekki: local iron crafts.
Iizaka Spa
Kodai Gangu, Nihonmatsu: local crafts.

On Hokkaido

Hakodate
Chiaki-kan, in Horai-cho: handmade Japanese confections.
Noboribetsu
Kagetsu Do, Hyotan Ame: Japanese sweets, gifts and souvenirs.
Akan National Park
Rakan, on Route 240: local crafts.
Akan Kohan Visitor Centre: local crafts.

Within Kansai

Ise
Akafuku Honten, near Ise Naiguu: Japanese confections, souvenirs.
Nara
Ikeda Gankohdo: Nara fans.
Somekawa Hakurokuen: Nara dolls.
Kyoto
Kawaramachi, main north-south street: **Matsuya**, Kawaramachi Dori Kyoto dolls.
Kiyamachi (parallels the Takase River, north–south): **Murakami Ju-honten**, at the end of 4-jo Dori: Japanese pickles; **Tachibana Syokai**, antiques.
Teramachi (downtown arcade), **Ippodo**: tea and accessories;

Kyukyodo: Japanese stationery; **Miyawaki Baisen-an**: fans.
Shijyo, main east-west street, **Erizen**: kimono and accessories; **Ichihara Heibei Shoten**: chopsticks; **Morita Wash**: paper crafts.
Arashiyama: Ishikawa Taki no Mise: bamboo crafts.
Kobe
Hon Takasagoya, Motomachi Dori 3-2-11: colourful gift items, souvenirs and Japanese confections.

In Southern Honshu

Himeji
Azumadou: Kawahara Shoutengai: Japanese confections.
Hagi
Ochadokoro: near Kikuya Yokocho: Japanese tea and confections.

On Shikoku

Tokushima
Fujiya: Japanese confections.
Aigura, Nishishinmachi Arcade: local crafts.
Kochi
Kitaura, Konyacho: dyed goods.
Tosa Mingei Ten: folk handicrafts.

On Kyushu

Nagasaki
Art Hata, in Kajiya-cho: original Nagasaki dolls.
Beppu Spa
Kishima: bamboo crafts.
Kagoshima
Satsuma Glass Kogei, near Shuseikan: local glass crafts.

On Okinawa

Naha
Hirugi, Keizairen Mingei Centre 2F, Kokusai Dori: Ryukyuan dishes, dances; crafts for sale.
Morita Sango no Mise, Kokusai Dori: Okinawan coral jewellery.
Okinawa City
Chuo Park Avenue: more than 100 shops and restaurants.

SPORTS

Spectator Sports

Sumo Tournaments

Six tournaments annually, each lasting for 15 days, are held in January, May and September in Tokyo, in March in Osaka, in July in Nagoya, and in November in Fukuoka. During the tournament, matches are televised daily from 4–6pm. Matches by junior wrestlers begin at about 10am; by senior wrestlers at 3pm on the first and the last days, and at 3.30pm on other days. Don't expect to sit close to the ring, or *dohyo*. These seats are expensive and are usually booked by large corporations or the very wealthy.

Tokyo
January, May and September: Kokugikan Sumo Hall, 1-3-28 Yokoami, Sumida-ku, Tokyo. Tel: 03-3623-5111. Near JR Ryogoku Station.
Osaka
March: Osaka Furitsu Taiikukaikan (Osaka Prefectural Gymnasium), 3-4-36 Namba Naka, Naniwa-ku, Osaka. Tel: 06-631-0121. Near Namba subway station.
Nagoya
July: Aichi Ken Taiikukan (Aichi Prefectural Gymnasium), 1-1 Ninomaru, Naka-ku, Nagoya. Tel: 052-971-2516. 15 minutes by car from Nagoya Station. Competition starts from 9.20am.
Fukuoka
November: Fukuoka Kokusai Centre Sogo Hall, 2-2 Chikuko-Honcho, Hakata-ku, Fukuoka. Tel: 092-272-1111.

Baseball

Often described as Japan's "second national sport", it remains a big game, though it is losing some popularity among the young. The season runs from April–October, peaking with the best-of-seven Japan Series between the Central and Pacific leagues.

Tokyo Dome
1-3-61 Koraku, Bunkyo-ku
Tel: 03-5800-9999
www.tokyo-dome.co.jp
Nicknamed the Big Egg, the stadium is home to the Yomiuri Giants.
Jingu Stadium
13 Kasumigaooka, Shinjuku-ku
Tel: 03-3404-8999
Home ground of the Swallows, this older, open-air stadium is probably more atmospheric than the Big Egg.
Koshien Stadium
Close to Koshien Station, this is the venue for the wildly popular All-Japan High School Baseball Championship, the city's summer highlight.
Osaka Dome
Home to the Kintetsu Buffalos team.
Fukuoka Dome
Hawks Town
Hi-tech stadium and home to the local Daiei Hawks team.

Horse Racing

Horse racing has become more fashionable and respectable of late. One of the few chances to gamble in Japan, schedules are available in English at the National Association of Racing website: www.jair.jrao.ne.jp

Oi Racetrack
2-1-1 Katsushima, Shinagawa-ku
Tel: 03-3763-2151
Tokyo Racecourse
1-1, 1-2 Hiyoshi-cho, Fuchu City
Tel: 042-363-3141

Martial Arts

Karate, aikido, jodo. *Kyudo* (archery), and *kendo* are well represented at the Nippon Budokan in Tokyo.

All-Japan Judo Federation
Kodokan Dojo, 1-16-30 Kasuga, Bunkyo-ku
Tel: 03-3818-4172 (English-speaking service)
All-Japan Kendo Association
Nippon Budokan, 2-3 Kitanomaru-koen, Chiyoda-ku
Tel: 03-3211 5804
Japan Karate Association
4F, Sanshin Building, 29-33 Sakuragaoka-cho, Shibuya-ku
Tel: 03-5459-6226
Japan Karatedo Federation
6F, 2 Nippon Zaiidan Building, 1-11-2 Toranomon, Minato-ku
Tel: 03-3503-6640
Nippon Budokan
2-3 Kitanomaru-koen, Chiyoda-ku
Tel: 03-3216-5100

Rugby

Rugby is quite popular in Japan, with a thriving corporate league, a good attendance at the Rugby World Cup and a keen following in universities.

Chichibu-no-miya Rugby Stadium
Kasumigaoka-cho, Shinjuku-ku

Soccer

The J-League now competes and fractionally outpaces baseball as the most popular spectator sport in Japan. The season runs Mar–Oct, with the Emperor's Cup in Dec.

National Stadium
Kasumigaoka, Shinjuku-ku
Tel: 03-3403-115
Ajinomoto Stadium
376-3, Nishimachi, Chofu City
Tel: 0424-40-0555
www.ajinomotostadium.com

Participant Sports

Golf

Some hotels offer golf packages, and this is probably the cheapest way to get onto the greens in Japan, which are otherwise very expensive. Driving ranges and putting greens, some under raised motorways or on department store rooftops, are easy to find.

Tokyo Metropolitan Golf Course
1-15-1 Shinden, Adachi-ku
Tel: 03-3919-0111

Ice Skating

This is a popular spectator sport, with exhibitions and shows at the

Sports Websites

Baseball	www.japanbaseball.com
Cycling	www.japancycling.org
Diving	www.divejapan.com
Football	www.jfa.or.jp/eng
Golf	www.golf-in-japan.com
Karate	www.karatedo.co.jp
Kendo	www.kendo.or.jp
Outdoors	www.outdoorjapan.com
Skiing	www.skijapanguide.com/index.php
Sumo	www.sumo.or.jp/eng/index
Surfing	www.japansurf.com

National Stadium in Tokyo.
Meiji Jingu Ice-Skating Rink
Gobanchi, Kasumigaoka, Shinjuku-ku
Tel: 03-3403-3456
Takadanobaba Citizen Ice-Skating Rink
4-29-27 Takabanobaba, Shinjuku-ku
Tel: 03-3371-0910

Fitness Centres

Chiyoda Kuritsu Sogo Taikukan
2-1-8 Uchi-kanda, Chiyoda-ku
Tel: 03-3256-8444
Open daily noon–5pm.
Fitness Club Esforta Roppongi
2F, Izumi Garden Terrace, 1-6-1 Roppongi, Minato-ku
Tel: 03-3560-3466
Open daily 9am–9pm
Minato-ku Sports Centre
3-1-19 Shibaura, Minato-ku
Tel: 03-3462-4151
Open Tues–Sun 9.15am–8pm.

Yoga

International Yoga Centre
5-30-6 Ogikubo, Suginami-ku
Tel: 090-4956-7996
Sun & Moon Yoga
Meguro Eki Mae mansion, Higashi Guchi Building, 3-1-5 Kami Osaki, Suite 204, Shinagawa-ku
Tel: 03-3280-6383

SIGHTSEEING TOURS

First-time visitors or those on a very tight schedule should consider taking a sightseeing tour in one of the major destinations such as Tokyo or Kyoto.

The **Japan Guide Association** (tel: 03-3213-2706; www.jga21c.or.jp/index_e.html) can put you in touch with an accredited tour guide. You can then negotiate the fee and itinerary with the guide. At some well-known sites, especially in Tokyo and Kyoto, you may be approached by volunteer guides. While their services are free, you should offer lunch as a gesture.

Bus Tours

Bus tours are usually reasonably priced and run from half day to full day and evening tours. Prices run respectively from ¥3,500–12,000. Tours can be booked through major hotels in the main historical cities.
Hato Bus Tokyo
Tel: 03-3435-6081
www.hatobus.co.jp
Reliable tour company offering half-day trips from ¥4,000.
Japan Gray Line Company
Tel: 03-3433-5745
www.jgl.co.jp/inbound
Tours prices range from ¥4,000–9,600, depending on length.
Sunrise Tours
Tel: 03-5796-5454
Run by the large Japan Travel Bureau, Sunrise offers tours of Toyo, Kamakura, Hakone, Osaka and Kyoto.

City Walking Tours

Tokyo

Get to know the back streets of Tokyo and their stories with English-speaking Mr Oka, a retired historian.
www.homestead.com/mroka

Kyoto

Peter Macintosh guides small groups through the mysteries of Kyoto's geisha world. Tel: 090-5169-1654.
www.kyotosightsandnights.com

River Tours

Tokyo Water Cruise
Tel: 03-5733-4812
www.suijobus.co.jpenglish/index.html
A delightful way to see Tokyo's Sumida River and its old bridges, many of them pre-war. Tours go to the Hama-Rikyu Garden and on to Odaiba.

Taxi Tours

Taxi tours are handy but expensive, even outside of the main sightseeing cities. Expect to pay between ¥26–50,000 for between 4 and 8 hours. Contact the JNTO *(see page 389)* for recommendations.

CHILDREN

Bringing children to Japan is a relatively easy task, given that the Japanese love kids and that the country is both safe and hygienic, with plenty of health and food products targeting toddlers to teens. There is plenty to keep children interested, though too many temples may tire even the most tolerant child. Overhead and subway trains and buses are free for kids under six; those aged 6–11 pay half price. Children under three go free on domestic flights, but have to share a seat with a parent; fares for kids aged 3–11 are half-price.

Hakuhinkan Toy Park
8-8-11 Ginza, Chuo-ku
Tokyo's top toy store.
Kiddyland
6-1-9 Jingumae, Shibuya-ku
Four floors of toys and electronics.
Osamu Tezuka Manga Museum
7-65 Mukogawa-cho, Takarazuka
Tel: 0797-812970
This Osaka museum features cartoon creation workshops.
National Children's Castle
5-31-1 Jingumae, Shibuya-ku
Tel: 03-3797-5665
Special interactive programmes for kids throughout the week.
Tokyo Disneyland
1-1 Maihama, Urayasu-shi, Chiba Prefecture
www.tokyodisneyresort.co.jp
Tickets for both Disneyland and Disney Sea can be bought on arrival, or from the Tokyo Disneyland Ticket Centre (Hibiya Mitsui Bldg, 1-1-2 Yurakucho, Chiyoda-ku; Tel: 03-3595-1777).
Tama Zoo
7-1-1 Hodokubo, Hino-shi
A natural-habitat zoo, with safari-park rides.
Universal Studios Japan
Tel: 06-4790-7000;
www.usj.co.jp/e_top.html
Movie-based themes, displays, special effects and rides at this Osaka park.

Kids Websites

www.tokyowithkids.com/index.html
www.jinjapan.org/kidsweb

The Magic Kingdom

Tokyo Disneyland is actually located in Chiba Prefecture just outside of the capital. Japan's most successful theme park celebrated its 20th anniversary in 2003. It's still inordinately popular so expect long queues for the more popular rides. Try to visit on weekdays or on the weekend before the 25th of the month, which is pay day in Japan. Disney Sea, offering underwater voyages, a Mediterranean-style port and much besides, was added to the complex in 2001. It requires a separate ticket. 1-4 Maihama, Urayasu City, Chiba Prefecture. Tel: 045-6833-777, www.tokyodisneyresort.co.jp. Take the Keiyo Line train to Maihama, then just follow the crowds.

A–Z

A Handy Summary of Practical Information, Arranged Alphabetically

Addresses

Finding an address in Japan can be tricky, even for taxi drivers. Especially in a city like Tokyo and Osaka, where addresses are written in a descending order *ku* (ward), then *cho* or *matchi* (district), followed by the *chome* (an area of a few blocks) designations. The English rendition of addresses, and the one used in this guide, would result in a location appearing like this: Regency Hotel, 5F, 4-9-11 Shibuya, Minato-ku. In Japan the ground floor equals the first. Floor numbers are often shown on the outside of the building.

If you are stuck, ask at the nearest police box, where they have detailed area maps, and are usually very helpful.

Bathhouses

Whether at a hot spring, a local *sento* (bathhouse), or at a traditional inn, the procedure for this quintessentially Japanese experience is the same. Disrobe, enter the bathroom (in public you hide your modesty with a small washcloth), and wash and rinse off thoroughly under a shower before easing into the hot bath – which is for soaking, not washing yourself. Don't pull the plug after you've finished; others will use the same water.

Budgeting for Your Trip

Japan has a reputation for being expensive, a legacy of the 1980s bubble economy years when the country was flush with cash. Compared to other Asian destinations, Japan remains expensive but, despite recent signs of a turnaround in its economy, 15 years of stagnation have left a dent in the cost-of-living index. Compared to European capitals, cities like Tokyo, Osaka and Kyoto begin to look quite affordable.

Budget accommodation can run from as little as ¥3,500 for a room in a modest inn or guesthouse, to over ¥50,000 in a top hotel. Food is exceptionally good value, and the choices are remarkable. A decent set lunch can cost as little as ¥650, less if you opt for a meal at a Japanese fast-food chain like Yoshinoya, the beef-bowl restaurants found in every Japanese city. American fast-food chains like McDonald's have dropped their prices in recent years to as little as ¥250 for a hamburger and coffee. Family restaurant chains are very good value, and provide free coffee refills. Convenience stores are good places for affordable snacks, lunchtime fillers like *onigiri*, instant *ramen* and *soba*.

Taxis are a major expense if you use them regularly, with base tariffs starting at ¥670. rising quickly if you get stuck in a traffic jam. Subway tickets are much more reasonable, with base fares starting at ¥140 for two or three stops. Rates are slightly different for each line.

Drinks at clubs and discos are generally cheaper to buy than at private bars and pubs. There is no tipping system in Japan, and prices quoted usually include a service charge and consumption tax, all of which makes a significant difference.

Business Hours

Officially, business is done on a 9am to 5pm basis, but this is in theory only. The Japanese will often do overtime till 8 or 9pm. In general, **government** offices are open from 8.30 or 9am to 4 or 5pm Monday to Friday, and from 9am to noon on the 1st and 3rd Saturday of the month. **Main post offices** are open 9am to 7pm Monday to Friday, 9am to 5pm on Saturday, and 9am to noon on Sunday and holidays. **Branch post offices** are open 9am to 5pm Monday to Friday. **Department stores** and larger shops open daily from 10am to 7.30 or 8pm, except that they tend to close twice or three times a month, which varies with each store. **Restaurants** are generally open for lunch from 11.30am to 2pm and for dinner from 5 to 9 or 10pm. **Major companies** and **offices** are open from 9am to 5pm Monday to Friday. Some are also open on Saturday mornings. Most **small shops** open between 9 and 11am and close between 6 and 8pm. Convenience stores are open 24 hours.

Business Travellers

When you meet a Japanese person, wait to see if she or he shakes your hand or bows, and then follow suit. Younger people are more comfortable with the handshake in general. Dressing smartly is part of doing business in Japan, something you should emulate.

The Japanese love of consensus, of trying to avoid confrontation wherever possible, is legendary, and can make doing business in Japan a frustrating experience. Don't expect rapid decisions, or a meeting to yield quick results. Long-term relationships are important to the Japanese business community, and these may take time to develop.

At meetings expect stiff formality to prevail, although a certain amount of small talk and civilities can break the ice. It may seem an elliptical approach, but circling around a topic before getting down to business is the norm. The pecking order for sitting is important: wait for others to decide this. The same applies to social situations like dinner.

The exchange of business cards is a vital ritual at first meetings. Make sure you have a good supply as they can go fast. If possible, have your cards printed on one side in *katakana* script, so that non-English speakers can pronounce it easily and do not jot down names or make notes on these cards. Don't be surprised or offended if you are asked questions regarding age, education, family background and company service. Identity and "proper" affiliation are very important in Japan.

Children

With a little advance planning Japan is a perfectly feasible place to bring children. There are many choices of activities, from amusement parks, children-oriented museums, zoos, aquariums and toy shops. When exploring Japanese cities with kids, try to avoid train rush hours, especially when using pushchairs.

Where public-toilet facilities are often inadequate in Japan, department stores usually have family rooms and play areas. Stores and malls are good places to eat, with plenty of set meals for children. Many of the bigger hotels offer baby-sitting services. See also Children's Activities *(page 380)*.

Babysitting Services

Hotels can sometimes arrange for babysitting but, failing that, there are several agencies in Tokyo that are recommended:

Japan Baby-Sitter Service, tel: 03-3423-1251. Open Mon–Fri 9am–6pm.
Poppins Service, tel: 03-3447-2100. Open Mon–Sat 9.30am–5.30pm.
Tom Sawyer Agency, tel: 03-3770-9530. Open Mon–Fri 9am–10.30pm.

Climate

When untravelled Japanese talk about living in a country that has four seasons – as if this is unique to Japan rather than countless temperate-zone land-masses – technically they are talking about an area which at the very most extends from parts of northern to certain areas of western Honshu island. These are the only regions that can truly be said to have four distinct seasons. This limited but culturally dominant belt, embracing both Tokyo *(see chart above)* and the former imperial capital of Kyoto, has influenced not only perceptions about the four seasons but almost every statement on Japanese culture.

Spring begins in the south, with the cherry blossoms coming out in Okinawa in February. Hokkaido, where the winter snow can linger well into April, will enjoy the blossoms in May. In general, May is a warm and pleasant month, while June sees the

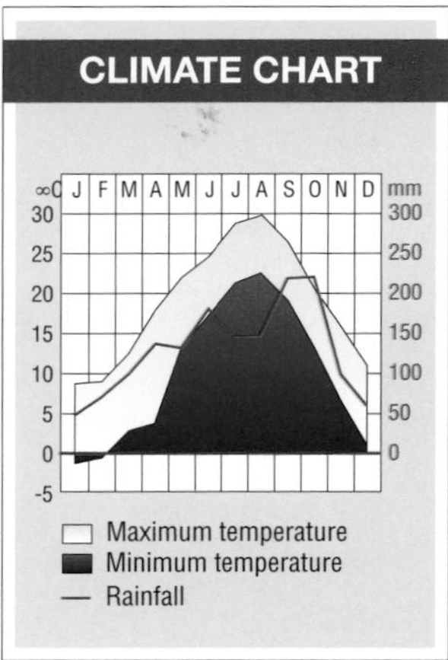

onset of the humid rainy season, known poetically as *tsuyu* (dew). This drizzly spell lasts about a month. Again, Hokkaido is exempt from this. Midsummer is hot and sticky, with the mercury rising into the mid and upper 30°C levels. Typhoons occur between August and October, though because of global climate change, these patterns are no longer fixed.

Many Japanese will say that October and November are the finest months to visit their country, the crisp, well-defined days of autumn, when the skies are often blue. Winter can be harsh in Hokkaido and the Japan Sea side of the country, with heavy snowdrifts. The winter of 2005/6 was particularly severe throughout the country. Clear skies and low humidity are the rewards of January and February, the coldest months. March is generally chilly, overcast and changeable. But again, bear in mind that, while one set of travellers will be enjoying the ski slopes of Hokkaido in that month, others may be taking their first tentative dip in the blue, coral waters of Okinawa.

Clothing

Although Japanese people place a great deal of importance on clothing and appearance in general, providing that clothes are clean, casual wear is perfectly in order for most occasions. In business situations, suits are definitely *de rigueur*.

The weather is relatively predictable, so dress for the season, bringing a thick jacket for winter, light cotton or linen clothes for the late spring and summer. A light jacket will usually suffice for spring and autumn. Check world weather reports for last-minute adjustments, though, before starting out on your trip.

Crime & Security

While the number of offences committed throughout Japan remains about one-eighth the number in the United States, crime has risen over the past decade, particularly among Japanese youth. Personal security is far higher than in Western countries, and visitors routinely comment on the fact that they never feel threatened walking in Japanese streets.

Theft of luggage and money is rare, although pickpockets have begun to work the Tokyo and Osaka subway trains. In recent years, the media has been full of reports of crimes committed by foreigners, especially Asian immigrants, though when closely examined, many of these turn out to be visa violations or activities connected to Japan's sex industry.

Organised crime, while often violent, is unlikely to affect the traveller or ordinary citizen as these are usually the result of turf disputes. The police generally turn a blind eye to prostitution, gambling, ticket touting, illegal immigration and the protection rackets operated by the *yakuza* gangs, only conducting crackdowns when inter-gang rivalry threatens the public domain.

If an incident occurs, report it to the nearest *koban* (police box). These are located in every neighbourhood, especially in busy areas and outside major railway stations. If possible go with an eye witness or a native speaker. For police contact details, *see Emergencies below*.

Women Travellers

Japan is not a dangerous place for women travellers on their own, although a certain amount of harassment, from which foreign women are not entirely excluded, does occasionally occur on crowded trains. The meaning of the term *seku-hara* (sexual harassment) is finally sinking in at the workplace, although Japan still lags behind Western countries in this regard, evident in degrading TV shows (not all late at night), tabloid papers, and the thinly veiled ads for prostitution services and manga books glorifying sexual violence towards women. Deplorable as this is, the situation will not improve as long as there remain thousands of women quite happy to humour these industries and profit from these forms of entertainment.

That said, it is safer to walk, travel, eat and drink anywhere in Japan than in most Western countries. Although red-light areas of large cities are inadvisable for women to walk alone in, two women together are unlikely to suffer anything worse than leering.

Customs Regulations

Japan strictly prohibits the import and use of narcotic drugs, firearms and ammunition. If caught in possession of any of these, the offender can expect no leniency. You can bring any currency, personal effects and valuables into Japan, but there is an official limit of ¥5 million that can be taken out.

You are also allowed to bring with you into Japan, free of tax, three 760-ml (25-fl oz) bottles of spirits, 400 cigarettes and 100 cigars or 500 g of tobacco, and 60 ml (2 fl oz) of perfume.

Disabled Visitors

In general, Japan is not user-friendly for the disabled and still lags behind most Western cities. Doors, lifts, toilets and just about everything else have not been designed for wheelchairs, nor are there any regulations regarding access for the disabled. It is a struggle for the disabled to get around Japan, but it can be done. Traditionally, the handicapped kept a low profile, as they were sometimes considered an embarrassment for the family. More recently, however, disabled people have become a more visible and accepted part of society.

Forget about using a wheelchair in train or subway stations, much less trains, during rush hour, 7–9am and 5–7pm. The crowds are just too thick, and too rude.

To arrange assistance – in advance – at **Tokyo Station**, call the JR English InfoLine at 03-3423-0111. They will make arrangements at Tokyo Station for you.

It is possible to reserve a special seat for wheelchairs on the *shinkansen*, or bullet train. Reservations can be made from one month to two days before departure. You must also reserve ahead to use the elevators for the *shinkansen* platforms.

In many stations, staff will help with escalators and lifts, although a wait of up to an hour may be involved.

Narita Airport's website (www.narita-airport.or.jp/en) has information for disabled travellers. The very comprehensive English-language guide, *Accessible Tokyo*, can be ordered in advance from the **Japanese Red Cross Language Service Volunteers** group (tel: 03-3438-1311; fax: 03-3432-5507) : 1-1-3 Minato-ku, Shiba Daimon; www.accessible.jp.org/tokyo/en

Club Tourism Division Barrier Free (tel: 03-5323-6915) has useful information about getting around Japanese cities. For help in emergencies or personal distress, telephone **Tokyo English Life Line** 03-5774-0992

Electricity

The power supply is 100 volts AC. Eastern cities in Japan, including Tokyo, run on 50 cycles, while those in the west such as Kyoto, Osaka and Nagoya, use 60 cycles. Sockets are two-pin and most hotels will have adaptors.

Embassies & Consulates

Australia, 2-1-14 Mita, Minato-ku. Tel: 03-5232-4111.
Canada, 7-3-38 Akasaka, Minato-ku. Tel: 03-5412-6200.
India, 2-2-11 Kudan-minami, Chiyoda-ku. Tel: 03-3262-2391
Ireland, No. 25 Kowa Bldg, 8-7 Sanbancho, Chiyoda-ku. Tel: 03-3263-0695.
New Zealand, 20-40 Kamiyamacho, Shibuya-ku. Tel: 03-3467-2271.
Singapore, 5-12-3 Roppongi, Minato-ku. Tel: 03-3586-9111.
United Kingdom, 1 Ichibancho, Chiyoda-ku. Tel: 03-5211-1100, fax: 03-5275-0346.
United States, 1-10-5 Akasaka, Minato-ku. Tel: 03-3224-5000.
US Consulate General in Osaka and Kobe, 2-11-5 Nishi-temma, Kita-ku, Osaka. Tel: 06-6315-5900.

Emergencies

Police: 110
Fire and ambulance: 119
Police info in English: 03-3501-0110
Emergency calls can be made from any phone without using coins or prepaid telephone cards.
Japan Hotline, information and help about everything, in English, weekdays 10am–4pm. Tel: 03-3586-0110.
For **hospital information**, call 03-5285-8181 in Tokyo (English spoken).

Entry Regulations

Visas and Passports

A proper visa is necessary for foreigners living in Japan and engaged in business or study. Passengers with confirmed departure reservations can obtain a stopover pass for up to 72 hours.

Japan has an agreement with 62 countries, whose nationals do not require visas for tourism purposes. They include: Australia, Canada, New Zealand, United States and most European countries (for stays of up to 90 days).

Visitors from Ireland and the UK may reside in Japan for up to 6 months providing they are not earning an income.

For further details and requirements for other nationalities, contact your nearest Japanese diplomatic mission or log on to www.mofa.go.jp.

Extension of Stay

Foreigners wishing to extend their stay in Japan must report, in person, to the Immigration Bureau within two weeks before their visa expiration. Present your passport, a statement with the reasons why you want an extension of stay, and documents certifying the reasons. The fee is ¥4,000.

Foreigners living in Japan must obtain a re-entry permit from the Immigration Bureau if they leave Japan and plan to return. Present, in person, your passport and certificate of alien registration (held by foreign residents in Japan) along with the appropriate re-entry form to the Immigration Office. Fees are charged for both single and multiple re-entry permits.

Those wishing to transfer visas to new passports must report to the Immigration Bureau in Tokyo. Present both old and new passports and certificate of alien registration.

Ministry of Foreign Affairs, www.mofa.go.jp
Information on the current rules and regulations regarding visas.

Tokyo Regional Immigration Bureau
5-5-30, Konan, Minato-ku, Tokyo
Tel: 03-5796-7112

Hakozaki Immigration Branch Office, Tokyo City Air Terminal, 42-1 Nihombashihakozaki, Chuo-ku.
Tel: 03-3664-3046. Open Mon–Fri 9am–noon, 1–5pm. (Near the Royal Park Hotel.)

Yokohama Regional Immigration Bureau. Tel: 045-681-6801.

Osaka Immigration Information.
Tel: 06-774-3409. Visa/Immigration Information in Osaka. English spoken. Open Mon–Fri 9.30am–noon, 1pm–4.30pm.

Automated Immigration Info.
Tel: 03-3213-8141. Usage: with a touch-tone phone, enter 2 for English. Dial the code number for the information you want (about 800 available). The code list is available at immigration/ward offices.

Alien Registration

Foreigners planning to stay in Japan for more than three months are required to register at the ward office in their residing area. The application must be made in person within 90 days. The applicant must have his/her passport containing the appropriate visa and two photographs (3 cm x 4 cm).

If the alien registration card has been lost or defaced, report to the ward office within 14 days. Take your passport and two new photographs and you will be issued a new one. For visitors under 16 years of age, applications may be made by a parent or legal guardian by producing the applicant's passport. No photograph is necessary. Ward office hours are Mon–Fri 8.45am–5pm and Sat 8.45am–12.30pm.

Tokyo Metropolitan Government, Tokyo Daisan Chosha, 3-5-1 Marunouchi, Chiyoda-ku, Tokyo. Tel: 03-3211-4433. English service is available on Mon and Thur 1–4pm.

The above information regarding alien status and visas is general and subject to change. For further information contact your appropriate embassy, consulate or the Japan Immigration Bureau.

Etiquette

At work and in most formal situations, the Japanese may seem a very reticent and reserved people, lacking in spontaneity or personality. There are books and theories explaining this behaviour, but it only provides one side of the picture. Japanese (especially men) can become extremely raucous when drinking and often let out their real opinions and feelings after a few drinks. The next morning in the office, all is forgotten. Intentionally.

On the crowded trains you will find yourself being pushed and bumped around. You do not need to be polite here; just push along with everyone else. It is often said that the Japanese are only polite with their shoes off, which means that they are polite and courteous with people they know well and would be indoors with (where shoes are almost always removed).

For the Japanese, the distinction between inside and outside the home is important. Inside the entrance to all homes (and some restaurants) is an area for removing shoes. You then step up into the living area, wearing slippers or in your stockinged feet. (Slippers are never worn on *tatami* mats, however, only socks and bare feet.) Taking shoes off keeps the house clean, besides being more relaxing, and it also increases the amount of usable space, since you can sit on the floor without worrying about getting dirty. The toilet, however, is one area of the house that is considered dirty, so separate slippers are provided for use there.

The custom of bowing has, in many cases, become somewhat a conditioned reflex. Foreigners, in general, are not expected to bow, and this is especially evident if a Japanese person first reaches out to shake hands.

As to punctuality and keeping appointments, the Japanese have a reputation for not being very punctual. At several of the famous meeting places (in Tokyo, in front of Ginza's Sony Building or at the Hachiko entrance to Shibuya Station, as examples) you can observe people waiting for someone, often for an hour or more.

After several apologies and explanations, everything is usually forgotten and forgiven.

The way the Japanese usually speak and express themselves gives a very good picture of their culture. Direct statements of fact are most often avoided as this implies that the speaker has a superior knowledge, and this is considered impolite. Therefore, much beating about the bush is done, which often leads to misunderstandings and seems like a waste of time to foreigners, but this must be taken into consideration when dealing with the Japanese.

In their own language, the Japanese are adept at reading between the lines and interpreting deft nuances of words and tone.

In any case, whatever happens, foreigners, who are blisfully unaware of these points, are usually forgiven for any breach of etiquette, so there's no need to spend time worrying about what is right and wrong. The cardinal rule is to try to be courteous at all times. Japanese behaviour in general is situational, and the Japanese themselves often do not know the right thing to do in any given situation. "It all depends on the situation," remarks the smart aleck, but it's often fun for everyone involved when one of "us" makes a slip. Sometimes it actually helps to break the ice and put everyone in a more relaxed mood.

Gay & Lesbian Travel

Unlike other developed countries, gay leanings in Japan are still kept very much under wraps. This is not to say that it is invisible. Gay and transvestite celebrities often appear on TV, and there has been a recent boom in comic books and films with gay themes, especially popular with young women. Tokyo's Shinjuku ni-chome district is the undisputed centre of the gay scene in Japan. There are over 300 gay bars and clubs located around its central street, Naka-dori. Outside of Tokyo and Osaka, the gay scene is very difficult to gain access to. *Badi* is Japan's premier gay publication, but there are classified ads and occasional coverage of the scene in the magazines *Metropolis* and *Tokyo Journal*.

Gay Websites

www.gnj.or.jp
A support and friendship group that also runs advertisements and discussion groups.
www.utopia-asia.com/tipssjapn.htm
General coverage of gay life in Japan, with club and venue listings.

Gay Venues

Advocates Bar
7F, Tenka Bldg, B1F, 2-18-1, Shinjuku, Shinjuku-ku
Tel: 03-3358-8638
With a sister establishment,
Advocates Café
just around the corner, is a popular meeting place for both Japanese and foreigners.
Kinswomyn
Daiichi Tenka Bldg, 3F, 2-15-10, Shinjuku, Shinjuku-ku
Tel: 03-3354-8720
A women-only club. Very popular.
Kinsmen
2F, 2-18-5, Shinjuku, Shinjuku-ku
Tel: 03-3354-4949
The male-only counterpart to Kinswomyn.
Jinya
2-30-19, Ikebukuro, Toshima-ku
Tel: 03-5951-0995
A welcoming spot, and a good alternative to the Shinjuku scene. Non-gays are also warmly welcomed.

Guides & Travel Agencies

Guides and Escorts

Japan Guide Association, Shin Kokusai Building 9F, 3-4-1 Marunouchi, Chiyoda-ku, Tokyo. Tel: 03-3213-2706, fax: 03-3213-2707.
Japan Federation of Licensed Guides, 2-1-10 Kamitakada, Nakamo-ku, Tokyo. Tel: 03-3319-1665, fax: 03-3319-1960.

Goodwill Guides

Goodwill Guides are volunteers who assist overseas visitors. All volunteers are registered with the JNTO. With over 40,000 members, the guides are affiliated with 74 groups throughout Japan, and guides are available in over two dozen regions to offer local information or guide you on walking tours.

Tokyo: 03-3201-3331
Yokohama: 03-3201-3331
Kyoto: 075-861-0540 and 075-371-5649
Osaka: 06-635-3143
Nara: 0745-74-6800 and 0742-45-5920
Nikko: 0288-54-2027
Sendai: 022-275-3796
Himeji: 0792-72-3605
Kurashiki: 086-424-7774
Fukuoka: 092-725-9100
Kagoshima: 099-224-3451

Travel Agencies

The JNTO website (www.jnto.go.jp/eng) lists travel agencies in Canada, the US and the UK that offer trips to Japan. The following agencies, listed by the JNTO, offer travel services for foreign travellers:
Japan Travel Bureau (JTB). Tel: 03-5345-5577, fax: 03-5620-9502. web2.jtb.co.jp/eng/index.html
Kinki Nippon Tourist Co., Kanda-Matsunaga-cho, Chiyoda-ku, Tokyo 101. Tel: 03-3255-6535, fax: 03-3251-1113. www.knt.co.jp/kokusai/top.htm
Kyoto Tourist Information Center, 9th floor of Kyoto Station. Tel: 075-344-3300.
Nippon Travel Agency, Shimbashi Ekimae Bldg, 2-20-15 Shimbashi, Minato-ku, Tokyo 105. Tel: 03-3572-8716, fax: 03-3574-9610. www.nta.co.jp/english/index.htm
Japan Gray Line, Pelican Bldg, 3-3-3 Nishi-Shimbashi, Minato-ku, Tokyo 105. Tel: 03-3595-5948.
JTB Traveland, 43–20 Minami Ikebukuro 2-chome, Toshima-ku, Tokyo 171. Tel: 03-3983-0251.
Toppan Travel Service, Towa-Hamamatsucho Bldg. 7F, 2-6-2 Hamamatsucho, Minato-ku, Tokyo 104. Tel: 03-5403-2500, fax: 03-5403-2504.
Osaka Visitors Information Center, Shin-Osaka Station, JR. Tel: 06-6305-3311.
Okinawa Tourist Service, 1-2-3 Matsuo, Naha, Okinawa 900. Tel: 098-862-1111, fax: 098-861-7965.

Health & Medical Care

In general, levels of hygiene are very high, and it is very unlikely that you will become ill as a result of eating or drinking something. The tap water, though heavily chlorinated, is drinkable. Most food is of a high standard. However, because the Japanese place so much emphasis on presentation and how food looks, there is wide use of chemical fertilisers in Japan, and therefore it is not recommended to eat the skins of fruits and some vegetables.

Medical Services

Try to remember that you are in Japan and must be prepared to adapt to the Japanese system. Although some doctors may speak English, the receptionist and nursing staff will not, so it is advisable to bring along a Japanese-speaking friend or someone who can speak both languages. Most hospitals and clinics do not have appointment systems, so you have to be prepared to wait your turn, however frustrating that may be. Here is a list of hospitals and clinics in Tokyo where you would have no problem in being understood or treated. They all have different hours and administrative systems.

Hospitals in Tokyo

International Catholic Hospital (Seibo Byoin), 2-5-1 Nakaochiai, Shinjuku-ku. Tel: 03-3951-1111. Open Mon–Sat 8–11am. Closed Sun and 3rd Sat.
Red Cross Medical Centre (Nisseki), 4-1-22 Hiroo, Shibuya-ku. Tel: 03-3400-1311. Open Mon–Fri 8.30–11am, Sat 8.30–10.30am. Closed Sun.
St Luke's International Hospital (Seiroka Byoin), 10-1 Akashicho, Chuo-ku. Tel: 03-3541-5151. Open Mon–Sat 8.30–11am. Closed Sun.
International Clinic, 1-5-9 Azabudai, Minato-ku. Tel: 03-3582-2646. Open Mon–Fri 9am–noon, 2.30–5pm; Sat 9am–noon. Closed Sun.
Tokyo Adventist Hospital (Tokyo Eisei Byoin), 3-17-3 Amanuma, Suginami-ku. Tel: 03-3392-6151. Open Mon–Sat 8.30–11am.
Toho Fujin Women's Clinic, 5-3-10 Kiba, Koto-ku. Tel: 03-3630-0303. Open Mon–Sat 1–5pm. Closed Sun.
Hospital Hotline (English): in Tokyo, tel: 03-3212-2323.
Tell-Tokyo English Lifeline: in Tokyo, tel: 03-5774-0992.

Pharmacies

Most Western-style, over-the-counter medicines are hard to find in Japan, and when they are available, prices are high. Pharmacists can help you with Japanese or Chinese remedies. It's best to bring your own preferred cold and allergy medicines with you. But note that many popular brands, like Sudafed, contain small amounts of amphetamine-like drugs and are illegal in Japan.

Note that while pharmacies stock useful regular medication and may be able to advise you on coping with minor problems, they do not dispense prescription drugs. Prescriptions can only be obtained

through a hospital or clinic after a consultation. The medicine will be issued to you on the same premises.
American Pharmacy, Marunouchi Building (basement), Chiyoda-ku. Tel: 03-3271-4034. Open Mon–Sat 9.30am–8pm, Sun 10am–6.30pm.
Boots the Chemist, 6-5-3, Jingumae, Shibuya-ku. Tel: 03-3708-6011. Open Mon–Fri 11am–8.30pm, Sat–Sun 11am–9pm.
Koyasu Drug Store Hotel Okura, Hotel Okura Main Bldg, 1F2-10-4, Toranomon, Minato-ku. Tel: 03-3583-7958. Open daily 8.30am–9pm.
National Azabu Supermarket Pharmacy, 4-5-2, Minami-Azabu, Minato-ku. Tel: 03-3442-3495. Open daily 9.30am–7pm.
Roppongi Pharmacy, 6-8-8, Roppongi, Minato-ku. Tel: 03-3403-8879. Open daily 10.30–2am.

Dentists

Harry K. Okamoto DDS, 7-9-7, 5F, Akasaka, Minato-ku. Tel: 03-3505-5910.
Ojima Dental Clinic, 2-7, Ichigaya-Tamachi, Shinjuku-ku. Tel: 03-3268-8818.
Royal Dental Office, 4-10-11, 2F, Roppongi, Minato-ku. Tel: 03-3404-0819.
Tokyo Clinic Dental Office, 4-10-11, 4F, Roppongi, Minato-ku. Tel: 03-3404-0819.
Tokyo Clinic Dental Office, 32 Mori Bldg, 2F, 3-4-30, Shiba-Koen, Minato-ku. Tel: 03-3431-4225.

Optical Care

Fuji Optical Service International, 1-6-1, Otemachi Bldg, 1F, Otemachi, Chiyoda-ku. Tel: 03-3214-4751.
International Vision Center, 3-3-13, 3F, Kyowa Gotankan Bldg, Kita-Aoyama, Minato-ku. Tel: 03-3497-1491.
Nozaki Eye Clinic, 2-9, Sakuragaoka-machi, Kasuya Bldg, Shibuya-ku. Tel: 03-3461-1671.

Internet & Email

If you're carrying a laptop or PDA and already have an ISP in your home country, check to see if they have a local phone number in Japan to make a connection; many do.

For those who must have their own connection in Japan while travelling, **Global OnLine** offers a modified account that costs approximately ¥500 per month for 5 hours, with additional per-minute costs after 5 hours. Local access numbers throughout Japan. In English, tel: 03-5334-1720, fax: 03-5334-1711. Email: sales@gol.com.

An account may be set up from anywhere using their website: http://home.gol.com/index_e.html.

Internet Cafés in Tokyo

Telephone rates have dropped dramatically in Japan, making surfing the net more affordable. While 24-hour manga cafés are very competitive, the cheapest deal is from Yahoo! Japan who, together with Starbucks, have set up branches in Tokyo and elsewhere. Below are some cafés in Tokyo:
Laputa City, 1-14-14 Shibuya, Shibuya-ku. Tel: 03-3407-2011.
Manga Hiroba, Chuwa Roppongi Bldg, 2F, 3-14-12 Roppongi, Minato-ku. Tel: 03-34997-1751
Marunouchi Café, 1F Fuji Bldg, 3-2-3 Marunouchi, Chiyoda-ku. Tel: 03-3212-5025; www.marunouchicafe.com.
Yahoo Café, Garden Square, 5-11-2 Jingumae, Shibuya-ku. Tel: 03-3797-6821.

Internet Cafés in Other Cities

Fukuoka
Kinko's, 1F, Daiichi Seimi Bldg, 1-4-1 Hakata-eki-mae. Tel: 092-473-2677
Hiroshima
I Love You, 6F, Futaba Bookshop, south exit Hiroshima Station.
Kagoshima
Best Denki Kagoshima, 1-5 Kajiya-cho. Tel: 099-223-2291
Kyoto
Kyoto Prefectural International Centre, 9F Kyoto Station Building. Tel: 075-342-5000
Kobe
Kinko's, 1F, Kobe Isuzu Recruit Building, 4-2-2 Kuomi-dori.
Kumamoto
Kumamoto City International Centre, 4-8 Hanabatacho. Tel: 096-359-2121
Matsumoto
Multimedia & Information Centre, 5F, AER Building. Tel: 022-724-1200
Matsyama
Matsyama Youth Hostel, 22-3 Himezuka Otsu, Dogo. Tel: 089-933-6366
Naha
Netbox, Tsubokawa-dori, 3F above Mister Donuts. Tel: 098-946-2833
Sapporo
Bon de Bon, Paseo Shopping Centre, basement of Sapporo Station. Tel: 011-213-5726.

Left Luggage

If possible, carry as little luggage as possible when travelling in Japan. Trains and stations, especially, are not designed for travellers with more than a small overnight bag. If you're thinking of making all your Tokyo train connections while hauling several large bags – forget it. The train/subway map looks neat and tidy, but station connections are serious hikes with no trolleys or porters available, and seemingly endless stairs. Hotels, of course, will usually store luggage for guests heading off on adventures.
International Airports. For security reasons, bombs in particular, the international airports have no coin lockers. There are cloakrooms, however, at international airports. While staff may not speak English, forms are bilingual and the staff will know why you're standing there.
ABC Skypartners: between the South Wing and the Central Bldg. ¥400 or ¥800 per day per bag, with no time limit for storage. Open 7am–10pm.
GPA (Green Port Agency): South Wing, 1F and 4F. ¥400 per day per bag, 30 day limit. Open 7am–10pm.
Train and subway stations. Most train and subway stations have coin lockers of varying sizes for ¥200 to

Lost Property

The Japanese are quite honest about handing in found items. If you've lost a wallet packed with cash, a camera, or an overnight bag, chances are it will be safe.
JR trains: Items left on trains will usually be kept for a couple of days at the nearest station. After that, they are taken to one of the major stations to be stored for five more days. Enquiries can be made in Japanese to lost-and-found centres at Tokyo Station 03-3231-1880, or Ueno Station 03-3841-8069. In English, enquiries can be made with the JR East Infoline 03-3423-0111, weekdays 10am–6pm.
Subways: On the Toei trains, or on Tokyo city-operated buses, enquire about lost property at terminals the same day, or call the lost-and-found centre, on 03-3812-2011 (Japanese only), weekdays 9am–6pm.
Taxis: All taxi companies in Tokyo report unclaimed items to a single centre, the Tokyo Taxi Kindaika Centre. Tel: 03-3648-0300 (Japanese only).
Police: As a last resort, contact the police. The Tokyo Metropolitan Police Department maintains an absolutely immense lost-and-found centre, with everything from forgotten umbrellas (zillions of them) to bags full of cash. Tel: 03-3814-4151, weekdays 8.30am–5.15pm. English spoken sometimes, Japanese mostly.

¥500 per day, depending on station and size of the locker. Time limit is 3 days. After that, contents are removed. You'll have no problem finding lockers; Japanese use them as a habit and convenience.

Cloakrooms for large bags are located at several main JR stations. Luggage can be stored for up to two weeks, ¥400 per day per bag for the first five days, ¥800 per day per bag for each additional day.

Tokyo Station, outside Yaesu south exit, 8.30am–6pm.
Ueno Station, in front of central exit, 8am–8pm.
Shin Osaka Station, outside the central exit, 5am–10pm.
Kyoto Station, Karasuma central exit and Hachijo central exit, 8am–8pm.

Maps

The JNTO in Tokyo and elsewhere provide lots of adequate maps, including walking and hiking tours. Nippon Kokuseisha publishes a comprehensive **Great Map of Japan**. Kodansha's **Tokyo City Atlas: A Bilingual Guide** is highly detailed and very useful. There is a similar atlas on Osaka and Kyoto. **Kyoto Information Map** provides a very detailed layout of the city in English and Japanese. **Kyoto Transportation Guide** has excellent mini area maps, train and bus routes. The **Insight Fleximap** to Tokyo is laminated and immensely durable.

Media

Television

There are several terrestrial TV channels. Two are from the quasi-national **Japan Broadcast Corporation** (NHK) and the other five are private-sector commercial networks. NHK also broadcasts on two satellite channels, plus a hi-definition TV channel. A small percentage of the programmes – including news bulletins – is bilingual, offering English on the sub-channel. Ask your hotel reception which button to press to see if the programme has this service.

Overseas networks CNN, ABC and BBC are available on satellite and cable TV at most large hotels.

Radio

The main foreign-language radio station is **Inter FM** (76.1 Mhz), which broadcasts news and music mainly in English. **J-Wave** (81.3 Mhz) also has some shows in English. The **Far East Network** (81.0 Mhz), broadcast by the US Armed Forces, airs music, news, US sports and some National Public Radio shows.

Newspapers

There are two daily newspapers in English. The *Japan Times* (www.japantimes.co.jp) is the premier English-language paper and the oldest, followed by *The Daily Yomiuri*. The *Nikkei Weekly* (www.nikkei.co.jp) is a financial digest.

Magazines

Several interesting English-language magazines are published in Japan. These tend to fall into two categories: events magazines and those focusing on Japanese culture. Of the first group, look out for the quarterly *Tokyo Journal*, the city's oldest events, issues and culture magazine, *JSelect* and *Metropolis*, a free weekly. *Kansai Time Out* covers the western region of Japan. *The Japan Journal* covers business quarterly *J@pan.Inc* is an internet- and business-related monthly magazine. Several online magazines are up and running *(see page 390 for listings)*.

Money

The unit of currency is the yen (¥), and the coins are ¥1, ¥5, ¥10, ¥50, ¥100 and ¥500. Bills are ¥1,000, ¥2,000, ¥5,000 and ¥10,000. Japanese stores, services and merchants are legally forbidden to accept foreign currencies. You can buy yen at foreign exchange banks and other authorised money changers on presentation of your passport. At the international airports at Narita and Osaka, the banks are open 24 hours. Traveller's cheques can only be cashed at banks and major hotels, and are not accepted elsewhere.

Credit Cards

Major credit cards, such as American Express, Diners Club, MasterCard and Visa, are accepted at establishments in and around Tokyo and Osaka/Kyoto, and there is no surcharge for their use. Unfortunately, acceptance is sporadic. Even at establishments displaying acceptance of Visa or MasterCard, for example, it is often quite difficult for a merchant to get approval for a credit card issued by a non-Japanese bank. If they refuse your card, don't get testy. Carry lots of cash instead, just in case.

American Express, Toranomon Mitsui Bldg, 3-8-1 Kasumigaseki, Chiyoda-ku. Tel: 03-3220-6100. Card member services: 0120-020-222 (toll-free). Lost/stolen card: 0120-376-100 (toll-free)
Diners Club, Senshu Bldg, 1-13-7 Shibuya, Shibuya-ku. Tel: 03-3499-1181.
MasterCard. Tel: 00531-113-886.
Visa. Tel: 0120-133-173 (toll-free).

Banks

Despite the wide use of computers and on-line systems, Japanese banks are often slow and inefficient in many fields. Especially when transferring money in or out of the country, you can expect the process to take a long time and to be costly. Also, small neighbourhood branches are often not able to process any international transactions. In order to send money out of the country, or cash foreign cheques, you will find it much easier to go to a major branch, where someone *may* be able to speak English and usually understand what you want to do. (An exception is Citibank, which has aggressively shaken up the way banks in Japan do business. If you are a Citibank customer elsewhere, your chances in Japan are much, much better.)

Banks open Mon–Fri 9am–3pm for normal banking. Cash dispensers (ATMs) are everywhere in Japan, even in convenience stores. The problem is that many of them can't be used for cash advances on cards issued abroad. The messages emitting from the machines will usually be in Japanese. The exceptions are big cities like Tokyo, Osaka and Kyoto, where international dispensers have been introduced, a trend that is likely to spread. For the time being though, carry plenty of cash with you.

Foreign Banks

Bank of America, 1-12-32 Akasaka, Minato-ku. Tel: 03-3587-3164.
Bank of Korea, Hibiya Park Bldg, 1-8-1 Yurakucho, Chiyoda-ku. Tel: 03-3213-6961.
Barclays Bank, 2-2-2 Otemachi, Chiyoda-ku. Tel: 03-5255-0011.
Chase Manhattan Bank, 1-2-1 Marunouchi, Chiyoda-ku. Tel: 03-3287-4000.
Citibank, Chiyoda-ku. Tel: 0120-223-773 (toll-free).
Commerzbank A.G., Nippon Press Centre Bldg, 2-2-1 Uchisaiwaicho, Chiyoda-ku. Tel: 03-3502-4371.
Commonwealth Bank of Australia, 1-1-3 Marunouchi, Chiyoda-ku. Tel: 03-3213-7311.
Crédit Lyonnais, Hibiya Park Bldg, 1-8-1 Yurakucho, Chiyoda-ku. Tel: 03-3217-1111.
Crédit Suisse, 1-11-30 Akasaka, Minato-ku. Tel: 03-3589-3636.
Lloyds TSB Bank, Akasaka Twin Tower, New Tower (5F), 2-11-7 Akasaka Minato-ku. Tel: 03-3589-7700.

Standard Chartered Bank, 3-2-3 Marunouchi, Chiyoda-ku. Tel: 03-3213-6541.
Union Bank of Switzerland, Yurakucho Bldg, 1-10-1 Yurakucho, Chiyoda-ku. Tel: 03-3214-7471.

Tipping

No tipping remains the rule in Japan, except for unusual or exceptional services. Porters at large stations and airports charge a flat rate of around ¥300 per piece of luggage. Taxi drivers don't expect any tips, nor do hotel staff. The only exception are country inns where it is the custom to hand a ¥1,000 note discreetly to the maid who takes you to your room and serves a welcome tea and sweets.

Photography

Although there are no limitations on what you can photograph, beyond the obvious taboos of military installations, you should use your discretion in religious sites, particularly when there are rites and rituals taking place.

Camera shops are plentiful as virtually every Japanese is an avid amateur photographer. Digital, slide, and print film, and developing, are widely available throughout Japan. You may even come across disposable cameras sold from vending machines. Moderately priced film can be purchased in the big camera and electronic shops like Yodabashi Camera, Laos and Sakuraya. Otherwise, there are camera shops, convenience stores and station kiosks.

Postal Services

There are nearly 30,000 post offices in Japan, which means they are ubiquitous. In addition to postal services, post offices offer savings services; in fact, the post office is Japan's largest holder of personal savings. Postal services are efficient and fast, but expensive for both international and domestic post.

For daytime opening hours, *see Business Hours*. For night owls, there's a 24-hour window at the **Tokyo Central Post Office**, on the Marunouchi side of Tokyo Station. Tel: 03-3284-9539. For 24-hour, 365-day international mail services, there's a special **Tokyo International Post Office** *(kokusai yubin kyoku)*, also near Tokyo Station and for foreign mail only: 2-3-3 Otemachi, Chiyoda-ku.

International express mail: Larger post offices offer EMS services; for some reason, the isolated post offices outside of the major cities of Tokyo and Osaka may require that an account be opened, though it's just a formality. If language is proving to be a problem in getting a package sent via EMS, this could be the reason.

International parcel post: foreign parcel post cannot exceed 20 kg per package to any international destination. For heavier packages or those that exceed certain size or content restrictions (which vary by country), a commercial courier service must be used *(see addresses below)*.

Postal information (English-language), tel: 0570-046-111; www.post.yusei.go.jp/english.

Pornography?

Magazines and videos showing any pubic hair are technically forbidden in Japan. This issue of films and magazines displaying pubic hair is a curious one. Photographs in *Playboy* magazine, for example, are literally sanded to obliterate pubic hair, but maybe only every other photo.

Yet at convenience stores like 7-Eleven, teenage boys can buy magazines with very explicit photographs or manga illustrations. Likewise, films sometimes will have fuzzy spots or electronic mosaics floating over offending parts. Other films are shown untouched. For most Westerners, whether bringing in offending material or not, Japanese offerings are more brusque and offensive.

Courier Services

DHL, 1-37-8 Higashi Shinagawa, Shinagawa-ku, Tokyo. Tel: 0120-392-580, fax: 0120-5479-5844.
Federal Express, Kyodo Bldg, 1st Floor, 16 Ichibancho, Chiyoda-ku, Tokyo. Tel: 0120-003-200 (toll-free), fax: 0120-5275-7712.

Public Holidays

1 January: *Ganjitsu* (New Year's Day)
2nd Monday, January: *Seijin no Hi* (Coming-of-Age Day)
11 February: *Kenkoku Kinen no Hi* (National Foundation Day)
Around 21 March: *Shumbun no Hi* (Vernal Equinox Day)
29 April: *Midori no Hi* (Greenery Day)
3 May: *Kempo Kinembi* (Constitution Memorial Day)
4 May: *Kokumin no Kyujitsu* (bank holiday)
5 May: *Kodomo no Hi* (Children's Day)
Third Monday in July: *Umi-no-Hi* (National Maritime Day)
Third Monday in September: *Keiro no Hi* (Respect-for-the-Aged Day)
Around 23 September: *Shubun no Hi* (Autumnal Equinox Day)
2nd Monday, October: *Taiiku no Hi* (Sports Day)
3 November: *Bunka no Hi* (Culture Day)
23 November: *Kinro Kansha no Hi* (Labour Thanksgiving Day)
23 December: *Tenno Tanjobi* (Emperor's Birthday)
25 December: *Kokumin no Kyujitsu* (bank holiday)

If a holiday falls upon Sunday, the following Monday will be a "substitute holiday".

Holidays to Avoid

There are three periods of the year when the Japanese travel and holiday en masse. You would be wise not to make any travel plans during this time:
New Year: from around 25 December to 4 January
Golden Week: from 29 April to 5 May
Obon: a week around 15 August.

Public Toilets

Apart from major hotels and some train stations, most toilets in Japan are of the Asian squatting type, which takes some getting used to, but are supposed to be the most hygienic (no part of your body actually touches them) and physiologically best. In Tokyo and other major cities, they are slowly being replaced with Western-style toilets. By law, every coffee shop and restaurant, etc, must have its own toilet, or access to one in the same building. Toilets in train stations and other large places are often dirty and smelly.

If you can't find a public toilet your best bet is to find a large department store which will have all the necessary facilities.

New hi-tech toilets with push-button control panels are on the increase. There are special enhancements such as heated seats, hot-air dryers, and a device that plays the sound of flushing water to conceal any embarrassing noises.

Religious Services

Protestant

Ginza Church, 4-2-1, Ginza, Chuo-ku. Tel: 03-3561-0236.

Baptist

International Baptist Church,

2-9-9, Yakumo, Meguro-ku. Tel: 03-3461-8425.

Lutheran

St Paul International Lutheran Church, 1-2-32, Fujimi-cho, Chiyoda-ku. Tel: 03-3461-3740.

Catholic

Azabu Church, 3-21-6, Nishi-Azabu, Minato-ku. Tel: 03-3408-1500.
Franciscan Chapel Center, 4-2-37, Roppongi, Minato-ku. Tel: 03-3401-2141.

Anglican Episcopal

St Alban's Church, 3-6-25, Shiba-Koen, Minato-ku. Tel: 03-3431-8534.

Telephones

Japan's country code: 81
Domestic area codes:
Fukuoka: 092
Hiroshima: 082
Kagoshima: 0992
Kyoto: 075
Nagasaki: 0958
Nagoya: 052
Naha: 098
Osaka: 066
Sapporo: 011
Sendai: 022
Tokyo: 03
Yokohama: 045

To use the public telephones, which come in a variety of colours and styles, just insert a ¥10 coin and dial the number desired. (¥10 for two minutes.) Yellow and green phones accept ¥100 coins, which make them more convenient for long-distance calls, but no change is returned for unused portions.

Most common are the green phones, all taking prepaid telephone cards and some taking only prepaid cards, no coins. Telephone cards can be obtained at any Nippon Telegraph and Telephone (NTT) office, KDD telecom company office, many shops, kiosks and virtually any convenience store, or through special vending machines near telephones.

Domestic calls, expensive over 60 km (37 miles), are cheaper at night and on weekends and holidays by as much as 40 percent.
NTT Information, domestic telephone directory information, in English. Weekdays 9am–5pm. Tokyo, tel: 03-5295-1010. Narita, tel: 0476-28-1010. Yokohama, tel: 045-322-1010. Hiroshima, tel: 082-262-1010.
City Source, free English telephone directory from NTT. Tel: 03-5256-3141, fax: 03-5256-3148. Osaka, tel: 06-571-7866, fax: 06-571-4185.
Japan Hotline (NTT/KDD), broad-based, hard-to-find phone numbers. Tel: 03-3586-0110. Mon–Fri, 10am–4pm.

Toll-Free Numbers

Domestic telephone numbers that begin with "0120" or "0088" are toll-free, or "freephone", calls.

International

A number of foreign companies such as AT&T and call-back companies have been revolutionising international phon e service in Japan. Western-style hotels, of course, usually offer the standard IDD capabilities. Elsewhere, the situation is changing so quickly that it's best to ask around for the current conditions.

International calls can be made only from specially marked – in English and Japanese – green telephones; look for an IDD sticker on the phone or booth. Increasingly, dark-grey card phones are appearing in hotels, public places and at airports. They have analogue and digital computer connections, with small screens displaying operating instructions in both Japanese and English.

To make a **person-to-person**, **reverse charge** (collect), or **credit-card** call from anywhere in Japan through KDD, the dominant international telecom company, simply dial 0051.
KDD Information, international telephone information, in English: 0057 (toll-free).
Using KDD Telecom:
AT&T: 00539 111
Sprint: 00539 131
MCI: 00539 121
Using IDC Telecom:
AT&T: 0066 55111
Sprint: 0066 55888
MCI: 0066 55121

Telephone Cards

The Japanese love prepaid cards, and telephone cards – not coins – are the primary form of payment for public telephones. These cards come in a number of different denominations and are for sale just about everywhere, including from vending machines. Companies and groups have customised cards printed for promotions and gifts. Collecting telephone cards is a big thing in Japan. There are actually two types of prepaid cards available: NTT (domestic) and KDD (international). The cards are slightly different sizes and can only be used in the appropriate phone.
Note: touts on the street, usually illegal immigrants overstaying their visas, will try to hustle cards at large discounts. These are definitely counterfeit and may not work in phones. This is a persistent problem around Shibuya, Ueno and Ueno Station.

Mobile Phones

Since the deregulation of the mobile-phone industry about seven years ago, Japan has gone from having one of the lowest rates of use to one of the highest.

Japan uses two mobile-phone systems: PDC and CDMA. If you come from a country that uses the more common GSM system found in Asia, UK, Europe, Australia and New Zealand, your phone will not work here. Check with your home service provider if unsure, as you will have to rent a handset that hooks up with the local network. Japan's international airports all have mobile phone counters, and the rentals are very reasonable. The largest of the several operators is **NTT Docomo**. Tel: 0120-005-250; www.nttdocomo.com.

Most mobile phone numbers begin with 090.

Telegrams

Domestic: 115
Overseas: 03-3344-5151
Central Post Office
Domestic: 03-3284-9539 (Japanese)
International: 03-3284-9540 (Japanese)

For telegram enquiries, tel: Tokyo, 03-3346-2521; Yokohama, tel: 045-671-4347.

Time Zone

Japan is GMT +9 hours; EST (New York) +14 hours; and PST (Los Angeles) +17. Japan does not have summer daylight savings time, although the idea is periodically mooted, and then dismissed in deference to the nation's farmers, a powerful electoral lobby.

Tourist Information

Tourist Offices

The Japan National Travel Organisation (JNTO) is an excellent source of information on visas, culture, accommodation, tours, etc. You can log on at: www.japantravelinfo.com and www.jnto.go.jp

JNTO Overseas Offices
Australia: Level 7, 36–38 Clarence Street, Sydney NSW 2000. Tel: 02-9279-2177, fax: 02-9279-3166. www.jnto.org.au
Canada: 481 University Ave, Suite

306, Toronto, Ont. M5G 2E9. Tel: 416-366-7140, fax: 416-366-4530, e-mail: info@jntoyyz.com.
Hong Kong: Suite 3704-05, 37/F, Dorset House, Taikoo Place, Quarry Bay. Tel: 2968-5688, fax: 2968-1722.
United Kingdom: 5th Floor, 12/13 Nicholas Lane, London EC4N 7BN. Tel: 020-7398-5670, fax: 020-7626-0224, www.seejapan.co.uk
United States:
Los Angeles: 515 Figueroa Street, Suite 1470, Los Angeles, CA 90071. Tel: 213-623-1952, fax: 213-623-6301, e-mail: info@jnto-lax.org
New York: One Rockefeller Plaza, Suite 1250, New York, NY 10020. Tel: 212-757-5640, fax: 212-307-6754, e-mail: visitjapan@jntonyc.org

Tourist Information Centres

Tokyo, 10th Floor, Tokyo Kotsu Kaikan Building, 2-10-1 Yurakucho, Chiyoda-ku, Tokyo 100-0006, Tel: 03-3201-3331. Open daily 9am–5pm, telephone-only service on 1 Jan .
Narita TIC, Terminal 1: North Wing, 1st floor (Arrivals). Tel: 0476-30-3383; Terminal 2: Main Building, 1st floor (Arrivals). Tel: 0476-34-6251. Open daily 9am–8pm.
Kyoto Office (TIC): 2nd floor, JR Kyoto Station, Shimogyo-ku, Kyoto 600-8216. Tel: 075-343-6655. Open daily 8.30am–7pm.

Tourist Information

Tokyo: Tel: 03-3201-3331
Narita: Tel: 0476-24-3198
Kyoto: Tel: 07-5371-5649
Nagoya: Tel: 052-541-4301
Yokohama: Tel: 04-5441-7300
Sendai: Tel: 022-222-4069
Sapporo: Tel: 011-213-5088

Teletourist Service

The Teletourist Service offers recorded information in English on events currently taking place that might be of interest to travellers. Tel: 03-3503-2911.

Local Tourist Websites

There are now a number of useful local websites to help you plan your visit. The links below are full of advice on what to see and suggestions of where to stay, plus the latest news on local events and festivals in each area.

Kyoto City Tourist and Cultural Information System: www.pref.kyoto.jp/visitkyoto/en
Osaka Tourist Guide: www.tourism.city.osaka.jp/en
Hokkaido Tourist Association: www.visit-hokkaido.jp/en
Koyasan Tourist Association: www.shukubo.jp/eng
Kyushu Tourism Promotion Organization: www.welcomekyushu.com
Okinawa Conventions and Visitors Bureau: www.ocvb.or/jp

Translators & Interpreters

Most languages are covered for translation or interpretation by the following companies, or check with a hotel business centre. Be aware that rates are not cheap.
ILC, Urban Point Sugamo Building 4F, 1-24-12 Sugamo, Toshima-ku, Tokyo. Tel: 03-5395-5561, fax: 03-5395-5566.
Adecco Japan, 45 Kowa Building 4F, 1-15-9 Minami Aoyama, Minato-ku, Tokyo. Tel: 03-3470-9300, fax: 03-3470-9334.

Useful Addresses

Organisations

American Center, ABC Kaikan, 2-6-3 Shibakoen, Minato-ku. Tel: 03-3436-0901.
American Chamber of Commerce, Bridgestone Toranomon Bldg, 3-25-2 Toranomon, Minato-ku. Tel: 03-3433-5381. www.accj.or.jp
Asia Centre of Japan, 8-10-32 Akasaka, Minato-ku. Tel: 03-3402-6111.
British Council, 1-2 Kagurazaka, Shinjuku-ku. Tel: 03-3235-8031.
Foreign Correspondents' Club, Yurakucho Denki Bldg, 20th Floor, 1-7-1 Yurakucho, Chiyoda-ku. Tel: 03-3211-3161.
Institut Franco-Japonais, 15 Ichigaya Funagawaracho, Shinjuku-ku. Tel: 03-5261-3933.
Italian Institute of Culture, 2-1-30 Kudan Minami, Chiyoda-ku. Tel: 03-3264-6011.
The Japan Foundation Library, Ark Mori Bldg, 20F, 1-12-32, Akasaka, Minato-ku. Tel: 03-5562-3527.
JETRO (Japan External Trade Organisation), 2-2-5 Toranomon, Minato-ku. Tel: 03-3582-5562.

Websites

Being A Broad: helpful data and insights for foreign women in Japan. www.being-a-broad.com
Chanpon: multicultural, pop and cute-culture Japan site. www.chanpon.org/
Cool Girls Japan: the latest fashion and street trends. www.coolgirlsjapan.biz
Insite: city-relevant articles and other information of an original or offbeat nature. www.insite-tokyo.com
Japan.com: good general site on Tokyo and Japan travel, business and technology. www.japan.com
Japan 101: huge site with articles on a wide range of Japan topics. www.japan-101.com
Japan-guide.com: extensive travel data, including an online shopping mall. www.japan-guide.com
Japan National Tourist Organisation: excellent links and travel info. www.jnto.go.jp
The Japan Times: a good online site for Japan's oldest English-language newspaper, which has nearly everything covered. www.japantimes.co.jp
NTT Townpage: NTT's on-line telephone book in English along with useful information. www.english.itp.ne.jp
Outdoor Japan: regularly updated site on the great outdoors including live weather forecasts and activity guides. http://outdoorjapan.com
Skiing Hokkaido: all the skiing information and resort details from Hokkaido. www.skiing-hokkaido.com
Stanford University: scholarly links for the more high-brow surfer. http://jguide.stanford.edu
Sumo Fan Magazine: online fan magazine. www.sumofanmag.com
Superfuture: trendy site for shopping, restaurants, bars and forthcoming events. www.superfuture.com
Tokyo Consumer Prices: if you would like to research the potential cost of your trip before going to Japan, check out this extensive guide. www.pricechecktokyo.com
Tokyodoko: a portal site offering access to good reference material on the capital. www.tokyodoko.com
Tokyo Food Page: updates on food, sake and beer. Tips on the best places to eat in Tokyo, plus some great recipes. www.bento.com
Tokyo Life Navigator: good site to research the city before coming. www.ima-chan.co.jp/guide/submr100/sub104.htm
Tokyo Subway Maps: a site for keeping up with Tokyo's ever-growing subwaysystem. www.tokyometro/jp/e
Tokyo Q (www.tokyoq.com) has the best restaurant and nightlife postings.
Superfuture (www.superfuture.com) is a trendy site for shopping, restaurants, bars and forthcoming events.
Yokoso: information and photo galleries on Japan that are regularly updated. www.japanwelcomesyou.com

Weights & Measures

Japan follows the metric system, except in cases governed by strong tradition. For example, rice and sake are measured in units of 1.8 litres and rooms are measured by a standard *tatami* mat size. Ancient measures are also used for carpentry in Shinto temples and for making kimono.

LANGUAGE

UNDERSTANDING THE LANGUAGE

The visitor will have few language problems within the confines of airports and the major hotels, but outside these the going can get tough. Quite apart from being unable to communicate verbally, the hapless visitor will also have the disconcerting experience of being almost totally illiterate.

The written language is made up of three different sets of characters: two simple home-grown syllabaries, *hiragana* and *katakana*, consisting of 46 characters each; and the much more formidable Chinese ideograms, *kanji*. Knowledge of just under two thousand of these is necessary to read a daily newspaper.

While the enormous effort required to memorise this number of *kanji* (it takes the Japanese most of their school career to do so) is clearly unjustifiable for those with only a passing interest in the language, a few hours spent learning the two syllabaries would not be time wasted for those who can afford it.

Hiragana can be useful for identifying which station your train has stopped at; the platforms are plastered with *hiragana* versions of the station name so that children who have not yet learned *kanji* can see where they are. Station names are usually (but not always) posted in roman script *(romanji)* as well, but not always as obviously. *Katakana* is used to transliterate foreign words. Western-style restaurants often simply list the foreign names for the dishes on their menus in *katakana*.

Pronunciation

With its small number of simple and unvarying vowel sounds, the pronunciation of Japanese should be easy for those who speak Western languages, which are rich in vowel sounds, and Japanese has nothing like the tonal system of Chinese.

Vowels have only one sound. Don't be sloppy with their pronunciations.

a – between fat and the u in but
e – like the e in egg
i – like the i in ink
o – like the o in orange
u – like the u in butcher

When they occur in the middle of words between voiceless consonants (ch, f, h, k, p, s, sh, t and ts), i and u are often almost silent. For example, *Takeshita* is really pronounced *Takesh'ta* while *sukiyaki* sounds more like *s'kiyaki*.

In spite of the seemingly simple pronunciation of Japanese, a lot of foreigners manage to mangle the language into a form which is almost impossible for the native speaker to understand. It is mainly intonation that is responsible for this. It would be untrue to claim that the Japanese language has no rise and fall in pitch but it is certainly "flatter" in character than Western languages.

It is important to avoid stressing syllables within words; whereas an English speaker would naturally stress either the second or third syllable of *Hiroshima*, for example, in Japanese the four syllables should be stressed equally.

Another problem lies in long (actually double) vowel sounds. These are often indicated by a line above the vowel, or simply by a double vowel. To pronounce these long vowels properly, it is simply necessary to give the vowel sound double length.

Numbers

Counting is very complicated in Japanese. Counting up to ten on their fingers, the Japanese will use general numbers, which are: *ichi, ni, san, shi* (or *yon*), *go, roku, shichi* (or *nana*), *hachi, ku* (or *kyuu*), *juu*. If they are counting bottles, they will say: *ip-pon, ni-hon, sam-bon, yon-hon, go-hon*... The suffix will change according to what is being counted. Categories of counter include flat objects (stamps, paper, etc.), long thin objects (pens, bottles, umbrellas) and people. You will be fairly safe with the following "all purpose" numbers below, which don't need suffixes:

one *hitotsu*
two *futatsu*
three *mittsu*
four *yottsu*
five *itsutsu*
six *muttsu*
seven *nanatsu*
eight *yattsu*
nine *kokonotsu*
ten *too*

If you want five of something, point at it and say, *itsutsu kudasai*. Or count on your fingers or write the number down. Thankfully the counter system only applies to numbers 1–10; after 10 the general numbers are used for all things.

Words & Phrases

Essential Phrases

Do you speak English?
eego ga dekimasu ka?
Please write it down
kaite kudasai
Pardon? *sumimasen*
I understand *wakari mashita*

I don't understand/I don't know *wakari masen*
Yes/No *hai/iie*
OK *ookee*
please *onegai shimasu*
Thank you (very much) *(doomo) arigatoo*

Greetings

Good morning *ohayoo gozaimasu*
Hello (afternoon) *kon-nichi-wa*
Good evening *konban-wa*
Good night *oyasumi nasai*
Goodbye *sayoonara* (*shitsure shimasu* for formal occasions)
How are you? *ogenki desu ka?*
My name is... *...to moshimasu*
I'm Mr/Ms Smith *watashi wa Smith desu*
Are you Mr/Ms Honda? *Honda-san desu ka?*
I'm American *Amerika-jin desu*
I'm British *Igirisu-jin desu*
I'm Australian *Osturaraia-jin desu*
I'm Canadian *Kanada-jin desu*

Asking for Directions

Excuse me, where is the toilet? *sumimasen, toire wa doko desu ka?*
Excuse me, is there a post office near here? *sumimasen. Kono chika-ku ni, yubin-kyoku wa arimasu ka?*
on the left/right *hidari/migi ni*
bakery *pan-ya*
stationer's *bunboogu-ya*
pharmacy *yakkyoku*
bookshop *hon-ya*
supermarket *suupaa*
department store *depato*
restaurant *restoran*
hotel *hoteru*
station *eki*
taxi rank *takushii noriba*
bank *ginkoo*
hospital *byooin*
police station *kooban*

Out Shopping

This one *kore*
That one (near the other person) *sore*
That one (near neither of you) *are*
Do you have...? *...(wa) arimasu ka?*
How much is it? *ikura desu ka?*
I'll take this *kore o kudasai*

Boarding the Train

Ticket (office) *kippu (uriba)*
reserved seat *shitei seki*
unreserved seat *jiyu seki*
first-class car *guriin sha*
Which platform does the train for Nagoya leave from? *Nagoya yuki wa namban sen desu ka?*
Thank you (very much) *(doomo) arigato gozaimasu* (informally, *doomo* is enough)
Don't mention it *doitashimashite*
Thanks for the meal *gochisosama deshita.*

Here you are *doozo*
After you *doozo*
Of course, go ahead *doozo* (in answer to "May I...?")

Days/Time

(On) Sunday *nichi-yoobi (ni)*
(Next) Monday *(raishu no) getsu-yoobi*
(Last) Tuesday *(senshu no) ka-yoobi*
(Every) Wednesday *(maishu) sui-yoobi*
(This) Thursday *(konshu no) moku-yoobi*
Friday *kin-yoobi*
Saturday *do-yoobii*
Yesterday *kino*
Today *kyo*
This morning *kesa*
This evening *konya*
Tomorrow *ashita*
What time is it? *nan-ji desu ka?*

Months/Seasons

January *ichi-gatsu*
February *ni-gatsu*
March *san-gatsu*
April *shi-gatsu*
May *go-gatsu*
June *roku-gatsu*
July *shichi-gatsu*
August *hachi-gatsu*
September *ku-gatsu*
October *juu-gatsu*
November *juu-ichi-gatsu*
December *juu-ni-gatsu*

At the Hotel

Western-style hotel *hoteru*
business hotel *bijinesu hoteru*
love hotel *rabu hoteru*
Japanese-style inn *ryokan*
guest house *minshuku*
temple accommodation *shukuboo*
youth hostel *yuusu hosuteru*
I have a reservation *yoyaku shite arimasu*
Do you have a room? *heya wa arimasu ka?*
I'd like a single/double room *shinguru/daburu ruumu o onegai shimasu*
I'd like a room with ... *... tsuki no heya o onegai shimasu*
twin beds *tsuin beddo*
double bed *daburu beddo*
bath/shower *basu/shawa*
air-conditioning *eakon*
TV/telephone *terebi/denwa*
How much is it? *ikura desu ka?*
Can I see the room please? *heya o misete kudasai*
That's fine, I'll take it *kekkoo dsu, tomari masu*
No, I won't take it *sumimasen, yamete okimasu*

At the Restaurant

A table for two, please *futari onegai shimasu*
The bill, please *o-kanjoo onegai shimasu*

A question of grammar

Japanese **questions** are formed by adding the grammar marker *ka* (a verbal question mark) to the verb at the end of a sentence. In Japanese the verb always comes last, with the basic rule for word order within a sentence is subject – object – verb

Japanese **nouns** have no articles (a, an, the) and very few plural forms. Whether a noun is singular or plural is judged from the context.

Personal pronouns are rarely used in Japanese. For 'you', either use the person's family name + -*san*, or omit the pronoun completely if it's clear who you are addressing.

I *watashi;* **we** *watashi tachi*

Japanese do not usually use **first names**, but the family name, followed by *-san*, which can stand for Mr, Mrs, Miss or Ms.

tsukemono **pickled vegetables**
sashimi **raw fish served with soy sauce and horseradish** *(wasabi)*
sushi **rice balls with fish/seafood**
tempura **battered vegetables, fish or seafood**
okonomiyaki **pizza/savoury pancake**
chanko-nabe **chicken and vegetable stew often served to sumo wrestlers**
gyoza **meat or vegetable dumplings**
soba **buckwheat noodles**
udon **thick wheat-flour noodles**
tonkotsu **pork broth-based dish with Chinese** *(ramen)* **noodles**
tonkatsu **breaded deep-fried pork**
yakitori **grilled chicken on skewers**
sukiyaki **thin slices of beef and vegetables in aromatic sauce**
shabu-shabu **beef cooked in broth**
karee raisu **Japanese curry on rice**
teppanyaki **griddled meat/fish**
kamameshi **rice casserole**
biiru **beer**
ocha **green tea**
o-sake/nihonshu **sake**
hiya/hitohada/atsukan **cold/luke warm/hot**
mizu **water**
mineraru wootaa **mineral water**

Sightseeing

Where is the ...? *... wa doko desu ka*
art gallery *bijutsu-kan*
botanical garden *shokubutsu-en*
Buddhist temple *o-tera*
castle *o-shiro*
museum *hakubutsu kan*
Imperial palace *kookyo*
Shinto shrine *jinja*
Can you show me on the map? *kono chizu de oshiete kudasai*

FURTHER READING

History and Culture

Dogs & Demons: Tales From the Dark Side of Japan by Alex Kerr. Hill & Wang, 2001.
Embracing Defeat: Japan in the Aftermath of World War II by John Dower. Allen Lane/Penguin, 2000.
A Historical Guide to Yokohama by Burritt Sabin. Yurindo, 2002.
In Praise of Shadows by Jun'ichiro Tanizaki (translated by Thomas J. Harper and Edward Seidensticker. Tuttle, 1984.
Japanese Garden Design by Mark P. Keane. Charles E. Tuttle, 1996.
Low City, High City: Tokyo From Edo to the Earthquake by Edward Seidensticker. Tuttle, 1983.
A Modern History of Japan by James L. McClain. W.W. Norton & Co, 2002.
Pink Samurai by Nicholas Bornoff. HarperCollins, 1991.
Speed Tribes by Karl Taro Greenfeld. HarperCollins, 1994.
The Gardens of Japan by Teiji Itoh. Kodansha International, 1984.
The Life And Death of Yukio Mishima by Henry Scott-Stokes. Cooper Square Press, 1999.
Zen & Japanese Culture by Daisetz Suzuki. Charles E. Tuttle, 1988.

General

Bells of Nagasaki by Dr Takashi Nagai. Kodansha, 1964.
Confessions of a Yakuza by Junichi Saga. Kodansha International, 1991.
A Far Valley: Four Years in a Japanese Village by Brian Moeran. Kodansha International, 1985.
Green Tea to Go: Stories from Tokyo by Leza Lowitz. Printed Matter Press, 2004.
A Guide To Kyogen by Don Kenny. Hinoki Shoten, 1968.
Hokkaido Highway Blues by Will Ferguson. Cannongate Books, 1998.
Japan: A Bilingual Atlas. Kodansha, Tokyo, 2000.
Japanese Society by Chie Nakane. Penguin, 1970.
Looking for the Lost by Alan Booth. Kodansha, 1994.
My Asakusa: Coming of Age in Pre-War Tokyo by Sadako Sawara. Tuttle Publishing, 2000.
Pictures from the Water Trade: An Englishman in Japan by John David Morley. Abacus, 1985.
Sado: Japan's Island in Exile by Angus Waycott. Stone Bridge Press, 1996.
Southern Exposure: Modern Japanese Literature from Okinawa. Edited by Michael Molasky and Steve Rabson. University of Hawaii Press, 2000.
Sake Pure & Simple by John Guantner, Griffith Frost. Stone Bridge Press, 1998.
The Enigma of Japanese Power by Karel van Wolferen. Macmillan, Tuttle, 1993.
The Inland Sea by Donald Richie. Tuttle, 1971.
The Kabuki Guide by Masakutsu Gunji. Kodansha, 1987.
Tokyo by Donald Richie. Reaktion Books, 2000.
Tokyo: A Bilingual Atlas. Kodansha, Tokyo, 2005.
Tokyo: City of Stories by Paul Waley. Weatherhill, New York, 1991.
Tokyo: A Guide to Recent Architecture by Noriyuki Tajima. Ellipsis Publication, 1995.
Tokyo Stories: A Literary Stroll by Lawrence Rogers. University of California Press, 2002.
Tokyo: The City at the End of the World by Peter Popham. Kodansha International Ltd, 1985.
Tokyo Underworld by Robert Whiting. Vintage, 2000.

Send Us Your Thoughts

We do our best to ensure the information in our books is as accurate and up-to-date as possible. However, some mistakes and omissions are inevitable and we are ultimately reliant on our readers to put us in the picture. We welcome your feedback. especially your experience of using the book on the road and will acknowledge all contributions. We will offer an Insight Guide to the best letters received.

Please write to us at:
Insight Guides
PO Box 7910
London SE1 1WE
United Kingdom

Or email us at:
insight@apaguide.co.uk

Other Insight Guides

Other Insight Guides to this part of the world include: Beijing, China, Hong Kong, Shanghai, South Korea and Taiwan.

Itinerary based Insight Step by Step Guides highlight the best city walks and tours, with itineraries for all tastes. Destinations in this series include Beijing, and Hong Kong.

Insight Smart Guides pack information into an easily portable and convenient format arranged in handy A–Z sections. Smart Guides to destinations in this region include Beijing and Tokyo.

Insight Fleximaps are full-colour, laminated and easy-to-fold maps with clear cartography, and photography describing a place's top 10 sights. Titles in this series to destinations in this region include: Beijing, Hong Kong, Shanghai and Tokyo.

Art & Photo Credits

AFP/Getty Images 109, 183
Charlotte Anderson 28/29, 56
APA 65, 169, 176
Stuart Atkin 144T, 163, 172
Tibor Bognar/Alamy 79, 184, 252, 299, 300, 325L
Jon Bower/Alamy 89, 155R
British Museum 84
Demetrio Carrasco/Jon Arnold 9T
Cephas Picture Library/Alamy 156
Paul Chesley/Getty Images 6T
Chinzan-so Back flap top
Douglas Corrance 119
David Crausby/Alamy 81
Digital Archive Japan/Alamy 141, 165
Ryan David 171
Empics 110
Alain Evrard 245
Guy Fisher 52
Michael Freeman Front flap bottom
Getty Images 48, 80, 102,
Golden Gate Images/Alamy 291
Blaine Harrington 12/13, 256
Dallas & John Heaton 138, 269L
G.Hellier/jonarnold.com 260
Jeremy Hoare 62, 100, 145, 235
Jim Holmes Back cover left & spine
Hans Höfer 177
Jean Kugler Back flap bottom, 17, 24, 253T
Kyoto Imperial Collection 44
Hiroshe Isobe 21
Hiroshima Itsukushima-jinja 74
J Marshall – TribaleyeImages/Alamy 37, 276
J Montgomery/jonarnold.com 121
Carol Jopp/Global Press Agency 87R, 181, 185, 192, 196/197, 201, 250, 251
JTB Photo/Alamy 8T, 146, 207, 208, 209L/R, 210, 220, 221, 222, 261, 274, 287, 298, 325R, 348
Kanagawa Prefectural Museum 46
Catherine Karnow 63, 118, 151, 167, 170, 229, 322, 350
Christian Kober/Alamy 154, 332, 333
Ron Kucera 108
Jean Kugler Back cover centre & right, 96/97, 105, 153, 160/161, 202, 223, 224/225, 266, 278/279, 289
Lyle Lawson 178, 213
Matthias Ley 144, 214, 233, 237, 246, 247, 293, 294, 305
Mainichi Shimbun 31, 49
Stephen Mansfield 142, 143, 255, 286, 319
Iain Masterson/Alamy 8B, 9L, 114/115, 139, 155L, 206L, 263, 288, 324
Robert McLeod 126/127, 157, 166, 177T, 179, 180, 182, 206T, 268, 269R, 271, 330
Ben Nakayama 238, 306T, 316/317
Richard Nowitz 7T, 7R, 116, 120
Pacific Press Service/Alamy 104, 297
Papillo/Alamy 189
Photobank/Singapore 39, 147, 150, 150T, 152T, 241
Photo Japan/Alamy 195, 206R
Photo Resource Hawaii/Alamy 265
Carol Purcell 148
Reuters/Corbis 50
Peter G. Richelt 230
Miguel Rivas-Micoud 47, 137, 140, 149T, 164T
Robert Harding/Alamy 326
Ronald Grant Archive 90, 91
Scott Rutherford Front flap top, 14, 18/19, 20, 22, 23L/R, 25, 26, 27, 51, 53, 54/55, 57, 58, 59, 60, 61, 64, 66/67, 68, 69, 70, 71, 86, 98, 101, 111, 122/123, 152, 187, 188, 188T, 190, 193, 198, 203, 204, 204T, 205, 211, 212, 215, 217, 218, 218T, 219, 222T, 239, 253, 255T, 257, 267, 277, 280, 284, 290, 295, 301, 302/303, 304, 307, 308, 308T, 309, 310, 311, 312, 313, 323, 323T, 328T, 332T, 334, 336, 337, 338/339, 340, 341, 342T, 343L/R, 345T, 346, 349
Schnelter/Alamy 191, 194
Blair Seitz 248
Ken Straiton 124/125, 296, 306, 342, 345
Adrian Storey 7B, 9B
Jeremy Sutton-Hibbert/Alamy 174, 327
Toho Video 92
Toho/The Kobal Collection 94
Tokyo National Museum 30, 32, 33, 34, 35, 36, 38, 40, 41, 45, 72, 75, 76, 77, 88, 99, 170T, 256T
Travel Ink/Alamy 328
Paul Van Riel 82/83, 168, 173, 331
Rohan Van Twest /Alamy 87L
Gorazd Vilhar 42/43, 72, 87, 85, 117, 128, 143T, 146T, 232, 249, 259L/R, 272, 273, 329
Michael Webb 10/11, 103, 175, 228, 234, 236, 240, 258, 285, 290T, 292T, 294T, 320
Nick Wheeler 164
Chris Willson/Alamy 6B, 262, 275
Gregory Wrona 254
Joseph Zanghi 78

Picture Spreads

Pages 106/107: Top row left to right: Tokyo Fuji Art Museum/Bridgeman, Bognar/Alamy, Getty Images, Jeremy Hoare/Alamy. Centre Row: Ulana Switucha/Alamy, Frantisek Staud/Alamy. Bottom Row: John Ferro Sims/Alamy, Pacific Press Service/Alamy
Pages 112/113: Top row left to right: Mitchell Coster/Axiom, Mitchell Coster/Axiom, Mitchell Coster/Axiom. Centre row: Michael Macintyre, Robert Holmes, Michael Macintyre. Bottom row: Michael Macintyre, Mitchell Coster/Axiom.
Pages 158/159: Top row left to right: M Faiman, Paul Quayle/Axiom, Robert Holmes. Centre row: Jim Holmes/Axiom, Demetrio Carrasco. Bottom Row Jim Holmes/Axiom, Michael Macintyre, Jon Burbank, Robert Holmes.
Pages 242/243: Top Row left to right: Jim Holmes/Axiom, Scott Rutherford, Jim Holmes/Axiom, Robert Holmes. Centre row: Scott Rutherford, Jim Holmes/Axiom. Bottom Row: Michael Macintyre, Jim Holmes/Axiom, Scott Rutherford, Scott Rutherford.
Pages 314/315: Top row left to right: Robert Holmes, Michael Freeman, Jim holmes/Axiom. Centre row: Jim holmes/Axiom, Robert Francis, Robert Holmes. Bottom row: Scott Rutherford, Jim Holmes/Axiom, Michael Freeman, the Hutchison Library.

Maps Berndtson & Berndtson Productions and Mike Adams

INSIGHT GUIDE
JAPAN

Cartographic Editor **Zoë Goodwin**
Production **Linton Donaldson**
Design Consultants
Klaus Geisler, Graham Mitchener
Picture Research **Jason Carter**

Index

Numbers in italics refer to photographs

L

M

R

S

T

U

V–X

Y–Z

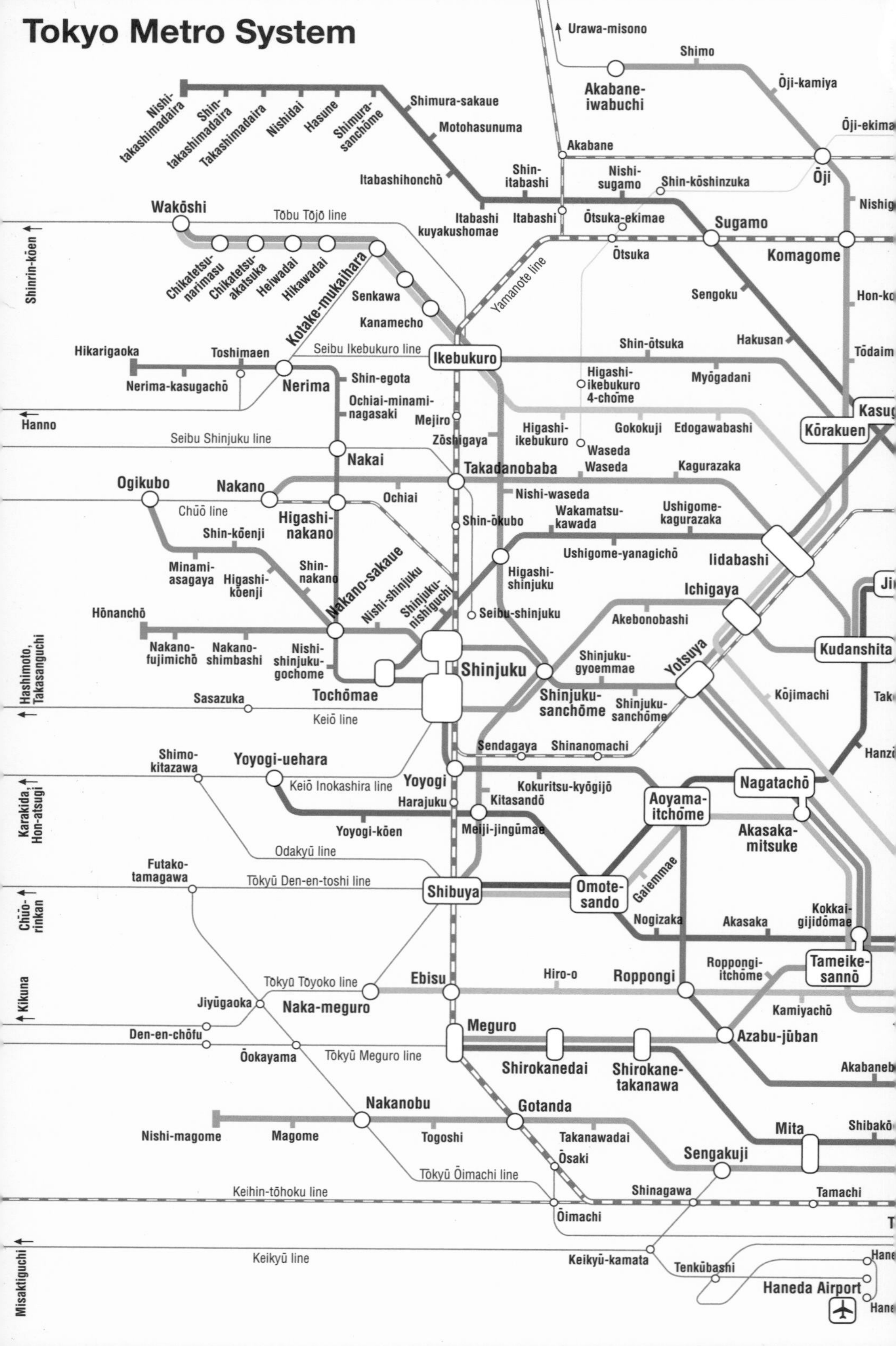
Tokyo Metro System
Urawa-misono
Shimo
Akabane-iwabuchi
Ōji-kamiya
Nishi-takashimadaira
Shin-takashimadaira
Takashimadaira
Nishidai
Hasune
Shimura-sanchōme
Shimura-sakaue
Motohasunuma
Itabashihonchō
Akabane
Ōji-ekima
Ōji
Shin-itabashi
Nishi-sugamo
Shin-kōshinzuka
Nishig
Wakōshi
Tōbu Tōjō line
Itabashi kuyakushomae
Itabashi
Ōtsuka-ekimae
Sugamo
Komagome
Shinrin-kōen
Chikatetsu-narimasu
Chikatetsu-akatsuka
Heiwadai
Hikawadai
Kotake-mukaihara
Ōtsuka
Yamanote line
Senkawa
Kanamecho
Sengoku
Hon-ko
Hikarigaoka
Toshimaen
Seibu Ikebukuro line
Ikebukuro
Shin-ōtsuka
Hakusan
Tōdaim
Nerima-kasugachō
Nerima
Shin-egota
Higashi-ikebukuro 4-chōme
Myōgadani
Hanno
Ochiai-minami-nagasaki
Mejiro
Kasug
Kōrakuen
Seibu Shinjuku line
Zōshigaya
Higashi-ikebukuro
Gokokuji
Edogawabashi
Waseda
Nakai
Takadanobaba
Waseda
Kagurazaka
Ogikubo
Nakano
Ochiai
Nishi-waseda
Chūō line
Higashi-nakano
Shin-ōkubo
Wakamatsu-kawada
Ushigome-kagurazaka
Shin-kōenji
Ushigome-yanagichō
Iidabashi
Minami-asagaya
Higashi-kōenji
Shin-nakano
Nakano-sakaue
Nishi-shinjuku
Shinjuku-nishiguchi
Higashi-shinjuku
Ichigaya
Hōnanchō
Seibu-shinjuku
Akebonobashi
Hashimoto, Takasanguchi
Nakano-fujimichō
Nakano-shimbashi
Nishi-shinjuku-gochome
Shinjuku
Shinjuku-gyoemmae
Yotsuya
Kudanshita
Tochōmae
Shinjuku-sanchōme
Shinjuku-sanchōme
Kōjimachi
Sasazuka
Keiō line
Sendagaya
Shinanomachi
Shimo-kitazawa
Yoyogi-uehara
Yoyogi
Kokuritsu-kyōgijō
Nagatachō
Karakida, Hon-atsugi
Keiō Inokashira line
Harajuku
Kitasandō
Aoyama-itchōme
Akasaka-mitsuke
Yoyogi-kōen
Meiji-jingūmae
Odakyū line
Futako-tamagawa
Tōkyū Den-en-toshi line
Chūō-rinkan
Shibuya
Omote-sando
Gaiemmae
Nogizaka
Akasaka
Kokkai-gijidōmae
Tameike-sannō
Roppongi-itchōme
Tōkyū Tōyoko line
Kikuna
Jiyūgaoka
Naka-meguro
Ebisu
Hiro-o
Roppongi
Kamiyachō
Den-en-chōfu
Meguro
Azabu-jūban
Ōokayama
Tōkyū Meguro line
Shirokanedai
Shirokane-takanawa
Akabaneb
Nakanobu
Gotanda
Nishi-magome
Magome
Togoshi
Takanawadai
Mita
Shibakō
Sengakuji
Ōsaki
Tōkyū Ōimachi line
Keihin-tōhoku line
Shinagawa
Tamachi
Ōimachi
Keikyū line
Keikyū-kamata
Tenkūbashi
Misaktiguchi
Haneda Airport